OS X and iOS Kernel Programming

Ole Henry Halvorsen
Douglas Clarke

OS X and iOS Kernel Programming

ISBN-13 (pbk): 978-1-4302-3536-1

ISBN-13 (electronic): 978-1-4302-3537-8

President and Publisher: Paul Manning
Lead Editor: James Markham
Technical Reviewers: Phil Jordan and Graham Lee
Editorial Board: Steve Anglin, Mark Beckner, Ewan Buckingham, Gary Cornell, Morgan Ertel, Jonathan Gennick,
    Jonathan Hassell, Robert Hutchinson, Michelle Lowman, James Markham, Matthew Moodie, Jeff Olson,
    Jeffrey Pepper, Douglas Pundick, Ben Renow-Clarke, Dominic Shakeshaft, Gwenan Spearing, Matt Wade,
    Tom Welsh
Coordinating Editor: Debra Kelly
Copy Editors: Scribendi Inc. and Kim Wimpsett
Compositor: Bytheway Publishing Services
Indexer: SPI Global
Artist: SPI Global
Cover Designer: Anna Ishchenko

Distributed to the book trade worldwide by Springer Science+Business Media New York, 233 Spring Street, 6th Floor, New York, NY 10013. Phone 1-800-SPRINGER, fax (201) 348-4505, e-mail orders-ny@springer-sbm.com, or visit www.springeronline.com.

For information on translations, please e-mail rights@apress.com, or visit www.apress.com. Apress and friends of ED books may be purchased in bulk for academic, corporate, or promotional use. eBook versions and licenses are also available for most titles. For more information, reference our Special Bulk Sales–eBook Licensing web page at www.apress.com/bulk-sales.

Any source code or other supplementary materials referenced by the author in this text is available to readers at www.apress.com. For detailed information about how to locate your book's source code, go to www.apress.com/source-code/.

To my wife and best friend, Jennifer,
and my children, Desmund and Isabel.
—Ole Henry Halvorsen

To my parents, who encouraged my
interest in computing from an early age.
—Douglas Clarke

Contents at a Glance

Contents

xiii

About the Authors

■ **Ole Henry Halvorsen** is currently a senior software engineer at a leading manufacturer of professional video equipment, where he works on drivers and software for high-end HD video hardware for Mac, Linux, and PC. He was part of the team that created some of the earliest video hardware devices for both USB 3.0 and Thunderbolt. He holds a bachelor's degree in network computing and a master's degree in information technology from Monash University, Australia. He formerly worked as an R&D engineer at Silicon Graphics (SGI) where he worked on NAS and SAN storage technologies and solutions for supercomputing and high-performance computing.

When not spending time with his family, he enjoys programming for the kernel, iOS, Linux, and the Web, as well as reading, watching movies, playing games, and keeping fit.

■ **Douglas Clarke** has been developing for the Macintosh professionally for 15 years. He has spent most of his career working with hardware and developing device drivers, and he has written drivers for Mac OS 9, Mac OS X, and Windows. His first exposure to the I/O Kit came a year before the initial release of Mac OS X, and he has been working with it continually since. He currently develops drivers to support real-time video applications. He graduated with a degree in computer science from Monash University in Australia.

About the Technical Reviewers

▓ **Phil Jordan** graduated from the University of York, UK, with an MPhys in physics with computer simulation. He then worked on the core technology team at Kuju London, extending and improving the in-house engine and tools used for the game Battalion Wars 2 on the Nintendo Wii. After moving to Vienna, he started his own software development contracting business, doing game and engine programming and building mobile, web, and custom business apps.

Using his experience of working closely with game console hardware, he has written open source kernel drivers for Mac OS X and Linux. He is now working on a kernel driver for getting the most out of solid-state disks.

▓ **Graham Lee** is a self-appointed "security boffin" who specializes in security on the Mac and smartphone and tablet platforms. He has written antivirus and disk encryption software for the Mac and consulted or contracted on numerous Cocoa and Cocoa Touch applications. Graham also speaks and writes on Apple-related security issues. He maintains a blog at `http://blog.securemacprogramming.com`. He lives in Oxford, UK, and in his spare time wonders where his spare time went.

Acknowledgments

The writing phase of this book started shortly after my beautiful Isabel and Desmund were born; in hindsight, it wasn't the greatest time to start a project of this scale. I was about to reconsider; however, my wife Jennifer, always being supportive, insisted I follow through. I cannot thank her enough for the superhuman effort she put in to allow me to work on this book. Caring for a baby is not easy under any circumstance, let alone twins! I am extremely proud of her, and I consider my part of this book our joint achievement.

Early on I was also fortunate to have my mother-in-law stay and help out, which made my life a lot easier and allowed me to focus on completing the first draft. Also thanks to my father-in-law, who had to endure without a decent home-cooked meal for quite some time. Similarly thanks to my brother-in-law for providing invaluable help to my wife and me in times of need. I'm also grateful to other members of my family, my friends, and my colleagues who provided help, encouragement, or ideas. I also owe thanks to my own parents for encouraging me to follow my own path and pursue my interests.

I would also like to thank the editorial team at Apress for the guidance, support, and help throughout this project. Likewise, I would like to thank the technical reviewers, Phil Jordan and Graham Lee, for their excellent guidance and their amazing ability to spot even the subtlest of errors. I would also like to mention Barry Naujok, Ian Costello, and Tim Serong for helping me answer questions in relation to networking and memory management. Last but not least, thanks to Doug for all his hard work and for making this book possible at all.

Thanks again to everyone involved!

Ole Henry Halvorsen

Introduction

Kernel development can be a daunting task and is very different from programming traditional user applications. The kernel environment is more volatile and complex. Extraordinary care must be taken to ensure that kernel code is free of bugs because any issue may have serious consequences to the stability, security, and performance of the system. This book covers the fundamentals necessary to begin programming in the kernel. We cover kernel development from a theoretical and practical point of view. We cover concepts fundamental to kernel development such as virtual memory and synchronization, as well as more practical knowledge. The book primarily focuses on Mac OS X, however the XNU kernel is also used by iOS, and hence the theoretical material in this book will also apply to it. By far the most common reason for doing development within the kernel's execution environment is to implement a device driver for controlling internal or external hardware devices. Because of this, much of the focus of this book is centred on the development of device drivers. The primary framework for device driver development in the XNU kernel is I/O Kit, which we cover extensively. As theory becomes boring quickly we have provided working code samples which you can play with to learn more or use as a starting point for your own drivers.

We hope you have as much fun reading this book as we have enjoyed writing it.

Who Is This Book For?

The book was written for anyone interested in Apple's iOS and Mac OS X operating systems, with a focus on practical kernel development, especially driver devel. Regardless of whether you are a hobbyist, student, or professional engineer, we hope to provide you with material of interest. While the focus is on kernel programming and development, we will cover many theoretical aspects of OS technology and provide a detailed overview of the OS X and iOS kernel environments. The aim of the book is to provide the knowledge necessary to start developing your own kernel extensions and drivers. We will focus in particular on the I/O Kit framework for writing device drivers and extensions, but we will also cover general knowledge that will give you a deeper understanding of how I/O Kit interacts with the OS. If you are mainly interested in developing OS X or iOS user applications, this book may not be for you. We will not cover Cocoa or any other framework used for developing end-user applications. This book covers kernel-programming topics such as driver and kernel extension development on Apple's OS X and iOS platform.

Some knowledge of operating system internals will be useful in understanding the concepts discussed in this book. Having completed an introductory computer science or engineering course will be a helpful starting point. Additionally, knowledge of at least one programming language will be required in order to understand examples throughout the book. Since we focus on I/O Kit, which is written in a subset of C++ called Embedded C++, it would be highly beneficial to have some experience with C++ (or at least C) to make the most of this book. The book does not cover general programming topics or theory. We will briefly cover some fundamentals of OS theory to provide a context for further discussions.

Book Structure

The following is a brief description of each chapter in this book:

Chapter 1, Operating System Fundamentals. Details the functionality of an operating system and its role in managing the computer's hardware resources. We describe the purpose of device drivers and when they are needed, and introduce the differences between programming in the kernel environment as compared to standard application development.

Chapter 2, Mac OS X and iOS. Provides a brief overview of the technical structure of XNU, the kernel used by Mac OS X and iOS.

Chapter 3, Xcode and the Kernel Development Environment. Provides an overview of the development tools provided by Apple for Mac OS X and iOS development. The chapter ends with a short "Hello world" kernel extension.

Chapter 4, The I/O Kit Framework. Introduces the I/O Kit framework that provides the driver model for Mac OS X and its object-oriented architecture. We explain how the I/O Kit finds the appropriate device driver to manage a hardware device. We demonstrate a generic device driver to illustrate the basic structure of any I/O Kit driver.

Chapter 5, Interacting with Drivers from Applications. Explains how application code can access a kernel driver. We demonstrate how to search and match against a specific driver as well as how to install a notification to wait for the arrival of a driver or a particular device. We will show how an application can send commands to a driver and watch for events sent by the driver.

Chapter 6, Memory Management. Provides an overview of kernel memory management and the different types of memory that a driver needs to work with. We describe the differences between physical and kernel virtual addresses and user-space memory. We also introduce the reader to the concepts such as memory descriptors and memory mapping.

Chapter 7, Synchronization and Threading. Describes the fundamentals of synchronization and why it is a necessity for every kernel driver. We discuss the usage of kernel locking mechanisms such as IOLock and IOCommandGate and their appropriate use. We explain how a typical driver requires synchronization between its own threads, user-space threads, and hardware interrupts. We discuss the kernel facilities for creating kernel threads and asynchronous timers.

Chapter 8, USB Drivers. Introduces the reader to the architecture of USB and how a driver interfaces with them. We provide an overview of the I/O Kit USB API and the classes it provides for enumerating devices and transferring data to or from a USB device. We also discuss steps needed to support device removal and provide an example to show how a driver can enumerate resources such as pipes.

Chapter 9, PCI and Thunderbolt. Provides an overview of the PCI architecture. We also describe the concepts that are unique to PCI drivers, such as memory-mapped I/O, high-speed data transfer through Direct Memory Access (DMA), and handling of device interrupts. We give an overview of the IOPCIDevice class that the I/O Kit provides for accessing and configuring PCI devices. We also discuss the related and more recent Thunderbolt technology.

Chapter 10, Power Management. Describes the methods that drivers need to implement in order to allow the system to enter low power states such as machine sleep. We also describe advanced power management that a driver can implement if it wishes to place its hardware into a low power state after a period of inactivity.

Chapter 11, Serial Port Drivers. Describes how to implement a serial port driver on Mac OS X. We introduce relevant data structures such as circular queues and techniques for managing data flow through blocking I/O and notification events. We show how a user application can enumerate and access a serial port driver.

Chapter 12, Audo Drivers. Discusses how system-wide audio input and output devices can be developed using the IOAudioFamily framework. We demonstrate a simple virtual audio device that copies audio output to its input.

Chapter 13, Network Drivers. Describes how a network interface can be implemented using the IONetworkingFamily. We also cover how to write network filters to filter, block, and modify network packets. The chapter concludes with an example of how to write an Ethernet driver.

Chapter 14, Storage Drivers. Covers the storage driver stack on Mac OS X that provides support for storage devices such as disks and CDs. We describe the drivers at each layer of the storage stack, including how to write a RAM disk, a partition scheme, and a filter driver that provides disk encryption.

Chapter 15, User space USB Drivers. Describes how certain drivers can be implemented entirely inside a user application. We describe the advantages to this approach and also when this may not be applicable.

Chapter 16, Debugging. Contains practical information on how to debug drivers, as well as common problems and pitfalls. It will enable a reader to work backwards from a kernel crash report to a location in their code, a common scenario facing a kernel developer. We will discuss the tools OS X provides to enable this, such as the GNU debugger (GDB).

Chapter 17, Advanced Kernel Programming. Explores some of the more advanced topics in kernel programming, such as utilizing SSE and floating point or implementing advanced driver architectures.

Chapter 18, Deployment. Concludes the book by describing how to distribute a driver to the end user. We cover the use of the Apple installation system for both first-time installation and upgrades. The chapter includes practical tips on how to avoid common driver installation problems.

CHAPTER 1

Operating System Fundamentals

The role of an operating system is to provide an environment in which the user is able to run application software. The applications that users run rely on services provided by the operating system to perform tasks while they execute, in many cases without the user—or even the programmer—giving much thought to them. For an application to read a file from disk, for example, the programmer simply needs to call a function that the operating system provides. The operating system handles the specific steps required to perform that read. This frees the application programmer from having to worry about the differences between reading a file that resides on the computer's internal hard disk or a file on an external USB flash drive; the operating system takes care of such matters.

Most programmers are familiar with developing code that is run by the user and perhaps uses a framework such as Cocoa to provide a graphical user interface with which to interact with the user. All of the applications available on the Mac or iPhone App Store fit into this category. This book is not about writing application software, but rather about writing kernel extensions—that is, code that provides services to applications. Two possible situations in which a kernel extension is necessary are allowing the operating system to work with custom hardware devices and adding support for new file systems. For example, a kernel extension could allow a new USB audio device to be used by iTunes or allow an Ethernet card to provide an interface for networking applications, as shown in Figure 1-1. A file system kernel extension could allow a hard disk formatted on a Windows computer to mount on a Mac as if it were a standard Mac drive.

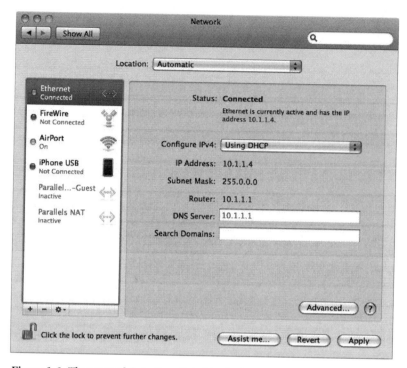

Figure 1-1. The network interfaces listed in the Mac OS X system preferences represent network kernel extensions.

An important role of the operating system is to manage the computer's hardware resources, such as memory and the CPU, and peripherals, such as disk storage and the keyboard. The collection of hardware devices that the operating system needs to support varies greatly from machine to machine. The hardware configuration of a MacBook Air is very different to that of a Mac Pro, although they both run the same operating system. To allow the operating system to support multiple hardware configurations without becoming bloated, the code required to support each hardware component is packaged into a special type of kernel extension known as a driver. This modularity allows the operating system to load drivers on demand, depending on the hardware that is present on the system. This approach also allows for drivers to be installed into the system by vendors to support their custom hardware. The standard installation of Mac OS X comes with over one hundred drivers, of which only a subset is needed to run a particular system.

Developing a kernel extension is very different from writing an application. The execution of an application tends to be driven by events originating from the user. The application runs when the user launches it; it may then wait for the user to click a button or select a menu item, at which point the application handles that request. Kernel extensions, on the other hand, have no user interface and do not interact with the user. They are loaded by the operating system, and are called by the operating system to perform tasks that it could not perform by itself, such as when the operating system needs to access a hardware device that the kernel extension is driving.

To help with the security and stability of the system, modern operating systems, such as Mac OS X, isolate the core operating system code (the kernel) from the applications and services that are run by the user. Any code that runs as part of the kernel, such as driver code, is said to run in "kernel space." Code that runs in kernel space is granted privileges that standard user applications do not have, such as the ability to directly read and write to hardware devices connected to the computer.

In contrast, the standard application code that users work with are said to run in "user space." Software that runs in user space has no direct access to hardware. Therefore, to access hardware, user code must send a request to the kernel, such as a disk read request, to request that the kernel perform a task on behalf of the application.

There is a strict barrier between code that runs in user space and code that runs in the kernel. Applications can only access the kernel by calling functions that the operating system publishes to user space code. Similarly, code that executes in kernel space runs in a separate environment to user space code. Rather than using the same rich programming APIs that are available to user space code, the kernel provides its own set of APIs that developers of kernel extensions must use. If you are accustomed to user space programming, these APIs may appear restrictive at first, since operations such as user interaction and file system access are typically not available to kernel extensions. Figure 1-2 shows the separation of user space code and kernel space code, and the interaction between each layer.

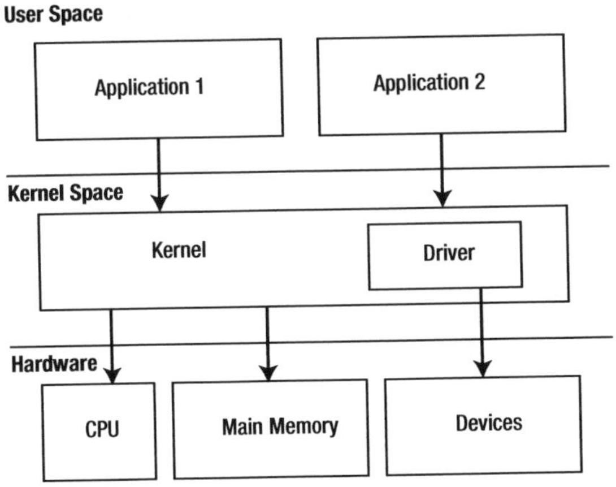

Figure 1-2. The separate layers of responsibility in a modern operating system

An advantage of forcing applications to make a request to the kernel to access hardware is that the kernel (and kernel driver) becomes the central arbiter of a hardware device. Consider the case of a sound card. There may be multiple applications on the system that are playing audio at any one time, but because their requests are funneled through to a single audio driver, that driver is able to mix the audio streams from all applications and provide the sound card with the resulting mixed stream.

In the remainder of this chapter, we provide an overview of the functionality provided by the operating system kernel, with a focus on its importance in providing user applications with access to hardware. We begin at the highest level, looking at application software, and then digging down into the operating system kernel level, and finally down into the deepest level, the hardware driver. If you are already familiar with these concepts, you can safely proceed to Chapter 2.

The Role of the Operating System

As part of the boot sequence, the operating system determines the hardware configuration of the system, finds any external devices connected to USB ports or plugged into PCI expansion slots, and initializes them, loading drivers along the way, if necessary.

Once the operating system has completed loading, the user is able to run application software. Application software may need to allocate memory or write a file to disk, and it is the operating system that handles these requests. To the user, the involvement of the operating system is largely transparent.

The operating system provides a layer of abstraction between running applications and the physical hardware. Applications typically communicate with hardware by issuing high-level requests to the operating system. Because the operating system handles these requests, the application can be completely unaware of the hardware configuration on which it is running, such as the amount of RAM installed and whether the disk storage is an internal SSD or an external USB drive.

This abstraction allows application software to be run on a wide variety of different hardware configurations without the programmer having to add support for each one, even if new hardware devices are created after the program has been released.

Application developers can often ignore many of the details of the workings of a computer system, because the operating system abstracts away the intricacies of the hardware platform on which the application is running. As a driver developer, however, the code that you write becomes part of the operating system and will interface directly with the computer's hardware; you are not immune to the inner-workings of a system. For this reason, a basic understanding of how the operating system performs its duties is necessary.

Process Management

A user typically has many applications installed on his or her computer. These are purely passive entities. The programs on disk contain data that is needed only when the program is run, consisting of the executable code and application data. When the user launches an application, the operating system loads the program's code and data into memory from disk and begins executing its code. A program being executed is known as a "process." Unlike a program, a process is an active entity, and consists of a snapshot of the state of the program at a single instance during execution. This includes the program's code, the memory that the program has allocated, and the current state of its execution, such as the CPU instruction of the function that the program is currently executing, and the contents of its variables and memory allocations.

There are typically many processes running on a system at once. These include applications that the user has launched (such as iTunes or Safari), as well as processes that are started automatically by the operating system and that run with no indication to the user. For example, the Time Machine backup service will automatically run a background process every hour to perform a backup of your data. There may even be multiple instances of the same program being executed at any one time, each of which is considered a distinct process by the operating system. Figure 1-3 shows the Activity Monitor utility that is included with Mac OS X, which allows all of the processes running on the system to be examined.

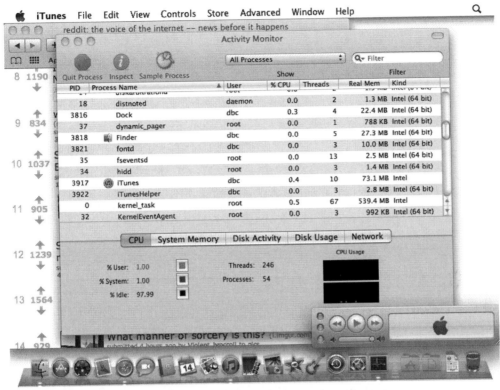

Figure 1-3. Activity Monitor on Mac OS X showing all processes running on the system. Compare this to the Dock, which shows the visible user applications.

Process Address Spaces

Although there are typically many processes running at any one time, each process is unaware of the other processes running on the system. In fact, without explicit code, one process cannot interact or influence the behavior of another process.

The operating system provides each process with a range of memory within which it is allowed to operate; this is known as the process's address space. The address space is dynamic and changes during execution as a process allocates memory. If a process attempts to read or write to a memory address outside of its address space, the operating system typically terminates it, and the user informed that the application has crashed.

Although protected memory is not new, it is only within the last decade that it has been found on consumer desktop systems. Prior to Mac OS X, a process running under Mac OS 9 was able to read or write to any memory address, even if that address corresponded to a buffer that was allocated by another process or belonged to the operating system itself.

Without memory protection, applications were able to bypass the operating system and implement their own inter-process communication schemes based on directly modifying the memory and variables of a different process, with or without the consent of that process. This was also true for operating system structures. For example, Mac OS 9 had an internal global variable that contained a linked list of every GUI window that was open. Although this linked list was nominally owned and manipulated by the operating system, applications were able to walk and modify the list without making any calls to the operating system.

Without memory protection, an operating system is susceptible to bugs in user applications. An application running on a system with memory protection can, at worst, corrupt its own memory and structures, but the damage is localized to the application itself. On a system without memory protection, such as Mac OS 9, a bug in an application could potentially overwrite the internal structures of the operating system, which could cause the system to crash entirely and require a reboot to recover.

It is worth noting that on a modern operating system such as Mac OS X, the kernel has an address space of its own. This allows the kernel to operate independently of all running processes. On Mac OS X, a single address space is used for both the kernel and all kernel extensions that are loaded. This means that there is nothing protecting core operating system structures from being inadvertently overwritten by a buggy driver. Unlike a user process, which can simply be aborted, if this situation occurs in the kernel, the entire system is brought down and the computer must be rebooted. This type of error presents itself as a kernel panic on Mac OS X, or the "blue screen of death" on Windows. For this reason, developers of kernel extensions need to be careful with memory management to ensure that all memory accesses are valid.

Operating System Services

With a modern operating system, there is a clear separation between the functions performed by the operating system and the functions performed by the application. Whenever a process wishes to perform a task such as allocating memory, reading data from disk, or sending data over a network, it needs to go through the operating system using a set of well-defined programming interfaces that are provided by the system. System functions such as malloc() and read() are examples of system calls that provide operating system services. These system calls may be made directly by the application or indirectly through a higher-level development framework such as the Cocoa framework on Mac OS X. Internally, the Cocoa framework is implemented on top of these same system calls, and accesses operating system services by invoking lower-level functions such as read().

However, because user processes have no direct access to hardware or to operating system structures, a call to a function such as read() needs to break out of the confines of the process's address space. When a function call to an operating system service is made, control passes from the user application to the privileged section of the operating system, known as the kernel. Transferring control to the kernel is usually performed with the help of the CPU, which provides an instruction for this purpose. For example, the Intel CPU found in modern-day Macs provides a syscall instruction that jumps to a function that was set up when the operating system booted. This kernel function first needs to identify which system call the user process executed (determined by a value written to a CPU register by the calling process) and then reads the function parameters passed to the system call (again, set up by the calling process through CPU registers). The kernel then performs the function call on behalf of the user process and returns control to the process along with any result code. This is illustrated in Figure 1-4.

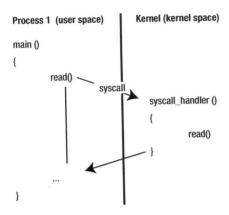

Figure 1-4. The flow of control in a system call

The kernel is a privileged process and has the ability to perform operations that are not available to user processes, but are necessary for configuring the system. When control transfers to the kernel, such as following a system call, the CPU enters a privileged mode while kernel code is executed and then drops back to restricted privileges before returning to the user process.

Since the kernel executes at a higher privilege level than the user process while it is executing a system call on behalf of the process, it needs to be careful that it doesn't inadvertently cause a security breach. This could happen if the kernel were tricked into performing a task that the user process should not be allowed to do, such as being asked to open a file for which the user does not have read permission, or being provided with a destination buffer whose address is not within the process's address space. In the first case, although the kernel process itself has permission to open any file on the system, because it is operating on behalf of a lesser-privileged user process, the request needs to be denied. In the second case, if the kernel were to access an invalid address, the result would be an unrecoverable error, which would lead to a kernel panic.

Kernel errors are catastrophic, requiring the entire system to be rebooted. To prevent this from occurring, whenever the kernel performs a request on behalf of a user process, it needs to take care to validate the parameters that have been provided by the process and should not assume that they are valid. This applies to system calls implemented by the kernel and, as we will see in subsequent chapters, whenever a driver accepts a control request from a user process.

Virtual Memory

The RAM in a computer system is a limited resource, with all of the running processes on the system competing for a share of it. When there are multiple applications running on a system, it is not unusual for the total amount of memory allocated by all processes to exceed the amount of RAM on the system.

An operating system that supports virtual memory allows a process to allocate and use more memory than the amount of RAM installed on the system; that is, the address space of a process is not constrained by the amount of physical RAM. With virtual memory, the operating system uses a backing store on secondary storage, such as the hard disk, to keep portions of a process address space that will not fit into RAM. The CPU, however, can still access only addresses that are resident in RAM, so the operating system must swap data between the disk backing store and RAM in response to memory accesses made by the process as it runs.

At a particular time, a process may only need to reference a small subset of the total memory that has been allocated. This is known as the working set of the process and, as long as the operating system keeps this working set in RAM, there is negligible impact on the execution speed imposed by virtual memory. The working set is a dynamic entity, and it changes based on the data that is actively being used as the process runs. If a process accesses a memory address that is not resident in RAM, the corresponding data is read from the backing store on disk and brought into RAM. If there is no free RAM available to load the data into, some of the existing data in RAM will need to be swapped out to disk beforehand, thus freeing up physical RAM.

Virtual memory is handled by the operating system. A user process plays no part in its implementation, and is unaware that portions of its address space are not in physical RAM or that data it has accessed needed to be swapped into main memory.

A consequence of virtual memory is that the addresses used by a process do not correspond to addresses in physical RAM. This is apparent if you consider that a process's address space may be larger than the amount of RAM on the system. Therefore, the addresses that a process reads from and writes to need to be translated from the process's virtual address space into a physical RAM address. Since every memory access requires an address translation, this is performed by the CPU to minimize the impact on execution speed.

Operating systems typically use a scheme known as "paging" to implement virtual to physical address translation. Under a paged memory scheme, physical memory is divided into fixed-sized blocks known as page frames. Most operating systems, including both Mac OS X and iOS, use a frame size of 4096 bytes. Similarly, the virtual address space of each process is divided into fixed-size blocks, known as pages. The number of bytes per page is always the same as the number of bytes per frame. Each page in a process can then be mapped to a frame in physical memory, as shown in Figure 1-5.

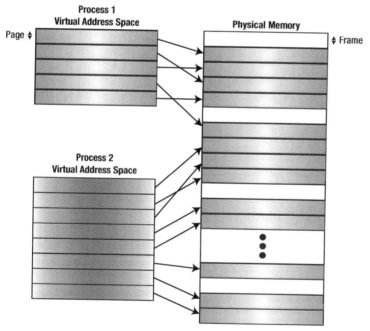

Figure 1-5. The pages in a process's address space can be mapped to any page frames in memory.

Another advantage of virtual memory is it allows a buffer that occupies a contiguous range of pages in the process's virtual address space to be spread over a number of discontiguous frames in physical memory, as seen in Figure 1-5. This solves the problem of fragmentation of physical memory, since a process's memory allocation can be spread over several physical memory segments and is not limited to the size of the longest contiguous group of physical page frames.

As part of launching a process, the operating system creates a table to map addresses between the process's virtual address space and their corresponding physical address. This is known as a "page table." Conceptually, the page table contains an entry for each page in the process's address space containing the address of the physical page frame to which each page is mapped. A page table entry may also contain access control bits that the CPU uses to determine whether the page is read-only and a bit that indicates whether the page is resident in memory or has been swapped out to the backing store. Figure 1-6 describes the steps that the CPU performs to translate a virtual address to a physical address.

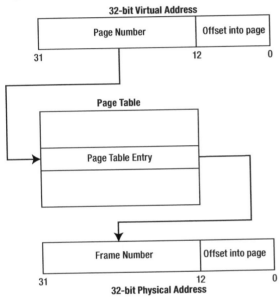

Figure 1-6. Virtual to physical address translation for a 32-bit address with a page size of 4096 bytes (12 bits)

If a process accesses a memory address that the CPU cannot translate into a physical address, an error known as a "page fault" occurs. Page faults are handled by the operating system, running at privileged execution level. The operating system determines whether the fault occurred because the address was not in the process's address space, in which case the process has attempted to access an invalid address and is terminated. If the fault occurred because the page containing the address has been swapped out to the backing store, the operating system performs the following steps:

1. A frame in physical memory is allocated to hold the requested page; if no free frames are available in memory, an existing frame is swapped out to the backing store to make room.

2. The requested page is read from the backing store into memory.

3. The page table for the process is updated so that the requested page is mapped to the allocated frame.

4. Control returns to the calling process.

The calling process re-executes the instruction that caused the fault, but this time around, the CPU finds a mapping for the requested page in the page table and the instruction completes successfully.

An understanding of virtual memory and paging is essential for kernel developers. Although the kernel handles requests on behalf of user applications, it also has an address space of its own, so parameters often need to be copied or mapped from a process's address space to the kernel's address space. In addition, kernel code that interfaces to hardware devices often needs to obtain the physical address of memory. Consider a disk driver that is handling a read request for a user process. The destination for the data read from disk is a buffer that resides in the address space of the user process. As with the CPU, the hardware controlled by the driver can write only to an address in main memory, and not to a destination in the backing store. Therefore, to handle the read request, the driver needs to ensure that the user buffer is swapped into main memory and remains in main memory for the duration of the read operation. Finally, the driver needs to translate the address of the destination buffer from a virtual address into a physical address that the hardware can access. We describe this in further detail in Chapter 6.

It's worth noting that although iOS provides a page table for each process, it does not support a backing store. At first, it may seem that this completely defeats the purpose of paging. However, it serves two very important purposes. First, it provides each process with the view that it has sole access to memory. Second, it avoids problems caused by the fragmentation of physical memory.

Scheduling

Another resource that is under high contention in a computer system is the CPU. Each process requires access to the CPU in order to execute, but typically, there are more active processes wanting access to the CPU than there are CPU cores on the system. The operating system must therefore share the CPU cores among the running processes and ensure that each process is provided regular access to the CPU so that it can execute.

We have seen that processes run independent of each other and are given their own address spaces to prevent one process from affecting the behavior of any other process. However, in many applications, it is useful to allow two independent execution paths to run simultaneously, without the restriction of having each path run within its own address space. This unit of execution is known as a "thread." Multiple threads all execute code from the same program code and are run within the same process (and hence share the same address space), but otherwise run independently.

To the operating system, a thread is the basic unit of scheduling; the operating system scheduler needs to look at only the active threads on the system when considering what to schedule next on the CPU. For a process to execute, it must contain at least one thread; the operating system automatically creates the initial thread for a new process when it begins running.

The goal of the scheduler is twofold: to prevent the CPU from becoming idle, since otherwise a valuable hardware component is being wasted, and to provide all threads with access to the CPU in a manner that is fair so that a single thread cannot monopolize the CPU and starve other threads from running. To do this, a thread is scheduled on an available CPU core until one of two events occurs:

- A certain amount of time has elapsed, known as the time quantum, at which point the thread is preempted by the operating system and another thread is scheduled. On Mac OS X, the default time quantum is 10 milliseconds.

- The thread can no longer execute because it is waiting for the completion of an operation, such as for data to be read from disk, or for the result of another thread. In this case, the scheduler allows another thread to run on the CPU while the original thread is blocked. This prevents the CPU from sitting idle when a thread has no work to do and maximizes the time that the CPU is spent executing code. A thread can also voluntarily give up its time on the CPU by calling one of the sleep() functions, which delay execution of the current thread for a specified duration.

One reason for adding multiple threads to an application is to allow it to execute concurrently across multiple CPU cores so that the application's execution can be sped up by dividing a complex operation into smaller steps that are run in parallel. However, multithreading has advantages even on a computer with a single CPU core. By rapidly switching between active threads, the scheduler gives the illusion that all threads are running concurrently. This allows a thread to block or sit in a tight loop with negligible impact on the responsiveness of other threads, so a time-consuming task can be moved to a background thread while leaving the rest of the application free to respond to user interaction.

A common design used in applications that interface with hardware is to place the code that accesses the hardware in its own thread. Software code often has to block while it is waiting for the hardware to respond; by removing this code from the main program thread, the program's user interface is not affected when the program needs to wait for the hardware.

Another common use of threads occurs when software needs to respond to an event from hardware with minimal delay. The application can create a thread that is blocked until it receives notification from hardware, which can be signaled using techniques discussed in later chapters. While the thread is blocked, the scheduler does not need to provide it with access to the CPU, so the presence of the thread has no impact on the performance of the system. However, once the hardware has signaled an event, the thread becomes unblocked, is scheduled on the CPU, and it is free to take whatever action is necessary to respond to the hardware.

Hardware and Drivers

In addition to managing essential hardware resources such as the CPU and memory, the operating system is also responsible for managing hardware peripherals that may be added to the system. This includes devices such as the keyboard and mouse, a USB flash drive, and the graphics card. Although the operating system is responsible for managing these devices, it does so with the help of drivers, which can be thought of as plug-ins that run inside the operating system kernel and allow the system to interface to hardware devices.

The code to support a hardware device can be found in two places: on the device itself (known as firmware) and on the computer (known as the driver). The role of the driver is to act on behalf of the operating system in controlling the hardware device. Driver code is loaded into the operating system kernel and is granted the same privileges as the rest of the kernel, including the ability to directly access hardware.

The driver has the responsibility of initializing the hardware when the device is plugged into the computer (or when the computer boots) and of translating requests from the operating system into a sequence of hardware-specific operations that the device needs to perform to complete the operating system's request.

The type of requests that a driver will receive from the operating system depends on what function the driver performs. For certain drivers, the operating system provides a framework for driver developers. For example, a sound card requires an audio driver to be written. The audio driver receives requests from the operating system that are specific to the world of audio, such as a request to create a 48 kHz audio output stream, followed by requests to output a provided packet of audio.

Drivers may also be built on top of other drivers and may request services provided by other drivers. For example, the driver of a USB audio input device uses the services of a lower-level generic USB driver to access its hardware. This relieves the developer from having to become intimate with the USB protocol, and the developer is instead free to concentrate on the specifics of his own device. As in the previous example, the audio driver receives requests from the operating system that represent audio stream operations, and in responding to these, the driver creates requests of its own that are passed to a lower-level USB driver. This allows a separation in the responsibility of each driver: The audio driver needs to concern itself only with handling audio requests and configuring the audio device, and the USB driver needs to concern itself only with the USB protocol and performing data transfers over the USB bus. An example of the way in which drivers can be layered is illustrated in Figure 1-7.

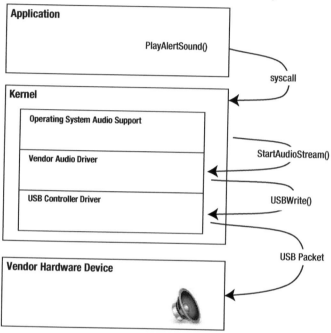

Figure 1-7. The chain of control requests in an audio request from application to hardware

Not all hardware fits into a specific class that is understood by the operating system. A specialized device, such as a 3D printer, is unlikely to have support from the operating system. Instead, the hardware manufacturer needs to write a generic driver for their hardware. As a generic driver, the operating system does not recognize the device as a printer and issue printing requests to it, but instead the driver is controlled by specialized application software, which communicates with the printer driver directly. The operating system provides a special system call to allow a user application to request an operation from a driver, known as an "i/o control" request, often shortened to "ioctl." An ioctl specifies the operation to be performed and provides the driver with parameters required by the operation, which may include a buffer to place the result of the operation. Although the ioctl request is implemented as a system call to the operating system, the request is passed directly to the driver.

Summary

The operating system is responsible for managing the hardware resources in a computer. It provides an abstract model of the computer system to user programs, giving the appearance that each program has full access to the CPU and the entire memory range. Programs that are run by the user cannot touch hardware without calling upon services provided by the operating system. In handling services that involve peripheral hardware devices, the operating system may need to call functions provided by the driver of that device.

In subsequent chapters, we will put the concepts we have covered here into practice. We will introduce you to the interfaces provided by Mac OS X to allow drivers to work with virtual and physical memory addresses, respond to requests from user applications, and communicate with PCI and USB devices.

CHAPTER 2

Mac OS X and iOS

Mac OS X is a modern Unix-based operating system developed by Apple Inc for their Macintosh computer series. OS X is the tenth incarnation of Mac OS.

OS X features a graphical user interface known for its ease of use and visual appeal. Apple has gained a cult-like following for their products, and any new feature addition to either OS X or iOS receives widespread attention. In addition to the regular edition of OS X, Apple also provided a server edition of OS X called Mac OS X Server.

The server version was later merged with the regular version in Mac OS X 10.7 (Lion). OS X was the successor to Mac OS 9, and represented a radical departure from earlier versions. Unlike its predecessors, OS X was based on the NeXTSTEP operating system. At present, there have been eight releases of Mac OS X, with the latest being Mac OS X 10.7, codenamed Lion. The Mac OS X releases to date are shown in Table 2-1.

Table 2-1. Mac OS X Releases to Date

Version	Name	Released
10.0	Cheetah	March 2001
10.1	Puma	September 2001
10.2	Jaguar	August 2002
10.3	Panther	October 2003
10.4	Tiger	April 2005
10.5	Leopard	October 2007
10.6	Snow Leopard	August 2009
10.7	Lion	July 2011

Mac OS X comes with a range of tools for developers, including Xcode, which allow the development of a wide range of applications, including the major topic of this book—kernel extensions.

For the end-user, OS X usually comes bundled with the iLife suite, which contains software for photo, audio, and video editing, as well as software for authoring web pages.

NEXTSTEP

OS X and iOS are based on the NeXTSTEP OS developed by NeXT Computer Inc, which was founded by Steve Jobs after he left Apple in 1985. The company was initially funded by Jobs himself, but later gained significant outside investments. NeXT was later acquired by Apple, and NeXTSTEP technology made its way into OS X. The aim of NeXT was to build a computer for academia and business. Despite limited commercial success relative to the competition, the NeXT computers (most notably the NeXTcube) had a highly innovative operating system, called NeXTSTEP, which was in many ways ahead of its time.

NeXTSTEP had a graphical user interface and command line interface like the current versions of OS X (iOS does not provide a user accessible command line interface). Many core technologies introduced by NeXTSTEP are still found in its successors, such as application bundles and Interface Builder. Interface Builder is now part of the Xcode development environment and is widely used for both OS X and iOS Cocoa applications. NeXTSTEP provided Driver Kit, an object-oriented framework for driver development, which later evolved into I/O Kit, one of the major topics of this book.

iOS was later derived from OS X, and it is Apple's OS for mobile devices. It was launched with the release of the first iPhone, in 2007, and at that point it was called iPhone OS, though it was later renamed iOS to better reflect the fact that it runs on other mobile devices, such as the iPod Touch, the iPad, and more recently the Apple TV. iOS was built specifically for mobile devices with touch interfaces. Unlike the biggest competitor, Windows, neither OS X nor iOS are licensed for use by third parties, and they can officially only be used on Apple's hardware products. A high-level view of the Mac OS X architecture is shown in Figure 2-1.

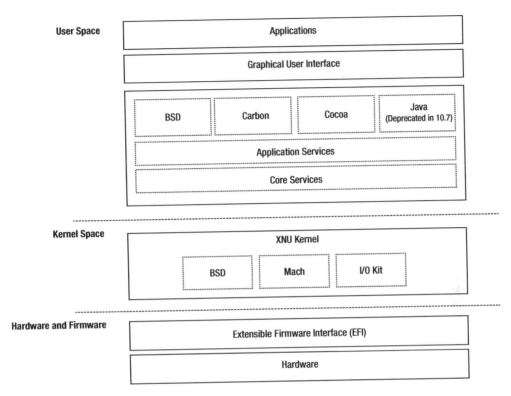

Figure 2-1. Mac OS X architecture

The core of Mac OS X and iOS is POSIX compliant and has since Mac OS X 10.5 (Leopard) complied with the Unix 03 Certification. The core of OS X and iOS, which includes the kernel and the Unix base of the OS, is known as Darwin, and it is an open source operating system published by Apple. Darwin, unlike Mac OS X, does not include the characteristic user interface, as it is a bare bones system, in that it only provides the kernel and user space base of tools and services typical of Unix systems. At its release, the only supported architecture was the PowerPC platform, but Intel 32 and 64-bit support was subsequently added as part of Apple's shift to the Intel architecture. Apple has thus far not released the ARM version of Darwin that iOS is based on. Darwin is currently downloadable in source form only, and has to be compiled. The Darwin distribution includes the source code for the XNU kernel. The kernel sources are a particularly useful resource for people wanting to know more about the inner workings of the OS, and for developing kernel extensions. You can often find more detailed explanations in the source code headers, or the code itself, than are documented on Apple's developer website.

The Darwin OS (and therefore OS X and iOS) runs the XNU kernel, which is based on code from the Mach kernel, as well as parts of the FreeBSD operating system. Figure 2-2 shows the Mac OS X desktop.

Figure 2-2. The Mac OS X desktop

Programming APIs

As you can see from Figure 2-1, OS X has a layered architecture. Between the Darwin core and the user application there is a rich set of programming APIs. The most significant of these is Cocoa, which is the preferred framework for GUI-based applications. The iOS equivalent is Cocoa Touch, which is principally the same, but offers GUI elements specialized for touch-based user interaction. Both Cocoa and Cocoa Touch are written in the Objective-C language. Objective-C is a superset of C, with support for Smalltalk style messages.

OBJECTIVE-C

Objective-C was the language of choice for application development under Mac OS X and iOS, as well as their predecessor, NeXTSTEP. Objective-C is a superset of the C language and provides support for object-oriented programming, but it lacks many of the advanced capabilities provided by languages like C++, such as multiple inheritance, templates, and operator overloading. Objective-C uses Smalltalk-style messaging and dynamic binding (which in many ways removes the need for multiple inheritance). The language was invented in the early 1980s by Brad Cox and Tom Love. Objective-C is still the de-facto standard language for application development on both OS X and iOS, although driver or system level programming is typically done in C or C++. Many core frameworks still use the *NS* (for NeXTSTEP) prefix in their class names, such as NSString and NSArray.

Other programming APIs include the BSD API, which provides application access to low-level file and device access, as well as the POSIX threading API (pthreads). The BSD layer, unlike Cocoa, does not provide facilities for programming applications with a graphical user interface. Mac OS X has another major API, called Carbon. Carbon is a C-based API that overlaps with Cocoa in terms of functionality. It originally provided some backward compatibility with earlier versions of Mac OS. The Carbon API is now deprecated in favor of Cocoa for GUI applications, but remains in OS X to support legacy applications, such as Apple's Final Cut Pro 7. The publically available version of Carbon remains 32-bit only, so Cocoa is needed for 64-bit compatibility. The fourth major API is Java, which has now also been deprecated. Java was removed from default installation in Mac OS X 10.7, although it is still provided as an optional install.

Graphics and multimedia are key differentiators that OS X and iOS offer over other operating systems. Both offer a rich set of APIs for working with graphics and multimedia. The core of the graphics system is the Quartz system. Quartz encompasses the windowing system (Quartz Compositor), as well as the API known as Quartz 2D. Quartz is based on the PDF (Portable Document Format) model. It offers resolution independent user interfaces, as well as anti-aliased rendering of text and graphics. The Quartz Extreme interface offers hardware-assisted OpenGL rendering of windows, where supported by the graphics hardware. Here's a short overview of some important graphics and multimedia frameworks:

- **Quartz:** Consists of the Quartz 2D API and the Quartz Compositor, which provides the graphical window server. Cocoa Drawing offers an object-oriented interface on top of Quartz for use in Cocoa applications.

- **OpenGL:** The industry standard API for developing 3D applications. iOS supports a version of OpenGL called OpenGL ES, a subset designed for embedded devices.

- **Core Animation:** A layer-based API integrated with Cocoa that makes it easy to create animated content and do transformations.

- **Core Image:** Provides support for working with images, including adding effects, cropping, or color correction.

- **Core Audio:** Offers support for audio playback, recording, mixing, and processing.

- **QuickTime:** An advanced library for working with multimedia. It allows playback and the recording of audio and video, including professional formats.

- **Core Text:** A C-based API for text rendering and layout. The Cocoa Text API is based on Core Text.

Supported Platforms

At its release, OS X was only supported on the PowerPC platform. In January 2006, Apple released version 10.4.4, which finally brought Mac OS X to the Intel x86-platform, as announced at WWDC 2005. The reason for transitioning away from the PowerPC platform was, according to Apple, their disappointment in IBM's ability to deliver a competitive microprocessor, especially for low-power processors intended for laptops. The transition to Intel was smooth for Apple, and indeed it is one of the few examples of a successful platform shift within the industry.

Apple provided an elegant solution, called Rosetta, which is a dynamic translator that would allow existing PowerPC applications to run on x86-based Macs (naturally with some performance penalties). Apple also provided developers with Universal Binaries, which allowed native code for more than one architecture to exist within a single binary executable (also referred to as fat binaries). While support for

PowerPC was discontinued, as of Mac OS X 10.6 (Snow Leopard), Universal Binaries is still used to provide 32-bit, and 64-bit x86 or x86_64, executables.

64-bit Operating System

Mac OS X 10.5 (Leopard) allowed, for the first time, GUI applications to be 64-bit native, accomplished through a new 64-bit version of Cocoa, which allowed developers to tap the additional benefits provided by the 64-bit CPUs found in the current generation of Macs. Applications based on the Carbon API are still 32-bit only. The subsequent release of Mac OS X 10.6 (Snow Leopard) took things one-step further by allowing the kernel to run in 64-bit mode.

While most applications and APIs were already 64-bit in Leopard, the kernel itself was still running in 32-bit mode. Although Snow Leopard made a 64-bit mode kernel possible, only some of the models defaulted to 64-bit, while other models required it to be enabled manually. Snow Leopard was the first release that did not include support for PowerPC computers, although PowerPC applications could still be run with Rosetta. Support for Rosetta was removed in Lion, along with support for the 32-bit kernel. While user space is able to support both 64-bit and 32-bit applications side by side, the kernel is incompatible with 32-bit drivers and extensions when running in 64-bit mode. A 64-bit kernel provides many advantages, and a larger address space means large amounts of memory can be supported.

iOS

iOS, or iPhone OS 1.0 as it was initially called, was released in June 2007 (see Table 2-2 for iOS releases). It was based on Mac OS X and shared most of its fundamental architecture with its older sibling. It featured, however, a new and innovative user interface provided by the Cocoa Touch API (sharing many traits and parts with the original Cocoa), which was specifically designed for the iPhone's capacitive touch screen. In addition to Cocoa Touch, iOS had a number of other programming APIs, like the Accelerate framework, which provided math and other related functions, optimized for the iOS hardware. The External Accessory Framework allows iOS devices to communicate with third-party hardware devices via Bluetooth or the inbuilt 30-pin connector.

Table 2-2. iOS Releases

Version	Device	Released
iPhone OS 1.0	iPhone, iPod Touch (1.1)	June 2007
iPhone OS 2.0	iPhone 3G	July 2008
iPhone OS 3.0	iPhone 3GS, iPad (3.2)	June 2009
iOS 4.0	iPhone 4	June 2010
iOS 5.0	iPhone 4S	October 2011

At its launch, iPhone OS was not able to run native third party applications, but it could run web applications tailored to the iPhone, which could be added to the iPhone's home screen. An SDK for the iPhone was later announced at the beginning of 2008, which allowed development of third party applications. Unlike most computer platforms, however, Apple requires all iPhone applications to be submitted and pre-approved, and thus digitally signed, before a customer can install it through the App

Store. While many criticized the approach (and still do), it allowed Apple to weed out poorly written, slow, and malicious software, thereby improving the overall user experience, and ultimately the popularity of the platform. Unofficially, it has been possible to "Jailbreak" iOS and gain access to the underlying Unix and kernel environment, but this voids the warranty. Due to concerns about battery life, the iPhone was not able to properly multitask third-party applications until the release of iOS 4.0. iOS now supports the iPhone, iPod Touch, and iPad, and also runs on the latest generation of Apple TVs, which were previously based on OS X, running on Intel x86 CPUs. Apple does not support third party applications on the Apple TV at this time.

The XNU Kernel

The XNU kernel is large and complex, and a full architectural description is beyond the scope of this book (there are other books that fill this need), but we will, in the following sections, outline some of the major components that make up XNU and offer a brief description of their responsibilities and mode of operation. In most cases when programming for the kernel you will be writing extensions rather than modifying the core kernel itself (unless you happen to be an Apple Engineer or contributor to Darwin), but it is useful to have a basic understanding of the kernel as a whole, as it will give a better understanding of how a kernel extension fit within the bigger picture. Subsequent chapters will focus on some of the more important programming frameworks that the kernel provides such as I/O Kit.

The XNU kernel is the core of Mac OS X and iOS. XNU has a layered architecture consisting of three major components. The inner ring of the kernel is referred to as the Mach layer, derived from the Mach 3.0 kernel developed at Carnegie Mellon University. References to Mach throughout the book will refer to Mach as it is implemented in OS X and iOS and not the original project. Mach was developed as a microkernel, a thin layer providing only fundamental services, such as processor management and scheduling, as well as IPC (inter-process communication), which is a core concept of the Mach kernel. Because of the layered architecture, there are minimal differences between the iOS and Mac OS X versions of XNU.

While the Mach layer in XNU has the same responsibilities as in the original project, other operating system services, such as file systems and networking, run in the same memory space as Mach. Apple cites performance as the key reason for doing this, as switching between address spaces (context switching) is an expensive operation.

Because the Mach layer is still, to some degree, an isolated component, many refer to XNU as a hybrid kernel, as opposed to a microkernel or a monolithic kernel, where all OS services run in the same context. Figure 2-3 shows a simplified view of XNU's architecture.

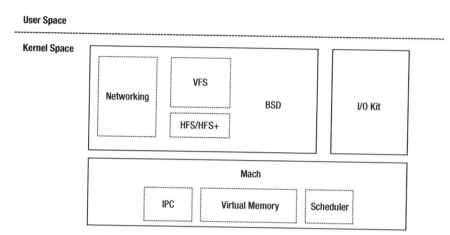

Figure 2-3. *The XNU kernel architecture*

The second major component of XNU is the BSD layer, which can be thought of as an outer ring around the Mach layer. BSD again provides a programming interface to end-user applications. Responsibilities include process management, file systems, and networking.

The last major component is the I/O Kit, which provides an object-oriented framework for device drivers.

While it would be nice if each layer had clear responsibilities, reality is somewhat more complicated and the lines between each layer are blurred, as many OS services and tasks span the borders of multiple components.

▪ **Tip** You can download the full source code for XNU at Apple's open source website:
http://www.opensource.apple.com.

Kernel Extensions (KEXTs)

The XNU kernel, like most, if not all, modern operating systems, supports dynamically loading code into the kernel's address space at runtime. This allows extra functionality, such as drivers, to be loaded and unloaded while the kernel is running. A main focus of this book will be the development of such kernel extensions, with a particular focus on drivers, as this is the most common reason to implement a kernel extension. There are two principal classes of kernel extensions. The first class is for I/O Kit-based kernel extensions, which are used for hardware drivers. These extensions are written in C++. The second class is for generic kernel extensions, which are typically written in C (though C++ is possible here, too). These extensions can implement anything from new network protocols to file systems. Generic kernel extensions usually interface with the BSD or Mach layers.

Mach

The Mach layer can be seen as the core of the kernel, a provider of lower-level services to higher-level components like the BSD layer and I/O Kit. It is responsible for hardware abstraction, hiding the differences between the PowerPC architecture and the Intel x86 and x86-64 architectures. This includes details for handling traps and interrupts, as well as managing memory, including virtual memory and paging. This design allows the kernel to be easily adapted to new hardware architectures, as proven with Apple's move to Intel x86, and later to ARM for iOS. In addition to hardware abstraction, Mach is responsible for the scheduling of threads. It supports symmetric multiprocessing (SMP), which refers to the ability to schedule processes between multiple CPUs or CPU cores. In fact, the difficulty of implementing proper SMP support in the existing BSD Unix kernel was instrumental in the development of Mach.

Interprocess communication (IPC) is the core tenet of Mach's design. IPC in Mach is implemented as a client/server system. A task (the client) is able to request services from another task (the server). The endpoints in this system are known as ports. A port has associated rights, which determine if a client has access to a particular service. This IPC mechanism is used internally throughout the XNU kernel. The following sections will outline the key abstractions and services provided by the Mach layer.

■ **Tip** Mach API documentation can be found in the osfmk/man directory of the XNU source package.

Tasks and Threads

A task is a group consisting of zero or more executable threads that share resources and memory address space. A task needs at least one thread to be executed. A Mach task maps one to one to a Unix (BSD layer) process. The XNU kernel is also a task (known as the kernel_task) consisting of multiple threads. Task resources are private and cannot normally be accessed by the threads of another task.

Unlike a task, a thread is an executable entity that can be scheduled and run by the CPU. A thread shares resources, such as open files or network sockets, with other threads in the same task. Threads of the same task can execute on different CPUs concurrently. A thread has its own state, which includes a copy of the processor state (registers and instruction counter) and its own stack. The state of a thread is restored when it is scheduled to run on a CPU. Mach supports preemptive multitasking, which means that a thread's execution can be interrupted before its allocated time slice (10ms in XNU) is up. Preemption happens under a variety of circumstances, such as when a high priority OS event occurs, when a higher priority thread needs to run, or when waiting for long I/O operations to complete. A thread can also voluntarily preempt itself by going to sleep. A Mach thread is scheduled independently from other threads, regardless of the task to which it belongs. The scheduler is also unaware of process parent-child relationships traditional in Unix systems (the BSD layer, however, is aware).

Scheduling

The scheduler is responsible for coordinating the access of threads to the CPU. Most modern kernels, including XNU, use a timesharing scheduler, where each thread is allocated a finite (10ms in XNU, as we've seen) time quantum in which the thread is allowed to execute. Upon expiration of the thread's quantum, it is put to sleep so that other threads can run. While it may seem reasonable and fair that each thread gets to run for an equal amount of time, this is impractical, as some threads have a greater need for low latencies, for example to perform audio and video playback. The XNU scheduler employs a priority-based algorithm to schedule threads. Table 2-3 shows the priority levels used by the scheduler.

Table 2-3. Scheduler Priority Levels

Priority	Level	Description
Normal	0–51	Normal applications. The default priority for a regular application thread is 31. Zero is the idle priority.
High Priority	52–79	High priority threads.
Kernel Mode	80–95	Range is reserved for high priority kernel threads, for example those used by a device driver.
Real-time	96–127	Real-time threads (user space threads can run in real-time).

The kernel organizes threads in doubly-linked lists. This collection of lists is known as the *run queue*. There is one list per priority level (currently 0–127). Each processor (core) in the system maintains its own run queue structure (osfmk/kern/sched.h):

```
struct run_queue {
        int             highq;              /* highest runnable queue */
        int             bitmap[NRQBM];      /* run queue bitmap array */
        int             count;              /* # of threads total */
        int             urgency;            /* level of preemption urgency */
        queue_head_t    queues[NRQS];       /* one for each priority */
};
```

A regular application thread starts with a priority of 31. Its priority may decrease over time, as a side effect of the scheduling algorithm. This will happen, for example, if a thread is highly compute intensive. By lowering the priority of such threads, it will improve the scheduling latency of I/O bound threads, which spend most of their time sleeping in-between issuing I/O requests, thus usually going back to sleep before their quantum expires, and thus allowing compute intensive threads access to the CPU again. The end result is improved system responsiveness.

To avoid getting into a situation where the thread's priority will be too low for it to run, the Mach scheduler will decay a thread's processor usage accounting over time, eventually resetting it, and thus a thread's priority will fluctuate over time.

The Mach scheduler provides support for real-time threads, although it does not provide guaranteed latency; however, every effort is made to ensure it will run for the required amount of clock cycles. A real-time thread may be downgraded to normal priority if it does not block/sleep frequently enough, for example if it is highly compute bound.

Mach IPC: Ports and Messages

A port is a unidirectional communications endpoint, which represents a resource referred to as an object. If you are familiar with TCP/IP networking, many parallels can be drawn between Mach's IPC and the UDP protocol, though unlike the UDP protocol, Mach IPC is used for more than just data transfers. It can be used to provide synchronization, or to send notifications between tasks. An IPC client can send messages to a port. The owner of the port receives the messages. For bidirectional communication, two ports are needed. A port is implemented as a message queue (though other mechanisms exist). Messages for the port are queued until a thread is available to service them. A port can receive messages from multiple senders, but there can be only one receiver per port.

Ports have protection mechanisms known as port rights. A task must have the proper permissions in order to interact with a port. Port rights are associated with a task; therefore, all threads in a task share the same privileges to a port. The following are examples of port rights: send, send once, and receive. The rights can be copied or moved between tasks. Unlike Unix permissions, port rights are not inherited from parent to child processes (Mach tasks do not have this concept). Table 2-4 shows the available port right types.

Table 2-4. Port Right Types (from mach/port.h)

Port Right Type	Description
MACH_PORT_RIGHT_SEND	The holder of the right has permission to send messages to a port.
MACH_PORT_RIGHT_RECIEVE	The holder has the right to receive messages from a port. Receive rights provide automatic send rights.
MACH_PORT_RIGHT_SEND_ONCE	Same as send rights, but only valid for one message.
MACH_PORT_RIGHT_PORT_SET	Receive (and send) rights to a group of ports.
MACH_PORT_RIGHT_DEAD_NAME	Denotes rights that have become invalid or been destroyed, such as after messaging a port with send once rights.

A group of ports are collectively known as a port set. The message queue is shared between all ports in a set. A 32-bit integer number addresses ports in the system. There is no global register or namespace for ports.

The Mach IPC system is also available in user space programs and can be used to pass messages between tasks or from a task to the kernel. It offers an alternative to system calls, though the mechanism uses system calls under the hood.

Mach Exceptions

Exceptions are interrupts sent by a CPU when certain (exceptional) events or conditions occur during the execution of a thread. An exception will result in the interruption of a thread's execution, while the OS (Mach) processes the exception. The task may resume afterwards, depending on the type of exception that occurred. Common causes for exceptions include access to invalid or non-existing memory, execution of an invalid processor instruction, passing invalid arguments, or division by zero. These exceptions usually result in the termination of the offending task, but there are also a number of non-erroneous exceptions that can occur.

A system call is one such exception. A user space application may issue a system call exception when it needs to perform a low-level operation involving the kernel, such as writing from a file, or receiving data on a network socket. When the OS handles the system call, it inspects a register for the system call number, which is then used to look up the handler for that call, for example read() or recv().

A task may also generate an exception if attempting to access paged out memory. In this case, a page fault exception is generated, which will be handled by retrieving the missing page from the backing store, or result in an invalid memory access. A task may also issue deliberate exceptions with the EXC_BREAKPOINT exception, which are typically used in debugging or tracing applications, such as Xcode, to temporarily halt the execution of a thread.

It is possible, of course, for the kernel itself to misbehave and cause exceptions. In this case, the OS will be halted and the *grey screen of death* will be shown (unless the kernel debugger is activated), informing the user to reboot the computer. Table 2-5 shows a subset of defined Mach exceptions.

Table 2-5. Common Mach Exception Types

Exception Type	Description
EXC_BAD_ACCESS	Invalid memory access.
EXC_BAD_INSTRUCTION	The thread attempted to access an illegal/invalid instruction or gave an invalid parameter (operand) to the instruction.
EXC_ARITMETHIC	Issued on division by zero or integer overflow/underflow.
EXC_SYSCALL and EXC_MACH_SYSCALL	Issued by an application to access kernel services such as file I/O or network access.
...	Other Mach exceptions are defined in mach/exception_types.h. Processor dependent exceptions are defined in mach/(i386,ppc, ...)/exception.h.

When an exception occurs, the kernel will suspend the thread which caused the exception, and send an IPC message to the thread's exception port. If the thread does not handle the exception, it's forwarded to the containing task's exception port, and finally to the system's (host) exception port. The following structure encapsulates a thread, task, or processor's (host) exception ports:

```
struct exception_action {
        struct ipc_port*        port;           /* exception port */
        thread_state_flavor_t   flavor;         /* state flavor to send */
        exception_behavior_t    behavior;       /* exception type to raise */
        boolean_t               privileged;     /* survives ipc_task_reset */
};
```

Each thread, task, and host has an array of the structure exception_action, which specifies exception behavior, one structure is defiend for each exception type (as defined in Table 2-5). The flavor and behavior fields specify the type of information that should be sent with the exception message, such as the state of general purpose, or other specialized CPU registers, and the handler, which should be executed. The handler will be either catch_mach_exception_raise(), catch_mach_exception_raise_state() or catch_mach_exception_raise_state_identity(). When an exception has been dispatched, the kernel waits for a reply in order to determine the course of action. A return of KERN_SUCCESS means the exception was handled, and the thread will be allowed to resume.

A thread's exception port defaults to PORT_NULL, unless a port is explicitly allocated, exceptions will be handled by task's exception port instead. When a process issues the fork() system call to spawn a child process, the child will inherit exception ports from the parent task. The Unix signaling mechanism is implemented on top of the Mach's exception system.

Time Management

Proper timekeeping is a vital responsibility of any OS, not only to serve user applications, but also to serve other important kernel functions such as scheduling processes. In Mach, the abstraction for time management is known as a clock. A clock object in Mach represents time in nanoseconds as a monotonically increasing value. There are three main clocks defined: the real-time clock, the calendar clock, and the high-resolution clock. The real-time clock keeps the time since the last boot, while the calendar clock is typically battery backed, so its value is persistent across system reboots, or in periods when the computer is powered off. It has a resolution of seconds and as the name implies, it is used to keep track of the current time. The Mach time KPI consists of three functions:

```
void clock_get_uptime(uint64_t* result);
void clock_get_system_nanotime(uint32_t* secs, uint32_t* nanosecs);
void clock_get_calendar_nanotime(uint32_t* secs, uint32_t* nanosecs);
```

The calendar clock is typically only used by applications, as the kernel itself rarely needs to concern itself with the current time or date, and doing so, in fact, is considered poor design. The kernel uses the relative time provided by the real-time clock. The time from the real-time clock typically comes from a circuit on the computer's motherboard that contains an oscillating crystal. The real-time clock circuit (RTC) is programmable, and wired to the CPUs' (every CPU/core) interrupt pins. The RTC gets programmed in XNU with a deadline of 100 Hz (using clock_set_timer_deadline()).

Memory Management

The Mach layer is responsible for coordinating the use of physical memory in a machine independent manner, providing a consistent interface to higher-level components. The virtual memory subsystem of Mach, the Mach VM, provides protected memory and facilities to applications, and the kernel itself, for allocating, sharing, and mapping memory. A solid understanding of memory management is essential to a successful kernel programmer.

Task Address Space

Each Mach task has its own virtual address (VM) space. For a 32-bit task, the address space is 4 GB, while for a 64-bit task it is substantially larger, with 51-bits (approximately 2 petabytes) of usable address space. Specialized applications, such as video editing or effects software, often exceed the 32-bit address space. Support for 64-bit virtual address space became available in OS X 10.4.

■ **Note** While 32-bit applications are limited to a 4 GB address space, this does not correlate with the amount of physical memory that can be used in a system. Technologies such as Physical Address Extensions (PAE) are supported by OS X and allow 32-bit x86 processors (or 64-bit processors running in 32-bit mode) to address up to 36-bits (64 GB) of physical memory; however, a task's address space remains limited to 4 GB.

A task's address space is fundamental to the concept of protected memory. A task is not allowed to access the address space, and thus the underlying physical memory containing the data of another task, unless explicitly allowed to do so, through the use of shared memory or other mechanisms.

KERNEL ADDRESS SPACE MANAGEMENT

The kernel itself has its own task, the kernel_task, which has its own seperate address space. Let's assume a 32-bit OS such as iOS. Some Unix-based operating systems, including Linux, have a design where the kernel's address space is mapped into each task's address space. The kernel has 1GB of address space available, while a task has 3GB available. When a task context switches into kernel space, the MMU (memory management unit) can avoid reconfiguring the translation lookaside buffer (TLB) with a new address space, as the kernel is already at a known location, thus speeding up the otherwise expensive context switch. The drawback, of course, is the limited amount of address space available for the kernel, as well as having only 3GB available for the task. In XNU, the kernel runs in its own virtual address space, which is not shared with user tasks, leaving 4GB for the kernel and 4GB for the user task.

VM Maps and Entries

The virtual memory (VM) map is the actual representation of a task's address space. Each task has its own VM map. The map is represented by the structure vm_map. There is no map associated with a thread as they share the VM map of the task that owns them.

A VM map represents a doubly-linked list of memory regions that is mapped into the process address space. Each region is a virtually contiguous range of memory addresses (not necessarily backed by contiguous physical memory) described by a start and end address, as well as other meta-data, such as protection flags, which can be any combination of read, write, and execute. The regions are represented by the vm_map_entry structure. A VM map entry may be merged with another adjacent entry when more memory is allocated before or after an existing entry or split into smaller regions. Splitting will occur if the protection flags are modified for a range of addresses described by an entry, as protection flags can only be set on VM map entries. Figure 2-4 shows a VM map with two VM map entries.

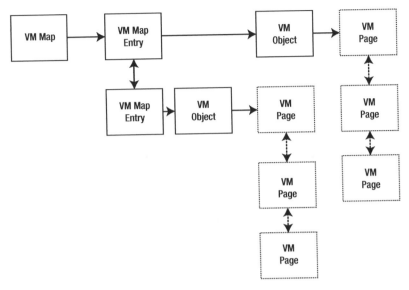

Figure 2-4. Relationship between VM subsystem structures

▓ **Tip** The relevant structures pertaining to task address spaces are defined in mach/vm_map.h and mach/vm_region.h in the XNU source package.

The Physical Map

Each VM map has an associated physical map, or pmap structure. This structure helps hold information on virtual to physical memory mappings being used by the task. The portion of the Mach VM that deals with physical mappings is machine dependent, as it interacts with the memory management unit (MMU), a specialized hardware component of the system that takes care of address translation.

VM Objects

A VM map entry can point to either a VM object or a VM submap. A submap is a container for other (VM map) mappings. A submap is used to share memory between addresses spaces. The VM object is a representation of the location, or rather how the described memory is accessed. Memory pages underlying the object may not be present in physical memory, but could be located on an external backing store (a hard drive on OS X). In this case, the VM object will have information on how to *page in* the external pages. Transfer to or from a backing store is handled by the *pager* discussed next.

A VM object describes memory in units of pages. A page in XNU is currently 4096 bytes. A virtual page is described by the vm_page structure. A VM object may contain many pages, but a page is only ever associated with one VM object.

PAGES

A page is the smallest unit of the virtual memory system. On Mac OS X and iOS, as well as many other operating systems, the size of a page is 4096 bytes (4KB). The page size is determined by the processor, as the processor, or rather its memory management unit (MMU), is responsible for virtual to physical mappings and manages the VM page table cache, also called a TLB. The page size of many architectures can be set by the operating system, and can be, for architectures such as the x86, up to 4 MB, or even a mixture between more than one page size. The operating system maintains a data structure called the page table, which contains one `struct vm_page` for each page-sized block of physical memory. The structure contains metadata, such as whether the page is in use.

When memory needs to be shared between tasks, a VM map entry will point into the foreign address space via a submap, as opposed to a VM object. This commonly happens when a shared library is used. The shared library gets mapped into the task's address space.

Let's consider another example. When a Unix process issues the fork() system call to create a child process, a new process will be created as a copy of the parent. To avoid having to copy the memory from the parent to the child, an optimization known as copy-on-write (COW) is employed. Read access to a child's memory will simply reference the same pages as the parent. If the child process modifies its memory, the page describing that memory will be copied, and a shadow VM object will be created. On the next read to that memory region, a check is performed to see if the shadow object has a copy of the page, and if not the original shared page is referenced. The previously described behavior is only true when the inheritance property of the original VM map entry from the parent is set to *copy*. Other possible values are *shared*, in which case the child will continue both the read and write operation to the original memory location. If the setting is *none*, the memory pages referenced by the map entry will not be mapped into the child's address space. The fourth possible value is *copy and delete*, where the memory will be copied to the child and deleted from the parent.

▓ **Note** Copy-on-write is also used by Mach IPC to optimize the transfer of data between tasks.

Examining a Task's Address Space

The vmmap command line utility allows you to inspect a process virtual memory map and its VM map entries. It clearly illustrates how memory regions are mapped into a task's VM address space. The vmmap command takes a process identifier (PID) as an argument. The following shows the output of vmmap executed with the PID of a simple Hello World C application (a.out), which prints a message and then goes to sleep:

```
==== Non-writable regions for process 46874
__PAGEZERO        00000000-00001000  [    4K] ---/--- SM=NUL  /Users/ole/a.out
__TEXT            00001000-00002000  [    4K] r-x/rwx SM=COW  /Users/ole/a.out
__LINKEDIT        00003000-00004000  [    4K] r--/rwx SM=COW  /Users/ole/a.out
MALLOC guard page 00004000-00005000  [    4K] ---/rwx SM=NUL
```

```
MALLOC metadata      00021000-00022000  [     4K] r--/rwx SM=PRV
__TEXT               8fe00000-8fe42000  [   264K] r-x/rwx SM=COW  /usr/lib/dyld
__LINKEDIT           8fe70000-8fe84000  [    80K] r--/rwx SM=COW  /usr/lib/dyld
__TEXT               9703b000-971e3000  [  1696K] r-x/r-x SM=COW  /usr/lib/libSystem.B.dylib
STACK GUARD          bc000000-bf800000  [  56.0M] ---/rwx SM=NUL  stack guard for thread 0
==== Writable regions for process 46874
__DATA               00002000-00003000  [     4K] rw-/rwx SM=PRV  /Users/ole/a.out
MALLOC metadata      00015000-00020000  [    44K] rw-/rwx SM=PRV
MALLOC_TINY          00100000-00200000  [  1024K] rw-/rwx SM=PRV  DefaultMallocZone_0x5000
MALLOC_SMALL         00800000-01000000  [  8192K] rw-/rwx SM=PRV  DefaultMallocZone_0x5000
__DATA               8fe42000-8fe6f000  [   180K] rw-/rwx SM=PRV  /usr/lib/dyld
__IMPORT             8fe6f000-8fe70000  [     4K] rwx/rwx SM=COW  /usr/lib/dyld
shared pmap          a0800000-a093a000  [  1256K] rw-/rwx SM=COW
__DATA               a093a000-a0952000  [    96K] rw-/rwx SM=COW  /usr/lib/libSystem.B.dylib
shared pmap          a0952000-a0a00000  [   696K] rw-/rwx SM=COW
Stack                bf800000-bffff000  [  8188K] rw-/rwx SM=ZER  thread 0
Stack                bffff000-c0000000  [     4K] rw-/rwx SM=COW  thread 0
```

The result has been trimmed for readability. The output is divided between non-writable regions and writable regions. The former, as you can see, includes the page zero mapping, which is read-only and will generate an exception if an application tries to write to memory addresses 0-4096 (4096 decimal = 0x1000 hex). This is why your application will crash if you try to dereference a null-pointer. The next map entry is the text segment of the application, which contains the executable code of the application. You will see that the text segment is marked as having a share mode (SM) of COW, which means that if this process spawns a child, it will inherit this mapping from the parent, thus avoiding a copy until pages in that segment are modified.

In addition to the text segment for the a.out program itself, you will also see a mapping for libSystem.B.dylib. On Mac OS X and iOS, libSystem implements the standard C Library and the POSIX thread API, as well as other system APIs. The a.out process inherited the mapping for libSystem from its parent process /sbin/launchd, the parent of all user space processes. This ensures the library is only loaded once, saving memory and improving the launch speed of applications, as fetching a library from secondary storage, such as a hard drive, is usually slow.

In the writable regions you can see the data segment of a.out and libSystem. These segments contain variables defined by the program/library. Obviously, these can be modified, so each process needs a copy of the data segment for a shared library, however it is COW, so no overhead is necessary until a process makes modifications to the mapping.

▪ **Tip** If you want to inspect the virtual memory map of a system process, such as launchd, you need to run vmmap with sudo, as by default your user will only be able to inspect its own processes.

Pagers

Virtual memory allows a process to have a virtual address space larger than the available physical memory, and it is possible for tasks running on the system to be combined, consuming more than the available amount of memory. The mechanism that makes this possible is known as a *pager*. The pager controls the transfer of memory pages to and from the system memory (RAM), to a secondary backing store, usually a hard drive. When a task that has high memory requirements needs to run, the *pager* can temporarily transfer (page out) memory pages belonging to inactive tasks to the backing store, thereby freeing up enough memory to allow the demanding task to execute. Similarly, if a process is found to be largely idle, the system can opt to page out the task's memory to free memory for current or future tasks. When an application runs, and it tries to access memory that has been paged out, an exception known as a page fault will occur, which is also the exception that occurs if a task tries to access an invalid memory address. When the page fault occurs, the kernel will attempt to transfer back (page in) the page corresponding to the memory address, and if the page cannot be transferred back, it will be treated as an invalid memory access, and the task will be aborted. The XNU kernel supports three different pagers:

- **Default Pager:** Performs traditional paging and transfers between the main memory and a swap file on the system hard drive (/var/vm/swapfile*).

- **Vnode Pager:** Ties in with the Unified Buffer Cache (UBC) used by file systems and is used to cache files in memory.

- **Device Pager:** Used for managing memory mappings of hardware devices, such as PCI devices that map registers into memory. Mapped memory is commonly used by I/O Kit drivers, and I/O Kit provides abstractions for working with such memory.

Which pager is in use is more or less transparent to higher-level parts, such as the VM object. Each VM object has an associated *memory object,* which provides (via ports) an interface to the current pager.

Memory Allocation in Mach

Some fundamental routines for memory allocation in Mach are:

```
kern_return_t kmem_alloc(vm_map_t map, vm_offset_t *addrp, vm_size_t  size);
kern_return_t kmem_alloc_contig(vm_map_t map, vm_offset_t *addrp,
                                vm_size_t size, vm_offset_t mask, int flags);
void kmem_free(vm_map_t map, vm_offset_t addr, vm_size_t size);
```

kmem_alloc() provides the main interface to obtaining memory in Mach. In order to allocate memory, you must provide a VM map. For most work within the kernel, kernel_map is defined and points to the VM map of kernel_task. The second variant, kmem_alloc_contig(), attempts to allocate memory that is physically contiguous, as opposed to the former, which allocates virtually contiguous memory. Apple recommends against making this type of allocation, as there is a significant penalty incurred in searching for free contiguous blocks. Mach also provides kmem_alloc_aligned() function, which allocates memory aligned to a power of two, as well as a few other variants that are less commonly used. The kmem_free() function is provided to free allocated memory. You have to take care to pass the same VM map as you used when you allocated, as well as the size of the original allocation.

The BSD Layer

Unlike Mach, which only provides a few fundamental services, the BSD layer sits between Mach and the user applications and implements many core OS functions, building on the services provided by Mach. In OS X and iOS, the BSD layer is running with the processor in privileged mode and not as a user task, as originally intended by the Mach project. The layer therefore does not have memory protection, and runs in the same address space as Mach and I/O Kit. The BSD layer refers to a portion of the kernel derived from the FreeBSD 5 operating system, and it is not a complete system in itself, but rather a portion of code originating from it.

The BSD layer provides services such as process management, system calls, file systems, and networking. Table 2-6 shows a brief overview of the services provided by the BSD layer.

Table 2-6. BSD Layer Services Overview

Service	Description
Process and User Management	Provides support for user (uid), group (gid), and process (pid) ids, as well as process creation (fork) and the Unix security model. POSIX threads and synchronization. Shared library support, signal handling.
File Management	Files, pipes, sockets, and POSIX IPC. The VFS, as well as the HFS, HFS+, ISO, and NFS file systems. Asynchronous I/O.
Security	Security auditing and cryptographic algorithms, such as AES, Blowfish, DES, MD5, and SHA-1.
Memory Management	The *vnode* file-based pager. Facilities for memory allocation. Unified Buffer Cache (UBC).
Drivers	Various drivers, including the console and other character device drivers such as /dev/null, /dev/zero, /dev/random, and RAM disk driver (/dev/md*).
Networking	TCP/IP 4&6, DHCP, ICMP, ARP, Ethernet, Routing and Firewall, Packet filters (BPF), and BSD sockets. Low-level network drivers are found in I/O Kit.
System Calls	Provides an API for granting user space applications access to basic/low-level kernel services such as file and process management.

The BSD layer provides abstractions on top of the services provided by Mach. For example, its process management and memory management is implemented on top of Mach services.

System Calls

When an application needs services from the file system, or wishes to access the network, it needs to issue a system call to the kernel. The BSD layer implements all system calls. When a system call handler executes, the kernel context switches from user mode to kernel mode to service a request by the application, such as to read a file. This API is referred to as the syscall API, and it is the traditional Unix API for calling functions in the kernel from user space. There are hundreds of system calls available, ranging from calls related to process control, such as fork() and execve(), or file management calls, such as open(), close(), read(), and write().

The BSD layer also provides ioctl() function (itself a system call), which is short for I/O control, and this is typically used to send commands to device drivers. The sysctl() function is provided to set or get a variety of kernel parameters, including but not limited to the scheduler, memory, and networking subsystems.

■ **Tip** Available system calls are defined in /usr/include/sys/syscall.h.

Mach traps are mechanisms similar to system calls, used for crossing the kernel/user space boundary. Unlike system calls that provide direct services to an application, the Mach traps are used to carry IPC messages from a user space client to a kernel server.

Networking

Networking is a major subsystem of the BSD portion of XNU. BSD handles most aspects of networking, such as the details of socket communication and the implementation of protocols like TCP/IP, except for low-level communication with actual hardware devices, which is typically handled by an I/O Kit driver. The I/O Kit network driver will interface with the network stack that is responsible for handling received buffers from the networking device, inspect them, and ensure they make their way down to the initiator, for example your web browser. Similarly, the BSD networking stack will accept outgoing data from an application, format the data in a packet, then route or dispatch it to the appropriate network interface. BSD also implements the IPFW firewall, which will filter packets to/from the computer according to policy set by the system administrator.

The BSD networking layer supports a wide range of network and transport layer protocols, including IPv4 and IPv6, TCP, and UDP. At the higher level we find support for BOOTP, DHCP, and ICMP, among others. Other networking-related functions include routing, bridging, and Network Address Translation (NAT), as well as device level packet filtering with Berkeley Packet Filter (BPF).

NETWORK KERNEL EXTENSIONS (NKE)

The Network Kernel Extensions KPI (kernel programming interface) is a mechanism that allows various parts of the networking stack to be extended. NKEs allow new protocols to be defined, and for hooks or filters to be inserted at various levels in the networking stack. For example, it would be possible to create a filter that intercepted TCP connections to a certain address by a certain application or user. It is also possible to temporarily block network packets, or modify them before transmission to a higher/lower level. NKEs originate from Apple and are not part of the traditional BSD networking stack, but, due to their nature, they are now intimately tied to it. NKEs are discussed in Chapter 13.

File Systems

The kernel has inbuilt support for a range of different file systems, as shown in Table 2-7. The primary file system used by Mac OS X and iOS is HFS+. It was developed as a replacement for the Mac OS file system HFS.

Table 2-7. File Systems Support by XNU

Name	Description
HFS+	The standard file system used by Mac OS X and iOS
HFS	Legacy Mac OS file system
UFS	The BSD Unix file system
NFS	Networked File System
ISO 9660 and UDF	Standard file systems used by CDs and DVDs
SMB	Server Message Block, a networked file system used to connect with Microsoft Windows computers
AFP	Apple Filing Protocol

HFS+ gained support for journaling in Mac OS X 10.2.2. Journaling improves the reliability of a file system by recording transactions in a *journal* prior to carrying them out. This makes the file system resilient to events such as a power failure or a crash of the kernel, as the data can be replayed after reboot in order to bring the file system to a consistent state.

HFS+ supports very large files, up to 8 EiB in size (1 Exbibyte = 2^{60} bytes), which is also the maximum possible volume size. The file system has full support for Unicode characters in file names and is case insensitive by default. Support for both Unix style file permissions and access control lists (ACLs) exists.

The Virtual File System

The virtual file system, or VFS, provides an abstraction over specific file systems, such as HFS+ and AFP, and makes it possible for applications to access them using a single consistent interface. The VFS allows support for new file systems to be easily added as kernel extensions through the VFS Kernel Programming Interface (KPI), without the OS as a whole knowing anything about its implementation. The fundamental data structure of the VFS is the vnode. The vnode is how both a file and a directory are represented in the kernel. A vnode structure exists for every file active in the kernel.

Unified Buffer Cache

The Unified Buffer Cache (UBC) is a cache for files. When a file is written to, or read from, it will be loaded into physical memory from a backing store, such as a hard drive. The UBC is intimately linked with the VM subsystem and the UBC also caches VM objects. The structure used to cache a vnode is shown in Listing 2-1.

Listing 2-1. The ubc_info Structure

```
struct ubc_info {
        memory_object_t         ui_pager;       /* pager */
        memory_object_control_t ui_control;     /* VM control for the pager */
        uint32_t                ui_flags;       /* flags */
        vnode_t                 ui_vnode;       /* vnode for this ubc_info */
        kauth_cred_t            ui_ucred;       /* holds credentials for NFS paging */
        off_t                   ui_size;        /* file size for the vnode */

        struct  cl_readahead*   cl_rahead;      /* cluster read ahead context */
        struct  cl_writebehind* cl_wbehind;     /* cluster write behind context */

        struct  cs_blob*        cs_blobs;       /* for CODE SIGNING */
};
```

Prior to the introduction of the UBC, the system had two caches, a page cache and a buffer cache. The buffer cache was indexed by a device and block number that addressed a chunk of data on the physical device, whereas the page cache performed caching of memory mappings.

The size of the UBC shrinks and grows dynamically depending on the needs of the system. If a file in the cache is modified, it is marked as dirty, to indicate that the cached copy differs from the original found on disk. Dirty entries are periodically flushed to disk. It is possible for a user space program to bypass UBC, and go directly to disk, by using the F_NOCACHE option of the *fcntl* system call, which may improve I/O performance for workloads that do not benefit from such caching, such as large sets of data that are unlikely to be reused.

The I/O Kit

The last major component that makes up XNU is the I/O Kit, which is an object-oriented framework for writing device drivers and other kernel extensions. It provides an abstraction of system hardware, with pre-defined base classes for many types of hardware, making it simple to implement a new driver, as it is able to inherit much of its functionality from a base class driver, achieving a high degree of code reuse. The I/O Kit framework consists of the kernel level framework, as well as a user space framework called IOKit.framework. The kernel framework is written in Embedded C++, a subset of C++, whereas the user space framework is C-based.

The I/O Kit maintains a database known as the I/O Catalog. The I/O Catalog is a registry of all available I/O Kit classes. Another database, the I/O Registry tracks object instances of classes in the I/O Catalog. Objects in the I/O Registry typically represent devices, drivers, or supporting classes, and are structured in a hierarchical manner, which mimics the way hardware devices are physically connected to each other. For example a USB device is a child of the USB controller it is connected to. The ioreg command line utility allows you to inspect the I/O Registry.

The I/O Kit is based around three major concepts:

- Families

- Drivers

- Nubs

Families represent common abstractions for devices of a particular type. For example, an IOUSBFamily handles many of the technicalities of implementing support for USB related devices.

Drivers are responsible for managing a specific device or bus. A driver may have a relationship with more than one family. In the case of a USB-based storage device, it might depend on the IOUSBFamily, as well as the IOStorageFamily. Nubs are interfaces for a controllable entity, such as a PCI or USB device, which a higher-level driver may use to communicate with the device.

As a kernel programmer, you will probably spend most of your time working with the I/O Kit, and thus much of this book will be devoted to it, and a full description of I/O Kit is provided in Chapter 4.

The Libkern Library

The libkern library, unlike Mach and BSD, which provide APIs for interacting with the system, provides supporting routines and classes to the rest of the kernel, and in particular the I/O Kit. That is, building blocks and utilities useful to the kernel itself, as well as extensions. The limited C++ runtime is implemented in libkern, which provides implementation for services such as the new and delete operators.

In addition to standard C++ runtime, libkern also provides a number of useful classes, the most fundamental being OSObject, the superclass of every class in I/O Kit. It provides support for reference counting, which works conceptually the same as NSObject in Cocoa, or Cocoa Touch in user space. Other classes of interest include OSDictionary, OSArray, OSString, and OSInteger. These classes, and others, are also used to provide a dictionary of values from the kernel extension's Info.plist.

The libkern library is not all about core C++ classes and runtime, as it also provides the implementation of many functions normally found in the standard C library. Examples of this are the printf() and sccanf() functions, as well as others such as strtol() and strsep(). Other functions provided by libkern include cryptographic hash algorithms (MD5 and SHA-1), UUID generation, and the zlib compression library. The library is also home to *kxld*, the library used to manage dynamically loaded kernel extensions.

Last, but not least, we find functions, such as OSMalloc(), for allocating memory and for the implementation of locking mechanisms and synchronization primitives.

■ **Note** The sources for libkern are found in the libkern/ and bsd/libkern/ directories in the XNU source distribution.

The Platform Expert

The platform expert contains an abstraction layer for the system. Parts of it are available as part of the public XNU source code distribution, but the remainder is implemented in the com.apple.driver.AppleACPIPlatform KEXT, for which no source code is available. The platform expert handles device enumeration and detection for the system bus. It can be seen as the driver for the motherboard. The platform expert is responsible for the initial construction of the I/O Kit device tree after the system boots (known as the I/O Registry). The platform expert itself will form the root node of the tree, IOPlatformExpertDevice.

Summary

In this chapter we have:

- Given an overview of the Mac OS X and iOS operating systems. We have discussed their general background and origin, with a particular focus on the kernel, the major topic of this book.

- Looked at the XNU kernel, which is the kernel for both OS X and iOS.

- Discussed the layered architecture of the XNU kernel, which consists of three major components: the Mach, the BSD, and the I/O Kit. The Mach layer can be seen as the inner ring, closest to the hardware, which provides services to the rest of the kernel. Services provided by the Mach layer include hardware abstraction, virtual memory, and task scheduling.

- Discussed the operation of the Mach scheduler, and the difference between tasks and threads. A task can be seen as a container for threads that share a common memory address space, as well as other resources, such as open files.

- Discussed Mach IPC, which is the mechanism used for communication within the kernel and the various layers it contains. Furthermore, we broke down the various components involved in providing virtual memory in Mach. Namely, the VM map, VM map entry, and VM objects.

- Discussed the role and operation of pagers.

- Discussed the BSD layer, which was derived from the FreeBSD operating system and runs on top of the Mach core, but in the same kernel address space. It provides the interface applications used to communicate with the kernel, most importantly the system calls. The BSD layer implements the networking stack, including TCP/IP and other protocols. It also provides support for file systems such as HFS+ that are implemented on top of the virtual file system layer (VFS), which is a unified interface for file systems.

- Discussed the I/O Kit, a C++ based kernel framework for writing device drivers and other extensions. The libkern library provides many utility functions and building blocks, including the set of classes that I/O Kit is built in top of, such as OSObject.

CHAPTER 3

Xcode and the Kernel Development Environment

Apple has a good track record of taking care of its developers and providing them with intuitive, user-friendly tools and APIs to develop for the Mac and iOS platforms. Anyone who has written application software for the Mac or iPhone will be familiar with the object-oriented Cocoa framework, which provides a rich set of interfaces to support graphical user interfaces and other services required by user applications. Likewise, kernel developers are provided with APIs that are designed to help with the tasks performed by a kernel extension. For driver development, Apple provides the I/O Kit, which is an object-oriented framework for interfacing with hardware. The following chapter discusses the tools and frameworks you will need to get started with kernel development and includes a tutorial for building and installing a simple kernel extension.

Language of Choice: C++

The C language has been the *de facto* system-level language for decades. Indeed, the language was originally developed as an alternative to writing non-portable assembly code specifically for the original Unix system. The XNU kernel and many Mac OS X core services are written in C, while the I/O Kit framework used for driver development is written in a subset of the C++ language. Apple chose C++ for the I/O Kit because it is an object-oriented language and therefore allows a driver model that abstracts the physical hardware connections. Apple did toy with the idea of an Objective-C-based framework for drivers, but finally settled on C++. Despite the widespread use of C++ for the development of application software, Mac OS X is still one of the few operating systems that allows and in fact encourages C++ code to be run in its kernel. However, this is not to say the Mac OS X kernel is immune from the same problems that make C++ code problematic in other kernels. To avoid some of these problems, Mac OS X kernel code must use a restricted subset of the features provided by C++, referred to as Embedded C++. The features that are not available include the following:

- Exceptions
- Multiple inheritance
- Templates
- Runtime type information

It is worth noting that, because Embedded C++ is a subset of the standard C++ language, any code written for Embedded C++ is compatible with a regular C++ compiler.

While technically possible to include these language features in the kernel, Apple decided to disable them because they can greatly increase the size of the compiled code, which in turn increases the memory footprint of the kernel. Support for exceptions was disabled not only because of the additional code size but also because failure to catch an exception would result in a kernel panic.

Although the standard runtime type information is disabled, the I/O Kit does provide its own limited implementation, which is discussed in the following chapter. Kernel developers also have access to a limited implementation of the C++ runtime library and with language support for templates disabled, the STL classes are unavailable.

As a general rule, C++ is used when writing kernel extensions based on the I/O Kit framework, whereas C is used for everything else, including implementation of file systems and low-level networking code.

Xcode

To begin developing a kernel extension, you will need to install Apple's development tools, known as Xcode. These are available from the Mac App Store. Installing the Xcode package adds a directory to the root level of your hard disk named "Developer," which includes everything that is required for both Mac OS X and iOS development, including the following:

- An integrated development environment (the Xcode application)

- Compilers for C, C++, and Objective-C

- A source code debugger

- The APIs and header files used for kernel and application development

- Profiling tools for measuring your code's execution time and identifying performance bottlenecks

- Utilities for examining the hardware devices connected to the system and the driver that has been loaded for each device

Of these tools, the Xcode application is the one in which you will spend most of your time when writing a kernel extension, since it provides the source code editor and a front-end to the compiler. Figure 3-1 shows the Xcode 4 user interface.

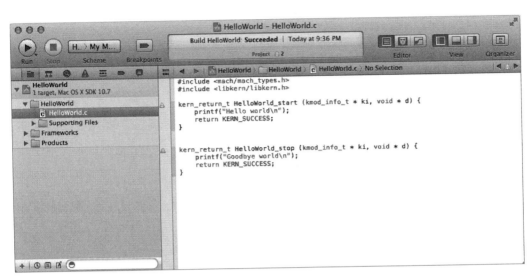

Figure 3-1. The Xcode 4 user interface

Under the hood, Xcode is a front-end to the command-line compiler and debugger. In fact, there is nothing to stop you from bypassing Xcode completely and building your kernel extensions by invoking GCC directly on the command line. However, as we will see in the next section, Xcode provides project templates that pass the appropriate compiler flags for building a kernel extension.

Previous versions of Xcode used the GCC compiler; however, starting from Xcode 4, an alternative and modern compiler based on LLVM is provided as the default compiler. The LLVM compiler is an open source project led by Apple that supports Objective-C, C, and C++. The goal of LLVM is to provide faster compile times than GCC and to provide tighter integration into IDEs, such as Xcode, by providing more legible warning and error messages and by allowing syntax highlighting and code completion to be driven by the semantic analysis performed by the compiler itself.

■ **Note** More information about Xcode, including information about how to obtain it, can be found at http://developer.apple.com/xcode.

"Hello World" Kernel Extension

To get started with kernel programming, let's begin by implementing a very simple example, the much beloved "Hello World" application or, in our case, kernel extension. First, launch Xcode and choose "Create a new Xcode project" from the welcome screen. This will present you with a list of templates for the new project. If you select the "System Plug-in" category, you will see that Xcode provides templates for both a "Generic Kernel Extension" and an "I/O Kit Driver." Although both templates create a kernel extension, an I/O Kit driver requires us to nominate a hardware device it will match against and will load only if that device is present. A generic kernel extension, on the other hand, is not a hardware driver and can be loaded any time by the user.

For this tutorial, we will create a project based on the "Generic Kernel Extension" template, so select that item and click the "Next" button. We are now asked for a product name and company identifier. The product name corresponds to the name of the executable file as seen by the user, so for this example, we will use "HelloWorld." The company identifier should be a reverse DNS style string for a domain name you or your company has registered. For this example, you are free to use "com.osxkernel," which is a domain registered for the purpose of this book. By appending the product name to the company identifier, Xcode creates a string that is guaranteed to be unique for the project and will not collide with the name of any existing kernel extension (the unique identifier for this tutorial would be "com.osxkernel.HelloWorld.")

■ **Note** The reverse DNS convention is used throughout Mac OS X in places where a unique identifier is required. We will see in later chapters that the I/O Kit uses a similar scheme to ensure the names of C++ classes are unique. Previous versions of Mac OS 9 used a unique four-character constant to identify applications, which required developers to register their chosen string with Apple. Using reverse DNS allows developers to generate their own unique identifier without having to register them with Apple.

After clicking the "Create" button, Xcode will generate a project for you, including an implementation file named "HelloWorld.c." You can examine the contents of the source file named "HelloWorld.c" by clicking on its icon in the left part of the project window. For this tutorial, modify the generated source code to include the header file <libkern/libkern.h> and to add two calls to printf(). The function named HelloWorld_start() will be called when our kernel extension is loaded and the function named HelloWorld_stop() will be called when the kernel extension is unloaded. When you have finished editing the file, the code should look like Listing 3-1.

Listing 3-1. The "HelloWorld.c" Tutorial

```
#include <mach/mach_types.h>
#include <libkern/libkern.h>

kern_return_t   HelloWorld_start (kmod_info_t * ki, void * d) {
    printf("Hello world\n");
    return KERN_SUCCESS;
}


kern_return_t   HelloWorld_stop (kmod_info_t * ki, void * d) {
    printf("Goodbye world\n");
    return KERN_SUCCESS;
}
```

As we mentioned in Chapter 1, the APIs used for writing kernel code are generally different to those available to user applications; this applies even to functions such as printf(). Rather than including the user space header <stdio.h>, the kernel has its own implementation of printf that is declared in the header file <libkern/libkern.h>. If you try to include <stdio.h> in a kernel project, the compiler will report that it cannot find the included header file.

As well as including the header file that defines the `printf()` function, we also need to link our kernel extension against the library that provides the actual implementation of `printf`. Rather than a compile-time linking, the kernel resolves any library dependencies of a kernel extension only when the kernel extension is loaded. To inform the kernel of our dependencies, we need to declare the libraries we wish to link against in our kernel extension's property list, a file that goes by the name "HelloWorld-Info.plist" in this tutorial project.

To modify the property list, click on the file named "HelloWorld-Info.plist" in the project window. Although the format of the file is text-based XML, Xcode contains a graphical editor for manipulating property list files, as shown in Figure 3-2. Add a new item to the `OSBundleLibraries` dictionary of your property list to include an item with the key name `com.apple.kpi.libkern` and the value `9.0.0` When you are finished, your property list should look identical to Figure 3-2.

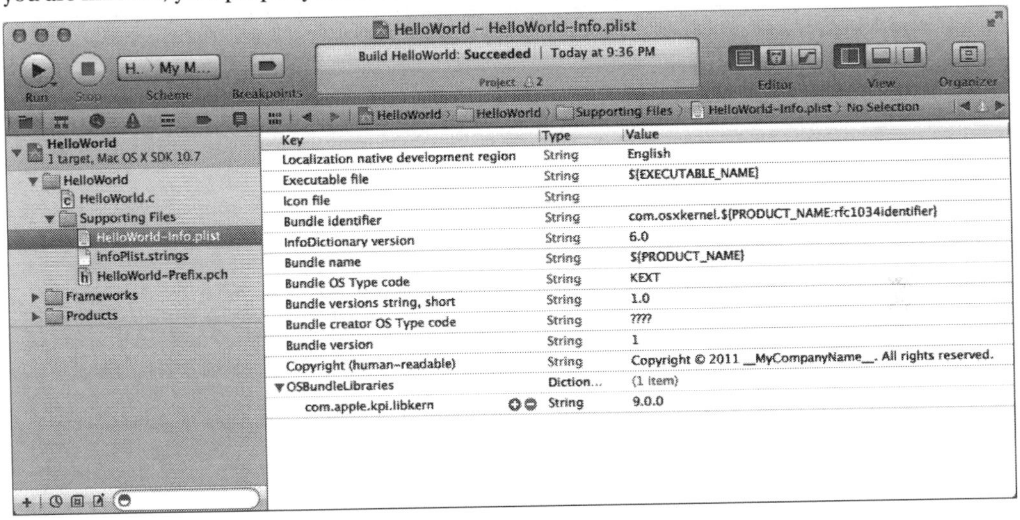

Figure 3-2. The graphical property list editor in Xcode

The XML that corresponds to the addition we made to the property list file is shown in Listing 3-2.

Listing 3-2. The Value of the OSBundleLibraries Entry for Our Tutorial Kernel Extension

```
<key>OSBundleLibraries</key>
<dict>
        <key>com.apple.kpi.libkern</key>
        <string>9.0.0</string>
</dict>
```

The project's property list is not used by the compiler (other than to perform some preprocessing, which replaces variables such as ${PRODUCT_NAME} with their actual value), but is intended for the kernel. The property list is copied to the compiled kernel extension and is read when the extension is loaded. The entry we added to the dictionary consists of a key-value pair; the key identifies a kernel library on which we depend and the value corresponds to the minimum required version of that library. In our case, we are informing the kernel that we require a library with the unique identifier `com.apple.kpi.libkern` and that we require version 9.0.0 or later of this library. The library identifier uses a reverse DNS prefix to ensure the name is unique; in this case, the prefix "com.apple" allows us to recognize the library as a standard library provided by Apple.

■ **Tip** The version of the library, in our case 9.0.0, is the version of the Mac OS X kernel, not the version of Mac OS X itself. Version 9.0.0 corresponds to Mac OS X 10.5.0. You can determine the version of the kernel on your machine by typing the command uname -r into Terminal.

■ **Note** You may have noticed that the project created from the Xcode template includes an item named "Kernel.framework" in the "Frameworks" group. This is not used by the linker when the project is built, but is simply included to help the developer by providing easy access to kernel headers.

The kernel extension project is now complete and is ready to be built. To do this, choose "Build" from the "Project" menu. You should not receive any build errors, but if you do, make sure the contents of your "HelloWorld.c" file match those shown in Listing 3-1.

Before we run this kernel extension, it is worth taking a moment to understand how the kernel knows which entry points to call, given that the two functions contained in the source file appear to be user-defined. As you may have suspected, Xcode gives us a gentle push and generates some of the boilerplate code for us automatically. In generating this code, Xcode uses two values that are defined in the project's settings, which define the kernel extension's start and stop routines. These values are shown in Figure 3-3. You are free to rename the entry points from HelloWorld_start and HelloWorld_stop, as long as you change the name of the functions defined in the source code and the values in the project build settings.

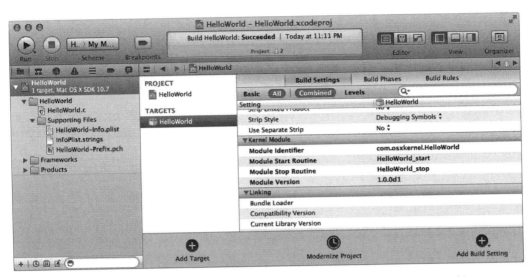

Figure 3-3. The project settings for the "Hello World" kernel extension

Following a successful compile of the project, Xcode will have created a kernel extension with the name "HelloWorld.kext." This file is packaged into a special file known as a KEXT bundle. If you are not familiar with bundles, they are essentially a directory that contains all the files required by the executable, but which the Finder presents to the user as a single file. Listing 3-3 shows the contents of the bundle created when we built the "Hello World" kernel extension.

Listing 3-3. The Contents of the HelloWorld.kext Bundle

```
HelloWorld.kext/
HelloWorld.kext/Contents/Info.plist
HelloWorld.kext/Contents/MacOS
HelloWorld.kext/Contents/MacOS/HelloWorld
HelloWorld.kext/Contents/Resources
HelloWorld.kext/Contents/Resources/en.lproj
HelloWorld.kext/Contents/Resources/en.lproj/InfoPlist.strings
```

The file named "Info.plist" should be familiar, since this is a copy of the property list we modified earlier (with some minor processing applied by Xcode along the way). The other file that deserves a mention is simply named "HelloWorld" and is located in the subdirectory of the bundle with the path "Contents/MacOS." This file contains the actual executable code of the kernel extension.

Loading and Unloading Kernel Extensions

A kernel extension is a code module that runs inside the operating system kernel. Having built our kernel extension, it now needs to be loaded into the kernel where it can be run. While Xcode is great for writing and building kernel extensions, it cannot be used for testing or debugging a kernel extension; in fact, for a kernel extension, the button named "Run" in the Xcode window will build the project only, but won't actually load or run the resulting output. Instead, kernel extensions on Mac OS X can be loaded one of two ways, automatically, by copying the kernel extension bundle to the directory /System/Library/Extensions, or manually through the command line.

To load the kernel extension, we first need to locate the compiled binary that was built by Xcode. By default, Xcode 4 will place the output from the compiler in a different location than the project directory that contains the source code, which can make it difficult to find the path to the kernel extension in order to load it on the command line. To locate the path in which Xcode has written the kernel extension, right-click on the product named "HelloWorld.kext," which displays a contextual menu, and select the item "Show in Finder," as shown in Figure 3-4.

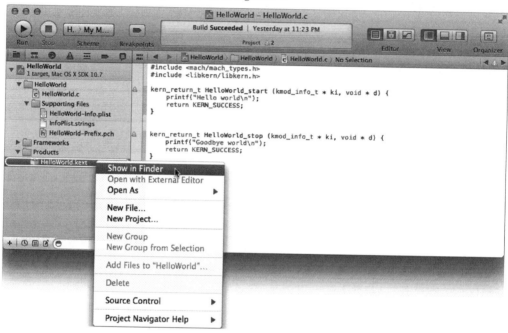

Figure 3-4. Locating the path to the built kernel extension

A kernel extension that is copied to the /System/Library/Extensions directory will be loaded when needed by the operating system. This could be when the system boots or, in the case of a driver, when a hardware device that requires the driver is connected to the computer. However, during development, it is typically more convenient to load the kernel extension manually from the command line.

For security, because a kernel extension is granted the same elevated privileges as the core operating system code, kernel extensions can only be installed or loaded by a user with administrative access to the system. As a further security measure, the system has strict requirements regarding the file permissions of the kernel extension's bundle and will refuse to load a kernel extension that does not meet these requirements, particularly the following.

- The KEXT bundle and all files and folders inside it must be owned by the user "root" (user id 0).

- The KEXT bundle and all files and folders inside it must be owned by the group "wheel" group id 0).

- The KEXT bundle and any directory inside it must have the permissions mask 0755 (rwxr-xr-x).

- All files inside the KEXT bundle must have the permissions mask 0644 (rw-r--r--).

When you build a kernel extension in Xcode, the KEXT bundle it produces will have the correct permission mask for the bundle and its contents, but user and group ownership will correspond to the user who ran the compiler. To correct the file ownership to that required by a kernel extension, you can use the following command in Terminal.

```
sudo chown -R root:wheel HelloWorld.kext
```

Note that if you change the ownership of the KEXT inside the Xcode build directory, Xcode will not have sufficient permission to overwrite the KEXT when the project is next built, which will result in a build error. To overcome this, you can copy the KEXT from the Xcode build directory to another directory (such as /tmp) before changing its ownership and loading it.

Mac OS X contains a number of command line utilities for the purpose of working with kernel extensions. Some of the commonly used commands include:

- kextload, which loads a KEXT into the kernel

- kextunload, which stops a loaded KEXT and unloads it from the kernel

- kextutil, which is a developer-oriented utility for loading KEXTs into the kernel and can provide diagnostic information detailing why a kernel extension failed to load and can produce symbols that are useful when debugging an active kernel extension

- kextstat, which displays a list of all KEXTs loaded into the kernel

With the exception of kextstat, which does not actively modify the state of the kernel, all these commands must be run with super-user permissions. This can be accomplished by prefixing commands with *sudo*.

We are now ready to load the "Hello World" kernel extension. To do this, run the following command in Terminal:

```
sudo kextload HelloWorld.kext
```

Although the "Hello World" kernel extension has been loaded and its start entry point called, you won't see the result of our call to printf in the terminal window. Instead, the output from calling the kernel's implementation of printf is written to a log file. To confirm the "Hello World" kernel extension was loaded, you can use the kextstat command, as follows:

```
kextstat
```

This will print a list of the running kernel extensions. Since the "Hello World" extension will be one of the most recent extensions to have been loaded, it should appear at the end of the list. An example of the output from kextstat is shown in Listing 3-4.

Listing 3-4. The Output from the kextstat Command, with Our Kernel Extension Highlighted

```
Index  Refs   Address           Size     Wired    Name (Version) <Linked Against>
  1     85   0xffffff7f80742000  0x683c   0x683c   com.apple.kpi.bsd (11.1.0)
  2      6   0xffffff7f8072e000  0x3d0    0x3d0    com.apple.kpi.dsep (11.1.0)
  3    110   0xffffff7f8074c000  0x1b9d8  0x1b9d8  com.apple.kpi.iokit (11.1.0)
  4    116   0xffffff7f80738000  0x9b54   0x9b54   com.apple.kpi.libkern (11.1.0)
  5    103   0xffffff7f8072f000  0x88c    0x88c    com.apple.kpi.mach (11.1.0)
...
130     0   0xffffff7f810ce000  0x51000  0x51000  com.apple.filesystems.afpfs (9.8) <129 7 6 5 4 3 1>
144     0   0xffffff7f807b8000  0x2000   0x2000   com.osxkernel.HelloWorld (1) <4>
```

Finally, we will unload the "Hello World" extension, which will result in the HelloWorld_stop() function being called and the kernel extension being unloaded from the kernel. This can be accomplished with the following command:

```
sudo kextunload HelloWorld.kext
```

Using Console to View Output

The resulting output from calling printf() in the kernel is written to a log file on disk. This log takes the format of a plain text file that allows it to be examined with the standard Unix commands tail and cat, passing the path to the logfile /var/log/kernel.log. Alternatively, the contents of the log can be inspected with an application included with Mac OS X named "Console," which can be found in the /Applications/Utilities directory. The Console application consolidates logs from a wide range of system services and applications, including the kernel logfile. A screenshot of the output from our tutorial viewed through Console is shown in Figure 3-5.

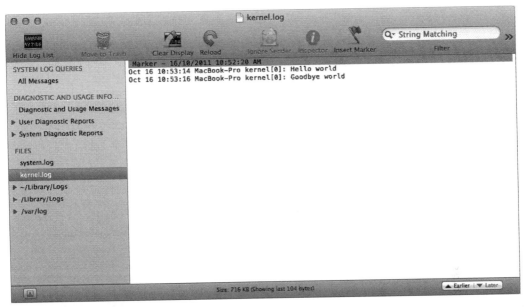

Figure 3-5. The output from a successful load and unload of our kernel extension, as shown in the Console utility

Although it may seem primitive if you are accustomed to source level debuggers from user-space development, being able to print debug output to the console remains one of the fundamental debug techniques for kernel code. You can find more information on debugging in Chapter 16.

Summary

Kernel extensions for Mac OS X are developed using the tools contained within the Xcode package provided by Apple. In this chapter, we created a tutorial "Hello World" kernel extension, showed how to import symbols from other kernel libraries, and introduced the command line utilities commonly used to load and work with kernel extensions.

CHAPTER 4

The I/O Kit Framework

Device drivers for Mac OS X are written using a framework known as the I/O Kit. The I/O Kit consists of header files and libraries that provide the services required by drivers, as well as header files and libraries that are used by user space code to locate a kernel driver and interact with it. There are two main parts of the I/O Kit:

- Kernel.framework

- IOKit.framework

Although it is slightly counterintuitive, the I/O Kit framework is designed for user space applications and not for developing I/O Kit drivers in the kernel. Instead, the Kernel framework contains the header files used for kernel space driver development. If you examine the contents of the Kernel framework, you will see that it contains a directory named IOKit that consists of the header files used for kernel space driver development. Another important directory in the Kernel framework is named libkern, which contains the foundation classes and types on which the kernel I/O Kit framework is built.

The user space I/O Kit framework serves two purposes. It provides user applications with functions for determining the hardware devices present on the machine on which it is running, functions for locating the appropriate driver for a particular hardware device, and functions for sending control requests and request statuses from that driver. These topics are further discussed in Chapter 5. In addition, the user I/O Kit framework provides the user space application the ability to communicate with certain hardware devices directly, removing the need for a kernel driver. This is possible for a select range of devices, most notably USB and FireWire devices that do not need to be shared between multiple running applications. We discuss this aspect of the I/O Kit in Chapter 15.

The I/O Kit Model

The I/O Kit is an object-oriented framework, thus it requires a language that provides an object-oriented programming abstraction. Apple chose to implement the I/O Kit in the C++ language, and consequently, drivers that are written for Mac OS X are developed in C++.

While the choice of C++ for driver development is unique among operating systems, it reflects the modern nature of Mac OS X. The initial version of Mac OS X was released in 2001, and Apple took the opportunity to design a completely new model for driver development. The choice of C++ reflects the state of both computer hardware and compilers when the I/O Kit was designed.

The choice of an object-oriented language has considerable advantages. Hardware in a computer system is, by its nature, an interconnected series of devices connected via a number of different buses. For example, a USB device may be connected to the internal USB hub of a keyboard, which itself is connected to the USB port on an iMac. Internally, the USB port is handled by a USB controller chip on the iMac's motherboard, which is connected to the motherboard's chipset controller via an internal PCI bus. By adopting an object-oriented driver model, the I/O Kit is able to mirror this same hardware connection through the driver objects.

The role of a driver is to enable the operating system—and ultimately the user—to take advantage of the services that are implemented by hardware. The operating system helps the driver by loading the driver when its hardware device is present, providing the driver with a way to access and interact with its hardware device, and by providing access points for the driver to plug its own services into the operating system.

■ **Note** The I/O Kit uses the term "nub" to describe a driver that provides services to other drivers. For example, the driver of a USB hub would be a nub because it provides services to the drivers of the USB devices that connect to it.

The choice of an object-oriented design serves the I/O Kit well. Each driver is implemented as a C++ class, which allows the I/O Kit to instantiate a new driver object for each instance of the hardware device present on the system. The driver's hardware device is accessed through an object known as the driver's "provider," which is provided to the driver at initialization. The I/O Kit will use a provider class that is appropriate for the hardware bus used by the device. For example, a USB device will have a provider class that is an instance of an IOUSBDevice, whereas a driver for a PCI card will have a provider class that is an instance of an IOPCIDevice. The different capabilities of these bus interfaces are abstracted by the different provider class types. For example, USB devices have a number of endpoints that data is transferred to or read from, so the IOUSBDevice class contains methods for reading or writing a data buffer to a specified endpoint. On the other hand, a PCI card is accessed by mapping a set of registers into the kernel's address space, which can then be read from and written to by the driver the same way in which it writes to any other memory address.

Lastly, drivers need a way to provide their services to the rest of the operating system. This is perhaps the area where the object-oriented design of the I/O Kit shines. The main class of the driver can be implemented as the subclass of one of the specialized classes provided by the I/O Kit for certain types of driver. For example, a driver that implements a serial port will subclass the standard IOSerialStreamSync class. Similarly, a driver that implements an audio output device will subclass the IOAudioDevice class.

The advantage of implementing a driver by subclassing is that your driver inherits the behavior and implementation from the parent class. There are certain operations that are common to every serial port and to every audio device, and this behavior is implemented by the superclass, saving driver developers from having to write boilerplate code. Developers can then concentrate on code that is specific to their particular hardware device. The superclass will call the driver when a device-specific action is required.

If you've implemented a driver for any other operating system, you have no doubt had to implement a dispatch routine that usually takes the form of one large switch statement in order to handle all the possible requests that the operating system may make and then calling the appropriate function in your driver that implements that request. The I/O Kit takes a different approach. Driver requests take the form of method calls. The driver simply needs to implement or override methods that are provided by its superclass. These methods are specific to the driver type. For example, a serial driver is concerned with transmitting bytes and receiving bytes over the serial port, so the IOSerialStreamSync class provides pure virtual methods enqueueData() and dequeueData() to be implemented by the subclass when these actions need to be performed.

For a specialized device, the I/O Kit may not provide a suitable superclass. For example, there is no suitable superclass provided by the I/O Kit to implement a driver for a specialized medical imaging device. The driver for such a device would be implemented by a class that subclasses from the generic IOService class. The IOService provides methods to manage the driver's lifecycle, including initialization and destroying the driver object.

Lastly, a driver may provide an interface to user space applications. In I/O Kit terminology, this is handled by implementing a class known as a "user client." The user client is a custom class implemented by the driver that subclasses the IOUserClient class. Whenever an application opens a connection to the driver, the I/O Kit instantiates a new user client object that handles all the requests coming from that application's connection to the driver. When the application closes that connection to the driver, or the application terminates (or crashes), the user client is destroyed. If an application opens multiple connections to the driver, the I/O Kit will instantiate as many user client objects as there are connections made.

Object Relationship

As we have seen, there are two important classes for an I/O Kit driver, one being the superclass that the main driver class inherits from and the other being the provider class that the driver uses to access its hardware. This design means that the functionality that the driver implements is separate from the way in which the driver's hardware device connects to the computer. For example, a driver that supports a PCI sound card and a driver that supports a USB audio output device will both inherit from the same IOAudioDevice superclass, and the operating system will interface to both drivers by making the same calls to each driver. After all, the operating system's audio subsystem shouldn't need to care how an audio output device connects to the computer.

This separation also encourages code reuse. A company that manufactures both PCI and USB based audio devices could potentially use the same driver for both devices, with the driver receiving a provider class that is of type IOPCIDevice or IOUSBDevice, depending on which of the two hardware devices is connected to the computer. Or, perhaps more conceivably, the hardware vendor could create its own superclass that implements the common functionality for both devices, which is itself a subclass of IOAudioDevice. The driver for the vendor's PCI and USB devices would need only a minimal implementation, with much of the common functionality coming from their custom superclass. Such an arrangement is shown in Figure 4-1.

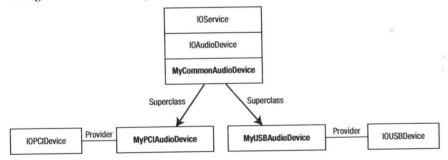

Figure 4-1. An example of the relationship between an I/O Kit driver and its superclass and provider class

The Info.plist File

The Macintosh platform has always supported a plug-and-play design for devices, which requires no configuration after installing the driver. Mac OS X, with the help of the I/O Kit, is no exception. Unlike the kernel extension that we developed in the previous chapter, which loads as soon as it is added to the system, a driver is loaded only when one of the devices that it supports is connected to the computer. In this way, even though there may be hundreds of drivers installed on a system, only those that correspond to hardware that is actually connected to the computer will be loaded and taking up memory.

In Chapter 3, we saw that a kernel extension requires a property list file to define such things as its entry points. The property list is even more important for a kernel extension that implements an I/O Kit driver. For an I/O Kit driver, the property list specifies the list of hardware devices that the driver is able to support. Each device supported by a driver contains its own "personality" in the property list, which consists of a "matching dictionary" that consists of an array that describes each hardware device to match against. The driver will be loaded only if one of the hardware devices described in its matching dictionary is connected to the computer.

One of the most important values contained in each matching dictionary is the "IOProviderClass," which defines the class type of the driver's provider, such as IOUSBDevice or IOPCIDevice. Whenever a new hardware device is connected to the computer, the I/O Kit creates an appropriate nub for that device, and then begins the process of finding a suitable driver for that nub. For example, a USB device connection is handled as follows:

1. The user connects a USB device to the computer.

2. A new instance of IOUSBDevice is created to represent the device.

3. The I/O Kit iterates over all drivers that contain a matching dictionary listing a provider class of IOUSBDevice.

4. The IOUSBDevice examines the entire contents of the matching dictionary for the driver.

5. If the requested properties of the matching dictionary correspond to the properties of the device, the driver is added to a list of potential drivers for the device.

Importantly, it is the provider class that decides whether a driver is suitable for a particular hardware device. It does this by examining the properties from a potential driver's matching dictionary; however, the particular properties that are used will be specific to the driver family. For example, a USB driver may match against a specific vendor ID and product ID of the USB device, or may match against a generic class of device such as any USB keyboard. A PCI device may be matched on the vendor ID and device ID specified in the device's PCI configuration space or against any PCI class, such as a network card or a display card.

Following the preceding steps, the I/O Kit has narrowed the list of drivers for the device down to an array of potential matches. To determine the best driver for the hardware device, the I/O Kit uses the notion of a "probe score" for each driver. Each driver nominates a probe score that provides a relative measure, in some way, of that driver's suitability for the device. The driver with the highest probe score is the one that is ultimately chosen to work with the device.

The driver's probe score can be set in two ways. One way is for a driver to provide a probe score in its matching dictionary. For example, a company that manufactures a custom USB keyboard could provide a driver whose matching dictionary matches against the exact product ID of the company's keyboard, with a probe score that is higher than the system's default keyboard driver. Another way that the probe score can be set is through "active matching," in which the I/O Kit instantiates each potential driver, temporarily attaches it to the hardware device, and provides it with a chance to interrogate the device and determine its probe score. During probe, the driver has full access to the hardware, so it can perform as much interrogation of the device as is required to determine its suitability to drive that device. The driver can adjust its probe score, or more commonly, can use the probe method to opt-out of matching against a device if it determines that it is unable to work with the connected hardware.

For example, a driver's implementation of probe could determine the version of firmware that is loaded on the device, and if the firmware is of a later version than that supported by the driver, it could refuse to load. Failing during the probe stage is more efficient than failing later on, when the driver has been selected as the driver for the device, because the I/O Kit does not need to continue on and start your driver, although, in both cases, the I/O Kit will continue by attempting to load the driver with the next highest probe score.

While in almost all cases only one driver is attached to a device, the I/O Kit does allow multiple drivers to be loaded for a single device. By adding an extra key to a driver's matching dictionary known as a "match category," the I/O Kit will load the driver with the highest probe score in each match category and attach it to the device. If no match category is given in the driver's matching dictionary, a default category is assumed.

The matching process is recursive, and drivers may themselves be nubs that act as a provider to other classes. For example, the driver for a PCI card that implements a USB host controller would match against an IOPCIDevice, but would create IOUSBDevice instances of its own to represent devices that have been connected to its own ports. In this way, the IOUSBDevice instances created by the driver would in turn become the provider class for other drivers, as shown in Figure 4-2. Rather than instantiate a class of type IOUSBDevice directly, a driver of this type would likely provide its own implementation of a class that inherits from IOUSBDevice, which is shown in Figure 4-2 as "MyUSBDevice."

Any driver that uses an instance of MyUSBDevice as a provider would talk to the provider through its standard IOUSBDevice interface, but the use of virtual methods would allow the MyUSBDevice implementation to override these methods and provide its own implementation.

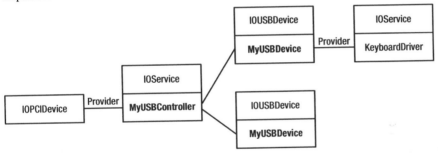

Figure 4-2. An example of a driver that is also a nub, creating objects that serve as the provider class to other drivers

Another example of a driver that acts as a nub, which is in fact a far more common scenario, is a driver that accepts connections from user applications. As mentioned earlier, for each connection that a user application makes to a driver, the I/O Kit instantiates a new object known as a "user client" to handle the control requests from the application and to pass them on to the driver. Like the main driver class, the user client class is also an I/O Kit service and it inherits from the same IOService base class as any other driver object. Each user client uses the main driver object as its provider class. Unlike the main driver, however, a user client doesn't need to go through the matching stage because the driver nominates the specific class name of its user client.

Listing 4-1. The Driver Personalities for a Hypothetical External Disk, Containing Matching Dictionaries for both FireWire and USB Connections

```
<key>IOKitPersonalities</key>
<dict>
        <key>MyExternalDiskFireWire</key>
        <dict>
                <key>CFBundleIdentifier</key>
                <string>com.mycompany.driver.MyExternalDiskDriver</string>
                <key>IOClass</key>
                <string>com_mycompany_driver_MyExternalDiskDriver</string>
                <key>IOProviderClass</key>
                <string>IOFireWireUnit</string>
                <key>Unit_SW_Version</key>
                <integer>1111</integer>
                <key>Unit_Spec_ID</key>
                <integer>2222</integer>
        </dict>
        <key>MyExternalDiskUSB</key>
        <dict>
                <key>CFBundleIdentifier</key>
                <string>com.mycompany.driver.MyExternalDiskDriver</string>
                <key>IOClass</key>
                <string>com_mycompany_driver_MyExternalDiskDriverUSB</string>
                <key>IOProviderClass</key>
                <string>IOUSBDevice</string>
                <key>idProduct</key>
                <integer>3333</integer>
                <key>idVendor</key>
                <integer>4444</integer>
                <key>IOProbeScore</key>
                <integer>9000</integer>
        </dict>
</dict>
```

Listing 4-1 shows the matching dictionary for a hypothetical external disk device that features both FireWire and USB connections. As such, it contains two entries in its matching dictionary, the first of which matches against a specific FireWire device, and another that matches against a specific USB device. The driver class com_mycompany_driver_MyExternalDiskDriver will be instantiated and given a chance to probe the device whenever a FireWire device with a unit software version of 1111 and a unit spec ID of 2222 is plugged in to the computer. Likewise, the driver class com_mycompany_driver_MyExternalDiskDriverUSB will be instantiated and given a chance to probe the device whenever a USB device with a product ID of 3333 and a vendor ID of 4444 is plugged into the computer. The USB device will have a default probe score of 9000, which should make it the preferred driver for this device.

The Driver Class

As we saw in the previous section, when the I/O Kit loads a driver, it does so by instantiating a class that is designated in the driver's property list. This class must be a subclass of the IOService class, either directly or by subclassing a class that is itself a child of the IOService class. The IOService class provides virtual methods that are called at various points during the lifetime of the driver—for example, when it is loaded and initialized, when it should probe its provider, and when the driver is stopped. Because these methods are declared as virtual methods in the definition of the IOService class, they can be easily overridden in the custom driver class that inherits from IOService.

At this point, it may be a good time to put what you have learned into practice by creating a simple I/O Kit driver. To begin, open Xcode and create a new project based on the "IOKit Driver" template. When prompted for a product name, enter "IOKitTest". You can use the company identifier "com.osxkernel", which is a domain name that has been registered for the purposes of this book. Xcode will create a project for you with two files, a C++ implementation file named "IOKitTest.cpp" and its corresponding header file named "IOKitTest.h".

Let's begin by declaring the class definition of our driver. Given that we are implementing a generic driver, and not one that provides specialized functionality such as a serial port or disk storage, we will define our driver's main class as a subclass of IOService and not one of the more specialized classes that the I/O Kit provides. Enter in the text from Listing 4-2 as the contents of IOKitTest.h.

Listing 4-2. The "IOKitTest.h" Tutorial

```
#include <IOKit/IOService.h>

class com_osxkernel_driver_IOKitTest : public IOService
{
        OSDeclareDefaultStructors(com_osxkernel_driver_IOKitTest)

public:
        virtual bool    init (OSDictionary* dictionary = NULL);
        virtual void    free (void);

        virtual IOService*      probe (IOService* provider, SInt32* score);
        virtual bool    start (IOService* provider);
        virtual void    stop (IOService* provider);
};
```

The contents of the header file should be fairly straightforward, with the possible exception of the macro OSDeclareDefaultStructors. As you will recall from Chapter 3, the I/O Kit is implemented in a subset of the C++ language that does not include exceptions and runtime type information. The macro OSDeclareDefaultStructors is needed as a consequence of both of these limitations; it provides the declaration of the class's constructor and destructor and metadata that provides the custom implementation of the I/O Kit's version of runtime type information. We discuss this in greater depth later in this chapter.

■ **Note** You may be wondering why we used such an elaborate name for our class. The kernel has a global namespace into which all symbols (including class names, functions, and global variables) exported by any active kernel extensions are loaded. The kernel will refuse to load an extension that contains symbols that collide with an extension that is already loaded, and so to avoid this, Apple recommends that all global functions, classes, and variables are decorated with a reverse-DNS naming scheme.

The implementation of the driver class should be placed in the file named "IOKitTest.cpp." The contents of this file are given in Listing 4-3.

Listing 4-3. The "IOKitTest.cpp" Tutorial

```cpp
#include "IOKitTest.h"
#include <IOKit/IOLib.h>

// Define the superclass.
#define super IOService

OSDefineMetaClassAndStructors(com_osxkernel_driver_IOKitTest, IOService)


bool com_osxkernel_driver_IOKitTest::init (OSDictionary* dict)
{
        bool res = super::init(dict);
        IOLog("IOKitTest::init\n");
        return res;
}

void com_osxkernel_driver_IOKitTest::free (void)
{
        IOLog("IOKitTest::free\n");
        super::free();
}

IOService* com_osxkernel_driver_IOKitTest::probe (IOService* provider, SInt32* score)
{
        IOService *res = super::probe(provider, score);
        IOLog("IOKitTest::probe\n");
        return res;
}

bool com_osxkernel_driver_IOKitTest::start (IOService *provider)
{
        bool res = super::start(provider);
        IOLog("IOKitTest::start\n");
        return res;
```

```
}
void com_osxkernel_driver_IOKitTest::stop (IOService *provider)
{
        IOLog("IOKitTest::stop\n");
        super::stop(provider);
}
```

■ **Note** It is a convention of the I/O Kit to define a macro named "super" as the name of the superclass of the current class. This allows a method to be delegated to the superclass implementation easily, as is shown in Listing 4-3.

Finally, we need to define the driver's matching dictionary and library dependencies through the Info.plist file. Add a new dictionary key named "IOKitTest" to the IOKitPersonalities dictionary that contains the following values:

Key	Type	Value
CFBundleIdentifier	String	com.osxkernel.${PRODUCT_NAME:rfc1034identifier}
IOClass	String	com_osxkernel_driver_IOKitTest
IOMatchCategory	String	com_osxkernel_driver_IOKitTest
IOProviderClass	String	IOResources
IOResourceMatch	String	IOKit

We also need to add two entries to the OSBundleLibraries dictionary:

Key	Type	Value
com.apple.kpi.iokit	String	9.0.0
com.apple.kpi.libkern	String	9.0.0

The final version of the project's property list is shown in Figure 4-3.

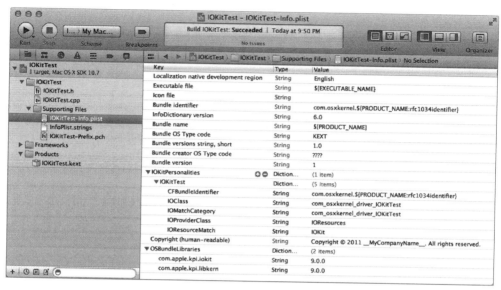

Figure 4-3. The property list, including the matching dictionary, for the IOKitTest tutorial

Given that the purpose of a driver is to control hardware, and that the I/O Kit will load a driver only when its hardware device is present, you may be wondering how it is possible to test this driver. Thankfully, the I/O Kit provides a special nub known as IOResources that can be used as the provider class of a driver that has no hardware device, such as the tutorial driver listed here. In a system, there will be multiple drivers matching against the IOResources nub, and so to allow more than one driver to attach itself to IOResources, the IOMatchCategory key in the driver's matching dictionary must be defined.

Since the I/O Kit allows a nub to have one driver attached to it per match category, specifying a unique category allows the driver to load and doesn't prevent other drivers from matching against the IOResources provider class after we have loaded. To complete the matching dictionary, we need to specify matching criteria that are unique for the provider class. If the provider class is a USB device, this may take the form of a USB product ID and vendor ID. In the case of our tutorial, the provider class is IOResources. A single key named "IOResourceMatch" is the matching criteria used by IOResources. In the sample driver's matching dictionary, this value is set to "IOKit". This tells the provider class to defer loading the driver until the IOKit subsystem has been fully loaded and initialized during system startup.

You can now build the IOKitTest project, which can be loaded using the same "kextload" command that was used in Chapter 3. If you open the "Console" utility and examine the contents of the "kernel.log" file, you should see that the various methods of the driver's class have been called.

The order in which the methods of the driver class are called is as follows:

1. init(). This method is guaranteed to be called before any other method in the class. Its purpose is the same as a constructor of a C++ class. A driver's init() method should first call the implementation provided by the superclass, and if this fails, it should abort immediately. This method is passed one parameter, a copy of the matching dictionary corresponding to the selected driver personality in the Info.plist file. If this method succeeds, it should return true; otherwise, it should return false.

2. probe(). This method is called during matching to give the driver a chance to examine the hardware device, which is passed to the method through the argument named "provider." Although the parameter "provider" is a pointer to an IOService, it can be cast to the more specialized provider class specified in the matching dictionary (such as IOUSBDevice). The driver's implementation of probe() should first call the superclass's implementation, and if this succeeds, perform any investigation of the hardware required to determine whether the driver is able to control it. If the driver is unable to control the hardware, it should return NULL from the probe() method; otherwise, it should return an instance of the IOService subclass that should control this device. In almost all cases, this method will return the current IOService instance ("this").

3. start(). If the previous call to probe() succeeded, and the driver has been chosen as being the best suited to control the hardware device (based on its probe score), its start() method is called. The implementation should first call the superclass's implementation of start(), and if this fails, it should abort immediately. The driver should use the start() method to configure the hardware for operation, and should initialize any resources that it needs while running. If for any reason the method fails and the driver is unable to go on to control the hardware, the method should return false. The I/O Kit will then provide the driver with the next highest probe score a chance to control the device.

4. stop(). This method isn't called until either the device is removed or the driver is manually unloaded. This method is the opposite of start(); any configuration or allocation that was performed in the start() method should be released when stop() is called. Finally, the implementation should call the superclass's implementation of stop().

5. free(). Finally, before the driver's object is destroyed, the I/O Kit calls its free() method. Its purpose is the same as a destructor of a C++ class. This provides the driver with a chance to release any resources that were allocated in its init() method. This method is called even if a driver was never selected as the best match for a particular device. The implementation should end by calling the superclass's implementation of free().

A consequence of limited exception support is that rather than using the traditional C++ approach of performing object initialization in the class's constructor and throwing an exception if an error occurs, the initialization of I/O Kit objects is performed in a custom method named "init," which returns a Boolean value to signal success.

IORegistryExplorer

Apple provides a very useful tool for visualizing the drivers loaded on a system, known as "IORegistryExplorer." This is included as part of the Xcode tools. IORegistryExplorer displays a graphical representation of the drivers that are currently loaded on the system and their relationship to other drivers. This relationship is shown as a hierarchical representation, with a provider class having a parent relationship to the clients that are connected to it.

IORegistryExplorer shows a representation of an entity known as the I/O Registry. If you're coming from a Windows background, don't confuse the I/O Registry with the Windows Registry. The I/O

Registry is a tree of I/O Kit objects that is created when the system is started, and then it dynamically grows or shrinks as hardware devices and their corresponding drivers are loaded or unloaded from the system. Unlike the Windows Registry, the I/O Registry is never written to disk or saved between reboots of the computer.

The IOService plane includes all objects in the I/O Registry. As such, it can be a little overwhelming when trying to locate a particular driver. To help find a particular driver in the I/O Registry, IORegistryExplorer provides a search field that can be used to filter the objects shown to those whose name matches a particular string.

IORegistryExplorer also displays the property table for each driver object. When the I/O Kit loads a driver, it initializes its property table to the contents of the matching dictionary that corresponds to the driver personality that was loaded; this corresponds to the OSDictionary object that was passed to the driver class's init() method. As the driver runs, it may manipulate its property list by adding or removing additional key/value pairs or by changing the value of a particular key. These changes are local to the driver instance (and so if the same driver is loaded multiple times for several devices in the system, they each have their own property table). Figure 4-4 shows IORegistryExplorer for the sample IOKit driver that we developed earlier.

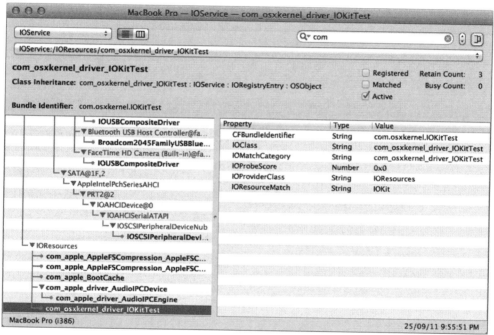

Figure 4-4. *IORegistryExplorer displaying the IOKitTest sample. The property table shown on the right was initialized from the contents of the driver's matching dictionary in its Info.plist file.*

Objects in the I/O Registry are organized into several planes. Each plane shows only those objects that share certain functionality. When launched, IORegistryExplorer will default to showing the relationship of objects in the "IOService" plane, which includes all objects in the I/O Registry. Some of the other planes that are commonly used include:

- IODeviceTree: This is a static plane that reflects the hardware configuration of the system; it does not change as hardware devices are connected to the system. The contents of the device tree largely depend on the system motherboard and will consist of a static snapshot of the computer's configuration at boot time, including PCI slots, built-in USB ports, and any hardware controllers that are on the motherboard, such as the CPU, memory, and USB controllers.

- IOPower. This plane shows all driver objects that have implemented power management and will receive notifications from the I/O Kit when the system is switching to a different power state such as when entering sleep mode.

- IOUSB. This plane shows all USB devices and hubs that are connected to the system. It includes the USB devices only; the corresponding driver that has been loaded for a device can be seen in the IOService plane.

The I/O Registry is also accessible on the command line through the tool "ioreg." Unlike IORegistryExplorer, which is available if the Xcode tools have been installed, ioreg is a standard part of a Mac OS X installation and is useful when debugging on an end-user's machine or any other system in which the developer tools are unlikely to be installed.

The Kernel Library: libkern

The runtime support and base classes on which the I/O Kit is built are implemented in a library known as libkern. The libkern library provides support that makes up for much of the functionality that is excluded in the embedded C++ language. The libkern library defines a class known as OSObject, which provides the base class that is used by all I/O Kit classes. Since the base driver class IOService is a subclass of OSObject, the main class of a driver will also be derived from OSObject. Any class that is derived from OSObject gets the following functionality:

- Runtime Type Information, which is implemented through custom macros provided by libkern. These macros provide functionality that includes

    - Type introspection, which is the ability at runtime to determine the type of an object or whether it is derived from a given base class

    - Dynamic casting, which is the ability to cast an object to the type of one of its derived classes (for example, to cast the provider class from an object of type IOService to IOUSBDevice)

- Object creation, including the ability to instantiate an object based on a string representation of its class name

- Object reference counting based on retain/release semantics

- Object tracking, that is, the ability to determine how many instances of a certain class have been instantiated but not yet released

OSObject

Some of the features provided by libkern should be very familiar if you have written user applications with Apple's Cocoa framework. In particular, the OSObject class can be thought of as the kernel equivalent of the NSObject class in Cocoa, and the dynamic type introspection capabilities are almost identical to their counterparts provided by the Objective-C runtime.

There is no requirement to use OSObject as the superclass for classes that are private to your driver, although you may find that the reference counting and object tracking that OSObject provides (without any extra work from you) is reason enough to adopt it.

Adopting OSObject as the base class involves the following steps:

1. Using the standard C++ syntax, declare your class to be a subclass of OSObject, or a class that is derived from OSObject (such as IOService). If you are subclassing from OSObject, you may need to include the header file <libkern/c++/OSObject.h>.

2. As the first line of your class's declaration (in your class's header file), include the macro OSDeclareDefaultDestructors(), passing the name of your class as its argument. This macro, among other things, declares the standard C++ constructor and destructor for your class, and so you should not add either to your class declaration. Instead, add a method named init() to your class to act as the constructor, and a method named free() to act as the destructor. You are free to add any arguments that your class requires to the init() method, as is shown in the following example.

```
class com_osxkernel_driver_MyObject : public OSObject
{
    OSDeclareDefaultStructors(com_osxkernel_driver_MyObject)
public:
    virtual bool    init (const char* name);
    virtual void    free ();
    ...
};
```

3. In the file that implements your class, place the macro OSDefineMetaClassAndStructors(), which takes two arguments, the name of the class, and the name of its direct superclass. The first few lines of an implementation file typically follow the pattern

```
#include "MyObject.h"

// Define super as a convenience macro to refer to the superclass
#define super OSObject

OSDefineMetaClassAndStructors(com_osxkernel_driver_MyObject, OSObject)
```

4. Provide an implementation of the methods init() and free(). These two methods play the role of the constructor and destructor, respectively, as shown in the following example.

```
bool com_osxkernel_driver_MyObject::init (const char* name)
{
    if (! super::init())
            return false;

    // Additional initialization
    return true;
}
```

```
void com_osxkernel_driver_MyObject::free ()
{
    // Release resources allocated in init()
    super::free();
}
```

Having defined an object that subclasses from OSObject, it can be instantiated in your code by calling the C++ new operator followed by the init() method. As a convenience, many classes provide a static method that performs both of these steps, and return a non-NULL object on success, as shown in Listing 4-4.

Listing 4-4. The Definition of a Static Helper Method to Construct a New Instance of a Custom Class

```
com_osxkernel_driver_MyObject*
        com_osxkernel_driver_MyObject::withName (const char* name)
{
    com_osxkernel_driver_MyObject*  me = new com_osxkernel_driver_MyObject;

    if (me && !me->init(name))
    {
            me->release();
            return NULL;
    }

    return me;
}
```

The lifetime of any object that is based on OSObject is determined by reference counting. When an object is first created, its reference count is initialized to 1. To free an object, rather than using the C++ operator delete (which the OSDeclareDefaultStructors macros declare as a protected method), your code should instead call the release() method. This method is implemented by the OSObject class and decrements the reference count of the object by 1. When the object's final reference is released, and the object's reference count becomes 0, the object is released and the free() method is called. If your code takes a pointer to an object that it needs to hold on to, it will need to extend the lifetime of that object to ensure that the object is not released while your code is holding a reference to it. This is done by calling the retain() method, which increments the reference count of the target object by 1. To prevent memory leaks, it is important that each call to retain() is matched with a call to release().

Any object that is derived from OSObject allows type introspection. To cast an object into another type, libkern provides a macro named OSDynamicCast(type, object), which performs the equivalent of the C++ operator dynamic_cast<type>(object). The macro verifies whether the object is derived from the requested class, and if so, a pointer to the object is returned; otherwise, the macro returns NULL. The most common use of dynamic casting is to safely convert an object from a base class to a more specialized class. For example, the driver's start() method is passed a pointer to its provider class as an IOService object. However, the provider is actually a more specialized class such as IOUSBDevice or IOPCIDevice, and a dynamic cast allows this conversion to be made safely. For example, a driver that controls a USB device will contain the following code in its start() method to convert the provider from an IOService to an IOUSBDevice:

```
IOUSBDevice* usbDevice = OSDynamicCast(IOUSBDevice, provider);
if (usbDevice == NULL)
{
        IOLog("Unknown provider class\n");
```

```
        return false;
}
```

The OSObject base class can also track the number of instances of each of its derived classes that have been instantiated but not yet released. This information is not only useful for the I/O Kit; it also provides an invaluable mechanism for tracking memory leaks. Internally, the I/O Kit uses the instance count of each class to ensure that it does not unload a kernel extension that has outstanding objects, which would lead to a kernel panic. When a kernel extension no longer has any outstanding instances for all classes that it defines, the kernel will unload that kernel extension. The number of instances of each OSObject-derived class can be examined through the command line tool "ioclasscount."

■ **Tip** If you open Terminal and run the command ioclasscount after loading the IOKitTest tutorial, you will see a single instance of the class com_osxkernel_driver_IOKitTest.

Container Classes

As well as defining the base class and providing a runtime environment for the kernel, libkern also defines a number of container classes to manage a collection of objects. The container classes provided by libkern include arrays, dictionaries, and both ordered and unordered sets. While all these containers can contain objects of varying types and can even contain objects of differing types within the same container, a container can contain only objects that are derived from the OSObject class.

■ **Note** If you are familiar with user space programming on Mac OS X, the libkern container classes are equivalent to NSMutableArray, NSMutableDictionary, and NSMutableSet, or the Core Foundation types CFMutableDictionary, CFMutableArray, and CFMutableSet.

To allow non-object scalar types such as Booleans, integers, and strings to be included in the container types, libkern provides the corresponding classes OSBoolean, OSNumber, and OSString for wrapping a bool, an integer value of up to 64 bits in length, and a C-string, respectively.

The handling of strings in libkern deserves special mention. The libkern library provides two classes for representing a string, OSString and OSSymbol (which is a subclass of OSString). The purpose of OSSymbol is not to provide a general wrapper for a string, but rather to hold string values that represent "symbols" in the kernel, such as commonly used keys in a matching dictionary. When a new instance of OSSymbol is created, the constructor checks for an existing OSSymbol object that contains the same string value, and if one is found, returns an instance of the existing object rather than creating a new instance. This means that for a given string value, there is at most one OSSymbol object representing that value. As a consequence, a dictionary that is keyed on OSSymbol values needs to compare the address of only two OSSymbol values rather than performing a more expensive string comparison.

All the container classes follow the same behavior with regard to object ownership. Any object added to a container is retained by that container class, and objects are released by the container class once they are removed from the container or the final reference of the container itself is released and so the container is deallocated. After inserting an object into a container, if the caller no longer requires its own reference to that object, it is free to release the inserted object since the container class will maintain a reference to the object.

After querying a container for an object that it contains, the caller should retain that object if there is any chance that the container could be released while the caller is still using the returned object. The libkern container classes do not increment the reference of their content objects before returning it to the caller (for example, the OSArray method getLastObject() will not increment the reference count of its last object before returning it to the caller).

It is important to note that the container classes do not provide any synchronization for use in a multi-threaded environment. That is not to say that they cannot be used in a driver that contains multi-threaded code, but rather that it is the caller's responsibility to add its own locking to ensure that calls to the container classes are serialized.

The container classes provided by libkern include the following:

- OSArray, which provides storage and retrieval of objects based on the index within the array

- OSDictionary, which provides storage and retrieval based on a provided string value (which is known as the "key")

- OSSet, which provides storage for objects and the ability to test whether an object is in the set

- OSOrderedSet, which provides storage that is sorted based on a provided comparison function and retrieval based on an index

All libkern container classes can be iterated over using the class OSCollectionIterator, as shown in Listing 4-5. When iterating over an OSDictionary, the objects returned by the iterator represent the keys of the dictionary, and not the values contained in the dictionary itself.

Listing 4-5. A Sample Function to Iterate Over the Objects Contained in an OSArray

```
void    IterateArray (OSArray* array)
{
        OSCollectionIterator*   iter;

        iter = OSCollectionIterator::withCollection(array);
        if (iter != NULL)
        {
                OSObject*       anObject;

                while ((anObject = iter->getNextObject()) != NULL)
                {
                        // Assume the array only contains string values:
                        // OSString* aString = OSDynamicCast(OSString, anObject);
                }

                iter->release();
        }
}
```

A special container object for drivers is their property table. This is a dictionary that contains a number of key/value pairs that are local to a particular driver instance. When a driver is loaded, the I/O Kit fills its property table with the entries of the matching dictionary from the driver's Info.plist file.

However, as the driver runs, it is free to add or remove additional values from its property table. A driver's property table is special because it can be accessed by user space applications, including IORegistryExplorer. This makes it a perfect means for passing small amounts of data, such as integer values, between the driver and user space.

Alternatively, a driver can write the values of certain important variables to keys in its property table, which can then be monitored in IORegistryExplorer (or a custom application) to track the state of the driver.

Summary

- The I/O Kit provides an object-oriented framework for developing drivers on Mac OS X.

- Drivers written using the framework inherit from a suitable base class that is chosen based on the functionality that the driver implements. The I/O Kit provides base classes for drivers such as audio input and output streams, serial ports, and disk devices.

- A driver accesses its hardware through an object known as its provider, which allows communication with hardware in a way that is natural to the bus on which the hardware is connected.

- A driver is loaded only when its hardware is present in the system, as described by matching criteria described in the driver's property list.

- The I/O Kit is built on top of a library known as libkern, which provides runtime support to the kernel by way of object instantiation, reference counting, and container classes.

CHAPTER 5

Interacting with Drivers from Applications

In the previous chapter, we learnt about I/O Kit drivers, which live in the kernel. On the other hand, the applications that users interact with live in user space. So, if the user is going to use the services provided by your driver, the kernel/user space boundary needs to be crossed.

Mac OS X provides several different mechanisms through which a driver can provide its services to user space applications. The method that a developer chooses to allow a particular driver to provide its services to user space applications is dependent on the type of functionality that the driver implements. For example, all serial ports, audio drivers, and storage devices have their own interface that is defined by the I/O Kit. This interface allows a user space application to work with these devices. An application will work with devices provided by any hardware vendor, provided that the vendor's driver implements the standard I/O Kit interface for that device. From a driver developer's point of view, using the common interface provided by the I/O Kit is in their best interest because it ensures that the driver is accessible to a large number of user space applications without forcing developers to adopt a custom interface for the driver. It also requires less work on your part.

A good example of this is a serial port driver. A Mac OS X user space application accesses serial ports through a character device that is represented by a file in the /dev path of the file system. To communicate over a serial device, a user application calls the same functions as it would to open, read, or write to any other file on the file system; that is open(), read(), and write(). In the kernel, a driver that provides a serial port will create an instance of the standard I/O Kit class IOSerialStreamSync. The I/O Kit's serial family will create a device node in the /dev directory, publishing the path of the node in the I/O Registry so that applications can find it. It will also pass requests from user applications to method calls in the driver's implementation, which is a subclass of the standard IOSerialDriverSync class. There was no work required by the driver developer in publishing its services to user space. This is illustrated in Figure 5-1.

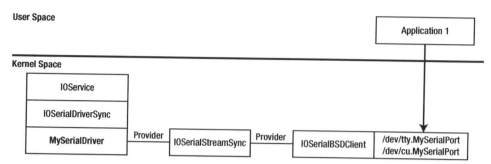

Figure 5-1. The classes involved in communicating with a serial port from a user space application. With the exception of MySerialDriver, all of the objects and their connections are created by the I/O Kit.

Not all driver developers are as fortunate as the developers of a serial port driver in having the I/O Kit take care of crossing the user space/kernel boundary. For a hardware device that provides custom functionality, the I/O Kit may not provide an appropriate client interface that your driver is able to use. In this case, your driver will need to implement a custom interface for user space applications to use when interacting with it. As we saw in Chapter 1, Mac OS X has a strict barrier between user space and the kernel. This places restrictions on the nature of how this interaction takes place. This chapter describes the methods provided by the I/O Kit to cross the user/kernel boundary and allow communication between user applications and a kernel driver.

The I/O Kit Framework

The user space API through which a process communicates with a kernel driver is provided by a framework known as "IOKit.framework," which will hereafter be referred to as the "I/O Kit framework." The I/O Kit framework allows a user space application to determine the hardware devices and kernel drivers that are present on the system, to watch for the arrival or removal of hardware that can be hot-plugged (such as USB devices), and to interact with I/O Kit drivers. The I/O Kit framework defines the data types that provide a user space representation of kernel objects and the functions that are needed to manipulate these kernel objects. Although the I/O Kit is a C++ based framework in the kernel, the user space I/O Kit framework is provided as a set of C-based functions, so it can be used by projects that are written in both C and C++ or by projects that are written in Objective-C, which is of particular importance for GUI applications.

The I/O Kit framework provides access to the kernel objects that are present in the I/O Registry, which can be examined with the IORegistryExplorer utility (see Chapter 4). The I/O Registry consists of kernel objects that represent hardware devices that are connected to the computer or drivers that have matched against connected hardware devices and have been loaded into the kernel. The objects in the I/O Registry can be created only within the kernel, including by kernel drivers, but the I/O Kit framework provides a way for applications in user space to examine the contents of the I/O Registry, including iterating the registry, determining the relationship between objects (for example, to determine which driver has been loaded against a particular hardware device), and to read and write the properties of an object in the I/O Registry.

The I/O Registry contains kernel objects that may represent either loaded drivers or connected hardware devices. This means that the functionality provided by the I/O Kit framework can be applied to both a driver and to a hardware device. In some cases, an application can directly manipulate a hardware device through its corresponding I/O Registry object without the need for a kernel driver; this is discussed in Chapter 15 for USB devices. The I/O Kit framework also allows an application to install a notification to watch for the arrival of a particular driver or hardware device.

Finding a Driver

The first step in communicating with a kernel driver from a user space application is to locate the running instances of the driver of interest. On a system such as Mac OS X, hardware devices can be plugged into the machine at any time and there may be several instances of a driver loaded if the user has connected multiple hardware devices that are supported by your driver. To handle these cases, the I/O Kit framework provides functions to not only iterate over all devices and drivers in the I/O Registry that match certain criteria, but also allows a callback function to be installed to watch for the arrival or removal of a driver or a device that matches certain criteria.

To locate a specific driver in the I/O Registry, the I/O Kit framework uses a matching dictionary that includes the properties of the driver or device that you are interested in. The beauty of the I/O Kit design is that the matching dictionary that a user space application uses to locate a driver or a hardware device takes exactly the same form as the matching dictionary found in the driver personality of a kernel driver's property list (see Chapter 4). In fact, the same code that the kernel uses to compare a driver's matching dictionary when deciding whether to load a driver against a device is the very code that is used to decide whether a device or driver is of interest to the application when comparing a user space application's matching dictionary.

As with the matching dictionary in a driver's property list, an application can create a matching dictionary that is as generic or specific as required. For example, depending on the properties you add to the matching dictionary, it could match against all USB devices or, by adding a specific USB vendor ID to the matching dictionary, against any USB device produced by a certain manufacturer. Adding a further USB product ID to the matching dictionary would allow it to match against only a specific USB device.

As an example, Listing 5-1 creates a matching dictionary that will match against any USB device and uses it to iterate over the I/O Registry, printing the name of all matching devices. To compile this sample, a new project in Xcode that is based on the Mac OS X application template named "Command Line Tool" is created. When prompted to name the project, enter "DriverIterator" and select "Core Foundation" as the project type. You will need to add the framework "I/OKit.framework" to the project; otherwise, you will receive a link error when the project is built.

The structure of the code should be fairly straightforward:

1. It creates a matching dictionary that specifies the properties of the hardware device or drivers that we are interested in. This example uses the helper function IOServiceMatching(), which creates a dictionary with a single entry for the IOProviderClass key with the specified value. This has the same effect as adding an IOProviderClass entry to the matching dictionary of a driver's property list; any kernel object that is a subclass of the specified class, IOUSBDevice in this example, will match against the dictionary.

2. It calls IOServiceGetMatchingServices() passing in the matching dictionary and receives as output an iterator that can be used to traverse all kernel objects in the I/O Registry that match the matching dictionary. The iterator represents the state of the system at the time that the function was called; once the iterator object has been created, it will not be modified, even if additional matching devices are added to the system.

3. The function IOIteratorNext() is called repeatedly, and on each call it returns the next object that matched the specified dictionary. When the final object has been received, any further calls to IOIteratorNext() will return 0. Any

object returned by the iterator has had its reference count incremented and needs to be released by the caller through a call to IOobjectRelease().

4. To refine this sample, the code excludes USB hubs and only lists the names of actual USB devices. This also allows the sample to demonstrate the type introspection functionality that user space applications can perform on kernel objects. To do this, the function IOobjectCopyClass() is called, which returns the object's class type as a CoreFoundation string. The matching dictionary will include all objects that are either instances of IOUSBDevice or instances of classes that are derived from IOUSBDevice, which includes the IOUSBHubDevice class. To exclude USB hub devices from the listing, this sample will ignore any objects whose class name is not an exact match of the string "IOUSBDevice."

Listing 5-1. Code To Iterate All Connected USB Hardware Devices

```
#include <CoreFoundation/CoreFoundation.h>
#include <IOKit/IOKitLib.h>

int main (int argc, const char * argv[])
{
        CFDictionaryRef     matchingDict = NULL;
        io_iterator_t       iter = 0;
        io_service_t        service = 0;
        kern_return_t       kr;

        // Create a matching dictionary that will find any USB device.
        matchingDict = IOServiceMatching("IOUSBDevice");

        // Create an iterator for all I/O Registry objects that match the dictionary.
        kr = IOServiceGetMatchingServices(kIOMasterPortDefault, matchingDict, &iter);
        if (kr != KERN_SUCCESS)
                return -1;

        // Iterate over all matching objects.
        while ((service = IOIteratorNext(iter)) != 0)
        {
                CFStringRef     className;
                io_name_t       name;

                // List all IOUSBDevice objects, ignoring objects that subclass IOUSBDevice.
                className = IOobjectCopyClass(service);
                if (CFEqual(className, CFSTR("IOUSBDevice")) == true)
                {
                        IORegistryEntryGetName(service, name);
                        printf("Found device with name: %s\n", name);
                }
                CFRelease(className);
                IOobjectRelease(service);
        }

        // Release the iterator.
        IOobjectRelease(iter);
```

```
        return 0;
}
```

■ **Note** The function IOServiceGetMatchingServices() is guaranteed to release a reference on the matching dictionary that is passed in. This is why the code in Listing 5-1 does not need to call CFRelease() on the CFDicionaryRef that it creates.

Listing 5-1 uses a function named IOServiceGetMatchingServices() to create a matching dictionary for kernel objects that the application is interested in. The first parameter to the function IOServiceGetMatchingServices() is a Mach port that is used for communicating between the user space process and the I/O Kit. In Mac OS X 10.2 and later, a convenience macro named kIOMasterPortDefault was introduced, although some of the Apple sample code still uses the pre-Mac OS X 10.2 approach of calling the IOMasterPort() function to obtain the I/O Kit's Mach port.

On a system such as Mac OS X, hardware devices can be plugged into the system at any time. The problem with the approach that we used in the previous section is that it requires the application to poll for a list of connected devices. A better approach is to have the I/O Kit notify your application whenever a device that you are interested in is connected to the computer. The I/O Kit framework provides an alternative approach in which the application specifies a matching dictionary and a callback function to be notified when an object that meets the matching dictionary is added to the I/O Registry. As with similar functions in Mac OS X, notifications from the I/O Kit framework are delivered using the standard event dispatch mechanism known as a "run loop."

The run loop is the fundamental means by which a Mac OS X or iOS application is notified of events from multiple sources without having to spend CPU time polling each source. The run loop is a Core Foundation object that monitors multiple "run loop sources." Whenever any of them generates an event that requires processing, the run loop dispatches the event to a registered callback function. Each thread on Mac OS X contains a run loop, including the main thread. The event loop on Mac OS X, which runs on the main thread, is simply a run loop that contains sources for keyboard and mouse events. For example, in response to the user clicking the mouse button, the main thread's run loop will awake and generate a Cocoa mouse down event for the application window in which the user clicked.

Listing 5-2 demonstrates how a command line utility can register to receive notifications whenever a USB device is connected to the computer. You will notice that the same matching dictionary can be used whether using a polling method or the notification callback.

Listing 5-2. Code To Watch for the Arrival of USB Devices

```
#include <CoreFoundation/CoreFoundation.h>
#include <IOKit/IOKitLib.h>

int main (int argc, const char * argv[])
{
        CFDictionaryRef          matchingDict = NULL;
        io_iterator_t            iter = 0;
        IONotificationPortRef    notificationPort = NULL;
        CFRunLoopSourceRef       runLoopSource;
        kern_return_t            kr;
```

```
    // Create a matching dictionary that will find any USB device
    matchingDict = IOServiceMatching("IOUSBDevice");

    notificationPort = IONotificationPortCreate(kIOMasterPortDefault);
    runLoopSource = IONotificationPortGetRunLoopSource(notificationPort);
    CFRunLoopAddSource(CFRunLoopGetCurrent(), runLoopSource, kCFRunLoopDefaultMode);

    kr = IOServiceAddMatchingNotification(notificationPort, kIOFirstMatchNotification,
        matchingDict, DeviceAdded, NULL, &iter);
    DeviceAdded(NULL, iter);

    CFRunLoopRun();

    IONotificationPortDestroy(notificationPort);

    // Release the iterator
    IOObjectRelease(iter);

    return 0;
}
```

To create a notification callback for device and driver objects that meet certain criteria, the code in Listing 5-2 performs the following steps:

1. A matching dictionary is created that describes the properties of the device that the application is interested in.

2. The function IONotificationPortCreate() is called to set up the communication channel through which the I/O Kit is able to deliver notification messages to the user space application.

3. Because we want to use a run loop to dispatch notifications to our application, we create a run loop source to represent the notification port and install that source on the current thread's run loop.

4. We then call IOServiceAddMatchingNotification() to associate the matching dictionary with the notification port (and run loop source). This function allocates and returns an iterator object, which plays an important role in the operation of notification messages. Following the call to IOServiceAddMatchingNotification(), the iterator contains all objects from the I/O Registry that match the matching dictionary. The I/O Kit framework won't deliver notifications for these devices, so we need to manually call our callback function, passing in the returned iterator. It's also important to do this because, until the end of the iterator is reached by calling IOIteratorNext(), no notifications will be delivered and the callback function will not be called. Similarly, the device callback must run through the iterator until the final object is reached. The caller must not release the iterator until the notification callback is no longer needed. As with the IOServiceGetMatchingServices() function, when IOServiceAddMatchingNotification() is called, it will always decrement the reference count of the matching dictionary. Therefore, if the caller requires the dictionary after installing the notification, it should manually retain the object beforehand.

5. Since this example is a command line utility, we need to manually run the run loop by calling CFRunLoopRun(). If this were a Cocoa-based application and we were installing the notification into the main run loop, the run loop would be started for us by the NSApplicationMain() function.

6. Finally, when the application exits, we destroy the notification port. This automatically removes the run loop source from the run loop into which it was added and releases the iterator object.

The callback function DeviceAdded is shown in Listing 5-3. You will notice that it is identical to the code that we used in the polling implementation. The iterator object that is passed to the callback function is the same object that is returned from the initial call to IOServiceAddMatchingNotification(). Because the same object is re-used for all devices that the notification informs us of, it is important that the callback does not release the iterator object, since the iterator must remain valid while the notification is installed.

Listing 5-3. Code To Watch for the Arrival of USB Devices

```
void DeviceAdded (void* refCon, io_iterator_t iterator)
{
        io_service_t            service = 0;

        // Iterate over all matching objects.
        while ((service = IOIteratorNext(iterator)) != 0)
        {
                CFStringRef     className;
                io_name_t       name;

                // List all IOUSBDevice objects, ignoring objects that subclass IOUSBDevice.
                className = IOObjectCopyClass(service);
                if (CFEqual(className, CFSTR("IOUSBDevice")) == true)
                {
                        IORegistryEntryGetName(service, name);
                        printf("Found device with name: %s\n", name);
                }
                CFRelease(className);
                IOObjectRelease(service);
        }
}
```

▩ **Tip** A common cause of problems with device notification callbacks is failing to empty the iterator by calling IOIteratorNext() until 0 is returned. Once the end of the iterator is reached, the iterator is re-armed and the callback is enabled.

For hardware devices that have a kernel driver, user space applications will control the hardware by sending control requests to the driver rather than interacting with the hardware device directly. In this case, the application isn't so much interested in the arrival of a particular hardware device as it is interested in when the driver for the hardware has loaded. This can be performed by creating a dictionary that matches the class name of the driver using the function IOServiceMatching(). For example, to create a dictionary that will match against the sample I/O Kit driver that was developed in Chapter 4, an application would use the following code:

```
IOServiceMatching("com_osxkernel_driver_IOKitTest");
```

The reverse-DNS naming scheme ensures that the driver's class name is unique, which means that any driver that matches the matching dictionary is guaranteed to be our driver.

Observing Device Removal

As well as watching for the arrival of devices, an application may wish to watch for a device being removed from the system, such as a USB device being unplugged. Unlike device arrival messages, which are delivered for any device that meets the criteria described by a matching dictionary, a device removal message is delivered only for a particular device that the application has registered an interest in. An application will typically register an interest in all devices that it has opened, since the application will want to respond to the removal of a device that it is accessing.

In our previous code examples, such as Listing 5-3, we obtained a reference to a driver object, read properties from the driver, and then released the driver object, all within the one function. It is far more common that an application will hold on to the driver object beyond the device arrival callback function, perhaps only releasing it when the application exits or the device is removed.

▧ **Note** In our previous examples, we were able to use the local variables of a function to hold the driver object, since the driver was released before we returned from the function. However, if an application wishes to use the driver object after returning from the function, it will need to allocate a structure on the heap to hold the driver state.

Having obtained a reference to a driver instance, an application can register to receive notifications when the driver's state changes, including when the driver has terminated in response to its hardware device being removed. This notification callback is installed by calling the function named IOServiceAddInterestNotification(), which is defined in the I/O Kit framework. As with the notification for device arrival, the application needs to provide a port on which the I/O Kit will signal the application when the driver's state has changed. This can be created with the function IONotificationPortCreate(), as was shown in Listing 5-2. If the application has already created a notification port for device arrival events, it can share that same notification port and its corresponding run loop source to receive device removal notifications. This is done by passing the existing notification port to the function IOServiceAddInterestNotification().

When the application receives a notification that a driver instance has terminated, it should release its reference to that driver and take any action that is necessary to inform the user that the device has been removed.

Listing 5-4 demonstrates a modification to the DeviceAdded() function from Listing 5-3 that creates a structure to represent an instance of a driver within the application and then installs a callback to receive notifications from the driver (such as driver termination).

Listing 5-4. Code Snippet Demonstrating How an Application Can Install a Callback Function To Receive a Notification When a Driver Terminates

```
#include <IOKit/IOMessage.h>

// Structure to describe a driver instance.
typedef struct {
        io_service_t    service;
        io_object_t     notification;
} MyDriverData;

// Notification port used for both device arrival and driver state changes.
IONotificationPortRef   gNotificationPort = NULL;

void DeviceAdded (void* refCon, io_iterator_t iterator)
{
        io_service_t            service = 0;

        // Iterate over all matching objects.
        while ((service = IOIteratorNext(iterator)) != 0)
        {
                MyDriverData*   myDriverData;
                kern_return_t   kr;

                // Allocate a structure to hold the driver instance.
                myDriverData = (MyDriverData*)malloc(sizeof(MyDriverData));
                // Save the io_service_t for this driver instance.
                myDriverData->service = service;

                // Install a callback to receive notification of driver state changes.
                kr = IOServiceAddInterestNotification(gNotificationPort,
                                        service,                        // driver object
                                        kIOGeneralInterest,
                                        DeviceNotification,             // callback
                                        myDriverData,           // refCon passed to callback
                                        &myDriverData->notification);

        }
}

void DeviceNotification (void* refCon, io_service_t service, natural_t messageType,
        void* messageArgument)
{
        MyDriverData*   myDriverData = (MyDriverData*)refCon;
        kern_return_t   kr;

        // Only handle driver termination notifications.
        if (messageType == kIOMessageServiceIsTerminated)
        {
                // Print the name of the removed device.
                io_name_t       name;
                IORegistryEntryGetName(service, name);
```

```
        printf("Device removed: %s\n", name);

        // Remove the driver state change notification.
        kr = IOObjectRelease(myDriverData->notification);

        // Release our reference to the driver object.
        IOObjectRelease(myDriverData->service);

        // Release our structure that holds the driver connection.
        free(myDriverData);
    }
}
```

Modifying Driver Properties

Once an application has located the driver object that it is interested in, it can interact with the driver and the hardware device that it controls. The I/O Kit framework provides two ways to interact with a driver from user space. One method requires the application to open a connection to the driver and then to use that connection to send control requests to the driver and receive status. A connection-based approach is necessary if the driver needs to maintain the state of a client or needs access control to ensure that only one client at a time can access the hardware device. This is discussed later in this chapter.

Another method, which is far simpler, is to allow an application to read and write key/value property values to the driver. The driver can perform certain types of operations without having to know which client sent the request, such as reading or writing driver preference values or configuring the settings of a hardware device. For example, the volume level of an audio device is a single value that could be read or written by any user application. When that value is set, the driver can reconfigure the hardware device for the new volume setting, regardless of which application set the value.

As we saw in Chapter 4, each I/O Kit driver contains a property table that is a dictionary of key/value pairs. A driver's property table is accessible from any user space application without restriction (which is how the I/ORegistryExplorer utility is able to display each driver's properties). Furthermore, an application can add new key/value pairs to a driver's property table and can modify the value of an existing property. This can be used to easily exchange small amounts of data between a user space application and a kernel driver. Since this approach is not connection based, the driver cannot modify its behavior for different user applications; every user application can access the same property table values. However, if there are multiple instances of the same driver loaded, each instance has its own property table. It should be noted that the driver's property table is volatile and will not be saved when the driver is unloaded.

Once an application has located the driver that it is interested in, the I/O Kit framework contains functions that make it very easy to read and write a driver's property table. The function IORegistryEntryCreateCFProperties() provides the calling application with a snapshot of the state of a driver's property table as a Core Foundation dictionary. If the application is interested in the value of a particular key, then the function IORegistryEntryCreateCFProperty() can be used. For example, suppose we wished to modify the callback function from Listing 5-3 so that it prints the name of the manufacturer for each USB device that is connected to the computer rather than printing the device name. The IOUSBDevice class makes the manufacturer string available through its property table with a key "USB Vendor Name." The code in Listing 5-5 shows the modified callback function, which reads the vendor name from the device's property table.

Listing 5-5. Reading the Property Table of a USB Device To Obtain the Device's Manufacturer String

```
void DeviceAdded (void* refCon, io_iterator_t iterator)
{
        io_service_t              service = 0;

        // Iterate over all matching objects
        while ((service = IOIteratorNext(iterator)) != 0)
        {
                CFStringRef      className;

                // List all IOUSBDevice objects, ignoring objects that subclass IOUSBDevice.
                className = IOObjectCopyClass(service);
                if (CFEqual(className, CFSTR("IOUSBDevice")) == true)
                {
                        CFTypeRef                    vendorName;

                        vendorName = IORegistryEntryCreateCFProperty(service,
                                CFSTR("USB Vendor Name"), kCFAllocatorDefault, 0);
                        CFShow(vendorName);
                }
                CFRelease(className);
                IOObjectRelease(service);
        }
}
```

As the code in Listing 5-5 shows, the property table is a very convenient way for a driver to publish information to user applications, such as a description of its hardware, the driver's current state, or debugging information. Another use of a driver's property table is to allow an application to pass small amounts of data to a driver. As an example, let's modify the sample I/O Kit driver that was developed in Chapter 4 to allow an application to specify a custom message to be printed when the driver is unloaded. We will do this by adding a string value to the property table under the key "StopMessage." This key will be added to the property table by a user space application but will be read from the property table by the kernel driver when it is being unloaded.

Let's begin by modifying the user space application. First, it needs to locate the I/O Kit driver that was written in Chapter 4. This can be done by creating the following matching dictionary:

```
matchingDict = IOServiceMatching("com_osxkernel_driver_IOKitTest");
```

Next, we will write string value "The driver has stopped" to the driver's property table and make it accessible under the key "StopMessage":

```
IORegistryEntrySetCFProperty(service, CFSTR("StopMessage"), CFSTR("The driver has stopped"));
```

That's all that is required from the user space application. In this example, we have chosen to use a string value, although the value of a driver's property may be any of the Core Foundation types CFString, CFNumber, CFBoolean, CFData, or a CFArray or CFDictionary containing objects of the supported Core Foundation types.

When a driver's property is set from a user space application, the method setProperties() in the corresponding driver object is called with a parameter containing a dictionary of the properties that have been set. The method setProperties() is defined in the IORegistryEntry class, but since every I/O Kit driver class is a subclass of IOService, which is itself a subclass of IORegistryEntry, every driver object can override this method. By default, the base class implementation of setProperties() does nothing. So unless your driver provides an implementation, any properties set on your driver by a user space application will be ignored.

The setProperties() method provides a driver with a chance to immediately respond to a value that has been set from a user space application. If the modified property requires the driver to reconfigure the underlying hardware device, the setProperties() method is the place in which this should be performed. For our sample driver, when an application changes the StopMessage property, we will have the driver update its property table and insert the provided string value. This will also make the property available so that it can be read by user applications, including I/ORegistryExplorer. The code to handle this is shown in Listing 5-6.

Listing 5-6. A Sample Implementation of the Driver's setProperties() Method

```
IOReturn com_osxkernel_driver_IOKitTest::setProperties (OSObject* properties)
{
        OSDictionary*    propertyDict;

        // The provided properties object should be an OSDictionary object.
        propertyDict = OSDynamicCast(OSDictionary, properties);
        if (propertyDict != NULL)
        {
                OSObject*               theValue;
                OSString*               theString;

                // Read the value corresponding to the key "StopMessage" from the dictionary.
                theValue = propertyDict->getObject("StopMessage");
                theString = OSDynamicCast(OSString, theValue);
                if (theString != NULL)
                {
                        // Add the value to the driver's property table.
                        setProperty("StopMessage", theString);
                        return kIOReturnSuccess;
                }
        }

        return kIOReturnUnsupported;
}
```

Finally, when the sample driver unloads, it should print the custom stop message if one was set from a user space application. This can be done by querying the driver's property table for the value of the key "StopMessage," as shown in Listing 5-7. In this example, we have chosen to write the property to the driver's property table. There is no requirement for a driver to handle the setProperties() method in this way. We could have saved the provided string value in an instance variable or, if the value was used to reconfigure hardware, we could have written the value to hardware in the setProperties() method, after which the driver would have no further need for the value and could discard it.

Listing 5-7. Using the Custom String Value That Has Been Set by the User Application

```
void com_osxkernel_driver_IOKitTest::stop (IOService *provider)
{
        OSString*        stopMessage;
```

```
        // Read a possible custom string to print from the driver property table.
        stopMessage = OSDynamicCast(OSString, getProperty("StopMessage"));
        if (stopMessage)
                IOLog("%s\n", stopMessage->getCStringNoCopy());

        super::stop(provider);
}
```

State-Based Interaction

Although the approach of getting and setting driver properties provides a very easy way to interact with a driver and a hardware device, it is rather inflexible, which makes it suitable only for very specific uses. The I/O Kit Framework provides another method for interacting with drivers from user space applications that is based on a connection between a user application and the driver. The use of a connection allows the driver to determine which user application a request has originated from and can therefore associate a state with the connection. (Alternatively, because an application can have multiple connections open to a driver, the driver can determine which connection a request is originating from.) This allows for the implementation of complex protocols and state-based control.

For example, a hardware device may be accessible to one user space application at a time, which requires an application to request exclusive access to the device. Having obtained exclusive access, it may then need to configure the device before reading or writing data. With a connection-based approach, the driver can allow control of the hardware to the client that has been granted exclusive access to the device and reject requests from other connections. Furthermore, it can ensure that a client cannot read or write data if that connection hasn't previously configured the hardware as required. The use of a connection also allows a driver to implement asynchronous operations. An application can send a request to the driver to begin a background operation and could then poll the driver to determine whether the transaction has been completed. Because the driver sees the request to begin the operation and each request to poll the status of the operation is being made from the same connection, it can use this to determine which operation the application is polling. Alternatively, the driver could use the application's connection to send a notification to the application when the background operation has completed and thus eliminate the need for the status to be polled.

In the kernel, each connection made to the driver from a user application is represented by a class known as IOUserClient. For each connection made to a driver, the I/O Kit instantiates an IOUserClient object, and that object is destroyed only when the application closes its connection to the driver or when the application terminates. All control requests that the application makes to the driver are handled by the user client object that represents that particular connection. A driver provides its own implementation of a class that subclasses from IOUserClient, adding any methods and instance variables that it needs to maintain the state of an application's connection.

The ingenuity of the I/O Kit design is that user client objects are themselves a driver object: the IOUserClient class inherits from IOService and, as with any other IOService instance, each user client has a provider class that, for a user client, is the instance of the driver that the application is controlling. An example of the relationship between a driver and its user client instances is shown in Figure 5-2.

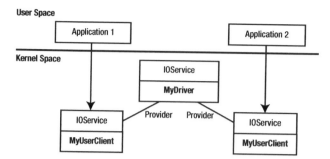

Figure 5-2. *The relationship between a driver object and its user client objects that provide the kernel-side representation of an application's connection to the driver.*

To establish a connection to a driver, an application simply has to call the function IOServiceOpen() as follows:

```
task_port_t     owningTask = mach_task_self();
uint32_t        type = 0;
io_connect_t    driverConnection;
kern_return_t   kr;
```

```
kr = IOServiceOpen(service, owningTask, type, &driverConnection);
```

In the preceding code, service represents the driver that the application wishes to connect to, which is found using the standard driver matching techniques described earlier, owningTask represents the running application, and type is an unsigned 32-bit integer whose value is interpreted by the driver in any way that it chooses. The driverConnection parameter is returned to the caller if the function completes successfully and represents the established connection to the driver. Any request that the application sends to the driver will be made by calling a function that takes this connection object as a parameter. When the application is no longer interested in controlling the driver, it makes a call to the function IOServiceClose().

When an application calls the function IOServiceOpen(), the operating system calls the specified driver object in the kernel, which handles the request. The driver's class receives the following method call:

```
IOReturn    DriverClass::newUserClient (task_t owningTask, void* securityID, UInt32 type,
OSDictionary* properties, IOUserClient** handler)
```

Many of the parameters to the newUserClient() method should look familiar. They are simply the values that the user space application passed to the IOServiceOpen() function. The kernel implementation of newUserClient() is responsible for instantiating a new user client object and returning it to the caller through the handler parameter. However, most drivers will never need to implement the newUserClient() method because an implementation that is suitable for nearly all uses is provided by the IOService base class. To take advantage of this standard implementation, all that a driver needs to do is add a string value to its property table with the key "IOUserClientClass." The value of this property is a string value that contains the class name of a driver's user client class. This can be done either by adding an entry to the driver's personality in the Info.plist file (because the driver's property table is initialized from the values in the Info.plist file) or by manually setting the property when the driver loads. For example, the driver in Figure 5-2 has a user client that is implemented by a class named MyUserClient and, as a result, would set its user client class with the following call:

```
setProperty("IOUserClientClass", "MyUserClient");
```

The standard implementation of newUserClient() will instantiate the driver's specified user client class and initialize the new user client, making the main driver class its provider.

Let's look at how we would implement a user client class for the tutorial I/O Kit driver that was developed in Chapter 4. The header file for a skeleton user client class for this driver is shown in Listing 5-8. You will notice that many of the methods that the user client implements are similar to the methods implemented by the main driver class, which is because the class IOUserClient is derived from the same IOService class that every driver is ultimately derived from. A user client therefore implements the same initialization and termination methods that any other driver class must implement.

Listing 5-8. The Header File for a Basic User Client Class

```
class com_osxkernel_driver_IOKitTestUserClient : public IOUserClient
{
        OSDeclareDefaultStructors(com_osxkernel_driver_IOKitTestUserClient)

private:
        task_t                          m_task;
        com_osxkernel_driver_IOKitTest* m_driver;

public:
        virtual bool    initWithTask (task_t owningTask, void* securityToken,
                                        UInt32 type, OSDictionary* properties);
        virtual bool    start (IOService* provider);

        virtual IOReturn        clientClose (void);
        virtual void    stop (IOService* provider);
        virtual void    free (void);
};
```

Along with the familiar methods start(), stop(), and free(), the user client provides an additional method that is part of a user client's object management, namely clientClose(). This method is called when the user space application has closed its connection to the driver, either through a call to IOServiceClose() or because the application has terminated or crashed. A driver should not trust a user space application to be well-written and to tidy up after itself before the user client is closed. Therefore, the clientClose() method is a good place for a driver to make sure that the hardware is returned to an idle state and ready for the next user space application that wishes to use it.

▪ **Tip** The IOUserClient class provides a method named clientDied(). A subclass can choose to implement this method if it needs to distinguish between a client connection closing as a result of the user space process terminating without calling IOServiceClose(). Since the default implementation of clientDied() simply calls clientClose(), most user client implementations can get by with an implementation of the clientClose() method which handles both cases.

The implementation of a sample user client class is shown in Listing 5-9. For brevity, the implementation methods of stop() and free() have been omitted because, for our basic user client, these methods are simply calling through to the implementation provided by the superclass.

Listing 5-9. The Implementation of a Basic User Client Class

```
// Define the superclass.
#define super IOUserClient

OSDefineMetaClassAndStructors(com_osxkernel_driver_IOKitTestUserClient, IOUserClient)

bool    com_osxkernel_driver_IOKitTestUserClient::initWithTask (task_t owningTask, void*
securityToken, UInt32 type, OSDictionary* properties)
{
        if (!owningTask)
                return false;

        if (! super::initWithTask(owningTask, securityToken , type, properties))
                return false;

        m_task = owningTask;

        // Optional:  Determine whether the calling process has admin privileges.
        IOReturn ret = clientHasPrivilege(securityToken, kIOClientPrivilegeAdministrator);
        if ( ret == kIOReturnSuccess )
        {
                // m_taskIsAdmin = true;
        }

        return true;
}

bool    com_osxkernel_driver_IOKitTestUserClient::start (IOService* provider)
{
        if (! super::start(provider))
                return false;

        m_driver = OSDynamicCast(com_osxkernel_driver_IOKitTest, provider);
        if (!m_driver)
                return false;

        return true;
}

IOReturn        com_osxkernel_driver_IOKitTestUserClient::clientClose (void)
{
        terminate();
        return kIOReturnSuccess;
}
```

There are several important points to note about the implementation of the three user client methods shown in Listing 5-9:

- In the initWithTask() method, we save the parameter owningTask to an instance variable. As we will see later in the chapter, this value is needed when we wish to access memory in the client's address space, such as when writing data from the driver to a buffer that has been allocated by the client process. The initWithTask() method is also an opportunity to determine the privileges of the calling process. Although not commonly needed, it is possible that the user client may wish to limit certain operations to tasks that are running with administrative privileges. For example, an Ethernet card could use this to prevent a non-privileged process from enabling promiscuous mode and having access to all network packets.

- The start() method is fairly straightforward, although it is worth noting that the provider class that is passed in as an argument is an instance to the main driver class. Since the user client's role is to accept control requests from a user space application and pass these requests on to the driver, the provider class will need a reference to the main driver class. This can be obtained by saving the provider class from the start() method to an instance variable.

- The clientClose() method is called in response to the calling process closing its driver connection by calling the IOServiceClose() function or otherwise terminating without closing its connection to the driver. The user client receives clientClose() before any other methods that are called as part of an IOService termination, such as stop() and free(). An implementation of clientClose() should release any resources that were allocated on behalf of the calling process and return the hardware to an idle state. Finally, it is important that the implementation calls the terminate() method, which begins the process of destroying the user client object.

The role of the user client is to act as an intermediary between all communications between an application in user space and a kernel driver. Requests from user space are identified by a 32-bit integer control code that is defined by the driver developer. Along with each request, the application can also provide parameters and receive results back from the control request. Having created the user client class, all that remains is for us to define an interface to expose the driver's functionality to user space applications. This interface will consist of two parts:

- A library of functions that can be called by user space applications that wish to take advantage of services provided by the kernel driver

- A number of methods in the user client class that correspond to each user function and that provide the kernel-side implementation of the interface

Both the library functions in user space and the user client methods in the kernel require only a basic implementation, since the functionality itself comes from the main driver class. The role of the functions in the user space interface is to encode the operation and its parameters and pass the request on to the driver. When the user client receives the request, its role is to decode the operation and parameters and to call the appropriate driver function that implements the requested functionality.

For our simple user client, we will define an interface that provides timing functionality to applications. The user space interface will implement the following functions:

```
kern_return_t   StartTimer (io_connect_t connection);
kern_return_t   StopTimer (io_connect_t connection);
kern_return_t   GetElapsedTimerTime (io_connect_t connection, uint32_t* timerTime);
kern_return_t   GetElapsedTimerValue (io_connect_t connection, TimerValue* timerValue);
```

```
kern_return_t   DelayForMs (io_connect_t connection, uint32_t milliseconds);
kern_return_t   DelayForTime (io_connect_t connection, const TimerValue* timerValue);
```

All driver interfaces have values and type definitions that are needed by both the user space implementation and the kernel's user client implementation. For the interface that we have defined, the shared definitions include the request codes and the definition of types, such as the TimerValue structure. To allow these definitions to be shared between both projects, such definitions are usually placed in a common header file that can be included by both the user space application and the kernel project. The shared definitions for our driver are shown in Listing 5-10.

Listing 5-10. The Contents of "TestDriverInterface.h" Containing Definitions That Are Required by Both the Kernel User Client and the User Space Interface.

```
typedef struct TimerValue
{
        uint64_t        time;
        uint64_t        timebase;
} TimerValue;

// Control request codes for user client methods.
enum TimerRequestCode {
        kTestUserClientStartTimer,
        kTestUserClientStopTimer,
        kTestUserClientGetElapsedTimerTime,
        kTestUserClientGetElapsedTimerValue,
        kTestUserClientDelayForMs,
        kTestUserClientDelayForTime,

        kTestUserClientMethodCount
};
```

▪ **Note** The interface by which IOUserClient dispatches a control requests to an appropriate handler was changed in Mac OS X 10.5 to support a 64-bit kernel. The new implementation is not backwards compatible with older versions of Mac OS X. This chapter describes the updated interface only.

The I/O Kit framework contains a number of functions that an application can use to invoke a method in a driver's user client. The choice of which function an application should use for a particular control request depends on the type of parameters that are required by the operation. For a request whose parameters are integer-based, the function IOConnectCallScalarMethod() is an appropriate choice since it allows a variable-sized array of 64-bit integers to be passed from the user process to the kernel user client and receives an array of 64-bit integers from the kernel driver containing the result of the operation:

```
kern_return_t   IOConnectCallScalarMethod(
                        io_connect_t            connection,
                        uint32_t                selector,
                        const uint64_t*         inputValues,
```

```
            uint32_t              inputCount,
            uint64_t*             outputValues,
            uint32_t*             outputCount);
```

The first argument to the function is a connection to a driver's user client, which the caller will have previously obtained by calling IOServiceOpen(). The next argument, selector, is the control code that is defined by the driver and describes which operation the user client should perform. This will be a value from the TimerRequestCode enumeration defined in Listing 5-10. The remaining arguments to the function allow the application to pass any parameters that are needed by the user client when it performs the operation and to receive any results back from the user client following the operation. Parameters that are labeled as inputs are provided by the calling application to the user client. Parameters that are labeled as outputs are returned to the application by the user client. The outputCount argument is both an input and an output argument; the caller initializes its value to the number of elements in the outputValues array, which tells the user client how many values it can safely write to the array. When the function completes, the number of values that were actually written to the outputValues array is returned in the value of outputCount. If the caller isn't expecting any values to be returned by the user client, it can simply pass NULL as the outputCount argument.

If a control request takes parameters of different types, it may be more natural to define a structure that combines all of the parameters that are provided to the user client and a structure to receive the result of the method. This is provided by the I/O Kit framework's IOConnectCallStructMethod() function:

```
kern_return_t   IOConnectCallStructMethod(
                    io_connect_t    connection,
                    uint32_t        selector,
                    const void*     inputStruct,
                    size_t          inputStructSize,
                    void*           outputStruct,
                    size_t*         outputStructSize);
```

A pointer to the structure containing the input parameters is provided through the inputStruct argument, and the size of the input structure in bytes is passed as the inputStructSize argument. As with the scalar function, the argument outputStructSize is both an input and an output argument. The caller initializes its value to the maximum size in bytes of the outputStruct buffer and, on completion, the user client returns through the outputStructSize argument the number of bytes written to the outputStruct buffer.

You may be wondering why the size of the returned structure would ever differ from the expected size of the output structure. The function IOConnectCallStructMethod() may be used to read a variable-length array or a variable-length string from the user client. In these instances, the caller doesn't know beforehand the number of bytes that will be returned. If the control request takes no input structure, then NULL can be passed as the inputStruct argument with an inputStructSize of 0 bytes. If the control request returns no output structure, then NULL can be passed for both the outputStruct and the outputStructSize arguments.

The I/O Kit framework also allows a mix of both scalar parameters and structure parameters for functions that have some integer-based input or output parameters, as well as requiring an input or output structure parameter:

```
kern_return_t   IOConnectCallMethod(
                    io_connect_t    connection,
                    uint32_t        selector,
                    const uint64_t* inputValues,
                    uint32_t        inputCount,
                    const void*     inputStruct,
```

```
        size_t              inputStructSize,
        uint64_t*           outputValues,
        uint32_t*           outputCount,
        void*               outputStruct,
        size_t*             outputStructSize);
```

Although the I/O Kit framework provides three functions for calling user client methods, the functions IOConnectCallScalarMethod() and IOConnectCallStructMethod() are merely convenience functions that are built on top of IOConnectCallMethod().

Given the three methods that the I/O Kit framework provides for calling user client methods, let's look at how we can implement the user space interface for our sample driver. The functions StartTimer() and StopTimer() pass no additional parameters to the user client, so they could be implemented by calling any of the three IOConnectCallXXX() functions. We have chosen to implement StartTimer() and StopTimer() using the IOConnectCallMethod() function. The user space implementation for StartTimer() is as follows:

```
kern_return_t   StartTimer (io_connect_t connection)
{
        return IOConnectCallMethod(connection, kTestUserClientStartTimer,
                          NULL, 0, NULL, 0, NULL, NULL, NULL, NULL);
}
```

The implementation of GetElapsedTimerTime() reads a 32-bit integer from the user client, and so it seems natural to implement it using the function IOConnectCallScalarMethod(). The integer type used to represent scalar values used by the I/O Kit is a 64-bit unsigned integer and not the 32-bit value that our caller is expecting so we need to thunk the result that is received from the user client through a temporary 64-bit variable. We don't check the value of scalarOutCount after the IOConnectCallScalarMethod() function completes, because we can trust our driver's implementation to have returned a single integer if the operation completes successfully.

```
kern_return_t   GetElapsedTimerTime (io_connect_t connection, uint32_t* timerTime)
{
        uint64_t                scalarOut[1];
        uint32_t                scalarOutCount;
        kern_return_t           result;

        scalarOutCount = 1;     // Initialize to the size of scalarOut array
        result = IOConnectCallScalarMethod(connection, kTestUserClientGetElapsedTimerTime,
                              NULL, 0, scalarOut, &scalarOutCount);
        if (result == kIOReturnSuccess)
                *timerTime = (uint32_t)scalarOut[0];

        return result;
}
```

Finally, let's take a look at the implementation of the function DelayForTime() in our user space library. This function passes its parameters to the user client through a structure, so we have implemented it using the function IOConnectCallStructMethod().

```
kern_return_t   DelayForTime (io_connect_t connection, const TimerValue* timerValue)
{
        return IOConnectCallStructMethod(connection, kTestUserClientDelayForTime,
                              timerValue, sizeof(TimerValue), NULL, 0);
}
```

All requests from a user space application will invoke a method named externalMethod() in the user client class, which has the responsibility of dispatching the appropriate method to handle the control request and unpacking the parameters that were provided by the user space application. The IOUserClient base class provides an implementation of externalMethod(); however, any user client that provides support for control requests should override the base class's implementation. Before looking any further into how a driver's user client should implement externalMethod(), it is worth taking a look at its interface:

```
IOReturn IOUserClient::externalMethod (uint32_t selector, IOExternalMethodArguments* args,
                    IOExternalMethodDispatch* dispatch, OSObject* target,
                    void* reference);
```

When the I/O Kit calls your class's implementation of externalMethod(), only the first two arguments will be filled in; the value of dispatch, target, and reference will all be set to NULL. The first argument, selector, is the 32-bit control code that specifies which operation the client application is requesting. The next argument, args, contains all of the scalar and structure parameters that the application passed to the user client. The definition of the IOExternalMethodArguments structure is shown in the following listing, with some fields omitted for clarity:

```
struct IOExternalMethodArguments
{
        ...
        const uint64_t*      scalarInput;
        uint32_t             scalarInputCount;

        const void*          structureInput;
        uint32_t             structureInputSize;

        IOMemoryDescriptor*  structureInputDescriptor;

        uint64_t*            scalarOutput;
        uint32_t             scalarOutputCount;

        void*                structureOutput;
        uint32_t             structureOutputSize;

        IOMemoryDescriptor*  structureOutputDescriptor;
        uint32_t             structureOutputDescriptorSize;
};
```

The fields of the IOExternalMethodArguments structure should look familiar since they are an almost perfect match of the arguments list of the user space IOConnectCallMethod() function. Two fields that deserve an explanation are structureInputDescriptor and structureOutputDescriptor. These fields are used to pass structures that are larger than 4096 bytes between the user process and the kernel driver. For structures that are smaller than the virtual memory page size, the I/O Kit will copy the entire structure between the user buffer and a kernel memory buffer. For larger buffers, the I/O Kit creates an IOMemoryDescriptor object to reference the buffer from the user process's address space directly. The IOMemoryDescriptor class is described in Chapter 6 "Memory Management."

Given that the first two arguments to externalMethod() provide the implementation with all the information that it requires to perform the requested operation, you may be wondering where the remaining three arguments fit in. The conventional approach taken by a driver's user client in implementing externalMethod() is to call the IOUserClient superclass's implementation, passing the values for selector and args that were provided to its method but filling in the dispatch, target, and reference arguments to describe the class method that should be called to handle the control request.

Although there is nothing to stop a driver from implementing externalMethod() without calling through to the superclass, the advantage of using the implementation provided by the IOUserClient class is that its implementation performs validation of the parameters that have been provided by the calling process. The validation performed by the IOUserClient is limited to ensuring that the user client has received the expected parameters from the calling process—for example, ensuring that the process has provided the correct number of scalar input and output parameters and that the size of structure parameters that has been provided by the process matches the size of the structures that the driver will be reading and writing. To do this, the IOUserClient's implementation of externalMethod() needs to know the parameters that the driver is expecting for a control request; this information comes from the IOExternalMethodDispatch structure that is passed to the superclass implementation through the dispatch argument. The type definition of IOExternalMethodDispatch is as follows:

```
struct IOExternalMethodDispatch
{
        IOExternalMethodAction          function;
        uint32_t                        checkScalarInputCount;
        uint32_t                        checkStructureInputSize;
        uint32_t                        checkScalarOutputCount;
        uint32_t                        checkStructureOutputSize;
};
```

The IOExternalMethodDispatch structure describes the callback function that should be invoked to handle the control request, the number of scalar input and output parameters, and the size of any input and output structure parameters that the callback function is expecting. For a callback function that can accept a variable number of scalar parameters or a variable-length structure, the constant kIOUCVariableStructureSize can be written to the corresponding field of the IOExternalMethodDispatch structure.

The callback function has the following signature:

```
typedef IOReturn (*IOExternalMethodAction)(OSObject* target, void* reference,
                        IOExternalMethodArguments* args);
```

You will notice that the arguments to the callback function correspond to three of the arguments of IOUserClient::externalMethod(), including target and reference. This is more than just a coincidence. When your driver calls through to the superclass implementation of externalMethod(), it validates the parameters that were provided by the user space process and, if the correct parameters were provided, it calls the specified handler function, passing the values of target, reference, and args to the callback. Since the callback function is a static method, it cannot access any instance variables of the user client through the "this" pointer. Therefore, the value of target should be set to the instance of the user client that will handle the control request or, if the control request will be handled by a method in a different class, target should be set to the instance of that class. The value of reference is free for the user client for passing arbitrary data to the callback function.

The entire process of handling a control request from a user space client, including the steps that are performed by the driver's custom user client implementation and the steps performed by the standard IOUserClient implementation, is described in the following pseudocode:

```
// Implementation provided by the driver's IOUserClient subclass
IOReturn              MyUserClient::externalMethod (selector, args, dispatch, target, reference)
{
        Use "selector" to determine which control request has been requested

        Initialize "newDispatch" to the appropriate callback function to handle the control
        request
        Initialize "newTarget" to the current MyUserClient instance
        Initialize "newReference" if we wish to provide additional data to the callback
        function

        Call the superclass:
        IOUserClient::externalMethod(selector, args, newDispatch, newTarget, newReference)
}

// Implementation provided by the I/O Kit's superclass
IOReturn              IOUserClient::externalMethod(selector, args, dispatch, target, reference)
{
        Check that the parameters provided by the user process through "args" match the
        parameters expected by the user client as described in "dispatch".

        If the parameters do not match, exit with the result kIOReturnBadArgument

        Otherwise, call the callback handler for this control request:
        dispatch->function(target, reference, args)
}
```

By convention, most drivers implement externalMethod() by adding a dispatch table to their user client class that contains the value of IOExternalMethodDispatch for each of the selector values that the user client accepts. For example, a possible dispatch table for our timer user client is shown in Listing 5-11.

Listing 5-11. The Dispatch Table for the Tutorial User Client Interface

```
const IOExternalMethodDispatch
com_osxkernel_driver_IOKitTestUserClient::sMethods[kTestUserClientMethodCount] =
{
        // kTestUserClientStartTimer    (void)
        { sStartTimer, 0, 0, 0, 0 },

        // kTestUserClientStopTimer     (void)
        { sStopTimer, 0, 0, 0, 0 },

        // kTestUserClientGetElapsedTimerTime   (uint32_t* timerValue)
        { sGetElapsedTimerTime, 0, 0, 1, 0 },

        // kTestUserClientGetElapsedTimerValue  (TimerValue* timerValue)
        { sGetElapsedTimerValue, 0, 0, 0, sizeof(TimerValue) },
```

```
            // kTestUserClientDelayForMs    (uint32_t milliseconds)
            { sDelayForMs, 1, 0, 0, 0 },


            // kTestUserClientDelayForTime  (const TimerValue* timerValue)
            { sDelayForTime, 0, sizeof(TimerValue), 0, 0 }
};
```

For convenience, we will be accessing items in the dispatch table using values from the TimerRequestCode enumeration as an index into the array, so it is important that the order of items in the dispatch table match the order of the request codes that were defined in Listing 5-10.

With a dispatch table defined, the implementation of our user client's externalMethod() becomes significantly easier, since nearly all of the values that it requires come straight from the dispatch table. A possible implementation is shown in Listing 5-12.

Listing 5-12. An Implementation of a Custom User Client's externalMethod()

```
IOReturn         com_osxkernel_driver_IOKitTestUserClient::
                 externalMethod (uint32_t selector, IOExternalMethodArguments* arguments,
                                 IOExternalMethodDispatch* dispatch, OSObject* target,
                                 void* reference)
{
       // Ensure the requested control selector is within range.
       if (selector >= kTestUserClientMethodCount)
           return kIOReturnUnsupported;

       dispatch = (IOExternalMethodDispatch*)&sMethods[selector];
       target = this;
       reference = NULL;
       return super::externalMethod(selector, arguments, dispatch, target, reference);
}
```

Finally, to complete our user client, let's take a look at the possible implementation for two of the selectors provided by our custom user client: GetElapsedTimerTime() and DelayForTime(). As we have seen, each selector that a user client implements has a corresponding callback function that is invoked to handle the selector. That callback function's arguments are passed through the IOExternalMethodArguments structure. It would be much easier to work with the parameters if they were instead passed as parameters to the function, so it is common for each control selector to have two method handlers: the static callback handler and an instance method that provides the actual implementation.

The static callback method unpacks the parameters from the IOExternalMethodArguments structure and passes them to an instance method in the user client class or the main driver class to perform the actual work. This arrangement is shown in Listing 5-13 for the implementation of the GetElapsedTimerTime() and DelayForTime() methods.

Listing 5-13. An Implementation of Two User Client Methods

```
IOReturn         com_osxkernel_driver_IOKitTestUserClient::
                 sGetElapsedTimerTime (OSObject* target, void* reference,
                                       IOExternalMethodArguments* arguments)
{
       com_osxkernel_driver_IOKitTestUserClient*      me;
```

```
    uint32_t                    timerTime;
    IOReturn                    result;

    me = (com_osxkernel_driver_IOKitTestUserClient*)target;

    // Call the method that implements the operation.
    result = me->getElapsedTimerTime(&timerTime);
    // Return the scalar result of the operation to the calling process.
    arguments->scalarOutput[0] = timerTime;

    return result;
}

IOReturn        com_osxkernel_driver_IOKitTestUserClient::
                sDelayForTime (OSObject* target, void* reference,
                                IOExternalMethodArguments* arguments)
{

    com_osxkernel_driver_IOKitTestUserClient*       me;

    me = (com_osxkernel_driver_IOKitTestUserClient*)target;
    return me->delayForTime((TimerValue*)arguments->structureInput);
}
```

Notice that we do not need to verify the size of the array scalarOutput in the implementation of sGetElapsedTimerTime() or the size of the buffer structureInput in the implementation of sDelayForTime(). This is because we can know that these parameters have been verified by the IOUserClient superclass's implementation of externalMethod(), which has compared the provided parameters against the driver's expected parameters. However, the actual implementation of getElapsedTimerTime() would verify that the client has previously started the timer by calling StartTimer() before attempting to read the timer's time.

▪ **Note** A driver's user client should always validate the value of parameters that it receives from a user process. The process may have been compromised or may be developed by a third party whose code provides parameter values that your driver does not expect to receive. Failing to reject illegal parameter values could cause your driver to kernel panic or could introduce vulnerabilities into the system.

Notifications from the Driver

The methods that we have implemented in the sample driver's user client are designed to be blocking functions; that is, the user process does not continue execution until the user client has completed the requested operation. For example, the method in our user client DelayForMs() would suspend the thread on which it was called until the specified delay has elapsed. While this may not be a bad thing for a function whose aim is to explicitly delay the calling thread, a user space application may not always wish to wait for a driver operation to complete, particularly if that operation may take an indeterminate amount of time or is dependent on an event over which the driver has no control, such as the arrival of data on a serial port.

Two approaches are used to overcome this problem. Unlike the Windows driver model, which, unless explicitly enabled, does not allow an application to send multiple control requests to a driver simultaneously, the I/O Kit allows as many threads to send requests to a user client as the application requires. This means that one solution for blocking operations is for the application to create a secondary thread on which to call blocking user client methods. This frees up the rest of the application to continue executing while the driver processes the request. The second approach is for the user client to implement asynchronous operations and notify the application when the operation completes through a callback function.

The I/O Kit framework makes it easy for a developer to turn an operation from a synchronous, blocking operation into an asynchronous operation. To see how it is done, let's extend the driver interface that we have developed in this chapter to include a function named InstallTimer(), which will delay for a specified period and then notify the application through a callback function. In this way, the InstallTimer() function can be thought of as an asynchronous implementation of our existing function DelayForTime().

The I/O Kit framework uses an implementation for asynchronous notifications that is very similar to the delivery of notifications for device arrival that was described at the start of this chapter (See Listing 5-2). In fact, the notifications received for device arrival can be thought of as a special asynchronous completion callback that is implemented by the I/O Kit framework itself. To initialize our driver library to support the delivery of completion callbacks, we need to create a notification port on which the kernel driver will signal the user space process when an operation has completed. This is done in the same way in which we created a notification port for the delivery of device arrival notifications, by calling the IONotificationPortCreate() function. Although this notification port will be allocated by the driver's user space library, it's good design practice to provide a function that allows the application to access the port so that the application can install the notification port on the run loop of its choice. A possible implementation of an accessor function for a driver's notification port is shown in Listing 5-14.

Listing 5-14. Allocating a Port on Which an Application Can Receive Notifications When an Asynchronous Operation Completes

```
IONotificationPortRef    gAsyncNotificationPort = NULL;

IONotificationPortRef    MyDriverGetAsyncCompletionPort ()
{
        // If the port has been allocated, return the existing instance.
        if (gAsyncNotificationPort != NULL)
                return gAsyncNotificationPort;

        gAsyncNotificationPort = IONotificationPortCreate(kIOMasterPortDefault);
        return gAsyncNotificationPort;
}
```

An application can then allocate and install the notification port in one of its run loops, as follows:

```
CFRunLoopSourceRef      runLoopSource;
notificationPort = MyDriverGetAsyncCompletionPort ();
runLoopSource = IONotificationPortGetRunLoopSource(notificationPort);
CFRunLoopAddSource(CFRunLoopGetCurrent(), runLoopSource, kCFRunLoopDefaultMode);
```

Having allocated a notification port on which the user space application can receive messages from the kernel driver, we now need to provide the port to our kernel driver so that it has a port on which it can signal the completion of asynchronous operations. The notification port is provided to the driver's user client on each asynchronous control request. The I/O Kit framework provides asynchronous variations of each of the IOConnectCallXXX() functions named IOConnectCallAsyncXXX(). The asynchronous form of these functions take additional arguments, including a notification port, a callback function, and a context parameter that is passed to the callback function.

In all regards, the asynchronous variation of the IOConnect functions behave identically to their synchronous counterparts; for example, IOConnectCallAsyncScalarMethod() passes an array of integer values to the user client and receives an array of integer values from the user client. As with the synchronous form of these functions, any output parameters are written as soon as the function returns and not when the asynchronous operation completes (the driver may still be handling the operation when the function returns).

To provide an example of how the asynchronous functions are used, let's examine the implementation of our sample InstallTimer() function. The user space code is shown in Listing 5-15.

Listing 5-15. The User Space Implemenation of an Asynchronous Control Request for Our Driver's InstallTimer() *Function*

```
kern_return_t   InstallTimer (io_connect_t connection, uint32_t milliseconds,
                   IOAsyncCallback0 timerCallback, void* context)
{
        io_async_ref64_t        asyncRef;
        uint64_t                scalarIn[1];

        // Set up the callback function.
        asyncRef[kIOAsyncCalloutFuncIndex] = (uint64_t)timerCallback;
        asyncRef[kIOAsyncCalloutRefconIndex] = (uint64_t)context;

        // Set up the input parameter.
        scalarIn[0] = milliseconds;
        return  IOConnectCallAsyncScalarMethod(connection, kTestUserClientInstallTimer,
                IONotificationPortGetMachPort(gAsyncNotificationPort),
                asyncRef, kIOAsyncCalloutCount,
                scalarIn, 1, NULL, NULL);
}
```

If you compare the preceding function to the implementation for DelayForTime(), you will notice that both functions have a lot in common and pass the same input and output parameters to the user client. The only difference between the two functions is the addition of the timerCallback and context arguments. The callback function and its context parameter are provided to the IOConnectCallAsync functions through the structure io_async_ref64_t, which is defined as an array of unsigned 64-bit integers. Because certain elements of the io_async_ref64_t array are used internally by the I/O Kit, an application should use the constants kIOAsyncCalloutFuncIndex and kIOAsyncCalloutRefconIndex to access the array, as shown in the example.

This is all that an application needs to do to perform an asynchronous operation. When the operation completes, the provided callback function will be notified and will execute on the run loop on which the application installed the run loop source. The callback function has the following signature:

```
typedef void (*IOAsyncCallback0)(void* context, IOReturn result);
```

Note that the "0" in IOAsyncCallback0 refers to the number of parameters from the driver that the function receives. These are separate from the output scalar count passed to the function IOConnectCallAsyncScalarMethod() and are specified by the kernel when the asynchronous operation is complete.

Of course, for an operation to be asynchronous, the kernel driver must ensure that it returns immediately from the user client but will continue to handle the requested operation in the background and signal the process when the operation completes. An asynchronous method call is received by the user client no differently than from any other method call and is dispatched by externalMethod() to a handler function that receives its arguments through an IOExternalMethodArguments structure. However, unlike a synchronous method, the IOExternalMethodArguments structure contains fields that are useful to an asynchronous operation, as shown in the following definition:

```
struct IOExternalMethodArguments
{
        ...
        mach_port_t             asyncWakePort;
        io_user_reference_t*    asyncReference;
        uint32_t                asyncReferenceCount;
        ...
};
```

By checking the value of asyncWakePort, the method that implements a control request can determine whether the user application invoked it through an asynchronous function call. If it is non-zero, an asynchronous operation was requested. Given that the handler function will perform the requested operation in the background (since an asynchronous control request should avoid blocking the calling application), it needs to save any values from the IOExternalMethodArguments structure that it will need to refer to while performing the operation. This includes copying any scalar and structure input parameter values that were provided by the caller (noting that the output values are returned to the calling application as soon as the user client returns and not when the asynchronous operation is completed). An important value from the IOExternalMethodArguments structure that needs to be saved is the asyncReference buffer, since this is used to signal the application when the operation has completed.

An example of how an asynchronous operation is performed is shown below in Listing 5-16.

Listing 5-16. The User Client Implementation of an Asynchronous Operation. This Implements the Kernel-side of the InstallTimer() Function.

```
// A structure to hold parameters required by the background operation.
struct TimerParams
{
        OSAsyncReference64              asyncRef;
        uint32_t                       milliseconds;
        OSObject*                      userClient;
};

IOReturn   com_osxkernel_driver_IOKitTestUserClient::
        sInstallTimer (OSObject* target, void* reference, IOExternalMethodArguments* arguments)
{
        TimerParams*    timerParams;
        thread_t        newThread;

        // Allocate a structure to store parameters required by the timer.
        timerParams = (TimerParams*)IOMalloc(sizeof(TimerParams));
        // Take a copy of the asyncReference buffer.
        bcopy(arguments->asyncReference, timerParams->asyncRef, sizeof(OSAsyncReference64));
```

```
    // Take a copy of the "milliseconds" value provided by the user application.
    timerParams->milliseconds = (uint32_t)arguments->scalarInput[0];
    // Take a reference to the userClient object.
    timerParams->userClient = target;
    // Retain the user client while an asynchronous operation is in progress.
    target->retain();

    // Start a background thread to continue the operation after returning to the caller.
    kernel_thread_start(DelayThreadFunc, timerParams, &newThread);
    thread_deallocate(newThread);

    // Return immediately to the calling application.
    return kIOReturnSuccess;
}

void    com_osxkernel_driver_IOKitTestUserClient::
               DelayThreadFunc (void *parameter, wait_result_t)
{
    TimerParams*    timerParams = (TimerParams*)parameter;

    // Sleep for the requested time.
    IOSleep(timerParams->milliseconds);
    // Send a notification to the user application that the operation has competed.
    sendAsyncResult64(timerParams->asyncRef, kIOReturnSuccess, NULL, 0);

    // The background operation has completed, release the extra reference to the
    // user client object.
    timerParams->userClient->release();

    IOFree(timerParams, sizeof(TimerParams));
}
```

Although there is a lot to take in from the preceding code, it is important to note the way that it allocates an object to hold the parameters that are required while the driver completes the requested operation on a background thread. To prevent the user client object from being released while the operation is in progress, the method increments its retain count when starting the operation and decrements its retain count when the operation completes. Finally, when the background operation has completed, the user client (or driver) signals the user application by calling sendAsyncResult64(). The final two parameters of sendAsyncResult64(), which are unused in this example, allow a driver to provide additional values to the application's callback function. For example, an asynchronous read operation could use this to return the number of bytes that it read.

Summary

- Nearly all drivers will need to expose their services to applications run by the user.

- To allow applications to interact with a kernel driver, the driver needs to cross the barrier that exists between user space code and kernel code. A driver written using the I/O Kit framework achieves this by implementing a class that derives from the IOUserClient class.

- Applications can iterate loaded kernel drivers or can install a callback function to receive notifications when drivers are loaded and unloaded.

- The I/O Kit provides several functions that allow a user application to request services provided by a driver, including by reading and writing driver properties, or by establishing a connection to the driver and sending control requests to the driver over that connection.

CHAPTER 6

Memory Management

Memory management in the kernel is significantly more complex than it is for a user space program. A user space program typically deals with a flat linear address space and can allocate memory in more or less arbitrary blocks without worrying about the source or arrangement of this memory. It has simple interfaces that typically take a size in bytes as an argument and deliver a yay or nay result, depending on the availability of the requested memory. At worst, the consequence of a failed allocation or misuse of memory is the termination of the offending process. However, things are not as straightforward in the kernel. The kernel has to deal with multiple memory spaces, including its own, as well as the mapping of memory between those memory spaces and physical memory. While user space programs deal with virtual memory, where the underlying physical arrangement is irrelevant, the kernel often needs to know whether the memory is contiguous and where it is located. This is because some hardware devices are unable to read from certain memory addresses or have specific requirements regarding the alignment of the memory, for example, because it can read only from memory that has been aligned to a 16-byte boundary or because it cannot read from addresses higher than 32-bit. However, the most obvious challenge of kernel memory management is to use as little as possible because it is a scarce resource, especially for embedded devices such as the iPhone or iPad. Incorrect use of memory in the kernel can lead to subtle and not so subtle consequences.

In this chapter, we aim to explain the various types of memory you will encounter as a kernel programmer, their purpose, and the most effective and safe use of memory. We also discuss mechanisms and methods for allocating and managing memory, as well as some low-level mechanisms used by the OS to manage memory. We will also look at how to perform memory mapping operations, where memory from one address space can be mapped into the address space of another task.

Types of Memory

The kernel deals with multiple types of memory, so understanding the difference is key to implementing a successful driver or kernel extension.

The types of memory can be categorized as:

- CPU physical address
- bus physical address
- user and kernel virtual addresses

In addition to the three types of memory addresses, the amount of addressable memory differs between architectures and can be from 32-bit to 64-bit. Memory may also be ordered differently depending on the architecture and can be of little or big endian.

The following sections will discuss the importance and usage of each type of memory as it applies to kernel programming.

CPU Physical Address

A physical address refers to the addressing system used by the CPU to access physical memory. Typically, physical addresses are hidden behind the Memory Management Unit (MMU) of the CPU. The MMU translates virtual addresses normally used by the kernel and user space into physical addresses. The physical address space is linear and goes from 0 to 0xffffffff (2^{32}) for 32-bit systems and 0 to 0xffffffffffffffff (2^{64}) for 64-bit systems. Access to physical memory is cached in smaller memory buffers, such as L1 and L2 caches typically contained on the CPU die.

It is generally unnecessary to deal directly with physical addresses, even when writing drivers.

PHYSICAL ADDRESS EXTENSIONS

Physical Address Extensions (PAE) is a feature developed by Intel to allow a larger physical address space, which works around the 4 GB memory limit on 32-bit systems. PAE is available on all versions of Mac OS X that support Intel processors (10.4.4 and higher). PAE expands available address space up to 36 bits (obviously, there are no 36-bit data types so addresses are represented with a 64-bit type), which allows it to address up to 64 GB of physical memory. However, PAE does not change the size of the virtual address space used by a process, which is still limited to 4 GB. While no process (or the kernel) can use more than 4 GB, the system collectively can use up to 64 GB.

Bus Physical Addresses

The introduction of 64-bit computing presented a challenge as legacy I/O buses such as PCI and PCI-X were unable to access memory addresses over 32-bit. To work around this, PowerPC G5-based Macs had an additional MMU on their *north bridge,* used for remapping memory from 64-bit addresses into 32-bit addresses the device can read from. This MMU is referred to as the Device Address Resolution Table (DART). The DART presents the translated memory as physical addresses to the device, however these addresses are translated and not the same physical address as the CPU use. Intel-based computers have similar capabilities known as I/O memory management unit (IOMMU), one of the virtualization technologies for directed I/O (VT-d).

A *bus physical address* appears to be a physical address to a hardware device, though in reality, it is a virtual address translated by the DART. If you are confused, don't worry; you rarely have to deal with these addresses. In fact, if you use I/O Kit, it will do all the required translations for you automatically if you use IOMemoryDescriptor, which is discussed later in this chapter. Drivers can use the IOPhysicalAddress type to handle physical addresses. The size of the type depends on the underlying architecture. Because of PAE, it may be 64-bit, even on 32-bit systems.

User and Kernel Virtual Addresses

Virtual addresses are linear addresses that are translated into physical addresses by a special chip on the CPU called the Memory Management Unit (MMU). Each user space process has its own memory address space, and for all intents and purposes it looks like a process owns all physical memory. It may use any memory location in its address space, even on addresses located beyond the amount of physical memory. The virtual address space appears linear to a process, although the memory that backs it may be fragmented.

In Mac OS X, the entire virtual address space is available for a process to use. On a 32-bit system this includes memory addresses from 0–4 GB. Operating systems such as Microsoft Windows or Linux use a split model, where the kernel is mapped into the virtual address space of each process. For example, on Windows (32-bit), user space virtual memory occupies addresses from 0 to 0x7FFFFFFF, whereas memory addresses reserved for the kernel go from 0x80000000 to 0xFFFFFFFF. Because the kernel is already mapped, the CPU doesn't have to change the page tables when a process context switches into kernel mode (an already expensive operation). The downside of this approach is that the kernel and user space processes have less address space available, and hence in the case of Windows, only 2 GB can be accessed at any given time by either the kernel or a user space process. On Linux, the split is typically 3 GB/1 GB, with only 1 GB available to the kernel (though everything in Linux is configurable and other configurations are also available). If the system has a GPU enabled, this typically comes with onboard memory of up to 1 GB, which has to be mapped into virtual address space and may result in some physical memory being unable to be used as the GPU's large frame buffer *shadows* it.

To avoid the shadowing problem, Mac OS X has completely separate address spaces for the kernel (4GB) and user space processes (4GB), but as mentioned the downside is more expensive context switching.

The 64-bit kernel introduced in Mac OS X 10.6 Snow Leopard solved the problem of limited address space once for all. In 64-bit kernels, the kernel address space is always mapped in. Mac OS X splits the address space so the upper 128 terabytes (!) are reserved for the kernel, while the lower 128 terabytes belong to the currently running user space task. Though the address space is shared with user space, tasks are not able to access kernel memory due to page protection flags.

A virtual memory address may not always be backed by a physical memory location, as memory may have been migrated to an external backing store, such as a hard drive, because it was infrequently used or because a running process required more memory than was available. If the CPU accesses an address and the memory for the address is not resident, it will result in a *page fault exception*. The *pager*, a component of the OS, will attempt to fetch the page containing the given memory address.

The first page (0–4 KB) of the virtual address space is inaccessible to a process and an exception will be generated if access is attempted.

The architecture agnostic type `IOVirtualAddress` can be used to handle virtual addresses in I/O Kit code. This type is, again, the alias of `mach_vm_address_t`, the type for virtual memory addresses in the Mach layer.

■ **Tip** For a more detailed discussion about virtual memory, see Chapter 1, or for details about the OS X and iOS implementation, see Chapter 2.

Memory Ordering: Big vs. Little Endian

Endianess refers to the ordering of the components of a binary word in memory. The ordering will be either little-endian or big-endian depending on the CPU architecture that is used. The effects of this can be illustrated with a simple C program, as shown in Listing 6-1.

Listing 6-1. Print the Byte Order of a 32-bit Word

```
#include <stdio.h>
#include <stdint.h>
int main(int argc, char *argv[])
{
        uint32_t word = 0xaabbccdd;
```

```
    uint8_t* ptr = (uint8_t*)&word;
    printf("%02x %02x %02x %02x\n", ptr[0], ptr[1], ptr[2], ptr[3]);
    return 0;
}
```

The result of executing on a system with little endinaness will be:

```
dd cc bb aa
```

While on a big endian system:

```
aa bb cc dd
```

As you can see, the ordering is reversed on little-endian systems. All current-generation Macs are little-endian, as the Intel x86/x86_64 processors are little-endian; so too are ARM-based iOS devices. The older PowerPC-based Macs were big-endian. Why should you care about big-endian then? Well, some hardware architectures or network protocols, such as TCP/IP, use big-endian; additionally, your driver or kernel extensions may have to be compatible with older Macs that are based on the PowerPC architecture. Furthermore, OS X has support for *Rosetta*, which emulates PowerPC applications on Intel-based Macs. It is possible your driver will be accessed by a *Rosetta* client task. Some user space APIs, such as the Carbon File Manager, also work with big-endian data structures.

The C pre-processor macros __LITTLE_ENDIAN__ and __BIG_ENDIAN__ are defined by the compiler and can be used to determine the byte order at compile time.

32-bit vs. 64-bit Memory Addressing

Modern Mac OS X systems are now 64-bit. By 64-bit, we mean the CPU's ability to work with addresses of a 64-bit width, including general-purpose registers, and the ability to use a 64-bit data bus and 64-bit virtual memory addressing.

THE INTEL 64 ARCHITECTURE

The Intel 64 (x86-64) architecture is an extension of the traditional Intel x86 instruction set, which enables it to operate in 64-bit mode and allows it to support large quantities of physical memory. While Intel invented the x86 compatible processors, this extension was originally created by AMD and was marketed as AMD64. Intel subsequently released their version of the 64-bit extensions, initially named EM64T and IA-32e, which provided compatibility with AMD's solution. Intel originally placed their bets on the designed-from-scratch IA64 (Itainum). IA64 ditched the legacy of x86. HP and other high-performance server vendors, such as SGI, pushed IA64 heavily but adoption was slow. Intel 64 / AMD64 remain the dominant architectures today. Intel 64-capable CPUs are found in all current-generation Macs. An x86-64 processor can operate in two modes, *long mode* or *legacy mode*. The former is the 64-bit mode and offers compatibility, which allows 32-bit and 16-bit applications to execute. The OS has to be 64-bit aware to operate in this mode. The latter is a 32-bit mode, for 32-bit only operating systems.

Table 6-1 shows the supported addressing modes and native pointer sizes of architectures supported by OS X and iOS.

Table 6-1. Memory Addressing for OS X and iOS Under Various Platforms

Architecture	64-bit kernel	64-bit apps	32-bit apps (in 64-bit mode)	32-bit kernel	Pointer size
32-bit PowerPC	No	No	N/A	Yes	4
64-bit PowerPC	No	Yes	Yes	No	8
32-bit Intel	No	No	N/A	No	4
64-bit Intel	Yes	Yes	Yes	Yes	8
iOS	No	No	Yes	Yes	4

Because it is possible for the kernel to be running in 32-bit mode while an application runs in 64-bit mode, great care must be taken when a 64-bit process exchanges data with the kernel, for example, through an ioctl() or an IOUserClient method. The same is true when running a 64-bit kernel and communicating with a 32-bit application. The problem is that 32-bit and 64-bit compilers may define data types differently. For example, the C data type long is 4 bytes wide in 32-bit programs and 8 bytes in a program compiled for a 64-bit instruction set.

Memory Allocation

The XNU kernel provides a rich set of tools for allocating memory. Kernel memory allocation is not as trivial and straightforward as the malloc()/free() interface found in user space libraries. Kernel memory allocation facilities range from high-level mechanisms analogous to the user space malloc() interface to direct allocation of raw pages. There are dozens of various functions for obtaining memory. Which one to use depends on the subsystem you are working within—for example, Mach, BSD, or the I/O Kit—as well as the requirements for the memory, such as size or alignment. Memory is arguably one of the most limited resources on a computer system, especially for the iOS platform, which has limited amounts of physical memory compared to most Mac OS X-based computers.

At the fundamental level, the kernel keeps track of physical memory using the structure vm_page. A vm_page structure exists for every physical page of memory. Available pages are part of one of the following page lists:

- *Active List:* Contains physical pages mapped into at least one virtual address space and have recently been used.

- *Inactive List:* Contains pages that are allocated but have not recently been used.

- *Free List:* Contains unallocated pages.

Getting a free page from the free list is done with the vm_page_grab() function or its higher-level interface vm_page_alloc(), which unlike the former, places the page in a vm_object as opposed to merely removing it from the free list. The kernel will signal the pageout daemon if it detects that the level of free pages falls behind a threshold. In this case, the pager will evict pages from the inactive list in a least recently used (LRU) fashion. Pages, which are mapped from an on-disk file, are prime candidates and can simply be discarded. The VM page cache and file system cache are combined on Mac OS X and iOS, which avoids duplication, and are collectively referred to as the Universal Buffer Cache (UBC). Pages originating from the file system are managed by the *vnode* pager, while pages in the VM cache are managed by the *default* pager.

The following sections will provide an overview of the various mechanisms for memory allocation available to kernel developers, as well as of their use and restrictions.

Low-Level Allocation Mechanisms

The kernel has several families of memory allocation routines. Each major subsystem, such as Mach, BSD, or I/O Kit, has their own families of functions. The VM subsystem lives in the Mach portion of the kernel, which implements the fundamental interfaces for allocating memory. These interfaces are in turn used to form higher-level memory allocation mechanisms for use in other subsystems such as BSD and I/O Kit.

For working in the Mach sections of the kernel, the kmem_alloc*() family of functions is used. These functions are fairly low-level and are only a few levels away from the raw vm_page_alloc() function. The following functions are available:

```
kern_return_t kmem_alloc(vm_map_t map, vm_offset_t* addrp, vm_size_t  size);
kern_return_t mem_alloc_aligned(vm_map_t map, vm_offset_t* addrp, vm_size_t size);
kern_return_t kmem_alloc_wired(vm_map_t map, vm_offset_t* addrp, vm_size_t size);
kern_return_t kmem_alloc_pageable(vm_map_t map, vm_offset_t* addrp, vm_size_t size);
kern_return_t kmem_alloc_contig(vm_map_t map, vm_offset_t* addrp, vm_size_t size,
                        vm_offset_t mask, int flags);
void kmem_free(vm_map_t map, vm_offset_t addr, vm_size_t size);
```

All the functions require you to specify a VM Map belonging to either a user space task or kernel_map. All the above functions allocate wired memory, which cannot be paged out, with the exception of kmem_alloc_pageable().

The Mach Zone Allocator

The Mach zone allocator is an allocation mechanism that can allocate fixed-size blocks of memory called zones. A zone usually represents a commonly used kernel data structure, such as a file descriptor or a task descriptor, but can also point to blocks of memory for more general use. Examples of data structures allocated by the zone allocator include:

- file descriptors
- BSD sockets
- tasks (struct task)
- virtual memory structures (VM Maps, VM Objects)

As a kernel programmer, you can create your own zones with the zinit() function if you have a need for frequent and fast allocation and de-allocation of data objects of the same type. To create a new zone, you need to tell the allocator the size of the object, the maximum size of the queue, and the allocation size, which specifies how much memory will be added when the zone is exhausted.

The kalloc Family

The kalloc family provides a slightly higher-level interface for fast memory allocation. The API would be familiar to those who have used the malloc() interface in user space. In fact, the kernel also has a malloc() function defined by the *libkern* kernel library, which again uses memory sourced by kalloc().

```
void* kalloc(vm_size_t size);
void* kalloc_noblock(vm_size_t size);
void* kalloc_canblock(vm_size_t size, boolean_t canblock);
void* krealloc(void** addrp, vm_size_t old_size, vm_size_t new_size);
void kfree(void *data, vm_size_t size);
```

Memory for the kalloc family of functions is obtained via the Mach zone allocator discussed in the previous section. Larger memory allocations are handled by kmem_alloc() function. Because memory can come from two sources, the kfree() function needs to know the size of the original allocation to determine its origin and to free the memory in the appropriate place. The kalloc family provides the API upon which fundamental memory functions in I/O Kit and the BSD layer are built. It is also the function used to provide memory for the C++ new and new[] operators for memory allocation.

The kalloc functions and variants, except kalloc_noblock(), may block (sleep) to obtain memory. The same is true for the kfree() function. Therefore, you must use kalloc_noblock() if you need memory in an interrupt context or while holding a simple lock.

The available zones can be queried; following is the trimmed output of the zprint command showing the zones used by the kalloc functions.

zone name	elem size	cur size	max size	cur #elts	max #elts	cur inuse	alloc size	alloc count
kalloc.16	16	660K	922K	42240	59049	30284	4K	256 C
kalloc.32	32	3356K	4920K	107392	157464	73407	4K	128 C
kalloc.64	64	4792K	6561K	76672	104976	75837	4K	64 C
kalloc.128	128	2732K	3888K	21856	31104	20571	4K	32 C
kalloc.256	256	4248K	5184K	16992	20736	15950	4K	16 C
kalloc.512	512	968K	1152K	1936	2304	1870	4K	8 C
kalloc.1024	1024	784K	1024K	784	1024	735	4K	4 C
kalloc.2048	2048	3396K	4608K	1698	2304	1586	4K	2 C
kalloc.4096	4096	2204K	4096K	551	1024	508	4K	1 C
kalloc.8192	8192	3160K	32768K	395	4096	383	8K	1 C
kalloc.large	41375	5697K	6743K	141	166	141	40K	1 C

There is one zone for each size up to 8 KB. Allocations smaller than 8 KB return an element from the smallest matching zone. It is not possible to partially allocate an element, so, for example, if you need 5000 bytes of memory, you will actually be allocated 8192 bytes (3192 bytes wasted per allocation!). Allocations greater than 8 KB are handled by the appropriate kmem_alloc() function instead of the zone allocator, but are nevertheless recorded in the virtual zone *kalloc.large*.

Memory Allocation in BSD

Memory allocation in the BSD subsystem is implemented by the following functions and macros:

```
#define MALLOC(space, cast, size, type, flags)  (space) = (cast)_MALLOC(size, type, flags)
#define FREE(addr, type)_   FREE((void *)addr, type)
#define MALLOC_ZONE(space, cast, size, type, flags)
                  (space) = (cast)_MALLOC_ZONE(size, type, flags)
```

```
#define FREE_ZONE(addr, size, type) _FREE_ZONE((void *)addr, size, type)

void* _MALLOC(size_t size, int type, int flags);
void _FREE(void *addr, int type);
void* _MALLOC_ZONE(size_t size, int type, int flags);
void _FREE_ZONE(void *elem, size_t size, int type);
```

Under the hood, the _MALLOC() function allocates memory using some variant of kalloc(), depending on the flags that are passed; for example, if non-blocking allocation is required, (M_NOWAIT) kalloc_noblock() is called. The _MALLOC_ZONE() function invokes the zone allocator directly instead of indirectly through kalloc(). Instead of using the general purpose *kalloc.X* zones, it allows you to access zones of commonly used object types, such as file descriptors, network sockets, or mbuf descriptors, used by the networking subsystem. The type argument is used to determine which zone to access. Although _MALLOC() also takes a type argument, it is ignored, except to check that the value is less than the maximum allowed. There are over a hundred different types defined. The flags parameter can be one of the following:

```
#define M_WAITOK          0x0000
#define M_NOWAIT          0x0001
#define M_ZERO            0x0004          /* bzero the allocation */
```

■ **Tip** MALLOC family of functions, along with zone types, are defined in sys/malloc.h.

The M_ZERO flag, if specified, will use the bzero() function to overwrite the memory with zeros before the memory is returned to the caller. If not, the memory will still have the contents written there by the last user or will contain random garbage if never used.

I/O Kit Memory Allocation

The I/O Kit provides a full set of functions for memory allocation. All the following functions return kernel virtual addresses, which can be accessed directly:

```
void* IOMalloc(vm_size_t size);
void* IOMallocAligned(vm_size_t size, vm_size_t alignment);
void* IOMallocPageable(vm_size_t size, vm_size_t alignment);
```

The corresponding functions for freeing memory are as follows.

```
void IOFree(void* address, vm_size_t size);
void IOFreeAligned(vm_size_t size);
void IOFreePageable(void* address, vm_size_t size);
```

The first function, IOMalloc(), is a wrapper for kalloc() and is subject to the same restrictions. Specifically, it cannot be used in an atomic context, such as a primary interrupt handler, as it may block (sleep) to obtain memory. Nor can IOMalloc() be used if aligned memory is required, as no guarantees are made. IOFree() is a wrapper for the kfree() function and may also block (sleep). It is also possible to deadlock the system if you call either IOMalloc() or IOFree() while holding a simple lock, such as OSSpinLock, as the thread may be preempted if either function sleeps. It could cause a deadlock if an interrupt handler attempted to claim the same lock. Furthermore, memory from IOMalloc() is intended for small and fast allocations and is not suitable for mapping into user space. Because the memory reserved for `IOMalloc()` comes from a small fixed-size pool, excessive use of `IOMalloc()` can drain this pool and panic the kernel if the pool is exhausted.

▓ **Caution** It is a bug to free memory allocated by, for example, `IOMallocAligned()` with `IOFree()`. Always use the free function corresponding to the original allocation function. Even if it works now (by accident), the mechanism could change in a future update and cause a crash.

`IOMallocAligned()` is subject to the same restrictions as `IOMalloc()`, but unlike `IOMalloc()`, it will return memory addresses aligned to a specific value. For example, if you need page-aligned memory you can pass in 4096 to get an address aligned to the beginning of a page. Following are some reasons for requesting aligned memory.

- Hardware cannot access memory that is not aligned to a specific boundary, or it does so slowly.

- Memory used in vector computation may be excessively slow from addresses not aligned to a specific byte boundary (typically 16 bytes for SSE).

- Memory will be used for mapping into a user space process. Since mapping is only possible for whole pages, you may wish to ensure the buffer starts on a page boundary.

- You want a data structure that is friendly to the CPU cache.

`IOMallocPageable()` allocates memory that can be paged, unlike the other variants, which always create memory that is wired and cannot be paged out. The restrictions that apply to `IOMalloc()` and `IOMallocAligned()` are also valid for `IOMallocPageable()`. Memory obtained by it cannot be used for device I/O such as DMA or in a code path that is not able to block/sleep without it being wired down first.

There is also a last variant, `IOMallocContiguous()`, that allocates memory that is physically contiguous. Its use is now deprecated. Apple recommends using `IOBufferMemoryDescriptor` instead.

Each of the memory allocation functions has a corresponding function to free the memory. It is important to call the right free function that matches the function you used for allocating the memory. Each of the variants source memory from different low-level mechanisms, hence they are not interchangeable. In fact, `IOMalloc()` may source its memory from more than one source. Larger allocations (>8 KB) may be allocated with `kmem_alloc()`; however, smaller allocations come from the *zone allocator*.

This happens to be the reason why you must pass in the size of the original allocation to the `IOFree*()` functions, as it is used to determine where the memory came from.

Allocating Memory with the C++ New Operator

The libkern library implements a basic C++ runtime, upon which I/O Kit is built. Memory allocation in C++ is typically done with the `new` and `new[]` operators for single objects and arrays, respectively. In libkern, the `new` operator is implemented internally by calling `kalloc()` to obtain memory. Because `kfree()` requires the size of the original allocation, libkern modifies the size passed to the new operator to include space for a small structure that can hold the size of the allocation, so that when the delete operator calls kfree(), it can retrieve the size in the four bytes preceding the address returned by new.

Memory allocated by new or new[] is always zeroed out, unlike most implementations of these operators in user space.

▪ **Tip** The implementation of the new, new[], delete, delete[] operators can be found in the XNU source distribution under libkern/c++/OSRuntime.cpp.

Memory Descriptors

Memory descriptors are implemented by the IOMemoryDescriptor class and is fundamental to working with memory in I/O Kit. The class also serves as a super class for other important memory-related classes, which we will discuss later in this chapter. Many parts of the I/O Kit accept an IOMemoryDescriptor as an argument. For example, the USB family uses the class to describe memory used for USB read and write requests.

The IOMemoryDescriptor describes the properties of a memory buffer or range of memory, but does not allocate (or free) the described memory. It contains metadata and allows some operations to be performed on the memory. It can describe virtual and physical memory. The class is versatile and can be used for a number of purposes. Consequently, there are also a number of ways to construct an IOMemoryDescriptor. A common way is to use the withAddressRange() method, as follows.

```
static IOMemoryDescriptor* withAddressRange(mach_vm_address_t address,
                                            mach_vm_size_t length, IOOptionBits options,
                                            task_t task);
```

- The first argument, address, is the start address of the memory buffer the descriptor should operate on.

- The length argument is the number of bytes of the buffer pointed to by address. The task argument specifies the task, which owns the virtual memory.

- The options argument specifies the direction of the descriptor in the event that it is used for I/O transfers. It may affect the behaviour of prepare() and complete(). The following flags are possible:

  - kIODirectionNone

  - kIODirectionIn

  - kIODirectionOut

  - kIODirectionOutIn

  - kIODirectionInOut

- The last paramter is the task that owns the memory. If the kernel owns the memory, you can pass kernel_task, which is a global variable pointing to the task_t structure for the kernel.

The **options** flags indicate the direction of an I/O transfer and may be used to determine if it is necessary to flush processor caches to ensure cache coherency.

If the descriptor is to be used for an I/O transfer you must first call its **prepare()** method, which will do the following:

- page in memory, if the underlying memory is paged out

- pin the memory down, so it cannot be paged out until the transfer is complete

- configure device address translation mappings if necessary

■ **Caution** Calls to prepare() **must** be balanced with a call to complete(). Care must also be taken not to call complete() unless prepare() was called first.

The **prepare()** method is not thread safe. However, it is valid to call **prepare()** multiple times, but you must then call **complete()** the same number of times. Calling the descriptors' **release()** method will not undo the effects of **prepare()** or call **complete()** for you, so **complete()** must be called before calling **release()**. If the descriptor is mapped into an address space, it will be unmapped automatically on **release()**. **IOMemoryDescriptor** can also be used to describe other types of memory, such as physical addresses. With physical addresses, the **prepare()** and **complete()** methods do nothing, but return successfully. Moreover, a physical memory descriptor is not associated with a task. The static member method **withPhysicalAddress()** can be used to construct an **IOMemoryDescriptor** for a physical segment, as in the following.

```
static IOMemoryDescriptor* withPhysicalAddress(IOPhysicalAddress address,

IOByteCount withLength, IODirection withDirection);
```

The IOBufferMemoryDescriptor

The **IOBufferMemoryDescriptor** is a subclass of **IOMemoryDescriptor**, but unlike its super class, it also allocates memory. It is currently the preferred way of allocating memory intended to be mapped to user space or for performing device I/O from a kernel-allocated buffer. However, the allocation method used internally depends on the size of the request and the options passed during construction. The **IOBufferMemoryDescriptor** is also the preferred way for obtaining physically contiguous memory. **IOBufferMemoryDescriptors** can be allocated by the static factory method **inTaskWithOptions()** or **inTaskWithPhysicalMask()**, as follows.

```
static IOBufferMemoryDescriptor* inTaskWithOptions(
    task_t                  inTask,
    IOOptionBits            options,
    vm_size_t               capacity,
    vm_offset_t             alignment = 1);

static IOBufferMemoryDescriptor* inTaskWithPhysicalMask(
    task_t                  inTask,
    IOOptionBits            options,
    mach_vm_size_t          capacity,
    mach_vm_address_t       physicalMask);
```

The inTask argument specifies which task the memory should be mapped to. For a kernel buffer, this should be set to kernel_task. If you specify another task identifier, the memory will be allocated and reachable in that task's address space. In addition to the flags and options available to IOMemoryDescriptor, the following options can be passed to control the allocation behavior.

- kIOMemoryPhysicallyContiguous allocates memory that is physically contiguous.

- kIOMemoryPageable allocates memory that can be paged out. All memory is non-pageable by default.

- kIOMemoryPurgeable applies only to pageable memory. If this option is specified, the memory pages can be discarded instead of paged out.

- kIOMemoryKernelUserShared should be specified if the memory will be mapped into the kernel and a user space task. It ensures memory will be page-aligned.

The second way to construct an IOBufferMemoryDescriptor is via the inTaskWithPhysicalMask(), which allows one to specify a bit mask used to restrict the physical address range of the buffer. This is mainly useful when allocating memory for DMA for a device unable to access certain address ranges. For example, some older devices may be unable to access physical memory over 32 bits.

It is generally frowned upon to request physically contiguous memory, particularly after the system has booted, as the memory becomes fragmented quickly. This would make it difficult to find free contiguous buffers, particularly larger ones. Requesting contiguous memory may also result in some memory being paged out to handle the request, which can take a long time. Hardware devices generally support scatter/gather operations, where multiple smaller buffers are chained together in a list and passed to the device, which then reads the list to work out where in physical memory to find its data. Thus, contiguous memory is often unnecessary.

Just like the IOMalloc() family of functions, IOBufferMemoryDescriptor may sleep, so it should not be called from interrupt contexts or while holding simple locks. In fact, IOBufferMemoryDescriptor uses IOMalloc() and IOMallocAligned() internally to allocate memory.

Other Memory Descriptors

IOMemoryDescriptor has a number of other related subclasses, as follows.

- IODeviceMemory is used to describe a range of memory mapped from a device.

- IOMultiMemoryDescriptor can be used to represent a larger contiguous buffer consisting of smaller IOMemoryDescriptor objects.

Mapping Memory

Mapping memory refers to the function of making a range of memory from one task available to another. At the lowest level, mapping is handled by the Mach VM subsystem, as discussed in Chapter 2. Memory mapping provides a fast way for tasks to share resources without copying memory, as mapping makes the same memory available between tasks. Writable mappings can be shared until a modification is made, in which case the copy-on-write (COW) optimization is used to copy only the memory that was modified. Memory mappings can occur in a variety of different ways, between multiple tasks, or from the kernel to a user space task or vice versa.

Mapping Memory from a User Space Task into Kernel Space

Mapping memory from a user space task is a common operation performed by a driver. Let's use the example of an audio device driver where an application wants to send us a data buffer containing audio samples for play out on a hardware device. To do this, the user task—that is, the audio player—passes us a memory pointer, which describes where in memory the buffer is located. In user space, the copying of memory is as simple as calling the memcpy() function.

Things are not so simple in the kernel. The address passed by the user task is meaningless to the kernel, as it is valid only within the task's private address space. In order to access the memory in the kernel, we need to create a mapping for the underlying physical memory of the buffer in the kernel's own address space. At the low level, this process happens by manipulating the kernel's VM Map. While it is possible to do this using the Mach low-level interfaces, it is most commonly performed with the help of the I/O Kit IOMemoryDescriptor and IOMemoryMap classes. Listing 6-2 shows the portion of our imaginary audio driver that copies memory from the user space audio player by mapping the memory buffer into the kernel's address space.

Listing 6-2. Mapping a User Space Buffer into the Kernel

```
void copyBufferFromUserTask(task_t userTask, void* userBuffer,
                            uint32_t userBufferSize, void* dstBuffer)
{
    uint32_t              bytesWritten = 0;
    bool                  wasPrepared = false;
    IOMemoryDescriptor*   memoryDescriptor = NULL;
    IOMemoryMap*          memoryMap = NULL;

    memoryDescriptor = IOMemoryDescriptor::withAddressRange
                            (userBuffer, userBufferSize,
                            kIODirectionOut, userTask);
    if (memoryDescriptor == NULL)
        goto bail;

    if (memoryDescriptor->prepare() != kIOReturnSuccess)
        goto bail;
    wasPrepared = true;

    memoryMap = memoryDescriptor->createMappingInTask
                    (kernel_task, 0, kIOMapAnywhere | kIOMapReadOnly);
    if (memoryMap == NULL)
        goto bail;

    void* srcBufferVirtualAddress = (void*)memoryMap->getVirtualAddress();

    if (srcBufferVirtualAddress != NULL)
        bcopy(srcBufferVirtualAddress, dstBuffer, userBufferSize);

    memoryMap->release(); // This will unmap the memory
    memoryMap = NULL;
```

```
bail:
    if (memoryDescriptor)
    {
        if (wasPrepared)
            memoryDescriptor->complete();
        memoryDescriptor->release();
        memoryDescriptor = NULL;
    }
}
```

To map the memory, we first create an IOMemoryDescriptor for the user space buffer. The IOMemoryDescriptor provides an interface to create the memory mapping, but it also allows us to pin the memory down while we copy from the buffer. This prevents the memory from being paged out to secondary storage or disappearing if the audio player should crash or the user exits the application while we are performing the copy.

■ **Note** You may have noticed the use of goto in the preceding method, which language purists often consider a bad practice. However, it is often used in kernel code and provides a convenient way of providing centralized cleanup if an error occurs, in lieu of exceptions that cannot be used in the kernel.

The actual mapping occurs with the invocation of the createMappingInTask() method:

```
IOMemoryMap* createMappingInTask(
    task_t                intoTask,
    mach_vm_address_t     atAddress,
    IOOptionBits          options,
    mach_vm_size_t        offset = 0,
    mach_vm_size_t        length = 0 );
```

■ **Tip** You can use IOMemoryDescriptor::map() method as a shortcut to create a standard mapping into the kernel's address space. Also beware that the overloaded variant of map() is deprecated in favor of createMappingInTask(), which was introduced in Mac OS X 10.5.

- The first argument, intoTask, is the task we want to create the mapping in. For our purposes, this is the kernel_task, though it would be possible to provide the task structure of another task, thereby making memory available from one task to another.

- The second argument, `atAddress`, is interesting as well. It specifies an optional destination address in the address space of `intoTask`. This allows the target task to locate the mapping at a fixed address. In our example, we don't really care where in our address space the mapping will be made; we just want one address to access it, so we pass in zero instead of a fixed address and set `kIOMapAnywhere` in `options`.

- The third argument, `options`, controls how the mapping will be performed using the flags described in the Memory Descriptors section, for example, read-only or read/write. Options also exist to control how the memory should behave in relation to the CPU cache. The following options can be set:

  - `kIOMapDefaultCache`, which specifies the caching policy for the mapping. It will disable the cache for I/O memory; otherwise, `kIOMapCopybackCache` is used.

  - `kIOMapInhibitCache`, which disables caching of this mapping.

  - `kIOMapWriteThruCache`, which uses write-thru caching.

  - `kIOMapCopybackCache`, which uses copy-back caching.

  - `kIOMapReadOnly`, which specifies the mapping will be read-only.

  - `kIOMapReference`, which is used when mapping an already existing mapping and will fail if the memory is not previously mapped.

  - `kIOMapUnique`, which ensures no previous mapping exists for the memory.

- The last two arguments are used to specify an optional offset and length into the buffer, if you want to map up only parts of it. However, note that mappings are a concept of the virtual memory system and operate on *pages*. You can map memory only in units of the page size (4096 bytes). The rounding happens internally and gives the illusion of working with byte boundaries.

The IOMemoryMap Class

The `createMappingInTask()` method in Listing 6-2 will return an instance of `IOMemoryMap` to represent the mapping. In our previous example, we call the `IOMemoryMap::getVirtualAddress()` method, which returns a value of the `IOVirtualAddress` type. The exact primitive data type of `IOVirtualAddress` depends on the architecture, but for 64-bit kernels, a 64-bit unsigned integer (`uin64_t`) is used and not a pointer type.

When we no longer need the mapping, we simply release the `IOMemoryMap` object, which takes care of unmapping. You may wonder why we do not call the `IOMemoryMap::unmap()` function to release the mapping. When you create a mapping, it is possible for another thread or the same thread to map the buffer again. While the mapping will of course only be created once, performing the mapping multiple times will increment an internal reference counter. However, calling `unmap()` will not simply decrement the reference count and remove the mapping if the count hits zero, it will destroy the mapping regardless of how many times it is referenced. This may lead to the kernel accessing an invalid address; hence, care should be taken when using `unmap()`. Simply calling `release()` for the map will decrement or remove the mapping if required. A collection of other interesting `IOMemoryMap` methods are described in Table 6-2.

Note that in the Listing 6-2 example, we could just as well have copied memory into the mapped buffer with some small modifications to create a writable mapping.

Table 6-2. IOMemoryMap Member Function Overview

Function	Description
getAddressTask()	Gets the task of the mapping.
getMemoryDescriptor()	Returns the memory descriptor this map was created from.
getPhysicalAddress()	Gets the physical address of the first byte in the mapping.
getPhysicalSegment()	Takes and offsets into the mapping and returns the address as well the length of the physical segment backing this virtual memory. The length may be the entire mapping if it is backed by contiguous memory.
redirect()	Allows the memory for the map to be swapped with new physical memory. This is done by supplying a new IOMemoryDescriptor and consequently, the mapping will be updated to point to the new physical memory owned by the passed descriptor. The redirect() function will only succeed if the memory map was created by kIOMapUnique. If NULL is passed in place of an IOMemoryDescriptor, any access to the memory range of the mapping by a user task will block until a valid memory descriptor has been supplied.
...	The full definition for the IOMemoryMap class can be found in IOMemoryDescriptor.h.

▓ **Note** It is not necessary to map memory into the kernel unless the kernel needs to actively modify it. If DMA is performed from a user space buffer and the data in the buffer does not have to be modified by the kernel, it is not necessary to map it into the kernel's address space, the buffer can be transferred directly to a hardware device. See Chapter 9 for more information about DMA.

Mapping Memory from the Kernel to a User Space Task

The previous sections showed how we can take memory allocated in user space and map that memory into the kernel's address space so the kernel can access it. While it is possible for the kernel to both read and write from the mapping, it may sometimes be desirable for a user space task to map kernel memory into its address space. It should be noted that Apple recommends against this practice for security and stability reasons and it should be avoided whenever possible. One possible reason for doing it might be the need to map device memory (for example, from a PCI device) to user space so it can access the device's registers.

In I/O Kit this form of memory mapping is usually done through the IOUserClient class. Available memory mappings should be returned via the clientMemoryForType() method. A generic example of how this can be achieved is shown in Listing 6-3.

Listing 6-3. Mapping Kernel Memory to User Space via IOUserClient

```
#define kTestUserClientDriverBuffer               0
IOReturn com_osxkernel_TestUserClient::
clientMemoryForType(UInt32 type, UInt32 *flags, IOMemoryDescriptor **memory)
{
    IOReturn ret = kIOReturnUnsupported;
    switch (type)
    {
        case kTestUserClientDriverBuffer:
            // Returns a pointer to an IOMemoryDescriptor or
            // if a hardware device, an IODeviceMemory pointer which is a
            // subclass of IOMemoryDescriptor
            *memory = driver->getBufferMemoryDescriptor();
            *memory->retain();
            ret = kIOReturnSuccess;
            break;
        default:
            break;
    }
    return ret;
}
```

Note that we need to call retain() on the IOMemoryDescriptor before returning it, as it will be released when the user client closes and we do not want the descriptor to be de-allocated as it is a shared resource owned by the driver. In this example, we call a hypothetical *driver* that, for the sake of the example, has a method called getBufferMemoryDescriptor() that returns an IOMemoryDescriptor for a kernel-allocated buffer (or it could even be device memory mapped into the kernel's address space). The type argument here is simply an integer and can be anything; the important thing is that the user space program that will access the memory knows the value so it can reference the right memory mapping.

In user space code, you can do the following to map the memory from the IOUserClient.

```
void* addressOfMappedBuffer = NULL;
int sizeOfMappedBuffer;
IOConnectMapMemory(openDeviceHandleHere,
                   kTestUserClientDriverBuffer,
                   mach_task_self(),
                   (vm_address_t *) &addressOfMappedBuffer,
                   &sizeOfMappedBuffer,
                   kIOMapAnywhere);
```

You may notice the similarity to creating a mapping in the kernel. The kIOMapAnywhere here signifies that we don't care where in our address space the mapping is made; the addressOfMappedBuffer argument will contain the address of the mapping if the call succeeds and can be used to access the mapped memory. If kIOMapAnywhere is not specified, the addressOfMappedBuffer argument is used to specify the preferred address for the mapping. The second last argument will tell us the size of the mapping. The smallest amount that can be mapped is a single page; therefore, if you map buffers smaller than 4096, it would allow a client to see the memory of the entire page the buffer is contained within, which could be a potential security problem.

Mapping Memory to a Specific User Space Task

The preceding example allows any task to map the memory and our driver code does not need to know which task the memory will be mapped to. However, if you know the specific task memory should be mapped to, you can use the approach from Listing 6-2. The difference is simply that the user space task identifier is passed to `IOMemoryDescriptor::createMappingInTask()` in place of `kernel_task`.

Apple recommends not mapping memory obtained from functions such as `IOMalloc()` and `IOMallocAligned()` (though it is possible using the latter) because they come from the zone allocator, which is intended for private and temporary allocations and not for sharing. The recommended way of mapping memory is to use the `IOBufferMemoryDescriptor`, a subclass of `IOMemoryDescriptor` that also allocates memory, as follows.

```
IOBufferMemoryDescriptor* memoryDescriptor = NULL;
memoryDescriptor = IOBufferMemoryDescriptor::withOptions(
    kIODirectionOutIn | kIOMemoryKernelUserShared, sizeInBytes, 4096);
```

An interesting parameter to note is `kIOMemoryKernelUserShared`, which indicates to the allocator that we wish to share the memory with a user task. We pass 4096 (the page size) to get page-aligned memory, as memory mappings can only be done on page-sized units.

Physical Address Mapping

Virtual memory addresses are only available to the CPU and are meaningless to a hardware device, which requires physical addresses. In order to communicate with hardware outside the CPU, we need to translate virtual memory from the kernel or a user space task into physical addresses the device can use to access information from RAM. This task is not always trivial as virtual memory is often fragmented. Let's look at an example, a 128 KB virtual memory buffer we want to send to a hardware device. The buffer can in the worst case consist of 32 individual 4 KB pages scattered anywhere throughout the system memory. Because of this, we cannot simply translate the address of the first byte of the buffer and tell the device the buffer is 128 KB long; we need to work out how many fragments the buffer consists of and instead send a list/array of addresses and lengths. This is often referred to as a scatter/gather table or list. The `IOMemoryDescriptor` and classes derived from it provide two methods to help with physical address translation, as follows.

- `getPhysicalAddress()`: Translates the address of the first byte to its physical address. This is mainly useful if the buffer is known to be contiguous.

- `getPhysicalSegment()`: Translates the address at a specified offset into the buffer and returns the length of the physical segment from that offset. For a contiguous buffer, this will always be the size of the buffer minus the offset.

■ **Caution** This method can cause a kernel panic if used improperly. See the following discussion for correct usage.

Note that there are two versions of getPhysicalSegment() depending on if you are using a 64-bit kernel or 32-bit kernel, as follows:

```
#ifdef __LP64__
    virtual addr64_t getPhysicalSegment( IOByteCount    offset,
                                         IOByteCount * length,
                                         IOOptionBits  options = 0 ) = 0;

#else /* ! __LP64__ */
    virtual addr64_t getPhysicalSegment( IOByteCount    offset,
                                         IOByteCount * length,
                                         IOOptionBits  options );

#endif /* ! __LP64__ */
```

For the 32-bit version (!__LP64__) the options argument must specify: kIOMemoryMapperNone or the method will panic for addresses over the 4 GB mark. A more flexible, safer and easier approach to memory translation is to use IODMACommand class, which works in conjunction with IOMemoryDescriptor. We discuss IODMACommand and this topic in much more detail in Chapter 9.

Summary

In this chapter, we have discussed:

- Types of memory addresses in use by the kernel. The kernel typically works with virtual addresses both for its own threads as well as those of user space tasks. Physical memory addresses are used between the CPU and memory, as well as hardware devices.

- The significance of 32-bit and 64-bit memory addressing and modes.

- How memory allocation is performed across the different kernel subsystems, Mach, BSD, and I/O Kit. In I/O Kit, the preferred mechanism is to use the IOMalloc*() functions or the IOBufferMemoryDescriptor.

- How the IOMemoryDescriptor and related subclasses are used by many parts of the I/O Kit to manage and describe memory buffers. The IOBufferMemoryDescriptor is one such subclass, which in addition to providing a memory descriptor also allocates memory in various forms, with alignment or even physically contiguous memory.

- How the IOMemoryMap class is used to manage memory mappings and allows the kernel to map a user space buffer into its virtual address space so memory can be manipulated by the kernel.

- How the IOUserClient class provides a useful method, clientMemoryForType(), which will handle the details of mapping a kernel buffer into user space.

- How the IOMemoryDescriptor provides methods such as getPhysicalSegment() that allow mapping of virtual memory addresses to physical addresses.

CHAPTER 7

Synchronization and Threading

As we have seen throughout this book, the role of a driver is to make the functionality that is provided by a hardware device available to the operating system and to user applications. This means that the code inside a driver may be called from any number of running applications at any time, depending on when an application wishes to request the services of the hardware device. In handling these requests, the driver runs in the thread context of the application that made the control call. In addition to these requests, the hardware itself can require servicing and may generate interrupts at arbitrary times that the driver must respond to. The end result for the driver developer is that driver code runs in a complex multithreaded environment, even without the driver creating any additional threads of its own.

The computer hardware on which a driver will execute will likely have multiple CPU cores. So, in addition to the driver code being preempted by an interrupt from the device or a request from a thread in another application, it's possible for your driver to be running on multiple cores simultaneously. This applies even to the interrupt service routine for your driver, which can run in parallel to the non-interrupt code of your driver on another CPU core.

As is the case with multithreaded application code, it's important that a driver provides synchronized access to its internal structures and any data that could potentially be read or written from multiple threads. How a driver provides the arbitration between multiple threads that are attempting to access its hardware is dependent on the type of device. Some hardware can only be accessed by one client at a time. For example, a serial port device will grant exclusive access to one user process at a time; the driver will make sure that an attempt by another process to open the serial port will be rejected. On the other hand, a disk device can expect to receive requests from multiple processes and, since the hardware itself can handle only one request at a time, it is the responsibility of the driver to queue the incoming requests and issue them to the disk device in a serial manner.

The I/O Kit provides several different mechanisms that a driver can use to implement a scheme that provides arbitrated access to its hardware while ensuring that the driver's internal structures remain valid in a multithreaded environment. This chapter assumes that you have a basic understanding of code synchronization and have previously written multithreaded application code.

Synchronization Primitives

Synchronization problems occur when code that is executing on two or more threads attempts to access a common resource or structure. A common synchronization problem for I/O Kit drivers arises when a driver needs to access its instance variables, since these are shared between all of the threads that the driver is executing. To give a concrete example, let's consider an actual example from the I/O Kit, namely, the OSobject base class's implementation of reference counting.

The OSObject class is the base class for all objects in the I/O Kit, and one of its roles is to maintain a reference count for each object instance and to release an object when its reference count is decremented to 0. A simplified version of the OSObject implementation, without the synchronization provided by the actual implementation, is shown in Listing 7-1.

Listing 7-1. A Possible Implementation of Object Reference Counting

```
void    Object::retain ()
{
        retainCount += 1;                    // An instance variable defined as an int
}

void    Object::release ()
{
        retainCount -= 1;
        if (retainCount == 0)
                this->free();
}
```

Although the preceding code looks correct and will run perfectly well if all calls to retain() and release() are made from a single thread, the code is not thread-safe and may fail if multiple threads were to simultaneously call retain() and release() for the same object. To understand the problem, it is necessary to examine the compiler output for the previous code. In this case, the assembler instructions that follow were generated when the implementation was compiled for the 64-bit Intel architecture under a Debug build. The code for retain() contains the following sequence of instructions:

```
        mov     eax, retainCount        ; Load retainCount into CPU register EAX
        add     eax, 0x1                ; Increment value in EAX
        mov     retainCount, eax        ; Write value in EAX to retainCount
```

And the code for release() contains the following sequence of instructions:

```
        mov     eax, retainCount        ; Load retainCount into CPU register EAX
        sub     eax, 0x1                ; Decrement value in EAX
        mov     retainCount, eax        ; Write value in EAX to retainCount
        mov     eax, retainCount        ; Load retainCount into CPU register EAX
        cmp     eax, 0x0                ; Determine whether the value of EAX is 0
        jne     skipFree                ; If EAX is not zero, jump over the next instruction
        call    free()                  ; Otherwise, call the free() method
skipFree:
        …
```

The cause of the problem in a multithreaded environment is that the C code both to increment and to decrement the instance variable retainCount compiles to three CPU instructions: the value held by the instance variable retainCount is loaded from memory into a CPU register, the value of the CPU register is either incremented or decremented, and the result is then written back to memory. Let's see what can happen if two threads were to call retain() simultaneously for the same object. For simplicity, let us assume that the code is executing on a machine with a single CPU core and that the operating system's scheduler preempts the first thread at the point where the initial mov instruction has been executed.

Thread 1	Thread 2
mov eax, retainCount	
	mov eax, retainCount
	add eax, 0x1
	mov retainCount, eax
add eax, 0x1	
mov retainCount, eax	

In this scenario, thread 1 will read the value of retainCount from memory into the EAX register. At this point, the operating system's scheduler preempts thread 1 and switches to thread 2 (after saving the state of thread 1's CPU registers). Thread 2 now runs and will read the same value of retainCount into the EAX register as was read by thread 1. It then increments the value and writes the incremented value back to memory. The operating system scheduler then preempts thread 2 and switches execution back to thread 1 after restoring the state of thread 1's saved CPU registers. Thread 1 now continues executing from where it left off, incrementing the *original* value of retainCount, and writing the result back to memory. Following this, retainCount has only increased in value by 1, even though the retain() method was called twice.

Note that this problem will only show up under specific conditions: Either the retainCount instance variable must be modified by two threads, with one preempting the other in the way illustrated, or the two threads must be running simultaneously on two CPU cores. A problem such as this, in which the result of executing code depends on the timing and the order in which the code runs, is known as a race condition. Race conditions can lead to problems that are very difficult to debug since the problem by its nature is timing-dependent and therefore may not occur every time the code is run. In fact, the code may appear to run perfectly fine during testing and it will only become apparent that the driver has problems when reports come in from users.

As well as being difficult to reproduce, race conditions can be very difficult to diagnose when they do cause problems. Take the example of the race condition outlined previously in which an object's retain count is incremented by 1, even though two calls to retain() were made. This wouldn't cause any immediate problems and the driver would continue to function as if nothing were wrong until much later, when the object is released. Since the object was retained twice, the calling code should be expected to release the object twice. However, since the value of the retain count is one less than the value it should be, the object will be destroyed while the driver still holds one reference to it. This means that, at some later time, the driver will try to access the object that it *thinks* it holds a reference to. But that object will have been destroyed and the driver will crash with an access to invalid memory. Note that the code that ends up crashing may be in a completely different function to the function that contains the race condition. As a result, tracing the cause of the bug back to retain() and release() will involve considerable sleuth work.

Atomic Operations

Since the race condition in the previous example was caused by the compiler generating a sequence of three instructions to increment and decrement the instance variable retainCount, one solution is to replace the compiler output from the sequence load-modify-store with a single instruction that performs an equivalent operation. In this way, there is no chance for the operation to be interrupted when execution is preempted by another thread. In reality, however, it may not always be possible to replace an operation with a single instruction. Instead, we use a sequence of instructions that behave as if they *were* a single instruction. This is referred to as an "atomic" operation because the result of the operation is the same as if the instruction sequence had executed as a single, indivisible group.

The implementation of an atomic operation requires support from the CPU. For example, the Intel CPU used in Macintosh computers provides an instruction to atomically add one value to another value in memory. However, this alone is not enough to make the operation atomic in a multiprocessor environment. So the Intel instruction set provides a LOCK prefix that prevents any other CPU in the system from accessing memory while the instruction is executing. Since the implementation of atomic operations relies on support that is specific to the CPU architecture, iOS devices, which use the ARM instruction set, require a different implementation for each atomic operation.

To make it easy to access atomic operations in driver code, the I/O Kit includes a number of functions that provide an atomic implementation of basic operations, such as integer addition, incrementing and decrementing a value, and bitwise operations. These functions are listed in Table 7-1, which are defined in the header file `<libkern/OSAtomic.h>`.

Table 7-1. Atomic Operations Provided By the Libkern Framework

Function	Description
OSIncrementAtomic(address); OSIncrementAtomic8/16/64(address);	Adds 1 to the signed 8-, 16-, 32-, or 64-bit value at the specified address. The original value prior to the increment is returned.
OSDecrementAtomic(address); OSDecrementAtomic8/16/64(address);	Subtracts 1 from the signed 8-, 16-, 32-, or 64-bit value at the specified address. The original value prior to the decrement is returned.
OSAddAtomic(amount, address); OSAddAtomic8/16/64(amount, address);	Adds the value in "amount" to the signed 8-, 16-, 32-, or 64-bit value at the specified address. The original value prior to addition is returned.
OSBitAndAtomic(mask, address); OSBitAndAtomic8/16(mask, address);	Performs a bitwise AND operation of the value in "mask" and the 8-, 16-, or 32-bit unsigned value at the specified address. The original value prior to the bitwise operation is returned.
OSBitOrAtomic(mask, address); OSBitOrAtomic8/16(mask, address);	Performs a bitwise OR operation of the value in "mask" and the 8-, 16-, or 32-bit unsigned value at the specified address. The original value prior to the bitwise operation is returned.

Function	Description
OSBitXorAtomic(mask, address); OSBitXorAtomic8/16(mask, address);	Performs a bitwise XOR operation of the value in "mask" and the 8-. 16-, or 32-bit unsigned value at the specified address. The original value prior to the bitwise operation is returned.
OSCompareAndSwap(oldValue, newValue, address); OSCompareAndSwapPtr(oldValue,newValue, address); OSCompareAndSwap64(oldValue, newValue, address);	If the value of the 32- or 64-bit integer at the specified address is equal to "oldValue", then "newValue" is written to the address. Otherwise, the value stored at the address is not modified. The function returns a Boolean that indicates whether newValue was written.
OSTestAndSet(bit, address);	Sets a bit within the byte at the specified address. Returns a Boolean that indicates whether the bit was already set.
OSTestAndClear(bit, address);	Clears a bit within the byte at the specified address. Returns a Boolean that indicates whether the bit was already clear.

With these functions at our disposal, we are now in a position to provide an implementation of retain() and release() that avoids the race condition that was present in the previous example. This is shown in Listing 7-2, which assumes that the instance variable retainCount is a 32-bit integer.

Listing 7-2. An Implementation of Object Reference Counting in a Multithreaded Environment

```
void    Object::retain ()
{
        OSIncrementAtomic(&retainCount);
}

void    Object::release ()
{
        uint32_t                originalValue;

        originalValue = OSDecrementAtomic(&retainCount);
        if (originalValue == 1)
                this->free();
}
```

If we go back and examine the original implementation in Listing 7-1 and the corresponding compiler output for the release() method, we can see that the code actually contained two race conditions. The conditional call to free() occurs when the value of retainCount has been decremented to 0. However, since the compiled code reloads the value of retainCount from memory before testing its value against 0, it's possible that two calls to release() both read the value 0 and the free() method is called twice for the object, which will likely result in a crash. To illustrate how this could occur, assume that one thread executing release() has decremented the retainCount from 2 to 1 and has written the decremented value back to memory. Also assume that, before it can reload the value of retainCount from memory and test whether its value is 0, the thread is preempted. Another thread now has a chance to run and, if it were to execute release(), the retainCount would be decremented from 1 to 0 and the object would be destroyed. When execution returns to the original thread, it will reload the value of retainCount, find that it is 0, and destroy the object a second time.

This race condition is avoided in Listing 7-2 by using the value returned by OSDecrementAtomic() to determine when the final reference count has been released. The function OSDecrementAtomic() returns the original value of its parameter before it was decremented. We know that if the original value was 1, the value of retainCount has now been decremented to 0 and the object can safely be destroyed.

One group of atomic operations that deserves special mention is the compare-and-swap family of functions. The compare-and-swap operation writes a value to a memory address but, importantly, the write will only take place if the value that is being overwritten is equal to some expected value that is provided by the caller. The result of the operation is a Boolean value that indicates whether the write succeeded. Importantly, for the purposes of synchronization, the entire operation is performed atomically.

The compare and swap function can be used to build more complex atomic operations. For example, suppose we wish to implement a function to perform a bitwise AND followed by a bitwise OR, with the overall operation being atomic. Clearly, we cannot simply call OSBitAndAtomic() followed by OSBitOrAtomic() because there is nothing to prevent the execution from being preempted between the two functions. With the OSCompareAndSwap() function at our disposal, we can implement a function that atomically performs a bitwise AND followed by a bitwise OR as follows:

```
uint32_t       AtomicBitAndOr (uint32_t andMask, uint32_t orMask, volatile uint32_t* address)
{
        uint32_t       oldValue;
        uint32_t       newValue;

        do {
                oldValue = *address;
                newValue = oldValue & andMask;
                newValue = newValue | orMask;
        } while (OSCompareAndSwap(oldValue, newValue, address) == false);

        return oldValue;
}
```

You will note that we have no synchronization at all while we perform the two bitwise operations. The reason that this implementation works and is atomic is because it uses the OSCompareAndSwap() function to ensure that the value at address hasn't changed from the original value on which we based our calculation of the new value to be written. If another thread had modified the value at address while this function was executing, then the OSCompareAndSwap() function would return false and would not perform the write. As a result, we would have to go back to the beginning of the loop and repeat the entire bitwise operation after re-reading the value at address. On this next attempt, we hope to have better luck in performing the operation without another thread modifying the value at address underneath us, although we will continue retrying until we successfully write the result to memory.

▓ **Note** All atomic operations, such as OSAddAtomic(), OSIncrementAtomic(), and OSBitOrAtomic() can be implemented using only OSCompareAndSwap(). In fact, a number of atomic functions provided by the libkern library are implemented this way, including all bitwise atomic operations and the 8-bit and 16-bit variations of each operation, which perform a compare and swap on the full 32-bit word containing the value being modified.

Locking

The use of atomic operations is a good solution for synchronizing access to a single variable. We often need to synchronize more complex sections of code, such as algorithms that rely on the value of multiple variables or functions that touch hardware. To remove the possibility of race conditions from these more complex areas of code, we rely on mutual exclusion; that is, any other thread that wishes to execute code which could interfere with the result of our operation is blocked until the operation is complete. The act of obtaining exclusive access is referred to as "acquiring a lock."

The basic idea behind locking is that any code that accesses a shared resource, such as the instance variables of a driver, will first acquire a lock before executing the code. It will then release the lock when it has finished accessing the shared resource. The important point about a lock is that it can be held by only one client at a time; any other thread that wishes to access the same shared resource will block when it attempts to obtain the lock and will remain blocked until the lock is released. Obtaining a lock will prevent any other thread that relies on the same lock from executing so it's good practice to hold a lock for as short a time as is needed.

The I/O Kit provides several different styles of locking mechanisms, each of which is appropriate in different situations. The locks provided by the I/O Kit include:

- IOSimpleLock, which implements a spin lock

- IOLock, which implements a traditional mutex

- IORecursiveLock, which implements a mutex that can safely be acquired multiple times from the thread that is holding the lock

- IORWLock, which implements a read/write lock that can be shared between multiple threads that need to read the shared resource but provides exclusive access to a thread that wishes to write to the shared resource.

Spin locks

The most basic implementation of locking is the spin lock, which can be implemented using nothing more than atomic operations (which may explain why the spin lock is known as IOSimpleLock in the I/O Kit implementation). A spin lock may consist of nothing more than a Boolean flag that indicates whether the lock is currently held by any thread. When a thread wishes to acquire the lock, the implementation determines whether the lock is held and, if not, performs an atomic set of the lock's flag. If the lock is held, then the function will simply repeatedly try to obtain the lock until the lock becomes available. An example implementation for a spin lock is shown in the following code. This implementation uses an unsigned 32-bit integer to represent the lock state, with a value of 0 indicating the lock is available and a value of 1 indicating that the lock is held.

```
typedef    uint32_t    MySpinLock;

void    MyAcquireSpinLock (MySpinLock* lock)
{
        // If the value of the lock is 0, set its value to 1.
        // Keep trying until the value of lock is successfully set.
        while (OSCompareAndSwap(0, 1, lock) == false)
              ;
}
```

A thread that holds a spin lock must be careful not to obtain the lock that it is currently holding a second time. If this were to happen, then the thread would attempt to acquire the lock and spin because the lock is not available. However, in this case, the thread will spin indefinitely since the only thread that can release the lock is blocked waiting for the lock. This situation is known as a deadlock.

The actual implementation of IOSimpleLock used by the I/O Kit is slightly more advanced than the example given, since it disables preemption of the running thread while the lock is held. This means that while a simple lock is held, the thread holding the lock will not be taken off the CPU on which it is running until the lock is released. Consequently, an IOSimpleLock should only be acquired for very brief periods (such as while a driver's instance variables are being updated) and should never perform an operation that may block the running thread, such as allocating memory or acquiring a mutex, since this could result in a deadlock.

Although it may seem that spin locks are an inefficient locking mechanism because a thread spends CPU cycles spinning if it cannot immediately obtain a lock, they can actually be more efficient than other locking mechanisms, provided that the lock is only held for short periods of time. On a machine with a single CPU, IOSimpleLock will never spin because, with thread preemption disabled, there is no possibility of lock contention (in effect, synchronization is provided by disabling thread preemption and preventing the execution of any other thread that may acquire the lock). On a multiprocessor system, disabling preemption when an IOSimpleLock is acquired does not prevent a thread running on another CPU from attempting to access the same lock (in fact, thread preemption is only disabled for the CPU core that has acquired the lock). However, providing that a spin lock is held for only a short period of time, the time spent by a thread spinning while it waits for the lock to become free will typically be much less than the overhead of blocking the thread had a mutex been used instead of a spin lock.

Unlike a mutex, an IOSimpleLock will never suspend the running thread. Instead it will spin until the lock becomes available. This makes IOSimpleLock perfect for providing synchronization between code that runs within a primary interrupt handler and non-interrupt code. In reality, this functionality is rarely needed within an I/O Kit driver since most drivers won't ever have to handle an interrupt directly and, if they do, most will defer the interrupt to a secondary interrupt handler. The I/O Kit provides other locking mechanisms that are appropriate for secondary interrupt handlers, which are discussed later in this chapter.

To provide synchronization with code that runs inside a primary interrupt handler, we need to make sure that code that acquires an IOSimpleLock at non-interrupt time is never preempted by code running inside an interrupt handler that attempts to acquire the same lock, since this would result in a deadlock. To solve this, the I/O Kit provides a function that disables interrupts for the running CPU before acquiring the spin lock and a counterpart that releases the spin lock and then re-enables interrupts. Just as disabling thread preemption guarantees that a thread holding an IOSimpleLock will not be preempted by another thread on the same CPU, disabling interrupts guarantees that a thread holding an IOSimpleLock will not be preempted by an interrupt handler on the same CPU. An interrupt may fire on another CPU on the system and may attempt to acquire an IOSimpleLock that is held by a thread on another CPU core (resulting in the interrupt handler spinning) but, because the thread is running on another CPU, it can continue to execute and will release the IOSimpleLock shortly afterwards.

A summary of the IOSimpleLock functions provided by the I/O Kit is given in Table 7-2.

Table 7-2. *Spin Lock Synchronization Functions Provided By the I/O Kit*

Function	Description
`IOSimpleLock*    IOSimpleLockAlloc(void);`	Allocates a new `IOSimpleLock` and returns a pointer to the initialized object or `NULL` on failure.
`void    IOSimpleLockFree(IOSimpleLock* lock);`	Deallocates an `IOSimpleLock` object that was allocated by `IOSimpleLockAlloc()`.
`void    IOSimpleLockLock (IOSimpleLock* lock);`	Acquires a simple lock, spinning if the lock is currently held by another client. When the function returns, preemption for the current CPU is disabled.
`boolean_t IOSimpleLockTryLock(IOSimpleLock* lock);`	Acquires a simple lock, but only if the lock is not already held. The function returns a Boolean that indicates whether the function was able to acquire the lock.
`void    IOSimpleLockUnlock(IOSimpleLock* lock);`	Releases a simple lock that has been acquired by either `IOSimpleLockLock()` or a successful call to `IOSimpleLockTryLock()`. Preemption for the current CPU is re-enabled.
`IOInterruptState IOSimpleLockLockDisableInterrupt (IOSimpleLock* lock);`	Acquires a simple lock and disables thread preemption and interrupts for the current CPU. This function is only needed for locks that are shared between interrupt context and thread context. The value returned by the function is required when releasing the lock to ensure that the CPU's interrupt state is restored to its original condition.
`void IOSimpleLockUnlockEnableInterrupt (IOSimpleLock* lock, IOInterruptState state);`	Releases a simple lock that has been acquired by `IOSimpleLockLockDisableInterrupt()`. Thread preemption is re-enabled and the interrupt state is restored to the parameter "state".

Mutexes

Although spin locks are efficient for certain applications, they are not suitable in cases in which a thread needs to hold the lock for a long time or when a thread performs an operation that may block while the lock is held, such as allocating memory or acquiring a second lock. In these cases, the use of a spin lock would be very inefficient, since any lock contention will result in a thread spinning continuously while it attempts to obtain the lock, which would prevent the CPU from performing any useful work. A mutex lock does not have this problem because a thread that attempts to acquire a mutex lock that is already taken will be suspended until the lock becomes available. Rather than spending CPU time spinning, the operating system is able to schedule another thread on the CPU. The I/O Kit provides support for mutex locks through an object known as an IOLock. Because a mutex may block if it cannot be acquired immediately, mutex locks cannot be used within an interrupt handler.

The functionality provided by IOLock is very similar to that provided by the POSIX mutex lock functions that are available to user space applications. You can use an IOLock in driver code in similar ways to how you would use a POSIX mutex in user space code. Unlike an IOSimpleLock, which shouldn't be held for long periods because it disables preemption (and possibly interrupts), a mutex has no such effect on the state of the CPU or operating system's scheduler. A thread holding a mutex will still be preempted by another thread once its time quantum has expired and a thread holding a mutex can still be preempted if the CPU needs to handle an interrupt. However, these points can be seen as advantages of using a mutex, since they mean that there are no restrictions on what operations can be performed while a mutex is held. While a mutex is held, a thread can allocate memory, map memory from user space into the kernel (which may result in memory paging), and can obtain another mutex (which is an operation that may block).

As with a spin lock, a thread that holds a mutex must be careful not to obtain a mutex that it is currently holding a second time. Otherwise, a deadlock will occur. At first, this may seem like an artificial problem, since it's simply a matter of ensuring that a thread doesn't attempt to obtain a lock that it is already holding. However, this can become complicated if the code that is executed while a lock is held calls other functions that may themselves call other functions that end up acquiring the lock.

For example, let's pretend that we have a function named ListEnqueue() that requires synchronization because it can be called from multiple threads. The ListEnqueue() function may be called from many locations in our project's codebase and some of the calling functions may already hold the synchronization lock but other calling functions nay not hold the lock. If our sample ListEnqueue() function were to acquire a lock to ensure that it is synchronized when called from functions that do not already hold the lock, we would introduce a deadlock when ListEnqueue() is called from functions that do hold the lock. This situation can be solved by using a recursive mutex.

Once a thread has acquired a recursive mutex, any code that runs on that same thread is able to reacquire the mutex multiple times without resulting in a deadlock. The shared resource is still synchronized, since any other thread that attempts to acquire the mutex will be blocked until all acquisitions made by the owning thread have been released. The I/O Kit provides support for a recursive mutex through the IORecursiveLock object.

A summary of the mutex operations provided by the I/O Kit is given in Table 7-3.

Table 7-3. Mutex Synchronization Functions Provided By the I/O Kit

Function	Description
IOLock* IOLockAlloc(void); IORecursiveLock* IORecursiveLockAlloc(void);	Allocates a new IOLock or IORecursiveLock and returns a pointer to the initialized object or NULL on failure.

void   IOLockFree(IOLock* lock);
 	
void   IORecursiveLockFree(IORecursiveLock* lock);
	Deallocates an IOLock object that was allocated by IOLockAlloc() or an IORecursiveLock object that was allocated by IORecursiveLockAlloc().

Function	Description

`void IOLockLock(IOLock* lock);`
 	
`void IORecursiveLockLock(IORecursiveLock* lock);`
	Acquires a mutex, blocking the calling thread if the lock is held by another thread. Once a thread has acquired a recursive lock, it can safely reacquire the same lock multiple times.

`boolean_t IOLockTryLock(IOLock* lock);`
 	
`boolean_t IORecursiveLockTryLock(IORecursiveLock* lock);`
	Acquires a mutex lock but only if the lock is not held by another thread. This function will never block the calling thread if the lock could not be acquired, but will return a Boolean that indicates whether the function was able to acquire the lock.

`void IOLockUnlock(IOLock* lock);`
 	
`void IORecursiveLockUnlock(IORecursiveLock* lock);`
	Releases a mutex that has been acquired by either IOLockLock() or a successful call to IOLockTryLock(). Or, for a recursive mutex, it releases a lock that was acquired by either IORecursiveLockLock() or a successful call to IORecursiveLockTryLock().

`boolean_t IORecursiveLockHaveLock (const IORecursiveLock* lock);`	Tests whether a recursive mutex is held by the calling thread. If the mutex has been acquired by the thread, then the value true is returned. If the mutex has either not been acquired or has been acquired by another thread, the value false is returned.

Condition Variables

As well as providing a mutex for exclusive access to a shared resource, the `IOLock` and `IORecursiveLock` objects provide support for a synchronization primitive known as a condition variable. A condition variable allows synchronization between multiple threads by providing a mechanism by which one thread can suspend its execution until a particular condition (or event) occurs.

As an example, let's consider the driver for a serial port. Our hypothetical driver will receive blocking read requests from a user space application. These requests will block and only return to user space once data has been received on the serial port. Rather than continually polling inside the driver until data is available, a better approach is to create a condition variable and suspend the thread so that it does not use any CPU time while it is waiting. When the driver receives data from hardware, it will wake any threads that are waiting on the condition variable. This is illustrated in the following sample code:

```
void    MyDriver::read (void* buffer, uint32_t* bytesRead)
{
        IOLockLock(m_lock);
        do {
                // Attempt to read from hardware
                *bytesRead = readFromHardware(buffer);

                // If no data available, sleep until the hardware receives data
```

```
        if (*bytesRead == 0)
        {
                int     result;

                result = IOLockSleep(m_lock, m_readEvent, THREAD_ABORTSAFE);
                if (result != THREAD_AWAKENED)
                        break;
        }
    } while (*bytesRead == 0);
    IOLockUnlock(m_lock);
}

void    MyDriver::DataAvailable ()
{
        // Wake any threads that are sleeping on m_readEvent
        IOLockWakeup(m_lock, m_readEvent, false);
}
```

In the preceding example, the read() method will attempt to receive any data from the hardware device, but if no data is available, then it will block the current thread until the hardware has data. When the hardware has data available, the DataAvailable() method is called (which could be called in response to a hardware interrupt) and any blocked thread is woken. Note that the entire contents of the read() method are protected by an IOLock. This ensures that all attempts to read data from the hardware device are serialized. Otherwise, a potential race condition would exist when the hardware signals the availability of data as multiple threads are awoken and simultaneously attempt to read data from the device. The behavior of IOLockSleep() is similar to that of its equivalent user space function pthread_cond_wait(). The first parameter is a lock that must be held by the caller; IOLockSleep() will atomically release the lock when it sleeps and reacquire the lock once the event has been signaled. In this way, the lock is not held while the thread is suspended.

The parameter m_readEvent is the condition variable; the waiting thread specifies the event that it is waiting on through the condition variable. The signaling thread indicates the event that has occurred by providing the same condition variable. A driver will define a number of condition variables that correspond to events that it uses to coordinate between its threads. Condition variables in the I/O Kit do not have a specific type, rather a condition variable is an arbitrary void* that uniquely identifies an event. A driver will usually use the address of an instance variable (such as the address of the lock itself) as a condition variable, since the use of an address guarantees that the value will be unique among multiple instances of the driver and other drivers in the system.

A summary of the condition variable synchronization operations provided by the I/O Kit is given in Table 7-4.

Table 7-4. Condition Variable Synchronization Functions Provided By the I/O Kit

Function	Description
int IOLockSleep(IOLock* lock, void* event, UInt32 interruptType);	Atomically unlocks the provided lock, which must be held by the caller, and waits on the specified event.
int IORecursiveLockSleep(IORecursiveLock* lock, void* event, UInt32 interruptType);	If the caller is running on a user space thread as part of a control request, the interruptType parameter specifies whether the sleep should be aborted if the user process receives a signal such as SIGHUP or SIGKILL. The lock is reacquired before the function returns.
int IOLockSleepDeadline(IOLock* lock, void* event, AbsoluteTime deadline, UInt32 interruptType); int IORecursiveLockSleepDeadline(IORecursiveLock* lock, void* event, AbsoluteTime deadline, UInt32 interruptType);	Performs a sleep on an event with a specified timeout parameter. If the event is not signaled before the specified time, the function will wake and return to the caller, with the lock reacquired.
void IOLockWakeup(IOLock * lock, void *event, bool oneThread); void IORecursiveLockWakeup(IORecursiveLock* lock, void* event, bool oneThread);	Signals that an event has occurred and wakes any threads that are sleeping on that same event. The parameter oneThread allows the caller to specify whether only one sleeping thread should be awoken or whether all threads that are sleeping on the event should be awoken.

The interruptType parameter that is provided to the sleep functions determines whether the function should return if the process that owns the thread receives a signal such as SIGHUP or SIGKILL. This is useful if the wait is being performed by a user client in response to a control request in which case the driver function will be running on a thread that was created by the user space application. Depending on the situation, the driver may wish to abort the wait if the process receives a signal, since the client process may have been terminated. The possible values for interruptType are:

- THREAD_UNINT specifies that the sleep should not be aborted by any signal

- THREAD_INTERRUPTIBLE specifies that the sleep may be aborted if a SIGKILL signal is received

- THREAD_ABORTSAFE specifies that the sleep may be aborted if any signal is received

Upon waking from a sleep, the function will return one of the following result values:

- THREAD_AWAKENED indicates the function returned normally and the event was signaled by a call to IOLockWakeup()

- **THREAD_TIMED_OUT** indicates that the event was not signaled by the specified deadline

- **THREAD_INTERRUPTED** indicates the user process that owns the thread on which the driver was sleeping received a signal

- **THREAD_RESTART** indicates that the wait operation should be restarted entirely

Read/Write Mutexes

One of the problems with a mutex is that allowing only a single thread to hold the lock can often be unnecessarily restrictive. In many cases, there is no reason why multiple threads should not be allowed to read a shared resource. It is only when a thread wishes to write to the shared resource or otherwise modify it that exclusive access is required. This problem is solved by a specialized type of mutex known as a read/write mutex.

The I/O Kit provides read/write mutexes through an object known as IORWLock. A read/write mutex can be used in a similar way to a standard mutex. The one distinction is the caller must determine whether it intends to read the shared resource (in which case it can share the mutex with other readers) or intends to write to the shared resource (in which case it requires exclusive access to the mutex). The I/O Kit provides two separate functions depending on the action that the calling code wishes to take.

A summary of the read/write mutex synchronization operations provided by the I/O Kit is given in Table 7-5.

Table 7-5. Read/Write Mutex Synchronization Functions Provided By the I/O Kit

Function	Description
IORWLock* IORWLockAlloc(void);	Allocates a new IORWLock and returns a pointer to the initialized object or NULL on failure.
void IORWLockFree(IORWLock* lock);	Deallocates an IORWLock that was allocated by IORWLockAlloc().
void IORWLockRead(IORWLock* lock);	Acquires a read/write mutex with the intention of reading the shared resource. The mutex may be shared with other readers but will block if the mutex is held by a writer.
void IORWLockWrite(IORWLock* lock);	Acquires a read/write mutex with the intention of writing to the shared resource. The caller is granted exclusive access to the shared resource and will block if the read/write mutex is held by any readers or writers.
void IORWLockUnlock(IORWLock* lock);	Releases a read/write mutex that has been acquired by either IORWLockRead() or IORWLockWrite().

■ **Note** The I/O Kit locking primitives are all built on top of Mach types. The I/O Kit contains functions to get at the underlying Mach locking types, including `IOSimpleLockGetMachLock()`, `IOLockGetMachLock()`, `IORecursiveLockGetMachLock()`, and `IORWLockGetMachLock()`. These functions can be useful to take advantage of behavior that is implemented at the Mach level but not exposed by the I/O Kit functions. For example, Mach read/write locks can be upgraded from shared read access to exclusive write access, but the I/O Kit provides no equivalent function.

Synchronizing Asynchronous Events: Work Loops

Synchronization within a driver becomes difficult if the driver needs to respond to asynchronous events such as hardware interrupts or timers. This adds an extra layer of complexity since, in addition to requiring synchronization between multiple threads of execution, the driver now has to contend with the synchronization of code that runs on multiple threads and code that runs in response to asynchronous events. To simplify the work required by the driver developer, the I/O Kit provides a class known as IOWorkLoop that creates a single thread on which all asynchronous events are handled. In I/O Kit nomenclature, this thread is known as a "work loop" and a driver registers any of its asynchronous event sources, such as interrupt handlers and timers, with an IOWorkLoop object.

For much of the time, the work loop thread will be idle, consuming no CPU time and simply waiting for an event to occur. Once an event occurs, the corresponding event source will signal the work loop. The work loop thread will wake up, handle the event, and then return to the sleep state. Since all events are handled on the same work loop thread, this design provides an elegant solution for synchronizing multiple sources within a driver. Another advantage of this design is that, since all event sources are handled on the same thread, the handler functions do not need to provide any additional locking because there is no possibility of multiple handlers running at the same time.

The work loop is an intrinsic part of every I/O Kit driver. The IOService class, which is the base class from which every driver object is ultimately derived, provides a method named getWorkLoop() through which a provider class can share its work loop with its child drivers. A driver can choose to use the IOWorkLoop object created by its provider class (by calling IOService::getWorkLoop()) or can opt to create its own IOWorkLoop object. If a driver expects to receive only the occasional asynchronous event and the latency of the event handler doesn't need to be kept to a minimum, then sharing the work loop of its provider class is an attractive approach. This will also simplify the code that forms the driver's constructor and destructor and eliminate the overhead of creating an additional kernel thread for the driver's own work loop. Drivers that handle hardware interrupts should create their own dedicated IOWorkLoop object since this guarantees minimum latency because the work loop is not shared with event sources from its provider driver.

A driver will typically initialize its work loop inside the driver's start() method. If a driver decides that it will share the work loop of its provider, then it can obtain a work loop in the following way:

```
m_workLoop = getWorkLoop();          // Implemented by the IOService superclass
if (m_workLoop == NULL)
        abort with error;
m_workLoop->retain();
```

If a driver decides that it will create a dedicated work loop of its own, then it can instantiate a new IOWorkLoop object as follows:

```
m_workLoop = IOWorkLoop::workLoop();
if (m_workLoop == NULL)
        abort with error;
```

If a driver instantiates its own IOWorkLoop object, then it should consider overriding the IOService method getWorkLoop() to expose its work loop to any child drivers of its own.

Having obtained an IOWorkLoop object, the driver next needs to register the event sources that it wishes to handle on the work loop thread. Event sources are objects that inherit from the IOEventSource base class. The I/O Kit provides specializations, including the IOInterruptEventSource class and the IOTimerEventSource class, for creating an event source for a PCI card's interrupt handler and a timer event, respectively. When an event source is instantiated, a callback function is provided, which will be invoked when the event requires servicing. The callback function is guaranteed to either be called from the work loop thread or to be synchronized with any code running on the work loop thread. An example of code to create an event source for a timer and add it to a work loop is given here:

```
m_timerEventSource = IOTimerEventSource::timerEventSource(this, TimerFiredFunc);
if (m_timerEventSource == NULL)
        abort with error;

result = m_workLoop->addEventSource(m_timerEventSource);
if (result != kIOReturnSuccess)
        abort with error;
```

▓ **Note** In the case of an interrupt handler, the callback that is run on the work loop thread corresponds to the secondary interrupt handler; the primary interrupt is still taken at the hardware interrupt level and will run in an arbitrary thread context.

A driver will typically specify a static method in its main driver class as the callback function of an IOEventSource. Although the arguments provided to the callback function differ depending on the type of event source that is being invoked, the first argument is always a pointer to an OSObject class that can be used to pass the driver's instance to the callback function. Depending on the complexity of the callback function, the implementation may either handle the event directly in the static class function or call through to an instance method of the driver.

IOCommandGate

One problem that remains is that a driver may need to synchronize code running on its own threads against event actions that run on the work loop thread. For example, consider the driver for a disk device that receives requests for read and write transactions from user space applications. Since the hardware can only service one transaction at a time, any additional transactions will be added to a queue and, whenever a transaction has completed (which is signaled through an interrupt), the driver will remove the next transaction from the head of the queue and service it. Since this hypothetical driver manipulates the transaction queue both from within its interrupt handler (which will run on the work loop) and from its user client, it requires some way of synchronizing code that runs on the work loop thread with code that runs in an arbitrary thread context.

To solve this problem, the I/O Kit provides a special event source known as a command gate, implemented by a class named IOCommandGate. A command gate is installed on a work loop like any other event source but, instead of generating events itself, it is used to execute an arbitrary callback function on the work loop thread. The IOCommandGate class contains a method named runAction() that takes a function pointer and runs that function such that it is synchronized with any other work loop event. A function that is executed through an IOCommandGate object is said to be a "gated" function. The gated function isn't actually run on the work loop thread. It is simply serialized against all other work loop sources, including other gated functions that are called through the same IOCommandGate. The command gate actually runs the function on whichever thread made the call to runAction(). This removes the overhead of a context switch to the work loop thread. An example of calling a function through an IOCommandGate is shown in the following code:

```
// Method called outside the gate
IOReturn MyDriver::startTransaction(Transaction* transaction)
{
        // Call the function StartTransactionAction through the command gate
        return m_commandGate->runAction((IOCommandGate::Action)StartTransactionAction);
}


// IOCommandGate::Action
IOReturn MyDriver::StartTransactionAction(MyDriver* self, Transaction* transaction)
{
        // This static method is synchronized against all work loop methods
        ...
        return kIOReturnSuccess;
}
```

In the previous example, we provided a single parameter to the action function, namely the argument "transaction". The IOCommandGate allows up to four parameters to be provided to an action function.

The IOCommandGate achieves its synchronization through a recursive lock. This allows a function that has been called through the IOCommandGate to call other functions through the same IOCommandGate without causing a deadlock. It also allows a gated function to sleep and wake on condition variables, using an approach that is similar to that discussed earlier in this chapter. The IOCommandGate class contains two methods for sleeping on a condition variable, one which will timeout after a specified period and one which will sleep until the condition variable is signaled. These two methods are described as follows:

```
IOReturn              commandSleep(void* event, UInt32 interruptType);
IOReturn              commandSleep(void* event, AbsoluteTime deadline, UInt32 interruptType);
```

The parameters event, interruptType, and deadline have the same meaning as the parameters of the same name that are passed to the functions IOLockSleep() and IOLockSleepDeadline() described in Table 7-4. As we saw in the section on "Condition Variables," a thread can only sleep on a condition variable if it is holding a synchronization lock. The same rule applies for the commandSleep() method, which must be called from a function that has been called through an IOCommandGate object.

To signal a command gate's condition variable when an event has occurred, the IOCommandGate class provides the following method that takes the same form as the IOLockWakeup() function described in Table 7-4:

```
void    commandWakeup(void* event, bool oneThread);
```

The IOCommandGate object provides all of the synchronization capabilities of an IORecursiveLock, including mutex locking and condition variable support. This allows a driver to use an IOCommandGate object instead of an I/O Kit lock for all of its synchronization. This can be useful if a driver needs a work loop to provide synchronization against asynchronous events; the driver can create an IOCommandGate and use the work loop throughout its implementation instead of creating additional locks.

Timers

The final event source that we will discuss is the IOTimerEventSource, which provides a basic, non-periodic timer. A common use of an IOTimerEventSource is for creating a watchdog timer to cancel operations that have not completed within a certain period of time.

When a timer is created, the caller provides a callback function that will be run when the timer expires. Like any other event source, a timer must be added to an IOWorkLoop object and its callback function will be run from a context that is synchronized to all other event sources installed on the work loop.

A timer can be initialized and added to an existing work loop as shown in the following code:

```
m_timer = IOTimerEventSource::timerEventSource(this, TimerFired);
if (m_timer == NULL)
        abort with error;

result = m_workLoop->addEventSource(m_timer);
if (result != kIOReturnSuccess)
        abort with error;
```

The method IOTimerEventSource::timerEventSource() instantiates a new IOTimerEventSource object. Its first parameter is a pointer to an OSObject, which is passed to the callback function, allowing it to access the driver object.

Next, the timer needs to be activated. This is done by specifying a timeout period from the current time until the timer fires. The IOTimerEventSource class provides methods to specify the timeout in milliseconds, microseconds, nanoseconds, or in arbitrary time units:

```
IOReturn        setTimeoutMS(UInt32 ms);
IOReturn        setTimeoutUS(UInt32 us);
IOReturn        setTimeout(UInt32 interval, UInt32 scale_factor = kNanosecondScale);
```

When the timer fires, the specified callback function will be run, which has the following signature:

```
void    MyDriver::TimerFired(OSObject* owner, IOTimerEventSource* sender)
{
}
```

Although the timer provided by IOTimerEventSource is not periodic, the timer's next timeout value can be set from within its callback function. You will notice that the IOTimerEventSource instance is provided as a parameter to the callback function, which allows the callback to easily re-install the timer. If the drift between subsequent firings of the timer needs to be avoided for a specific application, the IOTimerEventSource provides a wakeAtTime() method that allows the timeout to be specified as an absolute time. A periodic timer that does not drift over time can be created by specifying an absolute time each time the timer is reinstalled.

If a timer needs to be cancelled, for example, because the operation that a watchdog timer was guarding has successfully completed, the IOTimerEventSource class includes a method named cancelTimeout(). This method is also a synchronization point, and will guarantee that the timer's callback function will not be called by the time this method has returned.

Releasing Work Loops

When a driver is unloaded, it will need to release any work loop that it has created. This is a two-step process and involves removing event sources from the work loop and then releasing the IOWorkLoop object. The first part is usually performed by a driver in its stop() method, but the work loop itself is typically not released until the driver's free() method is called. A possible implementation follows:

```
void    MyDriver::stop(IOService* provider)
{
        // Remove and release the command gate event source.
        if (m_commandGate != NULL)
        {
                m_workLoop->removeEventSource(m_commandGate);
                m_commandGate->release();
                m_commandGate = NULL;
        }

        // Remove and release the timer event source.
        if (m_timer != NULL)
        {
                m_timer->cancelTimeout();
                m_workLoop->removeEventSource(m_timer);
                m_timer->release();
                m_timer = NULL;
        }

        super::stop(provider);
}


void    MyDriver::free()
{
        // Release the work loop
        if (m_workLoop != NULL)
        {
                m_workLoop->release();
                m_workLoop = NULL;
        }

        super::free();
}
```

Kernel Threads

Unlike a user space application, a driver doesn't have a main thread that is always running while the driver is active. Instead, a driver typically executes on existing threads in response to certain events. For example, when a user space process makes a control request through the driver's user client, the driver executes within the context of the calling thread owned by the user process. Similarly, when a driver's hardware generates an interrupt, the driver's secondary interrupt handler is executed from the work loop thread. Because a driver executes in response to such events, if a driver isn't handling an event, such as a control request or an interrupt handler, it will typically have no code executing on any thread in the system.

The lack of an equivalent of a main thread can be a problem for a driver, particularly if it needs to have code executing continually so that it can periodically poll its hardware device or if it wishes to perform a time-consuming operation such as downloading firmware to its hardware. In these cases, a driver can create its own kernel thread on which to continue executing code without tying up the thread of a user process or the work loop thread.

A good example of the use of a kernel thread is shown in Listing 5-16 from Chapter 5. In this example, a user space application made a control request to the driver to perform a delay operation. Rather than performing the delay within the context of the process thread, which would have blocked the calling process, the driver instead chose to create a background thread on which to perform the sleep operation. Once the delay had completed, the driver then signaled the user process with an asynchronous notification. This simple design pattern demonstrates how a driver can use a kernel thread to turn a synchronous operation that would block the thread from the calling process into an operation that appears to be asynchronous to the calling process.

The APIs for creating a kernel thread come from the lower-level Mach layer and are declared in the header file <kern/thread.h>. You should never need to include this header file directly though, since it is included by the header file <IOKit/IOLib.h>. If you look at the contents of IOLib.h, you will see that it contains a small number of threading functions, including support for creating a thread. Starting in Mac OS X 10.6, however, these functions have been deprecated by Apple in favor of the Mach functions.

The function kernel_thread_start() can be used to create kernel thread. Its prototype is given as follows:

```
kern_return_t   kernel_thread_start(thread_continue_t continuation, void* parameter,
                        thread_t* new_thread);
```

The argument "continuation" is actually a function pointer to the start routine of the newly created thread. If a thread was successfully created, the return value from kernel_thread_start() will be kIOReturnSuccess and the argument "new_thread" will contain a reference to the newly created thread, much like the reference that is returned by the user space function pthread_create(). The thread_t object that is returned isn't terribly useful to the caller, since there are very few public kernel APIs for thread manipulation. However, the thread_t value can be compared against the value returned by current_thread() to determine whether the active function is running on a particular thread.

In most cases, the caller immediately releases the thread_t object after successfully creating a thread; this does not impact the execution of the background thread itself. To release the thread_t object, the function thread_deallocate() should be used, which has the following prototype:

```
void    thread_deallocate(thread_t thread);
```

■ **Note** It is important that the thread_t object that is returned by kernel_thread_start() is released to prevent a memory leak.

The start routine for the thread has the following signature:

```
void    ThreadFunction (void* parameter, wait_result_t waitResult)
```

The first argument to the function, parameter, corresponds to the value that was passed to kernel_thread_start() and allows the creator of the thread to pass context to the thread's function. The second argument to the function, `waitResult`, is not useful for threads created through `kernel_thread_start()`; its presence is simply a consequence of the thread function being defined as the type `thread_continue_t`. Internally, the kernel makes use of the type `thread_continue_t` elsewhere and the value of `waitResult` is used in these cases.

Finally, once a thread has completed its operation and wishes to terminate, the thread function should call the function `thread_terminate()`, as demonstrated:

```
thread_terminate(current_thread());
```

Note that although it might seem that it is possible to terminate a background thread from another thread, this will fail with an error returned to the caller. The `thread_terminate()` function only allows the current thread to be terminated. To terminate a background thread, for example, when a driver is unloaded, the driver should instead signal the background thread that it needs to exit and allow the thread to terminate itself. This signaling can be done either by setting a Boolean flag that the background thread checks periodically or by setting a condition variable that the background thread sleeps on.

Summary

- A driver runs in a multithreaded environment.

- The methods of a driver class can potentially be called from an arbitrary thread. This means that, even if a driver creates no threads of its own, it cannot escape the need for synchronized access to its shared instance variables and hardware.

- The I/O Kit provides synchronization functions that a driver can use to prevent multiple threads from modifying shared data at the same time.

- A spin lock is a suitable synchronization mechanism for code that will hold the lock only for a short period of time or for code that will execute inside a primary interrupt handler.

- A mutex is a better choice if the lock will be held for longer periods, but it cannot be used inside a primary interrupt handler.

- To synchronize events that can occur at an arbitrary time, such as a hardware interrupt or a software timer, the I/O Kit provides a dedicated thread on which the handler for these events is run. This is known as the work loop thread and the I/O Kit ensures that all event sources that are installed on the work loop are executed in a serial manner.

CHAPTER 8

Universal Serial Bus

The Universal Serial Bus (USB) is a ubiquitous technology found in a wide variety of products, notably computer peripherals, including mice, keyboards, hard drives, and printers, as well as almost any other type of device or equipment that can be connected to a computer. The USB is a specification that defines the communication between a device, such as a printer or mobile phone, and a host controlled by a computer device, such as your Mac or iPad. The USB specification was developed in 1996 by a consortium of companies, including Compaq, DEC, IBM, Intel, Microsoft, NEC, and Nortel. The motivation was to replace a series of connectors with a universal connector, making it easier to connect external devices to personal computers. The USB specification is currently at version 3.0. Support for 3.0 is still emerging, and support for version 2.0 is by far the most ubiquitous at this time. Apple has yet to release hardware capable of supporting the latest USB 3.0 specification, but Apple computers have shipped with USB support since before OS X. The iOS series of devices are themselves USB devices, but they can also act as USB hosts. An example of this is the iPad, which can act as a host for USB devices, such as digital cameras.

USB is based on a master-slave system, where a controller (host) communicates with slave devices. A host commonly has a one-to-one relationship with a bus.

As a kernel programmer, if you are tasked with writing a driver for a hardware device, there is a major chance that it would be for a USB device. The good news (for us lazy programmers, anyway) is that you can get away without having a driver if your device conforms to one of the classes defined by the USB Implementers Forum (USB-IF). For example, keyboards and mice comply with the human interface device (HID) specification, which makes it unnecessary for a vendor to supply a driver, as the OS will already have a generic driver that can be used to communicate with these devices. However, the vendor could still elect to develop a driver—for example, if the device has advanced capabilities, such as additional customizable buttons on a mouse.

This chapter will provide a broad overview of the USB specification and architecture. The specification is much longer than this book, so obviously a detailed discussion is out of the question. We will instead focus on the parts that matter when implementing a driver for a USB device. We will also discuss the architecture of the USB subsystem provided by I/O Kit, as well as provide code for a fictional USB device driver. It is worth mentioning that USB drivers can be written both in the kernel and in user space. A kernel driver is generally needed when a driver/device can be accessed concurrently by many applications, or if the primary client of the driver is the kernel itself. Examples of devices typically implemented in the kernel are storage, networking, audio, and display drivers, whereas drivers for printers, mice, and keyboards may be handled fully or partially by a user space driver. In this chapter, we will focus on the USB in general, and on the implementation of kernel space drivers. A discussion about user space drivers is provided in Chapter 15.

USB Architecture

In a USB system, the host controller is the master and the USB devices are the subordinates. The USB topology is organized in a tree-like structure, which forms a bus, with the host controller being the root and the controller of the subordinated device. The host controller is responsible for coordinating activities on the bus, and a device is not able to perform I/O, or any other activity on the bus, without first being asked to do so by the host.

The tree structure branches out with the help of hubs, which allow connected devices to become part of the bus, and thus extend it, as a new branch. The subordinate devices of a hub can have other hubs connected to them— up to four levels deep is possible. The root hub is usually embedded into, and part of, the host controller itself. Figure 8-1 shows the USB topology for a MacBook computer.

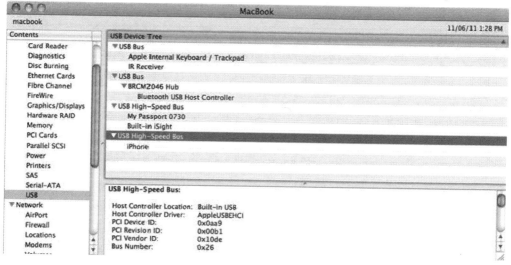

Figure 8-1. *System Information showing the USB topology of a MacBook, with external devices connected*

The system in Figure 8-1 has four built-in USB buses, but only two buses are actually connected to external USB ports. While most people associate USB devices with external devices, USB is often used to communicate with fixed internal devices in the computer system. The first two USB buses of the MacBook in Figure 8-1 are internal to the notebook, and are used to connect to the internal keyboard, the trackpad, and the IR Receiver. The second internal bus connects to the Bluetooth USB host controller. Both of these buses are USB 1.1 buses, which is fine because the devices connected to them all have low bandwidth requirements.

This MacBook has two external USB devices connected, an external hard drive and an iPhone, each connected to a separate physical USB port on the system. Although you would think that an external USB port has its own dedicated bus, this may not always be the case. As you can see in Figure 8-1, one of the buses has an additional USB device attached to it, namely the built-in iSight camera. The camera requires more bandwidth than the 1.1 USB buses/controllers can provide, so it is instead attached to one of the two USB 2.0 controllers, likely to avoid having a separate controller just for the iSight, saving space, parts, cost, and battery power. The downside is that an external device will share bandwidth with the iSight camera (when it is in use).

The exact USB topology will vary from system to system, and this is just one example of how it can be organized.

Each bus in a USB system can support up to 127 devices, including hub devices, which are also USB devices. Bandwidth on a USB bus is shared between the connected devices, so having a large number of active devices will incur a significant penalty, which is why it is now common to have physical USB ports on separate host controllers—each providing a bus, rather than having ports connected to a single controller.

A USB is designed to be hot-pluggable, which means that the system can handle the insertion or removal of any device at any time during operation, although, depending on the type of device, this may not necessarily be safe to do—the prime example is a hard drive, which, if unplugged at the wrong time, can lead to corruption of the drive's file system. From a developer's perspective, this means that your driver code needs to be designed to anticipate the arrival or removal of a device.

The USB specification also supports power for devices through the bus, a major advantage over older bus technologies, as this, for example, will allow you to charge an iPhone simply by plugging it in to your laptop, or to self-power a device such as a hard drive.

The key characteristics of the USB can be summarized as follows:

- Single connector type for all devices, designed to replace a variety of older connectors, such as the PS/2.

- Ability to connect many devices to the same connector.

- USB buses can be expanded with the help of hubs, supporting up to 127 devices per bus.

- Devices are hot-pluggable.

- Devices can be powered by the bus, which enables them to be charted or fully powered through the bus, depending on power requirements.

- Bandwidth is shared between devices on a bus.

- A USB device is a slave device and cannot initiate any activity on the bus without the permission of the host.

One key characteristic that sets the USB apart from traditional hardware architectures, such as the PCI, is that it does not directly generate system interrupts. The ability for a device to asynchronously notify the system of some event is essential for the operation of many types of common devices—for example, a network device that will notify the system each time a new network packet arrives, or a mouse or keyboard that relies on telling the system its current position or which key was pressed.

A USB device can still provide interrupt-like capabilities, but it is not able to directly interrupt a CPU in the same way that a PCI device can. To receive an interrupt from a USB device, an interrupt transfer has to be issued to the device. Once the transfer is issued, and an event occurs, such as the arrival of a network packet, the USB device is not simply free to signal the host controller—it has to be polled by the host controller. A USB device can only interact on the bus if told to do so by the host. The host controller provides a maximum latency guarantee for interrupt transfers. The lowest achievable latency is 125 microseconds. A device can specify the desired interval for interrupt polling in its endpoint descriptors.

It should be noted that although a USB device cannot directly interrupt a CPU itself, a USB host controller certainly can, and may do so in response to a completed interrupt transfer from a device. Most modern computer systems talk to USB controllers via PCI.

■ **Tip** The USB specifications are governed by the USB Implementers Forum (USB-IF), a not-for-profit organization. Their website can be found at http://www.usb.org.

USB Transfer Speeds

The first iteration of the USB standard supported two speeds: a low speed, at 1.5 Mbit/s, and a full speed, at 12 Mbit/s. Low speed devices are less susceptible to electromagnetic interference, and therefore these can be made cheaper, as they can be created using lower quality parts. This reduces the cost of simpler USB devices, which do not require the additional bandwidth needed for a full speed device. The USB 2.0 standard included the full speed mode, capable of operating at speeds up to 480 Mbits/s, while also being backward compatible with USB 1.0. This made the USB competitive with the Firewire specification, which at the time operated at 400 Mbits/s (see Table 8-1 for USB transfer speeds).

Table 8-1. USB Transfer Speeds

Name	Rate	Introduced In
Low-speed	1.5 Mbits/s	USB 1.0
Full-speed	12 Mbits/s	USB 1.0
High-speed	480 Mbits/s	USB 2.0
SuperSpeed	5.0 Gbits/s	USB 3.0

The USB 3.0 specification supports speeds up to 5 Gbits/s, and it was the fastest generally available external bus until Thunderbolt was released in 2011. Apple has so far not opted to include USB 3.0 compatible devices in its computers, although there are third party offerings available for Macs that support ExpressCard or PCI-Express.

Host Controllers

Host controllers are governed by separate specifications that determine how the computer system will communicate with the host controller. Modern systems typically embed the USB host controller on the motherboard's I/O controller (south bridge). Most host controllers have a PCI interface that is used by the system for communication with the controller. When a driver talks to a USB device, it does not do so directly—it talks to the host controller over PCI, although to the driver it looks as if it is communicating with the device directly, due to the object-oriented abstraction layer provided by the I/O Kit. The USB does not generate interrupts directly; however, the host controller uses both DMA and interrupts.

Typically, a 32-bit x86 system has only 16 interrupt lines, and often as few as 2–3 interrupt lines, available for use by external peripherals. The USB solves this problem, as the computer system needs only a single interrupt line to the USB host controller to communicate with all of the devices connected to the controller. The USB specifications standardize the way in which a host communicates with a USB device; however, there are several standards for how a computer system communicates with a host controller:

- *Universal Host Controller Interface (UHCI):* UHCI was developed by Intel. The UHCI specification supports USB 1.x devices at low and full speed.

- *Open Host Controller Interface (OHCI):* OHCI was developed by Microsoft and Compaq, among others, also for USB 1.x devices. The OCHI controller is *smarter* than UHCI, in that it has more logic embedded in the controller itself, as opposed to UHCI, which is simpler on a hardware level, but requires a more complicated host controller driver in the OS.

- *Enhanced Host Controller Interface (EHCI):* EHCI was created for USB 2.0 and supports 480 Mbits/s high-speed devices. The EHCI does not handle USB 1.x devices, so it needs to incorporate a UCHI- or OHCI-based controller to handle devices based on the 1.x series of specifications.

- *Extensible Host Controller Interface (xHCI):* xHCI was designed by Intel and supports the USB 3.0 specification. It was designed as a unified host controller, making EHCI, OHCI, and UHCI redundant.

It is not uncommon for a computer system to have several host controllers, each supporting a different host controller interface. For example, the MacBook in Figure 8-1 has two OHCI controllers and two EHCI controllers for USB 2.0 support. Mac OS X presently has controller drivers to support OCHI, UHCI, and EHCI, but not xHCI.

USB ON-THE-GO

An additional standard exists as part of the USB 2.0 specification, called USB On-The-Go (OTG). While embedded devices, such as mobile phones, typically act as USB (slave) devices, USB OTG allows for a role switch, with the mobile device itself acting as a USB host. The USB OTG only works between two devices and does not support hubs. The iPad is a good example of this, as the iPad can be connected to a computer system as a USB device. However, using a special adapter, the iPad can also act as a USB host, to which you can connect digital cameras or memory cards.

The USB Protocol

Unlike serial port devices, where there are no protocols (it's up to the application to implement one) and just streams of bits and bytes, the USB has a packet-based protocol. This is necessary as the bus is shared and there can be many devices connected to it, which has to be individually addressed. Unless you are a hardware engineer programming the firmware for a USB device, you don't really need to understand, or even know about, the specifics of how this communication occurs, but it may be helpful, in some cases, to have a basic understanding of how the communication happens at the protocol level, in order to debug problems.

The USB protocol is implemented between the host controller and the device, and it determines how data is transferred on the bus. A driver does not really have insight or influence over this process, as the details are handled by the electronics of the host and the device, and not the driver—unlike with networking, where many aspects of the communication protocol are under software control. In order to see or intercept what is actually crossing the wire, a USB packet analyzer is needed. A USB analyzer is a specialized (usually very expensive) device that can be connected between the device and the host to capture the traffic between them.

USB packets consist of 8-bit words in little-endian format (LSB). The USB protocol has four main packet types:

- *Token packet:* This acts a header, and tells the recipient what type of packet/data follows. The three types of token packets are IN, OUT, and Setup. The first two specify the direction of the packet and the last is used to initiate a control transfer. The direction is seen from the host side, so IN means a transfer from the device to the host, and OUT means a transfer from the host to the device.

- *Data packet:* This can carry arbitrary data, with 0–1024 bytes per data packet.

- *Handshake packet:* This is sent to acknowledge the successful (ACK) or unsuccessful (NAK) delivery of a packet, as well as to report stalls (STALL).

- *Start of Frame packet:* This is sent at regular intervals to synchronize data flow for isochronous transfer modes.

The layout of each packet type can be seen in Figure 8-2.

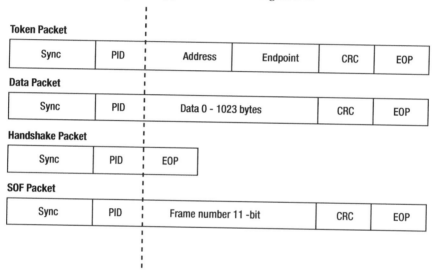

Figure 8-2. Layout of USB packet types

All USB packets start with the *sync* and *PID* (packet identifier) fields. The sync field precedes other data and can be used by the receiver for clock synchronization. The field is 8-bits for low and full speed devices, and 32-bits for high-speed devices. The PID (packet identifier) field allows the decoder to determine the packet type that follows it. Possible values for the PID field are shown in Table 8-2. The PID is 4-bits wide, though it is 8-bits in total. The last four bits are a check field containing a complement of the first four bits, which helps determine if the packet is valid and has not been corrupted.

Table 8-2. Possible Packet Identifier (PID) Values

Type	PID	Description
Token	0001	OUT Token
Token	1001	IN Token
Token	0101	SOF Token
Token	1101	Setup Token
Data	0011	DATA0
Data	1011	DATA1
Data	0111	DATA2
Data	1111	MDATA
Handshake	0010	ACK Handshake
Handshake	1010	NAK Handshake
Handshake	1110	STALL Handshake
Handshake	0110	NYET—Not yet
Other	1100	Preamble
Other	1100	Error
Other	1000	Split
Other	0100	Ping

Token packets are used for addressing a specific device. The address field specifies which device the packet is to or from, and is a number from 1–127, which addresses the device on the bus. A USB device may have several endpoints, which are independent communication channels, and the *endpoint* field specifies to which endpoint on a device the packet will be delivered. Endpoints are discussed later in this chapter.

All packet types have a CRC (Cyclic Redundancy Check—used to verify the integrity of the data) field. All packet types have a CRC field that is 5-bits wide, except data packets, which instead have a wider 16-bit CRC field.

The end of packet (EOP) field is used as a delimiter.

A USB transaction can consist of up to three data packets. Data packets are indicated by the PID field and can be one of the following: DATA0, DATA1, DATA2, and MDATA, though the latter two are used only for isochronous transfer modes. The PID field determines which of the data packets are transmitted, as shown in Table 8-2.

A data transfer from the host to a device might look like this:

1. Token Packet containing the address of the device and the endpoint. PID indicates an OUT transfer.

2. Data 0 Packet containing 1024 bytes of payload data.

3. Data 1 Packet containing 322 bytes of payload data.

4. Handshake Packet sent from the device to the host indicating the status of the transfer, such as ACK, NAK, or STALL.

Endpoints

Communication between a host controller and a USB device is based on the concept of endpoints. An endpoint is uni-directional, and the direction is either IN or OUT—that is, communication from the device to the host, or communication from the host to the device. The connection from a host controller to an endpoint is referred to as a pipe. There are two types of pipes: a *stream pipe*, which carries data, and a *message pipe*, which carries control requests. A USB device can support up to 32 endpoints, with a maximum of 16 IN endpoints and 16 OUT endpoints. Endpoint address 0 is special, reserved for device configuration. There are four different types of endpoints available:

- *Bulk endpoints:* These are used for transferring large amounts of data. Bulk transfers offer no guarantees about timely delivery or bandwidth, but do offer guaranteed delivery and error detection. Bulk transfers are not available for low speed modes. Hard drives, scanners, printers, and network cards typically use bulk transfers.

- *Control endpoints:* These are used for device configuration and status retrieval. Requests to a control endpoint are guaranteed delivery by using reserved bandwidth.

- *Interrupt endpoints:* These are intended for exchanging small amounts of time-sensitive data with guaranteed delivery.

- *Isochronous endpoints:* These provide guaranteed bandwidth, but not guaranteed delivery. Data is not re-sent if it is lost, which is ideal for video and audio applications.

USB Descriptors

A USB descriptor is used to describe a device's capabilities, type, requirements, and more. Descriptors are organized in a hierarchy consisting of the following main descriptor types:

- *Device Descriptor:* This contains the product ID (*idProduct*) and vendor ID (*idVendor*) of the USB device. There is only one device descriptor per device. It also contains information on how many descriptors follow it. Both the vendor ID and product ID are 16-bit integers. The vendor ID is assigned by the USB-IF. A vendor can choose any 16-bit value for the product ID. The vendor/product ID combination must be unique to avoid problems, as they are used to determine the correct drivers for a device. The device descriptor also contains two fields to indicate the type of device: *bDeviceClass* and *bDeviceSubClass*.

- *Configuration Descriptor:* This specifies an alternate configuration in which a device can operate. For example, a device might have two configurations: one configuration when it is self-powered and one configuration when it is bus-powered. The latter can operate in a limited mode that only allows a subset of overall functionality, or perhaps only provide the ability to program the device's firmware. Only one configuration can be active at any given time. The configuration descriptor may have several interfaces underneath it, and it is uncommon for a device to have more than one configuration descriptor.

- *Interface Descriptor:* This is a collection or group of endpoints that together perform a function. It can be useful to think of it as a logical subdevice. An interface may have zero or more endpoints. For example, in Figure 8-3, we see a multifunction USB device, which contains two interfaces: interface #0 is a printer, while interface #1 is a scanner device. Multiple interfaces may be active and operate simultaneously. Just like the device descriptor, the interface descriptor has fields to indicate the class of interface, which is given by *bInterfaceClass* and *bInterfaceSubClass*.

- *Endpoint Descriptor:* This describes the type (bulk, interrupt, isochronous, or control) and the direction (IN, OUT) of an endpoint.

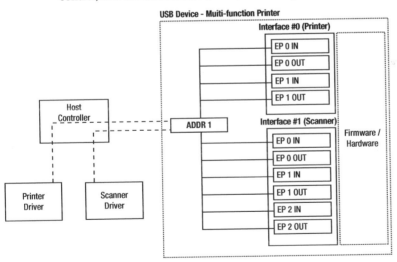

Figure 8-3. USB compound device with two interfaces

USB Device Classes

The USB descriptors contain class codes, which identify the class of a device to the system and can be used to identify the appropriate driver to load for the device. The class code may be specified in the device descriptor, the interface descriptor, or both. A class code of 00h specified in the device descriptor means that the actual class code should be read from the interface descriptors instead. There is also a subclass field that further narrows down the type of device. Table 8-3 shows a small subset of available class codes.

Table 8-3. A Subset of Standard USB Class Codes

Base Class	Descriptors Used	Type of device
0x00	Device	Class information is provided in interface descriptors.
0x01	Interface	Audio
0x03	Interface	Human Interface Device (HID), mouse, keyboard, trackpad etc.
0x08	Interface	Mass Storage, hard drives, thumb drives etc.
0xFF	Both	Vendor Specific

Many operating systems, including Mac OS X and iOS, provide default drivers for devices that conform to the standard classes, and therefore the OS can handle any mass storage or audio USB device without having to install a third party driver. It is still possible for a vendor to supply an optional driver for devices that provide additional capabilities not found in the generic driver supplied by the OS. For this, the I/O Kit matching system can be used to ensure that the more specific driver is matched, rather than the default driver.

▩ **Tip** The full list of class codes, as well as more detailed descriptions, can be found at http://www.usb.org/developers/defined_class.

I/O Kit USB Support

USB support in the I/O Kit is provided by the IOUSBFamily, which is a dynamically loadable KEXT, identified by the bundle identifier com.apple.iokit.IOUSBFamily. The USB family provides the central core of USB handling in the kernel and contains drivers for the host controllers, as well as abstraction classes for representing USB devices, interfaces, and pipes. The class hierarchy of the USB Family is shown in Figure 8-4.

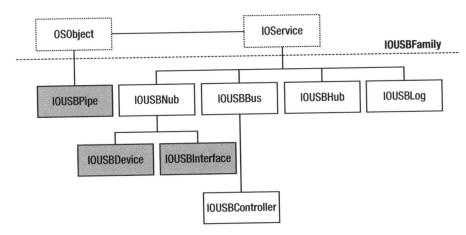

Figure 8-4. *IOUSBFamily class hierarchy*

Most of these classes are irrelevant if you only want to implement a driver for a USB device. The main classes used for USB driver development are shown in gray, in Figure 8-4, and include IOUSBPipe, IOUSBDevice, and IOUSBInterface, which we will discuss in detail later.

If you need to implement support for a new host controller, this can be done by inheriting from IOUSBController; however, kernel already provides drivers for UHCI-, OHCI-, and EHCI-compliant host controllers. Although not shown in Figure 8-4, these are subclasses of IOUSBController, and they are called AppleUSBUHCI, AppleUSBOHCI, and AppleUSBEHCI, respectively.

▓ **Tip** The USB Family is not part of the XNU source distribution, but is nevertheless available in source code form as a download from http://opensource.apple.com. The source package includes source for the entire USB Family, including the implementation of the UHCI, OCHI, and EHCI controllers. It also includes sample code for USB drivers, and how to enumerate and access USB devices from user space.

USB Device and Driver Handling

When a USB device is inserted, the USB Family will create an instance of the IOUSBDevice class, a subclass of IOService, and insert it into the I/O Registry. Exactly one instance of IOUSBDevice will be created for each device inserted onto the bus. The provider for an IOUSBDevice is the IOUSBController to which the device is attached. The IOUSBDevice class provides an abstraction of the USB device's device and configuration descriptors. Interface descriptors can be accessed from the IOUSBInterface class. The IOUSBDevice acts as a provider for IOUSBInterface classes, as seen in Figure 8-5.

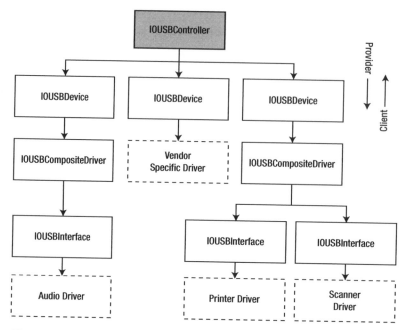

Figure 8-5. *USB device and driver provider relationships*

Figure 8-5 shows three USB devices and how they relate to their higher-level providers:

- *The driver on the left:* This is a driver for an audio device. You may have noticed that there is an additional driver between IOUSBDevice and IOUSBInterface called IOUSBCompositeDriver. This composite driver is matched against, and loaded for, any USB device that has its device class and subclass set to zero in its device descriptor and that has no other vendor specific driver matched against it. The name of the driver may suggest that it is only for composite drivers with multiple functions, but the driver is loaded even for devices with a single interface. The only function the composite driver performs is to select the device's active configuration (if it has multiple configuration descriptors), and then ensure that other drivers can be matched against the selected configuration's interfaces.

- *The driver in the middle:* This is a vendor specific driver attached directly to the IOUSBDevice nub. The IOUSBCompositeDriver was not loaded as the device class, and the subclass fields in the device descriptor were set to 0xFF/0xFF, indicating a vendor specific device, and a driver was properly matched against the device.

- *The driver on the right:* This has the same organization as on the left, with an IOUSBCompositeDriver attached to the IOUSBDevice nub. The composite driver will enumerate all device interfaces and ensure that they are made available for matching. In this case, there are two interfaces, each with an attached independent driver.

Loading USB Drivers

To have your driver loaded automatically when a device is inserted, you must configure your driver's Info.plist, as we learned in Chapter 4. As we saw in the previous section, a single driver may handle a USB device, or it may have several drivers, one for each interface (function) presented. For a USB device, a driver is matched against it using keys from the device's device descriptor. The I/O Kit follows the rules for driver matching set by the Universal Serial Bus Common Class Specification. The following combinations of keys are valid for matching a driver against a USB device:

- idVendor & idProduct & bcdDevice

- idVendor & idProduct

- idVendor & bDeviceSubClass & bDeviceProtocol (only if bDeviceClass == 0xff)

- idVendor & bDeviceSubClass (only if bDeviceClass == 0xff)

- bDeviceClass & bDeviceSubClass & bDeviceProtocol (only if bDeviceClass != 0xff)

- bDeviceClass & bDeviceSubClass (only if bDeviceClass != 0xff)

Each key represents an entry in the device's device descriptor. The bcdDevice field is used to store the device's revision number. If the bDeviceClass field is 0xff, it means the device class is vendor specific. A matching dictionary in Info.plist, which matches against a vendor ID, a product ID, and a revision number (bcdDevice), is shown in Listing 8-1.

Listing 8-1. Matching Dictionary for Matching Against Vendor ID, Product ID, and Device Revision

```
<key>MyUSBDriver</key>
<dict>
<key>CFBundleIdentifier</key>
    <string>com.osxkernel.MyUSBDriver</string>
    <key>IOClass</key>
    <string>com_osxkernel_MyUSBDriver</string>
    <key>IOProviderClass</key>
    <string>IOUSBDevice</string>
    <key>bcdDevice</key>
    <integer>1</integer>
    <key>idProduct</key>
    <integer>2323</integer>
    <key>idVendor</key>
    <integer>0001</integer>
</dict>
```

The entry must be located in the IOKitPersonalities section of your driver's Info.plist file to have any effect.

Devices that are not matched by the previous rules will be handled by the IOUSBCompositeDriver, which selects a device configuration, if the device has multiple configurations present, and then initiates matching against the device's interfaces instead. The keys that can be used to match against device interfaces are shown here:

- idVendor & idProduct & bcdDevice & bConfigurationValue & bInterfaceNumber

- idVendor & idProduct & bConfigurationValue & bInterfaceNumber

- idVendor & bInterfaceSubClass & bInterfaceProtocol (only if bInterfaceClass == 0xff)

- idVendor & bInterfaceSubClass (only if bInterfaceClass == 0xff)

- bInterfaceClass & bInterfaceSubClass & bInterfaceProtocol (only if bInterfaceClass != 0xff)

- bInterfaceClass & bInterfaceSubClass (only if bInterfaceClass != 0xff)

■ **Note** You cannot create your own combinations of keys; you have to use one of the combinations shown above for either an interface or a device. However, you can add several personalities to your driver, which can each match against a different combination, but it has to be one of the valid combinations.

Each key represents a field in an interface descriptor. The matching rules are ordered according to how specific they are. The last rule, for example, which matches against the interface class and subclass, is used by Apple's USB Mass Storage driver to match all devices that conform to that interface, regardless of vendor or product ID. The Info.plist for the Apple mass storage driver is shown in Listing 8-2 (though some keys unrelated to matching were trimmed for readability).

Listing 8-2. Matching Dictionary for Matching Against a USB Interface Class and Subclass

```
<key>IOUSBMassStorageClass6</key>
<dict>
    <key>CFBundleIdentifier</key>
    <string>com.apple.iokit.IOUSBMassStorageClass</string>
    <key>IOClass</key>
    <string>IOUSBMassStorageClass</string>
    <key>IOProviderClass</key>
    <string>IOUSBInterface</string>
    <key>bInterfaceClass</key>
    <integer>8</integer>
    <key>bInterfaceSubClass</key>
    <integer>6</integer>
</dict>
```

Unlike the example in Listing 8-1, the IOProviderClass is specified as IOUSBInterface, which will be the provider passed to your driver's start() method instead of IOUSBDevice.

USB Prober

Before we start looking at actual code, it is worth mentioning a highly useful tool called USB Prober. USB Prober is a utility that is bundled with the Xcode distribution. The USB Prober tool is shown in Figure 8-6.

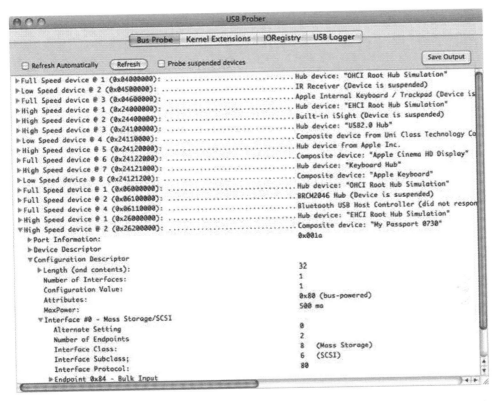

Figure 8-6. USB Prober utility

USB Prober allows you to probe available USB buses on your system and inspect the hierarchy of devices attached to each bus. It also allows you to inspect the device, configuration, interface, and endpoint descriptors. The *IORegistry* tab allows you to inspect the *IOService* plane of the I/O Registry as it pertains to USB devices, which is very useful during development of a USB driver, as it allows you to verify that your driver was matched correctly. USB prober can also perform USB specific tracing from the IOUSBFamily, which may be useful for debugging your driver in some cases. This requires some setup, including downloading the USB Debug Kit from Apple's developer website. The kit contains an alternate version of IOUSBFamily, which provides verbose logging. Access to the debug kit is restricted to members of the Mac developer program.

Driver Example: USB Mass Storage Device Driver

Let's put what we've learned so far into practice by putting together a simple USB-based driver, which will print log messages as various events occur. Now we could make a purely virtual driver, but that wouldn't be any fun, so let's instead create a driver that piggybacks on a real USB device so that we can see what happens when the device is plugged in and removed from the bus, but without interfering with the device's operation. The object-oriented nature of the I/O Kit makes it such that writing a device driver requires relatively little effort. Moreover, writing a device driver for a USB device is very similar to writing a driver for Firewire, PCI, or the virtual IOKitTest driver from Chapter 4.

To try this example, you need a thumb/flash drive or external USB hard drive. It doesn't have to be formatted for Mac, as we are not going to access the data.

▪ **Caution** It is recommended to try examples in this book on a Mac that is not being used to store important data. A kernel crash may corrupt your files or operating system. If you do not have a dedicated Mac for this purpose, ensure you have working backups of your data.

Our driver will be called MyFirstUSBDriver, and the class declaration is shown in Listing 8-3.

Listing 8-3. MyFirstUSBDriver.h: Class Declaration for MyFirstUSBDriver

```
#include <IOKit/usb/IOUSBDevice.h>

class com_osxkernel_MyFirstUSBDriver : public IOService
{
    OSDeclareDefaultStructors(com_osxkernel_MyFirstUSBDriver)

public:
    virtual bool init(OSDictionary *propTable);
    virtual IOService* probe(IOService *provider, SInt32 *score );
    virtual bool attach(IOService *provider);
    virtual void detach(IOService *provider);
    virtual bool start(IOService *provider);
    virtual void stop(IOService *provider);
    virtual bool terminate(IOOptionBits options = 0);
};
```

You will notice that the class is structurally nearly identical to the IOKitTest driver, with a few minor changes, which we will discuss later. The implementation of MyFirstUSBDriver is shown in Listing 8-4.

Listing 8-4. MyFirstUSBDriver.cpp: Implementation of MyFirstUSBDriver Class

```
#include <IOKit/IOLib.h>
#include <IOKit/usb/IOUSBInterface.h>
#include "MyFirstUSBDriver.h"

OSDefineMetaClassAndStructors(com_osxkernel_MyFirstUSBDriver, IOService)
#define super IOService

void logEndpoint(IOUSBPipe* pipe)
{
    IOLog("Endpoint #%d ", pipe->GetEndpointNumber());
    IOLog("--> Type: ");
    switch (pipe->GetType())
    {
```

```
        case kUSBControl: IOLog("kUSBControl "); break;
        case kUSBBulk: IOLog("kUSBBulk "); break;
        case kUSBIsoc: IOLog("kUSBIsoc "); break;
        case kUSBInterrupt: IOLog("kUSBInterrupt "); break;
    }
    IOLog("--> Direction: ");
    switch (pipe->GetDirection())
    {
        case kUSBOut: IOLog("OUT (kUSBOut) "); break;
        case kUSBIn: IOLog("IN (kUSBIn) "); break;
        case kUSBAnyDirn: IOLog("ANY (Control Pipe) "); break;
    }
    IOLog("maxPacketSize: %d interval: %d\n", pipe->GetMaxPacketSize(), pipe->GetInterval());
}

bool com_osxkernel_MyFirstUSBDriver::init(OSDictionary* propTable)
{
    IOLog("com_osxkernel_MyFirstUSBDriver::init(%p)\n", this);
    return super::init(propTable);
}

IOService* com_osxkernel_MyFirstUSBDriver::probe(IOService* provider, SInt32* score)
{
    IOLog("%s(%p)::probe\n", getName(), this);
    return super::probe(provider, score);
}

bool com_osxkernel_MyFirstUSBDriver::attach(IOService* provider)
{
    IOLog("%s(%p)::attach\n", getName(), this);
    return super::attach(provider);
}

void com_osxkernel_MyFirstUSBDriver::detach(IOService* provider)
{
    IOLog("%s(%p)::detach\n", getName(), this);
    return super::detach(provider);
}

bool com_osxkernel_MyFirstUSBDriver::start(IOService* provider)
{
    IOUSBInterface* interface;
    IOUSBFindEndpointRequest request;
    IOUSBPipe* pipe = NULL;

    IOLog("%s(%p)::start\n", getName(), this);

    if (!super::start(provider))
        return false;

    interface = OSDynamicCast(IOUSBInterface, provider);
    if (interface == NULL)
```

```
        {
            IOLog("%s(%p)::start -> provider not a IOUSBInterface\n", getName(), this);
            return false;
        }

        // Mass Storage Devices use two bulk pipes, one for reading and one for writing.

        // Find the Bulk In Pipe.
        request.type = kUSBBulk;
        request.direction = kUSBIn;
        pipe = interface->FindNextPipe(NULL, &request, true);
        if (pipe)
        {
            logEndpoint(pipe);
            pipe->release();
        }

        // Find the Bulk Out Pipe.
        request.type = kUSBBulk;
        request.direction = kUSBOut;
        pipe = interface->FindNextPipe(NULL, &request, true);
        if (pipe)
        {
            logEndpoint(pipe);
            pipe->release();
        }
        return true;
}

void com_osxkernel_MyFirstUSBDriver::stop(IOService *provider)
{
    IOLog("%s(%p)::stop\n", getName(), this);
    super::stop(provider);
}

bool com_osxkernel_MyFirstUSBDriver::terminate(IOOptionBits options)
{
    IOLog("%s(%p)::terminate\n", getName(), this);
    return super::terminate(options);
}
```

As you may see, there is very little logic in this driver, with the exception of logging when the various methods of our driver are called. The start() method will also attempt to find the bulk IN and bulk OUT endpoints, and log information about the endpoints. We will test the driver shortly, but first we have to create a matching dictionary so that the I/O Kit will know when to load our driver. The matching dictionary for MyFirstUSBDriver is shown in Listing 8-5.

Listing 8-5. Matching Dictionary for MyFirstUSBDriver

```
<key>IOKitPersonalities</key>
<dict>
    <key>MyFirstUSBDriver</key>
```

```
<dict>
    <key>bInterfaceClass</key>
    <integer>8</integer>
    <key>bInterfaceSubClass</key>
    <integer>6</integer>
    <key>CFBundleIdentifier</key>
    <string>com.osxkernel.MyFirstUSBDriver</string>
    <key>IOClass</key>
    <string>com_osxkernel_MyFirstUSBDriver</string>
    <key>IOMatchCategory</key>
    <string>com_osxkernel_MyFirstUSBDriver</string>
    <key>IOProviderClass</key>
    <string>IOUSBInterface</string>
</dict>
</dict>
```

The matching dictionary is more or less the same as the example in Listing 8-2. It will match against a USB interface rather than a USB device. We set bInterfaceClass to 8, which is the class code for mass storage devices, and we set bInterfaceSubClass to 6, which indicates that it uses the SCSI command set to communicate with the device (which doesn't necessarily imply that the drive/storage itself understands the SCSI protocol, but it is used to tunnel commands to the device over the bus, where another controller may translate it into, for example, ATA commands).

Because Apple's default IOUSBMassStorageClass matches against the same keys as us, we need to specify a match category so that our driver will also be loaded. We do this by adding the IOMatchCategory key. We set it to the name of our class, but it could be any string.

▪ **Tip** When you open a Info.plist file in Xcode, it is opening in the property list editor by default. If you wish to cut and paste to the property list, or you are curious about the format it is stored in, you can right-click the file and choose "Open as," and then choose "Source Code," which will present it in XML format.

There is one additional change we need to make to our driver's property list file, and that is to include our dependencies under the OSBundleLibraries dictionary; otherwise, the driver will fail to load. Dependencies can be found using the kextlibs tool. We used the following section to add a dependency to libkern and IOUSBFamily:

```
<key>OSBundleLibraries</key>
<dict>
        <key>com.apple.iokit.IOUSBFamily</key>
        <string>4.1.8</string>
        <key>com.apple.kernel.libkern</key>
        <string>6.0</string>
</dict>
```

We are now ready to load the driver, or rather to allow I/O Kit to load the driver for us. For the driver to load automatically, as the USB device is plugged in, it must be located in the directory /System/Library/Extensions, the standard location for all KEXTs.

When all is done, you should now be able to plug the device in. Before you do, however, you can bring up the Console application, and select kernel.log from the log list. Once you insert your compatible device, you should see the following entries being printed to the log in response to the insertion:

```
Jun 16 22:37:56 macbook kernel[0]: com_osxkernel_MyFirstUSBDriver::init(0x1361f900)
Jun 16 22:37:56 macbook kernel[0]: com_osxkernel_MyFirstUSBDriver(0x1361f900)::attach
Jun 16 22:37:56 macbook kernel[0]: com_osxkernel_MyFirstUSBDriver(0x1361f900)::probe
Jun 16 22:37:56 macbook kernel[0]: com_osxkernel_MyFirstUSBDriver(0x1361f900)::detach
Jun 16 22:37:56 macbook kernel[0]: com_osxkernel_MyFirstUSBDriver(0x1361f900)::attach
Jun 16 22:37:56 macbook kernel[0]: com_osxkernel_MyFirstUSBDriver(0x1361f900)::start
Jun 16 22:37:56 macbook kernel[0]: Endpoint #4 --> Type: kUSBBulk --> Direction: IN (kUSBIn)
maxPacketSize: 512 interval: 0
Jun 16 22:37:56 macbook kernel[0]: Endpoint #3 --> Type: kUSBBulk --> Direction: OUT
(kUSBOut) maxPacketSize: 512 interval: 0
```

The first five calls are part of the matching process. The first method attach() is used to connect our driver into the IOService plane of the I/O Registry, which in this case will attach us as a client of the IOUSBInterface nub, which again is the client of the IOUSBDevice we just plugged in. As we know from Chapter 4, the probe method is used for active matching, and allows us to further interrogate the device, or interface in this case, to determine if we are a match for it. I/O Kit then calls detach(), and the decision to which driver to load is made once all possible matches have been examined. It is usually not recommended to allocate any resources in attach() as it can be called multiple times. Usually, it is not necessary to override attach() or detach(), as the default ones provided by IOService are almost always sufficient. Once I/O Kit has selected our driver, which is guaranteed in our case (as we specified a unique IOMatchCategory), we will be getting a call to our attach() method again, and then finally the start() method of our driver. We can now use USB Prober to verify where in the hierarchy our driver was placed, as shown in Figure 8-7.

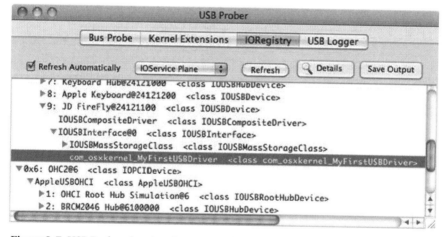

Figure 8-7. USB Prober showing the com_osxkernel_MyFirstUSBDriver attached to the IOService plane

You will notice that we are attached to the IOUSBInterface of the storage device, together with the IOUSBMassStorageClass driver, and that the USB device itself is managed by the composite driver IOUSBCompositeDriver.

Driver Startup

The implementation of our start() method in MyFirstUSBDriver is deliberately sparse because the IOUSBMassStorageClass driver is also managing the interface, and we do not wish to interfere with its use of the USB interface. We do a basic sanity check, which is commonly done in the start() method, to ensure that we get a provider that is of the type we expect. However, nothing is preventing you from writing a driver that can accept and work with multiple types of providers—for example, an IOUSBDevice and IOUSBInterface, or even an IOPCIDevice provider.

Here's an outline of the steps a USB driver typically must perform in its start() method:

- Verify that the IOService provider object passed to us is of the type we expect. We do this with the help of the OSDynamicCast() macro, which works with I/O Kit's runtime type identification system, and returns a pointer to the object if the cast is successful, or NULL otherwise.

- Store a pointer to the provider for later use.

- Attempt to open the provider by calling its open(IOService* forClient, …) method.

- If your driver is operating on an IOUSBDevice you may have to set the device's configuration. For IOUSBInterface-based drivers, the IOUSBCompositeDriver normally handles this. You can set the configuration using IOUSBDevice::SetConfiguration().

- Find and verify the interfaces you will use for a driver that has an IOUSBDevice provider. And search for the appropriate endpoints needed by your driver. More about this in the section "Enumerating Device Resources."

- Interrogate the device for status information, and perform the needed configuration of the device by issuing control requests to it.

- Allocate any driver specific resources you may need, for example I/O buffers or auxiliary classes needed by your driver.

- If your driver is a *nub* and intends to provide services to other drivers, it needs to allocate and register these. For example, in the case of IOUSBMassStorageClass it will allocate IOSCSILogicalUnitNub objects for each logical unit provided by the interface, and for each of these call registerService(), a method inherited from IOService. The method ensures that matching will begin for each IOSCSILogicalUnitNub object.

- If everything succeeds, start() should return true. If false is returned, the driver will obviously not be loaded, and the I/O Kit will try to load a new driver, if any, possibly one that "lost" and got a lower score previously. Be aware that stop() will not be called if you return false from start().

> ■ **Tip** To uninstall `MyFirstUSBDriver`, simply use the command: `sudo rm -rf`
> `/System/Library/Extensions/MyFirstUSBDriver.kext`

Handling Device Removals

USB devices and drivers must be able to cope with the removal of a device at any point in time. When the `IOUSBController` detects that a device is removed, it will propagate this information recursively down the driver stack. The first notification to a driver is made by calling its `terminate()` method. The following sequence of calls is the result of unplugging the mass storage device that MyFirstUSBDriver is attached to:

```
Jun 16 22:58:46 macbook kernel[0]: com_osxkernel_MyFirstUSBDriver(0xb4e6100)::terminate
Jun 16 22:58:46 macbook kernel[0]: com_osxkernel_MyFirstUSBDriver(0xb4e6100)::stop
Jun 16 22:58:46 macbook kernel[0]: com_osxkernel_MyFirstUSBDriver(0xb4e6100)::detach
```

Any incomplete I/O can be cancelled using `IOUSBPipe::Abort()` and can be done when the `terminate()` method gets called, or in the `willTerminate()` or `didTerminate()` methods if overridden by the driver.

The next step in the removal process is that the driver's `stop()` method will be called, which should reverse actions taken in the `start()` method. After that `detach()` and finally `free()` will be called, which should clean up all remaining resources.

If your driver is opened by a user application, for example through a `IOUserClient`, it will not be deallocated (the `free()` method will not be called) until the application releases its reference to the device. If the device happens to be re-inserted at this time, the application is not able to resume using the device, as a new instance of the driver is created each time a device is inserted. The application can handle this by using notifications, as described in Chapter 5.

Enumerating Interfaces

During a USB driver's `start()` method, it is usually necessary to find and configure the endpoints and interfaces that will be used by the device. If your driver is based on the `IOUSBDevice` provider, chances are that you need to search for one or more of the interfaces that will be used by your driver. This can be done using the `IOUSBDevice::FindNextInterface()` method:

```
virtual IOUSBInterface* FindNextInterface(IOUSBInterface* current,
                                          IOUSBFindInterfaceRequest* request);
```

The first parameter can be specified to start the search from an existing `IOUSBInterface` instance and ignore any interfaces before it. `NULL` can be specified to start the search from the first interface.

The second parameter is a structure of the type `IOUSBFindInterfaceRequest`:

```
typedef struct {
    UInt16 bInterfaceClass;
    UInt16 bInterfaceSubClass;
    UInt16 bInterfaceProtocol;
    UInt16 bAlternateSetting;
} IOUSBFindInterfaceRequest;
```

To find an interface, you can fill out the IOUSBFindInterfaceRequest structure with the desired properties for the interface.

- bInterfaceClass and bInterfaceSubClass can be filled in to search for an interface of a specific class and subclass. The values correspond to the codes in Table 8-3. The header file USBSpec.h in the IOUSBFamily source distribution define symbolic constants such as kUSBMassStorageInterfaceClass or kUSBPrintingClass.

- The bInterfaceProtocol specifies the protocol used by the interface. The field is meaningless without the class and subclass. A HID (Human Interaction Device) may for example specify the protocol as kHIDKeyboardInterfaceProtocol or kHIDMouseInterfaceProtocol.

- It is possible for an interface to have alternate versions of itself that uses a different set of endpoints, the bAlternateSetting field can therefore be set to request the specific interface desired.

Fields that does not matter can be set to kIOUSBFindInterfaceDontCare. Setting every field to this value will simply return the next interface regardless.

Listing 8-6 shows an extract from the Apple USB Ethernet driver which uses the FindNextInterface() method to search a USB device (IOUSBDevice) for an interface that supports Ethernet.

Listing 8-6. Searching a IOUSBDevice for a Interface (from USBCDCEthernet.cpp)

```
IOUSBFindInterfaceRequest        req;
IOUSBInterface*                  fCommInterface = NULL;

req.bInterfaceClass =     kUSBCommClass;
req.bInterfaceSubClass = kEthernetControlModel;
req.bInterfaceProtocol = kIOUSBFindInterfaceDontCare;
req.bAlternateSetting =  kIOUSBFindInterfaceDontCare;

fCommInterface = fpDevice->FindNextInterface(NULL, &req);
if (!fCommInterface)
{
    // not found
    ...
}
```

Enumerating Endpoints

An interface does not do anything useful by itself, so once the correct interface is retrieved by the driver, it must enumerate the interface's endpoints which are used for actual I/O. The enumeration/search is process is similar to that of finding an interface and is done with the IOUSBInterface::FindNextPipe() method:

```
virtual IOUSBPipe *FindNextPipe(IOUSBPipe *current, IOUSBFindEndpointRequest *request);
virtual IOUSBPipe* FindNextPipe(IOUSBPipe *current, IOUSBFindEndpointRequest *request,
        bool withRetain);
```

The first parameter if non-NULL tells the method to ignore pipes before it. The second parameter is a pointer to an IOUSBFindEndpointRequest:

```
typedef struct {
    UInt8 type;
    UInt8 direction;
    UInt16 maxPacketSize;
    UInt8 interval;
} IOUSBFindEndpointRequest;
```

- The type field can be kUSBControl, kUSBIsoc, kUSBBulk, kUSBInterrupt, or kUSBAnyType.

- The direction field must be set to kUSBOut, kUSBIn, or kUSBAnyDirn.

- The maxPacketSize field is the max packet size in bytes that endpoint zero supports, and should be 8, 16, 32, or 64. It can be set to 0 if irrelevant.

- The interval field can be used to search for an endpoint that has a specific polling interval. The polling interval only applies to isochronous and interrupts endpoints.

Listing 8-7 shows how the Apple USB Ethernet driver uses the FindNextPipe() method to enumerate endpoints.

Listing 8-7. Enumerating IOUSBPipe Instances for an Interface (from USBCDCEthernet.cpp)

```
IOUSBFindEndpointRequest          epReq;              // endPoint request struct on stack
…
// Open all the end points

epReq.type = kUSBBulk;
epReq.direction = kUSBIn;
epReq.maxPacketSize    = 0;
epReq.interval = 0;
fInPipe = fDataInterface->FindNextPipe(0, &epReq);
if (!fInPipe)
{
    …
    return false;
}
…
epReq.direction = kUSBOut;
fOutPipe = fDataInterface->FindNextPipe(0, &epReq);
if (!fOutPipe)
{
    …
    return false;
}
fOutPacketSize = epReq.maxPacketSize;
…
// Interrupt pipe - Comm Interface

epReq.type = kUSBInterrupt;
epReq.direction = kUSBIn;
fCommPipe = fCommInterface->FindNextPipe(0, &epReq);
```

```
if (!fCommPipe)
{
    ….
}
```

The driver in Listing 8-7 is a USB Ethernet driver. It uses three endpoints for its operation. The first is a bulk IN endpoint, which is used to read network data from the device. The second endpoint is a bulk OUT pipe, which is used to transmit packets to the device. The last end point is an interrupt IN endpoint, which is used to signal the arrival of a network packet and for notification of other events. In the following sections, we will look at how endpoints are used to perform I/O.

Performing Device Requests

Device requests are I/O requests to the default bi-directional default control pipe zero of the USB device, typically used for device configuration and accessing device registers. There are three classes of device requests:

- Standard USB requests: These are standard requests implemented by all device. An example of a standard device request is querying a device's status. A list of symbolic constants for standard requests can be found in USBSpec.h.

- Class specific requests: These are specific to a class of device. For example, an Ethernet device may provide a number of requests for configuring Ethernet related parameters.

- Vendor specific requests

To perform a device request, both IOUSBDevice and IOUSBInterface provide a special DeviceRequest() convenience method, which under the hood uses the IOUSBPipe object, representing the default pipe, to transmit the request. If you wish, you can enumerate the IOUSBPipe instance for the zero endpoint and use it directly as well. The method is declared as follows:

```
DeviceRequest(IOUSBDevRequest *request, UInt32 noDataTimeout,
          UInt32 completionTimeout, IOUSBCompletion *completion);
DeviceRequest(IOUSBDevRequestDesc *, UInt32 noDataTimeout,
          UInt32 completionTimeout, IOUSBCompletion *completion);
```

In order to send a request, you must create an IOUSBDevRequest or IOUSBDeviceRequestDesc structure and fill in the appropriate fields.

```
typedef struct {                    typedef struct {
    UInt8 bmRequestType;                UInt8 bmRequestType;
    UInt8 bRequest;                     UInt8 bRequest;
    UInt16 wValue;                      UInt16 wValue;
    UInt16 wIndex;                      UInt16 wIndex;
    UInt16 wLength;                     UInt16 wLength;
    void *pData;                        IOMemoryDescriptor *pData;
    UInt32 wLenDone;                    UInt32 wLenDone;
} IOUSBDevRequest;                  } IOUSBDevRequestDesc;
```

- The bmRequestType field: Is a composite field that specifies the type of request, the direction, the type, and the recpient. The field can be generated by using the USBmakebmRequestType(direction, type, recpient) macro with the following paramters:

    - The direction will be either kUSBIn, kUSBOut, or kUSBNone.

    - The type will be either kUSBStandard, kUSBClass, or kUSBVendor.

    - The recpient will be either kUSBInterface, kUSBEndpoint, or kUSBDevice.

- The bRequest field: This is a 8-bit value that selects the request to be performed.

- The wValue and wIndex: These can be used to pass arguments along with the request. Their meaning depends on the request. For interface and endpoint requests, the wIndex number specifies the index number of the endpoint/interface to which the request is addressed. You can get the index number by calling either IOUSBPipe::GetEndpointNumber() or IOUSBInterface->GetInterfaceNumber().

- The wLength field: This is the number of bytes for the pData field.

- The pData field: This is either a pointer to a memory buffer or an IOMemoryDescriptor. The pData pointer may be set to NULL if no additional data is needed for the request. The buffer will either be read from or written to, depending on the direction of the request. If an IOMemoryDescriptor is used you should call prepare() on it first to ensure the memory is paged in and pinned down until the request is completed. The memory may come from user space if a memory descriptor is used. If the void* variant is used, the pointer must be in the kernel's virtual address space.

- The wLenDone field: This should not be filled in, as it is used to return the number of bytes actually transferred.

Apart from the request parameters, the DeviceRequest() methods takes another three parameters.

- noDataTimeout: This is the timeout, in milliseconds, to wait before aborting the request if no data has been sent/received.

- completionTimeout: This specifies a timeout value for the entire command with data, and is also in milliseconds.

- completion: This is optional, and if specified it allows us to perform the request asynchronously, which may often be desired to avoid blocking the calling thread. We will discuss asynchronous requests in more detail later in this chapter.

Let's look at an example of how a device request can be issued, again using the Apple USB Ethernet driver as an example. The code in Listing 8-8 is called by the driver from a periodic timer and is used to get statistics and status information from the Ethernet device, such as collisions, dropped packets, incoming packets, etc.

Listing 8-8. Device Request for Downloading Statistics From An Ethernet Device (USBCDCEthernet.cpp)

```
STREQ = (IOUSBDevRequest*)IOMalloc(sizeof(IOUSBDevRequest));
if (!STREQ)
{
```

```
    ...
} else {
    bzero(STREQ, sizeof(IOUSBDevRequest));
    // Now build the Statistics Request
    STREQ->bmRequestType = USBmakebmRequestType(kUSBOut, kUSBClass, kUSBInterface);
    STREQ->bRequest = kGet_Ethernet_Statistics;
    STREQ->wValue = currStat;
    STREQ->wIndex = fCommInterfaceNumber;
    STREQ->wLength = 4;
    STREQ->pData = &fStatValue;

    fStatsCompletionInfo.parameter = STREQ;

    rc = fpDevice->DeviceRequest(STREQ, &fStatsCompletionInfo);
    if (rc != kIOReturnSuccess)
    {
        ...
        IOFree(STREQ, sizeof(IOUSBDevRequest));
    } else {
        fStatInProgress = true;
    }
}
```

The request in Listing 8-8 is performed asynchronously. Because the IOUSBDevRequest structure must persist until the request finishes, it must not be allocated on the stack, although this is fine for a synchronous request. The request performed in Listing 8-8 is directed to a specific interface, and it is a class specific request, which means it will work the same on all interfaces with the same class code. The wValue field of the request is an index number specifying the statistic that should be transferred.

Control Requests

Device requests, discussed in the previous section, are I/O to the default control pipe (zero). The DeviceRequest() method cannot be used for control endpoints other than the default. If we wish to perform requests to another control endpoint, we must use the IOUSBPipe::ControlRequest() method instead. There are four ControlRequest() methods available:

```
virtual IOReturn ControlRequest(IOUSBDevRequestDesc* request,
        IOUSBCompletion* completion = 0);
virtual IOReturn ControlRequest(IOUSBDevRequest* request, IOUSBCompletion* completion = 0);
virtual IOReturn ControlRequest(IOUSBDevRequestDesc* request,
        UInt32 noDataTimeout,
        UInt32 completionTimeout,
        IOUSBCompletion* completion = 0);
virtual IOReturn ControlRequest(IOUSBDevRequest* request,
        UInt32 noDataTimeout,
        UInt32 completionTimeout,
        IOUSBCompletion* completion = 0);
```

The two first methods use the exact same arguments as the DeviceRequest() method discussed earlier. The two last also support the noDataTimeout and completionTimeout parameters.

Performing I/O to Bulk and Interrupt Endpoints

Sending and Receiving data is performed with the help of the IOUSBPipe class, which represents an endpoint. The IOUSBPipe class presents a simple interface for performing I/O, which is reminiscent of how user space performs file I/O. USB does not utilize DMA directly, although the host controller does use DMA to transfer data, but the details of this are abstracted away from us. This also means that we do not need to worry about memory alignment, if the memory is physically contiguous, is in the correct address range, or translating memory addresses to physical addresses. We can also perform I/O from a user space buffer.

The IOUSBPipe class supports I/O to all endpoint types: control, bulk, interrupt, and isochronous. The methods for performing bulk and interrupt I/O are the Read() and Write() methods:

```
virtual IOReturn Read(IOMemoryDescriptor* buffer,
                      UInt32 noDataTimeout,
                      UInt32 completionTimeout,
                      IOByteCount reqCount,
                      IOUSBCompletion* completion = 0,
                      IOByteCount* bytesRead = 0);

virtual IOReturn Write(IOMemoryDescriptor* buffer,
                       UInt32 noDataTimeout,
                       UInt32 completionTimeout,
                       IOByteCount reqCount,
                       IOUSBCompletion* completion = 0);
```

- The buffer is an IOMemoryDescriptor containing the buffer for which data should be read or written. The memory descriptor should have its prepare() method called to ensure memory is paged in and pinned down. The memory may be in the kernel or a user task's address space.

- The noDataTimeout argument specifies the amount of time, in milliseconds, to wait for data transfer on the bus before the request is considered unsuccessful.

- The completionTimeout is the time to allow, in milliseconds, for the entire request to complete before it is considered unsuccessful.

- The reqCount is the amount of data, in bytes, that should be read or written. It must be less or equal to the size of the buffer, as returned by IOMemoryDescriptor::getLength().

- The *completion* parameter is a structure of the type IOUSBCompletion, and is used for asynchronous requests. The parameter can be specified as NULL to perform the request synchronously, in which case the call will block until the request is complete or times out. We will look at asynchronous I/O later.

- For the Read() method bytesRead will return the number of bytes that were read. It may be less than what was requested. The value is only set for synchronous requests.

Listing 8-9 shows example invocations of the Read() and Write() methods.

Listing 8-9. Examples of Synchronous Read() and Write() to a Bulk Pipe

```
UInt32 bytesRead;
IOMemoryDescriptor* readBuffer;
IOMemoryDescriptor* writeBuffer;
...
if (myBulkPipeIn->Read(readBuffer, 1000, 5000,
                       readBuffer->GetLength(), 0, &bytesRead) != kIOReturnSuccess)
{
    // Handle error
}
else
    IOLog("We read: %u bytes\n", bytesRead);

if (myBulkPipeOut->Write(writeBuffer, 1000, 5000,
                         writeBuffer->GetLength()) != kIOReturnSuccess)
{
    // Handle error
}
```

Since we didn't specify the `completion` argument for either method, they will both be executed synchronously, which means that the request will be executed in its entirety by the time the method returns control to us. Recall that all pipes are uni-directional, with the exception of the default control pipe, so the IN and OUT requests are performed on two separate pipes.

■ **Note** Another overloaded set of `Read()` and `Write()` exists that does not accept a `reqCount` parameter, but rather uses the `GetLength()` method of the `IOMemoryDescriptor`. These methods are now deprecated and should not be used.

The example in Listing 8-9 will also work for an interrupt endpoint. There is no special programming interface needed to work with interrupt endpoints. I/O is handled in the same way as with bulk endpoints. The difference is in behavior. An interrupt endpoint provides bounded latency and the host controller guarantees to poll the device for data no less often than what is requested in the endpoint's descriptor. The minimum-polling interval is 125 microseconds. Interrupt transfers use reserved bandwidth, which guarantees that the requests make it through even in the event that there are high amounts of activity on the bus. Unlike bulk transfers, interrupt transfers are not suitable for transferring large amounts of data and are limited to 8, 64, or, 1024 bytes for low-speed, full-speed, and high-speed, respectively. Note that interrupt endpoints are not related to system interrupts in any way. I/O to interrupt endpoints is performed in a normal kernel thread.

Dealing with Errors and Pipe Stalls

When an endpoint is unable to transmit or receive data due to an error, the host or device may set the HALT bit. Communicating with an endpoint in this state, or an endpoint with an error, will return a

STALL handshake packet. An error needs to be resolved before I/O can continue on the endpoint. The IOUSBPipe class provides two methods for clearing a pipe stall and allowing I/O to resume:

```
virtual IOReturn ClearStall(void);
virtual IOReturn ClearPipeStall(bool withDeviceRequest);
```

The second version clears the error (toggle bit) on the controller, but it does not send out a device request to the endpoint if withDeviceRequest is false. Both methods will cause outstanding I/O to be completed with the return code kIOUSBTransactionReturned.

Isochronous I/O

Isochronous transfers are continuous in nature and are suitable for use with devices, such as audio and video, where information is continuously streaming and there is a need for guaranteed bandwidth and bounded latency. Data integrity can be verified using a CRC, but corrupted data is never re-sent automatically. The amount of bandwidth needed by a device is specified in the isochronous endpoint descriptor. If the host controller is unable to guarantee enough bandwidth to support the device, which can happen if another device already has reserved bandwidth on the bus, the device may be unable to function. If the device is able to operate with less bandwidth, it can define alternate interface descriptors with more conservative requirements. Maximum payloads for isochronous transfers are as follows:

- High-speed devices have a maximum packet size of 1024 bytes.

- Full-speed devices have a maximum packet size of 1023 bytes.

- Low-speed devices do not support isochronous transfers.

Isochronous transfers use the concept of microframes. A microframe is 125 microseconds long. For high-speed devices, up to three packets can be transmitted per microframe, giving a maximum data-rate of 3 x 1024 x 8000 microframes per second = 24 MB/s. This is slightly lower than the maximum bandwidth possible over a bulk endpoint.

A microframe is represented by the IOUSBIsocFrame structure:

```
typedef struct IOUSBIsocFrame {
    IOReturn            frStatus;
    UInt16              frReqCount;
    UInt16              frActCount;
} IOUSBIsocFrame;
```

The structure describes how many bytes of data should be transmitted or received fromt the I/O buffer in each microframe. The frReqCount field is the amount of bytes requested, whereas the frActCount is the count actually transferred. The structure also contains a status field.

The methods for reading and writing to an isochronous endpoint are similar to those used to read and write from interrupt and bulk endpoints:

```
virtual IOReturn Read(IOMemoryDescriptor* buffer, UInt64 frameStart, UInt32 numFrames,
                IOUSBIsocFrame* frameList, IOUSBIsocCompletion* completion = 0);
virtual IOReturn Write(IOMemoryDescriptor* buffer, UInt64 frameStart, UInt32 numFrames,
                IOUSBIsocFrame *frameList, IOUSBIsocCompletion * completion = 0);
```

The methods take the following arguments:

- The **buffer** argument is a virtually contiguous buffer containing the data to be transferred. The memory descriptor should have its **prepare()** method called to ensure memory is paged in and pinned down for the duration of the transfer. There are no special requirements otherwise for the memory and it can be either user space or kernel memory.

- The **frameStart** argument specifies the index of the USB frame from which to start. One USB frame corresponds to 8 microframes.

- The **numFrames** argument is a count of the microframe descriptors contained in the **frameList** array.

- The **frameList** argument is a pointer to an array of **IOUSBIsocFrame** structures.

- An optional **completion** structure. If specified, this will perform the transfer asynchronously.

Asynchronous Requests

It is often necessary to perform requests to USB devices asynchronously—for example, when performing large bulk requests to a hard drive. Instead of having the caller thread blocked, the request can be handled by the USB controller, and it will notify us, through a callback method, when the request is completed.

To do this, you must supply an **IOUSBCompletion** structure to the **Read()**, **Write()**, **DeviceRequest()**, or **ControlRequest()** methods:

```
typedef struct IOUSBCompletion {
    void* target;
    IOUSBCompletionAction action;
    void* parameter;
} IOUSBCompletion;
```

- The **target** field is a pointer that can contain user-defined data. Often it is used to pass the pointer to the class that sent the request, so that you can cast the pointer back to the original class in the completion function.

- The **action** field is the actual callback, and should be a pointer to a function matching the **IOUSBCompletionAction** prototype. The method will be called once the request completes.

- The **parameter** field can carry an additional parameter, which will also be passed to the completion function.

The **IOUSBCompletionAction** callback has the following prototype:

```
typedef void ( *IOUSBCompletionAction)(void* target, void* parameter,
                                IOReturn status, UInt32 bufferSizeRemaining);
```

As you can see, the **target** and **parameter** fields of the **IOUSBCompletion** structure are passed directly to the callback. The callback will also get the **status** of the transfer, and the **bufferSizeRemaining** field will contain the number of bytes left to transfer if the request was not fully completed.

Asynchronous requests are completed on the IOUSBFamily work loop thread, which means that if you access data in the callback from your own driver, you must ensure that this access is properly synchronized.

Generally speaking, USB drivers never operate in a primary interrupt context, with the exception of the low latency versions of the isochronous Read() and Write() methods, which allows asynchronous isochronous I/O to have the completion callback called at primary interrupt time. In this case, extreme care needs to be taken to avoid calling code that may block. The use of low latency isochronous I/O should be used sparingly, and is generally not required even for audio and video drivers.

Summary

- At the time of writing, the Universal Serial Bus Specification exists in three major revisions, the latest being USB 3.0. USB 3.0, although emerging rapidly in the PC segment, has not yet been adopted by Apple, which at the time of writing only supports USB 2.0,

- A USB uses a shared bus topology, where up to 127 devices can be controlled by a single host. The host controller is the master of the bus, and controls all activity on the bus. A device is never allowed to use the bus without permission from the host.

- A USB device is described by a hierarchical structure of descriptors, which contain information about the class, type, capabilities, and requirements of the device.

- A USB device may consist of zero or more interfaces, which are groups of endpoints. An interface typically represents a logical device function, such as a printer or scanner.

- There are four types of endpoints: control, bulk, interrupt, and isochronous. Control transfers are used for device configuration and control. Bulk endpoints are used for applications such as hard drives or network devices. Interrupt endpoints provide bounded latency, but they can only transfer small amounts. Isochronous is ideal for video and audio applications that require guaranteed and predictable bandwidth, as well as low latency.

- The IOUSBFamily handles USB support in the kernel. The family implements support for common USB controllers. The three principal classes relevant to a driver developer are IOUSBDevice, IOUSBInterface, and IOUSBPipe. A USB driver can use either IOUSBDevice or IOUSBInterface as its provider.

- The IOUSBPipe provides an abstraction around endpoints. It has methods to deal with all four endpoints. It supports synchronous and asynchronous I/O.

CHAPTER 9

PCI Express and Thunderbolt

PCI (Peripheral Component Interconnect) is a high-speed bus developed by Intel, in the early nineties, to replace various older and slower bus technologies such as EISA, ISA, MCA, and VESA. The term PCI is often used to describe the family of technologies based on the original PCI specification. Throughout this chapter, when we refer to PCI, we refer to commonalities found in the PCI–based technologies; namely, PCI Express, Thunderbolt, and to a lesser extent ExpressCard. Most people associate PCI with expansion boards plugged into a computer, but it is worth noting that PCI is fundamental to many computer systems—even those without PCI slots, such as iMacs— that have internal PCI buses that connect the CPU to USB, Firewire, and SATA controllers. Recent PCI-based advancements (like Thunderbolt) allow the PCI bus to be extended outside of the computer, much in the same way as USB and Firewire.

PCI enjoyed widespread adoption and solved many of the problems found in older bus technologies; for example, it eliminated the need to configure jumpers on expansion cards, as resources such as memory regions and interrupts were configured automatically by the system BIOS and/or the OS itself.

PCI was extended by the PCI-X and PCI-X 2.0 standards, which allowed for a 64-bit bus width as opposed to the Legacy PCI's 32-bit bus width. PCI-X standards, having been succeeded by the PCI Express (PCIe) standard, have become obsolete. Unlike PCI-X however, PCIe uses a packet-based serial protocol, rather than the parallel interface characteristic of its predecessors. PCIe allows devices on a bus to have dedicated bandwidth instead of sharing bus bandwidth with other devices on the same bus. While PCIe and PCI are substantially different from an electrical and physical standpoint, they are backwards compatible from a software point of view; consequently, drivers require only minor (or no) changes to support newer standards.

As previously mentioned, there are myriads of PCI-related standards. We will discuss only technologies currently sold by Apple, which include PCIe, Thunderbolt, and ExpressCard. Thunderbolt is found in most 2011 or newer Macs. Thunderbolt and ExpressCard are based on PCIe technology and connect to the PCI host bridge. However, ExpressCard is being phased out in favor of Thunderbolt on all Macs, and is now found only in the 17" MacBook Pro. The Mac Pro is currently the only Mac to have physically accessible PCI Express slots after the XServe was discontinued.

This chapter begins with a discussion of the various PCI technologies that apply to the current generation of Macs. We will focus on the parts that are important to understand from a software point of view and necessary to build a functional driver for a PCI-based device. For example, we as programmers need not be concerned with how PCI functions at the electrical level. The second part of this chapter focuses on how we can interface with PCI-based devices in I/O Kit, how to match and configure them, read registers, and deal with the removal of devices. We will also address how to handle interrupts and perform DMA (Direct Memory Access), which are two typical tasks performed by a PCI-based driver.

PCI Express

PCIe was designed to replace PCI and PCI-X, as well as the AGP (Accelerated Graphics Port), a stopgap employed by graphics cards allowing for higher bandwidths not possible with PCI-X. PCIe uses uni-directional, point-to-point connections known as "lanes." This approach avoids the PCI and PCI-X's shared bus problem; although system designers could somewhat alleviate this issue by putting each physical PCI slot on its own dedicated bus. Still, PCIe is substantially faster than its predecessors.

So far, three revisions of the PCIe standard have been released. The second generation doubled the possible bandwidth for a single PCIe lane from 250 MB/s to 500 MB/s. The third revision doubled that and can handle up to 1 GB/s per lane. PCIe typically uses lane configurations of 1x, 4x, 8x, 16x, and 32x; although, the latter is less common, especially for physical slots. Slots for graphics cards/GPUs are typically 16x lanes wide, as they require massive amounts of bandwidth. The latest revision of the Mac Pro conforms to the PCIe 2.0 standard. The latest version of Mac Pro (5,1) has four 16x lane slots, but only slots 1 and 2 are able to operate at 16x, while slots 3 and 4 operate at 4x.

Thunderbolt

Thunderbolt, a relatively new technology, was initially developed by Intel and later adopted by Apple; the latter is currently the only vendor shipping Thunderbolt-enabled computers. Although the availability of devices is limited, several companies, including Blackmagic Design, Promise Technology, and Western Digital, have announced their support for the technology. Thunderbolt is an external expansion interface that allows PCIe and DisplayPort 1.1 to be tunneled over the same cable. A cable can carry two bi-directional channels of up to 10 Gbps of data, which amounts to a total bandwidth of 40 Gbps per cable. The channels are independent of each other, and it is not possible to aggregate the bandwidth between them. Thunderbolt is also able to provide up to 10 Watts of power to devices connected to the bus. The cable uses the Mini DisplayPort connector, which is indentical at both ends.

The current specification of Thunderbolt allows up to six devices to be daisy chained. Later revisions will showcase a tree-like topology similar to that of USB. However, unlike USB, Thunderbolt allows host-to-host connections like Firewire. Apple has also enabled a target disk mode using Thunderbolt, as well as the ability to boot the operating system from Thunderbolt attached storage. Due to the fact that Thunderbolt devices communicate directly with the PCIe host system, existing devices can be updated to support Thunderbolt with relatively few modifications to the hardware (ignoring the fact that an external case and possibly an external power source are needed). On the software side, very few changes are needed (devices are still managed by the IOPCIFamily); however, one requirement is that the driver must support being dynamically unloaded.

Thunderbolt makes it possible for the Mac Mini, iMac or MacBook series computers to access high-speed storage and storage area networks, as well as high-bandwidth uncompressed video capture, which was previously reserved for the high-end Mac Pro and Xserve.

ExpressCard

ExpressCard is an older expansion interface found in the MacBook Pro series. ExpressCard is being phased out in favour of Thunderbolt; however, laptops with both ExpressCard and Thunderbolt ports are available (at the time of writing). ExpressCard is the modern version of PCMCIA and is based on PCIe. The latest standard supports transfer speeds of up to 5 Gbps.

Configuration Space Registers

All PCI devices (including bridges) have a set of registers known as the configuration space. This space is a minimum of 256 bytes for conventional PCI devices, but on technologies based on PCI-X 2.0 and PCI Express, the configuration space is up to 4096 bytes long and is referred to as the extended configuration space. The first 48 bytes of the configuration space registers are shown in Figure 9-1.

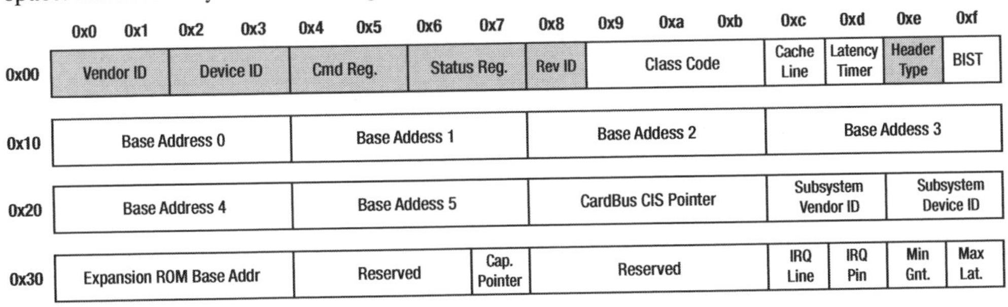

	0x0	0x1	0x2	0x3	0x4	0x5	0x6	0x7	0x8	0x9	0xa	0xb	0xc	0xd	0xe	0xf
0x00	Vendor ID		Device ID		Cmd Reg.		Status Reg.		Rev ID	Class Code			Cache Line	Latency Timer	Header Type	BIST
0x10	Base Address 0				Base Addess 1				Base Addess 2				Base Addess 3			
0x20	Base Address 4				Base Addess 5				CardBus CIS Pointer				Subsystem Vendor ID		Subsystem Device ID	
0x30	Expansion ROM Base Addr				Reserved			Cap. Pointer	Reserved				IRQ Line	IRQ Pin	Min Gnt.	Max Lat.

Figure 9-1. Standard PCI configuration space registers

The required registers are shown in gray; other registers are optional. The first 48 bytes are standardized and you will find the same layout regardless of whether the device is PCI, PCI-X, or PCIe-based. Many of the registers are no longer applicable because PCI Express is point-to-point based— it doesn't use a shared bus.

Let's look at the mandatory registers from Figure 9-1 in more detail.

- *Vendor ID:* Contains a 16-bit identifier unique to each hardware manufacturer. Vendor IDs are assigned by the PCI-SIG (special interest group) of each hardware manufacturer. Apple, for example, is assigned the vendor ID 0x106b. The combination of vendor ID and device ID is often used by operating systems to determine which driver to load for a device. 0xffff is not a valid vendor ID.

- *Device ID:* Also 16-bits wide. Unlike the vendor ID, the device ID can be assigned by the manufacturer and is not maintained in a central register.

- *Class Code:* A 24-bit register that holds the type classification for the device. The first 8 bits hold the base class. Examples of base classes include Unclassified (0x0), Mass Storage controller (0x1), Network Controller (0x2), Display Controller (0x3), etc. The next 8 bits hold the subclass. If the base class is a display controller, for instance, the subclasses might be VGA (0x0), XGA (0x1), or other (0x80). The remaining 8 bits are used to specify the program interface (register-level interface) of the device if more than one is possible. This is used for USB controllers to verify whether they comply with the UHCI, OHCI, EHCI, or XCHI interfaces, which are register-level specifications that determine how a driver should interact with a device.

- *Subsytem Vendor/Device ID*: Follows the same rules and assignments as the vendor and device IDs. The subsystem IDs are used to identify the chip, when many different manufacturers sell products using the same chip (OEM). Prime examples of this are Nvidia and ATI. They manufacture GPU chips that are subsequently used by third-party manufacturers to make the final product. The PCI configuration space of such a device contains the third-party's vendor ID and device ID, but uses either Nvidia or ATI as the subsystem vendor ID, as well as their device ID as the subsystem device ID. This allows ATI's and Nvidia's drivers to be used, even if they didn't manufacture the board directly.

- *Base Address 0-5*: Contains up to six I/O regions, which can be either I/O ports or memory regions. The latter is much more common. We will discuss I/O regions in more detail shortly. A base address is often abbreviated BAR (Base Address Register).

PCI in I/O Kit

PCI in the I/O Kit is handled by the IOPCIFamily, which, just like the IOUSBFamily, is implemented in its own KEXT. The IOPCIFamily is simpler than the IOUSBFamily in terms of the number of provided classes. This means there are fewer building blocks to help us out when implementing drivers. PCI is more low-level than USB from a driver point-of-view, and, as such, the writing of drivers for PCI devices is often more complex. Figure 9-2 shows the class hierarchy of the IOPCIFamily.

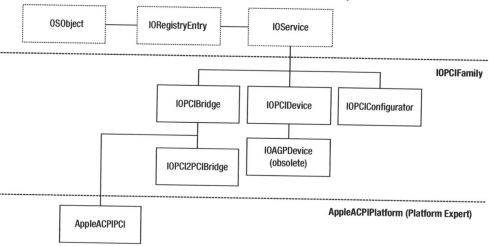

Figure 9-2. IOPCIFamily class hierarchy

The IOPCIDevice object acts a *nub* or provider for all PCI-based devices, including PCIe, Thunderbolt, and ExpressCard. An IOPCIDevice subclass called IOAGPDevice handles older AGP (Advanced Graphics Port)-based graphics cards; however, no Intel-based Macs feature AGP. In many cases, you only need to interact with the IOPCIDevice class from the IOPCIFamily. An instance of this object is provided for each PCI device in the system; similarly, an IOPCIBridge instance exists for each PCI bridge in the system. There are cases where a driver may need to interact with its bridge to read or write the bridge's configuration space. Although uncommon, it is also possible to create your own PCI bridge driver. We will discuss device and bridge access later in this chapter. The root PCI bridge (also known as the host bridge and root complex) is implemented by a subclass of `IOPCIBridge` called `AppleACPIPCI` class. This class is part of the Platform Expert implemented by the `AppleACPIPlatform` KEXT and controls access to all devices and bridges in the system. There is only one instance of this class. The `IOPCI2PCIBridge` class is the driver for PCI-to-PCI bridges.

▓ **Tip** As with the `IOUSBFamily`, the `IOPCIFamily` is not part of the *xnu* source distribution; rather, it is available as a separate download from `http://opensource.apple.com`. The source package contains the source code for the classes discussed above, as well as a sample PCI driver and source code for user space tools to dump information from a PCI device.

Matching and Loading Drivers

PCI drivers are commonly matched against properties found in their configuration space registers, such as the vendor ID, device ID, class, subsystem vendor ID, and subsystem device ID. Often, the latter two are needed if a PCI device is based on a generic chip.

Though the configuration spaces contain more fields, they cannot be matched against using a matching dictionary (property-based matching). If you need more advanced matching, your driver will have to override the `IOService::probe(IOProvider* service)` method, and you will have to examine the `IOPCIDevice` yourself to determine if your driver matches the device. The keys listed in Table 9-1 can be used for matching against PCI-based devices.

Table 9-1. Keys for Matching PCI Devices

Key	Description
IOPCIMatch	Match against vendor ID and device ID; if a match is not found, try to match against subsystem vendor ID and subsystem device ID.
IOPCIPrimaryMatch	Only match against vendor ID and device ID.
IOPCISecondaryMatch	Only match against subsystem vendor ID and subsystem device ID.
IOPCIClassMatch	Match against the PCI class code.
IONameMatch	Not PCI-specific; can be used to match against the name property.

Listing 9-1 shows the matching dictionary for a typical PCI device with a vendor ID or subsystem vendor ID of 0xabcd and a device ID or subsystem device ID of 0x1234.

Listing 9-1. Simple Matching Dictionary for a PCI Driver

```
<key>IOKitPersonalities</key>
<dict>
    <key>MyPCIDriver</key>
    <dict>
        <key>CFBundleIdentifier</key>
        <string>com.osxkernel.MyPCIDriver</string>
        <key>IOClass</key>
        <string>com_osxkernel_MyPCIDriver</string>
        <key>IOProviderClass</key>
        <string>IOPCIDevice</string>
        <key>IOPCIMatch</key>
        <string>0x1234abcd</string>
    </dict>
</dict>
```

The value is specified as a 32-bit hexadecimal string in little-endian format. The first four characters will represent the device ID and the last four characters will represent the vendor ID. It is worth noting that the value is of the string type and not an integer. The key IOProviderClass must have the value IOPCIDevice in order for the I/O Kit to pass your driver an IOPCIDevice instance. If you need to match against the vendor ID and device ID, you can substitute IOPCIMatch with IOPCIPrimaryMatch or, if you only wish to match the subsystem IDs, you can use IOPCISecondaryMatch.

If your driver handles multiple devices, this can be done as a space-separated list as follows:

```
<key>IOPCIMatch</key>
<string>0x1234abcd 0x1235abcd 0x1236abcd</string>
```

This will match device IDs 0x1234, 0x1235, and 0x1236 of vendor 0xabcd. If your driver supports a large family of devices, you can use masks to achieve the same effect, rather than enumerating each device separately.

```
<key>IOPCIMatch</key>
<string>0x1230abcd&0xfff0ffff</string>
```

■ **Note** If you are editing Info.plist directly, you must express the ampersand (&) as &amp, as the ampersand symbol is used to indicate an escape sequence in XML.

This will match every device ID beginning with 0x123X; for example, the range from 0x1230 to 0x123F, and a vendor ID of 0xabcd. Bits that should be ignored by the mask must be set to zero.

You can also match against the class register. To do this, you must specify the IOPCIClassMatch key. The class register is 3 bytes wide. However, to match against it, the I/O Kit requires you to specify a 4 byte value. The last byte is ignored. The following example matches display controllers (base class code 0x03):

```
<key>IOPCIClassMatch</key>
<string>0x03000000&amp;0xFF000000</string>
```

As all PCI devices are assigned names according to their devices and vendor IDs, it is also possible to use IONameMatch to match PCI devices as shown in Listing 9-2.

Listing 9-2. Matching Based on Name Property

```
<key>IONameMatch</key>
<array>
    <string>pciabcd,1234</string>
    <string>pciabcd,1235</string>
    <string>pciabcd,1236</string>
</array>
```

The previous approach is perhaps more readable, but the downside is that it is not possible to match against the subsystem vendor and device ID.

■ **Note** Remember to add a dependency to the IOPCIFamily in your driver's Info.plist file under the OSBundleLibraries section.

During system boot, drivers for PCI devices installed in a physical slot or embedded on the motherboard are loaded. Thunderbolt and ExpressCard drivers are loaded at boot-time or on demand as they are plugged in.

While Thunderbolt devices follow PCI devices' rules for identification, they need an additional change in order for the driver to load. In the driver's Info.plist file, under each personality specified, the following key needs to be set:

```
<key>IOPCITunnelCompatible</key>
<true/>
```

This tells the system that the driver is Thunderbolt-ready, and therefore, is safe to unload. It is possible for a Thunderbolt and a PCIe device to share the same device driver; however, PCI drivers may in many cases be written under the assumption that the driver/device will never be removed during operation. A driver will not be loaded against a Thunderbolt device unless this key is set.

THUNDERBOLT UNIQUE INDENTIFIER

All Thunderbolt devices have a device ROM (DROM) that contains an additional ID identifying the vendor, referred to as an Authority ID. This ID is part of a 64-bit UID number, which is unique for every Thunderbolt device, just like the MAC address of a network interface. The authority ID is assigned by the Thunderbolt naming authority (Intel) and not the PCI-SIG. At the time of writing, there are no publications explaining how to access this number from the I/O Kit, or if it can be used to match Thunderbolt devices.

Driver Example: A Simple PCI Driver

It's time to get our hands dirty. In order to demonstrate a PCI driver in action, we will take advantage of the IOMatchCategory key to allow the loading of a secondary driver for a device. We will load our driver against the display controller (graphics card/GPU) in this case, as it is a device guaranteed to be present on all Macs—even laptops—as they all use PCIe internally. We will use the following to match against the display controller:

```
<key>IOPCIClassMatch</key>
<string>0x03000000&amp;0xFF000000</string>
```

▓ **Caution** Be careful about making your own modifications to MyFirstPCIDriver, as it attaches to a device already controlled by another driver. Therefore, performing actions other than querying information may be unsafe and cause your system to crash or become corrupt.

Recall that 0x03 is a base class for display controllers. If you have more than one GPU, this will cause multiple instances of the driver to be instantiated—one per device.

Let's start with the class declaration for our driver, as shown in Listing 9-3.

Listing 9-3. MyFirstPCIDriver Class Declaration

```
#include <IOKit/IOLib.h>
#include <IOKit/pci/IOPCIDevice.h>

class com_osxkernel_MyFirstPCIDriver : public IOService
{
    OSDeclareDefaultStructors(com_osxkernel_MyFirstPCIDriver);

private:
    IOPCIDevice*        fPCIDevice;

public:
    virtual bool start(IOService* provider);
    virtual void stop(IOService* provider);
};
```

There should be few surprises here if you've followed earlier examples. We simply declare a sub-class of IOService and override the start() and stop() methods. Note that we include the file IOKit/pci/IOPCIDevice.h that contains the definition of the IOPCIDevice class.

The implementation of MyFirstPCIDriver is shown in Listing 9-4.

Listing 9-4. MyFirstPCIDriver Class Implementation

```
#include "MyFirstPCIDriver.h"

#define super IOService
OSDefineMetaClassAndStructors(com_osxkernel_MyFirstPCIDriver, IOService);
```

```
bool com_osxkernel_MyFirstPCIDriver::start(IOService * provider)
{
    IOLog("%s::start\n", getName());

    if(!super::start(provider))
        return false ;

    fPCIDevice = OSDynamicCast(IOPCIDevice, provider);
    if (!fPCIDevice)
        return false;

    fPCIDevice->setMemoryEnable(true);

    registerService();

    return true;
}

void com_osxkernel_MyFirstPCIDriver::stop( IOService * provider )
{
    IOLog("%s::stop\n", getName());
    super::stop(provider);
}
```

When a driver is matched successfully, either from the Info.plist dictionary or by invocation of the driver's probe() method, your driver will have its start() method called. As with the USB driver in chapter 8, we check to ensure that the provider that is passed to us is in fact of the right type (IOPCIDevice), which is good practice although it shouldn't happen if your Info.plist correctly specifies the IOProviderClass key.

If we have a valid IOPCIDevice, the next step is to enable the I/O resources of the device by calling the IOPCIDevice::setMemoryEnable(bool enable) method. This will set a toggle bit in the device's command register, letting it know that we want to access its resources. Finally, our driver calls registerService(), which will notify potential clients (possibly a higher-level driver) of our driver's arrival. We return true to indicate to the I/O Kit that the driver was loaded successfully.

We can now attempt to load MyFirstPCIDriver using the kextload utility. You can verify that it gets loaded correctly by checking kernel.log in Console.app or by searching for it using IORegistryExplorer as shown in Figure 9-3.

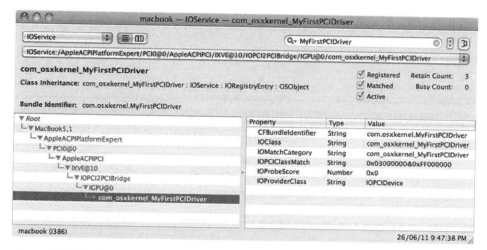

Figure 9-3. *IORegistryExplorer showing MyFirstPCIDriver loaded*

Accessing Configuration Space Registers

The IOPCIDevice class contains a number of helper methods that make it easy to access a device's configuration space registers. The following methods allow you to read and write configuration space registers.

```
virtual UInt8 configRead8(UInt8 offset);
virtual UInt16 configRead16(UInt8 offset);
virtual UInt32 configRead32(UInt8 offset);

virtual void configWrite8(UInt8 offset, UInt8 data);
virtual void configWrite16(UInt8 offset, UInt16 data);
virtual void configWrite32(UInt8 offset, UInt32 data);
```

There are three variants of read methods and three variants of write methods, which allow you to read or write an 8-bit value, a 16-bit value, or a 32-bit value from the offset specified. The offset parameter is a byte-offset into the configuration space and must be between 0-255. To read a device's device ID and vendor ID, we can do the following:

```
UInt16 vendorID = fPCIDevice->configRead16(0);
UInt16 deviceID = fPCIDevice->configRead16(2);
IOLog("vendor ID = 0x%04x device ID = 0x%04x\n", vendorID, deviceID);
```

The previous request could also be achieved by a single call:

```
UInt32 bothIDs = fPCIDevice->configRead32(0);
IOLog("vendor ID = 0x%04x device ID = 0x%04x\n", bothIDs >> 16, bothIDs & 0x0000FFFF);
```

The preceding call uses integer byte offsets, but the IOPCIDevice.h file specifies constants that can be used to address common register locations. So to make the code more readable, you can use kIOPCIConfigVendorID and kIOPCIConfigDeviceID instead of the hard coded values. The full list of available constants is shown in Listing 9-5.

Listing 9-5. Constants for Offsets of Common PCI Configuration Space Registers (IOPCIDevice.h)

```
enum {
    kIOPCIConfigVendorID = 0x00,
    kIOPCIConfigDeviceID = 0x02,
    kIOPCIConfigCommand = 0x04,
    kIOPCIConfigStatus = 0x06,
    kIOPCIConfigRevisionID = 0x08,
    kIOPCIConfigClassCode = 0x09,
    kIOPCIConfigCacheLineSize = 0x0C,
    kIOPCIConfigLatencyTimer = 0x0D,
    kIOPCIConfigHeaderType = 0x0E,
    kIOPCIConfigBIST = 0x0F,
    kIOPCIConfigBaseAddress0 = 0x10,
    kIOPCIConfigBaseAddress1 = 0x14,
    kIOPCIConfigBaseAddress2 = 0x18,
    kIOPCIConfigBaseAddress3 = 0x1C,
    kIOPCIConfigBaseAddress4 = 0x20,
    kIOPCIConfigBaseAddress5 = 0x24,
    kIOPCIConfigCardBusCISPtr = 0x28,
    kIOPCIConfigSubSystemVendorID = 0x2C,
    kIOPCIConfigSubSystemID = 0x2E,
    kIOPCIConfigExpansionROMBase = 0x30,
    kIOPCIConfigCapabilitiesPtr = 0x34,
    kIOPCIConfigInterruptLine = 0x3C,
    kIOPCIConfigInterruptPin = 0x3D,
    kIOPCIConfigMinimumGrant = 0x3E,
    kIOPCIConfigMaximumLatency = 0x3F
};
```

IOPCIDevice also provides a convenient method for setting individual bits of a register called setConfigBits().

A read request to a missing or malfunctioning device will return a value of 0xFFFF (0xFF or 0xFFFFFFFF for the 8 and 32-bit variants), which is an invalid device/vendor ID. So if this value is returned while reading either register it can be used to determine if a problem has occurred or if a Thunderbolt device has been unplugged.

Writing values to the configuration space is simple but there are a few things to note. Many areas of the configuration space are read-only. For example, the device ID and vendor ID are programmed into the device's PCI controller firmware. Also note that it is not possible to determine if a write to a register location succeeded; you would have to read back the register or another that was affected by the write transaction in order to determine its success.

■ **Note** If your driver needs to maintain compatibility with PowerPC-based systems, be aware that the PCI config space is stored in little-endian format, however IOPCIDevice handles byte swapping for you.

A number of methods of IOPCIDevice, such as *setMemoryEnable()*, are simply convenient abstractions that perform the appropriate configuration space reads or writes on your behalf. I/O to configuration space is forwarded by an IOPCIDevice to its parent (an IOPCIBridge in most cases) until it reaches the root bridge, which is implemented by the Platform Expert, as the exact details are system dependent.

Accessing the Extended Configuration Space

You may have noticed an inconsistency with the I/O functions in the previous section. We saw earlier that the extended configuration space is 4096 bytes. How do you address offsets greater than 255 when the config*() functions take a UInt8 type for the offset argument? The answer is the following family of methods.

```
UInt32 extendedConfigRead32(IOByteCount offset);
UInt16 extendedConfigRead16(IOByteCount offset);
UInt8 extendedConfigRead8(IOByteCount offset);

void extendedConfigWrite32(IOByteCount offset, UInt32 data);
void extendedConfigWrite16(IOByteCount offset, UInt16 data);
void extendedConfigWrite8(IOByteCount offset, UInt8 data);
```

The methods have the same interface as is shown above. However, they use the wider data-type IOByteCount for the offset parameter to allow access to offsets greater than 255.

Searching for Capabilities Registers

Because capability registers are not located at a fixed offset, the process of finding a capability register involves searching for a capability ID and then reading the next byte to determine the length of the capability, which also tells you the offset of the next capability. This process is followed moving down the list until the right capability is located. Fortunately, we do not need to write this code manually as the IOPCIDevice class provides two helper methods to locate capabilities:

```
virtual UInt32 findPCICapability(UInt8 capabilityID, UInt8* offset = 0 );
virtual UInt32 extendedFindPCICapability(UInt32 capabilityID, IOByteCount* offset = 0 );
```

The following demonstrates how to fetch the PCIe link status register, which contains the number of active lanes (bits 4-9) and the link speed (bits 0-3) for the device.

```
IOByteCount offset = 0;
if (fPCIDevice->extendedFindPCICapability(kIOPCIPCIExpressCapability, &offset))
{
        UInt16 value = fPCIDevice->extendedConfigRead16(offset + 0x12);
}
```

The method will return the capability ID (kIOPCIExpressCapability in this case) or zero if the capability with the specified ID could not be found. The output argument offset is used to store the offset of the found capability. Once the capability is found we can read the link status register by adding 0x12 (18) to the offset.

PCI I/O Memory Regions

PCI devices may have up to six I/O regions. Each region contains either I/O memory or I/O space (ports). The latter is seldom used in new devices as I/O ports are generally a very slow way of performing I/O and can only be accessed using special in/out CPU instructions. Some legacy devices, such as IDE controllers, may have both I/O ports and memory and can be controlled by either. On the other hand,

I/O memory is more efficient and also easier to access, as it can simply be mapped into the system's memory space and accessed like regular memory. I/O memory is commonly referred to as Memory Mapped I/O (MMIO). This concept is not to be confused with mapping of memory between virtual address spaces or the mapping of files in memory (mmap).

Access to and from mapped device memory can be cached by the CPU if the region has the memory prefetchable bit set.

How is a device controlled through a memory region? That is entirely up to the device. For example, one region could be used for control and status registers, while a second region could be used to read or write data, for example input video from a camera. If you are reading this in electronic form, then this very text may be continuously written to the memory region representing the frame buffer of your graphics card. Just like USB, there are a number of standardized interfaces for PCI-based devices as well. An example of this is VGA compatible graphics cards, which allow for the basic operation of a graphics card using a known interface including memory regions and/or ports. Standardized interfaces for IDE, SATA, and PCI-based USB controllers also exist, enabling an operating system to use its default driver for any device that complies with such an interface.

Because PCI is "plug and play," I/O resource for a PCI device is configured automatically by the kernel/EFI (or BIOS in traditional PCs), in contrast to the obsolete ISA bus, where jumpers had to be physically placed to select the base I/O addresses and interrupt line for each device separately in an attempt to avoid resource conflicts.

When a device is configured, each region present in the configuration space will be configured with its own address range. The size of the range depends on the device.

When a device is configured, it will be assigned a physical memory address range by the system. As you can see from Figure 9-1 there is no register for storing the size of each memory region. So how does the system know how big each region is? The size of a memory region is determined by the system by setting all bits in one of the base address slots in the configuration space and then reading back the value. A region must be of a size that is a power of two. Devices, if they support it, can combine two BARs to form a 64-bit address.

Before the system or a driver can access any of the I/O regions, they need to be enabled by toggling a bit in the device's command register. We already saw how this was done in MyFirstPCIDriver by calling fPCIDevice->setMemoryEnable(true) in the driver's start() method.

Enumerating I/O Regions

To discover available memory regions of a PCI device (there may be up to six), let's modify MyFirstPCIDriver to dump some additional information about the device in its start() method, by adding the code in Listing 9-6 after the call to setMemoryEnable().

Listing 9-6. Enumerating PCI I/O Memory Regions

```
for (UInt32 i = 0; i < fPCIDevice->getDeviceMemoryCount(); i++)
{
    IODeviceMemory* memoryDesc = fPCIDevice->getDeviceMemoryWithIndex(i);
    if (!memoryDesc)
        continue;
    #ifdef __LP64__
        IOLog("region%u: length=%llu bytes\n", i, memoryDesc->getLength());
    #else
```

```
        IOLog("region%lu: length=%lu bytes\n", i, memoryDesc->getLength());
    #endif
}
```

If you compile and load the driver, you should see something like the following printed in the kernel.log:

```
Apr 1 11:06:18 macbook kernel[0]: com_osxkernel_MyFirstPCIDriver::start
Apr 1 11:06:18 macbook kernel[0]: region0: length=16777216 bytes
Apr 1 11:06:18 macbook kernel[0]: region1: length=268435456 bytes
Apr 1 11:06:18 macbook kernel[0]: region2: length=33554432 bytes
Apr 1 11:06:18 macbook kernel[0]: region3: length=128 bytes
Apr 1 11:06:18 macbook kernel[0]: region4: length=131072 bytes
```

Your output may differ depending on your system model and graphics card (you may even have multiple). In this case, the largest region (256 MB) is region 1, which is the graphics card's frame buffer.

Mapping and Accessing Device Memory Regions

The previous section showed us how we can obtain information about available I/O memory regions. We need to do some more work before we can actually access data from the regions. Furthermore, in most real-world drivers, it is unnecessary to explicitly enumerate the regions, as a driver usually knows exactly which regions, if not all that it needs to map. The following IOPCIDevice method can be used to map a BAR region directly:

```
virtual IOMemoryMap * mapDeviceMemoryWithRegister(UInt8 reg, IOOptionBits options = 0);
```

The following is an example of its use.

```
IOMemoryMap *bar0Map = fPCIDevice->mapDeviceMemoryWithRegister(kIOPCIConfigBaseAddress0);
IOMemoryMap *bar1Map = fPCIDevice->mapDeviceMemoryWithRegister(kIOPCIConfigBaseAddress1);
if (bar0Map)
{
    UInt8 *address = (UInt8*)bar0Map->getVirtualAddress();
    // do something with address
}
...
```

If you have already obtained an IODeviceMemory (subclass of IOMemoryDescriptor) object by calling getDeviceMemoryWithIndex() as in Listing 9-6, you can simply call the map() method which does the same thing. In fact, that is exactly what mapDeviceMemoryWithRegister() does under the hood. Once an IOMemoryMap object is obtained, you can call the getVirtualAddress() method to obtain a kernel virtual address which can be used to access the mapping. The returned pointer can be read and written to in the same way as regular memory assuming it points to I/O memory and not I/O space.

When a driver is done accessing the memory it should call the unmap() method.

Accessing I/O Space

I/O Space consists of a 16-bit address space and is an older way of communicating with devices. I/O ports were also used for communication with serial and parallel ports in older computers, so it is not specific to PCI, but rather a way for an external device (to the CPU) to interface with the processor. I/O

Space ranges assigned to a device can be accessed and mapped just like memory regions by using mapDeviceMemoryWithRegister() and getDeviceMemoryWithIndex(). The difference however, is that you cannot simply access the pointer returned by getVirtualAddress() as above directly. You have to use one of the following methods.

```
virtual void ioWrite32(UInt16 offset, UInt32 value, IOMemoryMap* map = 0);
virtual void ioWrite16(UInt16 offset, UInt16 value, IOMemoryMap* map = 0);
virtual void ioWrite8(UInt16 offset, UInt8 value, IOMemoryMap* map = 0);
virtual UInt32 ioRead32(UInt16 offset, IOMemoryMap* map = 0);
virtual UInt16 ioRead16(UInt16 offset, IOMemoryMap* map = 0);
virtual UInt8 ioRead8(UInt16 offset, IOMemoryMap* map = 0);
```

Using I/O space in new devices is frowned upon, due to poor performance and the limited address space it provides. Accessing mapped memory can take as little as 1 CPU cycle, while accessing a port can take as many as 100 cycles on certain architectures.

Before I/O space can be accessed, it needs to be enabled in the device's command register. IOPCIDevice provides the setIOEnable() method for this purpose.

Handling Device Removal

Thunderbolt and ExpressCard devices may be unplugged during operation. Therefore, drivers that handle these devices need some additional modifications over traditional PCI drivers, which are usually not written with removal of the device in mind. Improper handling of device removal may lead to hanging applications, system crashes, or disruptions to system stability or performance. For Thunderbolt devices, removal is not an exceptional condition so a driver must be able to cope with the removal of the device.

▓ **Caution** Storage devices with mounted file systems may NOT be unplugged without the user first "Ejecting" (unmounting) the file system. Failure to do so may result in loss or, in the worst-case scenario, corruption of the file system. Thunderbolt based storage drivers should call:

setProperty(kIOPropertyPhysicalInterconnectLocationKey, kIOPropertyExternalKey) early in the driver's start() method to indicate to the I/O Kit that the storage is externally connected.

While it may seem complicated to handle device removals, the I/O Kit was designed specifically to allow removal of devices. The IOService class handles a lot of the heavy lifting for us automatically.

Your driver may detect the first sign that a device has been removed if it receives the value 0xffffffff (assuming a 32-bit read) while reading a value from memory mapped I/O (MMIO) or PCI configuration space registers. Of course the value might actually be valid for some registers, however you can read an alternate register or memory location that you know is guaranteed never to contain that value to confirm if the device is unresponsive. The driver may detect this condition before the I/O Kit messages the driver informing it that the device has been removed. If a driver determines that a device is removed, it should cease all access to mapped memory and the configuration space as further requests will result in timing out requests, which can take up to several milliseconds and may affect overall system performance. Apple recommends funneling all accesses to MMIO through a single method, as follows:

```
UInt32 com_osxkernel_MyFirstPCIDriver::readRegister32(UInt32 offset)
{
    UInt32 res = 0xffffffff;
    if (!fDeviceRemoved)
    {
        res = OSReadLittleInt32(fBar0Address, offset);
        if (res == 0xffffffff)
            fDeviceRemoved = true;
    }
    return res;
}
```

The method will prevent further accesses to registers once the device has been removed. We can now use the member variable fDeviceRemoved in other parts of the driver to prevent operations that will communicate with the hardware.

The I/O Kit handles device removal in three phases:

1. The bus controller (PCI root) will call the terminate() method on its client *nub*, which will message its clients again and so forth until it reaches the bottom of the stack. An IOService object that overrides the message() method will also receive a kIOServicesIsTerminated message. The driver is now considered inactive and cannot be enumerated or attached to by new clients. Existing clients holding the driver open will still remain active.

2. Drivers in the stack will have their willTerminate() method called, and thereafter didTerminate(). This process happens in reverse order, so clients will call their providers instead of the other way around, until it reaches the original provider that initiated the call to terminate() in the first place. Remember that these methods are optional, and you can choose to implement these based on your driver's needs. In response to having its willTerminate() method called, a driver should clear all queued requests and cancel in-flight I/O such as unfinished DMA transfers.

3. The last phase of the removal will call the drivers stop() method, then detach() which will remove it from the I/O Registry. If the driver's retain count reaches zero, the driver will be deallocated and its free() method will be called.

If a user plugs the same device back again, a new instance of the driver will be allocated. Any applications accessing the driver at the time will still be attached to the old instance of the driver. To handle this situation, the application must install a notification to detect when the driver/device is removed or added to the system. Because a driver instance is not reused when a device is reinserted, it doesn't need to return to its default state once it has handled a device removal. However, it is important it properly release and free any used resources, as the new instance will reallocate or reclaim those which could result in a memory leak or the new driver instance not coming up properly.

▒ **Tip** Xcode supplies a command-line tool called `ioclasscount` that prints instance counts for `OSObject` derived classes and can be used to help debug memory leaks related to device removals. See Chapter 16 for more information.

Interrupts

Interrupts provide a mechanism for PCI and other hardware devices to signal the CPU asynchronously when an event of interest occurs, such as when a key on a keyboard is pressed or when the position of the mouse is moved or its buttons clicked. A web camera might send an interrupt every time a new video frame becomes available, which will allow its driver to know when the new frame can be read from its mapped memory region. Interrupts save the CPU from polling each device to determine if new data is available. Legacy PCI devices used dedicated interrupt pins that were physically wired from the PCI card/slot to a pin on the CPU. More modern Thunderbolt and PCIe-based technologies use message-signaled interrupts (MSI), avoiding the need for dedicated physical lines between a device and the CPU or interrupt controller chip. Traditional PCI cards had four interrupt pins, which limited the amount of interrupts that could be used for a device. MSI however allow for up to 32 interrupts per device. While MSI is electrically different from traditional interrupts, they do appear to function identically from a driver's point of view.

When a CPU receives an interrupt, it puts the currently running thread to sleep, even if the thread belongs to the kernel itself. When the interrupt occur the CPU will try to locate an Interrupt Service Routine (ISR) for the interrupt that was triggered.

The ISR gets routed to the driver that "owns" the device. It is possible for legacy interrupt based devices to share interrupt lines. In this case, the driver will need to interrogate the device, usually by reading a memory mapped register to determine if its device raised the interrupt.

MSI interrupts are never shared, although it is still good practice to anticipate this scenario. Interrupts are not always generated just from hardware devices such as PCI. Interrupts are also sent by the system timer, which is used to drive OS services such as the scheduler.

While an ISR runs, the CPU handling the interrupt will disable other interrupts, which means that nothing will execute on the CPU until the ISR has completed.

As you can imagine, it would not be ideal for system performance if a driver performed large amounts of work in the ISR callback. In fact, it is highly recommended that a driver do nothing but acknowledge the interrupt. If the interrupt is not acknowledged, it may cause the ISR to go off continuously, which would affect both performance and stability. When an ISR runs, this is often referred to as the *primary interrupt context*. To improve system performance, most OSs, including OS X and iOS, have mechanisms to defer handling of interrupts to a kernel thread at a later time. This is often referred to as the *secondary interrupt context*. It is in the secondary interrupt context (thread) that the real work of handling an interrupt is performed, such as copying incoming packets from a network. The primary handler usually acknowledges the interrupt and then, if there is work to do, signals the secondary handler.

In the primary context, it is not possible to do an operation that blocks or sleeps, which includes most memory allocation routines and holding locks other than spin locks. This is because blocking/sleeping is performed by giving up access to the CPU and temporarily yielding in favor of some other thread. However, the ISR is not associated with a task or thread descriptor. Therefore, the scheduler is not able to schedule the ISR back again as it is fired directly by the CPU.

The secondary interrupt handler has no such restrictions and can happily allocate memory and block waiting for locks to become available. This is possible under OS X and iOS, but some operating systems may run the secondary handler (also called bottom half, the primary being the top half) in a context that does not allow this.

While OS X and iOS impose fewer restrictions for what you can do in a secondary interrupt handler, it still has to be very efficient.

Handling of primary interrupts cannot be done by a user space program. If a user space program needs to know when an interrupt occur, it would need to be signaled by the driver instead.

In OS X, all primary interrupts are routed to CPU 0 (core) and secondary interrupts are spread across all cores, which allows multiple drivers to run in parallel. Because secondary interrupts run in a separate kernel thread (high priority), it can be scheduled like any other thread and thus run while interrupts are enabled. Interrupt mechanisms are conceptually simple to implement. However, they can be complicated by their parallelism if data is shared between the primary and secondary handler, and also by user threads that may call into the driver that needs to access the same data. Great care needs to be taken to ensure that there are no deadlocks and also to reduce contention between the various threads of execution. This ensures that no thread will have to wait excessively to gain access to needed resources. For more information on synchronization, refer to Chapter 7.

▓ **Note** The term primary interrupt is sometimes referred to as direct interrupt, and secondary interrupts as indirect interrupts.

I/O Kit Interrupt Mechanisms

The preferred way to handle both primary and secondary interrupts in I/O Kit is through the work loop system. However, direct handling is also possible. If you are unsure about how work loops operate, check out Chapter 7 for more details. There are three main mechanisms available to handle driver interrupts. Figure 9-4 shows how the three different mechanisms respond to primary interrupts.

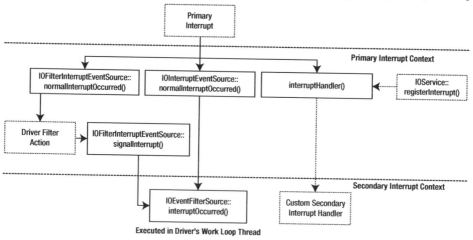

Figure 9-4. I/O Kit mechanisms for handling device interrupts

- IOInterruptEventSource: The standard and easiest way to handle device interrupts. You simply register a handler method, which is executed in the secondary interrupt context. Your driver never has to deal with primary interrupts. Interrupts will be disabled from the provider until the interrupt handler has completed, thus guaranteeing single-threaded handling of the interrupt, as another handler cannot run in parallel. IOInterruptEventSource is the preferred way of handling interrupts.

- IOFilterInterruptEventSource: Shown on the left in Figure 9-4, it is a subclass of IOInterruptEventSource and provides more flexibility. It allows a custom filter action to be supplied. This filter action is invoked in primary interrupt context and allows a driver to interrogate a hardware device to see if it really has an interrupt. If the interrupt is shared between several devices or the device is a complex or multi-function device with many possible interrupts or have requirements for very low latency, this method is recommended. The secondary interrupts are scheduled based on the return value of the installed filter action (routine).

- IOService::registerInterrupt(): The last method is to use IOService::registerInterrupt() to register a C function that will be invoked during primary interrupt. This method does not use the driver's work loop and provides no means to invoke a secondary interrupt handler. If secondary interrupts are required, the mechanism for handling them would have to be implemented manually.

Registering to Receive Interrupts

As with many things in the I/O Kit, registering interrupts is simple and most of the heavy lifting is handled internally by the I/O Kit and the Platform Expert. We do not have to worry about assigning an IRQ number or interrupt routing because that is automatically handled. A typical block of code demonstrating how to register a driver to receive interrupts from its provider (IOPCIDevice) with a primary interrupt filter is shown in Listing 9-7.

Listing 9-7. Creating a Filtering Interrupt Event Source

```
bool MyFirstPCIDriver::start(IOService * provider)
{
    ...
    IOWorkLoop *workLoop = (IOWorkLoop*)getWorkLoop();
    if (!workLoop)
        return false;

    IOFilterInterruptEventSource* interruptSource =
        IOFilterInterruptEventSource::filterInterruptEventSource(this,
                (IOInterruptEventAction) &MyFirstPCIDriver::interruptOccurred,
                (IOFilterInterruptAction) &MyFirstPCIDriver::interruptFilter,
                provider, 0);

    if (workLoop->addEventSource(interruptSource) != kIOReturnSuccess)
            return false;
    ...
}
```

There are four steps involved:

1. Obtain or allocate an IOWorkLoop instance.

2. Allocate the event source, which is done using the factory method filterInterruptEventSource(). We pass five parameters:

    - A pointer to ourselves,

    - A pointer to the secondary interrupt handler interruptOccurred() method

    - The filter action method that will be executed in primary interrupt context.

    - The last argument is the interrupt index number of the provider and can be specified if a provider has more than one interrupt type. For example, the provider may support Message Signaled Interrupts (MSI) in addition to shared interrupts.

    - The index of the interrupt type. See the section "Enabling Message Signaled Interrupts" for details.

3. Add the event source to the IOWorkLoop instance using addEventSource().

4. The last step is to enable the event source, as it is disabled by default, even after it is added to the work loop. To start receiving interrupts, simply call interruptSource->enable().

It is important to make sure the driver is fully initialized and ready to receive interrupts before this is called or, if possible, ensure interrupts are deactivated on the hardware itself until the driver is ready to process them.

To register an IOInterruptEventSource, the process is nearly identical and is shown in Listing 9-8.

Listing 9-8. Creating an Interrupt Event Source

```
IOWorkLoop *workLoop = (IOWorkLoop*)getWorkLoop();
if (!workLoop)
        return false;

IOInterruptEventSource* interruptSource =
        IOInterruptEventSource::interruptEventSource(this,
                (IOInterruptEventAction) &MyFirstPCIDriver::interruptOccurred,
                provider, 0);

if (workLoop->addEventSource(interruptSource) != kIOReturnSuccess)
        return false;
...
```

The only difference is that it doesn't accept a filter action, as is the case with *IOFilterInterruptEventSource.*

Enabling Message Signaled Interrupts

If you need to be sure that Message Signaled Interrupts (MSI) is used, you must first enumerate the index of the MSI interrupt type. In Listings 9-7 and 9-8, we simply passed 0 to get the first interrupt type of the provider, which may or may not be MSI capable, depending on the device. The following method will enumerate available interrupt types of the provider and return the index of the MSI interrupt type, which can then be passed in as the index argument to IOInterruptEventSource::interruptEventSource():

```
int com_osxkernel_MyFirstPCIDriver::findMSIInterruptTypeIndex()
{
    IOReturn ret;
    int index, source = 0;

    for (index = 0; ; index++)
    {
        int interruptType;
        ret = fPCIDevice->getInterruptType(index, &interruptType);
        if (ret != kIOReturnSuccess)
            break;

        if (interruptType & kIOInterruptTypePCIMessaged)
        {
            source = index;
            break;
        }
    }
    return source;
}
```

Handling Primary Interrupts

Let's have a look at the implementation of the primary interrupt filter and how to schedule the secondary interrupt handler. A Primary interrupt filter for an audio device might look something like shown in Listing 9-9.

Listing 9-9. Primary Interrupt Filter Method

```
bool com_osxkernel_MyAudioPCIDriver::interruptFilter(OSObject* owner,
IOFilterInterruptEventSource * src)
{
    bool scheduleSecondaryInterrupt = false;

    com_osxkernel_MyAudioPCIDriver* me = (com_osxkernel_MyAudioPCIDriver*)owner;

    uint32_t registerContents = me->readRegister(kHardwareInterruptRegisterOffset);
    if (registerContents & kAudioInputInterruptBit)
    {
        scheduleSecondaryInterrupt = true;
        me->fAudioInputInterruptPending = true;
    }
    else if (registerContents & kAudioOutputInterrupt)
    {
        scheduleSecondaryInterrupt = true;
        me->fAudioOutputInterruptPending = true;
    }
```

```
      return scheduleSecondaryInterrupt;
}
```

The method accepts two arguments. The first is an OSObject pointer, which value was passed during construction of the IOFilterInterruptEventSource instance. We used the this pointer to pass ourselves. The reason for this is that the interruptFilter() function is a static class member, as regular member functions cannot be used as function pointers in C++. We simply cast the owner argument back to a type of our driver class to retrieve our instance. We are also passed an instance of the event source.

■ **Caution** It may be tempting to put debug statements in the primary interrupt handler to see if it triggers or that the right registers are set in hardware with IOLog(). Do NOT do this. It is a very bad idea. Did we mention it was a bad idea? Your system will crash.

Because the filter function runs in primary interrupt context, it is unsafe to call most parts of the I/O Kit framework, including memory allocation functions and most locking functions. You should also avoid doing I/O or other long-winded operations in primary interrupt context. In the hypothetical example shown in Listing 9-9, we are handling interrupts for a bi-directional audio device that has two interrupts, one for each direction. In our filter, we first read the device's interrupt register. If either of the interrupts are set, we set the variable scheduleSecondaryInterrupt to true, which we use as a return value. A return of true means we want the secondary interrupt handler to run, and a return of false means that our device wasn't interrupting. This either means we are sharing an interrupt line with another device, which was the one that raised the interrupt, or it could be a false interrupt due to malfunctioning hardware or interference. If we return true from the filter, our device's interrupt will be disabled until the secondary handler is scheduled and it completes its execution. This ensures that an interrupt is serialized so our driver doesn't need to worry about locking between the primary and secondary handlers, as they never run in parallel.

There are some cases where this behavior is undesired, and we can prevent the interrupt from being disabled by modifying our interrupt filter to always return false, which will ensure the interrupt doesn't get disabled, but that also prevents the secondary interrupt from being scheduled. However, we can manually schedule it as follows instead:

```
bool com_osxkernel_MyFirstPCIDriver::interruptFilter(OSObject* owner,
IOFilterInterruptEventSource * src)
{
…

…

      if (scheduleSecondaryInterrupt)
            src->signalInterrupt();
      return false;
}
```

This will have the effect of allowing the device to issue primary interrupts, even if our secondary interrupt handler is already running. In the case of our audio device, this may allow concurrent processing of input and output interrupts.

Handling Secondary Interrupts

The secondary interrupt handler is the same regardless if it is used with an IOInterruptEventSource or an IOFilterInterruptEventSource. The prototype is similar to that of the primary interrupt filter function, but has an additional parameter that contains the index of the interrupt source of the provider, if a provider has more than one interrupt. Our audio device has only one interrupt, and we need to read the device's register to determine which events were signaled. If the device had several interrupts, we could instead differentiate this by looking at the intCount parameter. A very simplistic implementation of the secondary interrupt handler for our imaginary audio device is shown in Listing 9-10.

Listing 9-10. Secondary Interrupt Handler Method

```
void com_osxkernel_MyAudioPCIDriver::interruptOccurred(OSObject* owner,
IOInterruptEventSource* src, int intCount)
{
    com_osxkernel_MyFirstPCIDriver*    me;
    me = (com_osxkernel_MyFirstPCIDriver*)owner;

    if (me->fAudioInputInterruptPending)
            me->handleAudioInputInterrupt();         // Start next DMA
    if (me->fAudioOutputInterruptPending)
            me->handleAudioOutputInterrupt();        // Start next DMA
}
```

We detect which interrupt that was pending and execute driver methods for handling the interrupts. The methods may, for example, signal a user application that data is now available and setup a new DMA transaction to fill another buffer. The reason why we use the instance variables fAudioInputInteruptPending and fAudioOutputInterruptPending rather than re-reading the interrupt status register from Listing 9-9 is that many hardware devices will automatically clear the interrupt register once the register is read, which also serves to acknowledge the interrupt.

The secondary interrupt handler may run in parallel to user space threads calling our driver, so it is important to have proper synchronization in place to guard shared data. Note that the secondary interrupt handler itself runs on the driver's work loop, which is single-threaded, so two secondary interrupt handlers are guaranteed not to run in parallel.

Direct Memory Access

Direct Memory Access (DMA) is a concept that allows a device to transfer data to or from system memory without the involvement of the CPU, leaving it free to perform other tasks, which has a significant impact on overall system performance, as I/O transfers are typically very slow relative to the CPU. DMA also allows for so-called zero-copy, in that we can transfer memory from a user space buffer directly to a device without any memory copies. PCI doesn't have a central DMA controller, but uses the concept of bus mastering, which allows the device to take control over the bus and initiate transfers. The IOPCIDevice class offers the setBusMasterEnable() method, which gives the device permission to act as a bus master. DMA transfers are directional. When the CPU wishes to transfer data from system memory to a device, this is referred to as *outbound* DMA, whereas transfers from a device to the system memory are referred to as *inbound* DMA.

There are no standard I/O Kit classes for controlling DMA to PCI devices as each device may implement DMA differently (the DMA function of a device is often referred to as a DMA engine). However, in most cases, the process is very similar. A device may support several concurrent DMA transfers and each transfer is said to have its own DMA channel. The concept of a DMA transfer is simple. For an outbound DMA transfer, the following steps typically occur.

1. The driver needs to identify the memory buffer to be transferred and pin the memory.

2. The driver will inform the device of the location (physical address) and size of the memory, which is typically done by writing the values to a register.

3. The driver will toggle a bit in one of the device's registers to indicate that it should start the DMA.

4. The device will transfer the contents of the buffer directly from system memory without the involvement of the CPU. It sets another register bit to indicate the completion of the transfer and raise an interrupt.

5. The driver will handle the interrupt, check if the DMA completion bit is set, and possibly prime another DMA transaction if there are more data to send.

The process of setting up and handling an inbound DMA transfer is the same. The only difference is that the device writes to the buffer instead of reading from it. We still need to tell the device the memory location where the data is and we still get an interrupt once the transfer is done. For a device like a storage device, the driver always initiates I/O, and it will control when to read and when to write data. However, devices such as network controllers are slightly different, in that data may arrive on the device asynchronously in response to an external event. In this case, the device will raise an interrupt and set a flag in its registers so the driver knows that the device has data in its input buffer. The driver will then prime a new DMA buffer and start a transfer to empty the device's input buffer. Once the device has completed the transaction, it will raise another interrupt to inform the driver that the transfer has completed.

While DMA is simple from a conceptual point of view, it is complicated by the following factors:

*   Memory caching on the CPU can cause coherency issues because data written by the CPU may be held in a cache on the CPU and not be committed to system memory straight away. If a DMA transfer is started at this time, the device may read the incorrect data, the previous contents of the RAM, or simply garbage. On Intel systems, this issue is handled automatically by hardware and does not require a driver to intervene. For PowerPC processors, I/O Kit provides the IOFlushProcessorCache() function which flush the CPU caches to system memory ensure that the device will see the correct memory contents. The function exists but does nothing on Intel based systems.

*   On 64-bit platforms (or when PAE is used), some older PCI-based hardware devices may be unable to access memory addresses greater than 32-bit. Two strategies exist for handling these situations. The poorest, in terms of performance, uses a bounce buffer that is located at an address range the device can access. Contents of an I/O buffer located at addresses over 32-bit would have to be copied to the new buffer before the device can access the data. The second approach involves using special hardware circuitry found on modern computers that can dynamically remap any memory location into a "virtual" physical address that the device can access.

- Although, from a user application's point of view, memory appears to be contiguous, user space memory is composed of physical pages that may be scattered across RAM. Let's say an application wants to output a buffer containing a large HD video frame to a video device. Because the frame is severely fragmented in physical memory, it is not enough to simply tell the device the address and size of a single buffer. We need to tell it about all the fragments that make up the video frame. So instead of a telling the device a location and size of a buffer, we instead provide it with a buffer containing a list of locations for each fragment. This buffer is known as a scatter/gather list. We will discuss this concept in more detail shortly.

Most of the complexity from a driver's point of view exists in setting up and preparing the memory buffer for transfer. There are a number of steps to perform. The buffer needs to be pinned down, as a page-out operation on the underlying memory could be disastrous, particularly if the transfer is directed to a storage device. Since some devices can only access memory situated in a 32-bit physical address range, we need to ensure that the physical memory backing our buffer is located in a range the device can access, or we have to ensure it will be copied or remapped. We then need to work out the individual segments of physical memory that our buffer is backed by and capture each segment's physical address and length to create a scatter/gather list. Things may be complicated further depending on the capabilities of the device, if it has special requirements for alignment, or limits on the length of individual segments. Figure 9-5 shows a simple scatter/gather list.

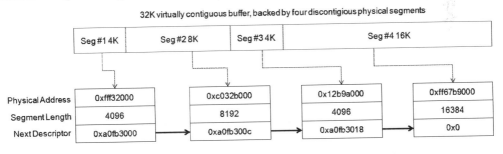

Figure 9-5. Simple scatter/gather list

An actual implementation might be more complex and have additional data associated with each descriptor, but we have kept it simple to illustrate the concept. Figure 9-5 shows how a 32K virtual buffer is composed of four physical segments of different lengths. The scatter/gather list is an array of DMA descriptor elements, each containing a pointer to the next descriptor in the list. Each element has an address and length of the physical segment it represents. When a DMA transfer is started, we can simply tell the device the location of the first descriptor, and the device will read memory from the first descriptor and then follow the next pointer to the next descriptor element until the end of the list, which is terminated by a NULL pointer in this case. Some devices may have S/G lists that connect the last descriptor to the first creating a circular buffer for continuous (streaming) DMA.

In Figure 9-5, we are using a data structure, which in computer science and engineering parlance is known as a singly linked list. It would perhaps be simpler to just implement the list as a standard array. However, the singly linked list approach is more flexible as the S/G list itself can effectively be scatter-gathered, as each DMA descriptor element doesn't necessarily need to be adjacent to each other in memory either.

Translating Physical Addresses to Bus Addresses

Modern computer systems may take advantage of a special memory management unit (MMU) referred to as the IOMMU, or I/O Memory Management Unit. The IOMMU is similar to the system MMU that provides virtual to physical memory translation for the CPU, but the IOMMU differs in that it provides translation to a hardware device instead. When an IOMMU is involved a hardware device will use addresses provided by the IOMMU instead of using physical addresses directly. The term *bus address* is typically used to avoid confusion with physical addresses. Figure 9-6 shows how the IOMMU interacts with a system conceptually.

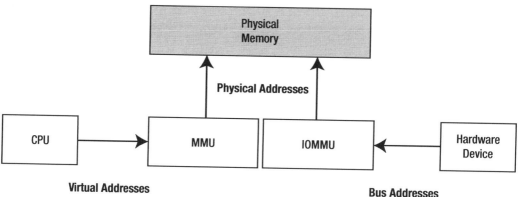

Figure 9-6. IOMMU address translation

When an IOMMU is not used, a hardware device will use the same physical addresses as the CPU. The IOMMU offers many advantages that range from security to performance and solves some of the issues discussed earlier, such as DMA transfers to older devices that are limited to 32-bit addressing. The IOMMU can remap memory, even if the physical memory is located at high memory addresses, so that the device can access the memory. This helps system performance, as the only other solution for this problem is to have a "bounce buffer" that we can copy to and perform DMA from, should the original buffer be located at an address inaccessible to the device. From a security/stability point of view, the IOMMU works like protected/virtual memory does between tasks. PCI devices normally have full access to hardware, so if a driver or device is malfunctioning, it is possible for it to corrupt random parts of memory. The IOMMU can map up a limited aperture and prevent access to addresses outside that window. The IOMMU is traditionally used for virtualization on PC servers as it allows hardware to be shared without interference between virtual machine instances and prevents rogue drivers from performing DMA transfers to parts of memory belonging to other VM instances, which poses a serious security problem.

Mac OS X will take advantage of the IOMMU where present. An IOMMU would be represented by a subclass of the IOMapper class, so you can search for that in IORegistryExplorer to determine if your system has one. Fortunately, we never have to deal with the IOMMU directly. Classes like IOMemoryDescriptor and IODMACommand (discussed later in this chapter) take care of setting this up internally, and we can remain blissfully unaware if the address from functions, such as getPhysicalAddress(), is a bus address mapped by the IOMMU or an actual physical address. Though there should be few reasons to do so, you can implement your own subclass of IOMapper to handle address translation yourself, and supply this to classes such as IODMACommand. IOMMUs were typically only found in high-powered workstations and servers, but are now also found in consumer grade platforms such as Intel's Core i7.

Preparing Memory for DMA

Before a DMA transfer can occur, there are a few things that need to be done to prepare the memory for transfer. The first is to ensure the memory is paged into resident memory, and that the memory pages backing the buffer are locked (pinned) so they will not be paged-out during the DMA transfer. To achieve this, you need to create an IOMemoryDescriptor for the buffer. The memory descriptor must be constructed with the task the buffer belongs to, kernel_task if the kernel owns the buffer, otherwise the task pointer of a user space process. If the direction of transfer is known at this time, you can pass that while constructing the descriptor. The direction will be kIODirectionOut, if memory is to be transferred to the device, and kIODirectionIn, if memory is to be transferred from the device. There is also kIODirectionInOut, which can be used for buffers that need to be used for transfers in either direction. It is important to specify the correct direction as it may have implications for cache-coherency as discussed above.

If you need to DMA from a kernel buffer, the recommended way is to use IOBufferMemoryDescriptor, which is a subclass of IOMemoryDescriptor that also allocates memory for you.

The prepare() method of IOMemoryDescriptor takes care of paging in memory and pinning it down. You can optionally pass the direction of the DMA transfer to prepare() if it wasn't specified at the time the descriptor was initialized.

■ **Caution** Calls to IOMemoryDescriptor::prepare() must be matched with a call to IOMemoryDescriptor::complete(). It is a bug to call complete() on a descriptor that was not previously prepared or prepared unsuccessfully.

Building a Scatter/Gather List

There are several ways of building an S/G list. The most basic way is to use IOMemoryDescriptor::getPhysicalSegment() to enumerate the underlying physical segments as shown in Listing 9-11.

Listing 9-11. Retrieving Physical Segments from a Buffer

```
IOBufferMemoryDescriptor* fDMABuffer =
IOBufferMemoryDescriptor::inTaskWithOptions(kernel_task, kIODirectionOut, 1024 * 1024, 4096);
IOByteCount offset = 0;
while (offset < fDMABuffer->getLength())
{
    IOByteCount segmentLength = 0;
```

```
#ifdef __LP64__
    addr64_t address = fDMABuffer->getPhysicalSegment(offset, &segmentLength);
    // In a real driver, we would store the address and length in a S/G list.
    // We just log it here.
    IOLog("Physical segment: address 0x%llx segmentLength: %llu\n", address, segmentLength);
#else
    addr64_t address = fDMABuffer->getPhysicalSegment(offset, &segmentLength,
kIOMemoryMapperNone);
    IOLog("Physical segment: address 0x%llx segmentLength: %lu\n", address, segmentLength);
#endif
    offset += segmentLength;
}
```

The output of Listing 9-11 will produce something similar to what is shown here:

```
Jun 3 22:28:12 macpro kernel[0]:  Physical segment: address 0x13837000 segmentLength: 4096
Jun 3 22:28:12 macpro kernel[0]:  Physical segment: address 0x143b6000 segmentLength: 4096
Jun 3 22:28:12 macpro kernel[0]:  Physical segment: address 0x1c035000 segmentLength: 4096
...

...
Jul 3 22:28:12 macbook kernel[0]: Physical segment: address 0x14172000 segmentLength: 4096
```

In the preceding output, there were no contiguous segments so every segment consists of a separate page (4096 bytes). However, if we pass the kIOMemoryPhysicallyContiguous flag when we allocate the buffer, we get the following:

```
Jun 3 22:21:08 macpro kernel[0]:  Physical segment: address 0x5975000 segmentLength: 1048576
```

It's not a good idea to allocate memory contiguously in a driver; for a full discussion why, see the section on IOBufferMemoryDescriptor in Chapter 6. We do it here for demonstration purposes.

The approach in Listing 9-11 may work just fine depending on the capabilities of your device, but there are some problems with this technique:

- Some hardware devices have constraints on the maximum or minimum length of a physical segment it can handle in an S/G list.

- The device may require segments of a certain size, for example, page sized segments, so it will match the hardware's buffer. In this case we may need to break larger segments into smaller chunks manually.

- Many hardware devices work with big-endian addressing. Therefore, we need to manually byte swap the physical addresses to ensure that the device actually accesses the correct location.

The IODMACommand Class

The IODMACommand solves a number of the previously discussed problems associated with DMA. It can automatically divide segments to the correct size needed by the hardware, as well as ensure that devices only capable of 32-bit addressing are guaranteed to be in the correct range. This is achieved by using the IOMMU to remap addresses if an IOMMU is present, or by employing a workaround if not. It is also capable of providing 32-bit or 64-bit physical or bus addresses in little or big-endian format. The IODMACommand class supersedes the IOMemoryCursor class, which performs many of the same functions, but offers fewer options.

An instance of the IODMACommand can be constructed with the factory method withSpecification() as following.

```
static IODMACommand * withSpecification(
    SegmentFunction outSegFunc,
    UInt8 numAddressBits,
    UInt64 maxSegmentSize,
    MappingOptions mappingOptions = kMapped,
    UInt64 maxTransferSize = 0,
    UInt32 alignment = 1,
    IOMapper *mapper = 0,
    void *refCon = 0);
```

Let's look at the parameters in more detail. The first parameter is a function pointer to a function that is used to output segment information. You can write your own if you are supporting an esoteric hardware device, however, for most cases, you can use one of the supplied ones:

- kIODMACommandOutputHost32 outputs 32-bit addresses in host byte order

- kIODMACommandOutputBig32 outputs 32-bit addresses in big-endian format

- kIODMACommandOutputLittle32 outputs 32-bit addresses in little-endian format

- kIODMACommandOutputHost64 outputs 64-bit addresses in host byte order

- kIODMACommandOutputBig64 outputs 64-bit addresses in big-endian format

- kIODMACommandOutputLittle64 outputs 64-bit addresses in little-endian format

The next parameter, numAddressBits, allows you to specify the maximum number of address bits the hardware can address, which is not always 32-bit or 64-bit. It can, for example, be 36-bit or even less than 32-bit in some cases. If the value passed is greater than 32-bit, you must specify one of the 64-bit output segment functions.

If physical pages are located at an address higher than what the device can address, some or all pages may be copied to temporary pages that meet the address requirements, unless there is an IOMMU present. Needless to say extra copying is expensive and can be avoided if you DMA from memory allocated by an IOBufferMemoryDescriptor with the inTaskWithPhysicalMask() factory method, as it allows you to allocate memory with physical addresses that are in the range specified by a bitmask. This method can also be used to allocate memory directly into the address space of a user space task. This is useful as DMA to/from user space allocated buffers can be problematic, as there is no way to control how the memory is allocated.

The parameter maxSegmentSize should be set to the largest physical contiguous segment that a device can handle as a segment in a scatter/gather list. Zero can be passed if there are no such restrictions.

The mappingOptions parameter allows bypassing of the IOMMU if one is present in the system. The default is to use the IOMMU. The mapper parameter allows you to specify an alternate IOMapper instance to be used instead of the default.

The maxTransferSize is the total number of bytes that can be transferred per DMA transaction. For example, a hard drive may have 1MB cache buffer, so we would not want to transfer more information than what it can accept.

If the hardware has specific alignment requirements, this can be specified with the alignment parameter. If the supplied memory is not aligned properly, it may again result in the copying or remapping of memory.

Let's modify the previous example in Listing 9-11 that used IOMemoryDescriptor::getPhysicalSegment() to instead use IODMACommand as shown in Listing 9-12.

Listing 9-12. Generating a Scatter/Gather List Using IODMACommand

```
IOReturn com_osxkernel_MyFirstPCIDriver::prepareDMATransfer()
{
    IODMACommand*        dmaCommand;
    IOReturn                        ret = kIOReturnSuccess;

    dmaCommand = IODMACommand::withSpecification(kIODMACommandOutputHost64, 36, 2048,
                IODMACommand::kMapped, 0, 1);
    if (!dmaCommand)
    {
        return kIOReturnNoMemory;
    }

    // Will also prepare the memory descriptor.
    ret = dmaCommand->setMemoryDescriptor(fDMABuffer);
    if (ret != kIOReturnSuccess)
        return ret;

    UInt64 offset = 0;
    while (offset < fDMABuffer->getLength())
    {
        IODMACommand::Segment64 segment;
        UInt32 numSeg = 1;

        ret = dmaCommand->gen64IOVMSegments(&offset, &segment, &numSeg);

        IOLog("%s::gen64IOVMSegments() addr 0x%qx, len %llu bytes\n",
                getName(), segment.fIOVMAddr, segment.fLength);

        if (ret != kIOReturnSuccess)
            break;
    }

    //
    // Setup DMA transfer here for real hardware devices.
    //

    if (dmaCommand->clearMemoryDescriptor() != kIOReturnSuccess)
    {
        IOLog("Failed to clear/complete memory descriptor\n");
    }
```

```
        dmaCommand->release();
        return ret;
}
```

In the previous example, we created an IODMACommand with constraints on the maximum physical address bits we want to 36 bits, and the maximum physical segment size to a half page, or 2048 bytes. The output of this code gives something as follows:

```
kernel[0]: com_osxkernel_MyFirstPCIDriver::gen64IOVMSegments() addr 0x13b9d5000, len 2048
kernel[0]: com_osxkernel_MyFirstPCIDriver::gen64IOVMSegments() addr 0x13b9d5800, len 2048
kernel[0]: com_osxkernel_MyFirstPCIDriver::gen64IOVMSegments() addr 0x1335d4000, len 2048
kernel[0]: com_osxkernel_MyFirstPCIDriver::gen64IOVMSegments() addr 0x1335d4800, len 2048
kernel[0]: com_osxkernel_MyFirstPCIDriver::gen64IOVMSegments() addr 0x3f913000, len 2048
kernel[0]: com_osxkernel_MyFirstPCIDriver::gen64IOVMSegments() addr 0x3f913800, len 2048
kernel[0]: com_osxkernel_MyFirstPCIDriver::gen64IOVMSegments() addr 0x3b1d2000, len 2048
kernel[0]: com_osxkernel_MyFirstPCIDriver::gen64IOVMSegments() addr 0x3b1d2800, len 2048
kernel[0]: com_osxkernel_MyFirstPCIDriver::gen64IOVMSegments() addr 0x18b11000, len 2048
kernel[0]: com_osxkernel_MyFirstPCIDriver::gen64IOVMSegments() addr 0x18b11800, len 2048
....
```

You will notice first that we have some addresses that are greater than 32-bit, but still below our 36-bit specification, and that segments are now limited to 2048 bytes, even though the first segment is physically contiguous with the second.

Summary

In this chapter, we have discussed:

- A technology overview of the PCI related standards PCI Express, Thunderbolt and also the lesser-used ExpressCard standard.

- The PCI configuration space, which is used by the operating system to enumerate, control, and operate PCI–based devices. Later in the chapter, we also discussed how accessing these from a driver using I/O Kit provided functionality.

- PCI support in the I/O Kit with IOPCIFamily. The cornerstone of the kernel PCI layer is the IOPCIDevice class, which is used as a provider for PCI-based drivers.

- Thunderbolt devices are compatible with PCI and also represented by the IOPCIDevice class.

- How to create a matching dictionary for PCI-based devices so that a driver can be loaded automatically when the device is plugged in or at boot.

- How to access and use memory mapped I/O memory and regions.

- How to handle removal of externally connected devices, notably for Thunderbolt and ExpressCard.

- Interrupt handling in the I/O Kit for primary and secondary interrupts using IOInterruptEventFilter and related classes.

- Direct Memory Access and how to create scatter/gather lists for transferring large non-contiguous chunks of memory. We also discussed common problems related to DMA.

- The IODMACommand is used to help translate memory addresses into bus addresses and to help manage the complexity of building scatter/gather lists.

CHAPTER 10

Power Management

Power management has become a fundamental feature across all computing devices. Every platform that runs Mac OS X can be put into a lower power mode, and so power management is just as important for a desktop computer that is always connected to a power supply as it is for a laptop or an iPhone that is running from a battery.

Even a Mac Pro, for example, can be placed into "sleep" mode, which puts the computer and its connected peripherals into a low power mode. During sleep mode, the CPU is put into a suspended state, the computer's display is powered off, and the hard drive is spun down. If the computer has PCI expansion slots, these will be powered down during sleep, with only a small amount of auxiliary power provided to allow a PCI card to initiate waking the computer from sleep.

Not all drivers will need to handle power management events. Whether a driver needs to implement power management will depend on the capabilities of the device and where the device draws power from. For example, if the driver for a PCI device doesn't support power management, the system must maintain full power to its PCI slots when it enters sleep mode because a PCI card is powered from the computer's motherboard. This leaves the computer in a state called "doze", which is not a complete sleep mode. Note that if the power to PCI slots is suspended during sleep, any PCI devices will lose their configuration and must be reinitialized by their driver when the system wakes, which can only happen if the driver receives power management events.

As the example of a PCI card's driver demonstrates, the drivers for hardware devices play a role in the system's transition from one power state to another. Drivers can opt to receive a notification before the system goes into the low power sleep mode, at which time the driver can prepare its device for the new power state. Similarly, a driver can receive a notification when the system wakes from sleep, at which time the driver can restore its device to full operating functionality.

The I/O Registry Power Plane

Part of the complexities of power management is that the power state for one device usually cannot be looked at in isolation, since a device will typically be dependent on another device through which it draws power and, in turn, may have devices that are dependent on it for their power. Consider, for example, a PCI peripheral card that implements a USB host and provides USB ports. The card will be powered by the PCI bus and will provide power over the USB bus to devices that are connected to its ports. This has implications for the power management system; the PCI card can only enter a low power state if there are no USB devices connected to it or only if all of the USB devices connected to it are in a low power state themselves. Similarly, when the system is put to sleep, the PCI slot will lose power, and any USB devices that are connected to the card must be informed of the change in power state as well.

To model this power dependency, the I/O Kit maintains a tree that represents the power dependencies between hardware devices in the system. This tree is stored in its own section of the I/O Registry in a plane known as the "power plane." The power plane can be viewed using the IORegistryExplorer utility, as shown in Figure 10-1.

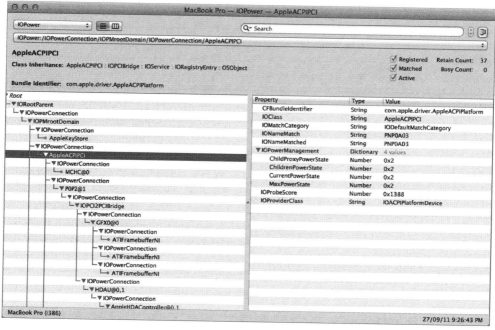

Figure 10-1. *A view of the power plane in IORegistryExplorer*

Each driver that supports power management is represented as a node in the power plane connected to the parent nodes, which represents devices that provide it power, and with children nodes, which represent devices that it provides power to. The parent of a device in the power plane is typically the driver's provider class (that is, the same object that the driver is connected to in the service plane of the I/O Registry), although this does not need to be the case.

The tree representation makes it very easy to visualize the power dependencies between devices in the system and to see which devices draw their power from a particular hardware device. The tree structure also provides an important role for the system itself, since it allows the system to determine which devices will be affected when the power state of one device changes.

Power Management in the I/O Kit

The system's power management, including transitions from one power state to another, is handled by the I/O Kit. Power management is performed by drivers that run in the kernel; user space drivers that can be written for hardware, such as USB devices, cannot play a part in the power management of that device. The I/O Kit provides support for power management in the IOService superclass from which all Mac OS X drivers are ultimately derived. This makes power management accessible to all drivers, providing that the driver has chosen to insert itself into the power plane.

The IOService also manages synchronization between a parent device and the children devices that depend on it for power. For example, before transitioning into a lower power state, the system will ensure that all children devices have transitioned to the lower power state before the parent device, on which they rely on for power, is sent a request to lower its power state. Similarly, when waking from sleep, the system will ensure that a parent device has become fully powered before sending a request to the dependent children devices to raise their power state.

Transitions from one power state to another are incredibly difficult because it can take some time for hardware to change to the new state. This can lead to situations where a power state transition is initiated while an existing power state transition is in progress. For example, a hard disk may spin down due to inactivity, but then a read request may immediately be made, requiring the disk to spin up again. The IOService class handles a lot of the details that would otherwise make power management difficult to implement. Each power state transition is serialized by IOService, and a driver will never receive a power request until it has finished handling its previous power request.

The support provided by the IOService class for power management means that a driver is free to concentrate only on the power management of its own device; the I/O Kit framework will take care of the details that would otherwise make power management difficult to implement.

Power state changes can be initiated by two sources. The system may request that a device be placed into a new power state in response to the computer being put to sleep, or a device (or its driver) may initiate a change of its power state. An example of a device initiating a transition to a lower power state is the computer display switching itself off when the computer hasn't been used for a period of time or a hard disk spinning down if it hasn't received a read or write request for some time

A driver can choose to implement support for either of these two types of power management; it can choose to respond to changes to system power, such as a sleep event, or it can volunteer to lower its power state itself, such as by spinning down its disk. Both of these cases are handled through the I/O Kit and are discussed in this chapter.

In general, power management is necessary for a device that not only has hardware support for being placed into a lower power state but also has the opportunity to be placed into a low power state due to the way that it is used. Depending on the type of hardware device that your driver manages, there may be little work to support transitions between various power states.

■ **Note** This chapter describes the work that a generic I/O Kit driver needs to take to handle power management requests. Certain I/O Kit driver families, such as the audio family, will add their driver to the power plane and respond to power management requests on behalf of the driver. Before adding power management support to your driver, you should check that your driver's superclass is not already handling power requests.

Responding to Power State Changes

The most basic level of power management support that a driver can implement is to opt-in to receive notifications for changes to the overall system power state. These include notifications before the system is put to sleep and a notification when the system wakes from sleep. This is particularly important for the driver of a PCI device, since these notifications need to be handled to allow the PCI bus to be powered down completely during system sleep.

The I/O Kit's power model is unique in that the framework doesn't dictate the set of power states that a driver must implement; rather a driver defines its own list of power states that match the capabilities of the device that it controls. At the very least, a driver must define two states: one in which the device is off, and another in which the device is fully operational. During the off state, the device consumes no power (and so draws no power from its parent in the power plane). In this state, the device is unusable. During the on state, the device is drawing power and all of its functionality is available to the user. When the system is put to sleep, the device is put into the off state, and when the system is awake, the device is put into the on state.

In addition to the off and on states, a driver can define power states that correspond to states in which, for example, the device is still powered but at a lower power state where it is still usable but with reduced capabilities. For example, the driver for an LCD monitor could create a power state to describe a mode in which the display is still running but the backlight has been dimmed.

Each power state that a device supports is described by a structure known as IOPMPowerState, which is defined in the header file <IOKit/pwr_mgt/IOPMpowerState.h>. The IOPMPowerState structure is defined as follows:

```
struct IOPMPowerState
{
        unsigned long    version;
        IOPMPowerFlags   capabilityFlags;
        IOPMPowerFlags   outputPowerCharacter;
        IOPMPowerFlags   inputPowerRequirement;
        unsigned long    staticPower;
        unsigned long    unbudgetedPower;
        unsigned long    powerToAttain;
        unsigned long    timeToAttain;
        unsigned long    settleUpTime;
        unsigned long    timeToLower;
        unsigned long    settleDownTime;
        unsigned long    powerDomainBudget;
};
```

The fields of this structure are described as follows:

- version: Holds the version of this IOPMPowerState structure, allowing the structure to be extended in future versions of the I/O Kit while maintaining backwards compatibility. As of Mac OS X 10.7, the structure is still at version 1; the header file provides a definition kIOPMPowerStateVersion1 that can be used.

- capabilityFlags: A bitmask of flags that describes the capabilities of the device in this power state. Possible flags are:

  - kIOPMPowerOn indicates that the device requires power from its parent and is able to provide power to its children.

  - kIOPMDeviceUsable indicates that the device is usable in this state.

  - kIOPMLowPower indicates that the device is running at a reduced power state compared to the kIOPMPowerOn state. The device may still be usable in this state, which can be indicated by setting both the kIOPMDeviceUsable and kIOPMLowPower bits. The device may or may not be able to provide power to its children while in the low power state.

  - kIOPMPreventIdleSleep is set to disable the system from going to sleep while this power state is active. Note that the user is still able to put the system to sleep (such as by selecting "Sleep" from the Apple menu). It only stops the system from automatically sleeping after a period of inactivity.

- kIOPMInitialDeviceState indicates that the device starts up in this state, and therefore the driver doesn't need to be sent a power request after being loaded. Note that the I/O Kit may decide to start the driver in a power state that doesn't have the kIOPMInitialDeviceState flag set, and in this case, the driver will receive a power request when it loads.

- outputPowerCharacter: A flag that describes the power that the device is able to provide to devices that depend on it for power while in this state. This can be either kIOPMPowerOn, to indicate that the device is able to power its children, or 0, to indicate that the device cannot provide power to its children.

- inputPowerRequirement: A flag that describes the power required by the device from its parent while in this state. This can be either kIOPMPowerOn, to indicate that the device requires its parent to provide it with power, or 0, to indicate that the device does not draw any power from its parent in this state.

- staticPower: The average power consumption of the device while in this state (in milliwatts). Note that if this value is unknown, a driver can provide a value of 0 for this field (as is done by many of the Apple drivers in the Darwin repository).

- unbudgetedPower: The power that this device draws from a separate power supply (and not from its parent) while in this state. This value is currently unused in Mac OS X, and so a driver can provide a value of 0 for this field.

- powerToAttain: The power that this device requires to transition into this state from the previous lower power state. This value is currently unused in Mac OS X, and so a driver can provide a value of 0 for this field.

- timeToAttain: The time required to transition the hardware into this state from the previous lower power state (in microseconds). If this value is unknown, a driver can provide a value of 0 for this field.

- settleUpTime: The time required for the power to settle after entering this state from the previous lower power state (in microseconds). If this value is unknown, a driver can provide a value of 0 for this field.

- timeToLower: The time required to transition the hardware from this state into the next lower power state (in microseconds). If this value is unknown, a driver can provide a value of 0 for this field.

- settleDownTime: The time required for the power to settle after leaving this state and entering the next lower power state (in microseconds). If this value is unknown, a driver can provide a value of 0 for this field.

- powerDomainBudget: The amount of power that the device is able to provide to its children while in this state. This value is currently unused in Mac OS X, and so a driver can provide a value of 0 for this field.

Each power state that a device supports is described by an IOPMPowerState structure. The device's driver creates an array of IOPMPowerState structures, each one of which corresponds to a device power state. Every driver that supports power management must contain a power state that corresponds to the off state (in which the device uses no power) and a power state that corresponds to the device's fully on state (in which the device is fully operational). The off state must be the first element in the driver's power state array, and the on state must be the final element in the driver's power state array. The driver can define as many power states as it needs to describe the distinct power states provided by its hardware device, with the only requirement being that the power state array must be sorted, starting with the off state, through the (optional) intermediate power states that require more power and are more functional, to the final state in which the device is running at its full power and is completely operational.

Because the I/O Kit provides support for power management within the IOService class from which every driver is ultimately derived, all drivers have the ability to take part in the power management of the system. To demonstrate this, we will add power management notifications to the simple IOKitTest sample that was developed in Chapter 4 (see Listing 4-2 and Listing 4-3).

To begin with, we need to define the power states that the device supports. This is typically done with a global array of IOPMPowerState structures that is defined at the top of the driver's implementation file. The example in Listing 10-1 shows a very basic set of power states that provide an off state and an on state.

Listing 10-1. *Defining a Set of Power States for a Driver*

```
enum {
    kOffPowerState,
    kOnPowerState,
    //
    kNumPowerStates
};

static IOPMPowerState gPowerStates[kNumPowerStates] = {
    // kOffPowerState
    {kIOPMPowerStateVersion1, 0, 0, 0, 0, 0, 0, 0, 0, 0, 0, 0},
    // kOnPowerState
    {kIOPMPowerStateVersion1, (kIOPMPowerOn | kIOPMDeviceUsable),
                          kIOPMPowerOn, kIOPMPowerOn, 0, 0, 0, 0, 0, 0, 0, 0}
};
```

When the I/O Kit makes a request to change to a new power state, the requested state will be identified by the index of that state in the gPowerStates array. Rather than referring to a power state by its index, we define an enumeration that allows us to give each power state a symbolic constant, which makes the driver code easier to read and maintain.

Having defined a set of power states, the IOService class, which provides the power management API, needs to be informed that our driver wishes to receive notifications when the system's power state changes. This is done in the driver's start() method, as shown in Listing 10-2.

Listing 10-2. *Registering a Driver for Power Management Support*

```
bool com_osxkernel_driver_IOKitTest::start (IOService *provider)
{
        if (super::start(provider) == false)
                return false;

        // Register driver for power management
        PMinit();
        provider->joinPMtree(this);
        registerPowerDriver(this, gPowerStates, kNumPowerStates);
```

```
        return true;
}
```

The call to the PMinit() method initializes instance variables in the IOService superclass that are needed only for a driver that implements power management. To receive power management notifications, the driver needs to be part of the power plane. This is done by the joinPMtree() method, which is called on the driver object from which our device obtains its power (in this case, our provider class) and takes as its argument the child driver (our instance). Finally, we call the registerPowerDriver() method to provide the I/O Kit with the array of power states that our driver supports.

A driver that registers for power management must make sure that it removes itself from the power plane before it is unloaded. If this is not done, the I/O Kit will attempt to send power notifications to your driver, even though it is no longer active, which could potentially result in a kernel panic. A driver removes itself from the power plane by calling PMStop(), which is shown in Listing 10-3.

Listing 10-3. Removing a Driver from the Power Management System

```
void com_osxkernel_driver_IOKitTest::stop (IOService *provider)
{
        PMstop();
        super::stop(provider);
}
```

Having inserted the driver into the power plane and registered it for power management events, the driver will receive power requests from the I/O Kit in response to changes in the system. When the system's power state changes, for example when the computer is put into a sleep state or wakes from sleep, the I/O Kit will choose one of the power states that the driver registered and request that the driver transition into that new state. These power requests are made to the driver through its setPowerState() method, which is a virtual method defined in the IOService base class. To receive these requests, a driver simply needs to provide its own implementation of setPowerState() in which to handle the change. A sample implementation is shown in Listing 10-4.

Listing 10-4. Responding to a Request to Change the Device's Power State

```
IOReturn com_osxkernel_driver_IOKitTest::setPowerState (unsigned long powerStateOrdinal,
IOService* device)
{
        switch (powerStateOrdinal)
        {
                case kOffPowerState:
                        // Save device configuration (if necessary) and prepare our hardware for
                        // sleep
                        // ...
                        break;
                case kOnPowerState:
                        // Bring our hardware out of sleep and initialize it with the saved
                        // configuration
                        // ...
                        break;
        }
```

```
        return kIOPMAckImplied;
}
```

The parameter named powerStateOrdinal describes the power state that the driver should place its device into. The parameter is expressed as an index into the array of power states that the driver passed to the registerPowerDriver() method during its initialization. In the case of our sample driver, we registered two power states that we handle in a switch statement.

The I/O Kit serializes calls to setPowerState(), so a driver can be sure that it will not receive a request to change power states while it is in the middle of handling an earlier power state transition. However, this does not guarantee that the driver won't receive a request to change power states while it is handling other operations that do not relate to power management. For example, a driver may be performing an asynchronous read operation when a power request is made to transition a driver to the sleep state. In this case, the driver must wait until the read operation has completed before powering down the hardware. This can be achieved by using the standard synchronization primitives that are provided by the I/O Kit. Most I/O Kit drivers will use the combination of a command gate and a work loop to provide synchronization, and so a driver could obtain the command gate in its setPowerState() method to ensure that power events are synchronized with the rest of the driver's code.

As of Mac OS X 10.5, the setPowerState() method is called on its own thread, and so a driver is able to perform actions in its implementation that may block or may otherwise take some time to complete. When the driver has successfully placed the hardware into the new power state, it should return with the result code kIOPMAckImplied.

If your driver will support versions of Mac OS X prior to Mac OS X 10.5, you should not perform blocking operations inside the setPowerState() method, but rather your driver should perform the tasks necessary to place the hardware into the new power state on a background thread. Instead of returning kIOPMAckImplied from the setPowerState() method, your driver should return a non-zero value that indicates the maximum time that your driver requires to place the hardware into the new power state (measured in microseconds). When your background thread has completed switching the hardware to the new device, it signals completion by calling acknowledgeSetPowerState(). Thankfully, none of this code is necessary if you are targeting Mac OS X 10.5 and later.

Requesting Power State Changes

So far we have looked at how a driver responds to requests from the system to change its power state in response to events such as the system being put into the sleep state. However, there are times when a driver may wish to initiate a change in the power state of its device independent of the overall power state of the system. For example, an LCD monitor may dim its backlight after a few minutes of inactivity, or a disk may spin down if it hasn't been accessed for some time.

A driver should use the I/O Kit's power management API even for power state changes that affect only the device that it is controlling. Doing so will not only ensure that any change of power state that is initiated by the driver is synchronized with power state changes requested by the system but it also allows your driver to take advantage of support provided by the I/O Kit for such tasks as installing a timer to monitor the device's activity and request a transition to a lower power state if the device is not accessed for a period of time. Lastly, if there are devices that rely on your hardware for their power, you will need to use the I/O Kit methods to transition your hardware's power so that any children devices are informed of possible changes to their input power.

There are three methods that can be called to change the current power state of a device:

- changePowerStateTo(powerStateOrdinal): Requests a change to the power state at the specified index in the registered power state array.

- `changePowerStateToPriv(powerStateOrdinal)`: Performs a similar function to the previous method, with the difference that this is a protected method in the `IOService` class, and so cannot be called by objects other than the driver itself.

- `makeUsable()`: Requests a power change to the highest power state supported by the driver. This method is typically called by another client of this driver (such as the driver's user client) to ensure that the device is fully functional before it makes further use of the device.

These three methods are implemented by the `IOService` class, and there is typically no need for a driver to override any of these methods. Internally, the implementation of the `makeUsable()` method calls through to the same code path as `changePowerStateToPriv()`, which means that each driver has two power states associated with it: the value requested through `changePowerStateTo()` and the value requested through `changePowerStateToPriv()`/`makeUsable()`.

The power state that the I/O Kit ultimately switches the device to is the maximum of the value requested by `changePowerStateTo()`, the value requested by `changePowerStateToPriv()`, and the maximum state that satisfies the requirements of any children that are dependent on the device for power. If the device has any children in the power plane that require power, then the parent device cannot be placed in a power state that has an `outputPowerCharacter` property that is not `kIOPMPowerOn`.

You may be wondering why the I/O Kit provides two nearly identical methods for setting a device's power state. The private method `changePowerStateToPriv()` allows a driver to set a minimum power level that cannot be affected by any clients of the driver, which only have the ability to call the public `changePowerStateTo()` method. A client may raise the power state above the level set by `changePowerStateToPriv()`, but the driver will never be placed into a power state lower than the value set by `changePowerStateToPriv()`. The one exception to this behavior is when the system is placed into the sleep state, at which time the device will be put into the lowest power state, overriding the power state that has been set through `changePowerStateToPriv()`. When the system wakes from sleep, it returns to the power state that was previously active.

By convention, a driver should set its power state through the protected method `changePowerStateToPriv()`. To remove any influence from the public power level, a driver should place a call to the public method `changePowerStateTo(0)` in its `start()` method after registering the driver for power management. Setting the public power state to 0 allows the power state that is requested by `changePowerStateToPriv()` to be applied without alteration (providing that the power requirements of any children devices can be satisfied).

Because the power state for the device is derived from three possible values, it is recalculated whenever the power state of one of its power children changes or a call it made to either the `changePowerStateTo()` or `changePowerStateToPriv()` method is called. If the calculated power state differs from the current power state of the driver, the I/O Kit will send the driver a request to change its power state. The driver will receive this request as described in the previous section of this chapter, "Responding to Power State Changes", and should respond to the request in the way previously described.

The methods `changePowerStateTo()`, `changePowerStateToPriv()`, and `makeUsable()` are all asynchronous, and may return to the caller before the device has transitioned to its new power state. The implication of this is that a driver that wishes to change its own power state (using, for example, the `changePowerStateToPriv()` method) should wait until its `setPowerState()` method is called before reprogramming its hardware to the new power state. A client that wishes to change the power state of another driver by calling a public method (such as `changePowerStateTo()` or `makeUsable()`) cannot assume that the device is running in the new power state when the method returns. Instead, it should register to receive notifications when the device's state changes. This is discussed in the section "Observing Device Power State Changes" later in this chapter.

Handling Device Idle

A common reason for a driver to lower the power state of its device is to reduce its power consumption when the device hasn't been accessed for a certain period of time. This involves creating a timer for the idle period of the device. If the timer expires and the device hasn't been accessed during that period, the driver places the device into a lower power state. After the device has been placed into a lower power state, the next time that the driver needs to access the device, it will need to place the hardware back in a usable state. Because these operations are common for all drivers that perform an idle power saving mode, this functionality is built into the I/O Kit and provided to driver developers through the IOService class.

There are two basic methods that a driver needs to call to let the I/O Kit track when its device has been idle and lower its power state.

- setIdleTimerPeriod(period): Installs a timer that expires after the specified number of seconds has elapsed.

- activityTickle(type, powerState): Is called by the driver before every access of the device, which informs the I/O Kit of the time at which the hardware was last accessed.

The method setIdleTimerPeriod() is typically called once, following the initialization of power management in the driver's start() method. Once called, the I/O Kit creates a timer that runs at the specified timeout period (in seconds). If the device hasn't been accessed during this period, the I/O Kit will lower the power state of the driver to the state below the driver's current power level. If the device remains inactive for the next idle period, the driver's power state is lowered again. In both cases, the driver receives a request to lower its power state through the same method, setPowerState(), that is used to deliver all power request changes, as described in the section "Responding to Power State Changes" earlier in this chapter. This continues until the device has been placed into the off state (power state 0).

When the device's power state is lowered as a result of inactivity, the I/O Kit sets the power state using the method changePowerStateToPriv(). Just as if the driver had called changePowerStateToPriv() itself, the new power state for the device cannot drop below the value set by the public method changePowerStateTo() or the power state required by the device's children. This means that the public power level that is set through changePowerStateTo() determines the minimum power state that the device can be placed in when idle. Typically, a driver that uses an idle timer will make a call to changePowerStateTo(0) in its start() method, thereby allowing the idle timer to take the device all the way down to the off state.

The idle timer requires the driver to inform the I/O Kit of every access to the hardware device, otherwise the idle timer will fire and lower the power state of the device while it is in use. To do this, the driver makes a call to the activityTickle() method when the device is used, typically at the start of each operation. The signature of the activityTickle() method is provided as follows:

```
bool    activityTickle(unsigned long type, unsigned long stateNumber);
```

The activityTickle() method takes two parameters, a type and a power state ordinal, that the caller uses to specify the minimum power level that the device must be in to handle the upcoming operation. The I/O Kit provides two pre-defined values for the type parameter in the header file <IOKit/pwr_mgt/IOPM.h>:

- kIOPMSubclassPolicy

- kIOPMSuperclassPolicy1

The type parameter defines which implementation should handle the activityTickle() request, either the driver itself (in which case kIOPMSubclassPolicy is passed) or the IOService superclass (in which case kIOPMSuperclassPolicy1 is passed). If the driver wishes to provide a custom implementation of activityTickle(), as well as passing kIOPMSubclassPolicy as the type parameter for each call to activityTickle(), it also needs to override the implementation of the activityTickle() method.

Most drivers, however, will be able to use the default implementation of activityTickle() provided by the IOService superclass. It's important that a driver that wishes to use the default implementation passes a value of kIOPMSuperclassPolicy1 for the type parameter of each call to activityTickle(), since the IOService implementation will ignore a request that has any other value passed as the type parameter.

The default implementation of activityTickle() will raise the power level of the device to the power state specified by the stateNumber parameter. Internally, the IOService class raises the device's power state by calling the changePowerStateToPriv() method, which the driver will receive through a call to its setPowerState() method. The Boolean value returned from the method indicates whether the device was already in the requested power state; a return value of true indicates that no power state transition was necessary, whereas a return value of false indicates that the power state of the device needed to be raised.

Since the activityTickle() method is asynchronous, it is important that the caller wait until the driver has completed the transition to the power state, and should not assume that the device is in a usable state when the activityTickle() method returns. The means by which a driver can observe power changes in a driver, including power changes in other driver objects, is explained in the next section.

Observing Device Power State Changes

The I/O Kit allows a driver to observe the power state of any device in the system and to receive notifications when the device's driver changes its power state. This can be used, for example, by a driver that is not part of the power plane but needs to interface with drivers that are power managed. Alternatively, these notifications allow a driver that initiates a change to its own power state through a method such as changePowerStateToPriv() or activityTickle() to determine when the power change has completed.

To receive notifications when another driver's power state changes, your driver must register for interest in that driver's power state. The IOService superclass provides two methods for doing this:

- registerInterestedDriver(IOService* driver)

- deRegisterInterestedDriver(IOService* driver)

Both of these methods are called on the driver object whose power state you are interested in observing. The parameter to the method is the driver that will receive the notifications, and so you will typically pass the "this" pointer. A driver can call either of these methods at any time to start and stop receiving notifications for changes to the power state of another driver. It is important that a driver deregister any notifications that are installed before it unloads; failure to do so could lead to a kernel panic.

When a driver has registered interest in another driver's power state changes, it will receive a notification before the device begins its transition to the new power state and another notification once the device has completed the transition to the new power state. These two notifications are delivered through the two methods described as follows:

- IOReturn   powerStateWillChangeTo(IOPMPowerFlags capabilities,

                        unsigned long stateNumber, IOService* whatDevice)

- IOReturn   powerStateDidChangeTo(IOPMPowerFlags capabilities,

unsigned long stateNumber, IOService* whatDevice)

These two notification methods are virtual methods that are implemented by the driver that wishes to receive the notifications. The notification powerStateWillChangeTo() is delivered before the observed driver's setPowerState() method is called. The notification powerStateDidChangeTo() is delivered after the observed driver's setPowerState() method is called. Both methods are passed an identical set of arguments. The capabilities argument is the value of the capabilityFlags bitmask from the IOPMPowerState that the observed driver is transitioning to. The stateNumber argument is the index of the power state that the observed driver is transitioning to. The whatDevice argument is the driver object whose power state is being changed.

After handling either notification, the driver should return a value of IOPMAckImplied. If your driver wishes to handle the notification asynchronously, it can return a non-zero value from the notification method that indicates the maximum amount of time (in microseconds) that the driver requires to complete the request. The driver can then continue processing the notification on a background thread; once the driver has completed the notification, it should call the method acknowledgePowerChange() to inform the I/O Kit that the notification has been handled. The method acknowledgePowerChange() can be called to acknowledge both the willChange and didChange notifications.

A driver that handles power management will automatically register for interest in itself, and so the two notification methods will be called for a driver that is responding to a change in its power state. Most drivers, however, will have no need to implement these two notification methods unless the driver is observing the state of another device, since a driver's own power changes should be handled within the setPowerState() method. Instead, for this purpose, the I/O Kit provides another notification method that is sent to a driver when its own power state has been changed and all of its children drivers have acknowledged the power change. To receive this notification method, a driver should implement the following virtual method:

void   powerChangeDone (unsigned long previousStateNumber);

The method is sent once the driver has handled the power state change (through the setPowerState() method) and all drivers that have registered an interest for the device's power state have been notified of the power change. The powerChangeDone() method provides a convenient way for a driver to determine when a power state change that it initiated has been completed and the device has become usable. It is important to note the parameter that is passed to the powerChangeDone() method is the power level that the device changed from and not the new power state of the device. To determine the power state that the device is currently in, the I/O Kit provides an accessor method named getPowerState(), as described as follows:

UInt32 getPowerState(void);

Putting It All Together

In this section, we combine what we have covered in this chapter into a single sample that demonstrates one way of structuring a driver that not only responds to power state changes from the system, but also lowers its own power state when the device has been idle for 5 minutes.

For demonstration purposes, the sample driver defines four power states consisting of the mandatory off and on states, as well as two lower power modes. The off and on state will be set by the power management system when the computer is put to sleep and woken from sleep. The two intermediate states are reached when the device has been left idle for a period; the driver sets up an idle timer in its start() method to lower the device's power state after a period of inactivity.

This sample also demonstrates one approach to synchronizing changes in the device's power state against hardware accesses that the driver makes while performing a requested operation. The driver includes a sample operation called myReadDataFromDevice(), which calls activityTickle() to ensure that the hardware is in a usable power state before attempting to perform the operation. However, since power state changes are asynchronous, the driver needs to wait until the device has fully transitioned to the new power state. The sample driver does this by sleeping on a condition variable that is signaled from the powerChangeDone() method.

Another synchronization problem that this driver needs to handle is that the device cannot be placed into a sleep state if the driver is handling outstanding operations. The sample driver uses an instance variable named m_outstandingIO to keep count of the number of outstanding operations that the driver is processing. If a request is made to lower the power state of the device, the setPowerState() method will wait until all outstanding operations have been completed before it removes the power to the hardware. While waiting for operations to complete, the driver needs to make sure that no further operations are started; this is done by setting the instance variable m_devicePowerState to a lower power state at the start of the setPowerState() method. This means that the m_devicePowerState instance variable will be in the reduced power state while we are waiting for operations to complete but, more importantly, it also means that a new operation, such as myReadDataFromDevice(), will sleep and wait for the device's power to transition to the on state.

The implementation of this sample driver is given in Listing 10-5 and Listing 10-6.

Listing 10-5. A Driver That Can Both Respond to Power State Changes and Can Control its Own Power State (header file)

```
#include <IOKit/IOService.h>

class com_osxkernel_driver_IOKitTest : public IOService
{
        OSDeclareDefaultStructors(com_osxkernel_driver_IOKitTest)


private:
        IOLock*          m_lock;
        unsigned long    m_devicePowerState;
        SInt32           m_outstandingIO;


protected:
        virtual void             powerChangeDone (unsigned long stateNumber);


public:
        virtual void             free (void);
        virtual bool             start (IOService* provider);
        virtual void             stop (IOService* provider);
```

```
        virtual IOReturn setPowerState (unsigned long powerStateOrdinal, IOService* device);

        IOReturn          myReadDataFromDevice ();
};
```

Listing 10-6. A Driver That Can Both Respond to Power State Changes and Can Control its Own Power State (implementation file)

```
#include "IOKitTest.h"
#include <IOKit/IOLib.h>

// Define the superclass
#define super IOService

OSDefineMetaClassAndStructors(com_osxkernel_driver_IOKitTest, IOService)

// Define our power states
enum {
    kOffPowerState,
    kStandbyPowerState,
    kIdlePowerState,
    kOnPowerState,
    //
    kNumPowerStates
};

static IOPMPowerState gPowerStates[kNumPowerStates] = {
    // kOffPowerState
    {kIOPMPowerStateVersion1, 0, 0, 0, 0, 0, 0, 0, 0, 0, 0, 0},
    // kStandbyPowerState
    {kIOPMPowerStateVersion1, kIOPMPowerOn, kIOPMPowerOn, kIOPMPowerOn, 0, 0, 0, 0, 0, 0, 0,
0},
    // kIdlePowerState
    {kIOPMPowerStateVersion1, kIOPMPowerOn, kIOPMPowerOn, kIOPMPowerOn, 0, 0, 0, 0, 0, 0, 0,
0},
    // kOnPowerState
    {kIOPMPowerStateVersion1, kIOPMPowerOn | kIOPMDeviceUsable,
                              kIOPMPowerOn, kIOPMPowerOn, 0, 0, 0, 0, 0, 0, 0, 0}
};


bool com_osxkernel_driver_IOKitTest::start (IOService *provider)
{
    if (super::start(provider) == false)
        return false;

    // Create a lock for driver/power management synchronization
    m_lock = IOLockAlloc();
    if (m_lock == NULL)
```

```
        return false;

    // Register driver for power management
    PMinit();
    provider->joinPMtree(this);
    makeUsable();                    // Set the private power state to the highest level
    changePowerStateTo(kOffPowerState);// Set the public power state to the lowest level
    registerPowerDriver(this, gPowerStates, kNumPowerStates);

    // Lower the device power level after 5 minutes of activity (expressed in seconds)
    setIdleTimerPeriod(5*60);

    return true;
}

void com_osxkernel_driver_IOKitTest::stop (IOService *provider)
{
    PMstop();
    super::stop(provider);
}

void com_osxkernel_driver_IOKitTest::free (void)
{
    if (m_lock)
        IOLockFree(m_lock);
    super::free();
}


IOReturn com_osxkernel_driver_IOKitTest::setPowerState (unsigned long powerStateOrdinal,
                                                IOService* device)
{
    // If lowering the power state, update the saved power state before powering down the
    // hardware
    if (powerStateOrdinal < m_devicePowerState)
        m_devicePowerState = powerStateOrdinal;

    switch (powerStateOrdinal)
    {
        case kOffPowerState:
        case kStandbyPowerState:
        case kIdlePowerState:
                // Wait for outstanding IO to complete before putting device into a lower
                // power state
                IOLockLock(m_lock);
                    while (m_outstandingIO != 0)
                    {
                            IOLockSleep(m_lock, &m_outstandingIO, THREAD_UNINT);
                    }
                IOLockUnlock(m_lock);

                // Prepare our hardware for sleep
```

```
                    // ...
                    break;
        }

        // If raising the power state, update the saved power state after reinitializing the
        // hardware
        if (powerStateOrdinal > m_devicePowerState)
            m_devicePowerState = powerStateOrdinal;

        return kIOPMAckImplied;
}

void com_osxkernel_driver_IOKitTest::powerChangeDone (unsigned long stateNumber)
{
        // Wake any threads that are waiting for a power state change
        IOLockWakeup(m_lock, &m_devicePowerState, false);
}


// *** Sample Device Operation *** //
IOReturn com_osxkernel_driver_IOKitTest::myReadDataFromDevice ()
{
        // Ensure the device is in the on power state
        IOLockLock(m_lock);
            if (activityTickle(kIOPMSuperclassPolicy1, kOnPowerState) == false)
            {
                    // Wait until the device transitions to the on state
                    while (m_devicePowerState != kOnPowerState)
                    {
                            IOLockSleep(m_lock, &m_devicePowerState, THREAD_UNINT);
                    }
            }

        // Increment the number of outstanding operations
        m_outstandingIO += 1;
        IOLockUnlock(m_lock);

        // Perform device read ...

        // When the operation is complete, decrement the number of outstanding operations
        IOLockLock(m_lock);
            m_outstandingIO -= 1;
            // Wake any threads that are waiting for a change in the number of outstanding
            // operations
            IOLockWakeup(m_lock, &m_outstandingIO, false);
        IOLockUnlock(m_lock);

        return kIOReturnSuccess;
}
```

In an actual driver, the method named myReadDataFromDevice() would be called in response to an action taken by the user that requires the hardware device to be accessed. As such, the method can be called irregularly and may be called at any time. Although we don't call the method myReadDataFromDevice() in the example in Listing 10-6, the code could be extended to add a user client to the driver, allowing a user space process to call the method myReadDataFromDevice().

Summary

- Every computer that runs Mac OS X has the ability to be placed in a low power mode known as "sleep". While in sleep mode, most hardware components are either powered down completely or are provided with only a reduced current.

- A device driver can register and respond to requests from the power management system to prepare its hardware for a loss of power before sleep and to restore the state of its hardware when the system is woken from sleep.

- The I/O Kit's power management API is implemented by the IOService base class. This makes it possible for every driver to provide support for power management.

- A driver may opt to lower the power state of its device independently of whether the computer is in the sleep mode. This can be useful for reducing the power consumption of the device when it has not been used for a period of time.

- A driver can observe the power state of any hardware device in the system. This can be used by a driver to receive a notification before a device changes its power state and a notification after the device has transitioned to its new power state.

CHAPTER 11

Serial Port Drivers

A serial port provides a basic communications interface for the purpose of getting low bandwidth data into and out of a computer. Although modern interfaces such as USB and FireWire have replaced many applications in which the traditional serial port was once used, the serial port driver is still well supported in modern day operating systems, including Mac OS X, despite the fact that Apple has not released hardware with a built-in serial port for over a decade.

There are several reasons for the longevity of the serial port. First, a serial port is simple and inexpensive to implement in hardware, making it a popular choice for hobbyists who are adding computer communications to their electronic projects. Second, it is a very flexible interface. The serial driver is concerned only with transferring data bytes between the serial port and the user space application. The driver plays no role in interpreting the data stream; it simply deals with the transmission of the data.

This leaves the user space application to implement the protocol of the connected device, which means that much of the work that would usually be done by a driver is instead left to the user space application. This means that a hardware vendor doesn't have to provide a driver for their device; they can simply publish the protocol describing the format of the data that they transmit over their serial port, and leave the implementation of the protocol for others. Devices that use serial ports include GPS receivers and barcode scanners. They are also commonly used to provide debugging output on hardware.

Serial ports are no longer found on Macintosh computers; they have been replaced by USB and FireWire ports. Serial devices, such as GPS receivers and barcode scanners, attach to a computer by USB, but they appear to the system as a USB-based serial port that a user space application can connect to. If you are interacting with a device that communicates over a serial port, in nearly all cases your application will be able to use an existing serial port driver. There are very few cases where you will need to implement your own serial port driver; even projects that use a USB-based serial port will use standard drivers to provide the serial port interface.

This chapter describes how a serial port driver is implemented within the I/O Kit, and how to read and write from a serial port in a user space application. The implementation of a serial port driver can be seen as a practical example of driver techniques, including implementing blocking calls, circular buffers, and synchronization and notification. Therefore, even if a serial port driver is not directly relevant to you, the concepts that we will cover can be applied to other drivers.

Mac OS X Serial Port Architecture Overview

On Mac OS X, serial ports have an interesting architecture. In the kernel, a serial driver is implemented using the object-oriented I/O Kit framework, but in user space it is accessed through the BSD layer, and the serial port is presented as a traditional UNIX device file. For each serial driver that is loaded in the kernel, the I/O Kit's serial family creates a corresponding device object in the /dev directory of the file system. To interact with a serial port, applications open the device file and read and write to it as if it were an ordinary file. This is an alternative to communicating with a driver through a user client; in fact, serial drivers don't have a user client. The advantage of this architecture is that it allows traditional UNIX applications that have been written using the POSIX APIs to access a serial port on Mac OS X without any changes to their code.

Although serial port drivers are not accessed through the I/O Kit framework from user space, they are still implemented in the kernel as a full I/O Kit driver. This means that a serial driver can take advantage of all of the features that the I/O Kit brings, including object-oriented design and dynamic driver loading and matching. The I/O Kit includes a family that is specific to serial devices, known as the IOSerialFamily. The IOSerialFamily, which is available through the Darwin open source project, contains the header files for the base classes that a serial port driver is derived from, as well as the implementation of the serial port subsystem of Mac OS X.

Figure 11-1 shows the various entities that are involved in handling communications over a serial port on Mac OS X. For this example, we have assumed that the serial port is implemented by a USB device (such as a USB to RS-232 adapter), which is why the leftmost provider object in the diagram is an IOUSBDevice.

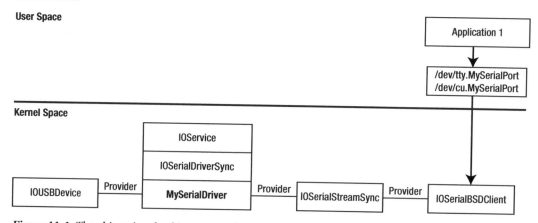

Figure 11-1. The objects involved in communicating with a serial port from a user space application

Starting in user space, an application connects to a serial port driver by opening a character device file from the /dev directory that corresponds to the serial port driver. Each serial driver has two entries in the /dev directory, one whose name begins with the prefix "tty." and another whose name begins with the prefix "cu.". The reason for this is largely historical and comes from a time when the serial port was the means by which a modem or a fax was connected to a computer. In this situation, the "tty" device was the dial-in device that was used to receive a call, and the "cu" was the callout device that was used to make a call.

A process that wished to receive a call would open the dial-in device; the open function would block until the carrier detect line was signaled, meaning that the modem had established a connection. However, to make an outgoing call, a process needed to be able to open the serial port without waiting for the carrier detect line, so it would open the callout device, which doesn't block on the carrier detect signal. When communicating with modern serial devices, given that most devices will not be connected to a phone line, Apple recommends opening the callout device.

The two device files in /dev are created by an I/O Kit class known as IOSerialBSDClient. This is a class that is provided by the IOSerialFamily and handles the kernel-side of operations that are made by a user space process on the device file. The IOSerialBSDClient handles any system call made by a user space process to operate on a serial port, including any of the following the functions: open(), close(), read(), write(), ioctl(), and select(). In this way, the IOSerialBSDClient can be thought of as playing the role of the user client for a serial driver (although it isn't derived from the IOUserClient class). Like a user client, the IOSerialBSDClient class is simply a conduit between a user space process and the kernel driver object. The class is responsible for handling the differences between blocking and non-blocking calls, but its main role is to translate function calls received from user space into method calls to the IOSerialStreamSync object.

The IOSerialStreamSync class is another class that is provided by the I/O Kit in the IOSerialFamily package. Its role is nothing more than a conduit between the IOSerialBSDClient and the implementation of the actual serial driver. In fact, for each method of the IOSerialStreamSync class, it calls a method of the same name in the IOSerialDriverSync class.

The IOSerialDriverSync class is a pure abstract interface that provides the base class for any serial driver on Mac OS X. It provides methods for reading and writing data, and for reporting changes in the state of the serial port, such as whether a carrier signal has been detected, the arrival of data on the serial port for reading, and whether the serial port can accept more bytes for transmission.

Finally, the last object that is involved in the serial driver stack is the provider class of the serial driver. In this example, we are assuming that the serial port is implemented by a USB-to-serial adapter, which is why the provider class has the type IOUSBDevice. Whenever the serial port driver needs to read data from the serial port or write data over the serial port, it will access the underlying hardware device through the IOUSBDevice instance.

The role of each class that plays a part in implementing a serial port driver is as follows:

- The serial port driver's provider class, IOUSBDevice in our example, performs the data transfer into and out of the computer to the serial port adapter.

- The main driver, which is a subclass of IOSerialDriverSync, manages the serial port's receive and transmit buffers, reading data from the hardware as it arrives, and writing data to the hardware when it is provided by user space.

- The IOSerialBSDClient manages interaction with user space applications.

Serial Port Drivers

Serial port drivers on Mac OS X are implemented by creating a class that is derived from the IOSerialDriverSync class. In this section, we describe the implementation of a serial port driver by walking through the source code of a driver provided by Apple for USB serial communication devices. Although it is unlikely that you will need to implement your own serial driver directly, this section can be seen as providing a working application of I/O Kit techniques and driver design, and many of the techniques used by the Apple USB serial driver can potentially be applied to other drivers that you will develop.

To follow along with this section, you may wish to download the source code for the serial port driver that we are discussing. The classes that play a part in the kernel serial driver stack are spread between the following two projects in the Darwin source code repository:

- The base classes, on which all serial drivers are built, including the implementation of the IOSerialBSDClient class, are contained within the IOSerialFamily project. To implement your own serial port driver, you would need only the classes contained within the IOSerialFamily project.

- The driver that loads against USB-based serial communication devices is contained within the project named AppleUSBCDCDriver. (USBCDC is an acronym for USB Communications Device Class.)

Given the number of supporting classes that are created to handle a serial port driver by the I/O Kit, it's instructive to understand how these classes are instantiated. When a USB device that implements the Communications Device Class is connected to a Mac, the USB host controller will create a new IOUSBDevice object to represent that device. When this IOUSBDevice object is published, it initiates the I/O Kit's driver matching process, which searches for an appropriate driver for the USB device. In this case, the I/O Kit will select the AppleUSBCDC driver, since its matching dictionary specifies that it should load against any USB device that supports the Communications Device Class. Note that the AppleUSBCDC driver is not a serial driver. It is a subclass of the generic IOService class, and its role is simply to configure the USB hardware for use as a serial device. It does this by iterating over the USB interfaces that the device supports and setting the active interface to one that provides communications support.

Once the AppleUSBCDC driver has configured the active USB device interface, the I/O Kit's USB family creates an IOUSBInterface object to represent the active interface. This kicks off another round of the I/O Kit's driver matching process, which searches for an appropriate driver for the IOUSBInterface object. For the purpose of this section, we will examine the implementation of the AppleUSBCDCDMM class, which will match against any IOUSBInterface object that implements a specific type of USB Communications Devices. This class is implemented in the file AppleUSBCDCDMM.cpp, and the class is declared in the file AppleUSBCDCDMM.h.

The AppleUSBCDCDMM class is a direct subclass of the IOSerialDriverSync class, so it is responsible for implementing the methods that are required for a serial port driver. To send and receive data over the hardware device, the AppleUSBCDCDMM class sends USB transfer requests to its provider class, which is an IOUSBInterface object.

Manually Instantiating a Driver Object

Until this point, the instantiation and loading of kernel objects has been fairly standard and has followed the same I/O Kit driver matching process that all drivers go through. However, a serial port driver is different from many drivers that you will write, in that it has a child driver. Thus, your serial port driver will act as the provider for another I/O Kit driver.

The child of a serial port driver is an object that inherits from the IOSerialStreamSync class (or a class that is derived from IOSerialStreamSync). For a serial port driver, its child driver isn't created through the I/O Kit's driver matching procedure; rather, the child driver object is explicitly instantiated and attached to the serial driver by the serial driver itself.

In the case of the AppleUSBCDCDMM driver, the child driver has the type IOModemSerialStreamSync, a class that inherits directly from the IOSerialStreamSync class. The AppleUSBCDCDMM class instantiates its child object in a method named createSerialStream(), which is called from the serial port driver's start() method. The method createSerialStream() is a custom method that is private to the AppleUSBCDCDMM class. A sample implementation of createSerialStream() that is based on the AppleUSBCDCDMM driver is shown in Listing 11-1.

*Listing 11-1. The Implementation of a Method to Create the IOSerialStreamSync Object of a Serial Port
Driver*

```
#include <IOKit/serial/IOModemSerialStreamSync.h>
#include <IOKit/serial/IOSerialKeys.h>

bool    MySerialDriver::createSerialStream()
{
        IOSerialStreamSync*    pChild;
        bool                   result;

        // Instantiate the child driver object
        pChild = new IOModemSerialStreamSync;
        if (pChild == NULL)
                return false;

        // Initialize the child driver
        result = pChild->init(0, 0);
        if (result == false)
                goto bail;

        // Attach pChild as a child device of ourself
        result = pChild->attach(this);    // Pass "this" as the child driver's provider
        if (result == false)
                goto bail;

        // Setup the properties used when naming the device file in /dev
        pChild->setProperty(kIOTTYBaseNameKey, "my_serial");
        pChild->setProperty(kIOTTYSuffixKey, "");

        // Allow matching of drivers that use pChild as their provider class
        pChild->registerService();

        // Fall-through on success
 bail:
        pChild->release();
        return result;
}
```

The code in Listing 11-1 provides an example of how a driver can instantiate its own child driver
explicitly, without having to create a property list file for the child driver and have the I/O Kit's matching
mechanism invoked. The three basic steps to creating a new driver object are: (1) allocating an instance
of the driver class by calling the C++ new operator, (2) initializing the returned object by calling its init()
method, and (3) attaching the driver object to its parent through the attach() method. The parameter
passed to attach() is the provider class of the child device, which will typically be the object that
instantiated the child driver.

You will notice that because the embedded C++ language used by the I/O Kit does not support
exceptions, to check whether the call to the C++ new operator has failed, we check to see if the returned
value is NULL. Note that we unconditionally release a reference to the child object before returning from
the method; if the call to attach() succeeded, the child driver object will be retained by the I/O Kit, so

the call to release() at the end of the method won't destroy the object but will release the reference to the object that we hold (preventing a leak). On the other hand, if the child driver failed in its init() method or couldn't be attached, we need to release (and destroy) the child driver object.

The IOModemSerialStreamSync class that is instantiated by the createSerialStream() method performs the role of a conduit between two classes, namely the IOSerialBSDClient class that handles operations on the serial port that are performed by user space applications, and the implementation of the serial port driver (MySerialDriver in the previous example). However, the serial port driver has no direct access to the IOSerialBSDClient class. To specify the name of the character device file that is created in the /dev directory, it needs to be able to pass certain parameters to the IOSerialBSDClient's initialization method. To do this, it sets two properties on the IOSerialStreamSync object before the IOSerialBSDClient class is created, and the IOSerialBSDClient object is then able to read these properties in its initialization.

The serial port driver calls the registerService() method on the IOSerialStreamSync object, which informs the I/O Kit that it should begin the matching procedure for the child device. Any driver that wishes to use the IOSerialStreamSync object as its parent (provider class) will be loaded. This is the means by which the IOSerialBSDClient class is loaded and attached to the IOSerialStreamSync object created by the serial port driver. The IOSerialFamily kernel module contains a matching dictionary for the IOSerialBSDClient class which matches against any IOSerialStreamSync object (or a class derived from IOSerialStreamSync).

■ **Note** In general, a driver that explicitly instantiates and attaches a child driver to itself should not need to call registerSerivce() for the child driver, since this will usually be taken care of by the child driver itself. However, in the case of the IOSerialStreamSync class, it does not register itself for driver matching, so after instantiating it we explicitly call its registerDriver() method.

When the IOSerialStreamSync class is registered with the I/O Kit, an instance of the IOSerialBSDClient class is created and attached, completing the set of driver objects that are required for a serial port. When the IOSerialBSDClient class is initialized, it creates two device nodes for the serial port in the /dev directory, one corresponding to the dial-in character device file and the other corresponding to the callout character device file. To determine the name to give these files, the IOSerialBSDClient class reads the value of the kIOTTYBaseNameKey and the kIOTTYSuffixKey properties and then creates two files using the format:

"tty." + kIOTTYBaseNameKey + kIOTTYSuffixKey

and

"cu." + kIOTTYBaseNameKey + kIOTTYSuffixKey

For the example in Listing 11-1, this results in a character device file with the name tty.my_serial for the dial-in device and a character device file with the name cu.my_serial for the callout device.

Implementing the IOSerialDriverSync Class

Serial drivers on Mac OS X must be derived from the IOSerialDriverSync class. The IOSerialDriverSync class is a pure abstract class that provides an interface that must be implemented by the serial driver. The methods that must be implemented by a serial driver are given in Listing 11-2.

Listing 11-2. The Interface of IOSerialDriverSync, Which Declares the Methods That Must Be Implemented by a Serial Port Driver

```
class IOSerialDriverSync : public IOService
{
        OSDeclareAbstractStructors(IOSerialDriverSync);

public:
        virtual IOReturn  acquirePort(bool sleep, void *refCon) = 0;

        virtual IOReturn  releasePort(void *refCon) = 0;

        virtual IOReturn  setState(UInt32 state, UInt32 mask, void *refCon) = 0;

        virtual UInt32    getState(void *refCon) = 0;

        virtual IOReturn  watchState(UInt32 *state, UInt32 mask, void *refCon) = 0;

        virtual UInt32    nextEvent(void *refCon) = 0;

        virtual IOReturn  executeEvent(UInt32 event, UInt32 data, void *refCon) = 0;

        virtual IOReturn  requestEvent(UInt32 event, UInt32 *data, void *refCon) = 0;

        virtual IOReturn  enqueueEvent(UInt32 event, UInt32 data,
                                bool sleep, void *refCon) = 0;

        virtual IOReturn  dequeueEvent(UInt32 *event, UInt32 *data,
                                bool sleep, void *refCon) = 0;

        virtual IOReturn  enqueueData(UInt8 *buffer, UInt32 size, UInt32 *count,
                                bool sleep, void *refCon) = 0;

        virtual IOReturn  dequeueData(UInt8 *buffer, UInt32 size, UInt32 *count,
                                UInt32 min, void *refCon) = 0;
};
```

You will notice that each method is provided with a parameter named "refCon". The refCon value can be used by a serial port driver to identify which serial port the method is operating on. The refCon value is actually specified by the serial port driver itself, and is passed to the IOSerialStramSync object at instantiation. In return, the IOSerialStreamSync class passes this refCon value back to the driver whenever it calls a method from the driver's class. In most cases, the refCon value is not needed, since any data that the serial port driver needs can be added as instance variables to the driver class. However, in the case of a serial port driver that manages hardware with multiple serial ports, such as a USB adapter with a COM1 and a COM2 port, the driver would need some way to identify which port is being referred to in a method call. To do this, the serial driver would create two instances of the IOSerialStreamSync class, one for each of its hardware ports, and provide a unique refCon value for each port.

The interface may appear to be daunting, but the methods can be broken into three categories:

- Methods that adjust the serial port's status and watch for changes in the serial port's state

- Methods that get or set properties of the serial port

- Methods that read and write data over the serial port

The following are brief descriptions of the methods defined by the IOSerialDriverSync interface:

- Opening and closing the serial port:
  acquirePort()
  releasePort()

- Managing a bitmask that represents the state of the serial port, and blocking the calling thread until a particular condition occurs. State bits describe such conditions as whether the serial port has been opened, whether data has been received over the serial port and is available for reading, and whether the serial port can accept bytes for writing:
  setState()
  getState()
  watchState()

- Setting properties of the serial port:
  executeEvent()
  enqueueEvent()

- Getting properties of the serial port:
  nextEvent()
  requestEvent()

- Writing data over the serial port:
  enqueueData()

- Reading data that has been received from the serial port:
  dequeueData()

One of the complexities in implementing the IOSerialDriverSync interface is that it requires careful synchronization. The interface methods may be called from multiple threads at any time, meaning that the implementation needs to make sure that each method is correctly synchronized to prevent such situations as the dequeueData() method returning data once the serial port has been closed. To further complicate matters, several methods may block the calling thread until a particular event occurs; this is particularly true of the watchState() method, which doesn't return until the serial port has entered a requested state. Both of these synchronization problems can be solved by using a mutex lock and a condition variable to signal changes in the serial port's state.

In the case of the AppleUSBCDCDMM driver, there is an even greater synchronization problem; the methods called through the IOSerialDriverSync interface need to be coordinated with callbacks that fire upon the completion of an asynchronous transfer over USB. This is necessary to prevent the completion callback for a USB write from placing data into a buffer at the same time that the dequeueData() method attempts to read out of that same buffer.

Although this description paints the picture of a very difficult synchronization problem, the I/O Kit design offers a surprisingly elegant solution. All USB completion callbacks are run on the USB work loop, so to synchronize serial port methods with USB code, the AppleUSBCDCDMM driver ensures that all serial port methods are handled on the USB work loop. This is performed as follows:

```
bool AppleUSBCDCDMM::start(IOService *provider)
{
        ...
        // Get the USB work loop (superclass will use the provider class' work loop)
        fWorkLoop = getWorkLoop();

        ...
        // Create a command gate and install it on the USB work loop
        fCommandGate = IOCommandGate::commandGate(this);
        fWorkLoop->addEventSource(fCommandGate);

        ...
}
```

For each serial port method, the AppleUSBCDCDMM driver calls each method through the command gate, ensuring that it is synchronized to the USB work loop. This is shown below for the implementation of releasePort():

```
IOReturn AppleUSBCDCDMM::releasePort(void *refCon)
{
        IOReturn        ret = kIOReturnSuccess;

        // Call the static method releasePortAction() on the work loop, which requires no
        // parameters
        ret = fCommandGate->runAction(releasePortAction);

        return ret;
}

IOReturn AppleUSBCDCDMM::releasePortAction(OSObject *owner, void *, void *, void *, void *)
{
        // Call through to the method releasePortGated()
        return ((AppleUSBCDCDMM*)owner)->releasePortGated();
}

IOReturn AppleUSBCDCDMM::releasePortGated()
{
        ...
        // Implementation of releasePort
        ...
}
```

The IOCommandGate also provides an object that a thread can sleep on and can be used to signal sleeping threads when an event occurs. As we will see, this provides a convenient means for implementing the serial port watchState() method.

Serial Port State

A central part of implementing the IOSerialDriverSync interface is managing the serial port's state. The serial port state is a bitfield of 32-bits that is used to report events, such as the arrival of data on the serial port, as well as to save the overall state of the port, such as whether it has been opened by a user space process or not. Although there are methods that are directly involved in manipulating the state bitmask, ultimately every method that the serial port implements from IOSerialDriverSync will need to access the serial port's state, even if for no other reason than to verify that the serial port has been opened before attempting to perform an operation.

The state bits are defined in the header file IOSerialStreamSync.h. The meaning of each bit is described as follows:

- PD_S_ACQUIRED indicates that the serial port has been opened and is in use by a user space application. This state bit is never set or cleared through the setState() method but rather is set in the acquirePort() method and cleared in the releasePort() method.

- PD_S_ACTIVE is set immediately following the acquisition of the serial port and is cleared immediately before the serial port is released. This state bit is never set or cleared through the setState() method; instead, the bit is set or cleared through the executeEvent() method, which uses an event type of PD_E_ACTIVE to manipulate this state bit.

- PD_S_TX_ENABLE and PD_S_RX_ENABLE are set to indicate that the serial port's transmit and receive interfaces are enabled. Most implementations, including the AppleUSBCDCDMM driver, set these bits when the serial port is opened and clear them when the serial port is closed, but otherwise make no other use of these state bits.

- PD_S_TX_BUSY and PD_S_RX_BUSY are set to indicate that the serial port driver is in the middle of sending data from its transmit buffer to the serial port hardware, or it is in the middle of reading data that has been sent over the serial port hardware into a driver buffer.

- PD_S_TX_EVENT and PD_S_RX_EVENT are two states that are used internally by the IOSerialBSDClient class to signal the beginning of a write or read operation. Although these state bits are unused by the serial driver, it needs to set the corresponding bit in setState() and allow a client to observe the bit through watchState() to ensure that the IOSerialBSDClient operates correctly.

A number of bits describe the status of the serial driver's transmit and receive buffers. The transmit buffer is used by the serial driver to hold bytes that it has been provided with through the enqueueData() method but that it has yet to send over the serial port hardware. The receive buffer holds bytes that the serial driver has read from the serial port hardware but has yet to pass on through the dequeueData() method. Following are descriptions of the serial driver buffer state bits:

- PD_S_TXQ_EMPTY and PD_S_RXQ_EMPTY indicate that the transmit buffer or receive buffer is empty and contains no bytes.

- PD_S_TXQ_LOW_WATER and PD_S_RXQ_LOW_WATER indicate that the number of bytes in the transmit buffer or receive buffer is below a "low water level." The AppleUSBCDCDMM driver sets the low water level to be one-third of the size of the overall transmit buffer or receive buffer.

- PD_S_TXQ_HIGH_WATER and PD_S_RXQ_HIGH_WATER indicate that the number of bytes in the transmit buffer or receive buffer is above a "high water level." The AppleUSBCDCDMM driver sets the high water level to be two-thirds of the size of the overall transmit buffer or receive buffer.

- PD_S_TXQ_FULL and PD_S_RXQ_FULL indicate that the transmit buffer or receive buffer is completely full and cannot accept any further data.

The header file IORS232SerialStreamSync.h defines status bits for the standard RS-232 signals. For example, definitions are provided for signals such as Clear To Send (PD_RS232_S_CTS) and Data Terminal Ready (PD_RS232_S_DTR). The state of software flow control, which uses the transmission of special XON and XOFF characters, is indicated through state bits PD_RS232_S_TXO and PD_RS232_S_RXO.

A serial port driver maintains a 32-bit integer that holds a bitmask of the state bits that describe the current state of the serial port. A serial driver must implement the following three methods to allow the serial port state to be manipulated: getState(), setState(), and watchState(). As well as being called by the IOSerialBSDClient class when it requires access to the state of the serial port, these three methods are called in the implementation of many other methods in the serial port class.

For example, the serial port method acquirePort(), which is called to open a serial port for exclusive access, and releasePort(), which is called to close the serial port, do so by setting the state bit PD_S_ACQUIRED. A possible implementation of the acquirePort() method is shown in Listing 11-3. This sample uses setState() to set the PD_S_ACQUIRED bit. If the serial port has already been acquired and the caller has requested that the method should block until the serial port becomes free, the implementation calls watchState() to wait until the PD_S_ACQUIRED state bit has been cleared.

Listing 11-3. A Sample Implementation of the acquirePort() Method. The Method Is Assumed to Have Been Called Through an IOCommandGate.

```
IOReturn        MySerialDriver::acquirePortGated (bool sleep, void* refCon)
{
        UInt32      state;
        IOReturn    rtn;

        // If the serial port is already acquired, wait until it is released
        while (m_currentState & PD_S_ACQUIRED)
        {
                // Abort if the caller has requested non-blocking operation
                if (sleep == false)
                        return kIOReturnExclusiveAccess;

                // Sleep until the acquired bit becomes clear
                state = 0;
                rtn = watchState(&state, PD_S_ACQUIRED, refCon);
                if (rtn != kIOReturnSuccess)
                        return rtn;
        }

        // Set the acquired bit and clear all other state bits
        setState(PD_S_ACQUIRED, 0xFFFFFFFF, refCon);

        // Serial port has been acquired, perform further initialization
        ...
```

```
        return kIOReturnSuccess;
}
```

A possible implementation of the releasePort() method, which uses setState() to clear the PD_S_ACQUIRED state is given in Listing 11-4.

Listing 11-4. A Sample Implementation of the releasePort() Method. The Method Is Assumed to Have Been Called Through an IOCommandGate.

```
IOReturn        MySerialDriver::releasePortGated (void* refCon)
{
        // Return an error if trying to release a port that hasn't been acquired
        if ((m_currentState & PD_S_ACQUIRED) == 0)
                return kIOReturnNotOpen;

        // Clear the entire state word, which also deactivates the port
        setState(0, 0xFFFFFFFF, refCon);

        return kIOReturnSuccess;
}
```

Often, the IOSerialBSDClient class, or even the serial port driver itself, needs to block the current thread until a particular state has become active or inactive. The serial driver provides this functionality through a method named watchState(). The events that the caller wishes to observe are described by two parameters. The "mask" parameter contains a bitmask of the state bits that the caller wishes to observe. The "state" parameter describes the corresponding value of each state bit that the caller wishes to observe. For example, if a bit is set in "mask", but not set in "state", the caller is interested in that state becoming inactive. If a bit is set in "mask" and also set in "state", the caller is interested in that state becoming active.

The watchState() method will return as soon as any of the observed state bits match the current state of the serial port. Upon return, the current state of the serial port is returned to the caller through the "state" parameter. If the serial port is closed while a thread is blocked in watchState(), the sleep will be aborted and the method will fail and return an error code to the caller, such as kIOReturnNotOpen. The following code gives an example of how watchState() can be used; this code will block until either the driver's transmit buffer becomes empty (PD_S_TXQ_EMPTY is set) or the hardware finishes a write to the serial port hardware (PD_S_TX_BUSY is clear):

```
UInt32          state;
IOReturn        rtn;

state = PD_S_TXQ_EMPTY;
rtn = watchState(&state, PD_S_TXQ_EMPTY | PD_S_TX_BUSY, refCon);
if (rtn != kIOReturnSuccess)
        handle error;
```

The implementation of the watchState() method is closely related to the implementation of the setState() method. As well as setting bits in the serial port state word, the setState() method is also responsible for waking any threads that are waiting for a particular state to be set. In Chapter 7, we introduced condition variables and saw how one thread could sleep on a condition variable and remain blocked until another thread signaled the condition variable to indicate that an event had occurred. This provides a mechanism that a serial port driver can use to suspend a thread in the watchState() method and to signal it from the setState() method when the observed state has changed.

When the setState() method is called, the serial driver updates a variable that maintains the current serial port state, and then signals all threads that are blocked in the watchState() method, allowing them to test whether the state on which they are waiting has become active. As an optimization, rather than waking up threads blocked in watchState() for every change to the serial port state, the AppleUSBCDCDMM driver maintains a union of all state bits that are being waited on across all current calls to watchState(), and will only unblock the threads if the value of a state bit that is being watched has changed.

A sample implementation of the setState() and watchState() methods is provided in Listing 11-5.

Listing 11-5. A Sample Implementation of the setState() and watchState() Methods. The Methods Are Assumed to Have Been Called Through an IOCommandGate.

```
IOReturn        MySerialDriver::setStateGated(UInt32 state, UInt32 mask, void* refCon)
{
        UInt32    newState;
        UInt32    deltaState;

        // Verify that the serial port has been acquired or is being acquired by this call
        if ((m_currentState & PD_S_ACQUIRED) || (state & PD_S_ACQUIRED))
        {
                // Compute the new state
                newState = (m_currentState & ~mask) | (state & mask);
                // Determine the mask of changed state bits
                deltaState = newState ^ m_currentState;
                // Set the new state
                m_currentState = newState;

                // If any state that is being observed by a thread in watchState() has changed,
                // wake up all threads asleep on watchState()
                if (deltaState & m_watchStateMask)
                {
                        // Reset watchStateMask; it will be regenerated as each watchStateGated()
                        // sleeps
                        m_watchStateMask = 0;
                        fCommandGate->commandWakeup((void*)&m_currentState);
                }

                return kIOReturnSuccess;

        }

        return kIOReturnNotOpen;
}

IOReturn        MySerialDriver::watchStateGated(UInt32* state, UInt32 mask, void* refCon)
{
        UInt32     watchState;
        bool       autoActiveBit = false;
        IOReturn   ret;
```

```
        // Abort if the serial port has not been acquired
        if ((m_currentState & PD_S_ACQUIRED) == 0)
                return kIOReturnNotOpen;

        watchState = *state;
        // If the caller is not waiting on the acquired or active state, register
        // interest in the active state so that we can abort if the serial port closes.
        if ((mask & (PD_S_ACQUIRED | PD_S_ACTIVE)) == 0)
        {
                watchState &= ~PD_S_ACTIVE;
                mask |= PD_S_ACTIVE;
                autoActiveBit = true;
        }

        while (true)
        {
                // Check port state for any bits that match the watchState value
                // NB. the '^ ~' is a XNOR and tests for equality of bits.
                UInt32    matchedStates = (watchState ^ ~m_currentState) & mask;
                if (matchedStates)
                {
                        *state = m_currentState;
                        // Abort if the serial port was closed and the caller didn't watch
                        // PD_S_ACTIVE
                        if (autoActiveBit && (matchedStates & PD_S_ACTIVE))
                                return kIOReturnIOError;
                        else
                                return kIOReturnSuccess;
                }

                // Add the bits we are sleeping on to watchStateMask
                m_watchStateMask |= mask;
                // Sleep until the serial port state changes
                ret = fCommandGate->commandSleep((void*)&m_currentState);
                if (ret == THREAD_INTERRUPTED)
                        return kIOReturnAborted;
        }

        return kIOReturnSuccess;
}
```

Note that the implementation of watchState() in Listing 11-5 will make sure that either the PD_S_ACQUIRED or PD_S_ACTIVE bits are being watched, and if not, will add an extra state to the mask to watch for the PD_S_ACTIVE bit becoming clear. This ensures that when the serial port is closed, all threads that are blocked in a call to watchState() will wake up and return to the caller. If the mask for serial port deactivation were not explicitly added, the blocked thread would never wake up, causing the serial port driver to deadlock.

Serial Port Events

The hardware serial port will need to be configured to match the settings used by the device on the other end of the serial connection. Configurable settings include parameters such as the baud rate at which data is sent, the number of bits in a data character, whether parity bits are transmitted, and the number of stop bits that are sent at the end of each character.

These serial port settings are determined by the user space process that has opened the serial port and are configured through functions such as tcsetattr() and tcgetattr(). These functions enter the kernel through the I/O Kit's IOSerialBSDClient class, which passes the individual configuration options to the serial port driver through its executeEvent() method.

The executeEvent() method is paired with the method requestEvent(), which is used by the IOSerialBSDClient class to query the current configuration of the serial port. The prototypes for the executeEvent() and requestEvent() methods are as follows:

```
IOReturn            executeEvent(UInt32 event, UInt32 data, void* refCon);
IOReturn            requestEvent(UInt32 event, UInt32* data, void* refCon);
```

The parameter "event" is an enumeration from IOSerialStreamSync.h and identifies the property that is being configured or queried. The parameter "data" is used to pass the new value for the property that is being set through executeEvent(), or the current value of the property that is being queried through requestEvent(). Most drivers implement the executeEvent() and requestEvent() methods with a large switch statement on the value of the event parameter. A description of the possible event types is given below in Table 11-1.

Table 11-1. Event Types Handled by executeEvent() or requestEvent()

Event	Description
PD_E_ACTIVE	This event is used to start or stop the serial port hardware. The data parameter is a Boolean value, with a non-zero value indicating that the serial port hardware should be started, and a value of zero indicating that the serial port hardware should be stopped. The driver should respond by changing the state of the hardware, and then setting or clearing the state bit PD_S_ACTIVE to reflect the state of the hardware.
	This property can be queried by requestEvent(), at which point the driver should return the current state of the hardware to the caller through the data parameter.
PD_E_TXQ_SIZE PD_E_RXQ_SIZE	The data parameter specifies the allocation size of the serial driver's internal transmit buffer or receive buffer. The buffer size is specified as the number of characters that the buffer can hold.
	This property can be both queried and set, although an implementation is free to ignore a caller's request to set this value.
PD_E_TXQ_LOW_WATER PD_E_RXQ_LOW_WATER PD_E_TXQ_HIGH_WATER	The data parameter specifies the number of characters in the serial driver's internal transmit buffer or receive buffer that is considered to be the low water level or high water level. This parameter governs the point at which the status bits PD_S_TXQ_LOW_WATER, PD_S_RXQ_LOW_WATER, PD_S_TXQ_HIGH_WATER, and PD_S_RXQ_HIGH_WATER are set.

Event	Description
PD_E_RXQ_HIGH_WATER	This property can be both queried and set, although an implementation is free to ignore a caller's request to set this value.
PD_E_TXQ_AVAILABLE PD_E_RXQ_AVAILABLE	The data parameter returns the number of additional characters that can be written to the driver's transmit buffer until it becomes full, or the number of characters that are currently held in the driver's receive buffer. This property can be queried, but not set.
PD_E_TXQ_FLUSH PD_E_RXQ_FLUSH	This event, specified through executeEvent(), indicates that the serial driver should discard all characters from its internal transmit buffer or receive buffer.
PD_E_DATA_RATE	This event is used to get or set the baud rate of the serial port. The value in the data parameter uses half-bits to express the speed, meaning that the baud rate, which is measured in bits, is found by dividing the value in of the data parameter by 2. There is also a PD_E_RX_DATA_RATE event that allows the baud rate used for data input to be specified independently, although most implementations will ignore this event.
PD_E_DATA_SIZE	This event is used to get or set the number of bits in each character sent over the serial port. The value in the data parameter specifies the data size in bits. There is also a PD_E_RX_DATA_SIZE event that allows the size of the data input to be specified independently, although most implementations will ignore this event.
PD_E_DATA_INTEGRITY	This event is used to get or set the parity of data sent over the serial port. The value in the data parameter will be one of the following values: PD_RS232_PARITY_NONE, PD_RS232_PARITY_ODD, or PD_RS232_PARITY_EVEN. There is also a PD_E_RX_DATA_INTEGRITY event that allows the parity of data input to be specified independently, although most implementations will ignore this event.
PD_RS232_E_STOP_BITS	This event is used to get or set the number of stop bits sent after each character has been sent over the serial port. This value in the data parameter is expressed in half-bits, meaning that a data value of 2 configures the serial port for 1 stop bit. There is also a PD_RS232_E_RX_STOP_BITS event that allows the stop bits of data input to be specified independently, although most implementations will ignore this event.

Event	Description
PD_E_FLOW_CONTROL	This event is used to pass on the flow control state that has been requested by the user space process. The value in the data parameter is a bitfield in which each bit corresponds to a bit from the user space termios structure. The following list gives the bits that are defined for the data value, along with the flag that each bit corresponds to from the user space termios structure: PD_RS232_A_TXO (equivalent to IXON) PD_RS232_A_XANY (equivalent to IXANY) PD_RS232_A_RXO (equivalent to IXOFF) PD_RS232_A_RFR (equivalent to CRTS_IFLOW) PD_RS232_A_CTS (equivalent to CCTS_OFLOW) PD_RS232_A_DTR (equivalent to CDTR_IFLOW)
PD_RS232_E_XON_BYTE PD_RS232_E_XOFF_BYTE	These events are used to get or set the start and stop characters that are used if software flow control is enabled.
PD_RS232_E_LINE_BREAK	This event takes a Boolean data value that specifies whether an RS-232 break condition is signaled on the transmit line.

In addition to the method executeEvent(), you will notice that the IOSerialDriverSync interface also defines a method named enqueueEvent() that is used for setting the properties of a serial port. There is a subtle difference between the two methods; a call to the executeEvent() method causes a change in the serial port's configuration to take effect as soon as the method is called, whereas a call to enqueueEvent() won't take effect until all of the characters that are currently in the serial driver's transmit buffer have been written to hardware.

Implementing the correct behavior of enqueueEvent() requires the serial driver to define a transmit buffer that consists of a queue of events and the data associated with each event. Then, each call to enqueueEvent() appends the pair of values {event, data} to the transmit queue. Similarly, character data for transmission also needs to be treated as an event and appended to the end of the transmit buffer. Whenever the transmit buffer is not empty, the serial driver pulls the next event off the queue, which is either an event that changes the configuration of the serial port or a character to be sent over the serial port.

A serial driver isn't required to adhere this closely to the correct implementation of enqueueEvent(). If you examine the source code for the AppleUSBCDCDMM driver, you will see that it implements enqueueEvent() by calling through to executeEvent(), which applies the requested change to the serial port's configuration immediately.

Similarly, the serial driver's receive buffer allows events to be inserted between data bytes read from the serial port. For the receive queue, events represent errors that have occurred while reading data from the serial port. Some of the errors that can be reported are described here:

- PD_RS232_E_RX_LINE_BREAK indicates that a break condition was detected by the receiver.

- PD_E_FRAMING_ERROR indicates that the character data was incorrectly framed. (The stop bit was not in the expected position.)

- PD_E_INTEGRITY_ERROR indicates a parity error was detected.

- PD_E_HW_OVERRUN_ERROR and PD_E_SW_OVERRUN_ERROR indicate that character data was not pulled from the hardware or the software buffers fast enough to prevent the buffer from filling and data being lost.

Before reading any data from the serial port, the IOSerialBSDClient class will make a call to the serial driver's nextEvent() method. If the next element in the serial driver's receive queue is an error event, nextEvent() will return the event type to the caller, and the caller will respond by calling the driver's dequeueEvent() method. Otherwise, if the next element in the serial driver's receive queue is a data byte that has been read from the serial port, it should return PD_E_EOQ.

As with the transmit side of the serial driver, it is not strictly necessary for a driver to fully implement the queuing of events in its receive queue. In fact, the implementation provided by the AppleUSBCDCDMM driver reports no events on its receive queue at all; its implementation of nextEvent() and dequeueEvent() will check that the serial port has been activated and, if so, will always return a value of kIOReturnSuccess. Note that kIOReturnSuccess has a value of 0, and therefore, corresponds to the event PD_E_EOQ, which also has a value of 0.

Serial Data Transfer

The remaining methods to be implemented from the IOSerialDriverSync interface are the data transfer methods. The serial driver will be provided with data to be transmitted over the serial port through the method enqueueData(), and the data that the driver has received from the serial port is provided to clients through the dequeueData() method.

When a user space process writes data to a serial port, it is first handled in the kernel by the IOSerialBSDClient class, which is responsible for passing the data on to the serial port driver. The IOSerialBSDClient will provide the data to the serial driver by calling its enqueueData() method, which has the following signature:

```
IOReturn  enqueueData(UInt8 *buffer, UInt32 size, UInt32 *count, bool sleep, void *refCon);
```

The data bytes to be sent are held in the buffer parameter, and the number of bytes to be sent is described by the size parameter. The typical design of a serial driver is to copy the data that has been provided into an internal buffer that it has allocated (known as the transmit buffer) and then return to the caller immediately. The driver will then continue handling the write request by transferring data from its transmit buffer to the hardware serial port asynchronously. Before returning from the enqueueData() method, the driver will return, through the count parameter, the number of bytes that it accepted; note that this is simply the number of bytes that the driver was able to copy to its transmit buffer, not the number of bytes that have been written over the hardware serial port. The sleep parameter allows the caller to request that, if the driver cannot accept all of the bytes that it has been provided, the driver should block and not return to the caller until all bytes have been copied to the driver's internal transmit buffer.

The current implementation of the IOSerialBSDClient will never request that the serial driver sleep if it cannot accept all of the data bytes that have been provided. Rather, it will make sure that it doesn't provide the serial driver with more data than it can accept, which is done by calling the driver's requestEvent() method with the event PD_E_TXQ_AVAILABLE. The IOSerialBSDClient will watch various states of the driver's transmit buffer to determine when the driver is able to accept more data, including the states PD_S_TXQ_LOW_WATER, PD_S_TXQ_EMPTY, and PD_S_TX_BUSY.

A sample implementation of the enqueueData() method is provided in Listing 11-6. Note that this implementation copies the data bytes to a transmit buffer that has been allocated by the serial driver, and then checks whether the hardware is currently writing data out on the serial port. If not, a hypothetical function named StartHardwareTransmit() is called which, although implementation specific, has the purpose of telling the hardware to begin sending data bytes from the driver's transmit buffer out over the serial port.

Listing 11-6. A Sample Implementation of the enqueueData() Method. The Method Is Assumed to Have Been Called Through an IOCommandGate.

```
IOReturn              MySerialDriver::enqueueDataGated(UInt8* buffer, UInt32 size, UInt32* count,
                                      bool sleep, void* refCon)
{
        // Abort if the serial port has not been acquired
        *count = 0;
        if ((m_currentState & PD_S_ACTIVE) == 0)
                return kIOReturnNotOpen;

        // Copy the provided data to the driver's transmit buffer
        *count = AddToTransmitQueue(buffer, size);
        // Regenerate the status bits for the transmit buffer
        CheckQueues(refCon);

        // If no hardware transmission is in progress, begin outputting bytes from the driver's
        // buffer
        if ((m_currentState & PD_S_TX_BUSY) == 0)
                StartHardwareTransmit();

        // Block if the caller has requested we send all bytes before returning
        while ((*count < size) && sleep)
        {
                UInt32      state;
                IOReturn    ret;

                // Wait until the driver's transmit buffer falls below the low waterlevel,
                // and try again
                state = PD_S_TXQ_LOW_WATER;
                ret = watchState(&state, PD_S_TXQ_LOW_WATER, refCon);
                if (ret != kIOReturnSuccess)
                        return ret;

                // Copy further bytes to the driver's transmit buffer
                *count += AddToTransmitQueue(buffer + *count, size - *count);
                CheckQueues(refCon);
                if ((m_currentState & PD_S_TX_BUSY) == 0)
                        StartHardwareTransmit();
        }

        return kIOReturnSuccess;
}
```

The other part of data transfer is reading bytes that have been received from the hardware serial port. A serial driver will obtain data that has been received from its hardware device and copy it into its internal receive buffer. The exact means by which the hardware will notify the serial driver that data has been received will be implementation-specific, but may be signaled by a PCI interrupt or the completion of a USB transaction. The driver now needs to pass the received data on to the IOSerialBSDClient, which in turn will provide the data to a user space process.

The I/O Kit uses a pull model to return data from the serial driver to the IOSerialBSDClient class. The IOSerialBSDClient will call the driver's dequeueData() method to obtain data that has been received on the hardware serial port; the signature for this method is as follows:

```
IOReturn    dequeueData(UInt8* buffer, UInt32 size, UInt32* count, UInt32 min, void* refCon);
```

Upon receiving this method, the serial driver should copy data from its internal receive buffer to the provided parameter buffer. The parameter size describes the maximum number of bytes that the provided buffer can hold. The parameter count is used to return the actual number of bytes that were written to the provided buffer. The caller can request that the dequeueData() method block and not return to the caller until a minimum number of bytes are available; this is done by specifying a non-zero value in the min parameter, which provides the minimum number of bytes that the caller should return.

Rather than continually polling the dequeueData() method until data is available, the IOSerialBSDClient class will specify a minimum read size of 1 byte. The effect of this is to block in the call to dequeueData() but have the method return immediately as soon as the serial port has received data. The AppleUSBCDCDMM serial port driver implements this method by calling through to the watchState() method, and waiting until the PD_S_RXQ_EMPTY state is clear, indicating that data is available in the driver's receive buffer. An advantage of this design is that it ensures that the driver will unblock a wait in the dequeueData() method when the serial port is closed, since the watchState() method will abort if the PD_S_ACTIVE flag is ever cleared (which happens when the user process closes the serial port).

A sample implementation of the dequeueData() method is given in Listing 11-7. This implementation copies data out of the driver's internal receive buffer and into a buffer that has been provided by the caller of the method.

Listing 11-7. A Sample Implementation of the dequeueData() Method. The Method Is Assumed to Have Been Called Through an IOCommandGate.

```
IOReturn            MySerialDriver::dequeueDataGated(UInt8* buffer, UInt32 size, UInt32* count,
                                                     UInt32 min, void* refCon)
{
        // Abort if the serial port has not been acquired
        *count = 0;
        if ((m_currentState & PD_S_ACTIVE) == 0)
                return kIOReturnNotOpen;

        // Copy data from the driver's receive buffer
        *count = RemovefromReceiveQueue(buffer, size);
        // Regenerate the status bits for the receive buffer
        CheckQueues(refCon);

        // Block if the caller has requested a minimum number of bytes
        while ((min > 0) && (*count < min))
        {
                UInt32          state;
                IOReturn        ret;
```

```
        // Wait until the driver's receive buffer is not empty, and try again
        state = 0;
        ret = watchState(&state, PD_S_RXQ_EMPTY, refCon);
        if (ret != kIOReturnSuccess)
                return ret;

        // Copy further bytes from the driver's receive buffer
        *count += RemovefromReceiveQueue(buffer + *count, size - *count);
        CheckQueues(refCon);
    }

    return kIOReturnSuccess;
}
```

The sample implementations of enqueueData() in Listing 11-6 and dequeueData() in Listing 11-7 both call a hypothetical function named CheckQueues() after reading or writing to the internal transmit buffer or receive buffer. Although CheckQueues() is a hypothetical function, its role is one that is needed by any serial port driver. Its purpose is to examine the number of bytes held in the driver's internal transmit buffer or receive buffer, and to update the state flags that describe the driver's queues. These flags describe whether the transmit or receive queue is empty, full, contains fewer bytes than the low water level, or contains more bytes than the high water level. Since there may be threads that are waiting for the transmit buffer or receive buffer to reach a certain level, it is important that the serial port driver updates these status flags whenever it reads or writes to its internal buffers.

As well as being called from the methods enqueueData() and dequeueData(), as shown in Listing 11-6 and Listing 11-7, a serial port driver would also call the CheckQueues() function when data from the transmit buffer is removed and written over the hardware serial port, and when the hardware adds data that is has read from the serial port to the receive buffer. A sample implementation of the CheckQueues() method is provided in Listing 11-8.

Listing 11-8. A Sample Method to Update the Status Flags for the Driver's Internal Transmit Buffer. The Method Is Assumed to Have Been Called Through an IOCommandGate.

```
void MySerialDriver::CheckQueues(void* refCon)
{
        UInt32          usedSpace;
        UInt32          freeSpace;
        UInt32          newState;
        UInt32          deltaState;

        // Initialize newState with the state at function entry.
        newState = m_currentState;

        // Check the number of bytes used and free in the transmit buffer
        usedSpace = GetUsedSpaceInTransmitQueue();
        freeSpace = GetFreeSpaceInTransmitQueue();

        // Set the full/empty state for the transmit buffer
        if (freeSpace == 0)
        {
                newState |= PD_S_TXQ_FULL;
```

```
            newState &= ~PD_S_TXQ_EMPTY;
    }
    else if (usedSpace == 0)
    {
            newState &= ~PD_S_TXQ_FULL;
            newState |=  PD_S_TXQ_EMPTY;
    }
    else
    {
            newState &= ~PD_S_TXQ_FULL;
            newState &= ~PD_S_TXQ_EMPTY;
    }

    // Set the low/high waterlevel state for the transmit buffer
    if (usedSpace < m_txLowWaterlevel)
            newState |=  PD_S_TXQ_LOW_WATER;
    else
            newState &= ~PD_S_TXQ_LOW_WATER;

    if (usedSpace > m_txHighWaterlevel)
            newState |= PD_S_TXQ_HIGH_WATER;
    else
            newState &= ~PD_S_TXQ_HIGH_WATER;

    // Perform the same checks on the receive buffer
    ...

    // Update any changed state bits
    deltaState = newState ^ m_currentState;
    setState(newState, deltaState, refCon);
}
```

Accessing a Serial Port from User Space

To a user space application, a serial port driver is accessed as a standard character device in the /dev directory. This should be familiar territory for anyone who has accessed a serial port on any other UNIX system. Where the I/O Kit approach differs, however, is in how a user space application enumerates the serial ports that are present in a system. For many traditional UNIX applications, the user must specify the full path of the serial port's character file. The approach taken by Mac OS X is to shield users from the /dev directory, and to present available serial ports through a descriptive name. This is where the I/O Kit comes in.

Since a serial port is implemented by an I/O Kit driver, its driver object can be found by user space applications in the I/O Registry, as described in Chapter 5. Like all entries in the I/O Registry, the entry for a serial port driver contains a property table that can be used to obtain a descriptive name for the serial port, and a full path to the serial port's character device file. Having obtained the path to the serial port's device file, the user space application can then proceed to open and access the device, as would be done by a traditional UNIX program.

As with any application that wishes to locate a driver through the I/O Registry, the first step in finding a serial port driver is to create a matching dictionary. The role of a matching dictionary is to locate entries in the I/O Registry that meet certain criteria, and filter out all other entries. A user space process accesses a serial port not through the serial port driver itself, but rather through the driver's associated IOSerialBSDClient class. Therefore, to find serial ports in the system, a user space process just needs to create a matching dictionary to find all IOSerialBSDClient objects in the registry. This can be done as follows:

```
#include <IOKit/serial/IOSerialKeys.h>

CFMutableDictionaryRef    matchingDict;
matchingDict = IOServiceMatching(kIOSerialBSDServiceValue);
```

To further refine the matches, the user process can add the key kIOSerialBSDTypeKey to the matching dictionary, and limit the results to modem devices (serial drivers that created an IOModemSerialStreamSync object) or generic serial port devices (serial drivers that created an IORS232SerialStreamSync object). For example, to limit the matches to modem devices, a user space application would create the following matching dictionary:

```
matchingDict = IOServiceMatching(kIOSerialBSDServiceValue);
CFDictionarySetValue(matchingDict, CFSTR(kIOSerialBSDTypeKey), CFSTR(kIOSerialBSDModemType));
```

Having created a matching dictionary to locate the serial devices that it is interested in, the process is then able to iterate the registry for drivers that meet the criteria specified by that dictionary. All instances of IOSerialBSDClient contain registry properties that are specific to a serial port driver, namely:

- kIOTTYDeviceKey: a CFStringRef containing a descriptive name for the serial port

- kIOCalloutDeviceKey: a CFStringRef containing the full path to the callout character device file for the serial port

- kIODialinDeviceKey: a CFStringRef containing the full path to the dial-in character device file for the serial port

To show how these properties can be used, the code in Listing 11-9 demonstrates how to enumerate all serial devices in the system and how to open each device.

Listing 11-9. A Sample Application That Uses the I/O Kit to Enumerate all Serial Devices Present in the System and Find the Path of the Character Device for each Serial Port

```
#include <CoreFoundation/CoreFoundation.h>
#include <IOKit/IOKitLib.h>
#include <IOKit/serial/IOSerialKeys.h>
#include <sys/param.h>
#include <fcntl.h>
#include <unistd.h>

int main (int argc, const char * argv[])
{
        CFMutableDictionaryRef          matchingDict;
        io_iterator_t                   iter = 0;
        io_service_t                    service = 0;
        kern_return_t                   kr;

        // Create a matching dictionary that will find any serial device
        matchingDict = IOServiceMatching(kIOSerialBSDServiceValue);
        kr = IOServiceGetMatchingServices(kIOMasterPortDefault, matchingDict, &iter);
```

```
        if (kr != KERN_SUCCESS)
                return -1;

        // Iterate over all matching objects
        while ((service = IOIteratorNext(iter)) != 0)
        {
                CFStringRef         cfDeviceName;
                CFStringRef         cfCalloutPath;
                Char                deviceName[256];
                Char                calloutPath[MAXPATHLEN];
                Int                 fd;

                // Get the device name
                cfDeviceName = IORegistryEntryCreateCFProperty(service, CFSTR(kIOTTYDeviceKey),
                                        kCFAllocatorDefault, 0);
                CFStringGetCString(cfDeviceName, deviceName, sizeof(deviceName),
                                        kCFStringEncodingUTF8);
                CFRelease(cfDeviceName);

                // Get the character device path
                cfCalloutPath = IORegistryEntryCreateCFProperty(service,
                                        CFSTR(kIOCalloutDeviceKey), kCFAllocatorDefault, 0);
                CFStringGetCString(cfCalloutPath, calloutPath, sizeof(calloutPath),
                                        kCFStringEncodingUTF8);
                CFRelease(cfCalloutPath);

                // The I/O Registry object is no longer needed
                IOObjectRelease(service);

                // Proceed to open and use the device at "calloutPath" as usual
                printf("Found device %s at path %s\n", deviceName, calloutPath);

                fd = open(calloutPath, O_RDWR | O_NOCTTY | O_NONBLOCK);
                // Clear the O_NONBLOCK flag so subsequent I/O will block
                fcntl(fd, F_SETFL, 0);

                // Configure serial device with tcsetattr()
                // Read and write with read() / write()

                close(fd);
        }

        // Release the I/O Registry iterator
        IOObjectRelease(iter);

        return 0;
}
```

Summary

- A serial port provides a simple means of low-bandwidth data transfer between devices. Although you can no longer find an RS-232 or RS-422 serial port on modern Macs, many USB devices present themselves as a serial port, so support for serial port drivers is still part of the Mac OS X operating system.

- A user space application accesses a serial port through a device file in the /dev directory, as is standard for the UNIX environment.

- A serial port driver is implemented in the I/O Kit by implementing a subclass of the IOSerialDriverSync interface. This interface contains methods for opening and closing the serial port, configuring the port, and reading and writing data.

- The I/O Kit provides a class known as IOSerialBSDClient that publishes the serial port driver to user space applications. This class receives requests from user space applications to read and write to the serial port, and passes the requests on to the kernel serial port driver.

- The I/O Kit design allows a serial port driver to be implemented using the modern, object-oriented design of the I/O Kit, without having to deal with the legacy user space interface of a serial port device.

CHAPTER 12

Audio Drivers

Audio devices are among the most common peripherals attached to a computer apart from storage devices. They are used for everything from voice recorders to MP3 players, headsets with microphones, security systems, and DJ and professional recording systems. Many video devices also have audio capabilities and come with their own audio drivers that allow you to use the audio features of the device independently or together with the video features, for example, a web camera with a built-in microphone. The microphone will have its own audio driver, representing the microphone in the system as an audio device that can be used independently of the camera.

Programming drivers for audio devices present a few unique challenges. Audio devices have strict latency requirements and must be fed a constant stream of data to avoid holes or glitches during playback or recording. The human ear is extremely sensitive and can detect even small glitches in only a few samples worth of data. Furthermore, audio data cannot be excessively buffered, as this will cause an unacceptable delay. For example, suppose you were playing loud music and received a phone call. You would not be happy if it took five seconds from when you pressed the pause button until the music actually stopped. Similarly, if you were playing a game firing a gun, you would expect to hear the sound of the gun firing almost immediately, not several seconds after you pulled the trigger. Therefore, an audio device must minimize buffering in order to alleviate these effects.

While the preceding examples specifically mentioned playback, buffering must also be minimized when capturing audio with an input device. For example, if you had a telephone connected via the input device, you wouldn't want to hear the other person's voice several seconds late. Because an audio buffer must be kept small in order to keep the latency or lag down, it will also need to respond to the hardware with as little latency as possible to avoid situations where the audio producer overtakes the audio consumer, or vice versa, which would lead to audible distortions. Because of these constraints and the fact that an audio driver needs to respond to multiple clients, it is a prime candidate for a kernel-level driver.

Core Audio is the term used to describe the entirety of audio support under Mac OS X. This includes a myriad of user space APIs as well as the kernel KPI, implemented by the IOAudioFamily interface that will be the subject of this chapter.

An Introduction to Digital Audio and Audio Devices

Sound waves are analog by nature, and as we know, analog signals aren't easily stored or manipulated by a computer system that stores and processes information digitally. Other devices, such as CD, DVD, and Blu-Ray players, also operate with digital audio.

Digital audio information is mainly derived from an analog audio wave by a process known as Pulse Code Modulation (PCM). PCM works by sampling or taking a measurement of the analog audio wave at fixed intervals. The number of measurements taken per second is known as the sample rate. Audio on a CD is sampled at 44.1 kHz. Other sources, such as HD video, may use 48 kHz, which means there are

48000 measurements of the audio wave performed per second. Each measurement is known as a sample.

The sample is a measurement of the analog signal's amplitude at the time of the measurement, which is then quantized to a digital scale. The range of this scale is known as the bit depth or sample depth. For CD audio and many other applications, the bit depth is 16 bits, which gives each sample a possible value between −32768 and 32767. When a sample is taken, the value is converted into this scale by rounding it to the nearest integer value. The higher the sample rate and sample width, the more accurate the representation of the original audio wave.

As computer programmers, we rarely need to care about the conversion of a signal from analog to digital or vice versa, as that is handled by circuitry on the audio hardware (ADC/DAC). However, a programmer needs to be aware of what digital PCM samples represent and understand the significance of the sample rate and depth. PCM samples are typically stored with channels interleaved in memory, as shown in Figure 12-1.

Byte Offset	0x00	0x02	0x04	0x06	0x08	0x0A
Channel	Left	Right	Left	Right	Left	Right
	-3201	-1510	-3033	-1496	-2995	-1483

Figure 12-1. Buffer of interleaved 16-bit signed PCM samples

As you can see in Figure 12-1, the data corresponding to each channel are not stored sequentially but are interleaved in the buffer. The buffer above uses 16 bits per sample, which means that each sample occupies two bytes. A pair of left/right samples is referred to as a sample frame (or sample group). If there were more than two channels, for example, eight (as used by HDMI), a sample group would instead consist of channels 1–8. Most digital audio systems expect audio data in this format and usually this is how audio is stored in a file on a computer, assuming the audio is uncompressed. File formats such as MP3 compress the audio data; however, they have to decompress the audio back to interleaved PCM samples before it can be played back by the audio hardware. Audio at 44.1 kHz will give us 44100 sample frames per second. If the sample depth is 16 bits and there are two channels, we need 176.4 KB (44100 Hz * (16/8 bits) * 2 channels = 176400 bytes) of data to store a single second of audio. PCM samples aren't necessarily always 16 bits wide, however. The sample depth can also be 8, 20, 24, or 32 bits. Furthermore, samples can be stored as unsigned or signed, or even in floating point, which is the preferred audio format of Core Audio. Table 12-1 shows some commonly used PCM formats.

Table 12-1. Examples of PCM Sample Formats

Sample Depth	Sample Width	Storage Type
8	8	signed integer
16	16	signed integer
24	32	signed integer
32	32	signed integer
32	32	signed floating point

An audio device and driver usually revolve around the concept of a sample buffer. The sample buffer usually contains interleaved PCM samples (assuming there is more than one channel). The sample buffer is a circular buffer allocated by the driver. For audio playback, the hardware device usually continuously reads the buffer. The device will access the memory of the buffer directly via direct memory access (DMA) without involving the CPU and issue an interrupt at some fixed interval to let the driver know the current location the device is reading from. This is necessary so that whatever is producing the audio data can write to the correct location without interfering with the device. After a period has elapsed, we know that a certain number of samples have been played by the device. In this case, it is common for the driver to erase the played samples. This ensures that silence will be outputted rather than repeating previous data should the buffer wrap around to the start without any new audio being inserted into the buffer. In the case of audio input, the process is simply reversed. Instead of reading from the buffer, the device will be writing audio samples into the sample buffer. It will also issue an interrupt, letting you know when/where audio samples can be read.

Some audio devices may have multiple independent inputs and outputs. In this case, each input and output may have its own sample buffer. Mac OS X comes with a USB audio device driver so no third party driver is generally needed for devices that conform to the USB audio interface.

Core Audio

Core Audio is an umbrella term used to describe the collective audio support under Mac OS X and iOS. This support consists of a number of frameworks, including the CoreAudio.Framework itself. The audio architecture is shown in Figure 12-2.

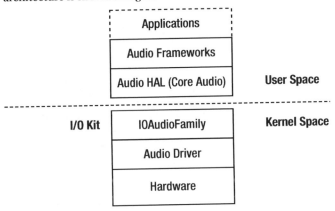

Figure 12-2. Mac OS X and iOS audio architecture

The core of the architecture is implemented in the Audio HAL (hardware abstraction layer), which acts as an intermediary between the frameworks, applications, and the audio hardware and driver. The current architecture exists to address a number of limitations with the previous audio architecture found in Mac OS 9. In OS 9, an application using an audio device wrote directly into the driver's double-buffered sample buffer. As a consequence, OS 9 could only handle audio output from a single application at a time. Furthermore, because of the direct access, the application had to write audio in a format supported by the audio device, which limited it to only support mono or stereo 16-bit PCM samples.

Under OS X and iOS, this limitation is removed. Instead of having an application talk directly to the driver, it instead interfaces with the Audio HAL. Core Audio takes care of combining audio from multiple applications and threads into a single buffer. Each application is free to choose any audio format supported by the HAL. The HAL will convert the audio buffer into 32-bit floating-point samples before handing the buffer to the driver. The driver is then responsible for converting the buffer from floating-point format to the native format supported by the audio hardware. The same is also the case for audio input. The driver is expected to convert incoming audio into 32-bit floating samples before the audio can be transferred back to the HAL. 32-bit floating-point format is used as it has a very high dynamic range, which ensures that precision will not be lost during conversion to or from another format.

While the Core Audio framework itself provides low-level access to audio drivers, Core Audio as the collective audio architecture provides numerous other frameworks built on top of it, such as follows:

- *Audio Toolbox* framework provides a diverse set of APIs for tasks such as audio clock synchronization, reading and writing of audio files, APIs for music playback, Audio conversion API, Audio graph API, and much more.

- *Audio Units* framework provides support for writing filters, such as equalizers and band-pass filters.

- *Core Audio Kit* framework allows the creation of Cocoa GUIs for Audio Units.

- *Core MIDI / MIDI Server* framework contains APIs for working MIDI.

- *OpenAL* is the Mac OS X implementation of the Open Audio Library.

I/O Kit Audio Support

The IOAudioFamily handles audio in the kernel and facilitates the creation of drivers for audio hardware. The responsibility of an audio driver is conceptually very simple; it merely transfers data to and from the hardware on behalf of clients (much like any hardware driver). It is also responsible for performing actions like muting, controlling the volume, or other configurable attributes. Core Audio uses 32-bit floating-point format as its native audio format and because not all devices will support this, a driver must handle conversion to and from a format the hardware is able to handle. Figure 12-3 shows the hierarchy of classes that make up the IOAudioFamily.

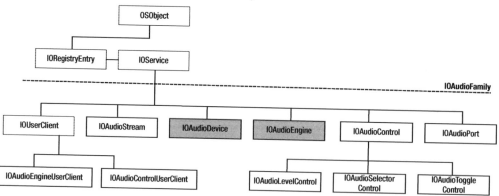

Figure 12-3. IOAudioFamily classes

Let's have a look at the role of each class in the family.

- The IOAudioDevice class serves as a central coordination point for an audio driver. It is responsible for attaching to a hardware provider and configuring and initializing the hardware. The class itself is not usually directly involved in the I/O of audio, which instead is the role of IOAudioEngine. The IOAudioDevice class also centralizes timing and synchronization services.

- The IOAudioEngine represents the DMA or I/O engine of an audio driver. Because an audio device can have many inputs and outputs that operate independently, it makes sense to encapsulate their behavior into their own class. If you look at the I/O Registry entries for the Apple built-in audio device on a Mac Pro, you will see the Apple audio driver has five instances of IOAudioEngine representing Line input, S/PDIF optical input, Headphone output, Line output, and S/PDIF optical output. An IOAudioEngine must allocate at least one IOAudioStream. The IOAudioEngine is an abstract class.

- The IOAudioStream represents a sample buffer. A sample buffer has a direction associated with it, which can be either input or output. It also has metadata that describes the formats it is capable of supporting, such as the numeric format of the contained samples, the sample rate, and the number of channels supported. The class is not abstract and can be instantiated directly. The class does not allocate memory for the sample buffer itself. It has to be told the location of the buffer. It is responsible for exposing the sample buffer to user space consumers. The audio stream also maintains an internal mix buffer where audio from multiple sources is mixed together into a single stream.

- The IOAudioControl class represents a tunable parameter of the device, such as the input volume, output volume, and mute. The IOAudioControl class is directly usable, but you can also subclass it yourself to create custom controls. Three subclasses of IOAudioControl exist, IOAudioLevelControl, IOAudioSelectorControl, and IOAudioToggleControl. A control may belong to the device itself, the engine, or an IOAudioPort.

- IOAudioPort can be used to represent a logical or physical port, such as Line out or Headphone out. The use of this class is not required for an audio driver.

- The Core Audio framework communicates with an IOAudioEngine through the IOAudioEngineUserClient, which allows it to interact with the engine's sample buffers for the purpose of playing back or capturing audio.

- The IOAudioControlUserClient serves as a user client for IOAudioControl instances and allows manipulation. This is how an application, such as *System Preferences*, can control volume or mute.

Implementing an Audio Driver

Now let's look at how a kernel audio driver can be implemented using the example project MyAudioDevice. We only show excerpts from this as it pertains to the topic in question; however, you can inspect the full source code of MyAudioDevice by downloading it from the Apress web site. For the sake of simplicity, we will make the driver as basic as possible. As there is no standardized widely available audio hardware we can build a driver for, we will build a virtual audio driver. The driver will have one output and one input so we can perform both functions. The driver will operate as a loopback device, which means that audio we play will be transferred from the output buffer to the input buffer. We leave it as an exercise for you, the reader, to do something more interesting, perhaps attach it to an actual audio device and forward audio data to or from it, or route audio to or from a network.

If everything works, we should be able to play a song using an application like iTunes and then capture the results using the audio recording feature of the QuickTime player. We will not be able to hear the audio as it plays, as it is not routed to a speaker. Additionally, the OS X sound preferences only allow output on a single device at a time, which prevents us from hearing the audio played on a different audio output. However, we will be able to hear the recording once we play it back again (after having selected an output other than our device). Once the driver is loaded, it should be visible under *System Preferences* ➤ *Sound*, as shown in Figure 12-4.

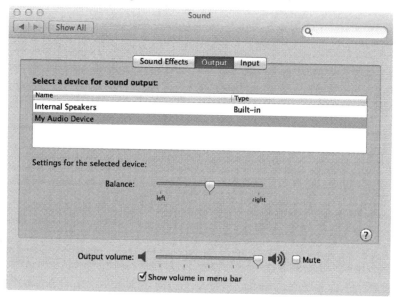

Figure 12-4. The Audio pane of System Preferences showing MyAudioDevice selected as the active output

The driver will be based on the example driver provided by the IOAudioFamily source code distribution called SampleAudioDevice. If you wish to learn more about audio drivers, you can look at its implementation as well as the second example, SamplePCIAudioDevice. Note that neither example is actually functional; rather, they serve as skeletons or starting points for a new driver, unlike MyAudioDevice, which is a working implementation of an audio driver.

In order to interface with the Core Audio system, our driver needs to implement an instance of IOAudioDevice. Note that it is entirely possible to implement a driver for an audio device without using the IOAudioFamily at all. The downside is that you would need to provide your own API for applications to access the device. Furthermore, existing applications would need modifications to be able to use your device because most applications depend on Core Audio or a framework that uses Core Audio instead.

Our driver will use IOAudioFamily. The architecture of MyAudioDevice and how it interacts with the classes of the IOAudioFamily can be seen in Figure 12-5.

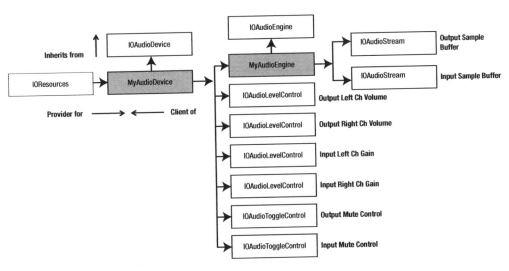

Figure 12-5. MyAudioDevice architecture

The virtual device will consist of a subclass of IOAudioDevice called MyAudioDevice. This will in turn allocate a single instance of the MyAudioEngine class, which is derived from IOAudioEngine. The main class will also allocate a number of IOAudioControl instances, which will be used to represent controls for adjusting the output and input volume levels for the left and right channels, as well as controls to mute the output and input. Because we do not have an actual hardware device, these controls will not do anything, but we implement them anyway for demonstration purposes. The MyAudioEngine class will represent the I/O engine in lieu of actual hardware. The class will allocate two IOAudioStream instances, one for the output sample buffer and one for the input sample buffer. When data enters the output buffer, we will simply copy the data over to the input buffer.

Driver and Hardware Initialization

IOAudioEngine primarily performs hardware initialization and its implementation is often quite minimalistic, as much of the complexity of an audio driver will be implemented as a subclass of IOAudioEngine. Nevertheless, the class performs some important tasks internally, such as providing a central IOWorkLoop and IOCommandGate, which are shared by subordinate classes such as IOAudioEngine and are used to serialize access to the driver and hardware. The IOAudioEngine class also provides a shared timer service that can be used by other objects in the driver. An object can register to receive timer events with the addTimerEvent() function, as follows:

```
virtual IOReturn addTimerEvent(OSObject *target, TimerEvent event, AbsoluteTime interval);
```

The target argument should be a pointer to the object that will be notified of the timer event. The interval specifies the frequency of the timer event in units of AbsoluteTime (nanoseconds). The event argument specifies the callback function. An audio driver may typically need several timer events, for example, to poll the status of an output connector to sense if a jack was connected.

The following steps are typically performed by an audio driver's IOAudioDevice subclass.

- Configure the hardware device's provider and enumerate any needed resources. For PCI or Thunderbolt, this means mapping device memory or I/O regions. For USB devices, enumerate interfaces and/or pipes.

- Configure the device for operation. For example, take it out of reset/sleep mode by accessing the device's registers or sending control requests.

- If your driver supports multiple audio chips or a chip with a varying number of DMA channels, inputs, or outputs, the driver will need to interrogate the device to work out its exact capabilities.

- Set the name and description of the audio device, which will identify it to Core Audio and user space applications.

- Based on information extracted from the device, create the appropriate number of IOAudioEngine instances, which in turn will allocate one or more IOAudioStream instances, along with associated sample buffers.

The header file for the MyAudioDevice class is shown in Listing 12-1.

Listing 12-1. Header File for the MyAudioDevice Class

```
#ifndef _MYAUDIODEVICE_H__
#define _MYAUDIODEVICE_H__

#include <IOKit/audio/IOAudioDevice.h>

#define MyAudioDevice com_osxkernel_MyAudioDevice

class MyAudioDevice : public IOAudioDevice
{
    OSDeclareDefaultStructors(MyAudioDevice);

    virtual bool initHardware(IOService *provider);
    bool createAudioEngine();

    // Control callbacks
    static IOReturn volumeChangeHandler(OSObject* target, IOAudioControl *volumeControl,
                        SInt32 oldValue, SInt32 newValue);
    virtual IOReturn volumeChanged(IOAudioControl *volumeControl, SInt32 oldValue, SInt32
                        newValue);

    static IOReturn outputMuteChangeHandler(OSObject* target, IOAudioControl *muteControl,
                        SInt32 oldValue, SInt32 newValue);
    virtual IOReturn outputMuteChanged(IOAudioControl* muteControl, SInt32 oldValue, SInt32
                        newValue);

    static IOReturn gainChangeHandler(OSObject* target, IOAudioControl* gainControl, SInt32
                        oldValue, SInt32 newValue);
    virtual IOReturn gainChanged(IOAudioControl* gainControl, SInt32 oldValue, SInt32
                        newValue);
```

```
    static IOReturn inputMuteChangeHandler(OSObject* target, IOAudioControl *muteControl,
                                SInt32 oldValue, SInt32 newValue);
    virtual IOReturn inputMuteChanged(IOAudioControl* muteControl, SInt32 oldValue, SInt32
                                newValue);
};

#endif
```

As you may have noticed, a number of the usual I/O Kit lifecycle methods, such as start() and stop(), are missing. This is because the super-class IOAudioDevice implements them for us. The start() method will take care of registering for power management and will then call the initHardware() method, which a driver should implement. Our class also implements a number of callbacks for audio controls, which we will discuss in more detail later in this chapter. The initHardware() is the preferred method for performing hardware-related initialization. Before the method returns, it should create at least one instance of an IOAudioEngine and activate it, which is done by calling the activateAudioEngine() method. The initHardware() method of MyAudioDevice is implemented as follows:

```
bool MyAudioDevice::initHardware(IOService *provider)
{
    bool result = false;

    IOLog("MyAudioDevice[%p]::initHardware(%p)\n", this, provider);

    if (!super::initHardware(provider))
        goto done;

    setDeviceName("My Audio Device");
    setDeviceShortName("MyAudioDevice");
    setManufacturerName("osxkernel.com");

    if (!createAudioEngine())
        goto done;

    result = true;

done:
    return result;
}
```

Since MyAudioDevice is not backed by a real hardware device, there is not much to do. We set the device name, a short name, and the manufacturer name, which will be used by Core Audio for various purposes. The device name will be visible in the OS X System Preferences. Strings set by an audio driver should be localized if possible because OS X is multi-lingual. If you have a descriptive string such as "Headphone Output" or "Microphone Input," these may not be meaningful to someone who doesn't speak English.

The final step of the function is to call an internal method called createAudioEngine(), which will initialize and create an instance of the IOAudioEngine subclass, MyAudioEngine. The method simply allocates an instance and then calls activateAudioEngine() on the created instance before returning. The method also creates the audio controls, as you shall see next.

> ■ **Note** Once `activateAudioEngine()` returns, you can call `release()` on the instance if you no longer need it, because it will be retained and released internally by the `IOAudioEngine` super class anyway.

Registering Audio Controls

An audio device will usually have one or more controllable attributes, such as the ability to adjust the volume level, mute, or perform some other adjustment. In order to make these controls visible to user space clients, an `IOAudioControl` is needed to describe each attribute. As previously mentioned, there are three subclasses of `IOAudioControl` provided by `IOAudioFamily`. The first is `IOAudioLevelControl`, which is used to control volume level. The control can also be used for creating any type of control that allows you to select a value out of a range. Following is an example of how to create and register a volume control for the left channel from Apple's `SampleAudioDevice` driver.

```
control = IOAudioLevelControl::createVolumeControl
                (65535,    // Initial value 0,
                 65535,                                      // min value
                 (-22 << 16) + (32768),                      // max value
                 0,                                          // -22.5 in IOFixed (16.16)
                 kIOAudioControlChannelIDDefaultLeft,        // max 0.0 in IOFixed
                 kIOAudioControlChannelNameLeft,
                 0,
                 kIOAudioControlUsageOutput);                // control ID - driver-defined
if (!control) {
    goto Done;
}

control->setValueChangeHandler(volumeChangeHandler, this);
audioEngine->addDefaultAudioControl(control);
control->release();
```

The volume control is created using the special factory method `createVolumeControl()`. The three first parameters of the method represent the initial volume value, the minimum value, and the maximum value. You may specify different values to match your hardware's register specification or you can translate the values in the callback to match the range expected by the hardware's volume control register. The two next parameters set the dB values the minimum and maximum values correspond to. The volume scale usually goes from 0.0 dB, which represents full volume, to some negative dB value. The volume is at its default level at 0.0 dB and is attenuated in order to lower the volume of the signal. The dB value is stored as a fixed-point value. The next parameter is the channel ID. We specify `kIOAudioControlChannelIDDefaultLeft` to indicate that this control is for the left stereo channel. The `IOAudioFamily` specifies constant names for other channels as well, such as `kIOAudioControlChannelIDDefaultCenter`, `kIOAudioControlChannelIDDefaultSub`, and `kIOAudioControlChannelIDDefaultLeftRear`. The channel definitions are declared in `IOKit/audio/AudioDefines.h`.

The next parameter is a string with a descriptive name for the channel. As with the channel ID, we use a predefined constant. The next parameter is an identifier that can be used by the driver to pass a value, which will not be interpreted by either `IOAudioFamily` or Core Audio. The last argument specifies what the control will be used for. In our case, we set it to `kIOAudioControlUsageOutput`, which indicates to Core Audio this is an output volume control. Other possible values are kIOAudioControlUsageInput, kIOAudioControlUsagePassThru, or kIOAudioControlUsageCoreAudioProperty.

Once a control is constructed successfully, you need to set the callback function, which will be invoked when the control is manipulated from user space. This callback must be a static member function, which can be implemented as follows:

```
IOReturn SampleAudioDevice::volumeChangeHandler(IOService *target, IOAudioControl
*volumeControl, SInt32 oldValue, SInt32 newValue)
{
    IOReturn result = kIOReturnBadArgument;
    SampleAudioDevice *audioDevice;

    audioDevice = (SampleAudioDevice *)target;
    if (audioDevice) {
        result = audioDevice->volumeChanged(volumeControl, oldValue, newValue);
    }
    return result;
}

IOReturn SampleAudioDevice::volumeChanged(IOAudioControl *volumeControl, SInt32 oldValue,
SInt32 newValue)
{
    IOLog("SampleAudioDevice[%p]::volumeChanged(%p, %ld, %ld)\n",
            this, volumeControl, oldValue, newValue);
    if (volumeControl) {
        IOLog("\t-> Channel %ld\n", volumeControl->getChannelID());
    }

    // Add hardware volume code change

    return kIOReturnSuccess;
}
```

The callback will provide a pointer to the control whose value was changed, which lets the same callback function service multiple controls. The callback will be passed the old value as well as the new value. For most hardware drivers, the method would then write the new value to a hardware register, which will have the effect of increasing or reducing the volume or performing some other action.

Either an IOAudioEngine instance or an IOAudioStream can have controls attached. In either case, you attach to the parent by calling the addDefaultAudioControl() method, as shown above. Mute controls are implemented similarly to volume controls, but using the createMuteControl() factory method instead, as follows:

```
// Create an input mute control
control = IOAudioToggleControl::createMuteControl(false,    // initial state - unmuted
                        AudioControlChannelIDAll,          // Affects all channels
                        kIOAudioControlChannelNameAll,
                        0,                                 // control ID - driver-defined
                        kIOAudioControlUsageInput);
```

Unlike the volume control, which operates on a single channel, the mute control in this case is specified to apply to all channels in this case.

Implementing an Audio Engine

The audio engine performs the actual I/O in an audio driver. An audio engine is implemented as a subclass of the abstract IOAudioEngine class. It controls the I/O behavior and handles the transfer of one or more related sample buffers. Many audio devices can drive multiple independent inputs and outputs at the same time; in this case, it is recommended to create more than one instance of IOAudioEngine, one for each I/O channel. The following steps are needed to implement an IOAudioEngine subclass:

- Override the initHardware() method to perform any additional hardware initialization needed.

- Allocate sample buffers and associated IOAudioStream instances.

- Implement the performAudioEngineStart() and performAudioEngineStop() methods to start and stop the I/O.

- Implement the free() method to clean up any used resources.

- Implement the getCurrentSampleFrame() method.

- Implement the performFormatChange() method to respond to change of format requests from Core Audio.

- Implement a mechanism to inform the super class of the timestamp of when the sample buffer wraps back to the beginning.

- Implement the clipOutputSamples() method for output streams and/or the convertInputSamples() method for input streams.

We will discuss the preceding steps in more detail in the following sections by examining the implementation of the MyAudioDevice example driver.

An IOAudioEngine subclass is started and stopped directly by Core Audio through the IOAudioEngineUserClient. Once started, the engine will continuously run through the sample buffer. The IOAudioEngine subclass is responsible for telling the super class when the buffer wraps around to the start of the buffer by taking a timestamp. The Core Audio framework uses the timestamp to accurately predict the position of the sample buffer. The audio engine will also ensure that played samples in the sample buffer are erased.

The header file for *MyAudioDevice*'s *IOAudioEngine* subclass is shown in Listing 12-2.

Listing 12-2. Header File for the MyAudioEngine Class

```
#ifndef _MYAUDIOENGINE_H_
#define _MYAUDIOENGINE_H_

#include <IOKit/audio/IOAudioEngine.h>

#include "MyAudioDevice.h"

#define MyAudioEngine com_osxkernel_MyAudioEngine

class MyAudioEngine : public IOAudioEngine
{
    OSDeclareDefaultStructors(MyAudioEngine)
```

```
public:
    virtual void free();

    virtual bool initHardware(IOService* provider);
    virtual void stop(IOService *provider);

    virtual IOAudioStream *createNewAudioStream(IOAudioStreamDirection direction,
                                    void* sampleBuffer, UInt32 sampleBufferSize);

    virtual IOReturn performAudioEngineStart();
    virtual IOReturn performAudioEngineStop();

    virtual UInt32 getCurrentSampleFrame();

    virtual IOReturn performFormatChange(IOAudioStream* audioStream, const IOAudioStreamFormat*
                                    newFormat, const IOAudioSampleRate* newSampleRate);

    virtual IOReturn clipOutputSamples(const void* mixBuf, void* sampleBuf, UInt32
                                    firstSampleFrame, UInt32 numSampleFrames,
                                    const IOAudioStreamFormat* streamFormat,
                                    IOAudioStream* audioStream);
    virtual IOReturn convertInputSamples(const void* sampleBuf, void* destBuf, UInt32
                                    firstSampleFrame, UInt32 numSampleFrames,
                                    const IOAudioStreamFormat* streamFormat,
                                    IOAudioStream* audioStream);

private:
    IOTimerEventSource*        fAudioInterruptSource;
    SInt16*                    fOutputBuffer;
    SInt16*                    fInputBuffer;
    UInt32                     fInterruptCount;
    SInt64                     fNextTimeout;

    static void                interruptOccured(OSObject* owner, IOTimerEventSource* sender);
    void                       handleAudioInterrupt();
};

#endif
```

I/O Engine Initialization

An IOAudioEngine has its own initHardware() method, which should be overridden to perform any I/O engine-specific hardware initialization, as well as allocation and initialization of other needed resources. Once the method returns, the engine should be ready to start I/O. performAudioEngineStart() can then be called to start the actual I/O. The initHardware() method gets called by the IOAudioDevice::activateAudioEngine() method in our case. Although IOAudioEngine derives from IOService, we do not override or call the start() method in this case. This is because the class is allocated and initialized by MyAudioDevice rather than by I/O Kit. The IOAudioEngine provides a default implementation of the start() method, which is hardwired to use an IOAudioDevice as its provider. Unlike start(), however, we do declare the stop() method. The stop() method can be implemented to reverse any action performed in initHardware(). The initHardware() method of our MyAudioDevice driver is shown in Listing 12-3.

Listing 12-3. The Implementation of initHardware() in MyAudioDevice

```
#define  kAudioSampleRate                        48000
#define  kAudioNumChannels                       2
#define  kAudioSampleDepth                        16
#define  kAudioSampleWidth                        16
#define  kAudioBufferSampleFrames                 kAudioSampleRate/2
// Buffer holds half second's worth of audio.
#define  kAudioSampleBufferSize                   (kAudioBufferSampleFrames * kAudioNumChannels *
                                                  (kAudioSampleDepth / 8))

#define  kAudioInterruptInterval                  10000000 // nanoseconds (1000 ms / 100 hz = 10ms).
#define  kAudioInterruptHZ                        100

bool MyAudioEngine::initHardware(IOService *provider)
{
    bool result = false;
    IOAudioSampleRate initialSampleRate;
    IOAudioStream*    audioStream;
    IOWorkLoop*       workLoop = NULL;

    IOLog("MyAudioEngine[%p]::initHardware(%p)\n", this, provider);

    if (!super::initHardware(provider))
        goto done;

    fAudioInterruptSource = IOTimerEventSource::timerEventSource(this, interruptOccured);
    if (!fAudioInterruptSource)
        return false;

    workLoop = getWorkLoop();
        if (!workLoop)
                return false;

    if (workLoop->addEventSource(fAudioInterruptSource) != kIOReturnSuccess)
        return false;

    // Setup the initial sample rate for the audio engine
    initialSampleRate.whole = kAudioSampleRate;
    initialSampleRate.fraction = 0;

    setDescription("My Audio Device");
    setSampleRate(&initialSampleRate);

    // Set the number of sample frames in each buffer
    setNumSampleFramesPerBuffer(kAudioBufferSampleFrames);
    setInputSampleLatency(kAudioSampleRate / kAudioInterruptHZ);
    setOutputSampleOffset(kAudioSampleRate / kAudioInterruptHZ);
```

```
    fOutputBuffer = (SInt16 *)IOMalloc(kAudioSampleBufferSize);
    if (!fOutputBuffer)
        goto done;

    fInputBuffer = (SInt16 *)IOMalloc(kAudioSampleBufferSize);
    if (!fInputBuffer)
        goto done;

    // Create an IOAudioStream for each buffer and add it to this audio engine
    audioStream = createNewAudioStream(kIOAudioStreamDirectionOutput,
                                fOutputBuffer, kAudioSampleBufferSize);

    if (!audioStream)
        goto done;

    addAudioStream(audioStream);
    audioStream->release();

    audioStream = createNewAudioStream(kIOAudioStreamDirectionInput,
                                fInputBuffer, kAudioSampleBufferSize);

    if (!audioStream)
        goto done;

    addAudioStream(audioStream);
    audioStream->release();

    result = true;
done:
    return result;
}
```

The first task the method performs is to allocate an IOTimerEventSource, used to simulate interrupts in lieu of hardware. We also set the description using the setDescription() method. This string will be visible to the user in several places, including in the sound pane of *System Preferences*, as show in Figure 12-4.

The next step is to set the sample rate of our engine. The sample rate is a property of the IOAudioEngine. Therefore, if the engine manages multiple streams, they must all have the same sample rate. In the case of MyAudioDevice, we set the current sample rate to kAudioSampleRate, which is defined as 48000 for a 48 kHz sample rate. We also need to define the number of samples our sample buffers will contain. If there are multiple streams in the same engine, the buffers must be of the same size. In MyAudioEngine, we use two streams, one for input and one for output. The number of samples contained in the buffer is set using the setNumSampleFramesPerBuffer() method. We currently set it to kAudioBufferSampleFrames, which is defined as the sample rate divided by two, corresponding to 24000 samples or half a second worth of audio. To calculate how many bytes 24000 samples correspond to, use the following formula:

```
24000 samples * 2 channels * (16 bits / 8 bits = 2 bytes) =  96000 bytes
```

This sample buffer size was chosen arbitrarily in our case; for a real world device, it will depend on the hardware's capabilities and often the size may be configurable. The buffer and other parameters

263

must be defined such that Core Audio doesn't write samples to a location before the hardware has had the chance to play them.

The setInputSampleLatency() and setOutputSampleLatency() methods can be used to indicate to Core Audio the time it takes from when samples were scheduled to be played until they actually start playing in hardware. Some hardware devices may have additional buffering or delay before the audio goes out on the DAC. You can also specify input and output latency together using setSampleLatency(). We set the latency to a single interrupt period (10 miliseconds) as we do not have any hardware delay, but we want to give Core Audio some headroom before reading and writing samples. We have 100 virtual interrupts per second and a sample rate of 48000, the delay corresponds to 480 samples. Again, we have simply chosen the value 100 Hz for simplicity; the rate of interrupts for an actual device is determined by the audio hardware.

We also have to allocate memory for the sample buffers. In MyAudioDevice, we are not performing DMA to a hardware device, so we simply allocate the input and output buffer using IOMalloc(). For a hardware-based driver, you need to either allocate IOBufferMemoryDescriptor or create a separate IOMemoryDescriptor for the buffer. The former is preferred. The buffers will then need to be prepared for DMA or I/O transfer. For DMA, you will need to translate the buffers' addresses into physical addresses so they can be read by the hardware or set up a scatter/gather table, all of which can be achieved using the IODMACommand class. Each buffer needs to be associated with an IOAudioStream, which coordinates client access to the buffer. The IOAudioStream instances are allocated using the method createNewAudioStream(), which is not a member of IOAudioEngine but is defined to avoid duplicating code. An IOAudioStream is added to the engine using the addAudioStream() method. Once the streams have been added, the reference can be released; the super class will take care of the final release.

Creating and Initializing Audio Streams

An IOAudioEngine needs at least one IOAudioStream in order to do anything useful. A stream is associated with exactly one sample buffer and describes the formats and sample rate supported by the buffer. A stream is either an output or an input stream. Under the hood, IOAudioStream handles the mechanics of getting data in and out from the sample buffer. Internally, it maintains a mix buffer, in which audio data from multiple clients is mixed together in a single stream before ending up in the final sample buffer destined for the hardware. Maintaining the mix and sample buffers are the most complicated tasks an audio driver performs, and it's all handled for us by the IOAudioStream class. For most cases, the default behavior of IOAudioStream should be sufficient; however, if your driver needs more advanced capabilities, you can override most methods in IOAudioStream to provide custom behavior. Shown below is the createNewAudioStream() method of MyAudioEngine responsible for creating the input and output stream.

```
IOAudioStream *MyAudioEngine::createNewAudioStream(IOAudioStreamDirection direction,
                                        void* sampleBuffer, UInt32 sampleBufferSize)
{
    IOAudioStream* audioStream;

    audioStream = new IOAudioStream;
    if (audioStream) {
        if (!audioStream->initWithAudioEngine(this, direction, 1)) {
            audioStream->release();
        } else {
            IOAudioSampleRate rate;
            IOAudioStreamFormat format = {
                2,                                              // num channels
```

```
                kIOAudioStreamSampleFormatLinearPCM,        // sample format
                kIOAudioStreamNumericRepresentationSignedInt, // numeric format
                kAudioSampleDepth,                          // 16-bit
                kAudioSampleWidth,                          // 16-bit
                kIOAudioStreamAlignmentHighByte,            // high byte aligned - unused
                                                            // because bit depth == bit
                                                            // width

                kIOAudioStreamByteOrderBigEndian,
                true,                                       // format is mixable
                0                                           // driver-defined tag - unused
                                                            // by this driver
            };
            audioStream->setSampleBuffer(sampleBuffer, sampleBufferSize);
            rate.fraction = 0;
            rate.whole = kAudioSampleRate;
            audioStream->addAvailableFormat(&format, &rate, &rate);
            audioStream->setFormat(&format);
        }
    }
    return audioStream;
}
```

The format of the sample buffer is described by the *IOAudioStreamFormat* structure. In the preceding case, we only added a single format and a single sample rate. You can define multiple supported formats and rates and add them by calling addAvailableFormat() for each defined format. The specification for our stream is Linear PCM signed integer samples at 16-bit depth/width in big-endian byte order. In most cases, bit depth and bit width are the same, such as for 16-bit samples. The depth specifies the number of bits used by the audio sample, whereas the width specifies the width in bits of the data word it's stored in. For example, this is used if you have 24-bit samples. A 24-bit sample occupies three bytes, which is awkward to work with and to align properly, so we instead use a 32-bit word to store each sample, which is more efficient in terms of performance (though it will waste eight bits per sample). If the width and depth do not match, the next field in the IOAudioStreamFormat structure must be set to either kIOAudioStreamAlignmentHighByte or kIOAudioStreamAlignmentLowByte to specify the alignment of the sample within the data word.

Handling Format Changes

Your IOAudioEngine will need to respond to requests from Core Audio to change the format of the engine's audio streams. Requests to change format are handled with the performFormatChange() method, which should be overridden as the default is a stub that simply returns an error. The Apple IOAudioFamily sample implements the format change method, as follows:

```
IOReturn SampleAudioEngine::performFormatChange(IOAudioStream *audioStream,
                                    const IOAudioStreamFormat *newFormat,
                                    const IOAudioSampleRate *newSampleRate)
{
    IOLog("SampleAudioEngine[%p]::peformFormatChange(%p, %p, %p)\n", this, audioStream,
newFormat, newSampleRate);

    // Since we only allow one format, we only need to be concerned with sample rate changes
    // In this case, we only allow two sample rates, 44100 and 48000,
```

```
        // so those are the only ones we check for.
        if (newSampleRate) {
            switch (newSampleRate->whole) {
                case 44100:
                    IOLog("/t-> 44.1kHz selected\n");
                    // Add code to switch hardware to 44.1khz
                    break;
                case 48000:
                    IOLog("/t-> 48kHz selected\n");
                    // Add code to switch hardware to 48kHz
                    break;
                default:
                    // This should not be possible since we only specified 44100 and 48000
                    // as valid sample rates
                    IOLog("/t Internal Error - unknown sample rate selected.\n");
                    break;
            }
        }
        return kIOReturnSuccess;
}
```

■ **Note** The performFormatChange() method will be called only for formats specified when IOAudioStreams were created.

Clipping and Converting Samples

Because Core Audio (Audio HAL) works with high-precision 32-bit floating-point samples, we must convert (unless supported natively by hardware) audio samples from floating-point format into a format the hardware can understand when outputting audio. Most audio hardware may only handle integer samples, as is the case with our virtual MyAudioDevice driver.

The IOAudioEngine subclass should override the IOAudioEngine::clipOutputSamples() method if the engine has an output IOAudioStream. Similarly, it will need to override the IOAudioEngine::convertInputSamples() method if it has an input IOAudioStream. The methods are responsible for converting audio data to or from the native format as well as to clip samples. Clipping refers to the process of checking each sample to ensure it is within the valid range. For example, a floating-point sample has to be in the range of –1.0 to 1.0, and values lower or higher must be clipped to the nearest valid value. The clipOutputSamples() method for MyAudioDevice is implemented as follows:

```
IOReturn MyAudioEngine::clipOutputSamples(const void *mixBuf, void *sampleBuf,
                                          UInt32 firstSampleFrame,
                                          UInt32 numSampleFrames,
                                          const IOAudioStreamFormat* streamFormat,
                                          IOAudioStream* audioStream)
{
    UInt32 sampleIndex, maxSampleIndex;
    float *floatMixBuf;
    SInt16 *outputBuf;
```

```
    floatMixBuf = (float *)mixBuf;
    outputBuf = (SInt16 *)sampleBuf;

    maxSampleIndex = (firstSampleFrame + numSampleFrames) * streamFormat->fNumChannels;

    for (sampleIndex = (firstSampleFrame * streamFormat->fNumChannels); sampleIndex <
maxSampleIndex; sampleIndex++)
{
        float inSample;

        inSample = floatMixBuf[sampleIndex];

        if (inSample > 1.0) {
            inSample = 1.0;
        } else if (inSample < -1.0) {
            inSample = -1.0;
        }

        // Scale the -1.0 to 1.0 range to the appropriate scale for signed 16-bit samples
        // and then convert to SInt16 and store in the hardware sample buffer
        if (inSample >= 0) {
            outputBuf[sampleIndex] = (SInt16) (inSample * 32767.0);
        } else {
            outputBuf[sampleIndex] = (SInt16) (inSample * 32768.0);
        }
    }
    return kIOReturnSuccess;
}
```

The method takes samples from the mix buffer containing the combined audio stream for all clients using our device, converts the samples, and transfers them into the final I/O buffer (fOutputBuffer). The method takes six arguments, as follows:

1. A pointer to the mix buffer, from which you should get samples.

2. The sampleBuf parameter is the sample buffer of the IOAudioStream given by the audioStream parameter.

3. firstSampleFrame is the offset into the buffers you should start from.

4. The numSampleFrames parameter is the number of samples you should convert and clip.

5. The streamFormat parameter is an IOAudioStreamFormat structure, which describes the current format of the audio stream.

6. A pointer to the IOAudioStream that owns the sample buffer.

The implementation of convertInputSamples() is very similar, only the reverse is done; convert to floating-point samples instead of from floating-point samples. Check the source code for MyAudioDevice to see its implementation. If your driver supports multiple audio formats, your clip functions will be more complicated than the preceding, which handle only conversion to 16-bit signed integer samples.

The MyAudioDevice implementation is taken from Apple's example driver and is intended to be as simple as possible for demonstration purposes. Because the method has to manipulate every channel of every sample frame, it is crucial that the method is as efficient as possible. To speed the code up, it would be possible to use a vector-based instruction set such as SSE to process multiple samples at a time. See Chapter 17 for information about how SSE instructions can be used in the kernel.

The clip and convert methods are the best location to manipulate the audio data should your driver need to perform any sort of adjustment, such as filtering certain frequencies. If you are implementing a virtual audio device, you can perform virtual volume level adjustments simultaneously by attenuating the samples to the desired level or muting them by zeroing each sample. Can you modify MyAudioDevice to do this?

The convertInputSamples() method is very similar to the output version, but one difference is that it should always write to the beginning of the destination, unlike clipOutputSamples(), which may start at an offset into the buffer.

■ **Tip** Consult the source of MyAudioDevice to see how the convertInputSamples() method is implemented.

Starting and Stopping the Audio Engine

The audio engine is started and stopped as needed by the Core Audio HAL. However, the start and stop actions don't relate to the *IOService* lifecycle methods start() and stop(), which are called once when the driver loads for the first time and once before the driver is about to unload. Instead, the IOAudioEngine class provides the performAudioEngineStart() and performAudioEngineStop() methods, which, unlike the aforementioned, start and stop audio I/O only. In MyAudioDevice, the performAudioEngineStart() method is implemented as follows:

```
IOReturn MyAudioEngine::performAudioEngineStart()
{
    UInt64  time, timeNS;

    IOLog("MyAudioEngine[%p]::performAudioEngineStart()\n", this);
    fInterruptCount = 0;
    takeTimeStamp(false);
    fAudioInterruptSource->setTimeoutUS(kAudioInterruptInterval / 1000);

    clock_get_uptime(&time);
    absolutetime_to_nanoseconds(time, &timeNS);

    fNextTimeout = timeNS + kAudioInterruptInterval;
    return kIOReturnSuccess;
}
```

The performAudioEngineStart() method should do two things, ensure the device starts playing or capturing in hardware and ensure the initial timestamp of the sample buffer(s) is set by calling the takeTimeStamp() function. We will discuss the purpose and meaning of the takeTimeStamp() method in the next section. In MyAudioEngine, we simply take the first timestamp and schedule the interrupt timer to timeout in 10 ms.

The performAudioEngineStop() will reverse the actions taken when the engine was started and disable interrupts so the device no longer performs I/O from the sample buffer and reset it into a state where it will be ready to run again. The MyAudioDevice driver implements the method as follows:

```
IOReturn MyAudioEngine::performAudioEngineStop()
{
    IOLog("MyAudioEngine[%p]::performAudioEngineStop()\n", this);
    fAudioInterruptSource->cancelTimeout();
    return kIOReturnSuccess;
}
```

The method simply cancels any further interrupts; however, the engine is left in a state where it is ready for I/O to be started again. When the driver is about to unload, its stop() method will be called and can be used to tear down anything performed in initHardware(). Audio streams and any controls attached to the class are cleaned up automatically by the super class. In our case, this leaves the stop() method looking much like performAudioEngineStop(), with the only additional step being to remove the interrupt source, as follows:

```
void MyAudioEngine::stop(IOService *provider)
{
    IOLog("MyAudioEngine[%p]::stop(%p)\n", this, provider);

    if (fAudioInterruptSource)
    {
        fAudioInterruptSource->cancelTimeout();
        getWorkLoop()->removeEventSource(fAudioInterruptSource);
    }
    super::stop(provider);
}
```

Engine Operation: Handling Interrupts and Timestamps

In an audio engine for a DMA-based device, there is actually not that much to do. The device will continuously read from the buffer for an audio output stream and write to the buffer for an audio input stream. The DMA engine will run more or less without any intervention once started. However, there is one very important task to perform, which is to inform the IOAudioEngine of the time when a sample buffer wraps around to the start and to keep track of how many times it has wrapped. It is critical that the timestamp is as accurate as possible. The information is used by the Audio HAL to keep track of the sample buffer position at any given time. This is important because Core Audio, unlike other audio architecture, does not receive direct notifications from the driver once an I/O cycle completes (i.e., the buffer wraps). Instead, it relies on the timestamps taken by the driver to predict the future position of the sample buffer. Taking a timestamp is achieved by calling the takeTimeStamp() method, which will store the current time in nanoseconds to an internal instance variable in the IOAudioEngine class (fLastLoopTime) and the loop count (fCurrentLoopCount).

In the performAudioEngineStart() method, it takes the initial timestamp once the I/O begins. You will notice it passed *false* as an argument, which ensures the loop count is not incremented since we have not yet completed any loops.

Therefore, at the basic level, assuming the hardware device issues an interrupt once it wraps around to the beginning of the buffer, an interrupt routine simply consisting of a call to takeTimeStamp() can be implemented. Some hardware devices allow the driver to program the rate of interrupts. In this case, you may want to count the interrupts and only call takeTimeStamp() once N interrupts have occurred. This is the case of MyAudioDevice, which is driven by a timer that "interrupts" every 10 ms. Our device operates at a rate of 48 kHz (48000 samples) and our buffer fits half a second of audio, which means it takes 500 ms before our buffer wraps back to the beginning; therefore, we want to count 50 interrupts (50 * 10 ms) before calling takeTimeStamp().The code for MyAudioDevice's interrupt handler is as follows:

```
void MyAudioEngine::interruptOccured(OSObject* owner, IOTimerEventSource* sender)
{
    UInt64      thisTimeNS;
    uint64_t    time;
    SInt64      diff;

    MyAudioEngine* audioEngine = (MyAudioEngine*)owner;

    if (audioEngine)
        audioEngine->handleAudioInterrupt();
    if (!sender)
        return;

    clock_get_uptime(&time);
    absolutetime_to_nanoseconds(time, &thisTimeNS);
    diff = ((SInt64)audioEngine->fNextTimeout - (SInt64)thisTimeNS);

    sender->setTimeoutUS((UInt32)(((SInt64)kAudioInterruptInterval + diff) / 1000));
    audioEngine->fNextTimeout += kAudioInterruptInterval;
}

void MyAudioEngine::handleAudioInterrupt()
{
    UInt32 bufferPosition = fInterruptCount % (kAudioInterruptHZ / 2);
    UInt32 samplesBytesPerInterrupt =
        (kAudioSampleRate / kAudioInterruptHZ) * (kAudioSampleWidth/8) * kAudioNumChannels;
    UInt32 byteOffsetInBuffer = bufferPosition * samplesBytesPerInterrupt;

    UInt8* inputBuf = (UInt8*)inputBuffer + byteOffsetInBuffer;
    UInt8* outputBuf = (UInt8*)outputBuffer + byteOffsetInBuffer;

    // Copy samples from the output buffer to the input buffer.
    bcopy(outputBuf, inputBuf, samplesBytesPerInterrupt);
    // Tell the buffer to wrap
    if (bufferPosition == 0)
    {
        takeTimeStamp();
    }

    fInterruptCount++;
}
```

In addition to taking timestamps whenever the buffer wraps, you are also required to implement the getCurrentSampleFrame() method, which should return the current position of the sample buffer. The sample position is used by IOAudioEngine to erase (set to zero/silence) samples that have already been played. The method is not required to return a 100% accurate position, but the position returned should be behind the hardware read head. Otherwise, you risk overwriting samples that have not yet been played, which again will result in pops, clicks, or other audio distortions. The buffer will be erased up to but not including the sample frame returned by the function. There are several ways of getting the position, such as reading it from a hardware register, using timestamps to calculate the position based on the sample rate, or using an interrupt count. MyAudioDevice uses the latter, as shown in the following example:

```
UInt32 MyAudioEngine::getCurrentSampleFrame()
{
    UInt32 periodCount = (UInt32) fInterruptCount % (kAudioInterruptHZ/2);
    UInt32 sampleFrame = periodCount * (kAudioSampleRate / kAudioInterruptHZ);
    return sampleFrame;
}
```

Additional Audio Engine Functionality

Previous sections have discussed the basic operation of the IOAudioEngine class. It does, however, have a number of other useful methods and capabilities. Some useful methods of IOAudioEngine we haven't discussed so far are outlined in Table 12-2.

Table 12-2. Summary of Additional IOAudioEngine Methods

Method	Description
virtual void clearAllSampleBuffers()	Zeros (silences) out all mix and sample buffers attached to the IOAudioEngine.
virtual void clientClosed(IOAudioEngineUserClient *client);	Called when a user space client closes the connection to the IOAudioEngine.
virtual IOReturn convertInputSamplesVBR(const void* sampleBuf, void* destBuf, UInt32 firstSampleFrame, UInt32 &numSampleFrames, const IOAudioStreamFormat* streamFormat, IOAudioStream* audioStream)	If overridden, provides an alternative to convertInputSamples() for returning a different number of samples from what was requested.
virtual IOReturn eraseOutputSamples(const void* mxBuf, void* sampleBuf, UInt32 firstSampleFrame, UInt32 numSampleFrames, const IOAudioStreamFormat* streamFormat, IOAudioStream* audioStream)	This is the method used internally by IOAudioEngine to erase the sample buffers. It is declared virtual so it is possible to override it if you need to alter how erasure is performed. You do not need to override this if you simply want to prevent erase from happening, as this can be achieved by calling setRunEraseHead(false).
virtual bool getRunEraseHead()	Returns true if the audio engine's erase process is active. See setRunEraseHead().
virtual const IOAudioSampleRate* getSampleRate()	Gets the current sample rate of the audio engine in samples per second.

Method	Description
`virtual const IOAudioEngineStatus* getState()`	Gets the state of the audio engine, which can be either kIOAudioEngineRunning or kIOAudioEngineStopped.
`virtual const IOAudioEngineStatus* getStatus()`	Returns a pointer to the internal status buffer of the audio engine. This is a structure that contains the current loop count and timestamps, as well as the location of the erase head.
`virtual void setClockDomain(UInt32 clockDomain = kIOAudioNewClockDomain)`	The method sets a property Core Audio can use to determine how an audio device clock is synchronized.
`virtual void setClockIsStable(bool clockIsStable)`	Used by Core Audio to determine how it should track the sample rate of the audio device. A device with an unstable clock source experiencing audio distortions may benefit from setting this to false.
`virtual void setInputSampleOffset(UInt32 numSamples)`	Sets the position in the sample buffer where Core Audio will read.
`virtual void setMixClipOverhead(UInt32 nexMixClipOverhead)`	This method can be called to hint to the IOAudioFamily the time taken by the mix and clip routine. The value should be a number between 1 and 99 and represents percentage of the sample buffer time.
`virtual void setOutputSampleOffset(UInt32 numSamples)`	Sets the position where Core Audio will write to in the sample buffer.
`virtual void setRunEraseHead(bool runEraseHead)`	Disable the erase process. For an engine that only does input, this is disabled by default.

Summary

In this chapter, we have covered the following areas:

- Digital audio and Pulse Code Modulation (PCM), which is a technique for converting an analog audio signal into a digital representation. We have also looked at how PCM samples are encoded and interleaved channel by channel.

- The Core Audio architecture, which collectively provides sound/audio support to Mac OS X and iOS. The cornerstone of Core Audio is the HAL, which coordinates the use of audio hardware on behalf of clients and allows multiple clients to access audio hardware simultaneously.

- The Core Audio HAL, which always uses 32-bit floating-point format to represent audio samples. A driver is therefore responsible for converting the native format of the hardware to or from this format.

- IOAudioFamily, which provides the kernel-level side of the audio architecture. The key classes of the family are IOAudioDevice, IOAudioEngine, and IOAudioStream.

- The IOAudioDevice class, which represents a hardware audio device in the kernel.

- The IOAudioEngine class, which represents a single I/O engine for which an IOAudioDevice may have more than one. The class is abstract. The audio engine class may have one or more IOAudioStreams associated with it.

- An IOAudioStream is used to represent a single sample buffer.

- The operation of an audio engine is conceptually simple, the engine simply needs to tell the super class (which again communicates with Core Audio/Audio HAL) when the device has wrapped to the beginning of the sample buffer and how many times this event has occurred.

CHAPTER 13

Networking

Network support in the kernel is implemented primarily in the BSD layer. The BSD flavors of UNIX are renowned for their robust and secure networking support. Consequently, code from the BSD networking stack has made its way into a wide variety of operating systems, including Mac OS X and iOS. While the networking support is primarily in the BSD layer, it has hooks into I/O Kit, which provides the interface for building hardware-based network drivers. A conceptual view of the kernel network architecture is shown in Figure 13-1.

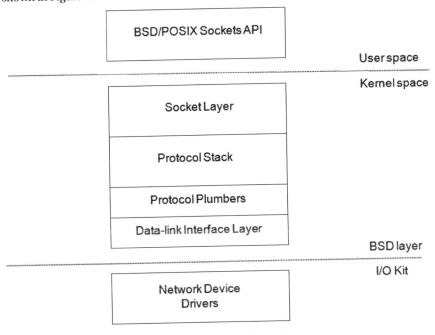

Figure 13-1. Conceptual view of the kernel network architecture

From a user space application's perspective, networking services are accessed through the BSD/POSIX socket API, with functions such as connect(), listen(), and bind(). However, the socket API is not only about networking. It also handles various forms of inter-process communication (IPC), such as UNIX domain sockets. Unlike most BSD versions, the XNU kernel also implements an in-kernel socket API (KPI). This KPI allows the kernel and KEXTs to use sockets much the same way as in user space applications. The key difference is that functions in the socket KPI are named with a "sock_" prefix. For example, the connect() function is named sock_connect() in the kernel KPI.

Higher-level APIs, like Core Foundation or Cocoa, build their network support on top of the socket API interface. The socket API communicates with the kernel through the standard system call interface. The socket layer shares many commonalities with the file system APIs; indeed, a socket is just a special type of file descriptor. In fact, the read() and write() system call functions can be used on socket descriptors as well.

The kernel part of the socket API is responsible for queuing and routing data to and from the appropriate protocol handler in the protocol stack, which handles the tasks of constructing network packets and dividing the data into appropriately sized packets, adding checksums, etc. It's in the protocol stack that TCP, UDP, and IP are handled. The protocol stack is also responsible for handling the details of routing, the firewall, and auxiliary protocols, such as ARP. Packets destined for external hosts end up in the interface layer of the BSD network stack. The interface layer again plugs into the network interface classes in the I/O Kit, which again communicates with a physical network device through its driver.

Four key data structures are used in the BSD network stack:

- The socket structure represents open sockets in user space or kernel space and is accessed using file descriptors from user space.

- The domain structure is used to describe protocol families, such as IP version 4 (PF_INET), IP version 6 (PF_INET6), or the local domain (PF_LOCAL/PF_UNIX).

- The protosw describes individual protocol handlers for each supported protocol, such as IPv4, IPv6, TCP, UDP, ICMP, IGMP, or RAW. Protocols accessible through the sockets interface, such as TCP and UDP, are referred to by the identifiers SOCK_STREAM and SOCK_DGRAM, respectively, when an AF_INET socket is used.

- The ifnet structure describes a network interface. Each interface listed by the command ifconfig, such as en0, en1, and lo0, is backed by an ifnet structure. An ifnet structure is also defined for each I/O Kit network driver. An I/O Kit driver doesn't need to interface with the structure directly, as the IONetworkInterface class provides an abstraction for it.

Another feature of the XNU kernel is the network kernel extensions (NKE) mechanism. NKE allows filters to be inserted at various levels of the network stack, such as in the sockets layer or IP layer. The NKE architecture allows you to write custom routing algorithms, and implement new protocols and virtual network interfaces. It can also be used for packet filtering and logging. Furthermore, the kernel supports the Berkeley Packet Filter (BPF), which allows raw network traffic to be routed to user space for analysis with tools such as tcpdump. We will look at the NKE system in more detail later in this chapter, as well as how to implement drivers for network devices in the I/O Kit.

To get the most out of this chapter, it is necessary that you have some understanding of networking, of concepts such as TCP/IP and Ethernet, and that you are familiar with the layers of the OSI model.

Network Memory Buffers

Network Memory Buffers, or mbufs, is a fundamental data structure in BSD UNIX systems, including Mac OS X and iOS. While it is mostly a concept of the BSD network layer, you will also encounter the mbuf data structure when writing I/O network drivers. The structure is used to represent network packets and their metadata. The structure is not exposed to user space. The mbuf structure is shown in Listing 13-1.

Listing 13-1. The mbuf Data Structure

```
struct mbuf {
    struct  m_hdr m_hdr;
    union {
        struct {
            struct  pkthdr MH_pkthdr;           /* M_PKTHDR set */
            union {
                struct  m_ext MH_ext;           /* M_EXT set */
                char    MH_databuf[_MHLEN];
            } MH_dat;
        } MH;
        char    M_databuf[_MLEN];               /* !M_PKTHDR, !M_EXT */
    } M_dat;
};
```

The complete mbuf structure is fixed size and is currently 256 bytes long. This size includes both the header and the data held by the structure. To get the number of bytes available for data storage: (256 – sizeof(struct m_hdr)). To describe larger packets, multiple mbufs are linked together in a linked list as shown in Figure 13-2.

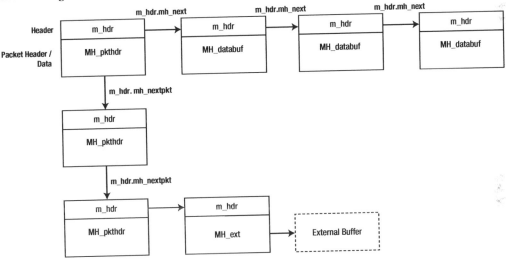

Figure 13-2. A chain of mbuf structures

A list of mbufs is called a chain. In Figure 13-2, a chain of three mbufs, each describing a packet, is shown. Each mbuf may contain chains of other mbufs making up the complete network packet.

To reduce overhead with large packets, mbufs can have their structure point to an external buffer instead of using the internal storage of the mbuf. An mbuf structure with an external buffer is referred to as a cluster. The MH_ext field is used to describe the external buffer. The mbuf header (m_hdr) is located at the start of the structure and contains the length of the mbuf's data, which is stored in the mh_len field. The header also contains the pointers for the next buffer in the chain, and the next entry in a list/or queue, which usually represent a new packet; however, mbufs can also be used for storage of other control information. The mh_type and mh_flags are used to determine the type and options of an mbuf—for example, whether it has an associated external buffer. If an mbuf represents the start of a packet, the MH_PKTHDR will be set, and if the mbuf has external data, the MH_EXT flag will be set, which means that it is safe to access the mbuf's MH_pkthdr or MH_ext structures.

Working with Memory Buffers

While the mbuf structure is found in many UNIX variants, the programming interface for working with them differs between platforms. The XNU kernel offers the mbuf KPI for working with mbufs. The idea of the KPI is to treat the mbuf as an opaque structure, which is only manipulated by KPI functions instead of accessing structure fields directly. This allows the mbuf implementation to change under the hood but still remain binary and source compatible with code that uses KPI. For this reason, when manipulating mbufs, we do not use the mbuf structure directly but rather use the handle mbuf_t as a reference.

▪ **Tip** The mbuf KPI header file is bsd/sys/mbuf.h. The full documentation for the KPI can be found at http://developer.apple.com/library/mac/#documentation/Darwin/Reference/KernelIOKitFramework/kpi_mbuf_h/.

Getting data in and out of mbufs can be achieved with the following functions:

```
errno_t mbuf_copydata(const mbuf_t mbuf, size_t offset, size_t length, void *out_data);
errno_t mbuf_copyback(mbuf_t mbuf, size_t offset, size_t length, const void *data, mbuf_how_t how);
```

It is not always possible to use bcopy() or similar functions directly, because data in mbufs may be scattered over several structures or external buffers. The preceding functions simplify this task significantly. However, if the buffer is known to be contiguous, the mbuf_data() function can retrieve the pointer to the data area of the mbuf. The mbuf_copydata() function copies data from an mbuf (chain) to the memory location pointed to by the out_data parameter, which should be large enough to hold length bytes.

The mbuf_copyback() does the reverse and allows you to copy data back to an mbuf. If the mbuf is not large enough, the function will grow the buffer by appending more mbufs to form a chain. The last parameter how should be either MBUF_WAITOK or MBUF_DONTWAIT, which indicates to the function whether it is allowed to block while allocating memory. In an interrupt routine or performance critical path, MBUF_DONTWAIT must be used and, generally, where possible, MBUF_DONTWAIT is preferred.

The mbuf KPI offers several ways to construct new mbufs as shown here:

```
errno_t mbuf_allocpacket(mbuf_how_t how, size_t packetlen, unsigned int *maxchunks, mbuf_t *mbuf);
errno_t mbuf_allocpacket_list(unsigned int numpkts, mbuf_how_t how,
                            size_t packetlen, unsigned int *maxchunks, mbuf_t *mbuf);
errno_t mbuf_tag_allocate(mbuf_t mbuf, mbuf_tag_id_t module_id,
                         mbuf_tag_type_t type, size_t length, mbuf_how_t how, void **data_p);
```

Following is a brief description of the preceding functions:

- mbuf_allocpacket() allocates a chain of mbufs with a leading packet header of the specified length. maxchunks is an input/output parameter that specifies the maximum length of the chain. If NULL is specified, there is no limit.

- mbuf_allocpacket_list() is identical to mbuf_allocpacket() but generates a list of mbuf chains instead.

- mbuf_tag_allocate() allocates an mbuf but also allows one to specify additional data *(tag)* that will be passed along with the mbuf as it travels through the stack. The tag can be retrieved again by using the mbuf_tag_find() function.

Besides allocating and copying data in and out of an mbuf, a common operation is to iterate through an mbuf chain using the mbuf_next() macro:

```
void walk_mbuf(mbuf_t mbuf_head)
{
    mbuf_t mb;
    unsigned char* data;
    size_t len;

    for (mb = mbuf_head; mb; mb = mbuf_next(mb))
    {
        data = (unsigned char*)mbuf_data(mb); // get pointer to data
        len = mbuf_len(mb);                    // get length of this segment
    }
}
```

Network Kernel Extensions

The kernel supports extending the network stack at multiple levels through the Network Kernel Extensions (NKE) mechanism. An NKE is no different from a regular KEXT; it is merely a term used to describe a KEXT that interfaces with or extends the network stack.

As such, NKEs are also dynamically loadable and unloadable at runtime. NKEs are not part of the I/O Kit, but located in the BSD layer. The NKE mechanism is unique to Mac OS X and not found in BSD UNIX flavors, such as FreeBSD.

An NKE can be used for many purposes. Some examples of use include, but are not limited to, the following:

- Custom firewall or security mechanisms, such as encryption

- Adding support for new protocols

- Adding support for new network interfaces

- Creating virtual network interfaces

- Creating custom routing schemes

- Delaying, modifying, inspecting, or blocking network packets

- Debugging network stack and drivers

An NKE typically utilizes one of the following KPI/filtering mechanisms:

- *Socket filter.* Allows filters to be inserted at various points in the socket layer, and can filter inbound and outbound traffic as well as out-of-band communication. It can filter most protocols supported by the socket API. It is possible to modify, delay, or reject traffic.

- *IP filter.* Allows filtering of IP version 4 and 6 traffic.

- *Interface filter.* Allows traffic to be monitored and modified on a specific network interface. Since this happens at the end of the stack, all protocols and traffic destined for that interface will be visible.

- *Interface KPI.* A programming interface for creating new network interfaces.

- *Protocol plumber.* Provides the glue that connects a network protocol to a network interface.

Kernel Control KPI

The kernel control interface <sys/kern_control.h> is a KPI that allows a KEXT to communicate bi-directionally with user space processes. This mechanism is often used in conjunction with NKEs to allow user space programs to control and configure a KEXT. A full discussion of the Kernel Control KPI is provided in Chapter 17.

Socket Filters

A socket filter is a powerful mechanism that allows intercepting of network and IPC traffic in the kernel's socket layer. The socket layer (and hence the socket filter) is situated between user space and the network protocol stack in the kernel. Because of this, socket filters cannot peek at the IP or TCP header of an outgoing network packet because that happens later in the processing chain. However, it is still possible to filter IP-based traffic using a socket filter, as metadata, such as the IP address the packet is destined for, is known. The same is true for incoming traffic. The protocol stack will strip header information before it enters the socket layer. In effect, we are seeing the reassembled data that will eventually be read by a user space application. Because of this, a socket filter is not suitable for use when information from protocol headers is required, and one should use the lower level IP or interface filters instead.

Another thing to note is that a socket filter cannot filter traffic from protocols that are not initiated through the socket API, because some auxiliary protocols are handled directly in the protocol stack. An example would be ARP and RARP requests, which are handled by the kernel and aren't usually initiated by a user application but rather happen as a side effect of some other type of traffic. The socket API is most commonly used by user space applications or libraries, however, as previously mentioned, a socket KPI also exists, allowing the kernel to use socket communication in much the same way as user space. Kernel-initiated sockets can also be filtered.

The socket interface isn't restricted to just filtering data packets. It can also intercept out-of-band communication, such as calls to socket-related system calls like bind() and listen().

A socket filter is registered by filling out desired callbacks in the sflt_filter structure, as shown in Listing 13-2.

Listing 13-2. The sflt_filter Structure Used to Register a Socket Filter (kpi_socketfilter.h)

```
struct sflt_filter {
        sflt_handle              sf_handle;
        int                      sf_flags;
        char                     *sf_name;
        sf_unregistered_func     sf_unregistered;
        sf_attach_func           sf_attach;
        sf_detach_func           sf_detach;
        sf_notify_func           sf_notify;
        sf_getpeername_func      sf_getpeername;
        sf_getsockname_func      sf_getsockname;
        sf_data_in_func          sf_data_in;
        sf_data_out_func         sf_data_out;
        sf_connect_in_func       sf_connect_in;
        sf_connect_out_func      sf_connect_out;
        sf_bind_func             sf_bind;
        sf_setoption_func        sf_setoption;
        sf_getoption_func        sf_getoption;
        sf_listen_func           sf_listen;
        sf_ioctl_func            sf_ioctl;
        struct sflt_filter_ext {
                unsigned int     sf_ext_len;
                sf_accept_func   sf_ext_accept;
                void             *sf_ext_rsvd[5];      /* Reserved */
        } sf_ext;
#define sf_len                   sf_ext.sf_ext_len
#define sf_accept                sf_ext.sf_ext_accept
};
```

As you can see, there are quite a few callbacks, but only a few, such as sf_attach and sf_detach, are mandatory. Non-mandatory callbacks not needed by a filter can be set to NULL. A socket filter can operate in two modes; which mode is used depends on the flags set in the sf_flags field. There are two possible values:

- SFLT_GLOBAL If set, the filter attaches itself to every socket that matches the protocol domain and protocol specified when the filter was registered. Once registered, the filter will be invoked for every new socket created matching the criteria.

- SFLT_PROG The filter will be activated, only if an owner of the socket specifically requests it, by using the SO_NKE socket option to the setsockopt() system call.

The first field of the structure sf_handle is used to identify the filter to clients when the filter is operating in programmatic mode (SFLT_PROG is set). It is also used to deregister the socket filter after use. The handle consists of a four-character sequence, which should be unique. Apple provides a registration process to apply for a unique character sequence called a creator code. The sft_name field is used for debug purposes and is commonly set to the bundle ID of the containing KEXT, but it can be anything.

A socket filter is registered with the system using the sflt_register() function.

Building an Application-Level Firewall Using Socket Filters

To better understand how the socket filter mechanism works, let's look at an example of what it can be used for. While Mac OS X ships with an application-level firewall already (ALF.kext), we will do a very simplistic version to demonstrate the power of socket filters. The AppWall architecture consists of an NKE KEXT, which contains the socket filter. AppWall will solve the problem of preventing unauthorized programs from accessing the network. The socket filter can also log information about data transferred in either direction for a specified program, without interfering with its operation. Because AppWall will be proof-of-concept, we will limit it to support IP version 4 using the TCP protocol.

Let's get started by defining the socket filter:

```
#define APPWALL_FLT_TCP_HANDLE        'apw0'       // codes should registered with Apple

static struct sflt_filter socket_tcp_filter = {
        APPWALL_FLT_TCP_HANDLE,
        SFLT_GLOBAL,
        "com_osxkernel_AppWall",
        appwall_unregistered,
        appwall_attach,
        appwall_detach,
        NULL,
...
        appwall_data_in,
        appwall_data_out,
        appwall_connect_in,
        appwall_connect_out,
        NULL,
...
};
```

■ **Tip** The unabridged source for AppWall will be made available on the publisher's website: www.apress.com.

Because of our requirements, we have left out a number of function pointers as NULL, as they are not relevant to our filter's design. If you wish, you can easily modify AppWall to implement these as well.

Let's have a look at how we register the filter:

```
kern_return_t AppWall_start (kmod_info_t * ki, void * d)
{
...
    ret = sflt_register(&socket_tcp_filter, PF_INET, SOCK_STREAM, IPPROTO_TCP);
    if (ret != KERN_SUCCESS)
        goto bail;

    add_entry("ssh", 1);    // block the ssh application.
    add_entry("nc", 0);     // log data from the nc application.

    g_filter_registered = TRUE;
...
}
```

For brevity, we have left out general housekeeping code, such as allocating locks or error handling. Once the sflt_register() function returns, the filter may be active and we may start seeing our callbacks invoked. Therefore, it is vital that any needed resources, such as locks, are initialized prior to registering the filter.

The sflt_register() function takes four arguments:

- The pointer to the socket filter structure, as mentioned earlier.

- The protocol domain, which we specify as PF_INET, which is the IP version 4 family.

- The type. We specify SOCK_STREAM, which refers to a full duplex stream-based socket.

- And finally the protocol, which we specify as IPPROTO_TCP.

▪ **Tip** The domain, type and protocol values are the same as those used in the user space socket API. Check the man 2 socket manual page for more details about available domains, types, and protocols.

If you wish to handle other protocols, such as UDP, a second call to sflt_register() is needed. Each registered filter needs its own unique handle, so you will need to declare a second structure for the UDP filter. If desired, the second structure may share some or all callbacks with the first.

The last step is to add some entries to our list of blocked/monitored applications using the AppWall add_entry() function. In a real NKE, you would most likely have a kernel control that allowed a user space utility to configure this instead of hard coding. The add_entry() function creates an appwall_entry structure, as shown in Listing 13-3.

AppWall Operation and Data Structures

Before we start implementing the filter callbacks, we need to declare data structures to store information collected from the filter. We declare the data structures in a shared header file, which can be used by a user space utility in the future, but for now, is only used by the AppWall KEXT. The data structure is shown in Listing 13-3.

Listing 13-3. AppWall Header File

```
#define BUNDLE_ID   "com.osxkernel.AppWall"

struct app_descriptor
{
    char name[PATH_MAX];
    unsigned long bytes_in;
    unsigned long bytes_out;
    unsigned long packets_in;
    unsigned long packets_out;
    int           do_block;
    int           outbound_blocked;
```

```
    int             inbound_blocked;
};

#if defined (KERNEL)
struct appwall_entry
{
    TAILQ_ENTRY(appwall_entry)   link;
    struct app_descriptor        desc;
    int                          users;
};
#endif

#endif
```

The first structure `app_descriptor` is used to hold the name of an application to be blocked or monitored. Entries with the `do_block` field set to non-zero are blocked, whereas a zero value means we will simply collect and report statistics for it.

We use the name of the application and not a process indentifier (PID) to track every instance of that program. While this is not secure, because you can bypass by renaming the executable, it is fine for the sake of example.

The field `do_block` will be non-zero, if we wish to block this particular application; if it is zero, we will instead collect statistics only. If we see a socket from an application for which no `appwall_entry` exists, our filter will ignore it.

Attaching and Detaching the Filter

The attach (`sf_attach`) and detach (`sf_detach`) functions are called whenever our filter attaches itself to a socket. This happens either because the client that owns the socket specifically request that we attach or for a global filter, when the socket is created. It is not possible to attach to a socket that is already established.

Because a filter may intercept a high volume of sockets, the callbacks should avoid doing any heavy processing, as it may impact the system's network performance. AppWall was designed for demonstration and to be as simple as possible, not as a high-performance socket filter.

Let's look at the implementation of the attach callback in AppWall:

```
static   errno_t appwall_attach(void** cookie, socket_t so)
{
    errno_t                  result = 0;
    struct appwall_entry*    entry;
    char                     name[PATH_MAX];

    *cookie = NULL;

    proc_selfname(name, PATH_MAX);

    lck_mtx_lock(g_mutex);

    entry = find_entry_by_name(name);
    if (entry)
    {
```

```
        entry->users++;
        *cookie = (void*)entry;
        printf("AppWall: attaching to process: %s\n", name);
    }
    else
        result = ENOPOLICY; // don't attach to this socket.

    lck_mtx_unlock(g_mutex);

    return result;
}
```

We are passed two arguments: The first is a cookie parameter that we can use to assign per-socket data. The cookie pointer will be passed back to us in every callback. The second argument is an opaque reference to the socket itself. Since the socket is opaque, it must be accessed with the socket KPI.

RETRIEVING THE IP ADDRESS OF A SOCKET

The following example shows how to use the socket KPI to get the IP address the socket is bound to:

```
unsigned char addrstr[256];
struct sockaddr_in  addr;
sock_getsockname(so, (struct sockaddr*)&addr, sizeof(addr));
inet_ntop(AF_INET, &addr.sin_addr, (char*)addrstr, sizeof(addrstr));
printf("%s:%d\n", addrstr, ntohs(addr.sin_port));
```

When the appwall_attach() function gets called, we are executing in the context of the task that created the socket, and we can, therefore, call proc_selfname(), which returns the process name of the current task. Once we have a name, we search the global linked list of appwall_entry structures to see if we can find a match. If a match is found, we increment its users count, and assign to the cookie return argument.

All manipulation of the linked list is performed under a global mutex to protect against concurrent access. If a match is not found, we return ENOPOLICY. Any non-zero return code from the function will have the effect of preventing the filter from being attached to this socket (without affecting the sockets lifecycle) and, hence, no further callbacks will be seen for that socket.

If you have a socket_t handle, you can manually attach to the socket by calling the sf_attach() function.

The sf_detach() callback will be invoked when the filter should be detached from the socket, which occurs when a socket closes or as a result of the filter being unregistered with sflt_unregister(). The detach callback in AppWall is implemented as follows:

```
static void
appwall_detach(void* cookie, socket_t so)
{
    struct appwall_entry*      entry;

    if (cookie)
```

```
        {
            entry = (struct appwall_entry*)cookie;

            lck_mtx_lock(g_mutex);

            entry->users--;
            if (entry->users == 0)
            {
                printf("report for: %s\n", entry->desc.name);
                printf("=================================\n");

                if (entry->desc.do_block)
                {
                    printf("inbound_blocked: %d\n", entry->desc.inbound_blocked);
                    printf("outbound_blocked: %d\n", entry->desc.outbound_blocked);
                }
                else
                {
                    printf("bytes_in: %lu\n", entry->desc.bytes_in);
                    printf("bytes_out: %lu\n", entry->desc.bytes_out);
                    printf("entry->desc.packets_in: %lu\n", entry->desc.packets_in);
                    printf("entry->desc.packets_out: %lu\n",entry->desc.packets_out);
                }
                cookie = NULL;
            }
            lck_mtx_unlock(g_mutex);
        }
        return;
}
```

The function simply prints a report of how many times connections were blocked, or if the application was monitored, dumps statistics for how many bytes and packets were transmitted.

Handling Connections

A socket filter can intercept calls to the connect() system call for outgoing connections. The system call handler calls our filter by using the sf_connect_out filter function. The filter function is passed the following three arguments.

- The cookie

- A handle to the socket itself

- A sockaddr structure describing the intended destination of the socket

Returning non-zero from the callback will have the effect of propagating the error directly back to the caller of the connect() function (from kernel or user space) and will prevent the socket from being established without any packets going out on the network, which is how AppWall is able to block outgoing connections.

There is a catch here for UDP. UDP is connectionless and is not required to call connect() at all; it will do so only to set the default address for send() and recv(), which does not result in outgoing network traffic. Blocking UDP traffic can instead be done in the data out or in callbacks on a per packet basis.

The sf_connect_in function, on the other hand, is not called in response to a system call like sf_connect_out but called by a protocol handler just before a new connection is established. The sf_connect_in callback is currently only invoked for TCP and does not apply to UDP. (It's connectionless.)

As with the output filter, it is possible to reject the connection by returning non-zero, preventing it from being established and sending any further data to the socket. The sf_connect_in callback takes the same arguments as the output callback, but the sockaddr structure will describe the remote address instead. AppWall implements the sf_connect_in filter function as follows:

```
static  errno_t
appwall_connect_in(void* cookie, socket_t so, const struct sockaddr* from)
{
    struct appwall_entry*        entry;
    errno_t                      result = 0;

    entry = (struct appwall_entry*)cookie;
    if (!entry)
        goto bail;

    lck_mtx_lock(g_mutex);

    if (entry->desc.do_block)
    {
        printf("blocked incoming connection to: %s", entry->desc.name);
        if (from)
        {
            printf(" from: ");
            log_ip_and_port_addr((struct sockaddr_in*)from);
        }
        entry->desc.inbound_blocked++;
        result = EPERM;
    }
    lck_mtx_unlock(g_mutex);
bail:

    return result;
}
```

The function looks for a non-NULL cookie, and if one is present, checks if the application owning the current socket should be blocked.

Socket Data Input and Output

The real power of socket filters are in the sf_data_in and sf_data_out filter functions. They allow interception of incoming and outgoing packets. Packets seen by a socket filter's data functions are stripped of (or have not yet had attached) protocol header information, such as IP, TCP, or UDP headers. In the case of TCP and UDP, the information will represent the actual payload data, which will be delivered to or from a socket. If you need data from the protocol headers, you may wish to write an IP or interface filter instead. For incoming data packets, you can determine the network interface a packet received by calling mbuf_pkthdr_rcvif() on the mbuf. For outgoing packets, this information isn't available because the filter function executes before the packet is routed to a network interface. The sf_data_out function in AppWall is implemented as follows:

```
static  errno_t
appwall_data_out(void* cookie, socket_t so, const struct sockaddr* to, mbuf_t* data,
                 mbuf_t* control, sflt_data_flag_t flags)
{
    struct appwall_entry*      entry;
    errno_t                    result = 0;

    entry = (struct appwall_entry*)cookie;
    if (!entry)
        goto bail;

    lck_mtx_lock(g_mutex);
    entry->desc.bytes_out += mbuf_pkthdr_len(*data);
    entry->desc.packets_out++;

    if (entry->desc.do_block)
        result = EPERM;
    lck_mtx_unlock(g_mutex);
bail:
    return result;
}
```

The function accepts the following six parameters:

- The cookie containing the pointer to the appwall_entry structure.

- A socket_t reference to socket transmitting data.

- A sockaddr structure containing the address of the host to which the packet is destined. The argument is NULL for TCP packets, but set for UDP. The destination of a TCP socket can be determined at the time the connection is created (sf_connect_out).

- A pointer to an mbuf_t handle. Note that you cannot use the mbuf_t directly, as it is merely a handle, you have to use the mbuf KPI to extract data and information from it. Also note that the mbuf argument is a pointer, so it also functions as an output argument. It is possible to assign a different mbuf_t, which will be transmitted in lieu of the original.

- A pointer to an mbuf_t handle containing additional control data.

- The sixth parameter is used to indicate the type of data, such as normal, out-of-band or records data. There are two valid flags: sock_data_filt_flag_oob and sock_data_filt_flag_record. A value of zero indicates normal data.

In the AppWall case, the data in function is implemented in a similar way to the connect function by checking if the calling socket has a cookie attached, which in turn means that the packet should either be logged or blocked. We return EPERM to signal the caller that it should free the packet and halt further processing if the packet should be blocked (filtered). If you wish to keep the packet, but prevent it from progressing further, you can return EJUSTRETURN instead, which will prevent the caller from freeing the packet.

AppWall implements the data input function nearly identically. It will block an incoming packet by returning EPERM.

▓ **Tip** If you wish to learn more about socket filters, Apple provides a more comprehensive socket filter example, called: *tcplognke,* which can be found on their developer website. It shows how to log connections as well as how to swallow (delay) and re-inject packets at a later time. It also demonstrates some of the other filter functions we have not covered here and the user of the kernel control mechanism.

Internet Protocol Filters

Internet Protocol (IP) filters allow filtering and injection of incoming and outgoing IP packets. The IP filter mechanism works both for IPv4 and for IPv6. Because the IP operates at the network layer, there is no concept of connections or sessions, as that is handled by higher layer protocols and mechanisms. At the IP level, there are only packets going in and out. As a result, IP filters are significantly less complex than socket filters. The programming interface is similar to that of socket filters. An IP filter is defined by the structure ipf_filter:

```
struct ipf_filter {
    void*           cookie;
    const char*     name;
    ipf_input_func  ipf_input;
    ipf_output_func ipf_output;
    ipf_detach_func ipf_detach;
};
```

The structure consists of the following fields and callbacks:

- The cookie field is used to assign a pointer containing some data that should be passed along to all the filter functions.

- The name is used for debugging purposes and should be set to something identifying your filter/KEXT.

- The ipf_input and ipf_output fields define the actual filter functions, which will be called for incoming and outgoing IP packets, respectively.

- The ipf_detach function will be called when the filter is detached. Unlike a socket filter, which detaches when a socket close is terminated, IP filters need to be detached/removed explicitly by calling ipf_remove(). Note that the ipf_remove() function may defer removal of the filter if one of the filter functions are executing when the function is called. Therefore, you need to wait for the ipf_detach filter function to complete before a KEXT can be unloaded to avoid a kernel panic when the IP stack tries to call ipf_detach after it has been unloaded from memory.

A complete example of a minimal IP filter is shown in Listing 13-4.

Listing 13-4. MyIPFilter: Implementation of a Simple IP Filter

```
#include <mach/mach_types.h>
#include <sys/kernel_types.h>
#include <sys/systm.h>
#include <sys/kpi_mbuf.h>
#include <netinet/ip.h>
#include <netinet/kpi_ipfilter.h>

enum {
    kMyFiltDirIn,
    kMyFiltDirOut,
    kMyFiltNumDirs
};

struct myfilter_stats {
    unsigned long udp_packets[kMyFiltNumDirs];
    unsigned long tcp_packets[kMyFiltNumDirs];
    unsigned long icmp_packets[kMyFiltNumDirs];
    unsigned long other_packets[kMyFiltNumDirs];
};

static struct myfilter_stats g_filter_stats;
static ipfilter_t g_filter_ref;
static boolean_t g_filter_registered = FALSE;
static boolean_t g_filter_detached = FALSE;

static void log_ip_packet(mbuf_t* data, int dir) {
    char src[32], dst[32];
    struct ip *ip = (struct ip*)mbuf_data(*data);

    if (ip->ip_v != 4)
        return;

    bzero(src, sizeof(src));
    bzero(dst, sizeof(dst));
    inet_ntop(AF_INET, &ip->ip_src, src, sizeof(src));
    inet_ntop(AF_INET, &ip->ip_dst, dst, sizeof(dst));

    switch (ip->ip_p) {
        case IPPROTO_TCP:
            printf("TCP: ");
            g_filter_stats.tcp_packets[dir]++;
            break;
        case IPPROTO_UDP:
            printf("UDP: ");
            g_filter_stats.udp_packets[dir]++;
            break;
        case IPPROTO_ICMP:
            printf("ICMP: ");
            g_filter_stats.icmp_packets[dir]++;
```

```
        default:
            printf("OTHER: ");
            g_filter_stats.other_packets[dir]++;
            break;
    }
    printf("%s -> %s\n", src, dst);
}

static errno_t myipfilter_output(void* cookie, mbuf_t* data, ipf_pktopts_t options) {
    if (data)
        log_ip_packet(data, kMyFiltDirOut);
    return 0;
}

static errno_t myipfilter_input(void* cookie, mbuf_t* data, int offset, u_int8_t protocol) {
    if (data)
        log_ip_packet(data, kMyFiltDirIn);
    return 0;
}

static void myipfilter_detach(void* cookie) {
    /* cookie isn't dynamically allocated, no need to free in this case */
    struct myfilter_stats* stats = (struct myfilter_stats*)cookie;
    printf("UDP_IN %lu UDP OUT: %lu TCP_IN: %lu TCP_OUT: %lu ICMP_IN: %lu ICMP OUT: %lu
OTHER_IN: %lu OTHER_OUT: %lu\n",
            stats->udp_packets[kMyFiltDirIn],
            stats->udp_packets[kMyFiltDirOut],
            stats->tcp_packets[kMyFiltDirIn],
            stats->tcp_packets[kMyFiltDirOut],
            stats->icmp_packets[kMyFiltDirIn],
            stats->icmp_packets[kMyFiltDirOut],
            stats->other_packets[kMyFiltDirIn],
            stats->other_packets[kMyFiltDirOut]);

    g_filter_detached = TRUE;
}

static struct ipf_filter g_my_ip_filter = {
    &g_filter_stats,
    "com.osxkernel.MyIPFilter",
    myipfilter_input,
    myipfilter_output,
    myipfilter_detach
};

kern_return_t MyIPFilter_start (kmod_info_t * ki, void * d) {
    int result;

    bzero(&g_filter_stats, sizeof(struct myfilter_stats));
    result = ipf_addv4(&g_my_ip_filter, &g_filter_ref);

    if (result == KERN_SUCCESS)
```

```
                g_filter_registered = TRUE;

        return result;
    }

    kern_return_t MyIPFilter_stop (kmod_info_t * ki, void * d) {

        if (g_filter_registered)
        {
            ipf_remove(g_filter_ref);
            g_filter_registered = FALSE;
        }
        /* We need to ensure filter is detached before we return */
        if (!g_filter_detached)
            return KERN_NO_ACCESS; // Try unloading again.

        return KERN_SUCCESS;
    }
```

The filter will attach itself once the KEXT is loaded, and detach itself once it unloads. The filter will print the source and destination of each received IP packet to the console, as well as keep track of statistics for TCP, UDP, and ICMP packets, for which a summary is printed once the filter is detached.

The ipf_filter structure is registered using the ipf_addv4() function, which registers an IPv4 filter. IPv6 filters can be registered with ipf_addv6().

The ipf_input and ipf_output callbacks are invoked from the IP stack on arrival or departure of an IP packet. For incoming IP packets, the filter function will be called just before the packet gets processed by a higher-level protocol handler, such as TCP or UDP. If the IP packet was fragmented, it is reassembled before being passed to the filter function. For outgoing packets, the filter function will be called before the packet is fragmented. Normally, a packet would only be seen by a filter function once. However, there is one exception, which is if the packet uses an encryption scheme like IPSec, where an IP packet may contain another encrypted IP packet. In this case, the filter function will be called once for the encrypted packet and once for the decrypted payload.

IP filters work across interfaces, so you will see packets from and to all active interfaces in the system. If you need to know which interface the packet arrived from, this information can be obtained from the mbuf packet header. For outgoing packets, this information is not yet available, because routing of the packet to a network interface happens after the output filter function is called. This is by design, because it is possible for the filter function to alter the destination of a packet, as we will see shortly.

IP filters are not limited to examining packets; it is also possible to modify packets, reject them, and inject your own packets. To illustrate the power of IP filters, we can modify the ipf_output filter function from Listing 13-4 with a new version:

```
static errno_t myipfilter_output_redirect(void* cookie, mbuf_t* data, ipf_pktopts_t options)
{
    struct in_addr addr_old;
    struct in_addr addr_new;
    int ret;

    struct ip* ip = (struct ip*)mbuf_data(*data);
    if (ip->ip_v != 4)
        return 0;
```

```
addr_old.s_addr = htonl(134744072); // 8.8.8.8
addr_new.s_addr = htonl(167837964); // 10.1.1.12

// redirect packets to 8.8.8.8 to the IP address 10.1.1.12.
if (ip->ip_dst.s_addr == addr_old.s_addr)
{
    ip->ip_dst = addr_new;
    myipfilter_update_cksum(*data);
    ret = ipf_inject_output(*data, g_filter_ref, options);
    return ret == 0 ? EJUSTRETURN : ret;
}
return 0;
}
```

The preceding example will redirect all IP traffic to the public IP address (8.8.8.8) to an internal IP address on our network (10.1.1.12). We do this by examining the destination of the IP address and, if it matches our address, we modify the packet's destination to the new address. Because we have modified the packet, we need to re-inject it. This will have the effect of treating the modified packet as a new one and, hence, it will again pass through our filter. We can prevent the packet from being processed again by our filter by passing in the reference to our filter when we inject the packet, as shown in the preceding example.

Since we have re-injected the packet, we need to stop the original packet from progressing further, which we do by returning EJUSTRETURN. This will tell the caller to stop processing the packet without freeing it. To discard a packet completely, we can return a value other than zero or EJUSTRETURN, which will cause the caller to stop processing and also free the packet. These rules apply for both incoming and outgoing packets. When modifying an IP packet's header, we need to update its checksum (CRC) to prevent the packet from being discarded as corrupt. The IP checksum covers its own header, but not the payload. TCP and UDP checksums are calculated using some of the fields of the IP header, including the source and destination address. Consequently, UDP and TCP checksums also need to be recalculated if an IP header's address fields are modified. IP, TCP, and UDP checksums can be calculated for an mbuf_t using the function mbuf_inet_cksum(). See the myipfilter_update_cksum() function in the book sample project MyIPFilter for an example of how to update the checksums.

We can now test that our modified IP filter function works correctly using the ping command line utility:

```
$ ping 8.8.8.8
PING 8.8.8.8 (8.8.8.8): 56 data bytes
64 bytes from 10.1.1.12: icmp_seq=0 ttl=64 time=307.636 ms
64 bytes from 10.1.1.12: icmp_seq=1 ttl=64 time=2.513 ms
```

As you can see, we will now get replies from 10.1.1.12 instead of the original IP address. This happens to work with the ping utility, which uses a RAW socket. However, for a regular socket-based application like ssh, we also need to modify the source address of incoming packets to enable full two-way communication, otherwise, the IP stack will be confused when it gets unsolicited packets from the 10.1.1.12 host. You can modify the ipf_input filter function to modify incoming packets so that the source address is translated from 10.1.1.12 back to 8.8.8.8, thereby ensuring that the packet is directed to the right application (which still thinks we are talking to 8.8.8.8). This is conceptually similar to how Network Address Translation (NAT) technology is implemented. NAT is the technique used by Mac OS

X's Internet sharing feature or how the iPhone can share its 3G connection to other wireless devices. Refer to the full source code of the MyIPFilter example to see how we can modify a packet on input.

Although, in the previous example, we have only modified the destination address, it is possible to modify any part of the packet, including application layer data. It is also possible to completely replace a packet with a new one. The structure of a typical IP packet is shown in Figure 13-3.

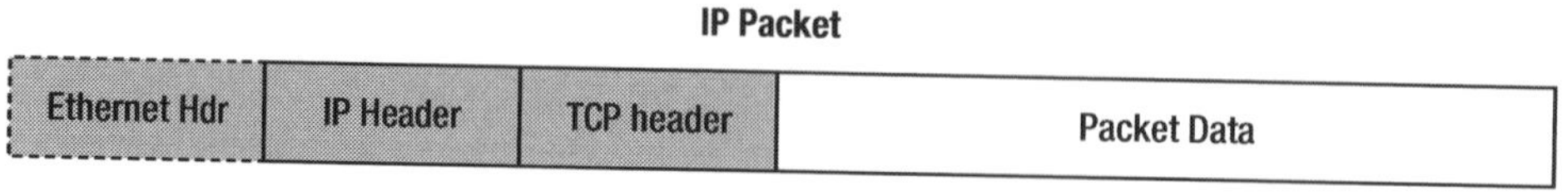

IP Packet

Figure 13-3. An Ethernet frame with an IP, TCP header, and data payload

In the case of both incoming and outgoing packets, a filter function will see the complete packet, but the packet data passed to the filter function will not include any data-link layer headers, such as an Ethernet header, because that will be processed before the packet enters the IP stack where our filter function gets called. Similarly for outgoing packets, the Ethernet, or other data-link layer header, will be attached after the packet goes through the filter function. Again, if you update any part of the packet, you must ensure that relevant checksums are updated as well.

Interface Filters

Interface filters are as close to the metal as we can get using a filtering mechanism. Interface filters operate just before and after a packet is sent or received by a network interface. If a packet is destined for a physical interface, as opposed to a loopback or virtual interface, it will likely be sent to an I/O Kit driver for physical transmission. An interface filter is bound to only one interface, unlike an IP or socket filter, which sees the aggregate packet flow of all interfaces in the system. If you need to filter packets on multiple interfaces, you must register multiple filters, one for each interface. The interface filter mechanism is very similar to that of socket and IP filters. As with socket filters, interface filters can also intercept out-of-band events, such as ioctl() messages sent to the interface—for example, requests to set or get the IP address, network mask, or MTU (maximum transfer unit). An interface filter can also trap events to the interface sent via the kernel event API. As with socket and IP filters, interface filters allow insertion, modification, rejection, and delay of packets. An interface filter is defined by the iff_filter structure:

```
struct iff_filter {
    void*           iff_cookie;
    const char*     iff_name;
    protocol_family_t iff_protocol;
    iff_input_func  iff_input;
    iff_output_func iff_output;
    iff_event_func  iff_event;
    iff_ioctl_func  iff_ioctl;
    iff_detached_func iff_detached;
};
```

All the filter functions are optional, and functions you do not care about can be left as NULL. Unlike an IP or socket filter, an interface filter will see all packets regardless of protocol, which will include protocols handled in the kernel, such as ARP. If your filter is interested only in IP packets, you can use the iff_protocol field to specify AF_INET for IPv4 or AF_INET6 for IPv6, which will ensure that the filter function will not be called for other protocols. It is only possible to specify protocol families, not individual protocols, like TCP or UDP. Furthermore, if your filter needs to examine IP packets, be aware that the IP packets may now be fragmented, and you will not have the opportunity to examine encrypted IP headers when IPSec is used. Listing 13-5 shows the implementation of a simple interface filter.

Listing 13-5. MyInterfaceFilter: A Simple Network Interface Filter

```
#include <libkern/libkern.h>
#include <sys/errno.h>
#include <sys/kpi_mbuf.h>
#include <mach/mach_types.h>
#include <net/kpi_interfacefilter.h>

#include <netinet/in.h>
#include <netinet/ip.h>
#include <net/ethernet.h>

static boolean_t g_filter_registered = TRUE;
static boolean_t g_filter_detached = FALSE;
static interface_filter_t g_filter_ref;

static errno_t myif_filter_input(void* cookie, ifnet_t interface, protocol_family_t protocol,
                        mbuf_t* data, char** frame_ptr)
{
    printf("incoming packet: %lu bytes\n", mbuf_pkthdr_len(*data));
    return 0;
}

static errno_t myif_filter_output(void* cookie, ifnet_t interface, protocol_family_t protocol,
                        mbuf_t* data)
{
    printf("outgoing packet: %lu bytes\n", mbuf_pkthdr_len(*data));
    return 0;
}
static void myif_filter_detached(void* cookie, ifnet_t interface)
{
    g_filter_detached = TRUE;
}

static struct iff_filter g_my_iff_filter =
{
    NULL,
    "com.osxkernel.MyInterfaceFilter",
    0,
    myif_filter_input,
    myif_filter_output,
    NULL,
    NULL,
    myif_filter_detached,
};

kern_return_t MyInterfaceFilter_start (kmod_info_t* ki, void* d)
{
    ifnet_t interface;
```

```
    if (ifnet_find_by_name("en1", &interface) != KERN_SUCCESS) // change to your own interface
        return KERN_FAILURE;

    if (iflt_attach(interface, &g_my_iff_filter, &g_filter_ref) == KERN_SUCCESS)
    {
        g_filter_registered = TRUE;
    }

    ifnet_release(interface);

    return KERN_SUCCESS;
}

kern_return_t MyInterfaceFilter_stop (kmod_info_t* ki, void* d)
{
    if (g_filter_registered)
    {
        iflt_detach(g_filter_ref);
        g_filter_registered = FALSE;
    }
    if (!g_filter_detached)
        return KERN_NO_ACCESS; // Don't allow unload until filter is detached.

    return KERN_SUCCESS;
}
```

Interface filters can be attached to a network interface using the iflt_attach() function. You can register a single iff_filter against multiple interfaces. A network interface is represented by the opaque type ifnet_t, which can be manipulated using the interface KPI (kpi_interface.h). In the preceding example, we use the interface KPI function ifnet_find_by_name() to obtain a reference to the network interface with the BSD name "en1," which, on a MacBook, corresponds to the Wi-Fi interface.

The iff_input filter function is called when an incoming packet is received by the interface. The callback takes five arguments:

- The cookie argument contains the pointer assigned to the iff_cookie field when the filter was registered.

- The ifnet_t argument is a reference to the network interface that received the packet. This is especially useful in case the same filter function handles filters attached to more than one network interface.

- The next parameter is the protocol family the incoming packet belongs to. Unless zero is specified for the iff_protocol field, this will always be the family you specified.

- The mbuf_t represents the buffer containing the packet data.

- The last argument, frame_ptr, is a pointer to the data-link frame header of the interface. The size and structure of the frame header varies depending on the network interface. For an Ethernet interface, the frame header consists of a source and destination MAC address as well as a 16-bit "ethertype" field, which determines the encapsulated protocol. The field will be 0x0800 for an Ethernet frame containing an IP packet. You can determine the length of the frame header for an interface by calling the ifnet_hdrlen(ifnet_t) function.

The output filter function iff_output is similar to the input function, but does not provide the frame header as a separate argument; rather the mbuf_t contains the entire frame including the data-link header, instead of pointing to the data after the data-link header. If we wish to examine the IP header of an incoming packet in an interface filter's output function, we need to first parse the data-link header to find the offset of the IP header. An example of this is shown here:

```
static errno_t myif_filter_output(void* cookie, ifnet_t interface, protocol_family_t protocol,
                                  mbuf_t* data)
{
    char                src[64], dst[64];
    unsigned char*      pktbuf = mbuf_data(*data);
    struct ether_header* eth = (struct ether_header *)pktbuf;

    if (ifnet_hdrlen(interface) != ETHER_HDR_LEN)
        return 0;

    if (ntohs(eth->ether_type) == ETHERTYPE_IP)
    {
        struct ip* iphdr = (struct ip*)(pktbuf + ETHER_HDR_LEN);
        inet_ntop(AF_INET, &iphdr->ip_src, src, sizeof(src));
        inet_ntop(AF_INET, &iphdr->ip_dst, dst, sizeof(dst));
        printf("outgoing packet: %lu bytes ip_src: %s ip_dst: %s\n",
               mbuf_pkthdr_len(*data), src, dst);
    }
    else
        printf("outgoing packet: %lu bytes\n", mbuf_pkthdr_len(*data));
    return 0;
}
```

The interface filter KPI does not provide functions for injecting incoming and outgoing packets. This is provided by the interface KPI instead. Outgoing packets can be injected using the function ifnet_output_raw() or using the function ifnet_input() to inject an inbound packet. For an example of how inet_output_raw() can be used, refer to the source code of the sample driver MyEthernetDriver discussed later in this chapter.

Debugging and Testing Network Extensions

Apart from the general techniques discussed in Chapter 16, "Debugging and Profiling," Mac OS X comes with some tools that allow debugging of network issues, the most notable of which are perhaps the command line tools tcpdump and netcat. The former utilizes the libpcap library, which again is built on top of the Berkeley Packet Filter (BPF) infrastructure, which is built into the kernel network stack. BPF can plug into each network interface and install hooks, which allow incoming and outgoing packets to be diverted to a character device file (/dev/bpfX) and can thereby be analyzed by tools such as tcpdump. The tcpdump utility allows you to view the packet flow live, or to capture it to a file for later analysis. A wide range of third party tools can work with the packet traces captured from tcpdump. If possible, the tcpdump utility will put the monitored interface into promiscuous mode. Promiscuous mode is a firmware feature of most network devices that tells it to forward packets, even if they are not addressed to its own hardware address. Newer versions of Mac OS X require root privileges in order to run tcpdump, even if promiscuous mode is disabled. Capturing packets from a busy network can be difficult due to the sheer amount of data. To address this, tcpdump takes advantage of the filtering capabilities of the BPF, which allows you to filter out packets based on a wide range of criteria ranging from the hardware address to the individual flags of the TCP header. The following is an example of tcpdump output:

```
$ sudo tcpdump -i en0
tcpdump: verbose output suppressed, use -v or -vv for full protocol decode
listening on en0, link-type EN10MB (Ethernet), capture size 65535 bytes
20:43:40.911558 IP 192.168.1.2.ipp > 192.168.255.255.ipp: UDP, length 237
20:43:51.113519 ARP, Request who-has 192.168.1.2 tell 192.168.1.3, length 28
20:43:51.113785 ARP, Reply 192.168.1.2 is-at 00:17:f2:0a:86:60 (oui Unknown), length 46
20:43:51.113831 IP 192.168.1.3 > 192.168.1.2: ICMP echo request, id 64769, seq 0, length 64
20:43:51.114004 IP 192.168.1.2 > 192.168.1.3: ICMP echo reply, id 64769, seq 0, length 64
20:44:11.911836 IP 192.168.1.2.ipp > 192.168.255.255.ipp: UDP, length 237
20:46:01.413453 IP 192.168.1.2.netbios-ns > 192.168.255.255.netbios-ns: NBT UDP PACKET(137):
QUERY; REQUEST; BROADCAST
20:46:01.451950 IP 192.168.1.2.netbios-dgm > 192.168.255.255.netbios-dgm: NBT UDP
PACKET(138)
```

The netcat utility has many uses. For network debugging, it is useful in its ability to create TCP- and UDP-based clients or servers, as it can be used to generate traffic in either direction for the purpose of testing. This is especially useful in the development of IP or socket filters as well as network interface drivers. The netcat utility can be invoked from the terminal with the nc command. The following example shows how to create a socket to listen for UDP traffic on port 4040:

```
$ nc -u -l 4040
```

You can connect to the server using nc on a different system:

```
$ nc -u 192.168.1.2 4040
Stuff typed here will be echoed back to the server
```

Networking in the I/O Kit

The IONetworkingFamily of classes represents the bottom part of the kernel network stack. As previously discussed, the I/O Kit is the preferred layer for implementing drivers for hardware-based network devices. The class hierarchy of the IONetworkingFamily is shown in Figure 13-4.

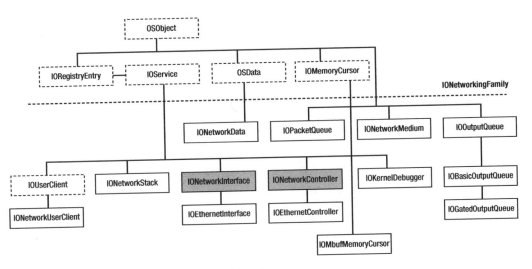

Figure 13-4. The IONetworkingFamily class hierachy

The family may look quite expansive, but many of the classes are auxiliary helper classes, and some, we do not need to worry about at all because they are only used internally in the family. The key classes in the family are the IONetworkController and IONetworkInterface. The former is used to represent a driver for network hardware, whereas the latter is used to interface with the data-link interface layer (DLIL) in the BSD layer. It serves as an adapter that allows I/O Kit network interfaces to be seen as BSD layer network interfaces, so you can use traditional UNIX tools, such as ifconfig, to configure the device. Let's have a look at the responsibilities of the individual classes:

- IOEthernetController is the base class for all Ethernet-based devices, including 802.11-based wireless devices. You would normally subclass this when writing a driver for an Ethernet or Wi-Fi-based device driver.

- IOEthernetInterface acts as a client of an IOEthernetController and provides the glue between the controller and the BSD networking layer. If you are implementing an Ethernet driver, you do not normally need to subclass IOEthernetInterface unless you have special requirements.

- IOKernelDebugger is a replacement driver, which will be used against an IONetworkController in lieu of an IONetworkInterface when the kernel debugger is active. You do not need to support this if you are writing a third party network driver.

- IOMbufMemoryCursor provides an object-oriented cursor around the mbuf structure, which allows translation of mbuf clusters to physical addresses for the purpose of DMA. Several specialized subclasses are available: IOMBufBigMemoryCursor, IOMbufDBMAMemoryCursor, IOMbufLittleMemoryCursor, IOMbufNaturalMemoryCursor.

- IONetworkController is the base class of IOEthernetController. You must subclass IONetworkController if you are writing a driver for a non-Ethernet compatible device.

- IONetworkData represents a fixed size data buffer used by IONetworkInterface to export interface data to user space, notably, usage statistics such as information about dropped packets and collisions.

- IONetworkInterface provides the glue to bind an IONetworkController to the BSD data-link layer (BDIL) and the rest of the network stack. The IONetworkInterface is an abstract class and must be re-implemented if your driver is based on IONetworkInterface.

- IONetworkUserClient is a subclass of IOUserClient, providing a user-client for IONetworkInterface.

- IOOutputQueue is a packet queue, which handles multiple producers and a single consumer (a device). Two specialized subclasses are available: IOBasicOutputQueue and IOGatedOutputQueue.

- IOPacketQueue implements a FIFO queue of mbufs synchronized by a spinlock.

You may have noticed the absence of any mention of 802.11x networking support. Apple does not publish a framework for development of wireless networking drivers. Apple's own AirPort drivers are located in the IO802Family.kext, but no source or header files are published for this. This does not preclude writing of wireless network drivers, but it does mean that you can't take advantage of pre-written classes, and you may have to provide your own IOUserClient and possible user space tools for configuration of the device. Apple's AirPort devices are subclasses of the private IO80211Controller, which, again, is a subclass of IOEthernetController. That being said all modern Macs have built-in wireless networking, so demand for third-party devices in this area is low.

Building a Simple Ethernet Controller Driver

Let's get our hands dirty with I/O Kit networking, by building a simple Ethernet driver. Since implementing a full working driver is highly complex and hardware-dependent, it is difficult to demonstrate in its entirety, and probably not that useful to someone having to implement a driver for a completely different device. We will instead focus on the fundamentals and on familiarizing ourselves with the tools an I/O Kit provides to aid in developing network drivers. We will do this by implementing a virtual Ethernet driver called MyEthernetDriver. The driver will demonstrate how core elements of an I/O Kit network driver are implemented and will show how packets flow through it to interact with the rest of the system. Figure 13-5 shows how MyEthernetDriver interacts with other I/O Kit classes.

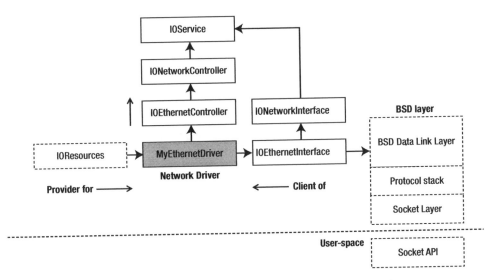

Figure 13-5. MyEthernetDriver: Interaction with I/O Kit and the network stack

In this case, MyEthernetDriver uses the IOResources nub as a provider, but for a real network device backed by a physical device, it would more probably use IOPCIDevice, IOUSBDevice, IOUSBInterface, or another *nub* representing a hardware device.

■ **Tip** If you are curious to see a network driver for a real device, the IOUSBFamily source distribution used to include the source code for AppleUSBCDCEthernet, which is the driver for devices that follow the USB Ethernet specification. The driver is not part of newer versions, but can still be found in older versions of IOUSBFamily at Apple's open-source website (opensource.apple.com). There is also source code available for a driver for the popular PCI based Realtek 8139 chipset called AppleRTL8139Ethernet. For an example of a network driver derived directly from IONetworkController, have a look at IOFireWireIP, which implements TCP/IP networking over FireWire.

The main driver class MyEthernetDriver will inherit from IOEthernetController, which again inherits from IONetworkController. The driver will also allocate an IOEthernetInterface instance, which will be used to interface with the network stack. The IOEthernetInterface class is not abstract and can be allocated and used directly.

The Design of MyEthernetDriver

To put the design of MyEthernetDriver into context, let's say we are employed to develop a driver for a new Ethernet device. The device will be a dongle that can be connected to a Mac's Thunderbolt port. As this is an emerging technology at this point, there is some delay in getting the needed parts, so we do not yet have access to a proper device. As much as we would all like to get paid to surf the net all day, we need to earn our bread and butter. So we get started on the driver without a working device. Our aim is to implement what can be done without having a hardware device. However, we quickly realize that a major component of the Ethernet device is going to be handling actual network I/O. While you can build a virtual device driver quite quickly, assign it an IP, and start talking to it, there is one major problem. Network packets destined to another interface or itself on the same host will not actually be forwarded to the device at all, but instead loop through the protocol stack without involving the I/O Kit driver. The I/O Kit was designed specifically to interface with actual hardware devices, so if you need a virtual network interface, the BSD layer is the best place for it.

Our solution to this problem will be to piggyback our virtual Ethernet device onto a real Ethernet interface and use it to send and receive packets on our behalf. The setup will look similar to the diagram in Figure 13-6.

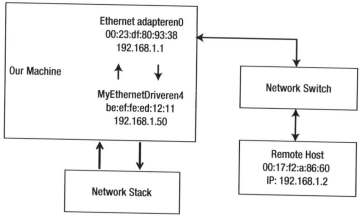

Figure 13-6. MyEthernetDriver test setup

When MyEthernetDriver receives a packet from the network stack, it will queue the packet and then transmit the packet out on the network using the interface *en0*, which is attached to a physical network switch. If you do not have a network switch, you can test this by using a straight through cat5 cable to connect directly to a remote machine. Each interface in the test setup is configured with its own IP address all on the same subnet. The network stack is responsible for framing the packet, so by the time MyEthernetDriver receives it, it will already have an Ethernet frame header attached, where the destination address will be 00:17:f2:0a:86:60 and the arbitrarily picked source address be:ef:fe:ed:12:11 of MyEthernetDriver. Most Ethernet based network devices allow sending a packet with a (fake) source address that differs from its own. Therefore, if everything is correctly configured, we should be able to receive the packet on the remote host received from MyEthernetDriver's MAC and IP address.

Getting the reply from the remote host back to our driver is somewhat more problematic, as the *en0* interface will most likely ignore a frame not addressed to itself. To work around this, we will simply enable promiscuous mode on *en0*, which will enable it to receive packets not destined to itself. We will then install an interface filter on the input queue for *en0* and check whether a packet is addressed to it, in which case, we leave it alone, or if it is addressed to MyEthernetDriver, steal it and divert it to its input queue instead. The end result is a virtual Ethernet bridge/switch. This is conceptually close to how virtual machine software, such as Parallels or VMWare fusion, enables a virtual machine guest's operating system to participate on the network in bridged mode. Because we have done this at the Ethernet level, the changes are completely transparent to higher-level protocols like IP, and we can even use an external DHCP server to obtain an IP address for our virtual interface.

This should leave us with a more or less working device driver, which, for all intents and purposes, is able to send and receive actual network traffic and provide a good approximation of a real device for us to play with. As much as possible, we will hide the fact that this bridging occurs from the driver by putting the code in a separate class called MyEthernetHwAbstraction. The class will handle communication with the "hardware" while the main driver will interface with I/O Kit. This design would allow us to quickly swap out the hardware abstraction class with one that talks to actual hardware instead. The design would also make it possible to subclass the abstraction class so that new variants of the hardware can be supported gracefully.

▨ **Note** MyEthernetDriver needs a wired Ethernet device to piggyback onto. This is because a wireless device generally does not allow packets to be transmitted with a source address different from its own. This is a limitation of the device's firmware.

The header file for MyEthernetDriver is shown in Listing 13-6.

Listing 13-6. MyEthernetDriver Header File

```
#ifndef MyEthernetDriver_h
#define MyEthernetDriver_h

#include <IOKit/assert.h>
#include <IOKit/IOTimerEventSource.h>
#include <IOKit/IOBufferMemoryDescriptor.h>
#include <IOKit/network/IOEthernetController.h>
#include <IOKit/network/IOEthernetInterface.h>
#include <IOKit/network/IOGatedOutputQueue.h>
#include <IOKit/network/IOMbufMemoryCursor.h>
#include <IOKit/network/IONetworkMedium.h>
#include <IOKit/IOUserClient.h>

#include "MyEthernetHwAbstraction.h"

class com_osxkernel_MyEthernetDriver : public IOEthernetController
{
    friend class com_osxkernel_MyEthernetHwAbstraction;

    OSDeclareDefaultStructors(com_osxkernel_MyEthernetDriver);
public:
    virtual bool init(OSDictionary* properties);
    virtual bool start(IOService* provider);
    virtual void stop(IOService* provider);
    virtual void free();

    virtual bool configureInterface(IONetworkInterface* netif);
```

```
    virtual IOReturn enable(IONetworkInterface* netif);
    virtual IOReturn disable(IONetworkInterface* netif);

    virtual IOReturn getHardwareAddress(IOEthernetAddress* addrP);

    // Allow our driver's Mac address to be set
    virtual IOReturn setHardwareAddress(const IOEthernetAddress* addrP);

    virtual UInt32 outputPacket(mbuf_t m, void* param);

    virtual IOReturn setPromiscuousMode(bool active) { return kIOReturnSuccess; }
    virtual IOReturn setMulticastMode(bool active) { return kIOReturnSuccess; }

    bool createMediumDict();

private:

    static void  interruptOccured(OSObject* owner, IOTimerEventSource* sender);

    IOTimerEventSource*      fInterruptSource;   // Simulate HW rx interrupt
    IOEthernetInterface*     fNetworkInterface;
    OSDictionary*            fMediumDict;
    IOWorkLoop*              fWorkLoop;

    IONetworkStats*          fNetworkStats;
    IOEthernetStats*         fEthernetStats;

    com_osxkernel_MyEthernetHwAbstraction* fHWAbstraction; // Low-level hardware access.
};

#endif
```

Driver Initialization and Startup

Network drivers follow the usual IOService lifecycle. Initialization of a driver and the device happens in the driver's start() method. For a typical device, the following steps may be performed:

1. Configure the device's provider and enumerate any needed resources. For PCI or Thunderbolt, this means mapping device memory or I/O regions. For USB devices, enumerate interfaces and pipes.

2. Configure the device for operation—for example, take it out of sleep state by accessing the device's registers or sending control requests.

3. Extract information from the device, such as the MAC address, and information about the device's capabilities, like supported media and speeds. Many Ethernet devices support the *Media Independent Interface* (MII) bus, which is a standard for accessing device status, information, and configuration in a consistent manner, decoupled from the part of the device that is concerned with physical transmission (usually referred to as the PHY). The MII registers contain information about the link status, supported network speeds, error reporting, and more. Gigabit or 10 Gigabit Ethernet devices are

supported by the GMII and XGMII specifications, respectively. MII, GMII, and XGMII are all IEEE standards. These standards do not, however, dictate how the DMA engine is implemented or how I/O to the device should occur.

4. Allocate and configure IOInterruptEventSource or IOTimerEventSources as needed, depending on requirements and underlying hardware. Many network devices use a software timer as a watchdog timer to continuously monitor the device for fault and attempt to reset the device should a fault occur.

5. Instantiate and register an instance of IOEthernetInterface, which will make our network controller visible to the BSD networking stack and the rest of the system.

The start() method for MyEthernetDriver is shown in Listing 13-7.

Listing 13-7. MyEthernetDriver's start() *Method*

```
bool com_osxkernel_MyEthernetDriver::start(IOService* provider)
{
    if (!super::start(provider))
        return false;

    fHWAbstraction = new com_osxkernel_MyEthernetHwAbstraction();
    if (!fHWAbstraction)
        return false;
    if (!fHWAbstraction->init(this))
        return false;

    if (!createMediumDict())
        return false;

    fWorkLoop = getWorkLoop();
    if (!fWorkLoop)
        return false;
    fWorkLoop->retain();

    if (attachInterface((IONetworkInterface**)&fNetworkInterface) == false)
        return false;

    fNetworkInterface->registerService();

    fInterruptSource = IOTimerEventSource::timerEventSource(this, interruptOccured);
    if (!fInterruptSource)
        return false;

    if (fWorkLoop->addEventSource(fInterruptSource) != kIOReturnSuccess)
        return false;

    IOLog("%s::start() -> success\n", getName());
    return true;
}
```

What needs to be done in the start() method is entirely dependent on the device's capabilities. In this case, we do not have a provider representing a hardware device, so we can bypass opening the provider. The next step performed is to allocate an instance of the class com_osxkernel_MyEthernetHwAbstraction and initialize it. The class contains code to interface with the hardware device, such as methods to read its registers and setup I/O transfers. In our case it instead contains code that allows us to piggyback on another device. This step is not technically required—you could easily all code in the main driver. However, we made the design decision so that in the future, when the "*MyEthernetDevice 2000 Pro*" becomes available, we can simply handle the hardware differences by inheriting from our existing hardware abstraction class. This allows the main driver to be kept clean and makes it easy to support several hardware variants with the same driver. We will look at the hardware abstraction class shortly.

After the "hardware" is initialized, we call the createMedium() function to publish details about which transmission standards and speeds our device support. We will discuss this process further in the next section.

The next method called is attachInterface(), which will return an instance of an IONetworkInterface class, which provides the glue that exposes our driver to the kernel network layer. In our case, the returned instance will be an IOEthernetInterface instance. If you need to subclass IOEthernetInterace for any reason, you can override IONetworkController::createInterface(), which is called by attachInterface() internally to allocate the overrided class instead. Before attachInterface() returns, it will also call IONetworkController::configureInterface(), which you can also override to perform additional configuration for the interface class. MyEthernetDriver implements the configureInterface() method as follows:

```
bool com_osxkernel_MyEthernetDriver::configureInterface(IONetworkInterface *netif)
{
    IONetworkData* nd;

    if (super::configureInterface(netif) == false)
        return false;

    nd = netif->getNetworkData(kIONetworkStatsKey);
    if (!nd || !(fNetworkStats = (IONetworkStats *)nd->getBuffer()))
        return false;

    nd = netif->getParameter(kIOEthernetStatsKey);
    if (!nd || !(fEthernetStats = (IOEthernetStats*)nd->getBuffer()))
        return false;

    return true;
}
```

The method obtains pointers to the interface's network statistics buffers, which will be used to record information about received/transmitted packets, collisions, and other events. The information is used by user space in several places, such as the network tab in the *Activity Monitor*.

To register an IOEthernetInterface instance with the system, we call its registerService() method.

Our final action before start() returns is to create an interrupt source. We simulate interrupts using an IOTimerEventSource, however, a hardware device would likely use IOFilterInterruptEventSource or IOInterruptEventSource to respond to actual hardware interrupts.

Most network drivers will also want to use a timer to provide watchdog functionality that periodically monitors the device for erroneous conditions, and check for things like the current link status, so that the network system and user space can be notified of events such as a cable being unplugged. Many drivers trigger their watchdog timer once every second.

Medium and Status Selection

The createMedium() method creates a dictionary that will publish details about the device's media capabilities to the BSD stack and user space. Most modern Ethernet devices can also support older Ethernet standards and transmission speeds. For example, the Ethernet device in a Macbook Pro can support the 1000BaseT, 100BaseTX and 10BaseT/UTP in full or half duplex modes with or without flow control. If the device and the driver support it, the media can be controlled via the UNIX command line tool ifconfig or via the *Network* pane in *System Preferences*. Most devices are able to auto-detect current media. Media capabilities are represented by the IONetworkMedium class. The implementation of the createMedium() class is shown in Listing 13-8.

Listing 13-8. Method for Publishing Details about Supported Ethernet Media

```
static struct MediumTable
{
    UInt32      type;
    UInt32      speed;
}

mediumTable[] =
{
    {kIOMediumEthernetNone, 0},
    {kIOMediumEthernetAuto, 0},
    {kIOMediumEthernet10BaseT | kIOMediumOptionFullDuplex,   10},
    {kIOMediumEthernet100BaseTX | kIOMediumOptionFullDuplex, 100},
    {kIOMediumEthernet1000BaseT | kIOMediumOptionFullDuplex, 1000},
};

bool com_osxkernel_MyEthernetDriver::createMediumDict()
{
    IONetworkMedium*  medium;
    UInt32                        i;

    fMediumDict = OSDictionary::withCapacity(sizeof(mediumTable) /
                                sizeof(struct MediumTable));
    if (fMediumDict == 0)
        return false;

    for (i = 0; i < sizeof(mediumTable) / sizeof(struct MediumTable); i++)
    {
        medium = IONetworkMedium::medium(mediumTable[i].type, mediumTable[i].speed);
        if (medium)
        {
            IONetworkMedium::addMedium(fMediumDict, medium);
            medium->release();
        }
    }

    if (publishMediumDictionary(fMediumDict) != true)
        return false;
```

```
medium = IONetworkMedium::getMediumWithType(fMediumDict, kIOMediumEthernetAuto);
setSelectedMedium(medium);
return true;
}
```

The method builds an OSDictionary containing the supported medium. The medium dictionary must be published with the method publishMediumDictionary() to advertise the driver's capabilities to the OS. If you want your driver to support manual selection of media, you need to override the IONetworkController::selectMedium() method. The default method will simply return kIOReturnUnsupported. Your driver can call setSelectedMedium() to inform the system of its medium selection. The setLinkStatus() method can be used to set the medium and the link status together. The link status flags are: kIONetworkLinkValid or kIONetworkLinkActive, which, for an Ethernet device, can be used to indicate whether a cable is connected, as well as if the device is active.

Configuring the Device Hardware Address

Ethernet networks use the Media Access Control (MAC) address, which should be a 48-bit globally unique address identifying the network controller. A MAC address conflict on the network may cause confusion to switches, hosts, and other networking gear. The MAC address is usually programmed into the device's EEPROM when it is being manufactured in a range assigned to each manufacturer by IEEE. Our driver needs to publish the MAC address to the networking stack and user space. The address serves no other purpose in user space other than to help uniquely identify the device for informational and configuration purposes. However, the networking stack does need to know the address to properly format outgoing packets and for address resolution for other protocols such as IP (ARP/RARP). The network stack will call the getHardwareAddress() function of our driver to get the MAC address. MyEthernetDriver implements it as follows:

```
IOReturn com_osxkernel_MyEthernetDriver::getHardwareAddress(IOEthernetAddress *addrP)
{
    addrP->bytes[0] = fHWAbstraction->readRegister8(kMyMacAddressRegisterOffset + 0);
    addrP->bytes[1] = fHWAbstraction->readRegister8(kMyMacAddressRegisterOffset + 1);
    addrP->bytes[2] = fHWAbstraction->readRegister8(kMyMacAddressRegisterOffset + 2);
    addrP->bytes[3] = fHWAbstraction->readRegister8(kMyMacAddressRegisterOffset + 3);
    addrP->bytes[4] = fHWAbstraction->readRegister8(kMyMacAddressRegisterOffset + 4);
    addrP->bytes[5] = fHWAbstraction->readRegister8(kMyMacAddressRegisterOffset + 5);

    return kIOReturnSuccess;
}
```

The getHardwareAddress() method is the only mandatory method (pure virtual) in the *IOEthernetController* and, hence, must be implemented. As we don't have a valid MAC address for MyEthernetDriver, we arbitrarily chose the address: be:ef:6c:8e:12:11. The implementation shows how you would likely fetch the MAC address from a device's registers.

If your device supports changing the MAC address to a user-defined value, you can override the setHardwareAddress() method. The method should write the new MAC address to the device's registers and return kIOReturnSuccess, if it was changed successfully. The default implementation will return kIOReturnUnsupported.

Enabling and Disabling the Device

Although the start method could fully prepare and make the device operational, the preferred way is to make the device active (that is, in a state where it can receive and transmit) when the driver's enable() method is called. Similarly, the device should become as dormant as it can, even sleep, if possible, when the driver's disable() method is called. A driver should do this because a user may elect to turn the device off at times, in which case, it should refrain from using resources, which again is important to ensure it doesn't drain a device's battery or waste energy. MyEthernetDriver's enable() method is shown here:

```
IOReturn com_osxkernel_MyEthernetDriver::enable(IONetworkInterface* netif)
{
    IOMediumType          mediumType = kIOMediumEthernet1000BaseT | kIOMediumOptionFullDuplex;
    IONetworkMedium*      medium;

    medium = IONetworkMedium::getMediumWithType(fMediumDict, mediumType);

    if (!fHWAbstraction->enableHardware())
        return kIOReturnError;

    setLinkStatus(kIONetworkLinkActive | kIONetworkLinkValid, medium, 1000 * 1000000);
    return kIOReturnSuccess;
}
```

The exact implementation is highly hardware-dependent, of course. In our case, the implementation will call into the hardware abstraction class, which will attach to the "slave" network interface we will use to enable transmission and reception of packets. For a real device, the method would likely bring the device out of sleep, and then enable interrupts. The implementation of the hardware abstraction enableHardware() method is shown here:

```
bool    com_osxkernel_MyEthernetHwAbstraction::enableHardware()
{
    bool success = true;

    fRxPacketQueue = IOPacketQueue::withCapacity();
    if (!fRxPacketQueue)
        return false;

    if (ifnet_find_by_name("en0", &interface) != KERN_SUCCESS) // change to your own interface
        return false;

    ifnet_set_promiscuous(interface, 1);

    if (iflt_attach(interface, &interfaceFilter, &gFilterReference) != KERN_SUCCESS)
        success = false;

    filterRegistered = true;
    return success;
}
```

The method will look for the device network interface *en0*, which should be an Ethernet device. It then puts the device into promiscuous mode, which is needed to ensure it will accept packets destined for MyEthernetDriver's MAC address. Finally, an interface filter is installed on the slave interface to intercept incoming packets. We will examine each incoming packet and divert packets addressed to us to our own input queue: fRxPacketQueue, while ignoring all other packets, and allow them to be processed by the original interface.

The disable() method should reverse the actions we performed when we enabled the device, and bring the device back into its original state. For our purposes, this means removing the interface filter so that we will no longer get incoming packets:

```
void    com_osxkernel_MyEthernetHwAbstraction::disableHardware()
{
    if (filterRegistered == true)
    {
        iflt_detach(gFilterReference);
        while (filterRegistered);

        ifnet_set_promiscuous(interface, 0);
        ifnet_release(interface);

        fRxPacketQueue->flush();
        fRxPacketQueue->release();
        fRxPacketQueue = NULL;
    }
}
```

Transmitting Network Packets

Now that we have successfully configured and prepared the device, we are ready to start doing some actual I/O. Networking I/O is conceptually very simple for a network driver. The network stack handles the heavy lifting of formatting the packet as well as determining that a packet is actually destined for our interface. Our driver need only be concerned with transmitting the raw bytes to the device. Packets are delivered to a driver via IONetworkController::outputPacket(), which your driver should override to receive packets from the network stack. The outputPacket() method of MyEthernetDriver is shown here:

```
UInt32  com_osxkernel_MyEthernetDriver::outputPacket(mbuf_t packet, void* param)
{
    IOReturn result = kIOReturnOutputSuccess;
    if (fHWAbstraction->transmitPacketToHardware(packet) != kIOReturnSuccess)
    {
        result = kIOReturnOutputStall;
    }
    return result;
}
```

▓ **Note** A driver should free the mbuf_t if a packet was accepted by the outputPacket() method. MyEthernetDriver does not need to do this because it passes the packet to another driver that will be responsible for freeing it.

An implementation should return kIOReturnOutputSuccess if the packet was handled successfully. If the hardware is busy and cannot accept another packet at this time, you can return kIOReturnOutputStall, which will retry the same packet again at a later stage. To drop packets, simply return kIOReturnOutputDropped. The outputPacket() method should not block or sleep.

By default, the outputPacket() method is called by the IONetworkInterface instance for the controller, unless an output queue was created manually by overriding the createOutputQueue() method, which should return a subclass of IOOutputQueue. It is highly recommended to implement an output queue (or provide your own queuing mechanism). If a queue is not present, you lose the ability to temporarily stall the queue, and you must handle the packet in your driver's outputPacket() method, otherwise it will be dropped. If the hardware is already busy transmitting packets at the time outputPacket() is called, the only way to handle this situation is to queue the packet until the hardware is ready again.

If you do implement a queue and it is stalled, the queue must be restarted when your hardware is ready to transmit packets again by calling IOOutputQueue::start(), or you will not receive further packets.

▪ **Note** Creating an output queue is highly recommended; however, MyEthernetDriver skips this step, as it transmits packets directly to another network interface, which implements its own queuing.

Creating a queue can be done by overriding the createOutputQueue() method. When a device is disabled, you should call flush() on the queue to remove any queued packets.

A typical network device will issue an (TX) interrupt whenever the hardware has put a packet (or packets) out on the wire, which also indicates there is now more room in its transmit buffer, or that a new DMA transaction can now be performed. You can notify the queue that the device is now ready for more data by calling the output queue's service() method. A side-effect of this will be another call to the driver's outputPacket() method, which will deliver a new packet, if one is available.

The transmitPacketToHardware() method from the preceding section is implemented as follows:

```
IOReturn    com_osxkernel_MyEthernetHwAbstraction::transmitPacketToHardware(mbuf_t packet)
{
    if (ifnet_output_raw(interface, 0, packet) != KERN_SUCCESS)
        return kIOReturnOutputDropped;

    // Raise an interrupt to the driver to inform it the packet was sent.
    fRegisterMap.interruptStatusRegister |= kTXInterruptPending;
    fDriver->fInterruptSource->setTimeoutUS(1);

    return kIOReturnSuccess;
}
```

The method will inject the received packet to the slave device's output queue. We simulate a hardware interrupt by setting the TX interrupt flag in our dummy interrupt register and then invoking our timer function to simulate an interrupt received from a hardware device a microsecond later.

The transmission of the packet to the hardware is again hardware-dependent. A PCI or Thunderbolt-based device is likely to use DMA. In this case, there are two options:

- The first is to have a pre-allocated physically allocated buffer; for example, one allocated with IOBufferMemoryDescriptor, using the kIOMemoryPhysicallyContiguous option, which an mbuf will be copied into and then DMA'ed to the hardware. Because an mbuf may consist of several chained buffers, it is important to ensure that you walk the chain with mbuf_next() so that all the segments can be copied into the DMA buffer.

- The second option, if the device supports it, is to create a scatter/gather list directly from the mbuf, using a variant of IOMbufMemoryCursor, which will avoid performing an extra copy. The cursor class takes care of generating the list of physical segments from the mbuf. Several IOMbufMemoryCursors subclasses exist; which one to use depends on the device and its limitations. For example, if you use a device that reads addresses in big-endian format, you can use the IOMbufBigMemoryCursor, which can be created with the withSpecification() factory method:

```
static IOMbufBigMemoryCursor* withSpecification(UInt32 maxSegmentSize,
UInt32 maxNumSegments);
```

The maxSegmentSize can be used to limit the size of individual scatter/gather list elements. Similarly, the maxNumSegments controls the length of the list.

Receiving Packets

Incoming packets arrive asynchronously from the network and a network driver's responsibility is to offload them from the hardware device when an RX interrupt occurs and deliver them to the network stack via its IONetworkInterface or IOEthernetInterface, in the case of an Ethernet driver. MyEthernetDriver's interrupt handler is shown in Listing 13-9.

Listing 13-9. Implementation of MyEthernetDriver's Interrupt Handler

```
void com_osxkernel_MyEthernetDriver::interruptOccured(OSObject* owner, IOTimerEventSource*
sender)
{
    mbuf_t packet;

    com_osxkernel_MyEthernetDriver* me = (com_osxkernel_MyEthernetDriver*)owner;
    com_osxkernel_MyEthernetHwAbstraction* hwAbstraction = me->fHWAbstraction;
    if (!me)
        return;

    UInt32 interruptStatus = hwAbstraction->readRegister32(kMyInterruptStatusRegisterOffset);

    // Recieve interrupt pending, grab packet from hardware.
    if (interruptStatus & kRXInterruptPending)
    {
        while ((packet = hwAbstraction->receivePacketFromHardware()))
        {
            me->fNetworkInterface->inputPacket(packet);
            me->fNetworkStats->inputPackets++;
        }
    }
```

```
        me->fNetworkInterface->flushInputQueue();
    }

    if (interruptStatus & kTXInterruptPending)
    {
        // Packet transmitted succesfully.
        me->fNetworkStats->outputPackets++;
    }
}
```

The interrupt handler is shared for RX and TX interrupts. To find out which interrupt occurred, we read the device's interrupt status register. Usually an interrupt status register is cleared on read, which will acknowledge and de-assert the interrupt. A quick note about the TX interrupt: we don't do anything other than record the packet as transmitted in our statistics structure, as we do not have a queue and also don't need to worry about setting up a new transaction.

When a packet is received, it needs to be transferred from an input buffer and passed to the IONetworkInterface class that was attached to the network controller driver. A packet is delivered to the network stack through the IONetworkInterface::inputPacket() method. The method accepts an mbuf_t. To get the data into an mbuf_t you can pre-allocate buffers using IONetworkController::allocatePacket(), which can then be used as a destination for the DMA of an incoming packet. An IOMbufMemoryCursor subclass can be used to handle translation of the mbuf data into physical addresses.

In the preceding example, we loop continuously until we have emptied the queue of incoming packets. A real hardware device may also receive multiple packets for a single interrupt. This process is often referred to as interrupt coalescing. Interrupt coalescing is necessary for modern network devices operating at speeds of 1 Gigabit or more, as network frames are often quite small and it would be inefficient to issue a hardware interrupt for every single packet received. Instead, the device may queue a number of packets in its onboard memory then issue an interrupt. Excessive queuing in hardware or by the driver should be avoided as it impacts latency, which may adversely affect some applications, such as real-time multiplayer games or audio/video conferencing. When inputPacket() is called, the packet is put in a queue internally by IONetworkInterface. We can drain this queue when we are ready by calling flushInputQueue(), which will forward packets to the BSD data-link layer for processing by protocol handlers.

Listing 13-10 shows the method that issues our pretend RX interrupt, once a packet has been retrieved from the slave device.

Listing 13-10. Method for Handling Incoming Packets from the Slave Device and Raising Virtual Interrupts

```
bool    com_osxkernel_MyEthernetHwAbstraction::handleIncomingPacket(mbuf_t packet,
                                                                     char** frameHdr)

{
    bool passPacketToCaller = true;
    bool copyPacket = false;

    struct ether_header *hdr = (struct ether_header*)*framePtr;
    if (!hdr)
        return false;

    // We only accept packets routed to us if it is addressed to our Mac address,
    // the broadcast or a multicast address.
```

```
if (memcmp(&fMacBcastAddress.bytes, &hdr->ether_dhost, ETHER_ADDR_LEN) == 0)
{
    copyPacket = true;
}
else if (memcmp(&fRegisterMap.address, &hdr->ether_dhost, ETHER_ADDR_LEN) == 0)
{
    passPacketToCaller = false; // Belongs to our interface.
    copyPacket = true;
}
else if (hdr->ether_dhost[0] & 0x01) // multicast
{
    copyPacket = true;
}

if (copyPacket)
{
    mbuf_t newPacket;
    newPacket = fDriver->allocatePacket((UInt32)mbuf_pkthdr_len(packet) + ETHER_HDR_LEN);

    if (newPacket)
    {
        unsigned char* data = (unsigned char*)mbuf_data(newPacket);
        bcopy(*framePtr, data, ETHER_HDR_LEN);
        data += ETHER_HDR_LEN;
        mbuf_copydata(packet, 0, mbuf_pkthdr_len(packet),data);

        IOLog("input packet is %lu bytes long\n", mbuf_pkthdr_len(packet));

        fRxPacketQueue->lockEnqueue(newPacket);
        fRegisterMap.interruptStatusRegister |= kRXInterruptPending;
        // Raise an interrupt to the driver to inform it of the new packet
        fDriver->fInterruptSource->setTimeoutUS(1);
    }
}
return passPacketToCaller;
}
```

In Listing 13-10, the packet is copied from the original packet in response to the input filter on the slave device being called, then queued using an IOPacketQueue that simulates the hardware receive buffer. We then raise an interrupt to the driver by first setting the RX interrupt pending flag in the status register, then setting the timeout of the interrupt timer function. When the interrupt handler runs, it will call receivePacketFromHardware(), which simply grabs a new packet from the queue under lock:

```
mbuf_t com_osxkernel_MyEthernetHwAbstraction::receivePacketFromHardware()
{
    if (!fRxPacketQueue)
        return NULL;
    return fRxPacketQueue->lockDequeue();
}
```

Taking MyEthernetDriver for a Test-Drive

If you wish to test MyEthernetDriver, it is best to do so on an isolated network segment or with the blessing of your network administrator because, unlike other samples, it will actively interact with your network. Before you test it, you should modify `MyEthernetHwAbstraction.cpp` so that it points to the Ethernet device you wish to use to transmit and receive on behalf of MyEthernetDriver.

You can load MyEthernetDriver by using `kextload`. Unlike an NKE, which has to be manually loaded, MyEthernetDriver uses `IOResources` as a provider so that it will be loaded automatically during boot, if installed to the proper location. For the purpose of testing the driver, it is recommended that you do not keep it in your systems extensions directory in case there is a problem. When the driver is loaded, you can verify its presence using `IORegisterExplorer`, as shown in Figure 13-7.

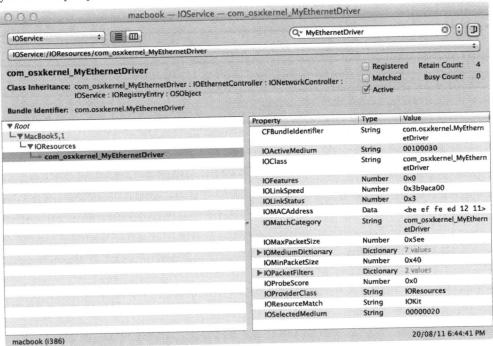

Figure 13-7. IORegisteryExplorer showing MyEthernetDriver attached to the IOResources nub

We should also be able to see the new network interface in System Preferences under the Network pane, as shown in Figure 13-8.

315

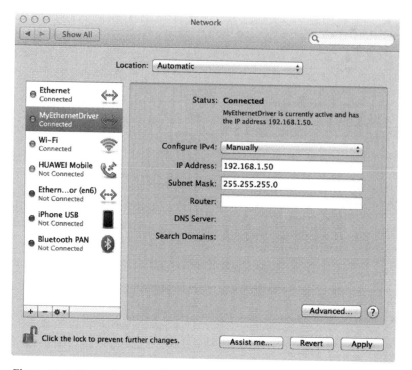

Figure 13-8. *Network pane in System Preferences showing the configuration options for MyEthernetDriver*

If you have a DHCP server on your network, you may see that MyEthernetDriver was automatically assigned an IP address. If not, you can manually configure an IP address using System Preferences or using the ifconfig command line tool:

```
$ sudo ifconfig en5 inet 192.168.1.50 netmask 255.255.255.0
$ ifconfig en5
en5: flags=8863<UP,BROADCAST,SMART,RUNNING,SIMPLEX,MULTICAST> mtu 1500
        ether be:ef:fe:ed:12:11
        inet6 fe80::bcef:feff:feed:1211%en5 prefixlen 64 scopeid 0x7
        inet 192.168.1.50 netmask 0xffffff00 broadcast 192.168.1.255
        media: autoselect (1000baseT <full-duplex>)
        status: active
```

Note that you may be assigned a different BSD network interface name, depending on how many interfaces you have installed on your system. In this case, *en5* is used. Provided that you have configured an IP address that is reachable by another host on the network, you should now be able to reach that host even if the slave interface is using a different IP/subnet. We can verify that it works correctly by using the ping utility on another host:

```
othermac$ ping 192.168.1.50
PING 192.168.1.50 (192.168.1.50): 56 data bytes
64 bytes from 192.168.1.50: icmp_seq=0 ttl=64 time=0.855 ms
64 bytes from 192.168.1.50: icmp_seq=1 ttl=64 time=0.588 ms
--- 192.168.1.50 ping statistics ---
2 packets transmitted, 2 packets received, 0.0% packet loss
round-trip min/avg/max/stddev = 0.588/0.722/0.855/0.133 ms


othermac$ arp -a
? (192.168.1.50) at be:ef:fe:ed:12:11 on en0 ifscope [ethernet]
? (192.168.255.255) at ff:ff:ff:ff:ff:ff on en0 ifscope [ethernet]
```

You will see that the other system has picked up the hardware address (MAC) of MyEthernetDriver and is not using the MAC of the slave interface to reach us.

Going back to the system with MyEthernetDriver installed, we can check the statistics for our interface to see the amount of packets and data it has transferred:

```
$ netstat -i -I en5
```

Name	Mtu	Network	Address	Ipkts	Ierrs	Opkts	Oerrs	Coll
en5	1500	<Link#7>	be:ef:fe:ed:12:11	61	0	67	0	0
en5	1500	192.168.1	192.168.1.50	61	-	67	-	-

Summary

In this chapter, we have looked at the kernel network filtering KPIs as well as how to implement a driver for an Ethernet controller. Some key points are as follows:

- The kernel network support is split into two parts: the BSD layer that implements support for all protocols and network services such as firewalls, and the I/O Kit, which provides facilities for writing drivers for network hardware.

- The kernel filtering KPI allows one to filter and manipulate network packets at various levels, including the socket, IP, and interface levels.

- The most important data-structure of the kernel network subsystem is the mbuf structure used to store network packets or other related data. In kernel extensions, mbufs can be manipulated using the opaque reference *mbuf_t* and the functions provided by the mbuf KPI. The concept of mbufs is used both in the BSD section of the kernel and in the I/O Kit.

- A socket filter allows interception of socket-based communication and out-of-band events. It can intercept incoming and outgoing data. Socket filters can be attached globally for every socket in the system, or programmatically per socket. With a socket filter, you can, among other things, modify, reject, or inject new packets.

- An IP filter is similar to a socket filter, but works at the IP layer. The IP filter will see all IP traffic in the system regardless of interface. It will also see IP packets that were not directly initiated through a socket.

- An interface filter allows a filter to be attached to a specific network interface. An interface filter can see all traffic to or from that interface regardless of protocol. It is possible to restrict seen packets to a specific protocol family, such as IPv4 or IPv6.

- The IONetworkingFamily provides the programming interfaces necessary to implement device drivers for network hardware. It includes classes for queuing and classes for abstracting the interface between the I/O Kit and the BSD layer.

- The IONetworkController class represents a network driver. A specialized class for handling an Ethernet compatible device is provided by IOEthernetController. The IONetworkInterface provides the glue that connects network devices to other parts of the kernel network system.

CHAPTER 14

Storage Systems

Storage devices encompass many types of devices, including hard disk drives, CDs and DVDs, USB flash drives, FireWire-based hard disks, and a file-based disk image that has been mounted as a virtual drive. For the user, a storage device appears as a volume on their desktop that they can read files from and write files to, but what the user doesn't see is the multiple drivers that work together in the kernel to make this possible.

The reason why storage devices require multiple drivers is a result of the myriad of different forms that a storage device may take. If you consider the difference between an external USB flash drive and an internal hard disk, both of which appear to the user as storage devices, you can appreciate the differences that need to be handled. For example:

- The interface through which a storage device is connected to the computer may be a USB or FireWire port (used for external storage devices), or through a SATA port (commonly used by the internal hard disk).

- The computer may control the storage device by sending SCSI commands, as is done for USB mass storage devices or FireWire SPB-2 drives, or by sending ATA/ATAPI commands to the AHCI interface, as is done for the internally connected SATA disks.

- The storage device may contain a single volume, or may be partitioned into multiple volumes.

- Each volume will be formatted with a file system chosen by the user, and may be HFS+ (the default file system used by Mac OS X), NTFS (the default file system used by Windows), or one of the many file systems that Mac OS X supports.

To handle all of these possible variations, the I/O Kit implements storage devices by building a layered stack of multiple drivers, where each layer is responsible for handling one aspect, such as the physical connection (USB, FireWire or SATA), the command protocol (SCSI or ATA/ATAPI), and the logical volume. Support for various file systems is provided by the Virtual File System layer (VFS layer), which, although a part of the kernel, resides in the BSD portion of the kernel and is located outside of the I/O Kit.

This modularity in the design of the I/O Kit's storage stack means that each layer of the driver stack is decoupled from the surrounding layers, and each driver needs to deal only with the functionality provided by its layer. This means that a new file system can be written without any knowledge of the types of storage devices on which the file system may reside, since the file system will never need to directly communicate with the disk device's hardware. Similarly, in writing a driver for a new type of storage device, the developer doesn't need to implement any details of the file system; instead, the disk can be formatted with any of the existing file systems supported by Mac OS X. The driver stack for a storage device is shown in Figure 14-1.

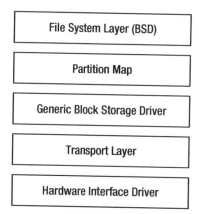

Figure 14-1. An abstract view of the drivers involved in supporting a storage device

It is not necessary to implement a driver in each layer. For example, to implement support for a new hard disk, you would need only to write a driver in the transport layer; the rest of the driver stack would match against your custom driver, and your new disk device would be presented to the user as a standard disk.

Transport Layer Drivers

The driver for a storage device is implemented in the I/O Kit as a transport driver that resides within the Transport Layer of Figure 14-1. Like any other I/O Kit driver, a transport driver will match against the provider class that represents its hardware device; the provider class is also the means by which the driver accesses the underlying hardware. For example, a storage device that is USB-based will have a provider class that is an instance of IOUSBDevice or IOUSBInterface.

The I/O Kit provides no restrictions on the superclass that a transport driver can be derived from, other than ultimately deriving from the IOService class, as is required by all I/O Kit drivers. This allows a transport driver a large degree of freedom, since it can use a set of methods that is natural for the communication protocol used by the disk device, rather than being forced to implement an interface that is imposed by the I/O Kit's storage family.

The lack of a common interface for transport drivers does provide a problem, since the upper layers of the driver stack, in particular, the generic block storage driver that sits immediately above the transport driver, has no common interface allowing it to call methods in the transport driver. To solve this, the I/O Kit defines a driver class known as IOBlockStorageDevice, which is a small lightweight "nub" driver that sits between the transport layer and generic block storage driver.

The role of the IOBlockStorageDevice class is to provide an abstract representation of the disk to the generic block storage driver, and to pass on all requests to the transport driver, which in turn implements the behavior that is specific to the disk device. The transport driver is responsible for defining a concrete subclass of the IOBlockStorageDevice class and instantiating it. An illustration of the relationship between the transport driver and the layers above and below it in the storage driver stack is shown in Figure 14-2, which uses the Apple AHCI driver as an example.

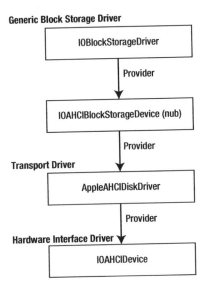

Generic Block Storage Driver

Figure 14-2. The relationship between drivers in the Apple AHCI storage driver stack

---

■ **Note** Since the I/O Kit puts no restrictions on how a transport driver should be implemented, the transport driver may be built from a stack of several drivers. Apple takes advantage of this in the drivers for devices that use the SCSI command set, including USB Mass Storage devices and FireWire devices. The drivers for these devices all make use of a common driver that implements the SCSI protocol.

The IOBlockStorageDevice Interface

The upper layers of the storage driver stack communicate with the transport driver through a class that is derived from the IOBlockStorageDevice interface. The IOBlockStorageDevice presents a view of the storage device as a linear array of logical blocks that can be either read from or written to by the caller. A logical block is the minimum number of bytes that the disk is capable of reading or writing, and a disk operation must operate on a multiple of blocks. Depending on the disk, the block size will be anywhere from 512 bytes to 4096 bytes. All operations performed by the IOBlockStorageDevice class work on a contiguous range of disk blocks.

The methods that must be implemented by a subclass of the IOBlockStorageDevice interface are described in Listing 14-1. The IOBlockStorageDevice class is not designed to provide a full implementation of the behavior of these methods; instead, it passes them on to its provider class, which is the transport driver within the storage driver stack.

Listing 14-1. The Methods to Be Implemented by a Subclass of the IOBlockStorageDevice Interface

```
class IOBlockStorageDevice : public IOService
{
        virtual bool            init(OSDictionary * properties);
        virtual IOReturn        doEjectMedia(void) = 0;
        virtual IOReturn        doFormatMedia(UInt64 byteCapacity) = 0;
        virtual UInt32          doGetFormatCapacities(UInt64 * capacities,
                                    UInt32   capacitiesMaxCount) const = 0;
        virtual IOReturn        doLockUnlockMedia(bool doLock) = 0;
        virtual IOReturn        doSynchronizeCache(void) = 0;
        virtual char*           getVendorString(void) = 0;
        virtual char*           getProductString(void) = 0;
        virtual char*           getRevisionString(void) = 0;
        virtual char*           getAdditionalDeviceInfoString(void) = 0;
        virtual IOReturn        reportBlockSize(UInt64 *blockSize) = 0;
        virtual IOReturn        reportEjectability(bool *isEjectable) = 0;
        virtual IOReturn        reportLockability(bool *isLockable) = 0;
        virtual IOReturn        reportMaxValidBlock(UInt64 *maxBlock) = 0;
        virtual IOReturn        reportMediaState(bool *mediaPresent,bool *changedState) = 0;
        virtual IOReturn        reportPollRequirements(bool *pollRequired,
                                    bool *pollIsExpensive) = 0;
        virtual IOReturn        reportRemovability(bool *isRemovable) = 0;
        virtual IOReturn        reportWriteProtection(bool *isWriteProtected) = 0;
        virtual IOReturn        getWriteCacheState(bool *enabled) = 0;
        virtual IOReturn        setWriteCacheState(bool enabled) = 0;
        virtual IOReturn        doAsyncReadWrite(IOMemoryDescriptor *buffer, UInt64 block,
                                    UInt64 nblks, IOStorageAttributes *attributes,
                                    IOStorageCompletion *completion) = 0;
        virtual IOReturn        requestIdle(void);
        virtual IOReturn        doDiscard(UInt64 block, UInt64 nblks);
        virtual IOReturn        doUnmap(IOBlockStorageDeviceExtent* extents,
                                    UInt32 extentsCount, UInt32 options);
};
```

The following sections describe the methods that a subclass of IOBlockStorageDevice needs to implement, and they are ordered by functionality. The first methods described each return a human readable description of the device to the user. These strings are used to help the user to identify the storage device that corresponds to a mounted volume. If the storage medium has not been formatted, no volume will be associated with the device, and these identification strings will be the only means the user has of ensuring that the device they are about to format is the device they think it is. Therefore, these strings should return a descriptive name that, for example, identifies the manufacturer of a USB flash drive or provides a description of the connection interface (such as "USB to SATA adapter"), allowing the user to easily identify the device. These strings appear in utilities such as "Disk Utility" and the system profiles produced by "System Information."

- getVendorString returns the name of the manufacturer of the storage device.

- getProductString returns a descriptive name of the product model.

- `getRevisionString` returns a string whose interpretation can be decided by the driver developer. This could be used to identify the firmware version running on the storage device, or it could provide an identification of the product design. Both values could also be included because the value is a string.

- `getAdditionalDeviceInfoString` is currently unused by the I/O Kit implementation, but could be queried from the driver by proprietary disk utility software.

The following methods are called to query the capabilities of the storage device:

- `reportRemovability` and `reportEjectability` both return similar information. A device is considered removable if the media may come and go while the driver is present. This means that the I/O Kit may periodically poll the transport driver to determine whether a disk is currently present. Furthermore, a device that is removable is considered ejectable if it can be removed through software control (such as a CD drive). If a device is not ejectable, the user can still "eject" through the Finder or Disk Utility, although Mac OS X will perform an unmount of the file system, but won't eject the media.

- `reportLockability` is called to determine whether the media in a removable drive can be "locked down" and prevented from being removed by the user. An example of locking a device is a CD drive that has an eject button on its front case that can be disabled (locked) when a CD is mounted.

- `reportPollRequirements` is called to determine whether the driver needs to be periodically called to check whether media has been inserted or removed, as opposed to the driver itself being able to generate a notification when media has arrived. If the device requires polling, the driver can return an additional flag through the `reportPollRequirements` method to indicate whether polling is expensive, for example, if media can be detected only by spinning up the device. The I/O Kit will poll a device only if it is not expensive.

- `reportMediaState` is called to determine whether there is media present in the device. This method is called once when the storage driver stack is created, to read the initial state of the hardware, and thereafter, only if the driver has indicated that it requires polling to determine the presence of media.

The following methods are called to query the capabilities of the media that is present. These methods are called whenever new media is detected.

- `reportBlockSize` should return the size in bytes of a disk sector (or block) for the device. A user space process can access this value through the ioctl `DKIOCGETBLOCKSIZE`.

- `reportMaxValidBlock` returns the capacity of the device, expressed in terms of the address of the final block of the device. Because disk blocks are indexed from 0, the maximum valid block is one less than the total block count of the device.

- `reportWriteProtection` is called to determine whether the media can be written to or is write-protected, in which case it will be mounted as a read-only volume. A user space process can access this value through the ioctl `DKIOCISWRITABLE`.

The following methods perform low-level formatting of the media. Not all devices can support low-level formatting. Even though these methods must be present in the implementation of the IOBlockStorageDevice interface, it is acceptable to return an error if the functionality is not provided.

- doGetFormatCapacities is called to obtain a list containing each size (in bytes) that the media can be formatted to. The storage to hold the result of this method is provided by the caller, and the method returns the actual number of items that were written to the list. The caller can provide a NULL pointer for the list storage if it wishes to determine the number of formats that the implementation supports, without receiving the actual list. A user space process can request this list through the ioctl DKIOCGETFORMATCAPACITIES.

- doFormatMedia is called to perform a low-level format of the device. If this functionality is not implemented, the method is free to return an error, such as kIOReturnUnsupported. A user space process can perform this action by sending the ioctl DKIOCFORMAT.

- The doDiscard method is called not to format the entire disk but rather to wipe blocks that no longer store data that is required by the file system. For a solid state disk, this method provides an opportunity to issue a TRIM command for the discarded blocks. A user space process can perform this action by sending the ioctl DKIOCDISCARD. This method was deprecated in later versions of Mac OS X 10.6 and has been replaced with the doUnmap method.

- The doUnmap method was introduced as a replacement for the doDiscard method. It performs a similar function, which is to release disk blocks that are not used by the file system. Unlike the doDiscard method, which is capable of releasing only a single physically contiguous run of disk blocks, the doUnmap method is provided with an array containing one or more ranges of disk blocks that are no longer in use. A user space process can perform this action by sending the ioctl DKIOCUNMAP.

The following methods allow software control over ejecting the media:

- doLockUnlockMedia is called to prevent the user from ejecting the media, such as disabling the eject button on the front of a CD drive. The method is passed a Boolean parameter that determines whether the driver should lock the media in the device (prevent user ejection) or unlock the media (allow user ejection).

- doEjectMedia is called to eject the media from the device. A user space process can perform this action by sending the ioctl DKIOCEJECT.

- requestIdle is called to place the disk in an idle state, such as spinning down a CD drive. While there is no corresponding method to take the device out of the idle state, the next read or write operation will implicitly do so. A user space process can perform this action by sending the ioctl DKIOCREQUESTIDLE.

Finally, and perhaps most importantly, are the following methods for reading and writing data to the device:

- doAsyncReadWrite is the generic data read and write method of the IOBlockStorageDevice interface. It takes as its parameters an IOMemoryDescriptor object that describes the source buffer (for a disk read) or the destination buffer (for a disk write), a contiguous range of disk blocks to read from or write to, and associated attribute flags. The IOMemoryDescriptor also serves to determine whether the requested operation is a read or a write; the driver calls the method getDirection() on the IOMemoryDescriptor object, and if the returned value is kIODirectionIn, a read operation has been requested. If the returned value is kIODirectionOut, a write operation has been requested. The disk operation is performed asynchronously, and when it completes, the caller is notified through a callback function that is provided.

- setWriteCacheState is called to enable or disable any hardware caching that the device has. The corresponding method getWriteCacheState returns the current state of the device cache.

- doSynchronizeCache is called to flush the contents of the hardware cache to the media. This is a synchronous method that should not return until the contents of the cache have been written to a disk. This method is also called in response to the ioctl DKIOCSYNCHRONIZECACHE from a user space process.

Building a RAM Disk Device

Having examined the methods that must be implemented to support the IOBlockStorageDevice interface, we can now take a look at how a simple RAM disk device can be implemented in Mac OS X. As with the driver for any disk device in the I/O Kit, we will split our driver into two classes: the transport driver class, which implements the functionality and communicates with the hardware device, and a class that implements the IOBlockStorageDevice interface, which acts as an interface between the transport driver and the device services layer of the storage driver stack.

As we have seen, the I/O Kit does not require the transport driver for a storage device to be written in any particular way or to subclass from any particular superclass. This allows the transport driver to be written in a way that is most natural for the type of hardware that provides access to the disk storage. For our RAM disk, the "hardware" controlled by the transport driver is nothing more than a memory allocation that provides the storage for the RAM disk. As we learned in Chapter 4, an I/O Kit driver that has no hardware device to match against will use the global IOResources class as its provider class. This will be the provider class of our RAM disk's transport driver. Since our transport driver is implemented as a generic driver, we will implement it as a subclass of the generic IOService class.

For simplicity, our RAM disk's transport driver will allocate the storage for the disk when it loads, and will not release it until the driver unloads. The storage is a fixed-size memory allocation. Our transport driver will also be responsible for instantiating the IOBlockStorageDevice object, which will provide the interface, through which the upper layer of the driver stack will communicate, with our transport driver. The header file for a RAM disk's transport driver is given in Listing 14-2.

Listing 14-2. The Header File of the Transport Driver for a RAM Disk Device

```
#include <IOKit/IOService.h>
#include <IOKit/IOBufferMemoryDescriptor.h>
```

```
class com_osxkernel_driver_RAMDisk : public IOService
{
        OSDeclareDefaultStructors(com_osxkernel_driver_RAMDisk)

private:
        IOBufferMemoryDescriptor*        m_memoryDesc;
        void*                            m_buffer;

protected:
    bool                     createBlockStorageDevice ();

public:
    virtual bool             start (IOService* provider);
    virtual void             free (void);

    virtual IOByteCount      performRead (IOMemoryDescriptor* dstDesc, UInt64 byteOffset,
                                        UInt64 byteCount);
    virtual IOByteCount      performWrite (IOMemoryDescriptor* srcDesc, UInt64 byteOffset,
                                        UInt64 byteCount);
};
```

The implementation of a RAM disk's transport driver is given in Listing 14-3.

Listing 14-3. The Implementation of the Transport Driver for a RAM Disk Device

```
// Define the superclass
#define super IOService

OSDefineMetaClassAndStructors(com_osxkernel_driver_RAMDisk, IOService)

#define kDiskByteSize            (16*1024*1024)  // Fix RAM disk size at 16MiB

bool com_osxkernel_driver_RAMDisk::start (IOService *provider)
{
        if (super::start(provider) == false)
                return false;

        // Allocate storage for the disk.
        m_memoryDesc = IOBufferMemoryDescriptor::withCapacity(kDiskByteSize,
                                                kIODirectionOutIn);
        if (m_memoryDesc == NULL)
                return false;
        m_buffer = m_memoryDesc->getBytesNoCopy();

        // Allocate an IOBlockStorageDevice nub.
        if (createBlockStorageDevice() == false)
                return false;

        return true;
}

void com_osxkernel_driver_RAMDisk::free (void)
```

```
{
        if (m_memoryDesc != NULL)
                m_memoryDesc->release();

        super::free();
}


IOByteCount com_osxkernel_driver_RAMDisk::performRead (IOMemoryDescriptor* dstDesc,
                                                  UInt64 byteOffset, UInt64 byteCount)

{
        return dstDesc->writeBytes(0, (void*)((uintptr_t)m_buffer + byteOffset), byteCount);
}

IOByteCount com_osxkernel_driver_RAMDisk::performWrite (IOMemoryDescriptor* srcDesc,
                                                  UInt64 byteOffset, UInt64 byteCount)

{
        return srcDesc->readBytes(0, (void*)((uintptr_t)m_buffer + byteOffset), byteCount);
}
```

The implementation of the RAMDisk class should be fairly straightforward. In its start() method, the transport driver allocates a memory buffer that provides the storage for the disk device. This buffer isn't released until the RAM disk driver is unloaded and its free() method is called. The RAMDisk driver class also defines two methods that provide access to the storage buffer, namely performRead() and performWrite().

As a general rule, the transport driver should be implemented in a way that matches the functionality and protocol of the device that it is controlling. The interface for the RAM disk in Listing 14-2 certainly meets this requirement, with its very simple set of methods. A consequence of this freedom is that the transport driver needs a nub driver, which implements the IOBlockStorageDevice interface, to accept method calls from the upper layers of the storage driver stack and to pass them on to the transport driver. In our sample RAM disk driver, this functionality is provided by a class named com_osxkernel_driver_RAMDiskStorageDevice, which is derived from the IOBlockStorageDevice interface.

A class that implements the IOBlockStorageDevice interface sits between the transport driver and the upper-layer drivers; it implements methods that are called by the upper-layer drivers, and in turn needs to call methods that are implemented in the transport driver. As such, it needs a reference to an instance of the transport driver class. This is usually done by making the transport driver the provider class of the IOBlockStorageDevice nub.

In our RAM disk driver, the transport driver directly instantiates the RAMDiskStorageDevice nub and attaches it to itself. Attaching the RAMDiskStorageDevice to the transport driver sets up the transport driver as the provider class of the RAMDiskStorageDevice. This process is implemented in a private method named createBlockStorageDevice(), which the transport driver calls from its start() method. The implementation of this is given in Listing 14-4.

Listing 14-4. Instantiating the IOBlockStorageDevice Nub from the RAM Disk Transport Driver

```
bool com_osxkernel_driver_RAMDisk::createBlockStorageDevice ()
{
        com_osxkernel_driver_RAMDiskStorageDevice*       nub = NULL;
        bool                      result = false;

        // Allocate a new IOBlockStorageDevice nub.
```

```
        nub = new com_osxkernel_driver_RAMDiskStorageDevice;
        if (nub == NULL)
                goto bail;

        // Call the custom init method (passing the overall disk size).
        if (nub->init(kDiskByteSize) == false)
                goto bail;

        // Attach the IOBlockStorageDevice to the this driver.
        // This call increments the reference count of the nub object,
        // so we can release our reference at function exit.
        if (nub->attach(this) == false)
                goto bail;

        // Allow the upper level drivers to match against the IOBlockStorageDevice.
        nub->registerService();

        result = true;

bail:
        // Unconditionally release the nub object.
        if (nub != NULL)
                nub->release();

        return result;
}
```

After instantiating the nub driver and attaching it as a client of the transport driver, it is important to call the method registerService() on the nub. This can either be performed by the implementation of the nub itself (such as in its start() method) or, as in this example, by the transport driver. The purpose of calling registerService() is to publish the IOBlockStorageDevice nub, allowing drivers to match against it, which begins the construction of the rest of the storage driver stack. The header file for the com_osxkernel_driver_RAMDiskStorageDevice nub driver is provided in Listing 14-5.

Listing 14-5. The Header File for the RAMDiskStorageDevice Nub Class

```
#include <IOKit/storage/IOBlockStorageDevice.h>

class com_osxkernel_driver_RAMDisk;

class com_osxkernel_driver_RAMDiskStorageDevice : public IOBlockStorageDevice
{
        OSDeclareDefaultStructors(com_osxkernel_driver_RAMDiskStorageDevice)

private:
        UInt64                         m_blockCount;
        com_osxkernel_driver_RAMDisk*  m_provider;

public:
        virtual bool     init(UInt64 diskSize, OSDictionary* properties = 0);

        virtual bool     attach(IOService* provider);
```

```
virtual void          detach(IOService* provider);

virtual IOReturn      doEjectMedia(void);
virtual IOReturn      doFormatMedia(UInt64 byteCapacity);
virtual UInt32        doGetFormatCapacities(UInt64 * capacities, UInt32
                          capacitiesMaxCount) const;
virtual IOReturn      doLockUnlockMedia(bool doLock);
virtual IOReturn      doSynchronizeCache(void);
virtual char*         getVendorString(void);
virtual char*         getProductString(void);
virtual char*         getRevisionString(void);
virtual char*         getAdditionalDeviceInfoString(void);
virtual IOReturn      reportBlockSize(UInt64 *blockSize);
virtual IOReturn      reportEjectability(bool *isEjectable);
virtual IOReturn      reportLockability(bool *isLockable);
virtual IOReturn      reportMaxValidBlock(UInt64 *maxBlock);
virtual IOReturn      reportMediaState(bool *mediaPresent,bool *changedState);
virtual IOReturn      reportPollRequirements(bool *pollRequired,
                          bool *pollIsExpensive);
virtual IOReturn      reportRemovability(bool *isRemovable);
virtual IOReturn      reportWriteProtection(bool *isWriteProtected);
virtual IOReturn      getWriteCacheState(bool *enabled);
virtual IOReturn      setWriteCacheState(bool enabled);
virtual IOReturn      doAsyncReadWrite(IOMemoryDescriptor *buffer, UInt64 block,
                          UInt64 nblks, IOStorageAttributes *attributes,
                          IOStorageCompletion *completion);
};
```

The implementation of the com_osxkernel_driver_RAMDiskStorageDevice class is provided in Listing 14-6. For brevity, methods with an empty implementation have been omitted.

Listing 14-6. The Implementation of an IOBlockStorageDevice Nub Class

```
#include <IOKit/storage/IOBlockStorageDevice.h>

// Define the superclass
#define super IOBlockStorageDevice

OSDefineMetaClassAndStructors(com_osxkernel_driver_RAMDiskStorageDevice, IOBlockStorageDevice)

#define kDiskBlockSize          512

bool com_osxkernel_driver_RAMDiskStorageDevice::init(UInt64 diskSize, OSDictionary*
    properties)
{
    if (super::init(properties) == false)
      return false;
    m_blockCount = diskSize / kDiskBlockSize;
    return true;
}

bool com_osxkernel_driver_RAMDiskStorageDevice::attach (IOService* provider)
```

329

```
    {
        if (super::attach(provider) == false)
          return false;
        m_provider = OSDynamicCast(com_osxkernel_driver_RAMDisk, provider);
        if (m_provider == NULL)
          return false;
        return true;
    }

    void com_osxkernel_driver_RAMDiskStorageDevice::detach(IOService* provider)
    {
        if (m_provider == provider)
          m_provider = NULL;
        super::detach(provider);
    }


    UInt32 com_osxkernel_driver_RAMDiskStorageDevice::doGetFormatCapacities(UInt64* capacities,
                                                        UInt32 capacitiesMaxCount) const
    {
        // Ensure that the array is sufficient to hold all our formats (we require 1 element).
        if ((capacities != NULL) && (capacitiesMaxCount < 1))
          return 0;                    // Error, return an array size of 0.

        // The caller may provide a NULL array if it wishes to query
        // the number of formats that we support.
        if (capacities != NULL)
          capacities[0] = m_blockCount * kDiskBlockSize;
        return 1;
    }

    char* com_osxkernel_driver_RAMDiskStorageDevice::getProductString(void)
    {
        return (char*)"RAM Disk";
    }

    IOReturn com_osxkernel_driver_RAMDiskStorageDevice::reportBlockSize(UInt64 *blockSize)
    {
        *blockSize = kDiskBlockSize;
        return kIOReturnSuccess;
    }

    IOReturn com_osxkernel_driver_RAMDiskStorageDevice::reportMaxValidBlock(UInt64 *maxBlock)
    {
        *maxBlock = m_blockCount-1;
        return kIOReturnSuccess;
    }

    IOReturn com_osxkernel_driver_RAMDiskStorageDevice::reportMediaState(bool *mediaPresent, bool
       *changedState)
    {
        *mediaPresent = true;
```

```
    *changedState = false;
    return kIOReturnSuccess;
}

IOReturn com_osxkernel_driver_RAMDiskStorageDevice::reportPollRequirements(bool *pollRequired,
    bool *pollIsExpensive)
{
    *pollRequired = false;
    *pollIsExpensive = false;
    return kIOReturnSuccess;
}

IOReturn com_osxkernel_driver_RAMDiskStorageDevice::reportRemovability(bool *isRemovable)
{
    *isRemovable = true;
    return kIOReturnSuccess;
}

IOReturn com_osxkernel_driver_RAMDiskStorageDevice::doAsyncReadWrite(IOMemoryDescriptor
    *buffer, UInt64 block, UInt64 nblks, IOStorageAttributes *attributes, IOStorageCompletion
    *completion)
{
    IODirection              direction;
    IOByteCount              actualByteCount;

    // Return errors for incoming I/O if we have been terminated.
    if (isInactive() == true)
      return kIOReturnNotAttached;
    // Ensure the block range being targeted is within the disk's capacity.
    if ((block + nblks) > m_blockCount)
      return kIOReturnBadArgument;

    // Get the buffer's direction, which indicates whether the operation is a read or a write.
    direction = buffer->getDirection();
    if ((direction != kIODirectionIn) && (direction != kIODirectionOut))
      return kIOReturnBadArgument;

    // Perform the read or write operation through the transport driver.
    if (direction == kIODirectionIn)
      actualByteCount = m_provider->performRead(buffer, (block*kDiskBlockSize),
                                     (nblks*kDiskBlockSize));

    else
      actualByteCount = m_provider->performWrite(buffer, (block*kDiskBlockSize),
                                     (nblks*kDiskBlockSize));

    // Call the completion function.
    (completion->action)(completion->target, completion->parameter, kIOReturnSuccess,
                       actualByteCount);

    return kIOReturnSuccess;
  }
```

Notice that although the transport driver for the RAM disk has no concept of a block size (since its minimum addressable unit was a byte), the IOBlockStorageDevice interface expresses the disk capacity in blocks, and operates on blocks when performing a read or write operation. For this reason, the nub driver's implementation defines an arbitrary block size of 512 bytes.

Finally, as with every I/O Kit driver, our RAM disk driver requires a property list that describes the requirements of the driver, including its matching dictionary. The IOBlockStorageDevice interface that the RAM disk driver implements is part of the I/O Kit's IOStorageFamily framework, so we need to explicitly include this dependency in the RAM disk driver's property list. This is done by adding an entry to the OSBundleLibraries section of the Info.plist file that references the kernel module com.apple.iokit.IOStorageFamily. In this sample, we import version 1.6 of the IOStorageFamily, which corresponds to the version that was included with Mac OS X 10.6.

■ **Note** Any kernel extension that implements a driver that is a part of the storage driver stack will need to include the IOStorageFamily as a dependency in its property list.

The property list for our sample RAM disk driver, including its matching dictionary and its library dependencies, is shown in Figure 14-3.

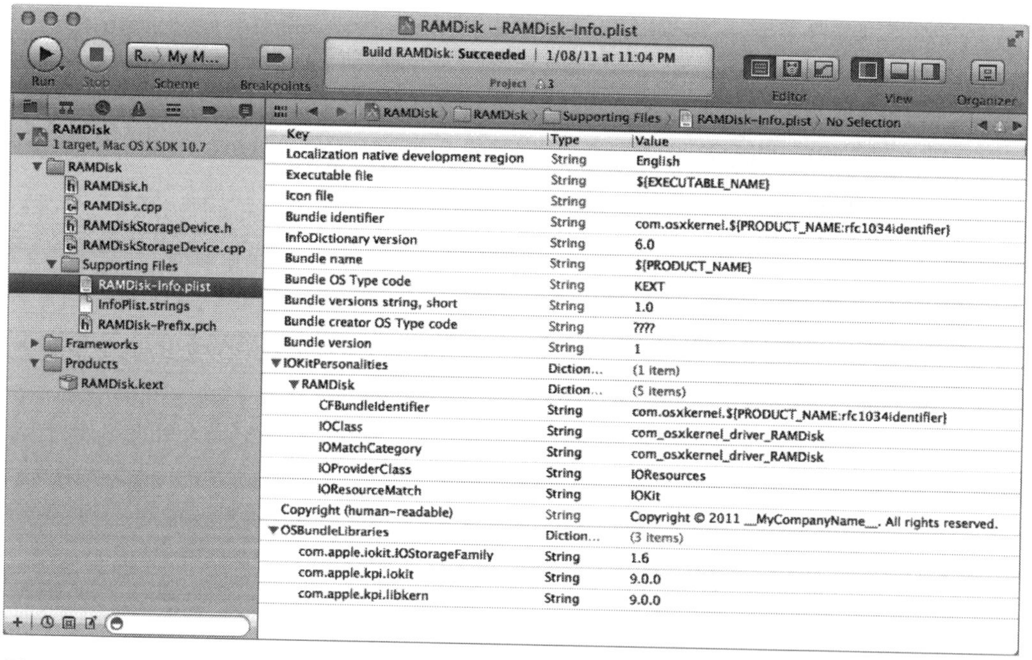

Figure 14-3. The property list for the sample RAM disk driver

After building the RAM disk driver and loading the resulting kernel extension, you will be presented with a dialog similar to that displayed in Figure 14-4. This does not indicate a problem with the device, but it does indicate that Mac OS X was unable to find a readable file system on the disk. Given that the disk has yet to be written to, this is an expected error.

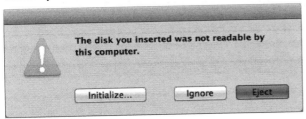

Figure 14-4. The standard Mac OS X dialog that is displayed when a disk is inserted that does not contain a readable file system

Clicking the "Initialize…" button in the dialog displayed in Figure 14-4 will launch the "Disk Utility" application, allowing the storage device to be partitioned and initialized with a file system. Before doing this, it is interesting to examine the state of the driver stack with the IORegisterExplorer utility. In addition to the RAMDisk transport driver and the RAMDiskStorageDevice nub, you will notice that the I/O Kit has constructed three drivers on top of the nub driver. The state of the driver stack is shown in Figure 14-5.

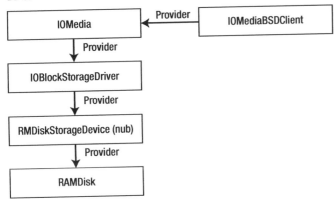

Figure 14-5. The driver stack that is created when a non-formatted storage device is loaded

The Disk Utility application allows a disk to be formatted and initialized for a file system. This process involves writing a partition table to the disk, which is required even if the disk contains only a single partition, and then writing a file system to that partition. To format a disk using Disk Utility, select the device from the list of disks on the left, and click the Erase tab. The name of the device that is displayed in Disk Utility is derived from the descriptive strings returned by the IOBlockStorageDevice nub, so in the case of the sample RAM disk, this results in a device with the name "RAM Disk Media."

By default, Disk Utility will write a GUID partition table to the disk and will use the Mac OS Extended file system, also known as the HFS+ file system. Disk Utility won't perform a low-level format of the volume, so the IOBlockStorageDevice method doFormatMedia does not need to be implemented. The process of initializing a volume is shown in Figure 14-6.

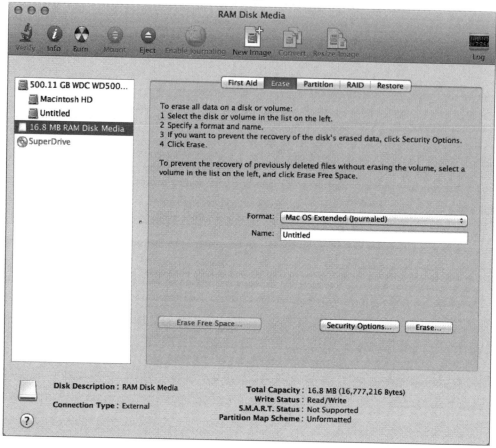

Figure 14-6. Initializing a new volume in Disk Utility

After a partition map and a file system has been written to the disk, the storage driver stack for the RAM disk will now contain three more drivers, as shown in Figure 14-7. On top of the IOMedia object that represents the entire disk is an I/O Kit class that represents the partition table that is present on the disk; in this case, it is the GUID partition table. Each partition has an IOMedia object that represents the logical volume of the partition.

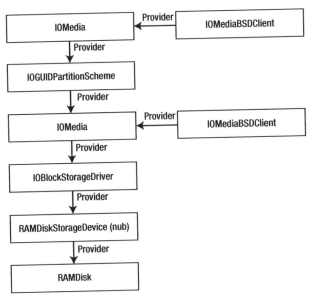

Figure 14-7. *The driver stack for a device that is partitioned with a GUID partition table containing a single partition*

When we implemented the driver for our RAM disk, all of the methods that we implemented were specific to accessing data from the device; it didn't need to provide any methods to handle partition schemes or file systems, or to make the device accessible to a user space process. All of this functionality is handled by classes provided by the I/O Kit's IOStorageFamily, in particular the IOBlockStorageDriver, IOMedia, and IOMediaBSDClient classes. The benefit of this design is that the functionality is largely common across all storage devices and can be implemented in shared classes, which removes the need for each storage device to rewrite the same functionality.

The IOBlockStorageDevice and IOBlockStorageDriver classes represent the disk drive hardware, and the IOMedia class represents the disk that is currently present in that drive. In the case of our sample RAM disk driver, or a USB flash drive, there will always be media present when there is a storage device; the two are inseparable. However, this does not always have to be true; a CD drive for example, will create an IOBlockStorageDevice (for which the I/O Kit will create a corresponding IOBlockStorageDriver), but unless there is a CD in the drive, there will be no IOMedia object in the driver stack.

The IOMedia class provides a logical representation of the disk. If the disk has been partitioned, a storage device will have multiple IOMedia objects, one for each partition, and another that represents the overall disk. In the case of a RAID, where a single volume has been created across multiple disks, there will be a single IOMedia object that represents the entire logical RAID volume.

Each IOMedia object in the kernel has an accompanying object known as the IOMediaBSDClient, which is responsible for making the logical disk available to user space processes. In most cases, a process won't need to interact with the disk driver directly. Rather, it will simply use the file system on the mounted volume to read and write files that are contained on that volume. In some cases, a user space process may need to read or write to the disk device directly or to send ioctl calls to the disk driver directly.

Following the convention of BSD, both a block device interface and a character device interface are created for every disk and every disk partition. The block device performs buffered I/O, with each read and write going through a buffer cache. When a process performs a read operation, the disk blocks that contain the accessed data are read from disk, placed into a buffer cache, and then copied into the destination buffer supplied by the user process. If a process reads a disk block that has recently been accessed, the data is likely to be present in the buffer cache, and the read request can be completed without having to access the disk.

The character device provides raw access to the disk storage, and doesn't go through the buffer cache. This means that every read or write to the device will result in a method call of the device's IOBlockStorageDevice interface, which will read or write directly into the process's buffer. As a consequence of this, all read and write operations performed to the character device must start on a disk block boundary, and the number of bytes transferred must be a multiple of the disk block size.

The block device and character device interfaces are created by the IOMediaBSDClient class. The block device interface can be accessed through the path /dev/diskN, and the character device interface can be accessed through the path /dev/rdiskN, where N is an integer to give the device a unique name.

After building and loading the RAM disk driver, a list of the disk devices that are present in the system can be examined by running the terminal command diskutil list. An example of the output from this command for the RAM disk device is shown in Listing 14-7. The interface disk1 corresponds to the entire storage device, and the interface disk1s1 corresponds to the HFS+ partition.

Listing 14-7. *The Output from the Command* diskutil list *for the RAM Disk Device*

```
/dev/disk1
   #:    TYPE                  NAME          SIZE        IDENTIFIER
   0:    GUID_partition_scheme               *16.8 MB    disk1
   1:    Apple_HFS             VolumeName    16.7 MB     disk1s1
```

Partition Schemes

A disk may be split into several smaller logical units, each of which appear as a separate disk to the user. Even if a hard disk only has a single partition it will contain a partition map, which lists the one or more partitions that have been created from the disk. Mac OS X provides support for many common partition schemes, including the GUID partition scheme that is the default on Mac OS X, the Master Boot Record that is still common on Windows, and the Apple Partition Map, which was the default partition scheme for Mac OS before the transition to Intel-based Macs.

Support for new partition schemes can be added to Mac OS X by writing an I/O Kit driver that is derived from the IOPartitionScheme class. A partition scheme driver loads whenever a disk is inserted, and scans the disk for a partition table that it recognizes. If a partition table that is supported by the driver is found, it creates an IOMedia object for each entry in the partition table, and attaches these IOMedia objects above it on the driver storage stack. The IOMedia objects created by the partition driver will describe only the section of the disk that is covered by the partition, and not the entire disk contents.

An IOMedia object can describe either the entire disk or a single partition consisting of a physically contiguous subset of blocks on the disk. When an IOMedia object is instantiated, its constructor takes a property that identifies whether the IOMedia object describes the entire disk or not. Although a partition driver will load against an IOMedia object, it will only load against one that describes the entire disk contents, because typically a partition table is not located within a partition.

After the partition scheme driver has successfully scanned a disk, the end result is the construction of a storage driver stack similar to that shown in Figure 14-7, with an IOMedia object that describes the entire disk's contents (the object above the IOBlockStorageDriver in the driver stack) and an IOMedia object for each partition (the object above the IOGUIDPartitionTableScheme in the driver stack).

It is worth noting that a partition scheme driver is responsible only for reading a partition table that already exists on the disk; the IOPartitionScheme class contains no methods for writing a partition table. A partition table could be created by providing a user space utility process that writes to the disk device directly.

Implementing a Sample Partition Scheme

In this section we will examine how the driver for a hypothetical partition map would be implemented in the I/O Kit. To begin with, let's examine the property list of the driver, in particular its matching dictionary, as shown in Listing 14-8.

Listing 14-8. A Sample Matching Dictionary from the Property List of a Partition Scheme Driver

```
<key>IOKitPersonalities</key>
<dict>
        <key>SamplePartitionScheme</key>
        <dict>
                <key>CFBundleIdentifier</key>
                <string>com.osxkernel.SamplePartitionScheme</string>
                <key>IOClass</key>
                <string>com_osxkernel_driver_SamplePartitionScheme</string>
                <key>IOMatchCategory</key>
                <string>IOStorage</string>
                <key>IOProviderClass</key>
                <string>IOMedia</string>
                <key>IOPropertyMatch</key>
                <dict>
                        <key>Whole</key>
                        <true/>
                </dict>
        </dict>
</dict>
```

There are three important aspects of the matching dictionary:

- It specifies a provider class of IOMedia, so whenever a new disk is inserted (and an IOMedia object is created to represent that disk), the partition driver will be given the chance to examine the contents of that disk for a supported partition table.

- The partition driver is interested only in an IOMedia object that represents the entire disk, since partition tables cannot be located within a disk partition. To narrow the match to IOMedia objects that represent an entire disk only, the matching dictionary uses the IOPropertyMatch key to specify that the I/O Kit should load the driver only against an IOMedia object that contains a property named "Whole" with the Boolean value of true. This is a standard property of IOMedia objects that specifies whether the object covers the entire disk, or a partition of that disk.

- The property list specifies an IOMatchCategory of IOStorage. This property appears in the property table of the partition driver, and is important for the correct construction of the storage driver stack. In particular, certain drivers will use the IOMatchCategory property to determine whether they are at the top of the driver stack, or whether the driver on top is also a part of the IOStorage stack.

Although a partition scheme driver is part of the storage driver stack, and is unloaded only after the disk is removed, the driver itself plays a role only when the disk is first inserted, when it is responsible for reading the partition table from the disk and instantiating an IOMedia object for each partition that it finds. As a driver that is derived from the standard I/O Kit class IOService, the partition scheme driver does this through the init(), probe(), and start() methods and on unloading through the stop() and free() methods.

The probe() method is of particular significance for an IOPartitionScheme driver. A partition scheme driver will be instantiated whenever a disk is added to the system, and it is up to the driver to determine whether the disk contains a supported partition table and, if not, to allow an IOPartitionScheme driver that is better suited to load instead. This is done through the standard IOService method probe(). In general, the purpose of the probe() method is to examine the hardware to determine whether the driver is able to support the device, and if so, to return an integer value that represents how well suited the driver is to the hardware. The driver with the highest probe score is the one that will be loaded by the I/O Kit.

In the case of an IOPartitionScheme driver, the role of the probe() method is to read enough of the disk to determine whether the partition table on the disk is supported by the driver and, if so, to go on to read the partition table entries. It isn't strictly necessary to read the entire partition table in the probe() method, but doing so prevents the need to rescan the partition table when the driver's start() method is called. The partition scheme drivers provided by Apple as a part of Mac OS X go one step further and actually instantiate an IOMedia object for each partition that is found in the probe() method.

If a disk contains a partition table that the partition scheme driver recognizes and the partition driver is selected by the I/O Kit as the most suitable driver, its start() method will be called. At this point, the partition scheme driver should create an IOMedia object for each partition entry and attach it to the storage driver stack.

A sample implementation of the probe() and start() methods is demonstrated in Listing 14-9. This driver is based on the partition scheme drivers that are included as part of the Darwin source code in the IOStorage family.

As with the partition drivers included in Darwin, the implementation in Listing 14-9 has a custom method named scan() to examine the disk, and if a supported partition table is found, to instantiate an IOMedia object for each partition and return the partition set to the caller through an OSSet object. If no IOMedia objects were found during the scan, the probe() method returns unsuccessfully, as indicated by a NULL result value, and the I/O Kit will continue searching for another partition scheme driver for the disk. If a supported partition table was found instead, the probe method saves the set of IOMedia objects representing each partition to an instance variable named m_partitions.

Listing 14-9. An Implementation of the probe() and start() Methods for a Partition Scheme Driver

```
#include <IOKit/storage/IOPartitionScheme.h>

// Define the superclass
#define super IOPartitionScheme

OSDefineMetaClassAndStructors(com_osxkernel_driver_PartitionScheme, IOPartitionScheme)
```

```
IOService* com_osxkernel_driver_PartitionScheme::probe(IOService* provider, SInt32* score)
{
        if (super::probe(provider, score) == NULL)
                return NULL;

        // Scan the IOMedia for a supported partition table.
        m_partitions = scan(score);

        // If no partition table was found, return NULL.
        return m_partitions ? this : NULL;
}

bool com_osxkernel_driver_PartitionScheme::start (IOService *provider)
{
        IOMedia*                partition;
        OSIterator*             partitionIterator;

        if (super::start(provider) == false)
                return false;

        // Create an iterator for the IOMedia objects that were
        // found and instantiated during probe.
        partitionIterator = OSCollectionIterator::withCollection(m_partitions);
        if (partitionIterator == NULL)
                return false;

        // Attach and register each IOMedia object (representing found partitions).
        while ((partition = (IOMedia*)partitionIterator->getNextObject()))
        {
                if (partition->attach(this))
                {
                        attachMediaObjectToDeviceTree(partition);
                        partition->registerService();
                }
        }
        partitionIterator->release();

        return true;
}
```

If the probe() method returns successfully and the I/O Kit doesn't find a better driver, our partition driver will be added to the storage stack and its start() method will be called. The role of a partition driver's start() method is to attach each of its IOMedia objects to the storage driver stack, where each IOMedia object represents a single partition entry on the disk. This is done through the IOService method named attach(), which inserts the IOMedia object into the service plane of the I/O Registry as a child of the partition driver (which is the provider class).

As well as inserting the IOMedia object into the service plane of the I/O Registry, it may also be necessary to insert the IOMedia object into the device plane of the I/O Registry. This is only needed if the partition could potentially be used as the boot volume on a PowerPC-based Macintosh. This is because the boot volume on a PowerPC-based Macintosh is identified through its location in the I/O Registry device plane, so the IOMedia object that represents the boot partition needs to have an entry in the device plane. The IOPartitionScheme superclass provides a method named attachMediaObjectToDeviceTree(), which will insert an IOMedia object into the I/O Registry's device plane.

The scan() method is a custom method that determines whether the disk contains a partition scheme that is supported by the driver and, if so, reads the partition table entries from the disk and creates a set of IOMedia objects that represent each partition. This requires the partition driver to be able to read the disk, which is performed through the driver's provider object. As specified in the driver's matching dictionary (see Listing 14-8), the partition driver's provider class is an IOMedia object that represents the entire disk. An example implementation of the scan() method is provided in Listing 14-10.

Listing 14-10. *A Method to Detect the Presence of a Sample Partition Table on a Disk and to Instantiate IOMedia Objects for that Partition Table*

```
OSSet*  com_osxkernel_driver_PartitionScheme::scan(SInt32* score)
{
          IOBufferMemoryDescriptor*      buffer        = NULL;
          SamplePartitionTable*          sampleTable;
1         IOMedia*                       media         = getProvider();
          UInt64                         mediaBlockSize = media->getPreferredBlockSize();
          bool                           mediaIsOpen   = false;
          OSSet*                         partitions    = NULL;
          IOReturn                       status;

          // Determine whether this media is formatted.
2         if (media->isFormatted() == false)
                  goto bail;
          // Allocate a sector-sized buffer to hold data read from disk.
3         buffer = IOBufferMemoryDescriptor::withCapacity(mediaBlockSize, kIODirectionIn);
          if (buffer == NULL)
                  goto bail;

          // Allocate a set to hold the media objects representing disk partitions.
4         partitions = OSSet::withCapacity(8);
          if (partitions == NULL)
                  goto bail;

          // Open the storage driver stack that (of which this partition driver is part)
          // for read access.
5         mediaIsOpen = open(this, 0, kIOStorageAccessReader);
          if (mediaIsOpen == false)
                  goto bail;

          // Read the first sector of the disk.
6         status = media->read(this, 0, buffer);
          if (status != kIOReturnSuccess)
                  goto bail;
          sampleTable = (SamplePartitionTable*)buffer->getBytesNoCopy();

          // Determine whether the first sector contains our recognized partition signature.
7         if (strcmp(sampleTable->partitionIdentifier, kSamplePartitionIdentifier) != 0)
                  goto bail;
```

```
     // Scan for valid partition entries in the partition map.
8    for (int index = 0; index < sampleTable->partitionCount; index++)
     {
9            if (isPartitionInvalid(&sampleTable->partitionEntries[index]))
                     continue;

             IOMedia*         newMedia;
10           newMedia = instantiateMediaObject(&sampleTable->partitionEntries[index],
                                         1+index);
             if ( newMedia )
             {
                     partitions->setObject(newMedia);
                     newMedia->release();
             }
     }

     // Release temporary resources.
11   close(this);
     buffer->release();

     return partitions;

bail:
     // Non-successful return; release all allocated objects.
12   if ( mediaIsOpen )        close(this);
     if ( partitions )         partitions->release();
     if ( buffer )             buffer->release();

     return NULL;
}
```

Corresponding to the numbered lines in Listing 14-10, the following is an overview of the steps performed in the listing:

1. We obtain a pointer to our provider class, which is an IOMedia object that represents the entire disk. All disk reads are performed through this object, which includes reading the partition table off the disk.

2. We check any properties of the disk's media before checking for a partition table. If the disk's media is not formatted, we abort the scan. This is also a suitable place to verify requirements, such as a minimum disk block size that may be required by the partition scheme.

3. All data that is read from the disk is written into an IOMemoryDescriptor as the destination. We therefore allocate an IOBufferMemoryDescriptor to hold the contents of the data that this method will read from the disk. Since this memory descriptor will be used in an operation that reads data from the disk, its direction must be set to kIODirectionIn.

4. We allocate an OSSet container to hold the collection of IOMedia objects that represent each partition that is found on the disk. Although the initial capacity

of the OSSet collection is 8 objects, the OSSet will automatically expand if more than 8 IOMedia objects are inserted.

5. The storage driver stack (of which the partition driver is a part of) is opened for read access. Since the partition driver will read the partition table from the disk, but not modify the disk contents, it only requires read access.

6. The first disk sector is read from the disk. This is typically the location of the partition table's header. The hypothetical partition scheme used in this sample stores its header in the first disk sector. The buffer parameter to the read() method specifies both the destination for the data that is read, and the number of bytes to read.

7. Based on the data read from the disk, the partition driver determines whether the disk contains a partition scheme that it supports. This code will be specific to the partition scheme; the hypothetical partition scheme used by our sample driver is identified through a string constant that is written to the first block on the disk. As such, the driver uses the strcmp() function to determine whether this string exists, and if it cannot be found, it assumes that another partition scheme exists on the disk and returns unsuccessfully.

8. The code iterates over each entry in the partition table that was read from the disk. This code will be specific to the partition scheme; the hypothetical partition scheme used in this sample stores the entire partition table in the initial disk sector.

9. The partition entry is verified. This may involve such checks as making sure that the starting block and length of the partition entry do not exceed the capacity of the disk.

10. A new IOMedia object is instantiated to represent the partition entry.

11. If the partition table was successfully scanned, the storage driver stack is closed (to balance the call to open() that was made earlier), and the set of IOMedia objects is returned to the caller.

12. If an error occurred, the code releases any resources that were partially allocated.

The implementation of the instantiateMediaObject() method that is called as a part of Step 10 is provided in Listing 14-11. This is a custom method that is defined by our partition scheme driver.

Listing 14-11. A Method to Instantiate IOMedia Objects That Represent an Individual Disk Partition

```
IOMedia* com_osxkernel_driver_PartitionScheme::instantiateMediaObject
                            (SamplePartitionEntry* sampleEntry, int index)
{
        IOMedia*        media           = getProvider();
        UInt64          mediaBlockSize  = media->getPreferredBlockSize();
        IOMedia*        newMedia;

1       newMedia = new IOMedia;
        if ( newMedia )
        {
```

```
          UInt64              partitionBase, partitionSize;

2         partitionBase = OSSwapLittleToHostInt64(sampleEntry->blockStart) *
                              mediaBlockSize;
          partitionSize = OSSwapLittleToHostInt64(sampleEntry->blockCount) *
                              mediaBlockSize;

3         if ( newMedia->init(partitionBase, partitionSize, mediaBlockSize,
              media->getAttributes(), false, media->isWritable()))
          {
4                 // Set a name for this partition.
                  newMedia->setName(sampleEntry->name);

                  // Set a location value (the partition number) for this partition.
                  char location[12];
                  snprintf(location, sizeof(location), "%d", index);
                  newMedia->setLocation(location);

                  // Set the "Partition ID" key for this partition.
                  newMedia->setProperty(kIOMediaPartitionIDKey, index, 32);
          }
          else
          {
5                 newMedia->release();
                  newMedia = NULL;
          }
      }
  }

6     return newMedia;
  }
```

Corresponding to the numbered lines in Listing 14-11, the following is an overview of the steps performed in the listing:

1. An IOMedia object is allocated using the C++ "new" operator.

2. The initial disk block number of the partition and the size of the partition are read from the partition table entry. A partition scheme will have a standard endianness that may differ from the native byte order of the host on which the driver is running, so it's important to use byte order macros such as OSSwapLittleToHostInt64() to make sure that the data is read correctly.

3. The allocated IOMedia object is initialized. The parameters of the IOMedia::init() method are provided here:

```
virtual bool init(UInt64              base,
                  UInt64              size,
                  UInt64              preferredBlockSize,
                  IOMediaAttributeMask attributes,
                  bool                isWhole,
                  bool                isWritable,
                  const char*         contentHint = 0,
                  OSDictionary*       properties  = 0);
```

The parameters base and size define the location of the partition on the disk, specified in bytes. Another important parameter is the Boolean parameter isWhole, which is set false to indicate that this IOMedia object represents a partition, and not the entire disk. The parameter contentHint describes the content of the partition, such as the file system that the volume uses. A description of the contentHint property is described in the following section.

4.   Various properties of the partition are set on the partition's IOMedia object. These include the partition name, and the location and partition IDs, both of which are derived from the index of this partition in the partition table.

5.   If the IOMedia object could not be successfully initialized, it is released.

6.   The initialized IOMedia object is returned to the caller or NULL if the object could not be successfully initialized.

Finally, when the driver for the partition scheme is unloaded, it must remove its IOMedia objects from the driver stack and release them. A partition driver may be unloaded because the disk has been ejected, or because the disk has been reformatted, in which case a new partition table may have been written to the disk, and potentially even a different partition scheme.

An example of the implementation of the stop() and free() methods for a partition scheme driver is shown in Listing 14-12. The stop() method removes each IOMedia object from the device plane of the I/O Registry, undoing the call to attachMediaObjectToDeviceTree() that the partition driver performed in its start() method. Before the partition driver is unloaded, its free() method is called, which releases the OSSet that holds the collection of IOMedia objects for each partition entry.

Listing 14-12. An Implementation of the stop() and free() Methods for a Partition Scheme Driver

```
void com_osxkernel_driver_PartitionScheme::stop(IOService* provider)
{
        IOMedia*                  partition;
        OSIterator*               partitionIterator;

        // Detach the media objects we previously attached to the device tree.
        partitionIterator = OSCollectionIterator::withCollection(m_partitions);
        if (partitionIterator)
        {
                while ((partition = (IOMedia*)partitionIterator->getNextObject()))
                {
                        detachMediaObjectFromDeviceTree(partition);
                }

                partitionIterator->release();
        }

        super::stop(provider);
}

void com_osxkernel_driver_PartitionScheme::free (void)
{
        if (m_partitions != NULL)
                m_partitions->release();
```

```
        super::free();
}
```

The Media Content Hint Property

As we saw in Listing 14-11, the initialization method of the IOMedia class takes a parameter named contentHint. Although this parameter is not interpreted by the IOMedia object, it plays a very important role in the construction of the driver storage stack. The contentHint parameter is a string value that describes the content that is contained by the IOMedia object on the disk. For an IOMedia object that represents an entire disk, the content hint may identify the partition scheme that the disk contains. For an IOMedia object that represents a single partition, the content hint may identify the type of file system that the volume uses. The content hint can also be used for a custom purpose; for example, a driver that provides disk encryption could use the content hint to describe the encryption scheme that has been used on the disk.

The content hint is not used to describe the content to the user, but rather to provide information that can be used by other drivers on the system. The contentHint parameter that is passed to the initialization method of the IOMedia class is set as an I/O Registry property on the IOMedia object. This makes the value of content hint accessible to other drivers in the storage stack, but more importantly, it provides a property that can be specified and matched against another driver's matching dictionary.

When we created our partition scheme driver, we specified an IOPropertyMatch item (see Listing 14-8), which limited the driver to matching against specific IOMedia objects. In the case of the partition scheme driver, we matched against only IOMedia objects that represented the entire disk. This was done by informing the I/O Kit that the partition driver should only match against an IOMedia object that contained a property named "Whole" with the value true. Similarly, a driver can add an IOPropertyMatch item to its matching dictionary that contains the key "Content Hint", and specify a value that contains the particular content type that the driver is interested in. This could be used, for example, to prevent a disk encryption driver from loading against IOMedia volumes that are not encrypted.

Another important use of the content hint property is to identify the correct file system driver to load for an IOMedia volume. Mac OS X will load a file system driver only if the content hint value of the IOMedia object identifies a supported file system.

Since the content hint value needs to be specified when an IOMedia object is initialized, any driver that instantiates an IOMedia object needs to know the content of the disk or partition that is represented by that object. For a partition scheme driver, the content hint will come from the partition table that is stored on the disk. For example, the Apple Partition Map contains a string value for each partition entry that is used as the content hint value directly. The GUID partition table contains a 128-bit GUID for each partition that identifies the file system and content of that partition. This GUID is converted to a string representation, which is then used as the content hint. This means that there may be multiple content hint values that identify a particular file system, so a file system driver must match against each possible value of the IOMedia's content hint that could identify its file system.

Media Filter Drivers

The top of the driver storage stack may contain one or more media filter drivers. A media filter driver, also known as a filter scheme driver, matches against an existing IOMedia object in the storage stack, and creates a new IOMedia object that represents the filtered media object. All read and write requests to the disk pass through the filter scheme driver, allowing the filter driver to manipulate the blocks that are read, or even to manipulate the data as it travels between the original IOMedia object and the filtered IOMedia object above it in the storage stack.

A filter scheme driver can be used to implement various types of functionality. For example, a filter driver could be used to implement block-level disk encryption by matching against an IOMedia object that represents an encrypted partition on the disk, and publishing an IOMedia object that represents the unencrypted partition that is used by the file system. Another use of a filter scheme driver could be to implement a RAID driver, which matches against multiple IOMedia objects, each of which represents an individual disk in the RAID set, and creates a single IOMedia object that represents the logical volume. The relationship between a filter scheme driver and the IOMedia objects that it controls, and the IOMedia object that it publishes, is shown in Figure 14-8.

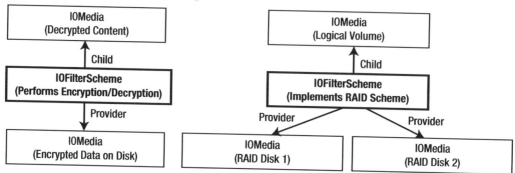

Figure 14-8. *The relationship between a filter scheme driver and its provider classes and the* IOMedia *objects that it creates for an encryption scheme (left) and a RAID driver (right)*

The partition scheme driver that was developed in the previous section can be thought of as a specialized form of a filter driver. Like a filter driver, the partition scheme driver loads against an existing IOMedia object and creates one or more IOMedia objects that represent the partitions on the disk. However, unlike the partition scheme, the general filter driver can have multiple provider classes, as in the case of the RAID driver shown in Figure 14-8. Another difference is that unlike a filter driver, a partition scheme driver typically isn't involved in handling each read or write request that is made through the IOMedia objects that it creates.

The I/O Kit provides a class known as IOFilterScheme that forms the superclass of any driver that implements a media filter scheme. A filter scheme driver will typically use the "Content Hint" property value of the IOMedia object that it matches against to restrict the filter scheme to loading only against an IOMedia object that the filter scheme can support. For example, the Apple software RAID driver formats each disk in the RAID set with the GUID partition table and, as such, each disk's IOMedia object contains a GUID as its "Content Hint" property. Apple has defined a GUID to indicate that the disk partition forms part of a RAID set, which the Apple RAID driver will match against. When the Apple RAID driver creates its child IOMedia object to represent the logical volume, it gives this IOMedia object a content hint that represents the file system that was written to the overall RAID set.

▪ **Note** File system drivers will load against only the top-level (leaf) IOMedia object in the driver storage stack. This means that, even though a filter scheme driver may match against an IOMedia object that contains a readable file system, and creates another IOMedia object with a readable file system, only the object above the filter scheme driver in the stack will be mounted on the user's desktop.

A Sample Filter Scheme for Encryption

Let's examine the implementation of a sample filter scheme driver by implementing a simple block-level encryption driver. The sample driver doesn't do anything sophisticated in terms of security–it simply implements a basic XOR encryption scheme–but it does demonstrate the structure of a filter scheme driver.

The filter scheme that we will develop will encrypt the contents of an entire partition, and our sample will require the disk to be formatted with the standard GUID partition table. To identify an encrypted partition, we will define a new GUID to describe the content of the partition, which we can generate using the command line tool uuidgen. Throughout this sample, we will use the GUID 8D7FD0BB-39A8-43C0-9432-F4E1A269F070, which our sample driver has defined to describe an encrypted disk partition that contains the HFS file system. Hereafter, we will use the term Encrypted_HFS_GUID in the chapter text instead of writing the GUID in full.

For this sample, we will use the standard GUID partition table, which means that the driver for the partition scheme in the storage driver stack will be the standard Apple GUID partition scheme driver. The Apple driver sets the "Content Hint" property of each partition's IOMedia object to the partition type GUID from the partition header on the disk. This means that the IOMedia object that our encryption filter driver wishes to load against will have a content hint of Encrypted_HFS_GUID. The encryption filter driver can ignore all other IOMedia objects, since it knows that they do not represent an encrypted partition. This requirement can be expressed in the filter driver's matching dictionary by adding an IOPropertyMatch key, as shown in Listing 14-13.

Listing 14-13. The Matching Dictionary from the Property List of a Sample Filter Scheme Driver That Implements Encryption

```
<key>IOKitPersonalities</key>
<dict>
        <key>SampleEncryptionFilter</key>
        <dict>
                <key>Content Mask</key>
                <string>Sample_Encrypted_Data</string>
                <key>CFBundleIdentifier</key>
                <string>com.osxkernel.SampleEncryptionFilter</string>
                <key>IOClass</key>
                <string>com_osxkernel_driver_SampleEncryptionFilter</string>
                <key>IOMatchCategory</key>
                <string>IOStorage</string>
                <key>IOProviderClass</key>
                <string>IOMedia</string>
                <key>IOPropertyMatch</key>
                <dict>
                        <key>Content Hint</key>
                        <string>8D7FD0BB-39A8-43C0-9432-F4E1A269F070</string>
                </dict>
        </dict>
</dict>
```

When a filter scheme driver loads, it may need to probe its IOMedia provider class to determine whether it contains content supported by the filter driver. If it does, it creates one or more IOMedia children objects that represent the filtered volume. These steps are similar to the implementation of the probe() and start() methods of the partition scheme driver shown in Listing 14-9. However, unlike the partition scheme driver, our sample encryption filter scheme driver can ignore the probe() method, since the driver's property list has been set up to ensure that the driver will load only against an IOMedia object whose "Content Hint" property contains our Encrypted_HFS_GUID type. Therefore, if the driver loads, we can assume that it is loading against an encrypted partition.

In our sample filter scheme driver's start() method, we need to create a new IOMedia object that represents the filtered disk contents; this is the IOMedia object through which we expose the unencrypted data to the rest of the system (such as the file system). As with a partition scheme driver, it's important that the filter driver correctly sets the contentHint parameter of any child IOMedia object that it creates, since this is the means by which the system is able to identify which file system (or even another filter scheme driver) to load against the IOMedia volume. In the case of our sample encryption filter, we have made the arbitrary design choice that it will encrypt an HFS file system, so the IOMedia child object that is published by the filter scheme will be created with a contentHint value of "Apple_HFS."

The implementation of the start() method for our sample encryption filter scheme is shown in Listing 14-14. Our sample filter scheme does not provide an implementation of the init() or probe() methods, because the implementation provided by the superclass is sufficient.

Listing 14-14. An Implementation of the start() Method for a Sample Filter Scheme that Provides Encryption

```
#include <IOKit/storage/IOFilterScheme.h>

// Define the superclass.
#define super IOFilterScheme

OSDefineMetaClassAndStructors(com_osxkernel_driver_SampleEncryptionFilter, IOFilterScheme)

bool com_osxkernel_driver_SampleEncryptionFilter::start (IOService *provider)
{
        if (super::start(provider) == false)
                return false;

        // Save a reference to our provider class, and verify that it is an IOMedia object.
        m_encryptedMedia = OSDynamicCast(IOMedia, provider);
        if (m_encryptedMedia == NULL)
                return false;

        // Create a child IOMedia object to represent the unencrypted data.
        m_childMedia = instantiateMediaObject();
        if (m_childMedia == NULL)
                return false;

        // Attach the unencrypted IOMedia object to the storage driver stack.
        if (m_childMedia->attach(this) == false)
                return false;
        m_childMedia->registerService();

        return true;
}
```

```
IOMedia* com_osxkernel_driver_SampleEncryptionFilter::instantiateMediaObject ()
{
        IOMedia*        newMedia;

        // Allocate a new IOMedia object.
        newMedia = new IOMedia;
        if ( newMedia )
        {
                // Initialize the child IOMedia object.
                // Nearly all of its parameters can be obtained from the provider class.
                if ( newMedia->init(0,                            // base
                                m_encryptedMedia->getSize(),
                                m_encryptedMedia->getPreferredBlockSize(),
                                m_encryptedMedia->getAttributes(),
                                false,                            // isWhole
                                m_encryptedMedia->isWritable(),
                                "Apple_HFS"))                     // contentHint
                {
                        // Set a location value (the partition number) for this media object.
                        newMedia->setLocation("1");
                }
                else
                {
                        newMedia->release();
                        newMedia = NULL;
                }
        }

        return newMedia;
}
```

The method named instantiateMediaObject() is a custom method defined by the SampleEncryptionFilter class and is responsible for creating a child IOMedia object to represent the unencrypted disk contents. Many of the properties of the child IOMedia object can come straight from the filter driver's encrypted IOMedia provider class. For a driver that implements block-level encryption, there is no need to modify properties such as the size of the volume and the size of a disk block for the child IOMedia object. In general, there is nothing to prevent a filter scheme driver from creating an IOMedia device of a different size or block size to that of its provider class, as may be required by the filter scheme of a RAID driver.

For our sample encryption driver, we need to intercept all read and write operations that are performed on the unencrypted child IOMedia object. Because our filter scheme sits between the unencrypted IOMedia object (the child object that we created) and the encrypted IOMedia object (our provider class), all read and write operations made on the child IOMedia object pass through our filter driver, so intercepting these operations involves nothing more than overriding the superclass implementation of the read() and write() methods.

In the case of a read operation, our encryption filter driver needs to pass the read request on to the encrypted IOMedia object and decrypt the data that is returned. This is complicated by the fact that the read is performed asynchronously, so the filter driver needs to provide completion callback to be notified when the read has completed. At this point, the data that was read back from the encrypted volume is decrypted, and the original read completion callback, as provided by the client that initiated the read, is called. The implementation of this is given in Listing 14-15.

Listing 14-15. An Implementation of the read() Method for a Sample Filter Scheme That Provides Encryption

```
void    com_osxkernel_driver_SampleEncryptionFilter::read (IOService* client,
                                    UInt64 byteStart,
                                    IOMemoryDescriptor* buffer, IOStorageAttributes* attributes,
                                    IOStorageCompletion* completion)
{
        ReadCompletionParams*    context;
        IOStorageCompletion      newCompletion;

        // Allocate a structure to hold state while the read
        // is being performed asynchronously.
1       context = (ReadCompletionParams*)IOMalloc(sizeof(ReadCompletionParams));
        if (context == NULL)
        {
                complete(completion, kIOReturnNoMemory);
                return;
        }

2       context->completion = *completion;
        context->buffer = buffer;
        context->buffer->retain();

        // Setup a callback function so that we will be notified
        // when the encrypted data has been read from disk.
3       newCompletion.target = this;
        newCompletion.action = readCompleted;
        newCompletion.parameter = context;

        // Perform a read of the encrypted data from disk.
4       m_encryptedMedia->read(client, byteStart, buffer, attributes, &newCompletion);
}

void    com_osxkernel_driver_SampleEncryptionFilter::readCompleted (void* target,
                                                    void* parameter,
                                    IOReturn status, UInt64 actualByteCount)
{
        ReadCompletionParams*    context = (ReadCompletionParams*)parameter;

        // Decrypt the data read from disk.
5       if (status == kIOReturnSuccess)
                status = decryptBuffer(context->buffer, actualByteCount);

        // If  either the read from disk or the decryption operation failed,
        // set the actualByteCount value to 0.
        if (status != kIOReturnSuccess)
                actualByteCount = 0;

        // Call the original caller's completion function.
```

```
6        complete(&context->completion, status, actualByteCount);

7        context->buffer->release();
         IOFree(context, sizeof(ReadCompletionParams));
}
```

Corresponding to the numbered lines in Listing 14-15, the following is an overview of the steps performed in the listing:

1. Since the read is performed asynchronously, any variables or state that is needed in the completion callback for the read need to be saved to a temporary structure. We use the IOMalloc() function to allocate a structure in memory to save anything that we need to pass to the completion callback.

2. The allocated context structure is initialized. One parameter that needs to be saved is the IOStorageCompletion structure provided by the caller; this contains the callback function that the caller wishes to be notified on when the read completes. We also save a reference to the IOMemoryDescriptor that the data from the disk is read into. Since we will be referencing this object in the callback, we retain it to prevent it from being released before the callback fires.

3. We set up an IOStorageCompletion structure to pass our own callback function to be notified when the asynchronous read completes.

4. We perform a read from the encrypted IOMedia object.

5. When the read completes, our specified callback function (readCompleted) will be called. If the read completed successfully, we decrypt the data that was read back from the encrypted IOMedia object.

6. We call the IOStorageCompletion callback that was provided by the caller, which notifies the caller that its buffer contains the decrypted data that it requested.

7. We release our reference to the IOMemoryDescriptor that we took, and release the structure that was allocated in Step 1.

The implementation of the encryption filter scheme's write operation is quite straightforward because it can perform the encryption before writing the resulting data to the encrypted IOMedia object. As such, even though the write is performed asynchronously, it doesn't need to replace the completion callback that was provided by the caller (unlike the read operation).

Rather than encrypt the data in-place, we allocate a new IOMemoryDescriptor to hold the encrypted data. This allows us to leave the caller's buffer unmodified, which is important because the write operation should not change the contents of the source buffer. Even though the write is performed asynchronously, the driver in the storage stack that performs the operation will retain the IOMemoryDescriptor buffer for the duration of the write. This allows us to release our own reference to the object immediately after issuing the write to the encrypted IOMedia object.

The implementation of the encryption filter scheme's write() method is provided in Listing 14-16.

Listing 14-16. An Implementation of the write() *Method for a Sample Filter Scheme That Provides Encryption*

```
Void    com_osxkernel_driver_SampleEncryptionFilter::write (IOService* client,
                                UInt64 byteStart,
                                IOMemoryDescriptor* buffer, IOStorageAttributes* attributes,
                                IOStorageCompletion* completion)
{
        IOMemoryDescriptor*             newDesc;

        // Allocate a buffer to hold the encrypted data and perform the encryption
        newDesc = encryptBuffer(buffer);
        if (newDesc == NULL)
        {
                // Return an error if a destination buffer could not be allocated.
                complete(completion, kIOReturnNoMemory);
                return;
        }

        // Perform a write of the encrypted data to the encrypted IOMedia object.
        m_encryptedMedia->write(client, byteStart, newDesc, attributes, completion);

        // Release our reference to the encrypted IOMemoryDescriptor
        newDesc->release();
}
```

Creating a Custom GUID Partition Table

The encryption filter scheme that we developed in the previous section will load only against an IOMedia object whose "Content Hint" property is a custom value that we have defined for the purposes of the sample filter scheme. To test out the driver, we need to create a GUID partition table that contains a partition entry with our custom GUID type.

This can be performed through various command line tools that are included with Mac OS X. For this tutorial we will create a volume containing a GUID partition table that we can use to test the encryption filter driver. The storage device for the encrypted volume will be provided by a disk image, which is a regular file that behaves as a virtual disk, and contains a file system (and possibly a partition scheme) that can be mounted as a volume on the Mac OS X desktop. Disk images provide a convenient way to test filter scheme and partition scheme drivers, since they can be easily created without having to format physical media.

This section provides a tutorial of some of the command line tools that can be used while developing drivers in the storage stack. In this section, we will create a disk image, write a GUID partition table that contains a single partition of our specified partition type, and write an HFS file system to our encrypted volume. All of these tasks will be performed through command line tools.

To begin, open the Terminal application. The first step is to create a blank disk image that will provide the storage for our media, and will play the role of a disk. The hdiutil command line utility is a tool for creating and manipulating disk image files. We can create a 25MiB blank disk image with the following command:

```
hdiutil create -megabytes 25 -layout NONE EncryptedImage.dmg
```

This will create a file named "EncryptedImage.dmg" in the current working directory, consisting of a 25MiB disk image. The option "-layout NONE" specifies that we do not want a partition table created on the disk image. Since the resulting disk image contains no partition map and no file system, it cannot be mounted. However, we can interact with the disk image by using the following command:

```
hdiutil attach -nomount EncryptedImage.dmg
```

With our understanding of how storage devices are implemented in the Mac OS X kernel, we are in a good position to examine what this command is doing behind the scenes. The "hdiutil attach" command will load the kernel driver supplied by Apple that manages disk images; this will be derived from the same IOBlockStorageDevice superclass that we used to implement the RAM disk. A storage driver stack will be constructed, consisting of a single IOMedia object that represents the entire disk image's contents. The IOMedia object will have a corresponding IOMediaBSDClient object, which will publish the device interfaces for the disk image in the /dev directory. This results in the creation of a block device, such as /dev/disk1 and a character device, such as /dev/rdisk1, through which the disk image can be accessed. The path to the block device that was created as a result of attaching the disk image is printed to the terminal output.

We can now read and write to the disk image through its block device interface, so the next step is to create a GUID partition table on the disk. The gpt command is a command line tool supplied by Apple with Mac OS X for creating and manipulating a disk's GUID partition table. We can create a GUID partition table on a blank disk with the following command. Make sure to replace the path /dev/diskN with the path to the device interface that corresponds to the attached disk image on your system.

```
gpt create /dev/diskN
```

This writes a GUID partition table that contains no partitions to the disk. We wish to create a single partition on the disk, so the next command will insert an entry into the disk's GUID partition table:

```
gpt add -t 8D7FD0BB-39A8-43C0-9432-F4E1A269F070 /dev/diskN
```

Although the "gpt add" command allows the partition size and initial block offset to be specified, if no partition range is specified, the utility will default to creating a partition that begins on the first unused range of disk blocks that it finds on the disk. This is perfect for our purposes, since it creates a single partition that fills the entire disk. The "-t" option can be used to specify the GUID type of the partition entry that is created. This allows us to create a partition entry that has our custom GUID type that we defined to identify an encrypted HFS volume. As a result of adding a partition to the disk, a new device interface is created that represents the partition. The path to the partition's block device interface is printed to the terminal output, and will take the form /dev/diskNs1.

■ **Note** BSD uses the term "slice" to refer to disk partitions. Therefore, disk2s1 refers to the first partition (slice) of the block device "disk2." The slice number comes from IOMedia object's location value. In our partition scheme driver and encryption filter scheme, we called the method setLocation() for each IOMedia object that we created. The string that we provided is used to generate the name of the device interfaces.

At the kernel level, creating a partition table on the disk resulted in the Apple-supplied IOGUIDPartitionScheme driver loading. This driver, in response to us having added a partition entry, will instantiate an IOMedia object to represent the partition. The partition's IOMedia object will have a "Content Hint" property that is equal to the custom GUID type that we gave the partition. At this point, we are ready to load our encryption filter driver. As you will recall, our filter scheme driver will load against any IOMedia object that has our custom content hint GUID. If we had not created a partition entry with the specified content type, our encryption scheme driver would not find a suitable IOMedia object to match against, and we would be unable to test our driver.

Our encryption filter scheme driver will create a new IOMedia object when it loads. This results in another block device being created, which will have an interface name similar to "diskNs1s1." This interface represents the unencrypted content of the disk partition. In the case of our sample encryption filter driver, the IOMedia object that it created was given a "Content Hint" property of Apple_HFS, which informs Mac OS X that the media contains the default HFS file system, and causes the HFS file system to be loaded for the unencrypted volume. However, at this stage, the disk partition is empty and doesn't contain any file system. We can create an HFS file system on the volume with the following command:

```
newfs_hfs -v MyVolumeName /dev/diskNs1s1
```

The option "-v" allows a volume name to be specified. In the preceding example, we are naming the HFS volume "MyVolumeName". Having written an HFS file system to the (unencrypted) volume, we can now mount the file system on the Mac OS X desktop. This can be done with the following command:

```
hdiutil mountvol /dev/diskNs1s1
```

This will result in a new volume appearing on the desktop. Because of the presence of our encryption filter scheme in the storage stack, any files written to the disk will be modified by our XOR encryption before the data is written to the disk image file. The disk image file itself is just a regular file, so the contents of each disk block can be examined by opening the .dmg file in any hex editor. This makes disk images a very useful means for debugging or verifying that a partition scheme driver, or a filter scheme driver, is operating correctly.

Having written a partition table and file system to the disk, the disk image can be mounted in the future by simply opening the disk image file. The I/O Kit will be able to automatically create the entire driver storage stack without any user involvement – from the transport driver for the disk image, the GUID partition scheme driver, the encryption filter scheme, and finally the HFS file system at the top of the stack.

Summary

- The functionality provided by a storage volume containing a file system is implemented through a stack of multiple drivers, each of which may be supplied by a different vendor. The driver at each level of the storage driver stack is responsible for performing a specific role.

- At the bottom of the stack is the transport driver, which interfaces directly with the hardware device that provides the data storage.

- The block storage driver provides an abstract representation of the storage device as a sequence of bytes that is organized into fixed-sized blocks and provides random-access to its data. The block storage driver sits above the transport driver in the driver stack.

- A partition driver is responsible for reading the partition table from a disk and creating a driver object to represent each logical volume that exists in the partition table. The partition driver sits above the block storage driver in the driver stack.

- The I/O Kit represents a logical volume through a driver object called IOMedia. Each IOMedia object can be accessed by a user space process through an interface in the /dev directory.

- The I/O Kit allows vendors to insert a filter scheme driver into the storage driver stack to intercept all read and write requests that are made to a disk. This can be used to implement a RAID driver, or to encrypt the data that is written to a disk.

- The file system driver sits at the very top of the storage driver stack. Although file system drivers read and write through the I/O Kit storage driver stack indirectly, they are actually part of the BSD layer of Mac OS X and are not part of the I/O Kit.

CHAPTER 15

User-Space USB Drivers

From a user's perspective, an application that requires a kernel driver detracts from the user experience. To begin with, driver installation involves writing to the "Extensions" directory, which requires administrative privileges. Therefore, the user needs to run an installer and enter the password of an administrative account, and then possibly restart before they can begin using the application. If, on the other hand, the application doesn't require a kernel driver, the installation procedure can be as simple as downloading an application from the Mac App Store.

In some cases, an application that would typically require a kernel driver can instead be written without the developer having to write any code that runs inside the kernel. Instead, the actions that would usually be performed by the driver can be done by the application. The advantage of this approach is that there is no kernel driver that needs to be installed, so the user doesn't need administrative privileges to install the application. Another advantage of moving the driver code out of the kernel and into the application is that any bugs that are present in the code can, at worst, crash the application, but they cannot cause a kernel panic that can bring down the entire system.

Not all hardware devices can be controlled through a user-space driver; for example, devices that contain a memory-mapped address range require a kernel driver. Similarly, devices that generate interrupts need a kernel driver, since only kernel code can execute at primary interrupt level. This means that all PCI and Thunderbolt devices need to be supported by a kernel driver. However, USB- and FireWire-based hardware devices are perfect candidates for a user-space driver. In this chapter, we discuss writing a driver that exists solely in user space for a USB device, without the need to write a kernel driver.

Not all USB and FireWire devices are suitable for a user-space driver. In particular, a driver that needs to create a device interface file in the /dev directory, such as a serial port driver or a storage device, needs a kernel driver. Also, a device that can be used by multiple applications simultaneously, or needs to be used by the system, such as an audio driver, should be written as a kernel driver. Thankfully, these cases are the exceptions, and most USB devices that require a custom driver can be controlled by a user-space driver.

Behind the Scenes

Having spent the initial chapters of this book describing the architecture of Mac OS X, and in particular stating that a modern operating system only allows hardware to be directly accessed from the kernel, you are probably wondering how this is consistent with a chapter describing user-space drivers.

Internally, user-space drivers do indeed require a kernel driver, but this is provided by the same IOUSBDevice and IOUSBInterface objects that would be used to interact with the USB device had the developer chosen to write a kernel driver for the hardware. To make these objects available to user-space applications, the IOUSBFamily publishes a user client for each instance of IOUSBDevice and IOUSBInterface that is created in the kernel.

The user client that is created for these classes is extremely generic and exists solely to expose the methods of the IOUSBDevice and IOUSBInterface class to user space. For example, the user client for the IOUSBDevice class contains methods for getting and setting the active device configuration, performing a device request, and iterating the device's interfaces. The user client for the IOUSBInterface class contains methods for reading and writing data to a specified endpoint.

An application doesn't need to call the methods from the user client class directly; instead, the I/O Kit framework provides a high level API to control the hardware. This API is known as IOUSBLib. The layering involved in a user-space USB driver is shown in Figure 15-1. The custom code a developer needs to write exists only in the application layer; the layers below are common libraries provided by Apple as part of Mac OS X.

Although it isn't necessary to have an understanding of how the IOUSBLib is implemented, a little knowledge will help you understand each of the steps that an application performs to find and interact with a USB device from user space.

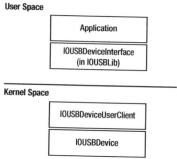

Figure 15-1. The layers through which a user-space driver accesses its USB hardware

The IOUSBLib Framework

The library used to write a user-space driver for a USB device is known as IOUSBLib, which is part of the I/O Kit framework (that is, the same framework a user-space application includes if it is communicating with a user client it defined itself).

The first task a user-space driver needs to perform is to watch for the arrival of the particular USB devices it is interested in. Since USB devices can be connected and disconnected from the computer at any time, there is no guarantee the device an application is interested in will be present when the application is launched. Therefore, it's a good idea for an application to install a notification callback that watches for the arrival of the USB devices it controls.

In Chapter 5, we saw how an application can create a matching dictionary to find each instance of a specified kernel driver. This same approach is used by an application that implements a user-space USB driver to locate the devices it will control. As in Chapter 5, we begin by creating a dictionary that specifies the class name of the driver objects our application is interested in matching against. For a USB device, this can be done as follows:

```
matchingDictionary = IOServiceMatching(kIOUSBDeviceClassName);  // "IOUSBDevice"
```

This matching dictionary is far too general for most applications since it will match against all USB devices connected to the computer, including the keyboard and mouse. An application is typically interested in only one particular USB device, so a matching dictionary such as this will be inappropriate.

We can narrow down the list of devices the matching dictionary satisfies by including the specific Product ID and Vendor ID of the USB device our application can support.

A sample function that will create a matching dictionary for a USB device of a specified Vendor ID and Product ID is shown in Listing 15-1.

Listing 15-1. Creating a USB Matching Dictionary

```
#include <IOKit/IOKitLib.h>
#include <IOKit/usb/IOUSBLib.h>
#include <CoreFoundation/CoreFoundation.h>

CFDictionaryRef          MyCreateUSBMatchingDictionary (SInt32 idVendor, SInt32 idProduct)
{
        CFMutableDictionaryRef  matchingDictionary = NULL;
        CFNumberRef             numberRef;

        // Create a matching dictionary for IOUSBDevice
        matchingDictionary = IOServiceMatching(kIOUSBDeviceClassName);
        if (matchingDictionary == NULL)
                goto bail;

        // Add the USB Vendor ID to the matching dictionary
        numberRef = CFNumberCreate(kCFAllocatorDefault, kCFNumberSInt32Type, &idVendor);
        if (numberRef == NULL)
                goto bail;
        CFDictionaryAddValue(matchingDictionary, CFSTR(kUSBVendorID), numberRef);
        CFRelease(numberRef);

        // Add the USB Product ID to the matching dictionary
        numberRef = CFNumberCreate(kCFAllocatorDefault, kCFNumberSInt32Type, &idProduct);
        if (numberRef == NULL)
                goto bail;
        CFDictionaryAddValue(matchingDictionary, CFSTR(kUSBProductID), numberRef);
        CFRelease(numberRef);

        // Success - return the dictionary to the caller
        return matchingDictionary;

bail:
        // Failure - release resources and return NULL
        if (matchingDictionary != NULL)
                CFRelease(matchingDictionary);

        return NULL;
}
```

■ **Note** An application can narrow the matching dictionary by adding any of the keys that could be placed in the property list of a kernel-based USB driver (see Chapter 8). For example, an application may include any of the keys idVendor, idProduct, bcdDevice, bDeviceSubClass, or bDeviceProtocol.

For a composite USB device, a driver may prefer to match against a particular interface rather than the entire USB device. A user-space driver is able to do this by creating a matching dictionary for a specific instance of an IOUSBInterface object. This is because the I/O Kit defines a user client for every instance of both the IOUSBDevice class and the IOUSBInterface class that is created in the kernel, which makes both of these classes available to user processes.

Having created a matching dictionary, an application is able to use the dictionary to iterate over all kernel objects that match its specifications or to install a callback to receive notifications when such a kernel object appears. This was described in Chapter 5. An example of a function to iterate over all kernel devices described by a given matching dictionary is given in Listing 15-2.

Listing 15-2. Finding and Iterating Over Devices That Satisfy a Matching Dictionary

```
void    MyFindMatchingDevices (CFDictionaryRef matchingDictionary)
{
        io_iterator_t           iterator = 0;
        io_service_t            usbDeviceRef;
        kern_return_t           err;

        // Find all kernel objects that match the dictionary.
        err = IOServiceGetMatchingServices(kIOMasterPortDefault, matchingDictionary,
                    &iterator);
        if (err == 0)
        {
                // Iterate over all matching kernel objects.
                while ((usbDeviceRef = IOIteratorNext(iterator)) != 0)
                {
                        IOUSBDeviceInterface300**       usbDevice;

                        // Create a driver for this device instance
                        usbDevice = MyStartDriver(usbDeviceRef);
                        IOObjectRelease(usbDeviceRef);
                }

                IOObjectRelease(iterator);
        }
}
```

The iterator for a matching dictionary, such as that shown in Listing 15-2, will return a number of io_service_t objects, each of which represents a kernel object. The io_service_t object is a user-space representation of an IOUSBDevice or IOUSBInterface object that resides in the kernel. Like any I/O Kit class, both IOUSBDevice and IOUSBInterface are each implemented by a C++ class. These classes contain a public interface that defines the methods through which a kernel driver interacts with a USB hardware device.

The IOUSBLib interface is implemented through a C++ class that wraps an io_service_t object representing either an IOUSBDevice or an IOUSBInterface. The user-space equivalent of the IOUSBDevice class is implemented by a class named IOUSBDeviceInterface and the user-space equivalent of the IOUSBInterface class is implemented by a class named IOUSBInterfaceInterface. The declaration of these classes can be found in the header file <IOKit/usb/IOUSBLib.h>. The code sample in Listing 15-3 demonstrates how a user-space application can instantiate an IOUSBDeviceInterface class from an io_service_t.

Listing 15-3. Instantiating an IOUSBDeviceInterface object from an io_service_t

```
IOUSBDeviceInterface300**       MyStartDriver (io_service_t usbDeviceRef)
{
        SInt32                  score;
        IOCFPlugInInterface**   plugin;
        IOUSBDeviceInterface300**  usbDevice = NULL;
        kern_return_t           err;

        err = IOCreatePlugInInterfaceForService(usbDeviceRef, kIOUSBDeviceUserClientTypeID,
                                        kIOCFPlugInInterfaceID, &plugin, &score);

        if (err == 0)
        {
                err = (*plugin)->QueryInterface(plugin,
                        CFUUIDGetUUIDBytes(kIOUSBDeviceInterfaceID300),
                        (LPVOID)&usbDevice);
                IODestroyPlugInInterface(plugin);
        }

        return usbDevice;
}
```

If the application had created a matching dictionary that specified an IOUSBInterface, each of the io_service_t values it receives would represent a kernel IOUSBInterface object and not an IOUSBDevice object. In this case, the user-space class the application would instantiate to represent the kernel object would be an IOUSBInterfaceInterface. This only requires one change to the parameters that are passed to two of the functions called in Listing 15-3. The call to IOCreatePlugInInterfaceForService would be called as follows.

```
err = IOCreatePlugInInterfaceForService(usbDeviceRef, kIOUSBInterfaceUserClientTypeID,
                                kIOCFPlugInInterfaceID, &plugin, &score);
```

Similarly, the call to QueryInterface on the returned plugin object would take the following parameters:

```
IOUSBInterfaceInterface300**            usbInterface = NULL;
err = (*plugin)->QueryInterface(plugin,
                CFUUIDGetUUIDBytes(kIOUSBInterfaceInterfaceID300),
                (LPVOID)&usbInterface);
```

Whether the application is instantiating an IOUSBDeviceInterface or an IOUSBInterfaceInterface, the structure of the code is the same. In both cases, the first step is to call the function IOCreatePlugInInterfaceForService(), which returns an object that has the type IOCFPlugInInterface. This object serves as a factory for instantiating the user-space I/O Kit classes and serves no purpose once this has been done. In fact, as Listing 15-3 shows, the object is released with a call to IODestroyPlugInInterface() as soon as the IOUSBDeviceInterface object has been created.

The IOCFPlugInInterface class contains a method named QueryInterface() that an application uses to receive a pointer to the IOUSBDeviceInterface or the IOUSBInterfaceInterface object. The IOUSBLib provides a way of versioning classes. This allows a future release of Mac OS X to extend a class, such as IOUSBDeviceInterface, to include additional functionality while maintaining backwards compatibility with applications that were written for an older version of the class.

When an application requests an interface, such as IOUSBDeviceInterface, it must also specify the version of that class it expects to receive. The version of the class is part of the class name; for example, IOUSBDeviceInterface300 identifies the version of the IOUSBDeviceInterface class included with the IOUSBFamily version 3.0.0. This was shipped with Mac OS X 10.5. A full set of the class names and their version, and the minimum version of the operating system required to support that class is provided in the IOUSBLib.h header file.

■ **Tip** As a general rule, the version of the IOUSBDeviceInterface and IOUSBInterfaceInterface classes you should use will be tied to the minimum version of Mac OS X your application needs to support. For example, an application that requires Mac OS X 10.5 or later should use IOUSBDeviceInterface300 and IOUSBInterfaceInterface300.

One aspect of the user client classes that can take some time to get used to is that IOUSBLib returns a pointer to the object pointer. This means that before calling a method from the object, the variable holding the interface requires an additional dereference. Another idiosyncrasy of the IOUSBLib classes is that each method requires a reference to the object to be passed as the first parameter. For example, consider the method QueryInterface() implemented by the IOCFPlugInInterface class, although you would expect to call the method with the following line of code:

```
plugin->QueryInterface(parameters);     // INCORRECT
```

Instead, because the "plugin" variable will have the type IOCFPlugInInterface** and is therefore a pointer to a pointer, the method must actually be called using the following structure:

```
(*plugin)->QueryInterface(plugin, parameters);
```

■ **Note** If you are familiar with Microsoft's Component Object Model (COM), you will instantly recognize the method name QueryInterface(). All IOUSBLib classes are based on the COM programming model and are derived from the base class IUnknown. The biggest impact of this design on an application using IOUSBLib is that all IOUSBLib objects are reference counted; they can be retained by calling the method AddRef() and can be released by calling the method Release().

Handling Asynchronous Operations

As we will see in our later discussion of IOUSBLib classes, many methods perform operations that complete asynchronously. All such asynchronous methods take two parameters, a pointer to a callback function and a parameter named "refcon" that allows the application to pass an arbitrary context value to its callback. The callback function has the following signature:

```
void    MyCallbackFunction (void* refcon, IOReturn result, void* arg0);
```

The first parameter, refcon, is the application's arbitrary context parameter. The second parameter reports the overall result of the operation; a value of kIOReturnSuccess indicates the operation completed successfully. The final argument, arg0, is provided by the IOUSBLib and is dependent on the type of operation performed. In this chapter, when we describe an asynchronous method, we will also describe the value passed by IOUSBLib to the callback function through the arg0 parameter.

Just as a kernel driver uses a work loop to synchronize its completion routines against other driver code, a user-space application can synchronize completion callbacks from IOUSBLib against the rest of its code using a run loop.

To begin, an application must create a run loop source for the IOUSBLib class that will be performing asynchronous operations. The IOUSBLib classes contain methods for creating either a run loop source or a mach port to receive asynchronous notifications; however, most applications will need to work only with the run loop source.

It's important to note the IOUSBLib classes provide a method with the prefix "Create" and with the prefix "Get"(such as CreateDeviceAsyncEventSource and GetDeviceAsyncEventSource). However, the "Get" method will only return an object that has previously been initialized through the "Create" method. An example function to create and install a run loop source that will be used to receive asynchronous notifications from the IOUSBDeviceInterface class is shown in the following snippet.

```
IOReturn    InstallRunLoopSourceForUSBDevice (IOUSBDeviceInterface300** usbDevice)
{
    CFRunLoopSourceRef          runLoopSource;
    IOReturn                    error;

    error = (*usbDevice)->CreateDeviceAsyncEventSource(usbDevice, &runLoopSource);
    if (error == kIOReturnSuccess)
            CFRunLoopAddSource(CFRunLoopGetCurrent(), runLoopSource, kCFRunLoopDefaultMode);

    return error;
}
```

An application is free to install the run loop source on the run loop of any particular thread it wishes, including the run loop for the application's main thread. The object ownership rules follow the same convention as all Core Foundation functions: If an application obtains an object from a "Create" method, it owns that object and is responsible for releasing it. If an application obtains an object from a "Get" method, it does not own a reference to that object, so if the application wishes to hold on to that object, it must explicitly retain the object first.

The IOUSBDeviceInterface Class

The IOUSBDeviceInterface class is a user-space class that provides equivalent functionality to the IOUSBDevice class used by kernel drivers. It's worth noting that although the user client class provides similar functionality to its kernel counterpart, it implements it through a different set of methods.

Therefore, a kernel USB driver written to work with the IOUSBDevice class cannot simply be brought into a user-space USB driver.

After obtaining a reference to the user-space IOUSBDeviceInterface, the first thing an application will need to do is to configure the USB hardware. The steps an application will take to do this will closely match those explained in Chapter 8 for a kernel driver. First, the application needs to obtain exclusive access to the USB hardware and prevent the hardware's configuration from being changed by another driver, which could either be another user-space driver or a kernel driver. This is achieved by calling the IOUSBDeviceInterface method USBDeviceOpen(), as follows:

```
error = (*usbDevice)->USBDeviceOpen(usbDevice);
```

If the error code returned from the method is kIOReturnSuccess, the application has been granted exclusive access to configure the hardware. If another application or driver has already obtained exclusive access to the hardware, the call to USBDeviceOpen() will fail with the error code kIOReturnExclusiveAccess and the application should abort all further access to the device, possibly reporting an error to the user.

When an application has finished using the device, it should relinquish its exclusive access to the hardware by calling the IOUSBDeviceInterface method USBDeviceClose(), as follows:

```
error = (*usbDevice)->USBDeviceClose(usbDevice);
```

What follows is a summary of the methods provided by the IOUSBDeviceInterface class that provide access to the information contained in the USB device descriptor. In this chapter, we describe the IOUSBDeviceInterface300 class, so some of the following methods will not be present in earlier versions of the IOUSBDeviceInterface class.

- GetDeviceClass, GetDeviceSubClass, and GetDeviceProtocol: Returns the device class (bDeviceClass), subclass (bDeviceSubClass), and protocol (bDeviceProtocol) from the USB device descriptor. Together, these three values define the function of the device based on values defined in the USB specification.

- GetDeviceVendor: Returns the USB Vendor ID of the device (idVendor).

- GetDeviceProduct: Returns the USB Product ID of the device (idProduct).

- GetDeviceReleaseNumber: Returns the device release number (bcdDevice).

- USBGetManufacturerStringIndex: Returns the index of the string for the device's manufacturer name (iManufacturer). To read the actual string from the device, an application must follow up by sending the standard device request "get descriptor" to read an entry from the device's string table.

- USBGetProductStringIndex: Returns the index of the string for the device's product name (iProduct).

- USBGetSerialNumberStringIndex: Returns the index of the string for the device's serial number (iSerialNumber).

- GetNumberOfConfigurations: Returns the number of configurations the device supports at its current speed (bNumConfigurations).

The following methods allow an application to read dynamic properties that relate to the current state of the USB device:

- GetDeviceAddress: Returns the address of the USB device, which is unique for the bus it is connected to.

- GetDeviceSpeed: Returns the speed of the device. Possible values include kUSBDeviceSpeedLow, kUSBDeviceSpeedFull, or kUSBDeviceSpeedHigh.

- GetLocationID: Returns a 32-bit value that uniquely identifies a USB device on the system, based on the USB hub and port the device is connected to. The Location ID won't change following a restart of the computer, but will change if the device is connected to another hub or port. Therefore, if the USB device provides a serial number string, it is a preferable way to track a device across reboots and disconnections.

- GetBusFrameNumber: Returns the current frame number of the USB bus to which the device is connected. The function also returns the system host time that corresponds to the time at which the kernel driver handled the request. The system time may fall anywhere within the returned USB frame.

- GetBusFrameNumberWithTime returns the current frame number of the USB bus to which the device is connected, but also returns the system host time that corresponds to the start of that frame. This method was introduced in later versions of the IOUSBDeviceInterface class and supersedes the method GetBusFrameNumber().

- GetBusMicroFrameNumber: Returns the current microframe number of the USB bus to which the device is connected. The function also returns the system host time that corresponds to the time at which the kernel driver handled the request (and so this method behaves like GetBusFrameNumber()).

The following methods provide a way for an application to reset the USB device:

- ResetDevice: Resets the USB device, returning it to the non-configured state.

- USBDeviceReEnumerate: Instructs the hub to which this device is connected to reset the port that this device is connected to. This is equivalent to disconnecting the device from the USB port and reconnecting it.

- USBDeviceSuspend: Despite the name of this method, it can either suspend or resume the port to which the USB device is connected, depending on the value of a Boolean parameter. If the method suspends the device, any outstanding transactions to the device will be aborted.

- USBDeviceAbortPipeZero: Aborts any outstanding transaction on the control endpoint.

The IOUSBDeviceInterface class provides the following methods to allow an application to send control requests to the device on endpoint zero:

- DeviceRequest: Is a synchronous method and will not return until the device request has completed. The device request is described by the same IOUSBDevRequest structure used by kernel USB drivers.

- DeviceRequestTO: Is a synchronous method that takes two timeout values, expressed in milliseconds. The method will return once the device has completed or a specified timeout period has elapsed (whichever comes first). The caller provides two timeout values. The device may stop sending or receiving data while handling the request, so one timeout value specifies the maximum amount of time to wait since the last data transfer before aborting the control request. The other timeout value specifies the maximum amount of time to allow for the control request to complete from start to finish. A control request is aborted if either of the specified timeout conditions occurs.

- DeviceRequestAsync: Is an asynchronous equivalent of the method DeviceRequest. The method takes a callback function the I/O Kit uses to notify the caller once the request has completed. It's important to note that a return value of kIOReturnSuccess from this method doesn't indicate the request completed successfully; rather, it indicates the operation was successfully started. The actual result of the operation will be returned through the callback function. The value of the arg0 parameter passed to the completion callback holds the number of bytes that were either read from the device or written to the device.

Listing 15-4 lists a sample function that uses the DeviceRequest method to read the manufacturer string from the USB string table. The function starts by calling USBGetManufacturerStringIndex to obtain the index of the manufacturer string. Next, the device request structure is prepared. The bmRequestType field specifies that the request is a data read (kUSBIn), is a standard request (as opposed to a request defined by the device class or is vendor-specific), and that the recipient of the request is the device (as opposed to an interface or an endpoint). Since the string table is treated as just another descriptor table by the USB Specification, the control request that is sent to the device to read a string is the kUSBRqGetDescriptor request. The wValue field indicates we are reading a string descriptor and also contains the index of the string to be read.

Finally, if the string data is successfully read from the device, the function creates a CFStringRef from the returned data, which is returned from the device with an encoding of UTF-16 little-endian.

Listing 15-4. *A Function That Demonstrates a Device Request Through the IOUSBDeviceInterface Class*

```
#include <IOKit/usb/IOUSBLib.h>
#include <IOKit/usb/USBSpec.h>
#include <CoreFoundation/CoreFoundation.h>

IOReturn                    PrintDeviceManufacturer (IOUSBDeviceInterface300** usbDevice)
{
        UInt8               stringIndex;
        IOUSBDevRequest     devRequest;
        UInt8               buffer[256];
        CFStringRef         manufString;
        IOReturn            error;

        // Get the index in the string table for the manufacturer.
        error = (*usbDevice)->USBGetManufacturerStringIndex(usbDevice, &stringIndex);
        if (error != kIOReturnSuccess)
                return error;

        // Perform a device request to read the string descriptor.
```

```
devRequest.bmRequestType = USBmakebmRequestType(kUSBIn, kUSBStandard, kUSBDevice);
devRequest.bRequest = kUSBRqGetDescriptor;
devRequest.wValue = (kUSBStringDesc << 8) | stringIndex;
devRequest.wIndex = 0x409;                 // Language setting - specify US English
devRequest.wLength = sizeof(buffer);
devRequest.pData = &buffer[0];
bzero(&buffer[0], sizeof(buffer));
//
error = (*usbDevice)->DeviceRequest(usbDevice, &devRequest);
if (error != kIOReturnSuccess)
        return error;

// Create a CFString representation of the returned data.
int            strLength;
strLength = buffer[0] - 2;                  // First byte is length (in bytes)
manufString = CFStringCreateWithBytes(kCFAllocatorDefault, &buffer[2], strLength,
                                      kCFStringEncodingUTF16LE, false);

// Print the manufacturer string.
CFShow(manufString);
CFRelease(manufString);

return error;
}
```

The following methods are used by an application to examine and set the device configuration, and to iterate the device's interfaces. These methods are usually called by an application to initialize the USB device when it is first detected:

- GetConfigurationDescriptionPtr: Returns a pointer to the descriptor for the specified configuration; note that although the caller receives a pointer to an IOUSBConfigurationDescriptorPtr structure, the buffer is owned by the IOUSBDeviceInterface object and should not be released by the caller.

- GetConfiguration: Returns the active configuration number of the device. Note that this is not the index of the configuration, but rather the value of bConfigurationValue from the active configuration description.

- SetConfiguration: Sets the active configuration of the device. The configuration is specified by passing the bConfigurationValue from the desired configuration description.

- CreateInterfaceIterator: Creates an iterator over the device's interfaces. Like its kernel equivalent, the caller provides an IOUSBFindInterfaceRequest structure that specifies the properties that returned interfaces must match.

Having examined the functionality provided by the IOUSBDeviceInterface class, we are now in a position to consider the steps an application will typically take to initialize a new USB device that has been attached to the system. A sample initialization function is given in Listing 15-5.

Listing 15-5. A Sample Function for Configuring a USB Device During Initialization

```
IOReturn        MyConfigureDevice (IOUSBDeviceInterface300** usbDevice)
{
```

```
UInt8                              numConfigurations;
IOUSBConfigurationDescriptorPtr    configDesc;
IOUSBFindInterfaceRequest          interfaceRequest;
io_iterator_t                      interfaceIterator;
io_service_t                       usbInterfaceRef;
IOReturn                           error;

// Get the count of the device's configurations.
error = (*usbDevice)->GetNumberOfConfigurations(usbDevice, &numConfigurations);
if (error != kIOReturnSuccess)
        return error;
// Ensure the device has at least one configuration
if (numConfigurations == 0)
        return kIOReturnError;

// Read the descriptor for the first configuration.
error = (*usbDevice)->GetConfigurationDescriptorPtr(usbDevice, 0, &configDesc);
if (error != kIOReturnSuccess)
        return error;

// Make the first configuration the active configuration.
error = (*usbDevice)->SetConfiguration(usbDevice, configDesc->bConfigurationValue);
if (error != kIOReturnSuccess)
        return error;

// Create an iterator over all interfaces in the active configuration.
interfaceRequest.bInterfaceClass = kIOUSBFindInterfaceDontCare;
interfaceRequest.bInterfaceSubClass = kIOUSBFindInterfaceDontCare;
interfaceRequest.bInterfaceProtocol = kIOUSBFindInterfaceDontCare;
interfaceRequest.bAlternateSetting = kIOUSBFindInterfaceDontCare;

error = (*usbDevice)->CreateInterfaceIterator(usbDevice, &interfaceRequest,
            &interfaceIterator);
if (error != kIOReturnSuccess)
        return error;

// Iterate over all interfaces.
while ((usbInterfaceRef = IOIteratorNext(interfaceIterator)) != 0)
{
        MySetupInterface(usbInterfaceRef);
        IOObjectRelease(usbInterfaceRef);
}
IOObjectRelease(interfaceIterator);

return kIOReturnSuccess;
}
```

The code in Listing 15-5 begins by setting the active configuration of the device to a known configuration, in this case the device's first configuration. This step is necessary because the device may have been used by another application before our application was launched, so the device may be in an unknown state.

Next, the application iterates over all interfaces in the active configuration. If we were interested in a particular interface, we could narrow down the list of interfaces returned by the iterator by specifying the desired class, subclass, protocol, or alternate setting for the interface. Obtaining a USB interface object is particularly important, since the only way an application can access the device's endpoints, other than the control endpoint, is through the IOUSBInterfaceInterface class.

The IOUSBInterfaceInterface Class

The IOUSBInterfaceInterface class is a user-space class that provides equivalent functionality to the IOUSBInterface class used by kernel drivers. An application can obtain a reference to an IOUSBInterfaceInterface class by iterating over the device's interfaces, as shown in Listing 15-5, or an application can obtain an IOUSBInterfaceInterface object directly by creating a matching dictionary that specifies the service name kIOUSBInterfaceClassName.

A USB interface contains one or more endpoints, which allow data to either be written to the device or data to be read from the device. A user-space USB driver is not limited in any way regarding the type of endpoints it is able to use; all endpoint types, including bulk, isochronous, and interrupt endpoints are available to a user-space driver. A user-space driver is able to achieve similar data bandwidth to that of a kernel driver, meaning that even applications that require large data transfers can be written in user space.

Whether an application uses the IOUSBDeviceInterface to iterate over USB interfaces or obtains a USB interface directly using a matching dictionary to create an iterator, the application will receive an io_service_t that provides a user-space representation of the underlying IOUSBInterface object in the kernel. Listing 15-6 demonstrates how to create an IOUSBInterfaceInterface object from the io_service_t object.

Listing 15-6. Instantiating an IOUSBInterfaceInterface object from an io_service_t

```
IOUSBInterfaceInterface300**      MyCreateInterfaceClass (io_service_t usbInterfaceRef)
{
        SInt32                    score;
        IOCFPlugInInterface**     plugin;
        IOUSBInterfaceInterface300**  usbInterface = NULL;
        kern_return_t             err;

        err = IOCreatePlugInInterfaceForService(usbInterfaceRef,
                kIOUSBInterfaceUserClientTypeID,
                kIOCFPlugInInterfaceID, &plugin, &score);
        if (err == 0)
        {
                err = (*plugin)->QueryInterface(plugin,
                        CFUUIDGetUUIDBytes(kIOUSBInterfaceInterfaceID300),
                        (LPVOID)&usbInterface);
                IODestroyPlugInInterface(plugin);
        }

        return usbInterface;
}
```

As with the USB device class, an application must obtain exclusive access to the USB interface object before it is able to transfer any data to or from an endpoint on the USB interface. This is achieved by calling the IOUSBInterfaceInterface method USBInterfaceOpen(), as follows:

```
error = (*usbInterface)->USBInterfaceOpen(usbInterface);
```

When an application has finished using the interface, it should relinquish its exclusive access by calling the IOUSBInterfaceInterface method USBInterfaceClose(), as follows:

```
error = (*usbInterface)->USBInterfaceClose(usbInterface);
```

The methods provided by the IOUSBInterfaceInterface class fall into two categories, those that either get or set the properties of the USB device or interface and those that relate to transferring data to or from one of the endpoints on the interface. What follows is a summary of the methods provided by the IOUSBInterfaceInterface class. In this chapter, we describe the IOUSBInterfaceInterface300 class, so some of the methods that follow will not be present in earlier versions of the IOUSBInterfaceInterface class.

Property Methods

The IOUSBInterfaceInterface class contains methods to both get and set properties relating to the interface and the USB device. Although some of these methods may seem to duplicate functionality provided by the IOUSBDeviceInterface class that was previously described, this is intentional, as it allows an application that has matched against the USB interface class and not the USB device class to still have access to common device functionality.

The following methods, although in the IOUSBInterfaceInterface class, relate to the USB device:

- GetDeviceVendor: Returns the USB Vendor ID of the USB device.

- GetDeviceProduct: Returns the USB Product ID of the USB device.

- GetDeviceReleaseNumber: Returns the device release number of the USB device.

- GetLocationID: Returns a 32-bit value that uniquely identifies a USB device on the system, based on the USB hub and port the device is connected to.

- GetDevice: Returns an io_service_t that corresponds to the kernel IOUSBDevice object. From this object, an application can instantiate an IOUSBDeviceInterface that represents the USB device.

- GetBusFrameNumber: Returns the current frame number of the USB bus on which the device is connected.

- GetBusFrameNumberWithTime: Returns the current frame number of the USB bus to which the device is connected and also returns the system host time that corresponds to the start of that frame.

- GetBusMicroFrameNumber: Returns the current microframe number of the USB bus to which the device is connected.

- GetFrameListTime: Performs a similar role to the IOUSBDeviceInterface method GetDeviceSpeed, although the device's speed is returned as the number of microseconds per USB frame at its current speed. A full speed device will return kUSBFullSpeedMicrosecondsInFrame (1000 microseconds), whereas a high speed device will return kUSBHighSpeedMicrosecondsInFrame (125 microseconds).

The following methods relate to getting and setting properties of the interface:

- GetInterfaceClass, GetInterfaceSubClass, and GetInterfaceProtocol: Return the interface class (bInterfaceClass), subclass (bInterfaceSubClass), and protocol (bInterfaceProtocol) from the USB interface descriptor. Together, these three values define the function of the interface based on values defined in the USB specification.

- GetConfigurationValue: Identifies the device configuration that contains this interface. The returned value is the bConfigurationValue from the active configuration's description.

- GetInterfaceNumber: Returns the zero-based index of this interface within the active configuration (bInterfaceNumber).

- GetAlternateSetting: Returns the active alternate setting of this interface (bAlternateSetting).

- SetAlternateInterface: Sets the active alternate setting for this interface. The alternate setting is specified by passing the bAlternateSetting value of the desired interface description.

- USBInterfaceGetStringIndex: Returns the index of the string for the interface description, which comes from the iInterface field from the interface descriptor.

Endpoint Data Transfer Methods

A USB interface can contain one or more endpoints from which data can be read from or written to. Unlike a kernel USB driver, the IOUSBLib contains no user-space object to represent the pipe to an endpoint; instead, all data transfers are made through the IOUSBInterfaceInterface class. An application can determine the endpoints present on an interface using the following methods:

- GetNumEndpoints: Returns the number of endpoints provided by the interface.

- GetEndpointProperties: Returns the type (bDescriptorType), maximum packet size (wMaxPacketSize), and polling interval (bInterval) of a specified endpoint. The endpoint is specified by three values—the alternate interface setting it is on, its endpoint number, and the transfer direction of the endpoint.

- GetPipeProperties: This method allows an application to specify the index of an endpoint from 0 up to and including the value returned by GetNumEndpoints, unlike GetEndpointProperties, which requires the caller to know the endpoint number and direction of an endpoint it is interested in. The endpoint at index 0 corresponds to the default control endpoint. The information returned by this method consists of almost all the data for an endpoint descriptor, including the endpoint's number, direction, type, maximum packet size, and polling interval (if an interrupt or isochronous endpoint).

- GetPipeStatus: Can be used to determine whether a specified pipe is stalled. This method will return kIOUSBPipeStalled if the pipe is stalled and kIOReturnSuccess otherwise. It will return kIOUSBUnknownPipeErr if the caller has specified an invalid pipe index.

- AbortPipe: Aborts an outstanding transaction from a specified pipe index. Any operations that are aborted will complete, with the result kIOReturnAborted.

- ResetPipe and ClearPipeStall: Although these two methods are identical, the use of ClearPipeStall is preferred. Either method is called by an application to reset an endpoint that has stalled. The endpoint's halt bit is cleared and its data toggle bit is reset.

- ClearPipeStallBothEnds: Is equivalent to ClearPipeStall, with the distinction that in addition to clearing the halt bit and resetting the data toggle on the host side, the halt bit is cleared on the device and the device's data toggle is reset. This ensures that, since both the host and device have been reset, there is no loss of data when data is next transferred to or from the endpoint.

To transfer data to or from an endpoint, an application must determine the pipe index that corresponds to the endpoint it wants to access. Although an endpoint address is constant, since it comes from a descriptor supplied by the device, the pipe index is assigned by the I/O Kit. Therefore, the only way to determine a pipe index for a given endpoint is to enumerate over each pipe contained within a USB interface. An example of this is given in Listing 15-7.

Listing 15-7. A Function to Find a Pipe Reference for a Bulk Output Endpoint

```
IOReturn        MyFindBulkOutEndpoint (IOUSBInterfaceInterface300** usbInterface,
                                       UInt8* pipeRef)
{
        UInt8           numEndpoints;
        UInt8           i;
        IOReturn        error;

        // Determine the number of endpoints in this interface.
        error = (*usbInterface)->GetNumEndpoints(usbInterface, &numEndpoints);
        if (error != kIOReturnSuccess)
                return error;

        // Iterate over all endpoints in the interface (skipping endpoint 0, the control
        // endpoint).
        for (i = 1; i <= numEndpoints; i++)
        {
                UInt8           direction, number, transferType;
                UInt16          maxPacketSize;
                UInt8           interval;

                error = (*usbInterface)->GetPipeProperties(usbInterface, i, &direction,
                                        &number,
                                        &transferType, &maxPacketSize, &interval);
                if (error != kIOReturnSuccess)
                        continue;

                // If we find a bulk output endpoint, return its pipe index the caller.
                if ((transferType == kUSBBulk) && (direction == kUSBOut))
                {
                        *pipeRef = i;
```

```
                return kIOReturnSuccess;
        }
}

    return kIOReturnNotFound;
}
```

Having determined the pipe index (referred to as the pipe reference by methods in IOUSBLib), an application can read or write data over the pipe. Which methods an application uses to manage a pipe will depend on the type of endpoint the pipe represents. The IOUSBInterfaceInterface class provides different methods depending on whether the pipe is connected to a control, bulk, interrupt, or isochronous endpoint.

The IOUSBInterfaceInterface class provides several methods for transferring data to or from an endpoint. Depending on the method called, the operation may complete synchronously or asynchronously. Other methods allow the caller to provide a timeout value that specifies the maximum amount of time to allow the operation to complete before aborting the request. Finally, there are methods that complete asynchronously and allow the caller to specify a timeout value.

The convention adopted by IOUSBLib is that a method completes synchronously unless the method contains "Async" in its name. An asynchronous method takes two extra parameters in addition to those passed to its synchronous counterpart—a callback function that runs when the operation completes and an arbitrary pointer that can be used to pass context information to the callback function.

A method that allows the caller to specify a timeout contains the letters "TO" in its name. The timeout value is described by two additional parameters that are passed to the method. The device may stop sending or receiving data while handling the request, so one timeout value specifies the maximum amount of time to wait from the last data transfer before aborting the operation. The second timeout value specifies the maximum amount of time to allow the operation to complete from start to finish. The request is aborted if either of the specified timeout conditions occurs.

The following methods are provided by the IOUSBInterfaceInterface class to perform a control transfer. These methods are similar to those provided by the IOUSBDeviceInterface class, with the exception that they each take an additional parameter, the pipe reference. If a value of 0 is passed for the pipe reference, the control request is sent to the default control endpoint, endpoint 0.

- ControlRequest: Performs a control request synchronously. This method takes an IOUSBDevRequest structure describing a control request, and sends it to the specified control endpoint.

- ControlRequestAsync: Performs a control request asynchronously. This method takes an IOUSBDevRequest structure and sends it to the specified control endpoint. When the request has completed, a callback function that was provided to the function is executed. The value of the arg0 parameter that is passed to the completion callback specifies the number of bytes that were either read from the device or written to the device.

- ControlRequestTO: Performs a control request synchronously and allows the caller to specify timeout parameters.

- ControlRequestAsyncTO: Performs a control request asynchronously, with a maximum time limit placed on how long the request is allowed to take.

A device is likely to use a bulk endpoint for its data transfer. As we saw in Chapter 8, bulk endpoints allow large amounts of data to be read or written to the device with high throughput and guaranteed data delivery, but with variable latency (depending on whether other devices are attempting to transfer data over the USB bus at the same time). The IOUSBInterfaceInterface class provides the following methods to allow an application to read and write buffers over a pipe to a bulk endpoint. The following methods are also applicable to transferring data over an interrupt endpoint:

- ReadPipe: Performs a data transfer synchronously from a bulk or interrupt endpoint on the USB device to an application-supplied buffer. The application's buffer is described by its address and the size of the buffer in bytes. The buffer size is also an output parameter; if the method completes successfully, the number of bytes that were read into the buffer is reported to the caller through the same size parameter.

- WritePipe: Performs a data transfer synchronously from an application-supplied buffer to a bulk or interrupt endpoint on the USB device. The application's buffer is described by its address and the size of the buffer in bytes.

- ReadPipeAsync: Performs a data transfer asynchronously from a bulk or interrupt endpoint on the USB device to an application-supplied buffer. When the transfer has completed, the provided callback function is passed the result of the operation and the number of bytes that were read from the device (which is passed through the arg0 argument).

- WritePipeAsync: Performs a data transfer asynchronously from an application-supplied buffer to a bulk or interrupt endpoint on the USB device. When the transfer has completed, the provided callback function is passed the result of the operation and the number of bytes that were written to the device (which is passed through the arg0 argument).

- ReadPipeTO: Performs a data transfer synchronously from a bulk or interrupt endpoint to an application buffer with a timeout value specified for the operation.

- WritePipeTO: Performs a data transfer synchronously from an application buffer to a bulk or interrupt endpoint with a timeout value specified for the operation.

- ReadPipeAsyncTO: Is an asynchronous equivalent of the ReadPipeTO method. When the transfer has completed or has timed out, a callback function that has been provided by the application is called.

- WritePipeAsyncTO: Is an asynchronous equivalent of the WritePipeTO method. When the transfer has completed or has timed out, a callback function that has been provided by the application is called.

An example of a function that reads data from a bulk endpoint using the asynchronous method ReadPipeAsyncTO is provided in Listing 15-8.

Listing 15-8. *A Function That Demonstrates the Use of the ReadPipeAsyncTO Method*

```
IOReturn        MyAsyncBulkRead (IOUSBInterfaceInterface300** usbInterface, UInt8 pipeRef)
{
        void*           dataBlock;
        const UInt32    noDataTimeout = 50;          // 50 ms
        const UInt32    completionTimeout = 500;     // 500 ms
        void*           refcon;
        IOReturn        error;

        // Allocate a buffer to hold the read data.
        dataBlock = malloc(kMyTransferSize);

        // Perform an asynchronous read, with specified timeout values.
        // We pass dataBlock to the callback function through the refcon parameter
        refcon = dataBlock;
        error = (*usbInterface)->ReadPipeAsyncTO(usbInterface, pipeRef, dataBlock,
                                        kMyTransferSize,
                                        noDataTimeout, completionTimeout,
                                        ReadCompletedCallback, refcon);

        // If the method returns an error, the callback will not be called.
        if (error != kIOReturnSuccess)
                free(dataBlock);

        return error;
}

void    ReadCompletedCallback (void* refcon, IOReturn result, void* arg0)
{
        void*           dataBlock = refcon;
        UInt32          byteCount = (UInt32)arg0;

        // If the read completed successfully, process any data that was read from the device.
        if (result == kIOReturnSuccess)
        {
                ProcessReadData(dataBlock, byteCount);
        }

        // Release the buffer that was allocated in MyAsyncBulkRead.
        free(dataBlock);
}
```

The remaining USB endpoint type is the isochronous endpoint. As we saw in Chapter 8, isochronous endpoints are designed for use by devices that transfer a stream of data that must be delivered in a timely manner with minimal latency, such as an audio or video data stream. The IOUSBLib provides full support for isochronous data transfers to a user-space application.

An isochronous pipe has guaranteed bandwidth on the USB bus. The device reports its bandwidth requirements and if the USB host is able to meet those requirements, the device is granted access to the USB bus. A full-speed device is able to transfer data over an isochronous pipe on every frame (once a millisecond), whereas a high speed or a super speed device is able to transfer data on each microframe (once every 125 microseconds).

As with the kernel implementation, an isochronous data transfer from an application is set up by filling out an array of IOUSBIsocFrame structures, which describe the number of bytes the application wishes to read or write over the isochronous pipe on each microframe (or frame, for a full speed device). The IOUSBIsocFrame structure is defined as shown below.

```
typedef struct IOUSBIsocFrame {
    IOReturn    frStatus;    // On return, the result for the transfer for this frame
    UInt16      frReqCount;  // The requested number of bytes to read or write on this frame
    UInt16      frActCount;  // On return, the actual number of bytes read or written on this
                             // frame
} IOUSBIsocFrame;
```

A read or write over an isochronous pipe will typically describe the transfer over several tens of milliseconds, with the application issuing a new isochronous transfer request whenever an outstanding request completes. The following methods are provided by the IOUSBInterfaceInterface class for performing transfers over an isochronous pipe:

- ReadIsochPipeAsync: Performs an asynchronous data transfer from an isochronous pipe. The data transfer is described by passing a buffer address to hold the data read from the device and an array of IOUSBIsocFrame elements that describes the maximum amount of data that can be accepted on each frame. The method takes a parameter named "frameStart" that determines the USB frame number on which the data transfer will begin, usually a USB frame shortly after the current frame. The current USB frame can be determined by calling the GetBusFrameNumber method. Once the transfer has completed, the callback function supplied by the application is called; the value of arg0 that is passed to the callback function is the address of the IOUSBIsocFrame array. The application can examine this array to determine the number of bytes that were actually read on each frame.

- WriteIsochPipeAsync: Performs an asynchronous data transfer to an isochronous pipe. The caller provides the address of a buffer containing the data to be written to the device and an array of IOUSBIsocFrame elements that describes the number of bytes to be transferred from the buffer on each USB frame. The method takes a parameter named "frameStart" that determines the USB frame number on which the data transfer will begin, usually a USB frame shortly after the current frame. The current USB frame can be determined by calling the GetBusFrameNumber method. Once the transfer has completed, a callback function supplied by the application is called; the value of arg0 that is passed to the callback function is the address of the IOUSBIsocFrame array.

- GetBandwidthAvailable: Returns the bandwidth that is available on the USB bus; this is the maximum bandwidth a device can allocate. The bandwidth is reported as the maximum number of bytes that can be allocated to an isochronous pipe for each frame (for a full speed device) or microframe (for a high speed device).

- `SetPipePolicy` : Allows an application to modify the bandwidth reservation of an isochronous or interrupt pipe. For an isochronous pipe, the maximum allowable packet size that can be transferred on a frame (for a full speed device) or a microframe (for a high speed device) can be changed. The packet size, however, cannot be set to a value larger than the maximum packet size in the device's endpoint descriptor. For an interrupt pipe, this method allows the maximum allowable packet size and the polling interval to be set. The packet size and polling interval, however, cannot exceed the values requested in the endpoint descriptor. If the initial bandwidth requested in a device's endpoint descriptor cannot be satisfied, the USB host will not allow data to be transferred over the isochronous pipe; this method can be used to assign a reduced bandwidth allocation to the pipe, allowing it to be used.

An example of a function that performs an isochronous read operation is given in Listing 15-9. Note that before issuing the request, the function initializes an array of `IOUSBIsocFrame` elements to describe the maximum number of bytes it can accept on each frame (or microframe, for a high speed device). Once the request has completed, the device is able to process the data that was received on each frame, which may be less than the maximum number of bytes requested.

The frame number on which the request begins is specified by the parameter "startFrame" which, in the example function, is determined by adding a fixed delay to the current frame. More generally, an application would typically set the initial frame number of an isochronous request to the final frame number of the previous isochronous request. In this way, the driver can read continually from the device without any gaps.

Listing 15-9. A Function That Demonstrates an Isochronous Data Transfer from a User-space Driver

```
const int       framesPerRequest = 512;
const int       bytesPerFrame = 1024;

IOReturn MyScheduleIsocRead (IOUSBInterfaceInterface300** usbInterface, UInt8 pipeRef,
                             void* destinationBuffer)

{
    UInt64          startFrame;
    AbsoluteTime    timeNow;
    IOUSBIsocFrame* frameList;
    void*           refcon;
    IOReturn        error;

    // Read the current frame number.
    // (Alternatively, we could issue this isoc request to follow
    // on from the previous request.)
    error = (*usbInterface)->GetBusFrameNumber(usbInterface, &startFrame, &timeNow);
    if (error != kIOReturnSuccess)
        return error;
    // Add an offset to the frame on which the request will start,
    // so it starts just ahead of the current frame.
    startFrame += 8;

    // Allocate an array of IOUSBIsocFrame elements.
    frameList = (IOUSBIsocFrame*)malloc(framesPerRequest * sizeof(IOUSBIsocFrame));
    // Set up the number of bytes to read on each frame of the isochronous request.
```

```
        for (int i = 0; i < framesPerRequest; i++)
            frameList[i].frReqCount = bytesPerFrame;

        // Perform the isochronous request.
        // We pass destinationBuffer to the callback function through the refcon parameter.
        refcon = destinationBuffer;
        error = (*usbInterface)->ReadIsochPipeAsync(usbInterface, pipeRef, destinationBuffer,
                                startFrame,
                                framesPerRequest, frameList, IsocReadCompletedCallback,
                                refcon);
        // If the method returns an error, the callback will not be called.
        if (error != kIOReturnSuccess)
            free(frameList);

        return error;
}

void IsocReadCompletedCallback (void* refcon, IOReturn result, void* arg0)
{
        uint8_t*            destinationBuffer = (uint8_t*)refcon;
        IOUSBIsocFrame*     frameList = (IOUSBIsocFrame*)arg0;

        // If the read completed successfully, process any data that was read from the device.
        if (result == kIOReturnSuccess)
        {
            for (int i = 0; i < framesPerRequest; i++)
            {
                if (frameList[i].frStatus == kIOReturnSuccess)
                {
                  UInt16            bytesRead;

                  // Process the data that was read on this frame
                  bytesRead = frameList[i].frActCount;
                  ProcessReadData(destinationBuffer, bytesRead);
                }

                // Calculate the starting address for the next frame's data
                destinationBuffer += frameList[i].frReqCount;
            }
        }

        // Release the frame list that was allocated in MyScheduleIsocRead.
        free(frameList);
}
```

Low-Latency Isochronous Transfers

Isochronous endpoints are typically used to transfer multimedia data, such as audio or video that is continually streamed to or from the USB device. An application that processes this data typically wishes to do so with minimal latency; for example, an application may wish to begin processing audio data that has been read from a microphone as soon as it is received by the USB device. One of the problems with the isochronous methods described previously is that the application must wait until the completion callback function is notified before it can begin processing the data that was read. If an application issues an isochronous request that spans 10 milliseconds worth of USB frames, this means there is a latency of at least 10 milliseconds from the start of the request until the application can begin to process the data that was read from the device.

As a solution to this, the IOUSBInterfaceInterface class contains low-latency isochronous transfer methods that give an application access to data as soon as it has been received by the device, even if the overall isochronous request hasn't completed. To do this, the I/O Kit updates the values of the frame list while the isochronous transaction is in flight; the values of frStatus and frActCount are written and available to the application during the transfer. Rather than waiting for the completion callback to fire, an application can periodically examine the values of its frame list and determine when new data is available to be processed. This can be done from a real-time thread in a user-space application, for example.

An application specifies how often the I/O Kit should update the frame list while the operation is in flight by specifying the number of milliseconds between updates (a value between 0–8). For example, an update frequency of 1 means the application's frame list will be updated by the I/O Kit every millisecond during the transfer. A value of 0 means the I/O Kit will not update the frame list until the end of the transfer, although the updated frame list will be available to the application as soon as the transaction has completed but before the application receives the completion callback.

To use low-latency isochronous transfers, the buffers used for the frame list array and to hold the source or destination data from the transfer must be allocated using methods provided by the IOUSBInterfaceInterface class. This allows the I/O Kit to ensure the buffers are available to both the kernel, which updates the buffers during the transfer, and the application, which reads the result during the transfer.

Note that instead of using the IOUSBIsocFrame structure to describe the transfer for a USB frame, the low-latency methods use the IOUSBLowLatencyIsocFrame structure. This structure includes an additional field, frTimeStamp, which holds the time at which the I/O Kit updated the structure's values.

The following methods are provided for low-latency isochronous transfers:

- LowLatencyCreateBuffer: Allocates a buffer used to hold either the source data for a low-latency isochronous write, the destination data for a low-latency isochronous read, or the array of IOUSBLowLatencyIsocFrame elements that describes an isochronous transfer. The application's intent for the buffer must be specified by providing one of the enumeration values— kUSBLowLatencyWriteBuffer, kUSBLowLatencyReadBuffer, or kUSBLowLatencyFrameListBuffer.

- LowLatencyDestroyBuffer: Releases a buffer that has previously been allocated by the method LowLatencyCreateBuffer.

- LowLatencyReadIsochPipeAsync: Performs a read from an isochronous endpoint on the USB device. The parameters to this method extend those of the method ReadIsochPipeAsync to include a parameter named updateFrequency that specifies how often the I/O Kit should update the frame list during the transfer (specified in milliseconds). The IOUSBLowLatencyIsocFrame array and the destination buffer must both have been allocated by the method LowLatencyCreateBuffer.

- `LowLatencyWriteIsochPipeAsync`: Performs a write to an isochronous endpoint on the USB device. The parameters to this method extend those of the method `WriteIsochPipeAsync` to include a parameter named `updateFrequency` that specifies how often the I/O Kit should update the frame list during the transfer (specified in milliseconds). The `IOUSBLowLatencyIsocFrame` array and the source buffer must both have been allocated by the method `LowLatencyCreateBuffer`.

Summary

- For certain types of devices, including USB devices, the I/O Kit makes it possible to forgo a kernel driver and implement the driver completely in user space. For the end user, this provides a much better experience.

- Not all USB devices are suitable for a user-space driver. A device that needs to be used by the system itself, such as a system-wide audio device or a USB storage device, must be implemented in the kernel.

- The I/O Kit provides a user-space library known as IOUSBLib that an application uses to interact with a USB device. The IOUSBLib provides a user- space equivalent to the `IOUSBDevice` and `IOUSBInterface` kernel classes, known as `IOUSBDeviceInterface` and `IOUSBInterfaceInterface`, respectively.

- An application can watch for the arrival and removal of the USB devices it supports by creating a matching dictionary and installing a notification callback, as described in Chapter 5. Once an application has been notified that a USB device or a USB interface it is interested in has been attached to the computer, it can instantiate an `IOUSBDeviceInterface` or `IOUSBInterfaceInterface` object to provide access to the USB hardware.

- The IOUSBLib provides full support for the functionality of a USB device to a user-space driver. All endpoint types are supported in user space, including control, bulk, interrupt, and isochronous transfers.

- An application can perform either synchronous or asynchronous operations with IOUSBLib. A callback is used to notify the application of the completion of an asynchronous request.

CHAPTER 16

Debugging

Debugging is part of the development process and the ongoing maintenance of a kernel level driver or extension. Therefore, having the skills and knowledge to debug the kernel effectively is an important part of a kernel engineer's job description. Although great care is taken during the development and quality assurance process, bugs are often unavoidable. This is partly because, once released, your driver is likely to run against hardware/software combinations that haven't been as well tested, if at all. For example, your driver may run on a faster or slower CPU than was tested initially, thus uncovering timing issues.

Many regard kernel debugging as a black art, and with good reason. When an application crashes, it can be dumped into the debugger and it then is often possible to pinpoint the exact code line that caused the problem. In the kernel, things are not that easy; although debugging with the GNU Debugger (GDB) is possible, it requires some setup and often two computers. Furthermore, crashes in the kernel can often manifest themselves in completely unrelated parts of your extension, making it hard to prove if your driver was involved. You may be lucky enough to extract information or attach a debugger after a crash; however, the memory may be corrupted and the values of data structures or the call stack may not be trustworthy.

If you are writing drivers for hardware devices, things may be even more complicated as malfunctioning devices (more common if using a prototype device) may also corrupt memory or cause the computer to lock up or crash. This sometimes makes it difficult to determine if it's a hardware or software problem.

In this chapter, we will look at various techniques and strategies to help debug common problems.

Common Types of Problems

There are many reasons why the kernel may crash or why other problems may happen. However, they are usually variations on common errors and once you know what class of problem you are dealing with, it makes it a lot easier to start examining your code for problems. Let's have a broad look at some of the problems you may encounter during kernel development.

- **Race Conditions:** A general class of bugs used to describe a problem where multiple threads of execution conflict with each other and the outcome depends on which thread gets there first. Race conditions are quite common and are often due to poor design or poor locking in multi-threaded environments. They can sometimes be tricky to reproduce and may be hiding a long time before discovery. Things go wrong when a particular sequence of events happen in a specific order, for example, because it is dependent on user input.

- **Deadlocks:** Happen when locking is poorly implemented and when one thread is waiting on an event or lock that will never happen, possibly because a second thread failed to release the lock after use. Once this happens, the condition can spread to new threads in the system also needing the lock. From a user's point of view, it can look like their application hangs and they may be unable to force quitting it because it is stuck waiting for an event in the kernel.

- **Lock Contention:** A performance problem, which happens when many threads need the same lock and spend excessive time waiting for the lock rather than doing anything useful. Lock contention is usually the result of poor design and can be prevented by implementing a proper locking scheme. The general rule is to lock access to data and not to code. Having large blocks of code protected may seem easier than fine-grained locking of shared data only; however, it will decrease performance and make it more likely for deadlocks to occur.

- **Access to Invalid Memory:** The most common cause for kernel panics. Unlike user space programs, which are aborted, the kernel simply panics if the CPU causes an invalid memory exception. If a debugger is enabled, the kernel will dump into the debugger instead of showing the grey screen of death on Mac OS X or rebooting, which is the behavior under iOS. Buffer overruns will sometimes cause an invalid memory exception, unless the buffer happens to be followed by valid memory, in which case silent memory corruption may occur.

- **Memory and Resource Leaks:** Can happen, for example, if a driver unloads and resources such as objects and buffers were not properly disposed of. It can also be that an extension allocates some memory each time it receives a request, but fails to free the memory after it is finished. The kernel has no garbage collection capabilities, so leaks can accumulate over time and cause a kernel panic.

- **Illegal Instruction/Operand:** These exceptions are issued by the CPU if it detects an invalid instruction or an invalid argument to an instruction. This can happen as the result of memory corruption or a poorly written driver that attempts to use features not present on the CPU, for example, using the SSE3 instruction set on machines that do not support it. You could also see this exception as a result of memory corruption.

- **Blocking in Primary Interrupt Context:** Results in a panic, as you cannot block during primary interrupt context. Blocking requires a scheduled thread, as blocking is implemented by putting the thread to sleep voluntarily. In this case the thread's state is saved and later restored when the scheduler determines it is time to run that thread again. A primary interrupt handler cannot be resumed; it must run to completion without being interrupted. Many kernel APIs may block under certain circumstances. For example, memory allocation may block if the system is low on memory, which will result in some memory being paged out to disk to free up memory for the request. Because of this, functions such as IOMalloc() or even IOLog() cannot be used during primary interrupt context.

- **Volunteered Panics:** Happen when the kernel voluntarily decides to crash because it has determined that something is about to go horribly wrong or an exceptional condition has occurred that it can't recover from. An example of this is if a memory allocation that cannot block fails. Your driver can panic the kernel by calling IOPanic(), which is a wrapper for the panic() function.

There are of course many other problems that can occur, but most are variants of the preceding typical ones.

Kernel Panics

A panic is the kernel's main defense mechanism for dealing with exceptional conditions, such as the preceding list of problems. Instead of attempting to keep going on a fault, the safest course of action is to terminate execution of the system immediately to avoid damage to the file system. When a Mac OS X system panics, the user is likely met by the multilingual panic screen, unless the kernel has been configured with debugging options instructing the user to restart the computer, as shown in Figure 16-1.

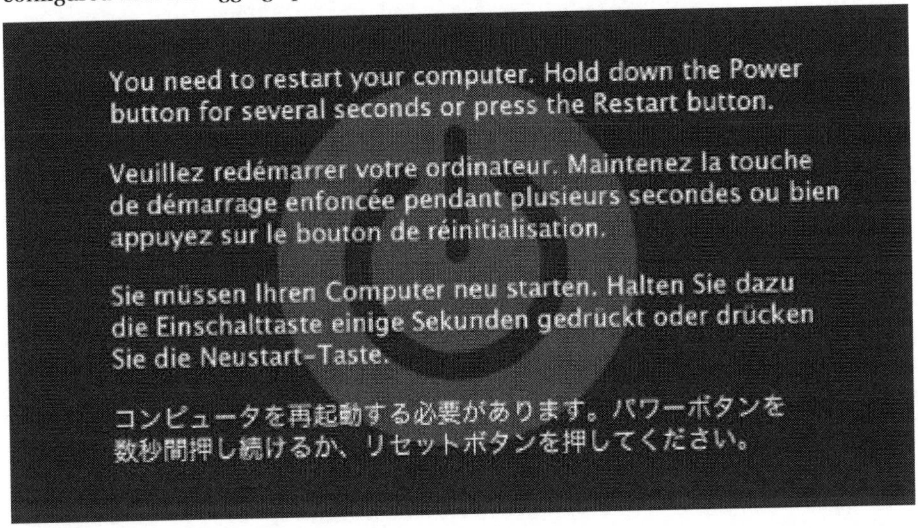

Figure 16-1. Mac OS X Panic Screen, the Mac OS X equivalent of Window's blue screen of death

Behind the scenes, the system will preserve a panic log, which contains a stack trace of the processor (core) the panic happened on. The panic log will be written to the system's non-volatile random-access memory (NVRAM) temporarily, as it is generally unsafe to access the file system after a system has panicked. After all, the purpose of the panic is not to annoy the user but to shut down the party before it gets out of hand and protect the file systems from damage.

Once the system boots again, the panic log is copied to the /Library/Logs/DiagnosticReports/ directory. The system will also show the crash reporter dialog window, which allows users to report the problem to Apple.

Debugging Mechanisms

There are many debugging techniques; which one to use typically depends on the nature of the problem at hand. Here, we will look at some of the techniques that can help aid in debugging kernel problems. Table 16-1 provides a brief overview of some of the mechanisms we will discuss in this chapter.

Table 16-1. Overview of Kernel Debugging Mechanisms

Name	Description
IOLog(), kprintf(), printf()	These carry out basic tracing to the system log (kernel.log). It is also possible to direct kprintf() over a FireWire connection or serial port (if available) to a remote system.
Remote debugging over Ethernet or FireWire using GDB	This allows you to attach the GDB to a remote system that is either crashed or halted. The protocol for remote debugging is called KDP (Kernel Debug Protocol) and is built in to the kernel, but must be enabled manually. The FireWireKDP implementation can also capture core dumps (mirror image of the system's memory).
Live debugging of a running kernel using GDB	This allows GDB to be attached to the kernel it is running on while the system is live.
KDB	This is an in-kernel debugger not built in to the kernel by default. It only works over a traditional serial port and is only found on Xserve servers (and Virtual Machine instances of OS X).
Remote core dumps over Ethernet	The *kdumpd* server can be configured to automatically download core dumps from crashed Macs on the network.

Most of the preceding debugging technologies are included by default, but are not always enabled in the kernel by default because they may cause interference with the running kernel or hardware devices, or may pose a security risk, as it may be possible to obtain sensitive contents of the target's memory.

Enabling debugging mechanisms or controlling the kernel's debug behavior can be done by setting kernel boot arguments. Boot arguments can be set in two ways, either by using the nvram command or by adding it to the boot arguments key in /Library/Preferences/SystemConfiguration/com.apple.Boot.plist. There are a heap of available boot arguments, but we are most interested in the *debug* argument, which controls debugger and system debug behavior. The argument is an integer value and can consist of the flags shown in Table 16-2.

Table 16-2. Flags for the Debug Boot Paramter

Name	Value	Description
DB_HALT	0x01	The kernel will halt at boot and wait for the debugger to be attached.
DB_PRT	0x02	This sends the output of printf() to the console.
DB_NMI	0x04	Makes the system drop into GDB on panic or when the power button or Command-Option-Control-Shift-Escape is pressed.
DB_KPRT	0x08	This sends the kprintf() output to the serial port (if available) or a FireWire remote log.
DB_KDB	0x10	This makes KDB the default debugger (requires building a custom kernel).
DB_SLOG	0x20	This outputs additional diagnostic info to the system log.
DB_ARP	0x40	This allows the debugger to issue ARP requests, allowing debugging across a router without configuring permanent ARP entries.
DB_KDP_BP_DIS	0x80	This allows older versions of GDB to attach to newer systems.
DB_LOG_PI_SCRN	0x100	This disables the graphical panic dialog shown in Figure 16-1.
DB_KDP_GETC_ENA	0x200	This is a prompt for c = continue, r = reboot, and k = enter KDB after a panic.
DB_KERN_DUMP_ON_PANIC	0x400	This triggers a core dump upon kernel panic.
DB_KERN_DUMP_ON_NMI	0x800	This enables a core dump upon an NMI event.
DB_DBG_POST_CORE	0x1000	This waits in the debugger after an NMI core dump.
DBG_PANICLOG_DUMP	0x2000	If set, a panic log is transmitted instead of a core dump.
DBPG_REBOOT_POST_CORE	0x4000	This initiates a reboot after a core/panic log dump.

The values form a bitmask and you can combine multiple values together by ORing them. For example, to enable NMI, disable the graphical panic screen and enter the debugger upon panic. We can combine the values so that:

```
0x04 | 0x100 = 0x104
```

The value can be set in the `com.apple.Boot.plist` or using the `nvram` command:

```
$ sudo nvram boot-args="original_contents debug=0x104"
```

To disable or remove debugging options, simply do the following:

```
$ sudo nvram boot-args="original_contents"
```

If you have existing boot arguments set, this command will overwrite them, so be sure to query the `boot-args` argument first to prevent overwriting them.

Recovering from Crashes During Boot

Your extension may be installed in the `/System/Library/Extensions` directory and get loaded automatically during system boot. If there is a problem that causes the extension to crash repeatedly during system boot, the system can be recovered in the following different ways.

- Boot in safe mode by holding the *shift* key down after you hear the startup tone and release the key when the Apple logo appears. This should ensure only essential kernel extensions (KEXTs) are loaded and you will be able to remove your KEXT so the system can boot manually.

- Attach the system to another computer and boot it in target disk mode using a FireWire or Thunderbolt cable by holding down the T key during boot. You should then be able to remove the offending extension form the system's disk.

- Boot into a different partition if one is available.

- If the offending KEXT is a driver for a piece of hardware, removing it from the system will likely prevent the driver from loading.

- Perform an NVRAM reset if you need to reset boot arguments.

If you are unsure what causes the crash, you can boot the system in verbose mode by pressing Command-V.

▨ **Tip** Details of startup key combinations supported by Intel-based Macs are available at `http://support.apple.com/kb/ht1533`.

Tracing with IOLog()

We have already seen tracing in action throughout this book. Tracing involves strategically placing `IOLog(...)` statements in your code to print variables and to test if conditional blocks are triggered. `IOLog()` output eventually ends up in the `kernel.log` file. The kernel has quite a limited buffer for storing messages from `IOLog()`, so if you write a large amount of long messages too quickly, the buffer will wrap and you may overwrite data before the *syslog* daemon has the chance to store it to the log. This may cause confusion and lead to incorrect assumptions when expected output is not seen.

Many functions of your driver may end up being called hundreds or even thousands of times per second, so printing a message on each invocation may be counterproductive. Although the logging daemon has features to coalesce identical messages, this falls apart if there are slight variations between them. It also does nothing to prevent the buffer wrapping around and potentially overwriting some messages.

You can change the size of the system log buffer that IOLog() writes into by re-compiling the kernel or using the much simpler way of adding the kernel flag msgbuf=n, where *n* is the size of the buffer in bytes, to the kernel's boot configuration property list com.apple.Boot.plist. This file is found in the /Library/Preferences/SystemConfiguration/ directory.

Even though a larger buffer may decrease the likelihood of data going missing, it doesn't prevent the log from being flooded with messages when printing from functions in the "hot path" of the driver. To avoid this, you can use variations of the technique shown in Listing 16-1.

Listing 16-1. Limiting IOLog Output

```
static uint32_t          conditionCount = 0;
com_osxkernel_MyDriver::driverMethod()
{
    ...
    if (someCondition)
    {
        conditionCount++;
        if (conditionCount % 1000 == 0)
            IOLog("condition has occurred: %u times\n", conditionCount);
    }
}
```

This will log the amount of times a condition occurs, but prints a message to the log only every thousandth time. If you wish to debug a primary interrupt filter, you can use a variant of this approach. However, the IOLog() call needs to be moved out of the primary interrupt filter routine to a place it can be safely called, for example, the secondary interrupt handler or a custom IOUserClient method.

If your driver has multiple instances, you may wish to print additional information so you can tell which instance is doing what. If you are in the context of an IOService, you can print the "*this*" pointer address to help uniquely identify each instance.

Should you always leave IOLog() statements in your driver code? Yes and no. Opinions differ on this, but it is definitely frowned upon for a driver to spam the system logs with unnecessary output that may hide other potentially important messages from other parts of the system. However, it may be acceptable to print a few messages about exceptional conditions. If you prefer to leave IOLog() statements in your code, you can prevent them from being outputted, using a conditional variable, which can be toggled on or off by a user space client. The problem with this is a slight increase in the executable size, as well as extra work to be done by the CPU in executing the conditional debug statements. The other approach is to use pre-processor directives, such as #ifdef DEBUG … #endif, so the statements will be compiled away from the resulting executable. Of course, there is also an option to leave most debug statements out entirely, which may make the code more readable. If a user reports a problem, the downside to the two last approaches is that there is no way to enable debugging once the driver is in the field, short of asking the user to install a debug version of the driver. A combination of all three is certainly also possible, but the general advice here is not to litter your code with debug logging, but to place them at strategic places where they are likely to be of use to you even for problems you didn't anticipate.

While tracing using IOLog() seems like a primitive approach, it is often very effective in finding bugs. Of course, this approach works best when the system doesn't actually crash so you can observe the behavior through the system log. However, if the system crashes, the *syslog* daemon will not be able to write the latest contents of the log buffer to the log file. Consequently, the output may be lost at the next reboot. There are ways to get around this, including remote tracing over FireWire, which is discussed later in this chapter.

Printing Stack Traces

The IOLog() function is good enough for many purposes; but in some cases, it is not enough to know a function is called. You also need to know the call stack that led to a call to your function as it may be called from multiple code paths. Printing the call stack can be achieved using the OSReportWithBackTrace() function, as demonstrated in Listing 16-2.

Listing 16-2. Using OSReportWithBackTrace() to Dump the Call Stack

```
void testFunc3() {
    IOLog("address of testFunc3: %p\n", &testFunc3);
    OSReportWithBacktrace("OSReportWithBacktrace() called from testFunc3()");
}
void testFunc2() {
    IOLog("address of testFunc2: %p\n", &testFunc2);
    testFunc3();
}
void testFunc1() {
    IOLog("address of testFunc1: %p\n", &testFunc1);
    testFunc2();
}
bool com_osxkernel_MyDebugDriver::start(IOService * provider) {
    testFunc1();
    ….
}
```

The code in Listing 16-2 should give the following results:

```
address of testFunc1: 0x9ac280
address of testFunc2: 0x9ac250
address of testFunc3: 0x9ac220
OSReportWithBacktrace() called from testFunc3()
Backtrace 0x9ac26f 0x9ac29f 0x9ac2ee 0x543f60 0x542137 0x5426e9 0x5443d5
    Kernel Extensions in backtrace (with dependencies):
        com.osxkernel.MyDebugDriver(1)@0x9ab000->0x9acfff
```

You may notice the printed addresses of the test functions are similar, but not the same as the ones printed in the back trace. The addresses printed by IOLog() are relative to the start of each function; however, in the back trace, you instead see the address of where each test function is calling the next test function. The OSReportWithBacktrace() function also prints the start and end addresses of any KEXTs involved in the back trace. We see our KEXT is loaded at the memory address 0x9ab000 and you may notice that testFunc1(), testFunc2(), and testFunc3() are all within the address range of the MyDebugDriver. Using this information, we can also work out the offset where a function is located within its executable image by subtracting the address of a function from the base address, for example, for `testFunc1()`: 0x9ac280 - 0x9ab000 = 4736 bytes. You can then use the GDB debugger with the *disassemble <offset>* command.

Remote Tracing over FireWire

It is possible to redirect output from the `krprintf()` function over a FireWire connection to another system. This method is more robust than using `IOLog()`, as log output will be preserved on the remote system in the event of a crash. Another advantage of this approach is that it is available in the very early boot process, which is useful for debugging a driver that's involved with the system boot process, such as storage and display drivers. It also allows debugging of shutdown and sleep events. Your driver does not need any special support or modifications to support outputting log information over FireWire.

Everything needed to configure remote logging over FireWire is already included in Mac OS X from versions 10.5 and above and there is no need to install additional KEXTs. You need two Macs to set this up. It is not necessary for both systems to run the same version of Mac OS X.

On the target machine, the machine you wish to send log output from, do the following.

```
$ sudo nvram boot-args="debug=0x8"
```

This boot option enables redirection of the `kprintf()` function so output will be mirrored to the FireWire interface as well as the system log. The system should be rebooted for this option to take effect. The next step is to connect a FireWire cable between the two systems. Unlike `IOLog()`, the `kprintf()` function is synchronous, which means by the time it returns, it will have transmitted the message over FireWire. The `kprintf()` disables interrupts until it completes, which can affect timing-related issues when used excessively. Because interrupts are disabled, the function may cause a crash if memory referenced by the functions arguments happens to be paged out.

▓ **Caution** It is recommended that both the target and debug machines have all other FireWire devices disconnected during debugging.

On the machine that will receive the debug output, run the `fwkpfv` command, which is the FireWire log viewer utility. If the target machine was connected correctly and the cable properly attached, you will receive debug output after a few seconds. The following example shows an extract from a session captured while the target machine boots:

```
Welcome to FireWireKPrintf. (viewer v2.6)
AppleFWOHCI_KPF: version 4.7.1 - init
u>626665 AppleFWOHCI_KPF: Time format-> Microseconds = 'u>clock_uptime_micro'
u>1141021 AppleUSBHub::setPowerState(0x4fbe200, 0 -> 4) took 301 ms
u>2065689 [Bluetooth::CSRHIDTransition] DeviceRequest error: e00002ed
u>2109928 AppleUSBHub::powerStateWillChangeTo(0x4f13200, AppleUSBHub, 4 -> 3) took 100 ms
u>2117294 AppleUSBHub::powerStateWillChangeTo(0x4f70e00, AppleUSBHub, 4 -> 3) took 100 ms
u>2130057 AppleUSBHub::powerStateWillChangeTo(0x4f70a00, AppleUSBHub, 4 -> 3) took 100 ms
...
...
...
```

```
u>20236388 Adding domain PPP (family 34)
u>24073549 kPEDisableScreen -1
u>24158956 kPEDisableScreen 1
u>25568081 initialize_screen: b=4645B000, w=00000690, h=0000041A, r=00002000, d=00000001
u>25568131 kPEEnableScreen 1
u>304129579 IOSCSIPeripheralDeviceType00::setPowerState(0x4fe3500, 3 -> 4) async took 351 ms
u>1070371211 IOSCSIPeripheralDeviceType00::setPowerState(0x4fe3500, 3 -> 2) async took 1153
ms
```

If you wish to log over FireWire from your own KEXT, you will have to use the kprintf() function to log with rather than IOLog(), which doesn't use kprintf internally but rather calls printf(), which only goes to the kernel log. A strategy to deal with this is to create your own wrapper function for IOLog() and kprintf() that calls the former for a release build and the latter for a debug build.

Listing 16-3 shows an example of how to log using kprintf().

Listing 16-3. Logging Messages to a Remote Machine over FireWire Using kprintf()

```
#include <kern/debug.h> // Declares kprintf()
bool com_osxkernel_MyDebugDriver::start(IOService * provider)
{
        kprintf("%s::start - Hello FireWire Listeners\n", getName());
        return true;
}
```

Running this yields the following on the remote system:

```
u>1071578492 com_osxkernel_MyDebugDriver::start - Hello FireWire Listeners
```

If the kernel crashes, you can also get the panic log through the FireWire log viewer. It is also possible to use FireWire to attach the GNU debugger remotely to the kernel, as we will see later in this chapter.

Remote Kernel Core Dumps

Mac OS X provides a mechanism for transmitting core dumps from a crashed (or hung) system to a remote machine over the network. A core dump is a binary image of the wired contents of the system's memory. By capturing a core dump, we can retain evidence of the exact state the system was in at the time of the crash and we can use this image with the GDB to get stack traces for all threads in the system and examine memory contents as well as kernel data structures.

Conveniently, everything you need to enable core dumps is already present in Mac OS X. Only minor configuration is required. On the dump server, the machine that receives the core dumps from crashed machines, you need to activate the *kdumpd* daemon, as follows.:

```
# sudo vi /System/Library/LaunchDaemons/com.apple.kdumpd.plist
```

Change the *Disabled* key from *true* to *false*. If you wish, you can also configure the directory where dumps will be located. The default is /PanicDumps. The *kdumpd* daemon is started as follows:

```
# sudo launchctl load /System/Library/LaunchDaemons/com.apple.kdumpd.plist
# sudo launchctl start com.apple.kdumpd
```

The server uses UDP on port 1069, so you should ensure there is no firewall between the target machines and the server. The target and server do not need to be running the same version of Mac OS X.

■ **Note** To use *kdumpd*, the target machine (the crashing system) needs to be connected to the network using Ethernet. It is not possible to use an AirPort device, as the driver for KDB (Kernel Debugging Protocol), which handles transmission of the dump, only works with Ethernet devices. When loaded, you can check where the kernel debugging driver is attached using IORegisteryExplorer and search for the driver named IOKernelDebugger.

The *kdumpd* daemon is able to receive core dumps from multiple machines and will archive each dump with the machine's IP address. If you work for a company that develops software that runs in the kernel, you can configure all your Macs to automatically send dumps to a central server when a crash occurs. This saves a lot of time when quality assurance testers encounter problems during testing, as engineering can simply start debugging the dumped image immediately.

■ **Caution** Care should be taken to only to use *kdumpd* in trusted networks, as memory contents of the crashed system are transmitted unencrypted over the network and may contain sensitive information, such as passwords and private keys.

Configuring the target machine is equally simple and is done by setting kernel boot arguments either in /Library/Preferences/SystemConfiguration/com.apple.Boot.plist or using the nvram command, as follows:

```
# sudo nvram boot-args="debug=0xd44 _panicd_ip=192.168.1.1"
```

The preceding instructs the kernel to dump core when it panics or if an NMI (non-maskable interrupt) event was triggered. The latter is highly useful in the cases where the system hangs completely and appears unresponsive but does not actually panic. In this case, you can use the power button on the computer to trigger the NMI event, which will start the core dump. During this time, the machine will be frozen and no processes will run. If the machine is responsive and you do this, the machine will simply resume as if nothing had happened after the core dump is transferred.

The *_panicd_ip* parameter specifies the IP address of the machine running *kdumpd*. If you plan on having a permanently running panic server, it is recommended this IP be static. It is not possible to use a hostname or DNS name for the server, as name resolution is not possible.

The following output will appear on the screen of the target machine if you press the power button:

```
Entering system dump routine
Attempting connection to panic server configured at IP 192.168.1.1, port 1069
Resolved 192.168.1.1's (or proxy's) link level address
Transmitting packets to link level address: 00:16:cb:a6:73:8b
Kernel map size is 4546437120
Sending write request for core-xnu-1699.22.73-192.168.1.2-2fe8a6d9
Protocol features: 0x1
Kernel map has 1389 entries
Generated Mach-O header size was 100224
```

The target machine will write dots (.) to the screen until the dump is complete. If it was an NMI event that triggered the dump, the system will resume; if it was a panic, the system will wait for a remote debugger to be attached.

KDB

The kernel supports an in-kernel debugger called KDB. KDB only supports debugging over the serial port. It is not included in the kernel build by default; therefore, you need to compile and install a custom kernel in order to use it. KDB has some applications for very low-level debugging where neither FireWire nor Ethernet is available. KDB requires a native serial port on the machine being debugged, which is only found on the now discontinued Xserve (although a serial port is available if Mac OS X is used under a virtual machine). For all intents and purposes, the GNU Debugger (GDB) is recommended; we only mention KDB here to avoid confusion with GDB.

Remote Debugging with GDB over Ethernet or FireWire

The kernel has support for using the GDB over Ethernet (IP/UDP) or FireWire connections. Again, this requires two computers running Mac OS X. While GDB is supported through Xcode, you cannot debug the kernel using Xcode; you will have to use the command-line interface. GDB is, however, part of Xcode. It is not necessary to install Xcode on the machine being debugged; it is only needed on the remote system (the client).

▓ **Note** Strictly speaking, it would be possible to use another operating system running GDB as the host to debug a Mac OS X target system. Although there is no documentation for doing this, some documentation suggests it is possible, however non-trivial, to configure.

The debugging support is built in to the kernel by default, unlike KDB. However, the debugging capabilities are disabled by default, but can easily be enabled by adding the appropriate boot arguments on the target machine, for example:

```
$ sudo nvram boot-args="debug=0x144 -v".
```

The "-v" (verbose) flag isn't strictly necessary. It has the effect of disabling the grey screen with the Apple logo during boot and instead showing a text console, commonly found on UNIX and Linux systems, which shows log messages as the system boots. Once the boot arguments have been set, the system needs to be rebooted for the changes to take effect.

Configuring the Host Machine

Setting up the target is straightforward. However, the host machine requires a little more preparation. Before you can start debugging, you need to download the correct Kernel Debug Kit for the kernel version used by the target system. Apple doesn't appear to publish a version for every build in a timely manner, so the target system would have to be downgraded or upgraded to match a published version of the Kernel Debug Kit. If you use the wrong version, GDB may fail to resolve the correct symbols and data structures and the results may be wrong and cause great confusion, for example, functions getting called that should not have.

■ **Tip** Kernel Debug Kits are not part of Xcode and can be downloaded from http://developer.apple.com/hardwaredrivers/download/kerneldebugkits.html. This page contains legacy versions, while newer versions are published in the *Downloads* ➤ *Developer Tools* section on the Apple developer site. This page is restricted to members of the Mac developer program (there's an annual fee to become a member).

The Kernel Debug Kit contains the following:

- Debug version of the kernel (mach_kernel)
- Debug version of I/O Kit families and selected KEXTs
- Symbol files
- Various scripts
- Macros for GDB

■ **Caution** Do not replace files on your system with files from the Kernel Debug Kit; they do not need to be installed on the target or host system. In fact, you do not need to install any files from the kit; you can access them directly through the mounted image.

You can replace the default kernel (mach_kernel) of a Mac OS X system with the debug version found in the Kernel Debug Kit. This will help you get more accurate results and stack traces, as optimization has been disabled.

If you have the sources for the XNU kernel installed on the host system, it is possible to link this with the debugger, which allows you to see source code instead of assembly code in the debugger, though this is often not needed if you are only debugging your own extension (in which case you can link the source for your own extension only).

Attaching to the Remote Target

If you have set the appropriate boot arguments with the `nvram` command on the target system and have the Kernel Debug Kit ready on the host machine, you can now trigger an NMI event on the target system by pressing the system's power button. This should cause the following text to appear on the top left corner of the screen:

```
Debugger called: <Button SCI>
ethernet MAC address: 00:16:cb:a6:74:8b
ip address: 192.168.1.1

Waiting for remote debugger connection.
```

Starting GDB and attaching to the remote target can be done using the following steps:

```
$ gdb -arch i386 /Volumes/KernelDebugKit/mach_kernel
```

The arch argument can specified if the debug host is running on a different architecture from the target system. For example, in this case, we are debugging a target running a 32-bit kernel on a system with a 64-bit kernel. You can also do the reverse by specifying *x86_64*.

```
(gdb) source /Volumes/KernelDebugKit/kgmacros
```

The preceding line will load specialized GDB macros, which will help you examine the state of the target system's kernel. You can, for example, dump a list of running tasks or threads. Type `help kgm` to get a full list of available macros.

To attach to the target, use the following:

```
(gdb) target remote-kdp
(gdb) attach 192.168.1.1
Connected.
(gdb)
```

The preceding will attach to the remote target so we can begin our debugging session. We can then start issuing commands, for example, `bt` to get a stack trace, which will look something like the following:

```
#0  Debugger (message=0xba97e4 "Button SCI") at /SourceCache/xnu/xnu-
1504.15.3/osfmk/i386/AT386/model_dep.c:867
#1  0x00ba8de3 in ?? ()
#2  0x00556636 in IOFilterInterruptEventSource::normalInterruptOccurred (this=0x4eab980) at
/SourceCache/xnu/xnu-1504.15.3/iokit/Kernel/IOFilterInterruptEventSource.cpp:140
#3  0x00b73a50 in ?? ()
#4  0x00b72ccd in ?? ()
#5  0x00b85fc5 in ?? ()
#6  0x00b89621 in ?? ()
#7  0x0056ac20 in IOSharedInterruptController::handleInterrupt (this=0x4e9cd80,
```

```
nub=0x4e9cd80) at /SourceCache/xnu/xnu-1504.15.3/iokit/Kernel/IOInterruptController.cpp:727
#8   0x00bcf5bb in ?? ()
#9   0x00b66213 in ?? ()
#10  0x00b71911 in ?? ()
#11  0x00580d96 in PE_incoming_interrupt (interrupt=73) at /SourceCache/xnu/xnu-
1504.15.3/pexpert/i386/pe_interrupt.c:65
#12  0x002ab432 in interrupt (state=0x4e9dd20) at /SourceCache/xnu/xnu-
1504.15.3/osfmk/i386/trap.c:511
#13  0x002a1c2e in lo_allintrs () at cpu_data.h:397
#14  0x00225bba in processor_idle (thread=0x10bff0, processor=0x4cf0dac) at
/SourceCache/xnu/xnu-1504.15.3/osfmk/kern/sched_prim.c:2982
#15  0x0022698c in thread_select (thread=0x5e407a8, processor=<value temporarily unavailable,
due to optimizations>) at /SourceCache/xnu/xnu-1504.15.3/osfmk/kern/sched_prim.c:1327
#16  0x002275b0 in thread_block_reason (continuation=0, parameter=0x0, reason=<value
temporarily unavailable, due to optimizations>) at /SourceCache/xnu/xnu-
1504.15.3/osfmk/kern/sched_prim.c:1856
#17  0x00227654 in thread_block (continuation=0) at /SourceCache/xnu/xnu-
1504.15.3/osfmk/kern/sched_prim.c:1875
#18  0x464debbc in ?? ()
```

The command will show the kernel stack, which is the sequence of function calls the CPU was executing at the time of the NMI event. We can see in this case that the last thing the system did before we halted it was to respond to the NMI interrupt. If you are curious what the other CPUs (cores) were doing at the time, you can issue the command showcurrentstacks, which will print a stack trace for each CPU (core) in the system.

You can now set breakpoints or examine the state of the kernel. Issuing the continue command will resume the kernel. We will look at how GDB can be used in more detail later in this chapter.

Debugging Using FireWire

In addition to Ethernet, the Kernel Debugging Protocol can also be used over FireWire, using the FireWireKDP mechanism. The fwkdp tool can be used to help set the appropriate debug parameters, but you can also set them manually. FireWireKDP is also compatible with logging over FireWire and can be used to transmit core dumps to a remote system.

To configure FireWireKDP on the target system, you can do as follows:

```
$ sudo fwkdp --setargs
FireWire KDP Tool (v1.3)
Boot-args helper mode:
*** Would you like to enable kernel core dumps? y|[n] > y
Setting boot-args with 'sudo nvram boot-args="debug=0xd46 kdp_match_name=firewire
_panicd_ip=1.2.3.4"'
Setting boot-args... done.
Restart for the nvram changes to take effect.
```

■ **Tip** The manual (man) page for fwkdp has more info.

On the host system, where you will run the debugger, you will need to run fwkdp as well. Be sure to start it in proxy mode. Once that is done, you can use GDB to debug in the same way as with Ethernet. The process of attaching to the remote target is nearly identical; the only major difference is that you attach to *localhost*, not the target's IP address. Once the target system is rebooted, you can enter the debugger by pressing the power button to generate an NMI event as before, which should give the following results on the target's screen:

```
Debugger Called: <Button SCI>
Entering system dump routine
Attempting connection to panic server configured at 1.2.3.4 port 1069
AppleFWOHCI_KDP: Darwin Kernel Version 10.8.0: Tue Jun 7 16:33:36 PDT 2011; root:xnu-
1504.15.3~1/RELEASE_i386
AppleFWOHCI_KDP: v4.7.3 configured as KDP sender/receiver.
Recevied a debugger packet, transferring control to the debugger
Transmitting packets to link level address: 00:1c:df:f7:e0:72
Kernel map size is 1187131392
Sending write request for core-xnu-1504.15.3-0.0.0.0-ff28cfb5
Kernel map has 850 entries
Generated Mach-O header size was 79932
Transmitting kernel state, please wait: ......
Total number of packets transmitted: 502848
Waiting for remote debugger connection.
Connected to remote debugger.
```

If all goes well, the fwkdp proxy running on the host will download the core file to its working directory. The core dump in the preceding example was named core-xnu-1504.15.3-0.0.0.0-ff28cfb5. After the core is downloaded, the remote system will wait for a debugger to be attached.

Live Debugging of a Running Kernel

A less known but powerful feature available in Mac OS X (since version 10.5) is the ability to attach the debugger to a running system. Live debugging requires you to enable support for the /dev/kmem character device file, which allows a user space process to read and write to the kernel's memory address space. You can enable support for /dev/kmem with the following command:

```
$ sudo nvram boot-args="kmem=1"
```

▓ **Note** The preceding command will clear existing boot arguments, so you would need to add this in addition to any other arguments you want, for example, to enable remote debugging or FireWire logging.

You can test if it worked by checking that the /dev/kmem file is present after a reboot. The process of attaching to the live kernel is similar to that of attaching to a remote target. The steps are as follows:

```
$ sudo gdb /Volumes/KernelDebugKit/mach_kernel
(gdb) target darwin-kernel
```

```
(gdb) source /Volumes/KernelDebugKit/kgmacros
Loading Kernel GDB Macros package. Type "help kgm" for more info.

(gdb) attach
Connected.
```

At this point, you can examine the state of the kernel, for example, using the showcurrentthreads command.

Live debugging is useful in a number of cases, for example, if an application using your driver hangs in the kernel while executing a user client method. You can attach to the kernel and find out where the issue is. You can also examine the memory of your driver and its data structures. Live debugging can only be used when the system is operational and cannot be used to debug a crashed or deadlocked system.

Debugging Using a Virtual Machine

If you do not have a second machine available, it is possible to perform kernel debugging using a virtual machine. Software such as VMWare Fusion or Parallels desktop allows another copy of Mac OS X to run virtualized. Enabling the kernel debug features on the virtual machine can be done by putting the desired boot arguments in the/Library/Preferences/SystemConfiguration/com.apple.Boot.plist. Debugging hardware drivers may not be possible under a virtual machine, as you cannot use PCI or Thunderbolt devices directly under a virtual machine. However, it is possible to assign USB devices to a virtual machine instance. Mac OS X Lion is able to run as a virtualized instance, however, prior to that, only the server version of Mac OS X could be virtualized.

Debugging in the Kernel Using GDB

There are several ways GDB can be used to debug the kernel or KEXTs loaded into it, such as:

- Remotely over Ethernet
- Remotely over FireWire
- On a captured core dump file
- On a Live live system
- Using a virtual machine

Additionally, a kernel can drop into the debugger in the following ways:

- Because of a kernel panic
- Manually triggered NMI event
- Because the DB_HALT option was set to halt the system at boot and enter the debugger
- Programmatically in code by calling the PE_enter_debugger() function

Programmatically entering the debugger is only possible with a remote debugging setup; live debugging cannot occur during boot, when the system is crashed, or halted with an NMI event, nor programmatically, as this stops the system until a remote debugger is attached and thereby the *gdb* instance running the debugging session as well.

Kernel GDB Macros

The *Kernel Debug Kit* comes with a wealth of helpful GDB macro functions, which greatly simplify the task of examining the kernel. The macros can help interpret common kernel data structures, such as task and thread descriptors, and memory-related data structures, such as VM maps. Furthermore, it provides functions for accessing PCI configuration space, I/O space, and un-translated access to physical memory. A small subset of available macros is shown in Table 16-3.

Table 16-3. Useful Kernel GDB Macros

Name	Description
showalltasks	Displays a list of all system tasks
showallthreads	Displays a list of all system threads
showallstacks	Prints stack trace for every single thread (be prepared for a massive amount of data)
showallkmods	Displays list of all loaded KEXTs and the addresses where they are loaded in memory
showallclasses	Shows all known classes, their size, and instance count
showregistry	Dumps the I/O Registry information to screen (similar to *ioreg*)
paniclog	Shows the panic log
systemlog	Shows the kernel log
showcurrentstacks	Shows the task/thread executing on each processor and stack trace
hexdump	Dumps HEX/ASCII from a memory address
pci_cfg_(read|write)(8|16|32)	Allows you to examine the state of a PCI device

Creating Symbol Information for KEXTs

Before you can debug your own KEXTs in GDB, you need to generate symbol information for the KEXT. Because a KEXT is dynamically loadable, we have no way of knowing where in memory it will be located. Although our KEXT includes symbol information, the addresses of functions and data are relative to the KEXT binary. The absolute address of a function in a KEXT will be the *kernel_load_address* + *relative_address* once the KEXT is loaded.

Fortunately, the Kernel Debug Kit gives us a helping hand by providing a small script that helps generate the final symbol table containing the absolute addresses within the kernel address space. The script is called createsymbolfiles and can be used as follows:

```
$ /Volumes/KernelDebugKit/createsymbolfiles -a i386 -s ./ MyDebugDriver.kext
MyDebugDriver.kext appears to be loadable (not including linkage for on-disk libraries).

Enter the hexadecimal load addresses for these extensions
(press Return to skip symbol generation for an extension):

com.osxkernel.MyDebugDriver: 0x9b9000
```

The load address can be found in several places, for example, with *kextstat*, as follows:

```
$ kextstat
Index Refs Address    Size    Wired    Name (Version) <Linked Against>
  126   0 0x9b9000   0x3000  0x2000    com.osxkernel.MyDebugDriver (1) <5 4 3>
```

In the preceding case, the KEXT had no additional dependencies; however, in a real world situation, a KEXT may have dependencies on one or more other KEXTs, such as an I/O Kit family, in which case you will be prompted to enter their addresses as well. If you are debugging a crash dump from a remote system or directly debugging a crashed system, the load address of your extension and any dependencies will be found in the panic log if your extension was involved in the crash. Note that your KEXT may be given a different address each time it loads, so you will need to regenerate the symbol information each time.

The above is enough to get us basic symbol information, but it is restricted to symbolic names of functions only and is not able to give us source code line information. You can get this by configuring your extension's debug information format, as shown in Figure 16-2.

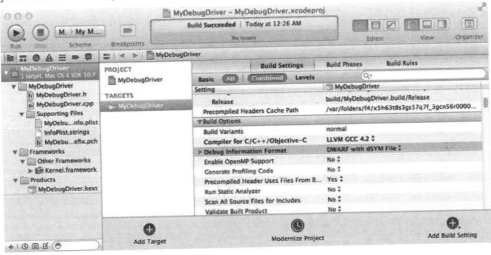

Figure 16-2. Setting the debug information format with Xcode

DWARF with dSYM creates a separate file for you containing a full set of symbols and information needed to map a code location back to a source code line. This information is normally embedded into an executable when doing a debug build; however, you can generate that information in an external file for release builds of the driver. It is good practice to archive this debug information for later use. This will make debugging easier if crashes should be reported by a user. The dSYM file (actually bundle) will be named MyDebugDriver.kext.dSYM in our case. The dSYM bundle should be placed together with the KEXT before the createsymbolfiles script is run.

Debugging KEXTs with GDB

In the following sections, we will analyze a crash caused by a hypothetical driver named MyDebugDriver. The header file specification for MyDebugDriver is shown in Listing 16-4.

Listing 16-4. MyDebugDriver Header File

```
class com_osxkernel_MyDebugDriver : public IOService
{
    OSDeclareDefaultStructors(com_osxkernel_MyDebugDriver);
public:
    virtual bool init(OSDictionary* dict);
    virtual bool start(IOService* provider);
    virtual void stop(IOService* provider);

    void testFunc1(UInt32 arg1, UInt32 arg2, UInt32 arg3, UInt32 arg4);
    void testFunc2(UInt32 arg1, UInt32 arg2, UInt32 arg3, UInt32 arg4);
    void testFunc3(UInt32 arg1, UInt32 arg2, UInt32 arg3, UInt32 arg4);

    static void  timerFired(OSObject* owner, IOTimerEventSource* sender);
private:

    IOTimerEventSource*     fTimer;
    int                     fVariable1;
    int                     fVariable2;
};
```

The driver starts a timer, from which testFunc1() is called, which in turn calls testFunc2(), which calls testFunc3(), which causes a kernel panic due to a null pointer dereference. Each function accepts four integers that have no significance (picked randomly) and are passed unchanged from the first function to the last. The values passed as arguments are 65261, 48879, 0, and 5380.

We have successfully generated a core dump from a crash system using the FireWire core dump mechanism and previously, we built symbol information for our driver using the correct load address. We are now ready to load it up in the GDB and get our hands dirty. The steps we need to perform to find the bug in our driver are as follows:

- Create a symbol file with the correct load address (see the last section)

- Start GDB and load the core dump

- Add symbol information from the kernel

- Load Kernel Debug Kit GDB macros

- Load our KEXT binary of MyDebugDriver into GDB

- Load symbol information for MyDebugDriver (if GDB cannot find them in the same location as the KEXT)

- Tell GDB the location of the source code for MyDebugDriver (optional)

Following is a complete debug session for MyDebugDriver:

```
$ gdb -c core-xnu-1504.15.3-0.0.0.0-fb3a74d3
GNU gdb 6.3.50-20050815 (Apple version gdb-1704) (Thu Jun 23 10:48:29 UTC 2011)
...
This GDB was configured as "x86_64-apple-darwin".
#0  0x002b1e3e in ?? ()
(gdb) add-symbol-file /Volumes/KernelDebugKit/mach_kernel
add symbol table from file "/Volumes/KernelDebugKit/mach_kernel"? (y or n) y
Reading symbols from /Volumes/KernelDebugKit/mach_kernel...Reading symbols from
/Volumes/KernelDebugKit/mach_kernel.dSYM/Contents/Resources/DWARF/mach_kernel...done.
done.
(gdb) source /Volumes/KernelDebugKit/kgmacros
Loading Kernel GDB Macros package.  Type "help kgm" for more info.
```

The preceding sequence of commands loads the core dump file, adds symbol information for the kernel from the Kernel Debug Kit, and finally loads the GDB macros, which must be loaded after the kernel symbol information to initialize properly.

We can now issue the backtrace command to see where the system crashed, as follows:

```
(gdb) backtrace
#0  0x002b1e3e in Debugger (message=0x5dd7fc "panic")
#1  0x0021b837 in panic (str=0x59e3d0 "Kernel trap at 0x%08x, type %d=%s, registers:\nCR0:
0x%08x, CR2: 0x%08x, CR3: 0x%08x, CR4: 0x%08x\nEAX: 0x%08x, EBX: 0x%08x, ECX: 0x%08x, EDX:
0x%08x\nCR2: 0x%08x, EBP: 0x%08x, ESI: 0x%08x, EDI: 0x%08x\nE"...) at /SourceCache/xnu/xnu-
1504.15.3/osfmk/kern/debug.c:303
#2  0x002abf6a in panic_trap [inlined] () at :1052
#3  0x002abf6a in kernel_trap (state=0x46ee3e10) at /SourceCache/xnu/xnu-
1504.15.3/osfmk/i386/trap.c:1001
#4  0x002a1a78 in trap_from_kernel () at cpu_data.h:397
#5  0x009ba0b7 in last_kernel_symbol ()
#6  0x009ba356 in last_kernel_symbol ()
#7  0x009ba3b8 in last_kernel_symbol ()
#8  0x009ba45b in last_kernel_symbol ()
#9  0x005571d5 in IOTimerEventSource::timeoutAndRelease (self=0x2a17b0, c=0x5022071) at
/SourceCache/xnu/xnu-1504.15.3/iokit/Kernel/IOTimerEventSource.cpp:122
#10 0x00230235 in thread_call_thread (group=0x863ea0) at /SourceCache/xnu/xnu-
1504.15.3/osfmk/kern/thread_call.c:848
```

Because we have not yet loaded our KEXT, symbols #5–#8 are showing up as bogus, as the debugger is unable to resolve the addresses of the functions to their symbolic names. To fix this, we will load the MyDebugDriver KEXT into GDB along with its symbol information, as follows:

```
(gdb) add-kext MyDebugDriver.kext
Reading symbols from com.osxkernel.MyDebugDriver.sym...Reading symbols from
MyDebugDriver.kext.dSYM/Contents/Resources/DWARF/MyDebugDriver...done.
(gdb) directory MyDebugDriver/
Source directories searched: MyDebugDriver:$cdir:$cwd
```

We have now loaded the driver along with its symbol information and informed GDB of the location where it should look for the source code of MyDebugDriver. The location of the kernel's own source code is hard wired into the debug kernel image. If you wish to show the source code in GDB, you need to create a symlink for the location where you downloaded the XNU source to the directory: /SourceCache/.

Let's try the backtrace command again with the KEXT and symbols loaded, as follows:

```
(gdb) backtrace
...
#5  0x009ba0b7 in com_osxkernel_MyDebugDriver::testFunc3 (this=0x4e80f80, arg1=65261,
arg2=48879, arg3=0, arg4=5380) at MyDebugDriver.cpp:14
#6  0x009ba356 in com_osxkernel_MyDebugDriver::testFunc2 (this=0x4e80f80, arg1=65261,
arg2=48879, arg3=0, arg4=5380) at MyDebugDriver.cpp:21
#7  0x009ba3b8 in com_osxkernel_MyDebugDriver::testFunc1 (this=0x4e80f80, arg1=65261,
arg2=48879, arg3=0, arg4=5380) at MyDebugDriver.cpp:27
#8  0x009ba45b in com_osxkernel_MyDebugDriver::timerFired (owner=0x4e80f80, sender=0xb63adc0)
at MyDebugDriver.cpp:64
...
```

That's much more readable. We have now identified the exact call stack and we can see which methods in our in our driver that was involved, down to the file and line number. We can also see the arguments that were passed to the methods and that they correspond to the values we picked earlier. Let's examine the crash further by jumping to the fifth stack frame, the location where the crash occurred, as follows:

```
(gdb) frame 5
#5  0x009ba0b7 in com_osxkernel_MyDebugDriver::testFunc3 (this=0x4e80f80, arg1=65261,
arg2=48879, arg3=0, arg4=5380) at MyDebugDriver.cpp:14
14                      thisWillNotWork->fVariable1 = arg3;
Current language:  auto; currently c++
(gdb) print thisWillNotWork
$1 = (com_osxkernel_MyDebugDriver *) 0x0
```

I think we found the problem! We are trying to assign a value to the member variable fVariable1 but the object is not initialized. We can also list the source code of testFunc3(), as follows:

```
(gdb) list com_osxkernel_MyDebugDriver::testFunc3,15
9    void com_osxkernel_MyDebugDriver::testFunc3(UInt32 arg1, UInt32 arg2, UInt32 arg3,
UInt32 arg4)
10   {
11       if (arg3 == 0)
12       {
13           com_osxkernel_MyDebugDriver *thisWillNotWork = NULL;
14           thisWillNotWork->fVariable1 = arg3;
15       }
```

Well, that would never work! We have found our bug, which appears to be triggered only when the third argument passed is set to zero.

If you only have symbol information and lack the debug information required to map addresses to a specific source code location, you can use the disassemble command in GDB to show a dump disassembly of the method from its address. Let's look at the disassembly of testFunc3(), as follows:

```
(gdb) disassemble 0x009ba0b7
...
0x009ba09f <testFunc3Emmmm+35>:     mov    %eax,-0x1c(%ebp)
0x009ba0a2 <testFunc3Emmmm+38>:     mov    -0x18(%ebp),%eax
0x009ba0a5 <testFunc3Emmmm+41>:     cmp    $0x0,%eax
0x009ba0a8 <testFunc3Emmmm+44>:     jne    0x9ba0ba <testFunc3Emmmm+62>
0x009ba0aa <testFunc3Emmmm+46>:     movl   $0x0,-0x20(%ebp)
```

```
0x009ba0b1 <testFunc3Emmmm+53>:     mov    -0x18(%ebp),%eax
0x009ba0b4 <testFunc3Emmmm+56>:     mov    -0x20(%ebp),%ecx
0x009ba0b7 <testFunc3Emmmm+59>:     mov    %eax,0x54(%ecx)
0x009ba0ba <testFunc3Emmmm+62>:     add    $0x18,%esp
...
```

While this looks very uninviting if you are not familiar with assembly, you will be able to infer a number of things by comparing the disassembly to the original source code. For example, the *cmp* instruction compares the value of the *eax* register against the constant value $0x0, which we can correctly guess corresponds to the if statement on line 11.

Although we have already found the source of the problem, let's pretend for a moment we are curious as to why a zero value was passed for the third argument. Perhaps our driver used an internal state to calculate the value passed to testFunc3(). In this case, we could continue our examination by looking at the state of the driver was in at the time of the crash. Because testFunc3() is a member method of the com_osxkernel_MyDebugDriver, we know that a pointer to the class instance is always passed automatically to the member function as the *this* pointer. We can dereference the this pointer address from the previous stack trace as follows:

```
(gdb) print *(com_osxkernel_MyDebugDriver*)0x4e80f80
$9 = {
  <IOService> = {
    <IORegistryEntry> = {
      <OSObject> = {
        <OSMetaClassBase> = {
          _vptr$OSMetaClassBase = 0x9baa00
        },
        members of OSObject:
        retainCount = 65537
      },
      members of IORegistryEntry:
      reserved = 0x4e71a40,
      fRegistryTable = 0xb693800,
      fPropertyTable = 0x503a400
    },
    members of IOService:
    reserved = 0x0,
    __provider = 0x4d17f00,
  .......
  },
  members of com_osxkernel_MyDebugDriver:
  fTimer = 0xb63adc0,
  fVariable1 = 2,
  fVariable2 = 4,
  static gMetaClass = {
    <OSMetaClass> = {
      <OSMetaClassBase> = {
        _vptr$OSMetaClassBase = 0x9ba980
      },
      members of OSMetaClass:
      reserved = 0xb63ba00,
      superClassLink = 0x85fac8,
      className = 0x4e5b5a0,
```

```
        classSize = 92,
        instanceCount = 1
    }, <No data fields>},
    static metaClass = 0x9ba000,
    static superClass = 0x9ba020
```

We can now examine the internal state of our driver instance and we can see the values of its member variables fVariable1 and fVariable2. We can also see how many instances of our class exist from the meta class information and determine the retain count of the driver.

Understanding Kernel Panic Logs

A panic log can be found in the /Library/Logs/DiagnosticReports/ directory after a crash or can be obtained by extracting it from a core dump or a remote GDB session to a crashed target. As a kernel programmer, you might be expected to analyze kernel panic logs sent from customers' computers, which you will rarely have, physical access to. Furthermore, the customer may be reluctant or unable to assist you in getting a core dump. It is therefore vital to be able to understand and extract as much information as possible from the logs. Let's start to look at the panic log and what information we can extract from it. A panic log for the MyDebugDriver crash discussed in the previous sections is shown in Listing 16-5.

Listing 16-5. Panic Log from MyDebugDriver Crash

```
panic(cpu 1 caller 0xffffff80002c268d): Kernel trap at 0xffffff7f81345570, type 14=page fault,
registers:
CR0: 0x000000008001003b, CR2: 0x0000000000000090, CR3: 0x0000000000100000, CR4:
0x0000000000000660
RAX: 0x0000000000000000, RBX: 0x0000000000000000, RCX: 0x0000000000000000, RDX:
0x000000000000beef
RSP: 0xffffff808e973e80, RBP: 0xffffff808e973ea0, RSI: 0x000000000000feed, RDI:
0xffffff801ab61100
R8:  0x0000000000001504, R9:  0x000000000000beef, R10: 0x0000000000000000, R11:
0x0000000000001504
R12: 0xffffff7f8134591a, R13: 0xffffff800c81d200, R14: 0xffffff800c81d200, R15:
0xffffff800b735880
RFL: 0x0000000000010246, RIP: 0xffffff7f81345570, CS:  0x0000000000000008, SS:
0x0000000000000010
CR2: 0x0000000000000090, Error code: 0x0000000000000002, Faulting CPU: 0x1

Backtrace (CPU 1), Frame : Return Address
0xffffff808e973b40 : 0xffffff8000220702
0xffffff808e973bc0 : 0xffffff80002c268d
0xffffff808e973d60 : 0xffffff80002d7a3d
0xffffff808e973d80 : 0xffffff7f81345570
0xffffff808e973ea0 : 0xffffff7f813458b6
0xffffff808e973ed0 : 0xffffff7f81345914
0xffffff808e973f00 : 0xffffff7f813459f4
0xffffff808e973f40 : 0xffffff800063bc61
0xffffff808e973f70 : 0xffffff800023dafc
0xffffff808e973fb0 : 0xffffff8000820057
    Kernel Extensions in backtrace:
```

```
        com.osxkernel.MyDebugDriver(1.0)[FF6F45C8-68F8-3150-9C43-
99A2F19B3FB1]@0xffffff7f81345000->0xffffff7f81348fff

BSD process name corresponding to current thread: kernel_task
Boot args: debug=0xd44 _panicd_ip=192.168.1.1 panicd_ip=192.168.1.1

Mac OS version:
11A511

Kernel version:
Darwin Kernel Version 11.0.0: Sat Jun 18 12:56:35 PDT 2011; root:xnu-
1699.22.73~1/RELEASE_X86_64
Kernel UUID: 24CC17EB-30B0-3F6C-907F-1A9B2057AF78
System model name: MacBook5,1 (Mac-F42D89C8)

System uptime in nanoseconds: 200305435891999
last loaded kext at 200285007562702: com.osxkernel.MyDebugDriver  1 (addr 0xffffff7f81345000,
size 16384)
last unloaded kext at 187374587106276: com.apple.driver.AppleUSBCDC    4.1.15 (addr
0xffffff7f8133d000, size 12288)
loaded kexts:
com.osxkernel.MyDebugDriver  1
com.apple.driver.AppleUSBDisplays    302.1.2
com.apple.driver.AppleIntelProfile  83
com.apple.filesystems.afpfs    9.8
```

The panic log in Listing 16-5 was generated on a different system than before. This system is running a newer version of Mac OS X Lion, which only runs the 64-bit version of the kernel. The panic log consists of the following elements:

- The type of panic/problem that occurred and the CPU (core) number it occurred on

- A dump of the CPU state (register values)

- Back trace of what the CPU was doing at the time of the crash

- Kernel extensions involved in the crash and their dependencies (none above)

- The name of the process (task) that caused the crash

- Kernel build and version numbers

- System model

- Information about recently loaded/unloaded KEXTs

- A complete list of KEXTs loaded

The first thing you may notice is that the panic was caused by a *page fault*, which gives us a clue about what to look for later in our code. It is often useful to look at the task that caused the problem as well. In this case, our driver was executing in kernel context (kernel_task) when the crash occurred and not on the behalf of a user space thread.

First let's look at the back race and try to prove that our driver was indeed involved. There is a very good chance that it was, as our driver is listed as being part of the back trace. You will also notice two addresses after our driver: 0xffffff7f81345000->0xffffff7f81348fff. This is the load address where the instructions and data for our KEXT were loaded into the kernel's address space. To determine which functions on the stack belong to our driver, we can simply look for addresses on the stack that are within that range. Four addresses can be identified—0xffffff7f81345570, 0xffffff7f813458b6, 0xffffff7f81345914, and 0xffffff7f813459f4.

We already know from earlier that they will most likely correspond to testFunc3(), testFunc2(), testFunc1(), and timerFired().

■ **Tip** In the previous back trace, the first address in the column is the address of the stack frame entry, while the second address is the return address, which is the point where execution returns to when the previous function call completes. It's the return address that is interesting to us in this case. You may notice that the stack frame addresses contain increasing addresses and are all within a single page in this case. If the values look random and all over the place, it is likely the stack frame has been corrupted and the back trace may then be useless as the information cannot be trusted.

Assuming we had no clue what functions the addresses corresponded to within our driver, we can employ a simple trick. By simply subtracting the address of one of the functions from the load address, we can determine the offset of the function in the executable image of the driver, as follows:

```
0xffffff7f81345570 - 0xffffff7f81345000 = 1392 bytes
```

We now know that the function is 1392 bytes from the start of the KEXT and assuming we have the executable image (the exact version and build that was involved in the crash) of the driver available, we can do the following:

```
$ gdb MyDebugDriver.kext/Contents/MacOS/MyDebugDriver
GNU gdb 6.3.50-20050815 (Apple version gdb-1704) (Thu Jun 23 10:48:29 UTC 2011)
This GDB was configured as "x86_64-apple-darwin"...
(gdb) disassemble 1392
Dump of assembler code for function _ZN27com_osxkernel_MyDebugDriver9testFunc3Ejjjj:
0x0000000000000540 <testFunc3Ejjjj+0>:     push    %rbp
0x0000000000000541 <testFunc3Ejjjj+1>:     mov     %rsp,%rbp
0x0000000000000544 <testFunc3Ejjjj+4>:     sub     $0x20,%rsp
0x0000000000000548 <testFunc3Ejjjj+8>:     mov     %rdi,-0x8(%rbp)
0x000000000000054c <testFunc3Ejjjj+12>:    mov     %esi,-0xc(%rbp)
0x000000000000054f <testFunc3Ejjjj+15>:    mov     %edx,-0x10(%rbp)
0x0000000000000552 <testFunc3Ejjjj+18>:    mov     %ecx,-0x14(%rbp)
0x0000000000000555 <testFunc3Ejjjj+21>:    mov     %r8d,-0x18(%rbp)
0x0000000000000559 <testFunc3Ejjjj+25>:    mov     -0x14(%rbp),%eax
0x000000000000055c <testFunc3Ejjjj+28>:    cmp     $0x0,%eax
0x000000000000055f <testFunc3Ejjjj+31>:    jne     0x576
<_ZN27com_osxkernel_MyDebugDriver9testFunc3Ejjjj+54>
...
End of assembler dump.
(gdb) info line *1392
```

```
Line 14 of "MyDebugDriver.cpp" starts at address 0x569
<_ZN27com_osxkernel_MyDebugDriver9testFunc3Ejjjj+41> and ends at 0x576
<_ZN27com_osxkernel_MyDebugDriver9testFunc3Ejjjj+54>.
```

And we have found the location of the crash! A full description of CPU registers is outside the scope of this book, but suffice it to say they contain a wealth of useful information. We will discuss how we can use register information to retrieve function arguments in the next section. The processor in the panic log was running in 64-bit mode. The x86_64 has a larger amount of registers available than i386 systems, and local variables are usually passed in general purpose registers instead of the stack.

■ **Tip** Technical Note 2063 discusses how to debug and understand kernel panics in much more detail and includes debugging panic logs from PowerPC systems:

http://developer.apple.com/library/mac/#technotes/tn2063/_index.html.

---

x86-64 Calling Conventions

A calling convention is a scheme for how functions are passed their arguments. The calling convention depends on the programming language, operating system, architecture, and compiler. Understanding the calling convention used can help us decode the register state when a crash occurs. For example, on Mac OS X running a 64-bit executable or kernel, the System V AMD64 ABI convention is used (note that Windows uses a different calling convention, so the register usage will be different). On Mac OS X for a 64-bit task, the register assignments for function call arguments are shown in Table 16-4.

Table 16-4. Register Usage for Function Paramters on x86_64

Argument	Register
First argument	RDI
Second argument	RSI
Third argument	RDX
Fourth argument	RCX
Fifth argument	R8
Sixth argument	R9
Vector/Floating Point arguments 0–7	XMM0–XMM7

If a function takes more than six arguments, the remaining arguments will be passed on the stack. One thing to consider when examining C++ code is that a non-static C++ member method always passes the *this* pointer as the first argument, so the actual first argument to the method is passed in *RDI* whereas the *this* pointer will be put in the register *RSI*.

Let's look at the registers in the panic log shown in Listing 16-5 and see if we can work out which arguments were passed to our function by examining the register state, as follows:

- RDI: 0xffffff801ab61100 (this pointer)

- RSI: 0x000000000000feed (decimal = 65261)

- RDX: 0x000000000000beef (decimal = 48879)

- RCX: 0x0000000000000000 (decimal = 0)

- R8: 0x0000000000001504 (decimal = 5380)

As you can see, the register contents from Listing 16-5 match exactly the four arguments passed to testFunc3(): 65261, 48879, 0, and 5380. We can also see that the first argument looks like a pointer and is likely to be the *this* pointer representing the current instance of MyDebugDriver.

Assuming testFunc3() was a longer and more complicated method and that the crash happened further down in the function, it is possible that the registers may have been reused and overwritten at the point of the crash. In that case, you may not be able to recover the original values of the arguments.

Diagnosing Hung Processes with Activity Monitor

The Mac OS X activity monitor shown in Figure 16-3 can be helpful in diagnosing kernel problems.

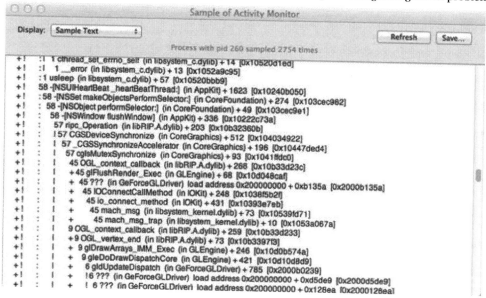

Figure 16-3. Sample process output from Acitivty Monitor

Any task shown in the Activity Monitor can be sampled (except the kernel_task), which will generate call graphs for all the threads of that task during the sample period. This is useful from a kernel debugging point of view in that you are able to see if a process has threads that are calling in to your driver through system calls like IOConnectCallMethod(). If a process is hung, force quitting it will start the Crash Reporter, which will give you a more detailed log, including the kernel stack of a thread if it is currently running in the kernel. The sample process function can also help you determine performance issues and find where an application is spending the most time.

Finding Memory and Resource Leaks

Preventing memory and resource leaks is particularly important for extensions that can be dynamically loaded and unloaded during runtime. A handy tool to detect leaks is the ioclasscount utility, which shows the instance count of each known class (loaded into the kernel). Typical output will look like the following:

```
CHUDUtils = 1
com_apple_AppleFSCompression_AppleFSCompressionTypeZlib = 1
com_apple_BootCache = 1
com_apple_driver_AudioIPCDevice = 1
com_apple_driver_AudioIPCEngine = 1
com_belkin_f2cd0007_adapter = 0
com_osxkernel_MyDebugDriver = 5
com_vmware_kext_KeyboardState = 1
com_vmware_kext_UsbDevice = 2
com_vmware_kext_UsbPortArbiter = 1
.....
```

It shows that our driver has been retained (retain()) five times. The driver's free() function will not be called until the retain count reaches zero, even if the hardware device it controls is removed. This will prevent the kernel extension from being completely unloaded. The retain count typically increases for each user space application that opens the driver, or it can increase because another driver or ancillary support class used by the driver calls retain() on it. Failure to balance a call to retain() with a call release() will result in a leak. The ioclasscount utility can be used without changes to kernel boot parameters; it is not installed on a system by default, but is installed as part of the Xcode distribution. It can be copied onto a system without Xcode for debugging purposes. A driver that has been unloaded and has all references to it released (retain count = 0) will be unloaded by the *kextd* daemon. Although the reference count has dropped to zero, it may take up to a minute for the KEXT to be fully unloaded.

If you are able to live debug the kernel using GDB, you can use macros such as showallclasses or showregistry, as follows:

```
(gdb) showallclasses
...
1   x    84 bytes com_vmware_kext_VmmonService
2   x    80 bytes com_vmware_kext_UsbDevice
1   x   104 bytes com_vmware_kext_UsbPortArbiter
1   x   136 bytes com_vmware_kext_UsbPortArbiterUserClient
1   x   132 bytes com_vmware_kext_KeyboardState
1   x    92 bytes com_osxkernel_MyDebugDriver
....
(gdb) showregistry
...
```

```
     +-o com_osxkernel_MyDebugDriver  <object 0x0703e680, id 0x1000007a9, vtable 0xcbc980,
!registered, !matched, active, busy 0, retain count 5>
...
```

■ **Tip** The zprint and showioalloc macros can further assist in tracking memory usage.

To further help debug reference counting bugs, it is possible to override OSObject::taggedRetain(const void *tag) and OSObject::taggedRelease(const void *). For example, print a message or print a back trace of the caller's stack to help identify where the leak comes from.

Summary

- Some common problems are likely to occur in the kernel, such as deadlocks and invalid memory accesses, which in turn can cause a kernel panic.

- A kernel panic is a defense mechanism against exceptional or erroneous conditions the kernel cannot recover from. It basically disables the system in order to prevent corruption of the file system or other file storage.

- Mac OS X provides a wide range of useful debugging mechanisms out of the box, ranging from a simple tracing and logging mechanism to the built-in support for remote kernel debugging.

- Mac OS X can be configured using the *kdumpd* to accept a core dump from a remote system when it crashes (or if triggered manually). The core dump consists of active/wired memory and can be loaded into GDB.

- The kernel can be debugged from a remote system over FireWire and Ethernet. This mechanism is built in, but not activated by default. Remote debugging can be enabled by setting the appropriate NVRAM parameters and flags.

- Apple usually provides a Kernel Debug Kit for each released build of Mac OS X. The kit contains scripts, a debug version of the kernel, and I/O Kit family KEXTs. The debug kit also contains macros for simplifying kernel debugging in GDB. The macros allow you to get information about call stacks and examine the kernel's key data structures. The kernel can also be live debugged with GDB while running from the same machine.

- To debug your own KEXT, you have to generate debugging symbols for it. Because a KEXT is dynamically loaded in the kernel, we need to generate the correct symbol addresses for a KEXT. The Kernel Debug Kit provides the createsymbolfiles script to help with this.

- A kernel panic log contains a lot of useful information we can use to backtrack and find the location that caused the crash.

- The ioclasscount tool tracks instance counts of classes in *I/O Kit* and can be used to detect memory leaks or other problems.

CHAPTER 17

Advanced Kernel Programming

This chapter covers miscellaneous topics that are of interest to more advanced kernel programmers. We'll discuss how Streaming SIMD Extensions (SSE) and floating point can be used in the kernel. (SIMD is short for Single Input Multiple Data.) We will also examine strategies for dealing with drivers for multi-function devices, and discuss the implementation of I/O Kit families. We'll cover the kernel control KPI that can be used for user space communication with KEXTs such as Network Kernel Extensions (NKE) that does not use the I/O Kit. We also show how to work with and manipulate processes from the kernel, such as getting the process identifier (PID) of a process and sending signals to the process. Some drivers may need additional resources loaded from the file system, such as firmware images. This chapter provides a discussion of how these resources can be loaded using the OSKextRequestResource() function. The chapter concludes with a discussion of how a driver can send messages to a user space daemon using notifications.

SSE and Floating Point in the Kernel

Streaming SIMD Extensions (SSE) is the successor to MMX and is a special instruction set found on most modern Intel and AMD processors that allow common instructions such as *add, multiply,* and *shift* to be performed on arrays (vectors) of values instead of single values (scalar). This can greatly speed up many computation tasks, especially in areas such as digital signal processing, audio, graphics, and video. Normally the kernel is not a great place to perform heavy computation, but there are some areas where it is unavoidable—for example, in the case of audio drivers, which need to convert audio samples from multiple user space applications and mix them into a single buffer for output. Software implementations of the RAID-5 and RAID-6 algorithms are also examples of computations that may need to occur in the kernel and which can be optimized using SSE.

Traditionally, SSE and floating point have been non-trivial for use in kernel environments. Some operating systems, such as Linux, require you to explicitly save the floating point/SSE state and restore it after use; otherwise, a thread's floating point state may be overwritten. In Mac OS X, however, the kernel is free to use both floating point and SSE without needing to manually save and restore the registers' states. Normally, when a thread finishes its time-slice or is preempted in favor of another thread, the state of the CPU registers at the time when the thread stopped executing is saved to memory and subsequently restored when the thread continues execution. To optimize performance, the kernel only stores the general-purpose registers and not the floating point and SSE registers, as they are less frequently used. In fact, many programs will not use floating point or SSE at all. When a different thread attempts to use the registers, the CPU issues an exception/trap, which will save the previous contents and clear the registers for the new thread. When the orginal thread is about to resume execution, floating point and/or SSE registers will be restored to the previous state.

There are two ways of using SSE:

- By directly using the CPU instructions through the use of assembly or inline assembly.

- By using the intrinsic functions provided by GCC, which provides user-friendlier C function wrappers around most instructions. For SSE2, these are provided in the header file emmintrin.h, which is not part of the kernel framework. However, you can copy the file and include it in your project. This is possible as the functions are all inline and do not depend on any external libraries.

There are many revisions of the SSE instruction set. The latest major version is currently SSE4. Some older systems may not support SSE4, which became available in 2007. Attempting to execute SSE4 instructions on a CPU that doesn't support it will result in a kernel panic. To prevent this, you need to provide run-time detection of the CPU's capabilities prior to executing the SSE instructions, or target an older version such as SSE2, which predates all Intel-based Macs.

Multi-Function Drivers

USB and PCI devices may be composite devices that include multiple independent devices in which each device's separate driver can handle each function. Other devices may consist of one logical device handled by multiple drivers. Let's consider a modern graphics card with an HDMI output port as an example. HDMI is able to carry both audio and video, so it would be nice to provide an audio driver that allowed the device to be used with Core Audio. The device is a graphics card, so the hardware doesn't have the typical DMA engine of most audio hardware. Instead, audio data is sent along with video frames at regular vertical blanking intervals. This design means that the audio and video parts are intimately linked and need a shared state between them in order to operate. Since there is no clear separation, the driver can be structured as shown in Figure 17-1.

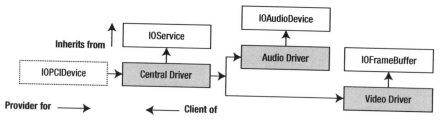

Figure 17-1. Multi-function driver

The design in Figure 17-1 uses a central driver, which coordinates the hardware and manages the provider. The central driver is used for matching against the hardware provider. The central driver then creates an audio driver based on the *IOAudioFamily* and a video/graphics driver based on the *IOGraphicsFamily*. There are two ways of managing the relationship of the subordinate drivers to the central driver:

- The central, audio, and video drivers can be in separate KEXTs. The central driver matches against the hardware resource, whereas the audio and video drivers will match against the central driver and use it as the provider.

- All drivers can be located in the same KEXT. The central driver would then need to manage the lifecycle of the subordinated drivers manually.

Writing I/O Kit Families

Until now we have looked at how to implement various forms of drivers, most of which interact with one or more family. In some circumstances, you may want to implement a family instead of a driver—for example, if you need to support a new bus technology or have a family of hardware devices that all depend on the same infrastructure or general services. A family can be characterized and differentiated from a driver by the following traits:

- A family usually consists of more than one IOService classes bundled together in a KEXT providing related services.

- A family can be thought of as the kernel analog of a user space shared library.

- A driver has a dependency on a family, not the other way around.

- A family is not loaded directly; it is loaded because a driver has expressed a dependency.

- A family does not have a matching dictionary and does not partake in either passive or active matching.

- Just like any other KEXT, a family is installed under /System/Library/Extensions.

There is no special API or approach to writing a family. It is simply done in the same way as any other driver. Apple recommends focusing on a good fundamental object-oriented design and allowing it to evolve naturally, rather than specifically setting out to create a family. A driver can express a dependency on a family (or any other KEXT) using the OSBundleLibraries key in its property list file. A driver cannot be loaded and linked into the kernel until all dependencies have been resolved and loaded first. The kextd daemon is responsible for performing this task. When a driver needs to be loaded, the kextd daemon will examine the driver's Info.plist file for its dependencies. If the Info.plist has incorrectly specified or has failed to list some dependencies, this will result in a link failure and the driver will not be loaded. In order to depend on a family, a driver has to list the family's bundle ID—for example, com.apple.iokit.IOAudioFamily—and version number—for example, 1.7.9fc8.

I/O Kit guarantees that a dependent family is loaded before the driver that depends on it, which is necessary, otherwise symbols in the driver would be left unresolved.

Since many of Apple's I/O Kit families are open-source code, it is possible to modify the families and replace the original versions with modified version. This is not recommended, however, as the family KEXT might be overwritten by a subsequent software update from Apple, which means that functionality of the modified KEXT might be lost. In some situations, modifying a family by inserting additional tracing might help you with debugging.

Extending a family is a better option than modifying it directly. Extending is easy, since most classes in I/O Kit families declare their methods as virtual, even if the class itself is non-abstract. There are many reasons why you might wish to do so. For example, if you were required to support a new type of USB controller not supported by the IOUSBFamily, you could create your own IOUSBController subclass to represent the new controller. The extended class can be compiled into the same KEXT as the driver that needs it, or in your own library/family KEXT. The IONetworkingFamily and other families were designed specifically to allow this form of extension.

Kernel Control KPI

The kernel control interface <sys/kern_control.h> is a KPI, which allows a KEXT to communicate bi-directionally with user space processes. The kernel control system lives in the BSD portion of the kernel and is therefore written in C and not C++ (I/O Kit uses C++).

The KPI is intended to allow a user space program to control and configure a KEXT. For example, let's say you had implemented a custom firewall NKE (Network Kernel Extension). You could then use the kernel control API to tell your firewall which addresses or ports it should block traffic from, as well as retrieving logs and statistics.

The KPI is relatively simple to use in both kernel space and user space. In fact, there is no special API required to use the kernel control mechanism for user space, because it is accessed via a regular socket. The getsockopt() or setsockopt() system call functions can be used to issue control requests from user space. The kernel control system may be compared to the ioctl() system call, but unlike the ioctl() system call the kernel control system is better suited for transferring large amounts of data across the kernel/user space boundary. Sending and receiving data are supported using the send() and recv() system call functions from user space. In the kernel, data transfers are handled using the mbuf data structure discussed earlier.

To use the kernel control interface, you must first register a new interface, which ensures that user space clients can find it and connect to it. This is accomplished by declaring and filling out a C structure containing callbacks for various events, as well as an identifying name. The C language is not object-oriented, and therefore "objects" are often represented by structures containing data and function pointers. The registration structure is shown in Listing 17-1.

Listing 17-1. The kern_ctl_reg Structure from <sys/kern_control.h>

```
struct kern_ctl_reg
{
    /* control information */
    char                    ctl_name[MAX_KCTL_NAME];
    u_int32_t               ctl_id;
    u_int32_t               ctl_unit;
    /* control settings */
    u_int32_t               ctl_flags;
    u_int32_t               ctl_sendsize;
    u_int32_t               ctl_recvsize;
    /* Dispatch functions */
    ctl_connect_func        ctl_connect;
    ctl_disconnect_func     ctl_disconnect;
    ctl_send_func           ctl_send;
    ctl_setopt_func         ctl_setopt;
    ctl_getopt_func         ctl_getopt;
};
```

Let's look at the fields of the structure in more detail:

- The ctl_name should be set to the bundle ID for the KEXT.

- The ctl_id field is used for additional addressing because a KEXT may have several kernel controls registered at once. The ctl_id field can be dynamically registered or assigned by Apple's developer technical support (DTS).

- The ctl_unit field is used only with a DTS-assigned ID. There are only two flags for the ctl_flags. The first is CTL_FLAG_PRIVILEGED, which if set means that a user space program must have root privileges in order to connect to the kernel control. The second flag is CTL_FLAG_REG_ID_UNIT, which should be set if using a DTS assigned ID.

- The ctl_sendsize and ctl_recvsize fields can be used to tune the size of the send and receive buffers for sending data using send() and recv().

The remaining fields are function pointers, which will be called when their corresponding events occur:

- The ctl_connect and ctl_disconnect callbacks will be called when a user space client connects or disconnects.

- The ctl_setopt and ctl_getopt callbacks are invoked when a client uses the setsockopt() or getsockopt() functions. These are often used to get or set configuration parameters. The next callback is ctl_send, which may be a bit confusing, as it's used not to send data but to receive data from a sending client. To actually send data, use the ctl_enqueuedata() function.

Kernel Control Registration

Let's look at an example (HelloKernControl) of how a kernel control interface is used. In this example, you will implement a very minimal kernel control with one get and one set operation. The get operation returns a string stored in the kernel. The set operation overwrites this string so that subsequent get operations return the new string instead. The following is an example of a filled out kernel control registration structure:

```
static struct kern_ctl_reg g_kern_ctl_reg = {
    "com.osxkernel.HelloKernControl",
    0,
    0,
    CTL_FLAG_PRIVILEGED,
    0,
    0,
    hello_ctl_connect,
    hello_ctl_disconnect,
    NULL,
    hello_ctl_set,
    hello_ctl_get
};
```

We use a dynamically assigned ID and specify that our kernel control will be accessible only by privileged clients (root). We defined four callbacks, but we leave the ctl_send callback as NULL because we don't support it in this example. The following is the code used to register and deregister the kernel control:

```
static boolean_t g_filter_registered = FALSE;
static kern_ctl_ref g_ctl_ref;

kern_return_t HelloKernControl_start (kmod_info_t* ki, void* d)
```

```
    {
        strncpy(g_string_buf, DEFAULT_STRING, strlen(DEFAULT_STRING));

        /* Register the control */
        int ret = ctl_register(&g_kern_ctl_reg, &g_ctl_ref);

        if (ret == KERN_SUCCESS)
        {
            g_filter_registered = TRUE;
            return KERN_SUCCESS;
        }
        return KERN_FAILURE;
    }

    kern_return_t HelloKernControl_stop (kmod_info_t* ki, void* d)
    {
        if (g_clients_connected != 0)
            return KERN_FAILURE;

        if (g_filter_registered)
            ctl_deregister(g_ctl_ref);

        return KERN_SUCCESS;
    }
```

You register the interface in the KEXT's start() function and deregister it in the stop() function, which will be called before the KEXT is unloaded. Because a kernel control often shares some data with user space, it is necessary to define a shared header file to store common declarations used by both the kernel and user space. The shared header file for HelloKernControl is shown in the following example:

```
#ifndef HelloKernControl_HelloKernControl_h
#define HelloKernControl_HelloKernControl_h

#define BUNDLE_ID "com.osxkernel.HelloKernControl"

#define HELLO_CONTROL_GET_STRING  1
#define HELLO_CONTROL_SET_STRING  2

#define DEFAULT_STRING            "Hello World"
#define MAX_STRING_LEN            256

#endif
```

Client Connections

The following are the implementation of the connect and disconnect callbacks:

```
static int hello_ctl_connect(kern_ctl_ref ctl_ref, struct sockaddr_ctl *sac, void** unitinfo)
{
    printf("process with pid=%d connected\n", proc_selfpid());
    return 0;
}
```

```
static errno_t hello_ctl_disconnect(kern_ctl_ref ctl_ref, u_int32_t unit, void* unitinfo)
{
    printf("process with pid=%d disconnected\n", proc_selfpid());
    return 0;
}
```

In the preceding example the hello_ctl_connect() function, logs the PID of the client that opened the kernel control. It is often necessary to maintain some per-client data structure. The data structure should be assigned to the unitinfo parameter—for example: *uinitinfo = myStructure;. The structure can now be retrieved in other callbacks. If you allocate memory when the client connects, you should free the memory in the disconnect callback. If you wish to refuse a client—for example, because only one client is allowed at a time, or the maximum number of clients is already connected—you can simply return an error code, such as EBUSY or EPERM.

Getting and Setting Options

Once a client is successfully connected, it can start issuing get/set option requests to the kernel control. The implementation of the control get function is as follows:

```
static int hello_ctl_get(kern_ctl_ref ctl_ref, u_int32_t unit, void *unitinfo, int opt,
                         void *data, size_t *len)
{
    int ret = 0;
    switch (opt) {
        case HELLO_CONTROL_GET_STRING:
            *len = min(MAX_STRING_LEN, *len);
            strncpy(data, g_string_buf, *len);
            break;
        default:
            ret = ENOTSUP;
            break;
    }
    return ret;
}
```

The opt argument comes from the client and specifies which option the client is interested in. A common approach is to create a shared header file, which contains option definitions that are shared between the KEXT and the user space program.

▨ **Caution** Be careful about sharing data structures, because the KEXT and the user space program may pad the structure differently. This can cause bugs, corruptions, or worse.

The preceding case only handles one option. This option is defined by HELLO_CONTROL_GET_STRING, which returns the string in the global g_string_buf variable shared between all clients. If you had allocated private data during the connect callback, you could retrieve it by casting the type of the data from the unitinfo argument.

To return the string to the client, you will copy it to the memory address given in the data argument. The len argument is an input/output argument and contains the length of the data buffer. Obviously, you must ensure that you do not write out of bounds. If you write to the buffer, you should modify len to reflect how many bytes were actually written.

The implementation of the set option function is very similar:

```
static int hello_ctl_set(kern_ctl_ref ctl_ref, u_int32_t unit, void* unitinfo, int opt,
                         void* data, size_t len)
{
    int ret = 0;
    switch (opt) {
        case HELLO_CONTROL_SET_STRING:
            strncpy(g_string_buf, (char*)data, min(MAX_STRING_LEN, len));
            printf("HELLP_CONTROL_SET_STRING: new string set to: \"%s\"\n", g_string_buf);
            break;
        default:
            ret = ENOTSUP;
            break;
    }
    return ret;
}
```

As with the control get option function, we are passed a buffer with data coming from user space and the length of the buffer in the data and len arguments. The data is not valid once the function returns, so you must copy any data you want to preserve.

Accessing Kernel Controls from User Space

The example in Listing 17-2 demonstrates how we can connect the kernel control interface described in the previous sections.

Listing 17-2. User Space Tool for Connecting to a Kernel Control Interface

```
#include <stdio.h>
#include <stdlib.h>
#include <strings.h>
#include <unistd.h>

#include <sys/socket.h>
#include <sys/ioctl.h>
#include <sys/kern_control.h>
#include <sys/sys_domain.h>

#include "HelloKernControl.h"

int main(int argc, char* const*argv)
{
    struct ctl_info ctl_info;
    struct sockaddr_ctl sc;
    char str[MAX_STRING_LEN];

    int sock = socket(PF_SYSTEM, SOCK_DGRAM, SYSPROTO_CONTROL);
        if (sock < 0)
        return -1;
```

```
    bzero(&ctl_info, sizeof(struct ctl_info));
    strcpy(ctl_info.ctl_name, "com.osxkernel.HelloKernControl");

    if (ioctl(sock, CTLIOCGINFO, &ctl_info) == -1)
        return -1;

    bzero(&sc, sizeof(struct sockaddr_ctl));
    sc.sc_len = sizeof(struct sockaddr_ctl);
    sc.sc_family = AF_SYSTEM;
    sc.ss_sysaddr = SYSPROTO_CONTROL;
    sc.sc_id = ctl_info.ctl_id;
    sc.sc_unit = 0;

    if (connect(sock, (struct sockaddr *)&sc, sizeof(struct sockaddr_ctl)))
        return -1;

    /* Get an existing string from the kernel */
    unsigned int size = MAX_STRING_LEN;
    if (getsockopt(sock, SYSPROTO_CONTROL, HELLO_CONTROL_GET_STRING, &str, &size) == -1)
        return -1;

    printf("kernel string is: %s\n", str);

    /* Set a new string */
    strcpy(str, "Hello Kernel, here's your new string, enjoy!");
    if (setsockopt(sock, SYSPROTO_CONTROL, HELLO_CONTROL_SET_STRING,
                   str, (socklen_t)strlen(str)) == -1)
        return -1;

    close(sock);

    return 0;
}
```

When the program in Listing 17-2 is executed, you should see the following results:

```
$ sudo kextload HelloKernControl.kext

$ sudo ./hello_tool
kernel string is: Hello World
$ sudo ./hello_tool
kernel string is: Hello Kernel, here's your new string, enjoy!
```

Working with Processes in the Kernel

The BSD portion of the kernel provides a KPI for getting information about active processes in the system. Note that the term *process* is used in BSD as opposed to *task*, which is used in the Mach portion of the kernel, though they really refer to the same thing.

KERNEL PRIVATE KPIS

If you are digging around in the kernel headers, you may come across the preprocessor directive KERNEL_PRIVATE. Functions or other symbols defined within these sections are not available for use by third-party kernel extensions, and attempting to use one even if the correct header is included will result in a failure to load that KEXT due to unresolved symbols. Apple's own KEXTs are able to access these symbols by adding a dependency to *com.apple.kpi.private*. If you add a dependency for this KPI in your own KEXT it will fail to load, as only Apple-signed KEXTs can use it.

You have already seen examples of how to get information about a process in the AppWall example in Chapter 13, where we used the proc_selfname() function to get the process name of the currently running process. If the function is called in a thread owned by the kernel, the kernel process name "*kernel_task*" will be returned.

If you need to know the PID of the currently running process instead of its name, you can call proc_selfpid(). You can also find the name of a process if you know its PID by using the proc_name(int pid, char * buf, int size); function. An overview of functions in the process KPI is outlined in Table 17-1.

Table 17-1. Functions for Process Manipulation (See sys/proc.h for Full List)

Function	Description
int proc_selfpid(void)	Returns the PID of the current process
int proc_selfppid(void)	Returns the PID of the current process's parent
void proc_signal(int pid, int signum)	Sends a signal (e.g. SIGTERM, SIGKILL) to the process with the specified PID
int proc_issignal(int pid, sigset_t mask)	Checks if any of the signals given by mask is pending for the process with the specified PID
int proc_isinferior(int pid1, int pid2)	Returns 1 if pid1 is subordinated to pid2
void proc_name(int pid, char * buf, int size)	Copies the process name into buf. If the name is shorter than size, it will be truncated.
void proc_selfname(char * buf, int size)	Same as preceding but for the current process

Function	Description
`proc_t proc_find(int pid)`	Gets the process handle of the process with the specified PID. This causes a reference to be added to the process, which must be released with `proc_rele()`.
`proc_t proc_self(void)`	Returns the process handle for the current process
`int proc_rele(proc_t p)`	Releases the process handle p
`int proc_pid(proc_t p)`	Returns the PID of process p
`int proc_ppid(proc_t p)`	Returns the PID of the parent process of p
`int proc_is64bit(proc_t p)`	Returns 1 if the process is running with a 64-bit address space
`int proc_exiting(proc_t p)`	Returns 1 if the process is exiting
`int proc_suser(proc_t p)`	Returns 1 if the process is running with superuser privileges

Loading Resources

The I/O Kit does not provide any classes or functions that provide a driver with access to the file system. This is a deliberate design decision, not an oversight in the I/O Kit design. In theory, a driver should not need to access files on disk. The driver's role is to respond to requests from the operating system to manage its own hardware device, and not to initiate requests of its own. In practice, however, there are many reasons why a driver may need to access data from the file system. One of the most common reasons is to read resource data, such as the firmware data for the driver's hardware.

Although the I/O Kit doesn't allow general file system access, it does provide a means for a driver to access files from the "Resources" directory inside the driver bundle. The I/O Kit's resource-loading API is defined in the header file `<libkern/OSKextLib.h>`. The API is asynchronous; a driver makes a request for the resource that it wishes to load and provides a callback function that the I/O Kit uses to notify the driver when the data is available.

We mentioned that the I/O Kit doesn't provide general file system access, but in addition to this, the I/O Kit itself doesn't have access to the file system. In order to load the resource file for a driver, the I/O Kit relies on a user space helper process, which reads the requested file on behalf of the I/O Kit and passes the file's contents back to the I/O Kit. The I/O Kit then notifies the driver that made the request.

Since the I/O Kit relies on a user space helper process to load resources, it is not possible to load resources in the boot process until the helper process has been launched. However, in most cases this does not cause a problem for the driver, since the I/O Kit will queue the request until the helper process is available to receive requests from the kernel.

A driver can request that the I/O Kit load a file from the driver's resources directory by calling the function OSKextRequestResource(). This function's definition is as follows:

```
OSReturn OSKextRequestResource(const char* kextIdentifier,
                               const char* resourceName,
                               OSKextRequestResourceCallback  callback,
                               void* context,
                               OSKextRequestTag* requestTagOut);
```

The first parameter, kextIdentifier, specifies the bundle identifier of the driver that contains the resource to load; this will almost always be the value specified by the CFBundleIdentifier key of the driver's Info.plist file. The second parameter, resourceName, is the name of the resource file to be loaded from the driver's bundle. The next two parameters are the callback function and an associated context argument that is passed to the callback function when the resource has been loaded. The final parameter, requestTagOut, is returned immediately to the caller and can be used to track the operation to load the resource.

If the call to OSKextRequestResource succeeds, the driver will be notified through its specified callback function when the request has completed. The completion callback has the following signature:

```
typedef void (*OSKextRequestResourceCallback)(OSKextRequestTag requestTag,
                                OSReturn result,
                                const void* resourceData,
                                uint32_t resourceDataLength,
                                void* context);
```

The first parameter provided to the callback, requestTag, identifies the resource that this completion callback refers to. The second parameter, result, informs the caller whether the operation was completed successfully. If the value of result is kIOReturnSuccess, the resource data has been successfully read from the disk and the next two parameters, resourceData and resourceDataLength, contain the contents of the requested resource file. The resourceData buffer is valid only within the callback, so if the driver wishes to refer to the resource data outside the callback, it must make a copy of the data. The final parameter, context, contains the value of the context parameter that was passed to the OSKextRequestResource function.

The remaining step is to add the resource file to the driver's bundle. Any resource loaded through the OSKextRequestResource function must be present in the "Resources" subdirectory of the driver's bundle. In most cases, this can be achieved by adding the file to the Xcode project for the driver. For file types other than source code, Xcode will default to copying the file to the bundle's resource directory when the project is built.

Beyond KEXT Resources

The resource loading functions discussed in the previous section are designed for a specific purpose. The I/O Kit functions provide a driver with read-only access to the contents of a file within its Resources directory. However, there are many situations where it is useful for a driver to access a file outside of its bundle and to write to a file on disk. For example, a driver that provides persistent settings will need some way to read those settings from a file on disk. It will also need a way to write those settings to disk.

Although the I/O Kit contains no functions that provide such functionality to a driver, its implementation of the resource loading functions provides us with a hint of how we might add such functionality to our own drivers. Just as the I/O Kit relies upon a user space daemon process to load resource files on behalf of the kernel, a driver can implement the reading and writing of its persistent settings from a file on disk by providing its own user space daemon process to handle requests on its behalf. This design, covered in the following section, opens up a more general solution that can be extended beyond driver preferences.

Notifications from Kernel Drivers

A general solution to the problem of accessing arbitrary file system items from a kernel driver is to implement a user space daemon process that acts as a helper process on behalf of the kernel driver. This process will handle requests from the driver, perform the specified operation, and then pass the result of the operation back to the driver. This approach can be extended beyond requests such as reading and writing files, and can be used to perform operations that are not possible within the kernel, such as displaying a dialog to the user. A good example of user interaction that originates from the kernel is the standard USB family, which presents a warning dialog if a device is connected that requires more power than the USB bus can deliver.

▪ **Note** The IOUSBFamily currently uses a deprecated interface known as the Kernel-User Notification Center to display alert messages, such as the lower power warning. The I/O Kit used to provide an API that allowed a driver to display a dialog box through a standard system daemon process. However, this API is now deprecated and a driver must now provide its own daemon process.

Any operation that a driver wishes to perform that is not possible within the kernel, such as writing to a file, displaying an error message, or even launching an application, can be performed through a user space daemon process. In effect, the driver code is split into two parts: the kernel driver and the user space daemon. This design uses the same techniques that were discussed in Chapter 5. However, instead of the user launching the user space process, the process will be a background daemon that is launched automatically by the system.

The user space daemon process and the driver work together to perform certain operations. Most of the time, the user space daemon is idle. It only acts when it receives a request from the kernel driver. There are three notifications that the user space daemon will need to respond to:

- The arrival of a new kernel driver

- The unloading of a kernel driver

- A request to perform an operation from a driver

Since the daemon process will be launched at system startup, it may be launched before its corresponding kernel driver has started. For this reason, the process should install a callback to receive notifications when its kernel driver is started or is stopped. In most cases, the daemon will have a one-to-many relationship with driver instances, and a single daemon will handle requests from all instances of its driver that are currently loaded.

A daemon can watch for instances of its kernel driver arriving and unloading by installing a matching dictionary for its driver, as described in Chapter 5. A process performs the same steps to do this whether it is a background daemon or an application with a user interface. The daemon process is able to communicate with its kernel driver by sending requests through the driver's IOUserClient class, using the functions from the I/O Kit framework that were described in Chapter 5.

In Chapter 5, you saw how a user space process can issue requests and send data to a kernel driver. This is important, since this is the approach that the daemon will use to send the results of an operation back to the kernel driver. Now, we'll cover how a process receives notifications from the kernel, such as a request to perform an operation on behalf of the driver—for example, display an error message to the user.

Communication from the kernel driver to the user space daemon occurs over a mach port. The following steps are involved in setting up a communication channel that a kernel driver can use to send a notification to a user space process:

1. The user space daemon locates an instance of its driver and opens a connection to the driver's user client by calling IOServiceOpen(), as described in Chapter 5.

2. The daemon creates a mach port that is able to receive notifications from the kernel driver. This is done using the function CFMachPortCreate(). The function accepts a number of arguments including a callback function, which is used to deliver notifications.

3. The daemon creates a run loop source for the mach port and installs the source into one of its thread's run loops. Later, when a notification is received on the mach port, the daemon's callback is run on the run loop thread.

4. The daemon passes the mach port to the kernel driver, using the function IOConnectSetNotificationPort(). In response, the driver's user client receives a call to its method registerNotificationPort().

5. In the kernel, the user client implements the virtual method registerNotificationPort(). The client receives the mach port that was created by the user space daemon and saves the value in an instance variable.

6. When the driver wishes to notify the user space daemon of an event, it calls the function mach_msg_send_from_kernel() and provides any data that it wishes to pass to the user space daemon.

7. In response, the daemon's callback function is invoked. The callback function receives any data that was passed from the kernel driver, and it handles the kernel's request. If the result of the operation needs to be passed back to the kernel, the user space daemon can do so by calling any of the methods defined by the driver's user client, as described in Chapter 5.

In the rest of this section, we'll go through an example of sending a notification from a kernel driver to a user space process. To begin with, you need to define a structure that will describe the data to be sent from the kernel driver to the user space daemon. This structure must begin with the mach_msg_header_t structure, since this describes the destination mach port within the user space daemon that will receive the data. Following the mach_msg_header_t field, the structure may contain a number of fields that allow arbitrary data to be sent along with the notification to the user space daemon. The definition of this structure must be accessible to both the user space daemon and the kernel driver, so it should be placed in a header file that can be included by both projects. The following is a sample definition for a structure that allows two integer parameters to be passed from the kernel to the user daemon:

```
typedef struct {
        mach_msg_header_t       messageHeader;
        uint32_t                customParameter1;
        uint32_t                customParameter2;
} MyNotificationMessage;
```

An example of the user space callback function that receives the notification sent from the kernel is given in the following listing. The parameter named msg contains the entire MyNotificationMessage structure, including the two arbitrary integers that were added. These extra fields that follow the message header can be used both to describe the operation that the driver wishes the user space daemon to perform and to pass additional parameters that are needed for the operation.

```
void    MyDriverRequestCallback (CFMachPortRef port, void *msg, CFIndex size, void *info)
{
        MyNotificationMessage* notify = (MyNotificationMessage*)msg;

        printf("Param 1 is %x, param 2 is %x\n", notify->customParameter1,
                notify->customParameter2);
}
```

The code snippet shown in Listing 17-3 demonstrates the steps that the user space daemon must take to install a mach port where it will receive notifications from the kernel driver. The first step is to allocate a mach port and a corresponding run loop source, and to install the mach port into its run loop. Next, the mach port is provided to the kernel driver. Whenever the driver wishes to send a notification to the user space process, that request is delivered over the provided mach port.

Listing 17-3. User Space Code to Install a Callback to Receive Notifications from a Kernel Driver

```
CFMachPortContext       portContext;
CFMachPortRef           notificationPort = NULL;
CFRunLoopSourceRef      runLoopSource = NULL;
kern_return_t           kr;

// Set up the CFMachPortContext structure that is needed when creating the mach port.
portContext.version = 0;
portContext.info = (void*)context; // Aribtrary pointer provided to the callback
portContext.retain = NULL;
portContext.release = NULL;
portContext.copyDescription = NULL;

// Create a mach port.
notificationPort = CFMachPortCreate(kCFAllocatorDefault, MyDriverRequestCallback,
&portContext,  NULL);
if (notificationPort)
{
    // Create a run loop source for the mach port.
    runLoopSource = CFMachPortCreateRunLoopSource(kCFAllocatorDefault, notificationPort, 0);
    // Install the run loop source on the run loop that corresponds to the current thread.
    CFRunLoopAddSource(CFRunLoopGetCurrent(), runLoopSource, kCFRunLoopDefaultMode);
}
```

```
// Pass the notification port to the driver.
kr = IOConnectSetNotificationPort(driverConnection, 0,
                          CFMachPortGetPort(notificationPort), 0);
```

The user space function IOConnectSetNotificationPort() results in a call to the driver's user client of the method registerNotificationPort(). This is a virtual method that is defined in the IOUserClient base class, but which needs to be implemented by each subclass. In the following sample implementation, the registerNotificationPort() method takes a copy of the mach port that corresponds to the user space process's notification port so that it can be used in the future whenever the driver wishes to signal the user space process.

```
IOReturn        com_osxkernel_driver_IOKitTestUserClient::
        registerNotificationPort (mach_port_t port, UInt32 type, io_user_reference_t refCon)
{
    m_notificationPort = port;
    return kIOReturnSuccess;
}
```

Having set up the process's notification port, the kernel driver is now able to signal the user space daemon when needed. This is typically performed through the IOUserClient subclass, since the notification port is specific to a particular user client. An example of a custom user client method that can be called to pass two arbitrary integers to the user space process is shown in Listing 17-4.

Listing 17-4. A Custom Method to Send a Notification from a Driver to a User Space Process

```
IOReturn        com_osxkernel_driver_IOKitTestUserClient::
        mySendNotification (uint32_t parameter1, uint32_t parameter2)
{
    MyNotificationMessage  notification;
    IOReturn               result;

    if (m_notificationPort == MACH_PORT_NULL)
        return kIOReturnError;

    // Set up the standard mach_msg_header_t fields.
    notification.messageHeader.msgh_bits = MACH_MSGH_BITS(MACH_MSG_TYPE_COPY_SEND, 0);
    notification.messageHeader.msgh_size = sizeof(MyNotificationMessage);
    notification.messageHeader.msgh_remote_port = m_notificationPort;
    notification.messageHeader.msgh_local_port = MACH_PORT_NULL;
    notification.messageHeader.msgh_reserved = 0;
    notification.messageHeader.msgh_id = 0;

    notification.customParameter1 = parameter1;
    notification.customParameter2 = parameter2;

    // Send the request to user space
    result = mach_msg_send_from_kernel(
                &notification.messageHeader, sizeof(MyNotificationMessage));

    return result;
}
```

Summary

This chapter covered:

- How to use floating point and SSE in the kernel. You learned that OS X, unlike other operating systems, does not require any special actions to support these activities.

- Strategies for writing multi-function drivers.

- The kernel control KPI is a BSD KPI that can be used for communicating between a kernel extension and user space. It is commonly used in conjunction with Network Kernel Extensions (NKE) but rarely used in I/O Kit.

- We covered the KPI for working with processes from the kernel. The KPI has functions for sending signals and getting the name and process identifier (PID) of a process.

- How a kernel extension can load external resources from its bundle and how to handle driver preferences.

- How a kernel extension can message and notify a user space process.

CHAPTER 18

Deployment

Thus far, we have provided background information and looked at the practical implementation of several types of drivers and kernel extensions. This chapter focuses on how we prepare our work for end–user delivery. Apple is known for providing user–friendly software (and hardware) solutions; both Apple and its customers have come to expect the same level of customer experience from third-party vendors. Frustrating customers or users with complex installation procedures is a good way to lose business to competitors on any platform. Deploying a piece of software like a kernel extension may seem easy at first, but there are a multitude of issues to consider, such as how to accommodate a wide range of different hardware and operating system versions. Many customers may be reluctant to upgrade. This is especially true for larger business or government installations— so, you may be required to support bleeding edge, as well as legacy operating system versions— all of which may have different features that require special handling. Besides the external factors, your software's distribution may be complicated. Rarely will you distribute only the KEXT itself; it often requires additional bundled software. For example, a computer graphics card may be delivered with a system preferences pane, a framework used to access the device's special features, applications for upgrading firmware, and perhaps bundled applications that show off the card's capabilities like games. You will also need to handle the possibility that a customer will upgrade or downgrade your software distribution.

While all this may seem daunting—and it is—there is hope. Apple, as usual, provides tools that simplify this process. For deployment, the tool of choice for more advanced software installation is PackageMaker. PackageMaker allows installation wizards to be created from an easy–to–use graphical user–interface. PackageMaker also has a command line utility feature, which can be used to integrate package building into a larger build system.

Installing and Loading Kernel Extensions

KEXT bundles will normally be installed in the system directory/System/Library/Extensions. You can keep KEXTs outside of this directory; however, you will then need to take care of loading the KEXT yourself by using the method outlined in the next section. The KEXT will still need to have the correct permissions set. A KEXT needs to be owned by the root user, belong to the wheel group, and have the permissions mask 0755 in order to be loadable by the KEXT daemon (*kextd*).

For I/O Kit-based drivers, the KEXT is usually loaded automatically by the KEXT daemon when its provider is registered in the I/O Registry (assuming the KEXT has a proper personality defined in its Info.plist file). A KEXT not associated with a hardware provider can load itself automatically at system startup by using the IOResources nub as a provider. For non-I/O Kit based KEXTs, such as NKEs or virtual network drivers, this will not be possible, as IOResources is not available for KEXTs outside the I/O Kit.

For non I/O Kit KEXTs, a Launch Daemon can be created. Launch Daemons and Agents are Apple's replacements for a number of traditional UNIX services including init.d, cron, and inetd. Agents are run as a user logs into the system based on that user's security permissions. Daemons, on the other hand, are system–wide and are generally run with root permissions. We can use a Launch Daemon to execute a shell script when the computer starts, which will in turn load our KEXT. To create a launch agent, simply define a plist file as shown in Listing 18-1.

Listing 18-1. Launch Daemon Property List File

```
<?xml version="1.0" encoding="UTF-8"?>
<!DOCTYPE plist PUBLIC "-//Apple Computer//DTD PLIST 1.0//EN"
        "http://www.apple.com/DTDs/PropertyList-1.0.dtd">
<plist version="1.0">
<dict>
    <key>Label</key>
    <string>com.osxkernel.launchd.HelloWorld</string>
    <key>ProgramArguments</key>
    <array>
        <string>/Library/Application\ Support/HelloWorld/loadkext.sh</string>
        <string>load</string>
    </array>
    <key>RunAtLoad</key>
    <true/>
</dict>
</plist>
```

This file should be installed to /System/Library/LaunchDaemon or ~/Library/LaunchDaemon, as com.osxkernel.launchd.HelloWorld.plist. The Launch Daemon will now trigger the loadkext.sh script during startup. The script itself can be implemented as shown in Listing 18-2.

Listing 18-2. UNIX Shell Script for Loading a KEXT

```
#!/bin/sh
COMMAND=$1

THEKEXT=/System/Library/Extensions/HelloWorld.kext

if [ -f "$THEKEXT" ]
then
    echo "KEXT does not exist"
    exit 1
fi
if [ "$COMMAND" = "load" ]
then
        kextload $THEKEXT
elif [ "$COMMAND" = "unload" ]
then
        kextunload $THEKEXT
fi
```

In some cases, it may be desirable to load the KEXT on demand, rather than at system boot. For example, in the case of a VPN (Virtual Private Network) application, it may come with a KEXT to handle a custom network level encryption scheme or install a virtual VPN interface. This KEXT is only needed for as long as the application remains active. Having it active wastes memory resources, and loading it at boot may potentially impact startup time. Furthermore, since the KEXT interacts with the network stack, it may actually get in the way and impact the system's network performance. In this case, the application may wish to load and unload the KEXT dynamically. This can be achieved by using a script like the preceding one. The application would need to run with root privileges in order to load and unload the KEXT. It is not a good idea, however, to make an entire application *setuid* root, as this can lead to a serious security problem. An alternative solution involves executing a minimal helper program using the AuthorizationExecuteWithPrivileges() API to temporarily escalate the privileges of the executed program. This will prompt the user for the computer's system password. It is possible to allow a KEXT to be loaded by a non–root user by modifying its plist file to include the following:

```
<key>OSBundleAllowUserLoad</key>
<true/>
```

While this will allow a non–privileged process or user to load the KEXT, root privileges are still required to unload the KEXT afterward. As such, the former technique is preferred and is also more secure, as users will have to approve the action explicitly.

KERNEL EXTENSIONS ON THE APP STORE

Apple does not currently permit applications to install KEXTs on either the Mac App Store or the iOS App Store (which doesn't have any means of building KEXTs without violating license agreements). If your application depends on a kernel extension, you would need to distribute it outside of the App Store. Mac App Store applications are not allowed to request root privileges either, which would be needed to install and load a KEXT. It is possible, however, to submit applications even though they may depend on a specific hardware device, but in this case you would need to talk to it through an approved user–space API (see Chapter 15 for details on how this can be done).

Loading Preferences and Settings

Many drivers may need some user–configurable per–device preferences or settings. For example, an audio device may have settings to control output volume level, which need to persist across system reboots. A driver cannot trivially access the file system (which is considered bad design anyway), so it cannot read the preferences from a file; however, An I/O Kit driver will have access to information stored in its plist file. The plist file is read-only and shared for all driver instances instantiated by a KEXT. Since a driver may create many instances, all which require different settings the plist file is unsuitable for this purpose.

Although you could implement your own scheme to put per–device settings in a plist file, it is not considered "good" design. Furthermore, it is difficult for an application to modify a plist file, as root privileges are usually required. Mac OS X does not offer a standardized mechanism or API for handling driver or KEXT preferences or settings. Therefore, if you need this capability, you must implement a user–space application to handle this for you. This can be done by installing a notification to wait for the device's arrival and then call the driver's user client using IOConnectCall*() functions to restore settings from a file. For information on how to install driver or device notifications, please refer to Chapter 5: "Interacting with Drivers from Applications."

If you are implementing a driver for a non–removable device, you can have your user space settings helper run at boot or start time using a Launch Daemon or a Startup Item. You will have to register for a notification for your driver to ensure that the helper doesn't run before your device has appeared. The process can exit once the device has appeared. If you have a removable–type device, such as a USB,

FireWire, or Thunderbolt, you may instead wish to implement a persistent daemon (Launch Daemon) that listens for device arrival and restore settings once a device is plugged in. If the settings are specific to an application that uses the driver or device exclusively, you can manage the settings from the application itself and optionally restore the settings to a previous state once the application exits. The helper program or daemon may be able to run with the privileges of a normal user if the user client or kernel control it interacts with permits it.

If your driver handles multiple instances of the same device, it may be a challenge to figure out which settings belong to which device—either the ordering may not be consistent across reboots—or USB devices may be plugged in in a different order, or into different ports. To combat this, you can use a unique serial number or another identifier the device may have. A network interface should have a unique MAC address; a USB device usually has a serial number or something similar. Thunderbolt devices are guaranteed (in theory) to have a globally unique identifier (UID).

Versioning Kernel Extensions

If your kernel extension is directly accessible to a user–space application, you may wish to provide a versioning system to prevent an older user–space application from accessing a newer kernel extension or vice versa. This is not necessary, for say, audio drivers or other drivers that use a system–supplied IOUserClient; however, in the case that it does not, your KEXT will essentially present an API to the application, which needs to be remain compatible. If the KEXT has been updated, an older application may break or even cause a crash. There is no standardized way to deal with this issue, and the solution is largely dependent on the nature of the KEXT and the applications that access it. One strategy is to include a version number in a shared header file:

```
//
// SharedHeaderFile.h
//
#ifndef Shared_Header_H_
#define Shared_Header_H_

const int KernelUserClientAPIVersion = 1001;

#endif
```

Since both the KEXT and the user application compile the KernelUserClientAPIVersion version number into their binary images, the user application can determine if the KEXT's version number matches that of its own. Every time the interface is changed; for example, if an IOUserClient method is added, removed, or changed, the version number must be updated to reflect this. If your KEXT presents an API available to third party developers, the best approach is to provide an API that takes care of this versioning internally rather than allowing developers access to the IOUserClient directly. This allows the interface between the kernel and user space to change without breaking existing applications; it even allows you to present the same API to a completely different driver or KEXT.

Testing and Quality Assurance

Testing a kernel extension can be a challenge. Modern computer systems and devices are usually very complex, and even if your component is fairly isolated from the rest of the system, unwanted side effects happen as result of it being another cog in the machinery. Proper testing, preferably conducted by those not directly involved in the engineering process, is essential—those directly involved may have preconceived notions of how the product works and fail to discover issues an end-user would. Testing kernel extensions is very dependent on the nature and type of the extension; so, providing an exhaustive list of things to test for is impossible. The following are some general suggestions:

- Test that the driver handles going to sleep and waking up. You can stress test this easily by using the SleepX tool included as part of Xcode. The application allows you to execute a script or external program every time the computer wakes up. You can also tune sleep intervals and the number of cycles you wish to test. It is extremely important that your driver handles sleep properly, especially for mobile devices and laptops, as having the driver still active means the CPU will need to be active—this will drain the system's battery and could even cause a laptop to overheat if it is operating with the lid closed.

- Test that the driver handles repeated loading and unloading with `kextload` and `kextunload`. You can test for reference leaks or memory allocation leaks using the `ioclasscount` and `ioalloccount` tools.

- Test applications that use the driver by performing common user tasks. For example, for an audio device, playback and capture audio with as many permutations of settings and formats as possible.

- Test on all supported platforms and operating systems, such as Macbook Pro, Mac Mini, iMac, Mac Pro or iPod, iPhone, and iPad. For Macs, be sure to test both 32-bit and 64-bit versions and all supported OS versions; e.g., Snow Leopard, Lion, etc.

- For hot–pluggable devices:

    - Test that drivers and devices continue to work correctly after repeated plugging and unplugging. You may wish to do a minimum of 100+ repetitions to be confident no issue will happen in the field.

    - Test that the driver handles the system going to sleep. The driver should also be prepared to handle the device being removed while the system was sleeping.

- Test 32-bit and 64-bit versions of a KEXT. If you support pre-Lion operating systems, you will want to provide universal binaries with support for both 32-bit and 64-bit systems.

- Test the installer package; make sure that all files are installed correctly—with the correct permissions, and in the correct location.

If a problem is discovered either during testing or reported by a customer, it is a good idea to have pre-archived symbol information and/or debug versions for every released KEXT, so you can quickly attempt to reproduce a problem and debug it. This may seem obvious to most people, but it does happen more often than you might think: someone passes on a release of a software component, such as a KEXT, without incrementing its version number. Every time a change is made and released/given to some external entity (or even the internal QA group), the version number should be unique, or you will quickly lose track and confuse everyone involved.

Packaging KEXTs and Software

PackageMaker is the preferred tool for packaging and distributing software consisting of multiple components. Unlike simple applications where every needed component is self–contained and embedded within the application's bundle, more advanced software distributions, such as those containing KEXTs, may need to install components to multiple locations on the file system. For example, a driver will need to place itself within the /System/Library/Extensions directory, and it may further contain helper programs to load preferences or upgrade firmware, which require Launch Agents or Daemons to be installed. PackageMaker is able to do this and more. The PackageMaker user interface is shown in Figure 18-1.

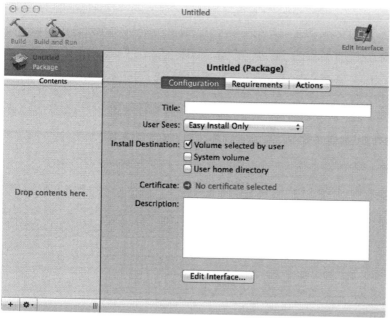

Figure 18-1. PackageMaker user interface

PackageMaker's output is a binary compressed package file with the extension ".*pkg*" that can be installed using the Installer.app program or the installer UNIX command, by executing something like the following:

```
sudo installer -pkg HelloWorld.pkg -target /
```

Installing using Installer.app brings up a GUI–based wizard that guides the user through the installation procedure. If the package has multiple optional sub-components, the user will have the opportunity to select or deselect them. The user can also change the target volume, where the package will be installed, provided that the package explicitly allows this, by setting the "Volume selected by user" option.

PackageMaker isn't just limited to placing software components in the file system. It can also check for system requirements and pre-requisites, including whether the operating system version is supported, or check if some other software component it depends on is present. It can also trigger custom UNIX scripts before and after the software is installed for each component. For hardware drivers, PackageMaker also allows you to verify that your device is present before the user is allowed to continue. This works for FireWire, PCI, and USB.

▓ **Tip** When packaging KEXTs for distribution, ensure that Xcode builds for the architectures you intend to support. By using the `file` command on the KEXT's binary, you can check which architectures it supports. You may also wish to ensure you are not distributing the debug version of your KEXT.

Building a Package for the Hello World Kernel Extension

Now, you can build a quick package for installing the sample Hello World KEXT. You will also need to install a Launch Daemon property lists file (Listing 18-1) and a shell script (Listing 18-2) that will be executed by the Launch Daemon, which will again load the KEXT. Before designing your own package, you will need to determine its components. For example, if you are distributing drivers for an audio device, you may wish to bundle the driver with some software that allows playback or capture of audio, and perhaps an SDK that other developers can use to write their own applications using the card. A developer may only want the driver, whereas an end–user may only want the bundled application and not the SDK, etc. In this scenario, you can create three sub-components: the driver, the application, and the SDK, and allow the user to select which components should be installed. For the HelloWorld package, you only need to add a single component.

To get started, open PackageMaker and chose "new" from the menu. You will then be prompted by a dialog, as shown in Figure 18-2.

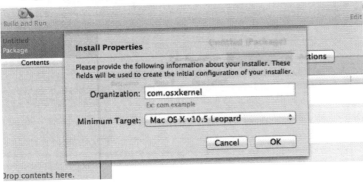

Figure 18-2. Install Properties dialog

The "Organization" field should be the reverse–DNS name of your organization. The value is used to identify the package and uniquely name it. The minimum target drop–down allows you to select the oldest OS version you wish to target. The package will refuse to install on versions older than the install target. Once you have entered your selection, you can give your package a title.

Adding Contents to the Package

You can now start adding files to your package. This can be done by either choosing "Project ➤ Add Contents . . ." from the main menu, or simply by dragging files into the left pane of PackageMaker. Figure 18-3 shows the content pane populated with the files required for the HelloWorld distribution.

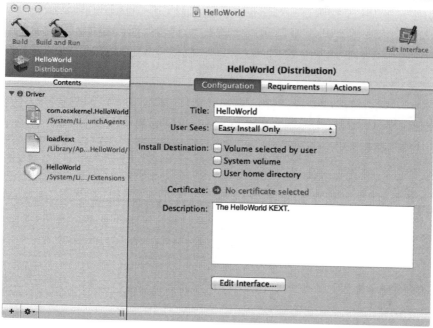

Figure 18-3. The HelloWorld distribution

Our HelloWorld package consists of only three files (shown on the left in Figure 18-3): The KEXT itself and two helper files to allow the KEXT to load at boot–time. When you drag or add some files to the package, PackageMaker will automatically create a *choice*, which, in this case, we have named "Driver." The choice represents a sub-component that can be individually selected by the user. However, if the "User Sees" field in the main pane is set to "Easy Install Only," a user will not be prompted to select individual components, even though there may be more than one. The "Installation Destination" selection allows you to set the location where the package will be installed. At this point, we do not check any of the options, as all of our files go into absolute paths. If the "Volume selected by user" is selected, the instillation wizard will ask which volume (hard drive) the user wishes to install to. It is recommended to allow this choice to give the user more flexibility—particularly for large software packages, which a user may wish to store on a second, larger data drive.

Configuring the Package

Choosing the "Edit Interface" option from the configuration pane in Figure 18-3 will bring up a view of how the package will be presented when opened with Installer.app. PackageMaker allows you to interactively edit text and set a background image. You can also add localizations for enabling instructions in other languages.

The main pane has three tabs, as shown in Figure 18-3. The "Requirements" tab allows for the configuration of requirements that are global to the whole package. You can also set requirements for choices individually, which would allow a user to install some components even if the system didn't meet the requirements for others. Requirements can be specified in the requirements editor, which has many pre-defined checks that can be configured. The following is a subset of available tests:

- Megabytes Available on Target

- Minimum CPU Frequency (HZ)

- Memory Available (Bytes)

- System OS Version / Target OS Version

- File Exists on System

- FireWire, USB, PCI Device Exists

- Result of Script

The last option, "Result of Script," is particularly useful when none of the pre-defined tests are suitable. You can write a shell script to perform your own tests and have the installer take action based on the return code of the script. You can also specify custom error messages that will appear if a requirements test fails. The "Actions" tab allows you to configure actions that can be performed automatically, either pre- or post-installation. For example, in the case of the HelloWorld package, we may wish to ensure that any previously installed HelloWorld.kext is unloaded before we install the new one. We can define this action as shown in Figure 18-4.

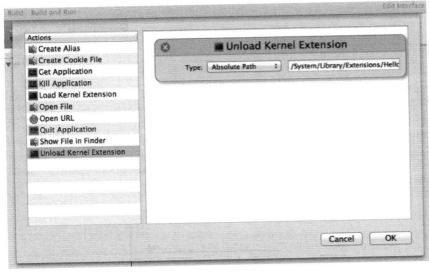

Figure 18-4. The action editor

In some cases, suppose you have a driver for a USB device: you may want to ensure that all applications using the device are killed before installing a new driver. An open application may prevent the driver from unloading properly. You may notice that there is no option for running a program or script; this can, however, be done on a per–file basis by selecting a file and choosing the "Scripts" tab.

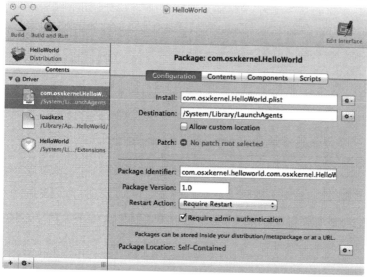

Figure 18-5. Configuration pane for individual packages

For now, we have used the term *Package* to refer to the entire project as a whole, but in PackageMaker terminology, we are actually referring to a distribution that consists of several smaller packages. The smaller packages are made up of the individual files or objects added to the distributions, such as KEXTs, application bundles, or PDF files. Each object has meta-data and version information associated with it.

Figure 18-5 shows the main configuration pane for a package added to the distribution. The "Install" field specifies the source location, whereas the "Destination" field specifies the location in the file system where the object will be installed. Selecting the "Allow custom location" option allows the user to specify an alternative location. Both the source and destination location can be a relative or absolute path. In most cases, the former is recommended. In the preceding example (Figure 18-5), we have used a relative location for the source file and an absolute path in the file system for the destination, as the file must go into that directory and cannot be relocated based on the user's preferences. The same will apply to the KEXT, which we require to be located in /System/Library/Extensions. A relative path is relative to the location of the PackageMaker project.

The "Patch" field allows you to specify an older version of the object you are installing, so that the installer can patch an existing file, rather than install a completely new file.

In the configuration pane, you can also specify a version number and identifier individually for each package. The "Restart Action" allows you to prompt users to restart their computers after the installation is complete. You may want to do this if you have Launch Agents or Daemons that must be started, or you have replaced a driver that is difficult reload (e.g., a storage or graphics driver) while the system is running. You can also require the user to logout or shutdown the system. The "Require admin authentication" checkbox will prompt the user for the administrator password before allowing the package to be installed. If you install files outside of the user's home directory, usually, you must specify this, as the installer does not have admin rights by default. Most KEXTs, particularly drivers, must be installed under /System, which is not normally writable by a regular user.

Finally, the "Package Location" field allows one to specify an alternate location where the package object file will be installed from; for example, you can specify an HTTP URL.

The "Contents" tab of a package is shown in Figure 18-6.

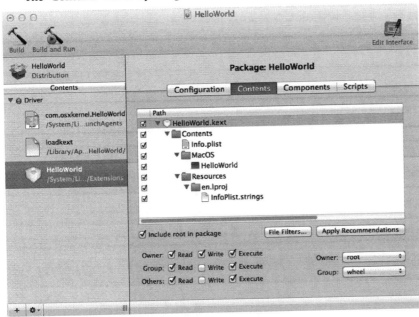

Figure 18-6. Contents tab of the package configuration pane

The "Contents" tab allows you to examine individual files of a package. Usually, packages consist of either a bundle or an individual file. A bundle can contain other bundles or arbitrary files within it. If you need to exclude some files, you can specify regular expression patterns to do so. For instance, the meta-data directories from a source code versioning system, such as Subversion, can be excluded with the pattern "Λ.svn$". You can also configure the file permissions the individual files should have once they are installed in the file system. The "Apply Recommendations" button will guess the correct permissions based on the file types and the intended destinations.

■ **Caution** Kernel Extensions are picky about their permissions and must be owned by the *root* user and the *wheel* group. Additionally, the owner must have read, write and execute rights, whereas the group should have only read and execute rights. This corresponds to the UNIX permissions mask 0755. Meta data files (such as the Info.plist file) do not need to have the executable bit set.

The "Scripts" tab allows for the defining of pre- and post-installation scripts for a package. These can be used to perform custom installation steps that cannot be defined by the "Actions" editor. You may wish to use a pre-install script to shut down daemons or applications before they are replaced with new versions. You can also clean up files that are no longer needed by the newer versions. The scripts are typically written in Bash or another scripting language. If you remove older files from your scripts, be careful about using the *"rm"* command, as your package may run with administrative privileges, and an incorrectly specified filename may lead to the wrong files or directories being deleted. As an example, consider the following: `rm -rf /System/Library/$MYKEXT`. If the $MYKEXT variable ends up being empty, the command will instead delete the /System/Library directory. A very unhappy customer will follow.

Building the Package

Once you have finished adding and configuring all the parts you want included in the distribution, you can build it by pressing the "Build" or "Build and Run" on the toolbar. The latter will open the package in `Installer.app` once the building finishes. During the build phase, the package will be validated and checked; if there are errors or warnings, you can correct them and rebuild the package. The end result will look something like Figure 18-7.

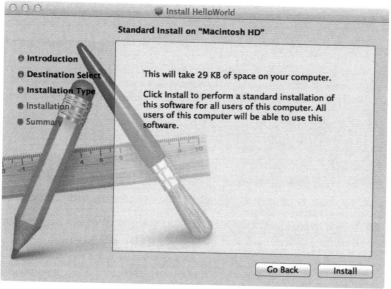

Figure 18-7. Package as presented when launched with Installer.app

The resulting package will be written to the filename `<Title>.pkg`. The package is compressed and not a bundle, so the contents cannot readily be inspected in Finder. When you save a PackageMaker project, it will be saved as a bundle named `<Title>.pmdoc`. The project bundle contains XML files that define the project. You can edit these with a text editor or automatically replace or update contents with a script during your product's build process. If you wish to build the package from the command line, you can do the following:

```
$ /Developer/Applications/Utilities/PackageMaker.app/Contents/MacOS/PackageMaker --doc
HelloWorld.pmdoc --version 2.0 --title 'HelloWorld'
```

The preceding command builds <Title>.pkg with a version number of 2.0.

Uninstalling Packages

Unfortunately, no mechanism exists for automatically uninstalling packages created with PackageMaker. To uninstall a package manually, you would need to identify the files installed by the package and delete them. You would also have to stop and remove any Launch Agents or Daemons installed by the package. A better option would be to provide your users with a script or program that performs the uninstall for them. PackageMaker are able to handle upgrades, however.

Summary

In this chapter, we have looked at the following:

- How the system loads I/O Kit kernel extensions automatically and how to manually load other types of KEXTs (such as Network Kernel Extensions) that are not loaded automatically. The latter is usually achieved using a Launch Daemon.

- Versioning the interface between a KEXT and user space is important in order to avoid breaking older/newer applications that run against it. One strategy to deal with this is to include a version number in a shared header file.

- Quality assurance and testing is an important part of the development cycle and is the last point of defense before software is distributed to a customer. It is important to properly test all aspects and usage patterns of the software on all supported platforms.

- The PackageMaker software is the preferred way of distributing more complex software packages on Mac OS X; i.e., things that include multiple components, such as KEXTs, helper daemons, and end–user applications.

- PackageMaker is a tool distributed with Xcode. PackageMaker can be used via a graphical user interface or the command line. Packages created with PackageMaker are installed using the Installer.app application.

- PackageMaker does not provide a mechanism for uninstalling packages.

Index

▓ O

▓ P, Q

▧ T

▧ U

22157224R00270

Made in the USA
San Bernardino, CA
09 January 2019